Each volume of this series of companions to major philoso-
phers contains specially commissioned essays by an international team of scholars, together with a substantial bibliography, and will serve as a reference work for students and
nonspecialists. One aim of the series is to dispel the intimi-
dation such readers often feel when faced with the work of a
difficult and challenging thinker.

Few thinkers are more controversial in the history of philosophy than Hegel. He has been dismissed as a charlatan
and obscurantist, but also praised as one of the greatest
thinkers in modern philosophy. No one interested in philosophy can afford to ignore him. This volume provides the most
comprehensive and up-to-date survey of Hegel's output. It
considers all the major aspects of his work: epistemology,
logic, ethics, political philosophy, aesthetics, philosophy of
history, philosophy of religion. Special attention is devoted
to problems in the interpretation of Hegel: the unity of the
Phenomenology of Spirit; the value of the dialectical
method; the status of his logic; the nature of his politics. A
final group of chapters treats Hegel's complex historical legacy: the development of Hegelianism and its growth into a
left- and a right-wing school; the relation of Hegel and Marx;
and the subtle connections between Hegel and contemporary analytic philosophy.

New readers and nonspecialists will find this the most
convenient, accessible guide to Hegel currently in print. Advanced students and specialists will find a conspectus of
recent developments in the interpretation of Hegel.

D08851095

THE CAMBRIDGE COMPANION TO
HEGEL

The Cambridge Companion to
HEGEL

Edited by Frederick C. Beiser
Indiana University

CAMBRIDGE
UNIVERSITY PRESS

PUBLISHED BY THE PRESS SYNDICATE OF THE UNIVERSITY OF CAMBRIDGE
The Pitt Building, Trumpington Street, Cambridge, United Kingdom

CAMBRIDGE UNIVERSITY PRESS
The Edinburgh Building, Cambridge CB2 2RU, UK   http://www.cup.cam.ac.uk
40 West 20th Street, New York, NY 10011-4211, USA   http://www.cup.org
10 Stamford Road, Oakleigh, Melbourne 3166, Australia

First published 1993
Reprinted 1993, 1995, 1996 (twice), 1998, 1999

Printed in the United States of America

Typeset in Trump Mediaeval

A catalogue record for this book is available from the British Library

Library of Congress Cataloguing-in-Publication Data is available

ISBN 0-521-38274-2 hardback
ISBN 0-521-38711-6 paperback

CONTENTS

v

CONTRIBUTORS

FREDERICK C. BEISER is Professor of Philosophy, Indiana University, Bloomington. He is the author of *The Fate of Reason: German Philosophy from Kant to Fichte* (Harvard University Press, 1987) and *Enlightenment, Revolution and Romanticism: The Genesis of Modern German Political Thought, 1790–1800* (Harvard University Press, 1992).

JOHN BURBIDGE is Professor of Philosophy, Trent University, Ontario, Canada. He has written many articles on Hegel and German philosophy and is the author of *On Hegel's Logic: Fragments of a Commentary* (Humanities Press, 1981).

LAURENCE DICKEY is Professor of History, the University of Wisconsin, Madison. He is the author of *Hegel: Religion, Economics and the Politics of Spirit, 1770–1807* (Cambridge University Press, 1987).

MICHAEL FORSTER is Professor of Philosophy, University of Chicago. He is the author of *Hegel and Skepticism* (Harvard University Press, 1989) and *Hegel's Idea of a Phenomenology of Spirit* (Harvard University Press, 1993).

PAUL GUYER is Professor of Philosophy at the University of Pennsylvania. He has published widely on Kant and other figures in German philosophy. He is the author of *Kant and the Claims of Taste* (Harvard University Press, 1979) and *Kant and the Claims of Knowledge* (Cambridge University Press, 1987). He is the general co-editor of the Cambridge Edition of the Works of Immanuel Kant (forthcoming) and the editor of the *Cambridge Companion to Kant* (1992).

vii

H.S. HARRIS is Distinguished Research Professor of Philosophy at York University, Toronto, Canada. He is the author of *Hegel's Development, Volume I: Toward the Sunlight, 1770–1801* (Oxford University Press, 1972) and *Volume II: Night Thoughts, Jena 1801–1806* (Oxford University Press, 1983).

PETER HYLTON is Professor of Philosophy at the University of Illinois – Chicago. He has published many articles on the history of analytic philosophy and is the author of *Russell, Idealism and the Emergence of Analytic Philosophy* (Oxford University Press, 1990).

ROBERT B. PIPPIN is Professor of Philosophy at the University of California, San Diego. He is the author of *Kant's Theory of Form* (Yale University Press, 1982) and *Hegel's Idealism* (Cambridge University Press, 1989).

JOHN TOEWS is Professor of History at the University of Washington. He is the author of *Hegelianism: The Path Toward Dialectical Humanism, 1805–1841* (Cambridge University Press, 1980).

THOMAS E. WARTENBERG is Professor of Philosophy at Mount Holyoke College. He has written widely on German philosophy. He is the author of *The Forms of Power: From Domination to Transformation* (Temple University Press, 1990) and the co-editor with Manfred Frank of *Feuerbach: Principles of the Philosophy of the Future* (Hackett, 1986).

KENNETH WESTPHAL is Professor of Philosophy at the University of New Hampshire. He has published many articles on Kant and Hegel and is the author of *Hegel's Epistemological Realism* (Kluwer, 1989).

ROBERT WICKS teaches philosophy at the University of Arizona. He has published articles in the fields of German philosophy and aesthetics. He is currently writing a book on Hegel's theory of aesthetic judgement.

ALLEN WOOD is Professor of Philosophy, Cornell University. He is general co-editor of The Cambridge Edition of the Works of Immanuel Kant (forthcoming). His books include *Kant's Moral Religion* (Cornell University Press, 1970), *Kant's Rational Theology* (Cornell University Press, 1981), *Karl Marx* (Routledge, Kegan & Paul, 1981) and *Hegel's Ethical Thought* (Cambridge University Press, 1990).

Introduction: Hegel and the problem of metaphysics

Few thinkers in the history of philosophy are more controversial than Hegel. Philosophers are either for or against him. Rarely do they regard him with cool detachment, weighing his merits and faults with strict impartiality. Hegel has been dismissed as a charlatan and obscurantist, but he has also been praised as one of the greatest thinkers of modern philosophy. As a result of these extreme views, Hegel has been either completely neglected or closely studied for decades.

Whether we love or hate Hegel, it is difficult to ignore him. We cannot neglect him if only because of his enormous historical significance. Most forms of modern philosophy have either been influenced by Hegel or reacted against him. This is true not only of Marxism and existentialism – the most obvious cases in point – but also of critical theory, hermeneutics and, if only in a negative sense, analytic philosophy. Hegel remains the watershed of modern philosophy, the source from which its many streams emanate and divide. If the modern philosopher wants to know the roots of his own position, sooner or later he will have to turn to Hegel.

Hegel demands our attention for more than historical reasons. If we consider any fundamental philosophical problem, we find that Hegel has proposed an interesting solution for it. He claimed that his system provides the only viable middle path between every philosophical antithesis. He held that it preserves the strengths, and cancels the weaknesses, of realism and idealism, materialism and dualism, relativism and absolutism, skepticism and dogmatism, nominalism and Platonism, pluralism and monism, radicalism and conservatism. Indeed, the more we study Hegel the more we find that his system seems to accommodate every viewpoint and to anticipate every objection. Of course, it is at least arguable that Hegel solved any of these problems. But can we safely ignore his claims to do so? Hegel's sheer presumption challenges us to make a closer study of his philosophy.

But if Hegel is important, he is also problematic. The Hegel renaissance, which began in the 1960s and continues today, has still not removed him from all suspicion. One of the chief reasons Hegel remains supsect lies with his notorious obscurity, which has put him at odds with the premium placed upon clarity in contemporary philosophy. Another, more important reason is Hegel's apparent indulgence in metaphysics, a subject that has been much discredited by the legacy of Kant and positivism. Hegel seems to fly in the face of every stricture upon the limits of knowledge, blithely speculating about such obscure entities as "spirit" and "the absolute." This image of the irresponsible metaphysician began with Russell's famous contention that Hegel's entire system rests upon a few elementary logical blunders.[1]

Not only contemporary philosophers have difficulty coming to terms with Hegel's metaphysics: Hegel scholars also remain deeply divided over its status and worth. Broadly speaking, there have been two antithetical approaches to Hegel's metaphysics. There is first of all the traditional historical approach, which accepts Hegel's metaphysics as a *fait accompli*, and which attempts to explain it by describing its relations to its historical antecedents. For example, Hegel's metaphysics is described as "inverted Spinozism," "dialectical neo-Thomism," or "monistic Leibnizianism." This approach can be found mainly in the older German studies of Hegel, especially those by Dilthey, Haym, Haering, Rosenkranz, and Kroner. Opposed to the historical approach is the more-modern positivistic approach, which tends to dismiss Hegel's metaphysics as a form of mysticism or speculation, but which values him for his many ideas in the fields of epistemology, ethics, politics, and aesthetics. According to this modern approach, we can find much of "philosophical significance" in Hegel, but it has nothing to do with his metaphysics, which is only the "mystical shell" of the "rational core." This approach to Hegel can be found in the Marxist tradition, in the Frankfurt school, and also in those recent studies that regard Hegel's philosophy simply as a form of "categorical analysis."[2]

Both of these approaches suffer from obvious difficulties. If the historical approach lacks a philosophical perspective, virtually inviting us to suspend our critical faculties, the positivistic approach has an anachronistic or tendentious conception of Hegel's "philosophical significance," relegating almost 90 percent of the actual Hegel to the dustbin of history. Apart from their separate difficulties, both approaches suffer from a common shortcoming: they fail to see that Hegel himself regarded metaphysics as a very problematic undertaking in need of legitimation, and that he accepted the Kantian challenge to metaphysics, insisting that "any future metaphysics that is to come forward as a science" must be based upon a critique of knowledge.

The main task of this introduction is to address the chief problem confronting the understanding and evaluation of Hegel's philosophy: the problem of metaphysics. It will do so by examining, if only in rough outline, Hegel's defense of metaphysics, his response to the Kantian challenge. If we investigate Hegel's own justification of metaphysics, we will be able to avoid the pitfalls of the traditional approaches to Hegel. We will not have to accept his metaphysics as a *fait accompli*, nor will we have to reject it as mysticism or speculation. Rather, we will be able to appraise it on its own merits, seeing whether it really does meet the Kantian challenge. The chief advantage of this approach is that we should be able to produce an interpretation of Hegel that is neither obscurantist nor reductivist, that neither regards his metaphysics as speculation about the supernatural nor reduces it to mere categorical analysis.

Any introduction to Hegel's metaphysics should answer four basic questions. 1) What does Hegel mean by "metaphysics"? 2) What does he mean by "the absolute"? 3) Why does he postulate the existence of the absolute? 4) How does he justify the attempt to know it in the face of Kant's critique of knowledge?

Before we examine Hegel's defense of metaphysics, we need some account of what he means by "metaphysics." The term is notoriously vague and ambiguous. It can refer to several different kinds of discipline: to an ontology, a study of the most general predicates of being; to a theology, a study of the highest being; or to a cosmology, a study of the first principles and forces of nature. Rather than defining his use of the term, however, Hegel refuses to adopt it. When he does use the term, it is almost always in a negative sense to refer to the antiquated doctrines and methods of the rationalist tradition, the metaphysics of Descartes, Leibniz, and Wolff, which had been discredited by Kant's critique of knowledge.[3] The term "metaphysics" had fallen into disrepute by the early 1800s, as Hegel himself noted,[4] so reviving it would have been impossible without invoking negative connotations. Nevertheless, even if Hegel avoided the term, he had a conception of philosophy that can only be described as "metaphysical." In his early Jena years, and indeed throughout his career, Hegel saw the purpose of philosophy as the rational knowledge of the absolute.[5] This conforms to one of the classical senses of the term "metaphysics," a sense given to it by Kant in the *Critique of Pure Reason:* the attempt to know the unconditioned through pure reason.[6]

If we define metaphysics as the knowledge of the absolute, we are still far from a clear understanding of its purpose and nature. For, to address our second question, what does Hegel mean by "the absolute"? Although Hegel himself never provides a simple definition of the term, one is given by his former philosophical ally, F.W.J. Schelling. According to Schelling, the absolute is that which does not depend upon anything else in order to exist or be conceived.[7] Both in its existence and essence, the absolute is independent of, or unconditioned by, all other things. In other words, the absolute is *causi sui,* that whose essence necessarily involves existence. The historical antecedent of this concept is Spinoza's definition of substance in the *Ethics:* "By substance, I mean that which is in itself, and is conceived through itself; in other words, that of which a conception can be formed independently of any other conception."[8] Making no secret of his debt to Spinoza, Schelling readily followed his definition by calling the absolute "the infinite substance" or, less eloquently, "the in-itself" (*das An-sich*).

Schelling and Hegel did not hesitate to draw Spinozistic conclusions from this definition of substance. Like Spinoza, they argued that only one thing can satisfy this definition: the universe as a whole. Since the universe as a whole contains everything, there will be nothing outside it for it to depend upon; for anything less than the universe as a whole, however, there will be something outside it in relation to which it must be conceived. With these Spinozistic arguments in mind, Schelling wrote in his 1800 *Presentation of My System of Philosophy:* "The absolute is not the cause of the universe but the universe itself."[9] Hegel too embraced Spinoza's conclusions. As late as the 1820s, he paid handsome tribute to the Spinozistic conception of the absolute: "When one begins to philosophize one must be first a Spinozist. The soul must bathe itself in the aether of this single substance, in which everything one has held for true is submerged."[10]

If we keep in mind Schelling's and Hegel's Spinozistic conception of the absolute, we can avoid some of the vulgar misconceptions surrounding their metaphysics. According to one common conception, metaphysics is a form of speculation about supernatural entities, such as God, Providence, and the soul. Such a conception has nothing to do with Schelling's and Hegel's metaphysics, however, for their metaphysics does not concern itself with a specific kind of entity. Their absolute is not a kind of thing, but simply the whole of which all things are only parts. No less than Kant, then, Schelling and Hegel warn against the fallacy of hypostasis, which treats the absolute as if it were only a specific thing.[11] Schelling and Hegel also insist that their metaphysics has nothing to do with the supernatural. Their conception of metaphysics is indeed profoundly naturalistic. They banish all occult forces and the supernatural from the universe, explaining everything in terms of natural laws.[12] They admired Spinoza precisely because of his thoroughgoing naturalism, precisely because he made a religion out of nature itself, conceiving of God as nothing more than the *natura naturans*.

It would be a mistake, however, to conceive of Schelling's and Hegel's metaphysics in purely Spinozistic terms. In the early 1800s Schelling developed a conception of the absolute as "subject-object identity" a conception whose ultimate meaning is *anti*-Spinozistic. What Schelling meant by describing the absolute as "subject-object identity" is *apparently* Spinozistic: the mental and physical, the subjective and objective, are only different attributes of a single infinite substance. Nevertheless, Schelling gave this doctrine a further meaning that would have made Benedictus turn in his grave. Contrary to Spinoza's rigidly mechanistic conception of the universe, Schelling conceived of the single infinite substance in vitalistic and teleological terms. Following Herder,[13] who insisted on breathing life into Spinoza's dead and frozen universe, Schelling saw substance as living force, "the force of all forces" or "primal force." According to Schelling's *Naturphilosophie*,[14] all of nature is a hierarchic manifestation of this force, beginning with its lower degrees of organization and development in minerals, plants, and animals, and ending with its highest degree of organization and development in human self-consciousness. The absolute is not simply a machine, then, but an organism, a self-generating and self-organizing whole.

Schelling thought he had good reason to conceive of the absolute in organic rather than mechanical terms. Only an organic conception of nature, he argued, agreed with all the latest results of the new sciences. The recent discoveries in electricity, magnetism, and biology made it necessary to conceive of matter in more dynamic terms. Rather than regarding matter as static, so that it acts only upon external impulse, Schelling felt it necessary to see it as active, as generating and organizing itself. Spinoza's more mechanical conception of the absolute was, then, only the product of the sciences of his day, which were now obsolete. Schelling also saw his vitalism as the solution to a problem that had haunted philosophy ever since Descartes: how to explain the interaction between the mind and body. According to Schelling, the mind and body are not distinct kinds of entity, but simply different degrees of organization and development of living force. Mind is the most organized and developed form of matter, and matter is the least organized and developed form of mind. Such a theory, Schelling argued, avoids the pitfalls of both dualism and mechanistic materialism. Since living force has to be explained in teleological terms, the mind is not merely a machine; and since force embodies itself only in the activity of matter, it is not a ghostly kind of substance.

Hegel inherited this organic conception of the absolute from Schelling in the early 1800s, the period of their collaboration on the *Critical Journal of Philosophy* (1802–04). Hegel accepted the broad outlines of Schelling's conception of the absolute. He agreed with Schelling's definition of the absolute: that which has an independent essence and existence. He also followed Schelling in conceiving of the absolute in organic terms, so that the mental and physical are only its attributes or degrees of organization and development. Nevertheless, even during their collaboration, Hegel began to have serious doubts about some of Schelling's formulations of the nature of the absolute. In his *Presentation of My System, Bruno,* and *Philosophy and Religion*,[15] Schelling sometimes spoke of the absolute as if it were nothing more than "subject-object identity," the single infinite substance or "the point of indifference" between the subjective and objective. But this limited way of speaking about the absolute suffers from a serious difficulty. If we conceive of the absolute as only subject-object identity *apart* from the apparant dualism between the subject and object in our ordinary experience – if we see it as only the infinite substance *without* its finite modes – then we seem to exclude the realm of the finite and appearance from it. Contrary to its definition, the absolute then becomes dependent in its essence, conceivable only in contrast to something it is not, namely the realm of appearance and finitude. Hence, in the preface to his *Phenomenology*, Hegel felt that it was necessary to correct Schelling's restricted formulation of the absolute. Since Schelling's absolute excluded its modes, which determine the specific characteristics of a thing, Hegel likened it to "a night when all cows are black." If we are to remain true to its definition, Hegel argued, then it is necessary to conceive of the absolute as the *whole* of substance *and* its modes, as the *unity* of the infinite *and* finite. Since the absolute must include all the flux of finitude and appearance within itself, Hegel called it "a Bacchanalian revel in which no member is not drunken."

Hegel's ridicule of Schelling should not blind us, however, to his deeper debts to his erstwhile colleague. All his life Hegel adhered to Schelling's organic conception of the absolute, attempting to work out some of its implications. What Hegel was objecting to in the preface of the *Phenomenology* was more Schelling's formulation of the absolute than his underlying conception. Although he vacillated, Schelling himself would sometimes conceive of the absolute in more Hegelian terms, explicitly including the realm of finitude within it.[16] When Hegel later insisted (in the preface to the *Phenomenology*) that the absolute is not only substance but also subject, he was not so much attacking Schelling as attacking Spinoza through Schelling. By conceiving of Spinoza's substance as living force, Schelling had laid the ground for seeing the absolute as subject. Hegel's philosophical development in his formative Jena years consisted not so much in a "break with Schelling" as in a persistent attempt to provide a better epistemological foundation for his views.[17]

Now that we have examined Schelling's and Hegel's conception of the absolute, we are in a much better position to understand their belief in the possibility of metaphysics. Because of their conception of the absolute, Schelling and Hegel believed they were justified in exempting their philosophy from much of Kant's critique of metaphysics. The target of Kant's critique – the victim of all the "amphibolies," "paralogisms," and "antinomies" – was the old metaphysics of the Leibnizian-Wolffian school. But this metaphysics was in the service of a deistic theology, which conceived of the absolute as a supernatural entity existing beyond the sphere of nature. Schelling and Hegel happily agreed with Kant that metaphysics in this sense is indeed impossible. They had, however, a different diagnosis of its impossibility: it is not because the supernatural is unknowable, as Kant thought, but because the supernatural does not exist. All of Kant's worries about the unknowability of the noumenal world were, in Schelling's and Hegel's view, simply the result of hypostasis, of conceiving of the absolute as if it were only a specific thing. If we conceive of the absolute in naturalistic terms, Schelling and Hegel argue, then metaphysics does not require the transcendent knowledge condemned by Kant. All that we then need to know is nature herself, which is given to our experience.

Schelling and Hegel were convinced of the possibility of their metaphysics chiefly because they regarded it as a form of scientific naturalism, as the appropriate philosophy for the new natural sciences of their day. They rejected any sharp distinction between the *a priori* and the *a posteriori*, insisting that their metaphysical principles be confirmed through experience. And, as we have already seen, they insisted on banishing all occult forces from nature and explaining everything according to natural laws. Although, to be sure, they conceived of the laws of nature in teleological rather than mechanical terms, they were adamant that the purposes of nature be conceived as internal to nature herself and not as imposed by some external designer. For Schelling and Hegel, then, the question of the possibility of metaphysics depended in no small measure upon the possibility of *Naturphilosophie* itself. We ignore this dimension of Schelling's and Hegel's philosophy only at the risk of positivistic anachronism.[18]

Seen in its proper historical perspective, Schelling's and Hegel's metaphysics should be placed within the tradition of vitalistic materialism, which goes back to Bruno and the early free-thinkers of seventeenth-century England.[19] This tradition attempted to banish the realm of the supernatural, yet it was not atheistic. Rather, it conceived of God as the whole of nature. Although it held that nature consists in matter alone, it conceived of matter in vitalistic rather than mechanistic terms. Matter was seen as dynamic, having self-generating and self-organizing powers.[20] The similarities with Schelling's and Hegel's metaphysics are apparent. But Schelling and Hegel should also be placed within this tradition because they shared some of its underlying moral and political values: a commitment to egalitarianism, republicanism, religious tolerance, and political liberty. If it seems strange to regard Hegel as a materialist, given all his talk about "spirit," then we must lay aside the usual mechanistic picture of materialism. We also must not forget that for Hegel, spirit is only the highest degree of organization and development of the organic powers within nature. If it were anything more, Hegel would relapse into the very dualism he condemns in Kant and Fichte. It is noteworthy that this materialistic element to Hegel's metaphysics was not lost on his contemporaries, who were quick to praise and damn him accordingly.[21]

If we consider Schelling's and Hegel's naturalistic conception of metaphysics, it might seem as if there is no point of conflict between them and Kant after all. It is as if Hegel engages in a kind of metaphysics that Kant himself would approve, a metaphysics of nature. But this would be a premature conclusion, one which misses the real point at issue between Kant and Hegel. For, in claiming that we can know nature as an organism, as a totality of living forces, Schelling and Hegel were flying in the face of Kant's strictures upon teleology in the *Critique of Judgement*. In this work Kant argues that we cannot confirm the idea of a natural purpose through experience, and that we attribute purposes to nature only by analogy with our own conscious intentions. The idea of an organism has a strictly heuristic value in helping us to systematize our knowledge of the many particular laws of nature. We cannot assume that nature *is* an organism, then, but we can proceed only *as if* it were one. In the terms of Kant's first *Critique*, the idea of an organism is not a "constitutive" but only a "regulative" principle. Rather than describing anything that exists, it simply prescribes a task, the organization of all our detailed knowledge into a system. Here, then, lies the basic sticking point between Kant and Hegel: Kant denies, and Hegel affirms, that we can know that nature *is* an organism.

We have now come to our third question: Why postulate the existence of the absolute? In other words, why give constitutive validity
to the idea of nature as an organism? Hegel's answer to this question
comes in his first published philosophical writing, his 1801 *Difference between the Fichtean and Schellingian Systems of Philosophy*.
The thesis of this early work is that there is a fundamental difference between Fichte's and Schelling's philosophy, and that Schelling's system is superior to Fichte's. Such a thesis would have been
news to Schelling himself, who had collaborated with Fichte for the
previous five years and regarded their positions as the same in principle. Hegel's tract was instrumental in effecting Schelling's break
with Fichte and forging the alliance between Schelling and Hegel.[22]
The essence of Hegel's argument for the superiority of Schelling's
system is that we can resolve the central outstanding problem of
Fichte's philosophy only if we assume the existence of Schelling's
absolute, that is, only if we give constitutive status to the idea of
nature as a living organism. To understand Hegel's argument, then,
we must first have some idea of Fichte's problem and of his difficulties in finding a solution to it.

The fundamental problem of Fichte's early philosophy, the *Wissenschaftslehre* of 1794,[23] began with the Transcendental Deduction of
Kant's *Critique of Pure Reason*. In this notoriously obscure secton of
his enigmatic masterpiece, Kant raised a question that would haunt
the entire generation after him: How is empirical knowledge possible if it requires a universality and necessity that cannot be verified
in experience? This problem arose in the context of Kant's dualistic
picture of the faculty of knowledge. According to Kant, empirical
knowledge requires the interchange between universal and necessary concepts, which provide the *form* of experience, and particular
and contingent intuitions or impressions, which supply the *matter*
of experience. While these concepts originate *a priori* in the understanding, a purely active and intellectual faculty, the intuitions are
given *a posteriori* to our sensibility, a purely passive and sensitive
faculty. The question then arose: If our *a priori* concepts derive from
the understanding, how do we know that they apply to the *a posteriori* intuitions of sensibility? Or, more simply, if these concepts do
not derive from experience, then how do we know that they are valid
for it? Kant's answer to this question – if we can summarize in a few
words the extremely involved and intricate argument of the Tran-

scendental Deduction – is that these *a priori* concepts apply to experience only if they are its necessary conditions. If they determine the very conditions under which we have representations, then they will indeed be valid for them, although they will have no validity beyond them.

Under the influence of some of Kant's early critics, Fichte quickly became dissatisfied with Kant's solution to the problem of the Transcendental Deduction. According to such early critics of Kant as J.G. Hamann, G.E. Schulze, and Salomon Maimon, the very manner in which Kant posed his problem made its solution impossible. Kant had postulated such a wide divide between the faculties of understanding and sensibility that there could not be any correspondence between *a priori* and *a posteriori* intuitions. If the understanding is a purely active intellectual faculty, whose activities are not in space and time, and if sensibility is a purely passive sensitive faculty, whose operations are in space and time, then how is it possible for these faculties to interact with one another? According to Maimon, one of Kant's sharpest critics, Kant's problems with the understanding-sensibility dualism were analogous to Descartes's problems with the mind-body dualism.[24] Just as Descartes could not explain how two such heterogeneous substances as the mind and body interact, so Kant could not explain how two such heterogeneous faculties as understanding and sensibility could cooperate with one another. Kant's dualism left his philosophy vulnerable to skeptical objections, for it seemed that his faculties could interact only in virtue of some mysterious pre-established harmony.

The main problem for philosophers after Kant, then, was to find some means of uniting Kant's disastrous dualisms. Philosophers searched for some higher power or source of the mind, of which the understanding and sensibility were only aspects or manifestations. They insisted upon raising a question that Kant himself refused to answer: How is the faculty of thought in general possible?[25] What makes the understanding and sensibility different functions of thought in general? Although it is well known that the overcoming of Kant's dualisms was a central objective of post-Kantian philosophy, this point is usually made in the context of Kant's moral philosophy, where Kant postulates a struggle between reason and desire. What we must see here, however, is that the overcoming of these dualisms was not only a moral imperative. Rather, it was also an epistemological one, since only in this way would it be possible to solve the problem of the Transcendental Deduction.

Recognizing the problematic status of Kant's dualisms, Fichte insisted that the only way to resolve the problem of the Transcendental Deduction was to postulate a principle of "subject-object identity."[26] According to this principle, all knowledge requires nothing less than the identity of the knower and the known. The subject who knows must be one and the same as the object that is known. We must postulate such a principle, Fichte argues, because any form of dualism leaves us prey to skepticism. If the subject and object are consciousness and the thing-in-itself, then we cannot step outside our consciousness to see if it corresponds to the thing as it exists prior to it. But if they are the concepts of the understanding and the intuitions of sensibility, then we cannot conceive how such distinct faculties interact. Hence the only means to avoid skepticism and to explain the possibility of knowledge, Fichte concludes, is to postulate some principle of subject-object identity.

Assuming that subject-object identity is a necessary condition of knowledge, under what conditions is it realized? Where is subject-object identity to be found? Fichte's answer is that only one kind of knowledge realizes the demanding conditions of subject-object identity: self-knowledge. Only in self-knowledge is the subject who knows one and the same as the object that is known. Hence, for Fichte, self-knowledge becomes the paradigm of all knowledge. If we can show that our knowledge of an object in experience really is only a form of self-knowledge, then we will be able to show how knowledge is possible. This strategy was perfectly summed up by the young Schelling when he was still a disciple of Fichte:

Only in the self-intuition of a mind is there the identity of a representation and its object. Hence to explain the absolute correspondence between a representation and its object, upon which the reality of all of our knowledge depends, it must be shown that the mind, insofar as it intuits objects, really intuits itself. If this can be shown, then the reality of all of our knowledge will be assured.[27]

Although Fichte followed Kant in spurning metaphysics, insisting that the very spirit of his philosophy was the limitation of knowledge to experience,[28] he never concealed the metaphysical dimensions of his principle of subject-object identity. These become apparent as soon as we raise the question "Who is the subjec subject-object identity?" It is clear that this subject cannot be the ordinary empirical or individual subject, a person like you or me, or like Jones, Bloggs, or Smith. Such a person does not know himself or herself in knowing empirical objects, which appear to be given and external. Indeed, it would be absurd to attribute to any individual or empirical subject the power to create all of his or her experience. Fichte is perfectly aware of this. He flatly rejects Berkeley's idealism, insisting that any successful idealism must explain the givenness and contingency of experience.[29] The subject of subject-object identity, Fichte maintains, is "the infinite" or "absolute" ego. This absolute ego, which comprises all of reality, creates its objects in the very act of knowing them. It is the divine intellect, the *intellectus archetypus* of Kant's third *Critique*.[30]

If the subject of subject-object identity is the absolute ego, it would seem as if Fichte is committed to an idealism where an absolute ego creates all of the reality of the external world. Then the finite ego's knowledge of an external object is really only its subconscious self-knowledge as an absolute ego. But this all-too-common picture of Fichte's idealism is a travesty, flying in the face of his strictures upon metaphysics. Fichte himself explicitly and emphatically rejected it.[31] Remaining true to the Kantian limits upon knowledge, Fichte insisted that the idea of the absolute ego should be read as a strictly regulative principle. We have no right to believe in the existence of the absolute ego, he argued, but we do have a duty to make it the goal of our moral action. According to Fichte, the idea of the absolute ego is not only a useful heuristic principle but is a necessary postulate of morality itself.[32] The moral law demands that we should become completely autonomous and independent agents, perfectly noumenal or intelligible beings subject to the laws of reason alone. We can fulfill this demand only if we gain complete control over nature, making it submit to our rational ends, for only then do we eliminate our sensible nature, which is subject to natural causes outside ourselves. Hence the moral demand for complete autonomy or independence requires that we strive to become like the absolute ego, a perfectly intelligible being that creates all of nature according to its reason.

True to his strictures against metaphysics, Fichte stressed that the absolute ego is a goal that we cannot realize. The finite ego cannot but ceasing to be finite and becoming God himself. the more the finite ego strives to gain control over g it conform to its rational ends, the more it *ap*-deal. Through its striving it can make the intelligible content perience increase as the sensible content decreases.

The underlying spirit of Fichte's 1794 *Wissenschaftslehre*, then, is profoundly pragmatic: knowledge is the result of action, not contemplation. We cannot refute the skeptic by theoretical reason, Fichte holds, because mere thinking cannot remove the subject-object dualism, which is the main obstacle to our knowledge. We can diminish this dualism and approach the subject-object identity required for knowledge, only by acting, only by striving to make nature conform to the demands of our reason. The only cure for skepticism is therefore action. Hence for Fichte, as for Marx after him, all the mysteries of transcendental philosophy are dissolved only in practice.

Such, in a nutshell, was the problem and doctrine of Fichte's 1794 *Wissenschaftslehre*, which became an inspiration for many thinkers in the mid-1790s. But sometime in late 1799 or early 1800, probably under the influence of their friend Hölderlin, Schelling and Hegel became dissatisfied with Fichte's solution to the problem of the Transcendental Deduction. The chief weakness of Fichte's solution, Schelling and Hegel argued, came from his giving the idea of the absolute a purely regulative status. If this idea is only a goal for action, and moreover a goal that we cannot ever attain, then how is empirical knowledge possible? It depends upon a condition that cannot be fulfilled, namely, subject-object identity. But the problem goes even deeper than this. It is not only that the process of striving cannot end; it cannot even begin. In other words, we cannot approach, let alone attain, the goal of subject-object identity. For if the finite ego and nature remain radically heterogeneous from one another – if the spontaneous activity of the ego is purely intellectual or noumenal and the sphere of nature is purely sensible or phenomenal – then the ego cannot even begin to act upon nature to bring it under its rational control. Hence Fichte's philosophy leaves the possibility of empirical knowledge hanging in the balance, still prey to skeptical objections.

We are now in a position to understand why Schelling and Hegel think we must give constitutive status to the idea of the absolute. If we give this idea a purely regulative status – if we assume that subject-object identity is only a goal for action – then we cannot explain the interaction between subject and object in our actual experience. We must assume, therefore, that subject-object identity exists, and moreover that it exists *within* the subject-object dualism we find in our experience. It is necessary to suppose, in other words, that when the finite ego knows an object that appears given and external to it, this is really only its subconscious self-knowledge as an absolute ego. This is the point behind Hegel's famous insistence that the absolute is not only subject-object identity but the identity of subject-object identity and subject-object non-identity. Only if subject-object identity exists within the subject-object dualism of our experience is it possible to explain the necessary conditions of empirical knowledge.

If we are to solve the problem of the Transcendental Deduction, Hegel argues in his *Difference,* then we must not only postulate the existence of subject-object identity. We must go a step further: we must conceive of subject-object identity along Schellingian lines. In other words, we must regard the absolute as a single infinite substance, whose nature consists in living force and whose attributes are the subjective and objective. The point of conceiving the absolute in this organic or vitalist manner, Hegel contends, is that only then will we be able to overcome Kant's disastrous dualisms. For if we conceive of all of nature as an organism, and the knowing subject as only part of it, then we can explain the interaction between subject and object. Rather than being heterogeneous substances or faculties, they will be only different degrees of organization and development of a single living force. The self-consciousness of the subject will be only the highest degree of organization and development of all the powers of nature, and inert matter will be only the lowest degree of organization and development of all the powers of the mind.

It should now be clear that Schelling's and Hegel's idea of the absolute was anything but an uncritical leap into metaphysics. Rather than ignoring the challenge of Kant's philosophy, their metaphysics was the only means to resolve its fundamental problem, namely, to explain how our *a priori* concepts apply to experience. Only if we remove Kant's strictures upon teleology, giving the idea of an organism a full constitutive validity, Hegel and Schelling argue, will we be able to surmount those Kantian dualisms that make it impossible to explain the possibility of knowledge. What this means, in more Kantian terms, is that we can provide a transcendental deduction of those metaphysical ideas. For we can show them to be not only useful fictions for systematizing our empirical knowledge but also necessary conditions for the possibility of experience itself.

It would be premature to conclude that Schelling and Hegel have completely satisfied the demands of Kantian criticism. Our fourth question still remains: How do we know the absolute? This question was especially pressing for Schelling and Hegel, who wished to avoid any relapse into the old metaphysical dogmatism. Like Kant and Fichte, they too insisted that we cannot have any knowledge beyond the limits of experience.[33] Nevertheless, they postulated the existence of the absolute, which is a necessary condition of our experience. How, then, does the necessary condition of our experience become the object of it? Who, indeed, has ever had an experience of themselves as an absolute ego? But if the idea of the absolute is not to be a transcendent hypostasis, then it is necessary to show, somehow, that it lies within our experience.

In the early 1800s Schelling developed an elaborate epistemology to justify and supply knowledge of the absolute. This was his theory of "philosophical construction" or "intellectual intuition." Acutely aware of Kant's challenge to metaphysics, Schelling had no wish to revive the old demonstrative methods of Leibnizian-Wolffian rationalism. Following Kant, he insisted that we cannot demonstrate the unconditioned through reasoning. He agreed with Kant that our *discursive* powers of conception, judgment, and demonstration cannot know the unconditioned, and that if they go beyond experience they will end in antinomies, amphibolies, and paralogisms. Nevertheless, Schelling refused to conclude that there could be no rational knowledge of the absolute. It is a mistake, he argued, to conceive of reason as a discursive power. Rather, it is a power of intellectual intuition or perception, which is distinct from both the empirical intuitions of sensibility and the discursive powers of the understanding. Such a power is not subject to Kant's strictures upon knowledge, Schelling argued, because these apply only to the discursive powers of the understanding when they attempt to go beyond the limits of experience. An intellectual intuition, however, is a kind of experience, a form of intuition or perception, so that it can provide the basis for a purely immanent metaphysics.

It is ironic that the inspiration for Schelling's theory of intellectual intuition came from Kant himself, and in particular from his theory of mathematical construction. In the *Critique of Pure Reason*, Kant argued that we demonstrate the truths of mathematical judgments by presenting them in intuition. For example, we show that two parallel lines do not intersect by drawing two equidistant lines on a chalk board. Schelling thought that this power of demonstrating mathematical truths revealed that we are in possession of a power of *a priori* intuition. Although Kant sharply distinguished between the methods of mathematics and philosophy, Schelling insisted upon extending the method of construction into philosophy itself. Accordingly, some of his major works of the 1800s proceed *more geometrico*, beginning with definitions and axioms and deriving theorems from them.

How, more precisely, does intellectual intuition give us knowledge of the absolute? Schelling sketched the mechanics of intellectual intuition in a work he wrote with Hegel in 1802, *Further Presentation of My System of Philosophy*.[34] We comprehend something through reason, Schelling wrote, when we see it in a whole. The task of philosophical construction is then to grasp the identity of each particular with the whole of all things. To gain such knowledge we should focus upon a thing by itself, apart from its relations to anything else; we should consider it as a single, unique whole, abstracting from all its properties, which are only its partial aspects, and which relate it to other things. Just as in mathematical construction we abstract from all the accidental features of a figure (it is written with chalk, it is on a blackboard) to see it as a perfect exemplar of some universal truth, so in philosophical construction we abstract from all the specific properties of an object to see it in the absolute whole. If we thus focus upon the object itself, abstracting from all its specific properties, we should also see its identity with the whole universe, for things differ from one another only through their properties.[35] Hence it is by perfectly grasping any particular thing that we arrive at a knowledge of the absolute, the whole in which all particular differences disappear.

In the early years of his collaboration with Schelling, Hegel too was a champion of intellectual intuition, which he saw as the indispensable organ of all philosophy. "Without transcendental intuition it is not possible to philosophize," he wrote in his *Difference*.[36]

Sometime in 1804, however, when Schelling left Jena, ending their collaboration, Hegel began to have serious doubts about intellectual intuition. It no longer seemed to provide an adequate foundation for knowledge of the absolute or a satisfactory response to the challenge of Kantian criticism. In some of the fragments Hegel wrote around this time,[37] and in some passages of the slightly later *Phenomenology of Spirit*,[38] Hegel came to several critical conclusions about intellectual intuition. First, the insights of intellectual intuition cannot be demonstrated against competing views. If the philosopher intuits his identity with all things, the man in the street sees them as external to himself. How, then, does the philosopher prove that his intellectual intuition is the correct vision of things? Second, we can identify the object of our intuition only by applying concepts to it, for it is only through concepts that we can determine what a thing is. Hence an intellectual intuition will be at best ineffable and at worst, empty. Third, the method of philosophical construction cannot explain the place of a particular in a whole because it abstracts from all its specific differences. The point, however, is to see how *these specific differences* are necessary to the whole and not to abstract from them, leaving the particulars outside the absolute. Fourth, an intellectual intuition is esoteric, the privilege of an elite few, whereas philosophy should be accessible to everyone.

Hegel's rejection of intellectual intuition made it imperative for him to find some discursive method by which to know the absolute. Only a conceptual and demonstrative knowledge would be exoteric, appealing to the intellect of everyone alike; and only it would be able to prove the philosopher's viewpoint against those of common sense. Yet this demand for a discursive knowledge of the absolute put Hegel at odds with Kant's critical strictures upon reason in the *Critique of Pure Reason*. Somehow, Hegel would have to show that, despite Kant's strictures, there can be a conceptual and demonstrative knowledge of the absolute. He would have to avoid the pitfalls of both intellectual intuition and the syllogistic method of the Leibnizian-Wolffian school.

Hegel's response to this challenge was his famous dialectic, which he began to sketch in the early 1800s, even during his collaboration with Schelling.[39] This dialectic is plain from Hegel's early plans for a "logic" that would demonstrate the viewpoint of absolute knowledge by beginning with the concepts of the understanding. This logic would show how the concepts of the understanding necessarily contradict themselves, and how their contradictions can be resolved only by seeing them as parts of a wider whole. More specifically, the dialectic would proceed through three stages. a) Some finite concept, true of only a limited part of reality, would go beyond its limits in attempting to know all of reality. It would claim to be an adequate concept to describe the absolute because, like the absolute, it has a complete or self-sufficient meaning independent of any other concept. b) This claim would come into conflict with the fact that the concept depends for its meaning on some other concept, having meaning only in contrast to its negation. There would then be a contradiction between its claim to independence and its *de facto* dependence upon another concept. c) The only way to resolve the contradiction would be to reinterpret the claim to independence, so that it applies not just to one concept to the exclusion of the other but to the whole of both concepts. Of course, the same stages could be repeated on a higher level, and so on, until we come to the complete *system* of all concepts, which is alone adequate to describe the absolute.

Although the early logic contained *en nuce* the germ of the dialectic, Hegel did not write his mature logic until after his Jena years. The plan for a dialectic leading to absolute knowledge was first completed in the *Phenomenology of Spirit*. The dialectic of the *Phenomenology* is different from that of the early logic, since it deals not with the concepts of the understanding but with the standpoints of consciousness. Nevertheless, the basic structure and purpose of the dialectic are the same. Hegel shows how the attempt by ordinary consciousness to know reality in itself ends in contradiction, and how this contradiction can be resolved only through rising to a more inclusive standpoint. The dialectic of ordinary consciousness consists in its *self*-examination, the comparison of its actual knowing with its own standard of knowledge. This self-examination essentially consists in two tests: the claim of ordinary consciousness to know reality itself is tested against its own standard of knowledge; this standard of knowledge is itself tested against its own experience. The dialectic continues until a standard of knowledge is found that is adequate to the experience of consciousness. This standard is, of course, that of subject-object identity itself.

It is especially in the *Phenomenology* that we find Hegel's attempt to legitimate metaphysics before the challenge of Kantian criticism. What Hegel attempts to provide in this work is nothing less than "a transcendental deduction" of absolute knowledge. Just as Kant attempted to provide a transcendental deduction of the concepts of the understanding by showing them to be necessary conditions of possible experience, so Hegel attempts to do the same for absolute knowledge. It is indeed striking that Hegel refers to his dialectic as "the experience of consciousness" and that he calls his phenomenology "the science of the experience of consciousness."⁴⁰ This was Hegel's way of meeting the critical challenge on Kant's own terms. The aim of the *Phenomenology* was to show the possibility, indeed the necessity, of a strictly immanent metaphysics based upon experience alone.

Of course, it was one thing for Hegel to sketch the plan for his dialectic and another for him to execute it. Surely, the Hegelian dialectic makes demands of a tall order, which perhaps can never be fulfilled. Yet there can be no doubt that the dialectic presented an original and ingenious solution to the problem facing Hegel: how to legitimate metaphysics in the face of the Kantian critique of knowledge. Even if Hegel's dialectic fails, we cannot accuse him of an uncritical indulgence in metaphysics. It should be clear by now that this would be only to beg important philosophical questions.

The essays in this volume attempt to introduce the modern student to the central topics and issues of Hegel's philosophy. They cover the whole range of his philosophy, his contributions to logic, epistemology, ethics, aesthetics, religion, and history. They also consider Hegel's historical significance, particularly the development of Hegelianism in the early nineteenth century, the influence of Hegel on Marx, and the problematic legacy of Hegel for analytic philosophy.

The first article, "Hegel's Intellectual Development" by H.S. Harris, introduces Hegel and places him in his historical context by providing a survey of his most formative period, the years in Tübingen and Jena before the publication of the *Phenomenology of Spirit* in 1806.

Five of the essays treat some of the classical problems in the interpretation of Hegel. The essay by Robert Pippin considers the question of the coherence of Hegel's *Phenomenology*. Ever since its publication, the structure of this work has been the source of puzzlement, since it divides into epistemological and historical halves, which have no apparent connection with one another. Pippin argues that the connecting link between these halves is provided by Hegel's attempt to provide a theory of social subjectivity.

The essay by John Burbidge discusses the problematic status of Hegel's logic. Is Hegel's logic a metaphysics, a transcendental system of categories, or a traditional formal logic? Burbidge contends that all these characterizations are partially correct, and that the guiding thread behind every aspect of Hegel's logic is his attempt to provide a general theory of reasoning about reasoning.

Tom Wartenberg deals with the troublesome question of Hegel's idealism, the precise characterization of which has created much dispute. Hegel's idealism has been described as the doctrine that "only minds and mental events exist" (Russell), but it has also been claimed that Hegel's philosophy is not idealism at all but a form of materialism (Lukács). Wartenberg maintains that there is a clear sense in which Hegel's philosophy is idealist, although not in the Berkelian or Kantian mould. Rather, Hegel's idealism is a form of conceptualism in that Hegel thinks that concepts determine the basic structure of reality.

Michael Forster examines perhaps the most controversial aspect of Hegel's thought, his dialectical method. Some scholars have denied that Hegel has such a method, while others dismiss it for committing elementary logical blunders. Forster argues that Hegel has, indeed, such a method, that it is not guilty of any simple fallacies, and that it plays several important roles in Hegel's thought.

Kenneth Westphal, while providing a general introduction to the structure of Hegel's *Philosophy of Right,* investigates Hegel's political views. Ever since the division of the Hegelian school into a left and a right wing, Hegel's philosophy has been seen as both radical and reactionary. By examining Hegel in his historical context, Westphal finds that it is more accurate to view Hegel as a liberal reformer who was anxious to steer a middle path between the extremes of revolution and reaction.

Another four essays discuss some central but less controversial aspects of Hegel's philosophy. Allen Wood analyzes Hegel's ethical theory, which he regards as neither teleological nor de-ontological, but as a theory about the conditions of self-actualization. Robert Wicks surveys Hegel's aesthetics, outlining Hegel's account of art history, his organization of the arts, his analysis of beauty, and his "end of art" thesis. Laurence Dickey attempts to explain the historical significance of Hegel's philosophy of religion by locating it in the context of his Berlin period (1818–1831). Only by placing Hegel's philosophy of religion in such a context, Dickey argues, can we determine what is characteristic of Hegel's position and rescue him from some of the stereotypes foisted upon him by his contemporaries. Finally, my own essay considers Hegel's historicism, the central role it plays in his philosophy, and the method, metaphysics, and politics behind it.

The last four essays consider either Hegel's historical influence or his problematic relation to other philosophers. Paul Guyer examines Hegel's polemic against Kant, arguing that it usually misses its target while obscuring their more important philosophical differences. Allen Wood considers Hegel's influence upon Marxism by focusing on the close affinities in their social and political theories. Investigating the question of Hegel's relationship to analytic philosophy, Peter Hylton concludes that Russell and Moore were reacting more to the legacy of Kant than Hegel. Finally, John Toews provides a general survey of the development of Hegelianism in Germany from 1805 to 1846.

If there is a common conviction behind all these articles, it is that Hegel's philosophy is important, both philosophically and historically, but that we still have a long way to go in appropriating the Hegelian legacy.

I wish to thank Allen Wood, Paul Guyer, Kenneth Westphal, Raymond Geuss, and Michael Hardimon for their advice in preparing this volume.

NOTES

1 Bertrand Russell, *Our Knowledge of the External World* (London: Unwin, 1914), 48–49 n. Cf. *History of Western Philosophy* (London: Unwin, 1961), 713–15.
2 See especially Klaus Hartmann's "Hegel: A Non-Metaphysical View" in *Hegel: A Collection of Critical Essays,* ed. Alasdair MacIntyre (Garden City, N.Y.: Doubleday, 1972), 101–24. A similar approach is followed by Alan White, *Absolute Knowledge: Hegel and the Problem of Metaphysics* (Athens: Ohio University Press, 1983), and by Terry Pinkard, *Hegel's Dialectic: The Explanation of Possibility* (Philadelphia: Temple University Press, 1988).

3 See, for example, Hegel's characterization of metaphysics in the *Enzyklopädie, Werke*, ed. E. Moldenahuer and K. Michel (Frankfurt: Suhrkamp, 1969–72), VIII, 93–106, §26–36.

4 See Hegel's essay "Wer denkt abstrakt," *Werke* II, 575. Cf. *Wissenschaft der Logik* V, 419.

5 See Hegel's *Differenz des Fichte'schen und Schelling'schen Systems der Philosophie, Werke* II, 25.

6 See *Critique of Pure Reason*, B 366–96, esp. B 395.

7 See Schelling, *Werke*, ed. Manfred Schröter (Munich: Beck'sche Verlag, 1927), III, 11; IV, 98, 115; *Ergänzungsband* II, 78, 128.

8 Spinoza, *Ethics*, Part I, def. 3.

9 Schelling, *Werke* III, 25, 32.

10 Hegel, *Werke* XX, 165.

11 This warning is especially apparent in the early writings of Schelling. See his *Vom Ich als Prinzip der Philosophie, Werke* I, 105, 130, and 167. One of the targets of Schelling's *Briefe über Dogmatismus und Kriticismus* is the attempt to justify belief in the existence of God as a regulative idea. See *Werke* I, 208–16. In his *Enzyklopädie* Hegel would later argue that the Kantian thing-in-itself is only the hypostasis of the abstract idea of pure being. See *Werke* VIII, 120–21, §44.

12 On Schelling's naturalism, see his *Erster Entwurf eines Systems der Naturphilosophie, Werke* II, 180. On Hegel's naturalism, see his statement that reason explains things according to their immanent necessity. *Enzyklopädie* VIII, 41, §1, and IX, 15, §246.

13 See Herder's *Gott, Einige Gespräche*, in Herder, *Sämtliche Werke*, ed. B. Suphan (Berlin: Weidmann, 1881–1913), XVI, 451–52. The young Schelling was an avid reader of Herder.

14 The essential works for Schelling's *Naturphilosophie* are his *Ideen zu einer Philosophie der Natur* (1797), *Von der Weltseele* (1798), and *Erster Entwurf eines Systems der Naturphilosophie* (1799).

15 See Schelling, *Presentation of My System*, §16, 33; *Werke* III, 17, 25–26; *Bruno, Werke* III, 140, 194; *Philosophy and Religion, Werke* IV, 25.

16 See *Bruno, Werke* III, 131–32; and *Jahrbücher, Werke* IV, 88.

17 On Hegel's relationship to Schelling in this respect, see the essay by H.S. Harris, Chapter 1, pp. 40–41, 42, 44, 45–46.

18 This is a pitfall of the approach developed by Hartmann and others. Seeing Hegel's philosophy as a form of categorial analysis does not explain the importance he or Schelling gave to *Naturphilosophie*, however respectable it might make them appear from a more contemporary perspective.

19 On this tradition, see Margaret C. Jacob, *The Radical Enlightenment: Pantheists, Freemasons and Republicans* (London: George, Allen & Unwin, 1981).

20 The *locus classicus* for this view of matter was John Toland's *Letters to Serena* (London: Lintot, 1704), pp. 163–239.

21 For some of these early reactions to Hegel, see Shlomo Avineri's article "Hegel Revisited" in *Hegel: A Collection of Critical Essays* (Garden City, N.Y.: Anchor, 1972), pp. 329–48, esp. 335, 337, 338, 339–40.

22 See Klaus Düsing, "Spekulation und Reflexion: Zur Zusammenarbeit Schellings und Hegels in Jena," *Hegel Studien* V (1969), 95–128.

23 The fundamental works of this phase of Fichte's thought are the *Grundlage der gesammten Wissenschaftslehre (Doctrine of Science)* trans. P. Heath and J. Lachs, (Cambridge: Cambridge University Press, 1981), *Über den Begriff der Wissenschaftslehre, Grundriß des Eigenthümlichen der Wissenschaftslehre* and *Vorlesungen über die Bestimmung des Gelehrten* (all translated by Daniel Breazeale in *Fichte: Early Philosophical Writings* (Ithaca, N.Y.: Cornell University Press, 1988).

24 See Maimon, *Versuch über die Transcendentalphilosophie, Gesammelte Werke*, ed. V. Verra (Hildesheim: Olms, 1965) II, 62–65, 182–83, 362–64.

25 See *Critique of Pure Reason* A xvii.

26 See Fichte, *Werke* IV, 1–2.

27 See Schelling, *Erläuterung des Idealismus der Wissenschaftslehre, Werke* I, 366.

28 See Fichte, *Werke* II, 333.

29 See Fichte, *Werke* I, 423, 438.

30 Kant, *Critique of Judgement* §76–77.

31 Fichte, *Werke* I, 270, 252–54, 277.

32 Fichte, *Werke* VI, 293–301.

33 Note, for example, Hegel's statement from the preface of the Phenomenology: "Consciousness knows and conceives nothing but what is in its experience.". *Werke* III, 38.

34 See Schelling, *Werke Ergänzungsband* I, 391–424.

35 Schelling adheres to Leibniz's principle of the identity of indiscernibles, according to which one thing differs from one another only in virtue of its properties. See his *Jahrbücher, Werke* IV, 114, 122.

36 Hegel *Werke* II, 42.

37 See, for example, the fragment "Anmerkung: Die Philosophie . . ." in *Jenaer Realphilosophie I: Die Vorlesungen 1803/04*, ed. J. Hoffmeister (Leipzig: Meiner, 1932), pp. 265–66, where Hegel anticipates the conclusions of the introduction to the *Phenomenology*. See also Hegel's *Wastebook, Werke* II, 543, 545, 548–49, 554, 559, 561.

38 Hegel *Werke* III, 20, 22, 71.

39 On the origins of Hegel's dialectic, see the essay by Michael Forster, in this volume.

40 Hegel *Werke* III, 80.

1 Hegel's intellectual development to 1807

Georg Wilhelm Friedrich Hegel was born in Stuttgart on 27 August 1770. He was the eldest son of a senior financial official in the administration of the duchy of Württemberg; the family belonged to the "notables" of the duchy. He was a serious and clever child. His mother (who gave him Latin lessons before he went to school) may have hoped he was destined for the Church; his father probably hoped for a successor in the civil service.

By the time his mother died in September 1783, Hegel was keeping a diary full of academic matters in which he practiced his Latin. He was first in his class every year at the Stuttgart Gymnasium. At about the time that he passed to the upper school (autumn 1784), Hegel began to organize his own private studies "encyclopaedically." He copied out long excerpts from the books that he read under headings and subheadings, which indicate a Baconian ambition to organize all knowledge under its proper "science." He continued this habit until after he entered the Theological Institute at Tübingen in October 1788. He never lost the habit of reading with pen in hand, and we have "excerpts" from all periods of his life; but at Tübingen he stopped writing his classificatory headings at the top of the page. Since he kept his schoolboy collection all his life, his biographer, Rosenkranz, was able to describe it in some detail. A small part of it survived and was printed by Gustav Thaulow in 1854 (see *Dok* . . . , pp. 54–166).[1]

When Hegel entered the seminary in October 1788, he was a typical product of the German Enlightenment – an enthusiastic reader of Rousseau and Lessing, acquainted with Kant (at least at second hand), but perhaps more deeply devoted to the classics than to anything modern. It is probable that he had already decided that he did

25

not want to enter the Church. (He had entered the seminary because he was eligible for a free education there as a stipendiary of the duke, and he signed an "obligation" to serve the duchy in the Church or the school system as directed by the Stuttgart Consistory.)

At Tübingen four students from the Stuttgart Gymnasium joined a class from the "cloister-schools" of the duchy who had already been under this same "obligation" for years. After the entrance examination, the two best students from the gymnasium, Hegel and Märklin, were placed in the ranking of the class just above Hölderlin. That was not pleasing to Hölderlin, but Hegel soon shared his grievance when, soon afterward, he and Märklin switched places and Hegel, who had been first for years, was placed second behind someone from his own school. C.P.F. Leutwein, the top student of the previous year, shared a study-room with Hegel in 1789–90. Leutwein later wrote that the "lasting wound" inflicted by this reversal was the original source of Hegel's academic ambitions in later years.[2] That is absurd. But the way Leutwein's recollection of the event does suggest that Hegel may have let everyone (including his teachers) know that his ambitions were not ecclesiastical. (Märklin came from a family of churchmen, and he eventually became a prelate.) When Hegel was (as he saw it) "punished" by his lowered ranking, he probably made a marked display of increased attention to the studies that he preferred. What he wanted to do was to leave the seminary and study law, which his father would not allow. Certainly the desire to escape from the Church formed an early bond between Hegel and Hölderlin.

The outbreak of the French Revolution caused great excitement in the seminary; the students took sides, calling themselves "royalists" or "patriots." We have reports that Hegel was both an impassioned and an effective orator in the "patriotic" cause. This is slightly surprising, because he was already known as a rather inadequate preacher, and he was never a good lecturer later. But in his writings we notice the same paradox: a vein of eloquence that breaks out when he is not hamstrung by his driving desire to articulate the necessity of some logical transition. Apparently the "glorious dawn" (as he called it later) loosed his tongue completely; he celebrated Bastille Day all his life.

One of the most prominent "patriots" in the seminary was the young Schelling, who had arrived in 1790 as the fifteen-year-old head of that year's class. In 1792 when the "patriots" held a concert and sang the Marseillaise, the duke's wrath fell upon Schelling, the German translator of that subversive anthem. Revolutionary sympathy seems to have been the first bond between Schelling and Hegel; certainly pure philosophy was not. For in later years when the bond had ruptured, when Hegel was famous, and Schelling had been overshadowed, he spoke of Hegel at the seminary in a way that fully confirms Leutwein's contention that Hegel was an "eclectic" who cared little for the new idealism of Kant, Reinhold, and Fichte.[3]

This is perhaps an appropriate juncture to note the nonphilosophical aspects of Hegel's scholarly eclecticism. His sister recorded his youthful joy in "physics" and his study of botany (as well as Sophocles) when he was at home on sick leave from the seminary. He followed an anatomy course in Tübingen, and he learned French and English there (although he probably began his study of modern languages during his school years in Stuttgart).[4]

But it was philosophical, religious, and moral studies that brought the students together. The seminary was quite a small community. Study groups pursued different interests, and the groups overlapped in various ways. The best students knew one another – and one another's interests – well. Leutwein could remember nearly fifty years later who the real 'Kantians' were. He did not include Hölderlin, and he explicitly excluded Hegel. Yet Hölderlin studied "Kant and the Greeks" obsessively, and although Hegel preferred Rousseau and Lessing, he studied Kant also. But the Greeks – especially Plato – came first with both of them.[5] The center of the radical Kantian group was a *Repetent* (i.e., a teaching assistant) named Karl Immanuel Diez. In opposition to the Professor of Theology G.C. Storr (who sought to use Kant's critical skepticism to make room for faith of a quite irrational kind), Diez exalted Kant as "the true Messiah" and regarded Jesus as the "betrayer" of pure reason.[6] Hegel and Hölderlin were not "Kantians" by Diez's standard, but they were serious students of Kant.

Hegel, Hölderlin, and other friends studied Jacobi's *Letters on Spinoza* (and other works) together, probably in 1790. As far as we know, this was when Hegel's lifelong fascination with Spinoza began and when Hölderlin adopted the *hen kai pan* (One and all) of Lessing's reported Spinozism as his "symbol." Hegel would certainly have read Herder's *God* at about this time. Probably he had already been reading Herder for some time, although the evidence for this claim is sparse.[7] The "identity" of rational necessity with rational freedom made quite a different impression on Hegel and Hölderlin than it did on Jacobi, and "pantheism" was for them a very different thing from "atheism." But the encounter with Jacobi's own doctrine of natural faith as the only answer to all the inevitable contradictions of the finite intellect proved to be of lifelong significance for Hegel.

Hegel's interest at this stage was focused on the problem of bringing the religious tradition of his culture to life. His inspiration came from Rousseau, whose Savoyard vicar taught that only the commitment of our hearts is truly free; from Lessing's *Nathan*, where "the spirit" and "the letter" were starkly opposed and a universal harmony of spirits was projected; but above all from his beloved Greeks, who had shown how reason and desire, religion and politics could be harmonized in actual social life. There was personal tragedy in the center of their picture but no thought of a necessary recompense for it in a life after death. Those who die in the cause of freedom cannot rationally ask for a better fate. They "live in the *Volk*" (as Hegel would say in 1802), and their immortality is in the memory preserved by the poets.

The anticipation of things that Hegel would say only ten years later helps us to understand the first essay that he wrote in 1793. In the "Tübingen fragment" (*G.W.* I.83–114; *T.W-A.* I. 9–44; *Sunlight*, pp. 481–504), all the influences mentioned above, (and some others, such as a Johannine mystical theology of the Logos which was shared by many of the pious patriots in the *Stift*)[8] can be observed mingling in a loose harmony, which required the surrender of all rigorism. Thus, the latest and newest influences detectable here are those of Kant's *Religion* and Fichte's *Critique of All Revelation*. Hegel's Kantian studies and discussions led him to admit both that "love is a pathological motive for action" and that "Empirismus is worth nothing at all in the establishment of principles." Yet "love is the fundamental principle of the empirical character" and "has something analogous to Reason in it." By "love" Hegel means not "refined self-love" but a commitment that loses itself in the "other" that is loved. This makes love the general name for all the feelings that can "come under the influence of Reason" (*G.W.* I, 100, 13–101. 20; *T.W-A.*, I, 29–30; *Sunlight*, p. 496). As Hegel understood it in

these early years, Reason was certainly a "principle of command."
But "Religion," with which all of Hegel's earliest manuscripts are
concerned, was a principle of persuasion. It seeks out and harnesses
every impulse that supports Reason, so that our inclinations harmonize with Reason and the imperative aspect of Reason disappears
from view.

Religion itself cannot exercise a commanding function without
becoming an external, or positive, authority. This externalization is
the death of true Religion, which knows no authority except the
internal command of our own Reason. The Lutheran Christianity of
the *Stift* was dissociated into a positive external authority, on the
one hand, and a purely private, emotional organizing power on the
other. It must be reintegrated into a public-spirited educational
power. The great advantage of Christianity was that, unlike the public religion of the Greeks, it was a religion of universal love and
brotherhood. In this sense, its doctrines were already "grounded on
universal Reason." If the principle of love is what appears, while
Reason remains the ground behind it, there is no need for "fancy,
heart and sensibility to go empty away" (*G.W.* I, 103, 19; *T.W-A.* I,
33; *Sunlight*, p. 499). The presiding spirit of this accommodation
between the sensible and the supersensible was Lessing's Nathan,
who tells the Friar, "What makes me to you a Christian, makes you
to me a Jew."[9] The universal Church of Reason becomes an "invisible Church" that is present in this world as a harmony of mutual
toleration. That we should all love one another in this sense is the
truly categorical imperative of Reason. What remains unclear is just
how "all the needs of life – the public affairs of the State" can be tied
in with this new religion (*G.W.* I, 103, 20–21; *T.W-A.* I, 33; *Sunlight*,
p. 499).

Lessing's opposition between the spirit and the letter is also the
key to Hegel's "harmony of the Gospels" (which we generally call
the "Life of Jesus"). There has been a general tendency to view this
essay as a "Kantian experiment," because the first formula of the
Categorical Imperative is firmly thrust into the place of the Golden
Rule (*G.W.* I, 221, 3–5 and Apparatus; Fuss and Dobbins, pp. 115–
16). But this is a mistake. That amendment was a deliberate updat-
ing of the "grounding of Religion in universal Reason." But if we
recall the militant practical rationalism of the "Kantian enragé"
Karl Diez, we can see at once that Hegel only wants to *harmonize*

the Gospel of Jesus with Kant. Hegel's Jesus is still the prophet of universal *love*. His mission is here presented as a campaign against what is called "fetish-faith" in the Tübingen fragment. He begins by setting aside the temptation to be a wonder-worker (Storr's Jesus). But his "brotherly love and forgiveness" is higher than the simple law-abiding spirit either of positive or of moral righteousness (the Kant of Diez). This is evident, even though the categorical imperative is called "the sum and substance of all moral legislation and of the sacred books of all peoples" and the precept "Love your enemies" is moderated into "If you cannot love your enemies, at least respect the humanity in them" (*G.W.* I, 217, 13–15; Fuss and Dobbins, p. 112). The fact that loving forgiveness is a higher attitude is clearly implied here by the concessive "at least." Once we grant that Hegel is defending Jesus against Diez, we can clearly see that the gospel of life as love (which Hegel developed three years later at Frankfurt) was already implicit in the climactic account of the Crucifixion in the essay of 1795. The "Pure Reason transcending all limits" that "is divinity itself" was never Kant's "pure Reason" (*G.W.* I, 207, 1; Fuss and Dobbins, p. 104).

Hegel went straight on from the rational justification of the Gospel to the question of how it had become the foundation for a "positive religion" (i.e., a faith that accepts the revelation of an external "law of God" and attaches itself to external fetishes of all kinds). The authority of Jesus as a new lawgiver originated (Hegel decided) in his being taken by his first followers as the Messiah – the "King of the Jews," as Pilate expressed it. This was completely contrary to Jesus' own gospel; but even when He was alive, He could not escape from the conceptual net of the Jewish tradition, and the dead Savior became the supreme fetish of the new faith.

The problem of why the world needed, and was willing to accept, this new fetish-faith had already engaged Hegel's attention. The triumph of positive Christianity came "once the Romans had lost their public virtue and their Empire was in decline" (*G.W.* I, 164, 1–3; *T.W-A.* I, 100; Fuss and Dobbins, p. 102). We can recognize here the influence of Gibbon (whom Hegel was reading in 1794). Eventually this answer to the problem of why "the imaginative religion of the Greeks" gave way to "the positive religion of the Christians"[10] develops into the *Gestalten* of the "Unhappy Consciousness" and "the World of *Bildung*" in the *Phenomenology*.

The "Positivity" essay was directed toward a genetic understanding of the sectarian and authoritarian Protestant church in which Hegel had been brought up. The "Kantian revolution" from which (like his less-eclectic friends) Hegel expected great things, represented the dawn of a new age. The Kantian "objectivity" of autonomous moral Reason must be put in the place of the ordinary objectivity of a positive law.[11]

This contrast between ordinary objectivity and objective validity as recognized by the subjective reason was of lifelong importance for Hegel. The development of a comprehensive theory of objectivity in which they are effectively reconciled is one of the best ways to characterize his mature system. But at this point, the acceptance of the Kantian view of Reason's objectivity was only the explicit recognition of an unsolved problem. The autonomy of Kantian reason is expressed in the subject's moral legislation for him or herself. The sovereignty of Reason, which the Greeks had intuitively recognized in imaginative form, had nothing to do with subjective legislation on the model of the Understanding. The Greeks were not "moral" in the modern way at all, so the restoration of Greek *Sittlichkeit* as a harmony of desire and self-assertion under the guidance of Reason was not the same as "respect for the moral law."

The battle for the soul of "Reason" between rational morality and imaginative freedom was about to be joined. In the first round the Greeks were bound to win, because the "stable man of understanding" (as Hölderlin called Hegel)[12] was about to rejoin his romantically inspired friend. In Switzerland (to which he went from Tübingen in 1793), Hegel pursued several lines of research that supported the cause of objectivity and his own interest in the positive sciences. (Only in his theory of religion and morals is "positivity" a "negative" concept.) He acquired a copy of Smith's *Wealth of Nations* (in English), enjoyed steady access to a library full of the masterworks of the Enlightenment, studied the financial system of the Berne administration (like a good son of his father), read Spinoza's *Tractatus Theologico-Politicus*, and translated the *Confidential Letters* of J.J. Cart with his own notes.[13] But from June 1796, when he knew that Hölderlin, already established in Frankfurt, was seeking a position for him there, the Greek ideal again dominated his thoughts. His essay on the differing religious imagination of the modern Germans and the ancient Greeks makes a passing reference to the way that even the slaves shared in the ancient city's cultural life. Like every revolutionary republican, Hegel regarded serfdom as an affront to the "dignity of man", so there is an implicit admission here that moral autonomy represents an advance over imaginative freedom (see *G.W.* I, 361, 15–21; *T.W-A.* I, 199; Knox, pp. 147–48). But the mystical reminiscence that dominates his *Eleusis* poem of August 1796 (*G.W.* I, 399–402; *Briefe* I, 38–40; Butler and Seiler, pp. 46–47) hails the presiding genius of the seven years that follow.

All of Hegel's work before the end of 1796 should be interpreted in terms of the rational canons laid down in the Tübingen essay. The ideal is a Platonic one, in which all aspects of human nature are harmonized under the control of Reason. In the celebrated fragment known as the "System-Programme" we are offered a new model, which is not so much different as clearer. Now the practical Reason of Kant and Fichte is made the critical preamble for an explicitly aesthetic religious ideal. Critical ethics, organized as a system of practical postulates, is to be applied to the politics of the modern nation-state regarded as an organic system of "estates." Then, on the basis of a new scientific "history of mankind," it will be shown that the problem of the present is the founding of a religion of freedom based on a "mythology of Reason." This theory goes in a circle, since the poetic mythology leads the popular consciousness toward the critical insight of the philosopher. So the primacy of philosophical Reason is not really upset (*Mythologie,* pp. 11–14; *T.W-A.* I, 234–36; *Sunlight,* pp. 510–12).[14]

As soon as Hegel arrived in Frankfurt, the peaceful evolution of the Tübingen canons in his "understanding" was radically disturbed. Hölderlin was already working with an "Identity" theory in which actuality was necessarily prior to possibility. The actual experience of "being" – the original unity of Subject and Object – is an intuition of the divine life that is enjoyed by the poet. The critical philosophy of a moral harmony that *ought* to exist (and hence must, at least, be "possible") can never be more than a reflective imitation of this actual intuition.[15] Hegel began, at once, to conceptualize both the "history of mankind" and the founding of his new "religion of freedom" in terms of this "philosophy of identity."[16]

As far as we can tell, the problem of the "forms of Union" in different cultures (especially biblical Judaism at different stages, archaic and classical Greece, medieval Germany, modern England, France, Germany, and Italy) dominated Hegel's thoughts until early 1800. The evidence is to be found not only in the datable manuscripts (where Judaism and primitive Christianity predominate, together with a few "theoretical" fragments) but also in the "fragments of historical studies" preserved by Rosenkranz, and in some lost studies of which he gives short reports.[17] We should understand that Hegel's interest in theology was always cultural rather than religious, and historical rather than dogmatic. When he turns his attention to Kant's *Metaphysics of Ethics* or Steuart's *Principles of Political Economy*, he is still concerned with the "form of union and division" in modern society.[18] The writing of a pamphlet on the Württemberg estates in 1798 probably was an interruption in the orderly progress of Hegel's studies caused by a practical political urgency of the moment. But the project for an essay on the "Constitution of Germany," although its inception at the end of 1798 was certainly stimulated by the Congress of Rastatt, was a natural fulfilment of one part of the project conceived more than five years earlier.

The founding of a new religion, Hegel argued theoretically in 1797, requires that "love" should be "made into an objective essence (*Wesen*) by the imagination," an "essence in which subject and object, freedom and nature, the actual and the potential, are united" (Hamacher, pp. 357–58; *T.W-A.* I, 242; *Clio*, VIII, 1979, pp. 260–61). His main project for the next year seems to have been to show how Jesus sought to do this in the context of the Jewish tradition. Abraham and Moses had bequeathed a "positive" religion, a religion of authority and law; and Kant and Fichte had only *internalized* the division between divine authority and finite sensibility that positive Christianity had inherited from that tradition. But Jesus had sought to create a new life in opposition to the whole positive (or divided) consciousness of the Infinite. He was "opposed to opposition." His love was not self-love – the desire for mastery and control – but a sense of unity with all life and with God, the "Father" of all life. The Johannine theology of the *Logos* here coalesces with the romantic pantheism of the *Hen kai pan* in a "union" that probably dates back to the Tübingen years. But now it is successfully conceptualized, and the figure of Jesus becomes the individuated *Gestalt* of this perfect *plerosis*, this "fulfilment" of the reflective ideal.

But in order to achieve this *plerosis*, Jesus was obliged to fly from the actual world and so to do violence to the integrity of life by refusing to live a natural life in order to preserve his unity with God. Thus he became a "beautiful soul" and the guilt of his "innocence" – the guilt of what he did not do – was as great as the guilt incurred by Oedipus for what he did do (*T.W-A*. I, 346–52; Knox, pp. 232–37; the comparison with Oedipus is mine). Against everyone (or every culture) that violates the integrity of life, the injured life rises as a "fate." Jesus, who preached forgiveness as the path of reconciliation with life, accepted and forgave his own fate. But the degeneration of his gospel into "positivity" was as natural and inevitable upon this view of it as upon the earlier one. So it is easy to see why Hegel could eventually turn back to the "Positivity" essay and find it necessary to revise only the first few pages (September 1800).

Reflection on the "fate" of Jesus, and on the inevitability of the positive aspects of the life from which he fled, caused Hegel to return to his "Spirit of Christianity" manuscript more than a year later with a new concept of *plerosis* that was better articulated. He had studied Kant's *Metaphysics of Ethics* before he began the first draft. Now he studied Steuart's *Principles* (and perhaps did some other "modern" studies) before he returned to Jesus and the Jews. The communism of the primitive Church he recognized as an impossible ideal. The "fate" of property – even though it introduced "division" into life – was one that could not be overcome. So in the revised version of his "Spirit of Christianity," the only version for which we have a printed text, Hegel developed and used the complex dialectical concept of an "infinite life" that does not just drown all memory of "division" but is reconciled with the necessity of finitude, and preserves the divisions *sublated* within itself. Hegel's mature conception of *Aufhebung* is visible for the first time in the revised version of the famous fragment on "Love."[19] (This is a "theoretical" fragment, but the fact that it was revised suggests that it belonged with "The Spirit of Christianity" in Hegel's plan. So it was not a merely *historical* study that he was preparing.)

The "infinite life" thus became the "Union of union and nonunion" which we meet in the so-called "System Fragment" of 1800. Most of this manuscript is lost, and we can only guess at what it contained. Almost certainly it was, in part, a theoretical treatise on the finite and the infinite, on philosophical "reflection" about "possibility" and religious "union" in actual experience; and quite certainly it ended with a sketch for the new "religion of freedom."[20] What else was in it we do not know, but we can be fairly sure that it did not contain "logic and metaphysics" (as some scholars have suggested). When he moved to Jena, Hegel's mind was fully occupied with the political aspect of his project, although he had begun to feel that it needed a "systematic" (i.e. a philosophical) form – as he says in his letter to Schelling of November 2, 1800.

At the beginning of 1799, Hegel's father died; within three months Hegel was in possession of a modest inheritance. He seems to have enjoyed some leisure in 1800; it may have been then that he occupied himself seriously with the philosophy of nature (or it may have been earlier, since he speaks of "giving wings to our physics" in the System Programme).[21] He certainly kept up with Schelling's publications, and he probably had the preliminary German version of his dissertation "On the Orbits of the Planets" in his papers when he moved to Jena.

In Jena he continued for some months to work on his "German Constitution" essay. But Schelling probably urged him into philosophical activity of a more academic type, and in a couple of months he produced his work *Difference between Fichte and Schelling* (July 1801). That essay demonstrated publicly his deep interest in the logical problems of post-Kantian idealism. So it was natural for Schelling (supported by some of his students) to suggest that Hegel should teach the "Logic and Metaphysics" of the new "Identity-Philosophy."[22]

Getting Hegel a licence to teach at Jena was slightly more difficult than expected because some of the faculty resented the 'Swabian invasion." The Latin dissertation had to be produced in a great hurry, and with the help of Schelling and some of his close friends, Hegel's university career began. It did not go well because he was a poor lecturer. Some courses that he announced did not take place; others – like the first "Logic" course – came to a rapid end because most of the small group of enrolled students defected.[23] After the *Difference* essay, Hegel's main impact in his first two and a half years at Jena was achieved anonymously with the *Critical Journal* – which everyone received as Schelling's voice, although Hegel wrote most of it.

In Hegel's own view, the one true philosophy is perennially present, and it had just been reborn from Kant's "deduction of the categories" in the speculative idealism of Fichte and Schelling. Speculation takes shape as a different "Identity" in different ages, because the culture of every age is dominated by a different antithesis of "division." The opposition that must be overcome is Kant's contrast between the noumenal and the phenomenal worlds, the antithesis between the Absolute and its "appearance." In Kant's practical philosophy, this takes the more traditional form of a contrast between "faith" and "knowledge." The Enlightenment destroyed the older "positive" faith, but Kant and Fichte resurrected it in a "rational" form. Fichte's "science of knowledge" overcame the dichotomy of finite and infinite theoretically (or "subjectively"), and his practical philosophy was the properly systematic shape of Kant's own moral theory (Faith and Knowledge, G.W. IV, 338; T.W-A. II, 321; Cerf and Harris, p. 85). Only a new philosophy of nature, like that which Schelling was constructing, could overcome the noumenal/phenomenal division properly. The Absolute must be comprehended as "life" – the "Identity of identity and nonidentity" (Differenz. G.W. IV, 64, 14; T.W-A, II, 96; Harris and Cerf, p. 156). This comprehension is a form of cognition – Spinoza's "intuitive science" – in which the forms of finite cognition are preserved through their connectedness in the Absolute. Critical logic drowns all of the intellectual categories in the Absolute, but Metaphysics resurrects them again in their absolute context.[24]

Kant's productive imagination is the primitive form of the "speculative Idea," and the "deduction of the categories" is a reflective "imitation" of the Identity of Reason. Hegel's "Transcendental Logic" (which is all that he produced for his first course) has now shown us how to connect the scattered comments in his critical essays. Reflective Understanding gives us the logic of inorganic nature; speculative logic reveals "God or Nature" as a living organism.[25]

The long critical review of Schulze reveals another important influence on Hegel's logic and metaphysics: the ancient Skeptics.[26] The origin of Hegel's "dialectical method" is complex. But in his own mature view he sees it as descending from Plato's Parmenides through the Academic tradition. He was a student of logic and philosophical method from his schooldays onward; and he was always conscious that his approach was different from the older methods of "analysis" and "synthesis," but he regarded it as the proper fulfilment of both.[27]

The best example of the method in its early form is the manuscript called the "System of Ethical Life," written at the end of 1802. It was based on Hegel's lectures on "Natural Law," and the published essay on *Natural Law* forms a sort of critical introduction for it. The sphere of "Ethical Life" (*Sittlichkeit*) is the real world in which humanity expresses its "nature." In the terms of the Identity Philosophy, this is simply the higher level of "Nature," and the "natural law" of the human world is part of the greater order of the "law of nature" as articulated in the inorganic world and in non-rational organic life. The first *Potenz of Sittlichkeit* (the basic "power" of ethical life which is to be "squared" and then "cubed") is the "relation" between free rational agency and its organic embodiment (including the suborganic environment upon which the living organism depends). Life begins as feeling, and it moves because the primitive feeling is one of lack. Consumption of some particular in nature produces enjoyment and finally satiation. This is the "subsumption" of the "concept" (nature as an order of particulars) under the "intuition" (of life). But is is all subrational. Reason begins when the order of nature is labored on, but preserved. The relation of absolute intuition (life) to absolute concept (natural order) now becomes systematically dialectical as the moments shift back and forth. Thus, in plant life the order of nature (the concept) subsumes the intuition (the organism); in animal life, the "subsumption" is in the opposite direction. The laboring desire must be subservient to this "real logic" of nature. But in the labor of educating rational selves, a perfect balance of "concept" and "intuition" is the final result. This pattern of a swaying balance that reaches equilibrium is the methodic movement that governs our philosophical comprehension. The overall emphasis of the "ethics of relation" is the "subsumption of intuition under concept," because an ethical "order of nature" is to be established (the family in control of its environment, producing fully formed citizens); and labor, as the negative of both intuition and concept (using up life-energy and transforming the natural order) is the moving principle of the whole.

In the second main *Potenz*, the free agency of life (the "intuition") is dominant. Here the interaction of families is observed as the evolution of "natural justice." The barbaric horde (intuitively aware of its own unity) is naturally conceptualized (self-consciously individuated) as the criminally selfish agent. The natural justice of tribal feuds is the equilibrated condition in which these negations reach their "totality", and we should note that only a community of ethically cultured tribes united for war can actually face and repel the intuitively unified horde. The ethical life of a constituted, free society is the *cubic* (three-dimensional) power of ethical life. Here we can recognize a model for modern national life.[28] Three classes (peasantry, nobility, and the bourgeoisie) are "governed" within a system of constituted justice.

The "system" ends with rough notes on the types of constitution. It fits fairly neatly into the four-part plan that we know Hegel presented to his hearers in 1801. Logic (i.e., Metaphysics as the Science of the Idea) is followed by Philosophy of Nature as the bodily realization of the Idea; then comes "Ethical Nature as the Real Spirit"; and finally "Religion as the resumption of the whole into one." The *System of Ethical Life* gives us part 3; and we know that Hegel's Natural Law lectures went on to the phenomenology of religion as the "biography of God."[29] It seems there was an agreement that Schelling would take care of all lecturing on part 2; and since Hegel ran parts 3 and 4 together in his "Natural Law" lectures, it is possible that he never made much formal use of the four-part division.[30]

After Schelling's departure from Jena, when Hegel began to lecture on the Philosophy of Nature himself, the division between "Nature" and "Spirit" at the finite level began to assume more importance than the division between finite and infinite Spirit (that is, between parts 3 and 4). After Schelling's departure, the influence of Fichte (with the radical Kantian antithesis between "Nature" and "Freedom") began to dominate Hegel's mind. It is possible to organize the surviving evidence regarding the 1803 "Outline of Universal Philosophy" into the four-part pattern.[31] But it is uncertain whether this reconstruction is correct; and even if it is, the new primacy of the standpoint of "consciousness" marks the advent of the Fichtean approach. We could argue that Hegel was too busy filling in the Philosophy of Nature – which he had never presented systematically before, and which was needed on *any* view of the "whole" – to concern himself for the moment with a new overall design.

The sequence of the manuscripts suggests that Hegel himself appreciated the full significance of admitting a radical breach between Nature and Spirit only gradually, and that what Rosenkranz called "the phenomenological crisis of the System"[32] did not properly begin until early in 1805. By September 1804 Hegel had put the often-

revised "Logic and Metaphysics" (which he had been promising to
publish since early in 1802) into its new shape, and he wrote confidently to Goethe about completing his "purely scientific treatment
of philosophy" during the winter (Letter 49, *Briefe* I, 84–85; Butler
and Seiler, p. 685). The confidence was necessary because Hegel was
in danger of being overtaken by Fries in the competition for a profes-
sorship. But the manuscript as we have it bears out Hegel's claims. It
is only about half finished, but the contrast between the part of the
Philosophy of Nature that Hegel wrote out and the comparative
chaos of the 1804 manuscripts (to which we must go for the theory
of the organism, and the Philosophy of Spirit) is truly remarkable.

The "Logic and Metaphysics" with which this manuscript begins
is the only one that we have from the Jena period. Hegel had been
working on it since October 1801, and it had gone through several
transformations. The "transcendental logic" of 1801 – in which the
"forms of finitude" are first sublated in speculation because they are
only an "imitation" and then in order to be reborn from Reason in
their true "metaphysical" shape – is recognizable as the logical *systema reflexionis* that was to give place to the metaphysical *systema
rationis* in 1802. But in the summer of 1804, Hegel tried to make a
single logical and metaphysical principle (probably the principle of
"ground," that is, the principle of "sufficient Reason") serve as the
fulcrum of his Logic and Metaphysics (see *G.W.* VII, 343–47). This
was only a few months before the "Logic and Metaphysics" of 1804/
5, where the Metaphysics begins from a "system of principles" in
which "sufficient Reason" is the climactic moment. So Hegel gave
up his experiment in simple unification quite rapidly. But we can see
from our manuscript that at some time (probably earlier) he had
already given up the parallelism of "reflection" and "speculation."
The critical logic of 1804 (probably) began with the Kantian (that is,
the reflective) categories of Quality and Quantity. Then (under "Relation") the Kantian triad of Substance, Cause, and Reciprocity (the
"Relation of Being") was followed by Concept, Judgment, and Syllogism (the "Relation of Thinking"). The transition to Metaphysics
proper is made through a chapter called "Proportion" that deals with
Definition, Division, and Cognition.

In the Metaphysics, the restoration of the "Ideas of Reason" that
were critically overthrown by Kant begins again, as soon as the
"system" of the "laws of thought" has been given its speculative

interpretation. Soul World, and God are the topics of the Metaphysics of Objectivity, and the Theoretical and Practical Ego (clearly of Fichtean provenance) lead us to "Absolute Spirit" in the "Metaphysics of Subjectivity." We have moved a long way from the triangulation of the Trinity, if that really *was* a "metaphysical" fragment (as Rosenkranz says, but as I find it almost impossible to believe).[33]

As far as the Philosophy of Nature was concerned, Hegel knew exactly what he was doing in this manuscript. But the way he speaks of the "self-cognition of the Earth" (*G.W.* VII, 280, 22–25, etc.) is a philosophical artifice, like the philosophical consciousness of the Absolute in the Logic of 1801 (Duesing-Troxler, p. 73, lines 13–22). It is reminiscent, still, of the "objective" use of "Intuition" and "Concept" in the *System of Ethical Life*. In the *Phenomenology* this "self-cognition of the Earth" will be carefully constructed in the first three chapters as the standpoint of *our* scientific observation before we embark upon the observation of the finite self-consciousness that "steps forth from the Earth" (as Hegel put it in 1804: *G.W.* VI, 269 [first draft]; Harris and Knox, pp. 207–8 [note 8]).

The real "phenomenological crisis" is marked by the sudden breaking off of a manuscript that was being prepared for the printer. The first sign of it is probably the comment in the "Waste-book": "Only after the history of consciousness does one know through the concept what one has in these abstractions: *Fichte's contribution.*"[34] We cannot date this exactly although nothing that we have from the *Wastebook* seems to be earlier than October 1804, but the book/manuscript was abandoned early in 1805. The revolution has several aspects. The "history of consciousness" replaces "critical logic" as the proper "introduction to philosophy;" and the speculative logic that enters in the place of "Metaphysics" is now conceived as a dialectical exposition of the most ordinary words in the vernacular language of everyday. Philosophy is to be given to the people, like the Bible, in its own tongue. The Latinate terminology of the academic tradition has always supported "formalism," and the spirit of "formalism" has now been reborn within the new speculative philosophy inaugurated by Schelling.[35]

It is important to realize that "Fichte's contribution" appeared to Hegel as the way to ensure that what we might call "Schelling's original insight" – the identity of thought and being – could be preserved. Hegel did not become a "Fichtean," but turned Fichte's method inside out by making the absolute reflection of the mind upon its own activity into the philosophical observation of the evolution of consciousness in history. The reflective method that results is entirely Hegel's own; and the bounds of its application are set by the "biography of God" that he originally worked out for his theory of "Natural Law." But the concept of "self-recognition in otherness," like the theory of subjective reason as "the category," comes from Fichte. In the language of the *Difference* essay, we might say that the theory of the "subjective subject-object" is now used to lead us up to the adequate logical theory of the subjectivity that is grounded in objective categories.

The "science of experience" is the great corrective for all varieties of "formalism." "Schematic formalism" foists an abstract schema upon us (as the deliverance of our supposed "intellectual intuition") and then arrays the levels of natural and spiritual development upon it mechanically. In Hegel's introductory science, by contrast, we watch the evolution of actual consciousness from stage to stage until it arrives at the philosophical consciousness of itself as the "for-itself" side of the Absolute Identity. In order to do this, the observed consciousness must traverse the whole range of our scientific experience. Hegel apparently believed that there was some kind of one-to-one correspondence between the categories of phenomenology and those of speculative logic. But we do not have the speculative logic of 1805, so we cannot say how he envisaged this parallel. It is a relic of the imitative parallelism between the reflective understanding and reason that he spoke of in 1801. It seems certain that he soon gave it up. For there is no sign of any such doctrine in the *Science of Logic*, although the *Phenomenology* is still regarded as the necessary introduction to speculative logic in that book (see *G.W.* XI, 20–21; *T.W-A.* V, 42–43; Miller, pp. 48–49).

On the side of content, there is a certain parallel between the "science of experience" and "speculative science" as a system because the whole of experience must be comprehended in both ways. When he published the *Phenomenology*, Hegel actually expected that the whole system of speculative philosophy would go into another volume of the same size.[36] In the *Encyclopaedia* he eventually achieved this aim, but the editions of 1827 and 1830 contained their own introduction, and the *Phenomenology* of 1807 was formally dispensed with. An introduction of some sort was pedagogically essential, and the whole conception of the *Encyclopaedia* made something much simpler than the "science of experience" necessary. Also, the changed political conditions meant that the *Phenomenology* could not be republished without some apology. Hegel's decision, in the last year of his life, to republish it with only slight revision and a formal reference to its different historical context seems to me to show that he regarded it as still valid.[37] So we can fairly say that with the appearance of the book in 1807, Hegel's intellectual development was, in all essentials, complete.

To test how far this is true, I will recapitulate briefly the structure of the "Real Philosophy" of 1805–6 and then, finally, summarize the account of his own development that Hegel gave to a lexicographer in 1824. The "system" exhibits, in 1805, the familiar tripartite structure: Logic, Philosophy of Nature, Philosophy of Spirit. The Logic (which is lost) was probably written out only schematically (since the course in summer 1806 began with the *Phenomenology* and dealt only with speculative logic in an outline way at the end).[38] The Philosophy of Nature begins with the concept of the "aether" as space. This "aether" is identical with the cognitive element of "absolute knowing," so Hegel's abiding commitment to Schelling's "Absolute Identity" is evident enough. From the three dimensions of Space, we pass to the single dimension of Time. Then Motion is treated as the "reality" of space and time. What is called the theory of "Mass" is conceptually identical with the "Absolute Mechanics" of the Berlin period, but it incorporates the theory of the Solar System (with which the later "Physics" begins).

The name "Physics" is used differently in 1805, and the conceptual order of development in the second section on "Shaping and Chemism" is rather different. (We should remember that Hegel went on struggling with the order and presentation of the Philosophy of Nature all his life.) In 1805 he moved from the theory of specific gravity and "fluidity" to "Chemism," and it is only in the "Total Process" that we hear about "physical bodies." But when we reach the theory of "the organic," the parallel is once again fairly close. The most interesting contrast is offered by the fact that although the living earth is treated as a "mineralogical organism," it is not called by that name. The section has no separate heading at all. The "Vegetable Organism" provides the stable foundation for the "Animal Process." In the *Encyclopaedia* we have "Terrestrial Organism" followed by "Plant Nature" and finally "Animal Organism." In 1805, "Animal Process" is the mediating phase through which we move to the organic totality of "Spirit."[39] In other words, the continuity of physical and ethical "nature" is still influential and important in Hegel's mind. For he has made the theory of the free organism into the logical completion of his "Philosophy of Nature." "Real Philosophy" still means for him the theory of the "Universe" of finite nature as the logical complement of "Transcendental Philosophy." He now wants to *compare* this Schellingian view with the Fichtean emphasis on the antithesis between "Nature" and freedom.

The *Philosophy of Spirit* is missing its first page. It begins with the sensible consciousness of a world intuited in space, but turns at once to the inward "treasury" of memory and develops the theory of language on that basis. From the Understanding we pass to "Will"; and it is obvious that the pattern of the *Phenomenology* is what is influential – Hegel does not yet have his developed theory of Subjective Spirit. But in the theory of "Actual Spirit" we have an account of "recognition" that leads to the theory of the family and of law. Here the incorporation of the movement of *Phenomenology* Chapter IV (with a point of arrival at the end of Chapter V) is clearly indicated – but without the "inequality" that makes the movement of the "science of experience" itself so long and arduous – so the necessary recurrence of "Phenomenology" as a normal phase of "subjective spirit" is clearly foreshadowed.[40] We can recognize the pattern of development in the *Encyclopaedia* if we ignore "Anthropology" and "Phenomenology" there and begin at "I C Psychology." But the whole argument still remains closer in spirit to the *System of Ethical Life*. Hegel lectured on "Natural Law" throughout the Jena period, and this exercised a powerful influence on his "Jena Philosophy of Spirit."[41]

"Civil Society" and "State" are both included under the heading "Constitution"; this is because the educational function of the "State" was more heavily emphasized in 1805 than it would be later. The genetic problem of how the State comes into existence is systematically extruded from the *Encyclopaedia*. (This is another reason why the *Phenomenology* cannot be dispensed with in the Berlin perspective.) But in 1805/6 "the State" is actually coming into being through the work of Napoleon. So although the many revisions in our manuscript were probably made after the first drafting of the *Phe-*

nomenology, the theory of world-history has not yet been pushed to the end of Hegel's political theory. The "estates" are all here in their mature shape, but Family, Civil Society, and State are all treated together as one education process. "Government," which becomes "the State" in the *Encyclopaedia*, is even called "The Self-Certain Spirit of Nature" (*G. W.* VIII, 276, 18; Rauch, p. 171).[42]

This is a sign that the Fichtean emphasis on the breach between "Nature" and (finite) Spirit has not yet triumphed completely in Hegel's mind over Schelling's Spinozist doctrine that the "finite" perspective is the order of "Nature" proper. "Absolutely free Spirit" dawns only with the "resumption of the whole into one" (which is here marked off as "C. Art, Religion and Science"). There can be no doubt that, from his first public appearance in the *Difference* essay as a champion of "Schelling's System" against Reinhold, right down to the drafting of the "Preface" when the text of the *Phenomenology* was in proof, Hegel saw himself as the true interpreter of the Identity Philosophy announced in Schelling's *Darstellung* of 1801. He was well aware that he had departed a long way from the visionary intuition of Schelling's *Bruno*. But he thought that "Science at its first beginning" (*G. W.* IX, 16, 6–8; *T. W-A.* III, 22–23; Miller, § 14) was bound to have a visionary quality, and that it should be defended against the degeneration into "Schematic formalism" which that invited. "Intuition" must be resolved into a truly *speculative* method of discursive reasoning. That was what he saw as the achievement of his *Phenomenology*. His new method owed a lot to the inspiration of Fichte, but his content was still the identity of "God and Nature."

What Hegel told the anonymous author of the article "Hegel" in the Brockhaus *Conversations-Lexikon* in 1824[43] (probably Amadeus Wendt) shows how he remembered the development discussed here (and at least how he wished it to be known then).[44]

At Tübingen (so Hegel said), he was "driven to study Kant's writings without laying those of Plato aside." This influenced his theological views; and as his view of philosophy broadened, so his interest in the natural sciences increased. (This last is a point that would never have been clear from the manuscript remains. We should always remember it, while trying not to depend too heavily upon this claim made thirty years later.)[45] The article does not even mention the social and theological studies of the Berne and Frankfurt years, but it does record the fact that Hegel's "idea of philosophy" had been "formed especially after a complete study of Fichte's "Science of Knowledge." The contemporary readers would take this to refer to his preparation for the *Difference* essay, but to us it appears as a disguised reference to the "Fichtean" context in which Hegel and Hölderlin (and other friends, notably Zwilling)[46] developed the "philosophy of Union". It also confirms the importance of "Fichte's contribution" to the genesis of Hegel's *Phenomenology*.

In the Jena period, says the article, Hegel was working toward the publication of a comprehensive work (for which the *Phenomenology* was to serve as the introduction). This would communicate to the world the point of view that was peculiar to Hegel (and divergent from that of Schelling), which he had developed for himself "through unbroken researches." When the anonymous author goes on (after his biographical sketch) to give an outline of this "original system," he says that

Hegel who had raised himself with Schelling to the recognition of the Absolute, diverged from Schelling first of all in this: that he did not believe he could presuppose the Absolute through an *intellectual intuition* in which Object and Subject coincide, but made the express requirement that the Absolute in Science, must also be found upon the *path* of Science, and consequently as the result [of the journey], if the Absolute is something true at all.

From this point onward the author summarizes the Preface and Introduction of the *Phenomenology*. I am inclined to believe that even there the summary is Hegel's, but I feel sure in any case that Wendt's knowledge that Hegel's resistance to Schelling's beginning with intellectual intuition was his *first* divergence comes from the biographical notes supplied by Hegel, because no one would have known (or even suspected) this from the published record available in 1824. Everyone knew, of course, that the "dark night in which all the cows are black" had occasioned the permanent breach between Hegel and Schelling, but not that Hegel had been struggling with the problem ever since he caused the decisive breach between Schelling and Fichte – as I think he did – through the *Difference* essay. I think that Hegel may very well have intended to cause the breach between Schelling and Fichte, or at least it was a matter of indifference to him. But if I am right, he did not intend to cause a breach between himself and Schelling. Both in the *Phenomenology* and for the rest of his life, he was trying to provide the philosophy of the Absolute Identity with a more adequate method, both of demonstration and of exposition. Probably the breach was inevitable, however, because Hegel *always* saw the Absolute Identity in a different light than Schelling. It came to him first as an aesthetic ideal that he shared with Hölderlin, and he formulated it methodically in response to the challenge posed by Fichte. For him, the process of our coming to know the Absolute was the very same motion of the Absolute's self-constitution.

NOTES

1 For the primary sources, the following texts are cited in this article:

Dokumente zu Hegels Entwicklung, edited by J. Hoffmeister. Stuttgart: Fromann, 1936 [*Dok.*].

Hegel in Berichten seiner Zeitgenossen, edited by G. Nicolin. Hamburg: Meiner, 198 [Nicolin].

Gesammelte Werke, edited by the Rheinisch-Westfaelischen Akademie der Wissenschaften. Hamburg: Meiner, 1988ff [*G.W.* plus volume, page, and line(s)].

Briefe von und an Hegel, edited by J. Hoffmeister and F. Nicolin, 4 vols in 5, Hamburg: Meiner, 1961–77 [*Briefe*].

Mythologie der Vernunft, edited by C. Jamme and H. Schneider. Frankfurt: Suhrkamp, 1984 [*Mythologie*].

Der Geist des Christentums, edited by W. Hamacher. Frankfurt: Ullstein, 1978 [Hamacher].

Schellings und Hegels erste absolute Metaphysik (1801–1802), Vorlesungsnachschriften von I.P.V. Troxler, edited by K. Duesing. Cologne: Dinter, 1988.

I have also given (where possible) the corresponding volume and page references in the *Theorie Werk-Ausgabe* (*T.W-A.*), edited by E. Moldenhauer and K-M. Michel, Frankfurt: Suhrkamp, 1970, and I have cited the best available English translations as follows:

"Religion ist eine . . ." (Tübingen Fragment), translated by H.S. Harris in *Hegel's Development I: Toward the Sunlight* (Oxford, 1972), pp. 481–507 [*Sunlight*].

Hegel: Three Essays, 1793–1795, translated by P. Fuss and J. Dobbins. Notre Dame: University of Notre Dame Press, 1984 [Fuss and Dobbins].

Hegel: Early Theological Writings, translated by T.M. Knox and R. Kroner. Chicago: University of Chicago Press, 1948 [Knox].

Hegel: Letters, translated by C. Butler and C. Seiler. Indianapolis: University of Indiana Press, 1984 [Butler and Seiler].

Hegel: Difference between Fichte's and Schelling's System of Philosophy, translated by H.S. Harris and W. Cerf. Albany: SUNY Press, 1977.

Hegel: Faith and Knowledge, translated by W. Cerf and H.S. Harris. Albany: SUNY Press, 1977.

Between Kant and Hegel (Selections from various authors), translated by G. di Giovanni and H.S. Harris. Albany: SUNY Press, 1985.

Hegel: System of Ethical Life and First Philosophy of Spirit, translated by T.M. Knox and H.S. Harris. Albany: SUNY Press, 1979.

Hegel: The Jena System, 1804–5: Logic and Metaphysics, translated by J.S. Burbidge and others. Montreal and Kingston: McGill–Queen's Univ. Press, 1986.

Hegel and the Human Spirit (Philosophy of Spirit, 1805/6), translated by L. Rauch. Detroit: Wayne State University Press, 1983.

Hegel: Phenomenology of Spirit, translated by A.V. Miller. Oxford: Clarendon Press, 1977.

For the works of Hölderlin, I have referred to the *Grosse Stuttgarter Ausgabe,* edited by F. Beissner and A. Beck. Stuttgart: Kohlhammer, 1943ff [*G.S.A.*].

2 The letter which Leutwein wrote during the last months of his life (1837/8, aged 69) can be found in *Hegel-Studien* III, 1965, pp. 53–57; or in Nicolin, pp. 10–13 (Report 8).

3 See, especially, Nicolin, reports 760 and 769: but compare also reports 552, 570, 581, 585, 630, and 634.

4 Christiane's recollections are in Nicolin, reports 1, 2, 12, and 15. For Hegel's study of the modern languages, see N. Waszek, *The Scottish Enlightenment and Hegel's Account of Civil Society* (Dordrecht, 1988). But Waszek is unduly skeptical about linguistic studies in Stuttgart, which are certainly suggested by Hegel's own *curriculum vitae* of 1804 (see *Briefe*, IV, 88). We possess one example of composition in French from the early years: see the "Fragments of Historical Studies" #16 (Rosenkranz, p. 532; trans. Butler in *Clio VII*, 1977, 130–31).

5 See the Conversations-Lexicon article – based on Hegel's own recollections – which is cited and discussed at the end of this essay (note 62, below).

6 See the summary account by Henrich in *Hegel-Studien* III, 1965, 276–82.

7 The clearest indication is in Hölderlin's letter of January 26, 1795 (*Briefe* I, 19).

8 The best testimony for this is in Heinrich's account of Leutwein's career and writings: see *Hegel-Studien* III, 1965, 43–50.

9 *Nathan the Wise*, Act IV, scene 7; see *G.W.* I, 92, 5–7; *Sunlight*, p. 487.

10 The antithesis comes from an internal heading in *Jedes Volk hat ihm* (mid-1796): see *G.W.* I, 365, 11–12; *T.W-A.* I, 202; Knox, p. 151n.

11 For Hegel's expectations, see Letter 11 (*Briefe* I, 23); Butler and Seiler, p. 35. For the Kantian conclusion added to the *Positivity* essay (in April 1796), see *G.W.* I, 349, 20 and 351, 24; *T.W-A.* I, 187–190; Knox, pp. 143–45.

12 Hölderlin, Letter 136, *G.S.A.* VI, 230, 42.

13 The translation became his first publication – anonymously – in 1798, soon after he arrived in Frankfurt.

14 For an argument that this fragment should be dated to December 1796, before Hegel actually went to Frankfurt, see my "Hegel and Hölderlin" in *Hegel: Origins and Legacies* (Montreal/Kingston: McGill–Queen's University Press, forthcoming).

15 See, especially, the fragment *Uber Urtheil und Seyn* (*G.S.A.* IV, 216–17; *Sunlight*, pp. 515–16).

16 See, especially, the fragment *Positiv wird ein Glauben genannt* (Hamacher, pp. 354–58; *T.W-A.* I, 239–43; *Clio* VIII, 1979, 258–61). If Schüler's order and dating is correct, then Hegel actually began with the historical problem of Jewish "positivity."

17 If Rosenkranz (pp. 12, 60) was right in thinking that the translation from Thucydides (now lost) belonged to the Berne period, then some of the "historical studies" may stem from 1796. At Frankfurt Hegel turned first to the Jews and Jesus.

18 It is to the great credit of Lukács, I think, that he was the first to grasp this point clearly.

19 *Welchem Zwecke denn* (Nov. 1797, revised at the end of 1798). A critical edition has been provided by C. Jamme (in *Hegel-Studien*, XVII, 1982, 9–23); we badly need a new translation from this text to replace the Knox rendering of Nohl's edition (Knox, pp. 302–8).

20 See *T.W-A.* I, 419–27 (or Knox, pp. 309–19) for the two surviving sheets. (The English version by Richard Kroner was revised by Knox himself.)

21 See the "System Fragment" (Nohl, p. 347; Knox, p. 311 at note 3) for signs of his interest in 1800.

22 For the conflicting testimonies, see K. Fischer, *Hegels Leben* (1911) II, 1201–2.

23 See Duesing-Troxler, pp. 12–14; also see the notes of Henry Crabb Robinson, printed by H. Marquardt, pp. 84, 345, and 347 (and cited by E. Behler, *Hegel-Studien* XV, 1980, 60–61).

24 Compare the "logic-outline" of 1801 with *Differenz and Faith and*

Knowledge (Rosenkranz, pp. 190–92; *G.W.* IV, 63–65, 354–56; Cerf and Harris, pp. 9–11, 107–9; Harris and Cerf, pp. 155–57).

25 Compare Duesing-Troxler, pp. 63–77, with *G.W.* IV, 12–13 and 15–19; also 327–31 (Harris and Cerf, pp. 89–90, 92–97; Cerf and Harris, pp. 69–75). See also the passage cited from the "Logic" fragments in *Night Thoughts*, p. 36.

26 The essay (*G.W.* IV, 197–238) is translated in Di Giovanni and Harris. The influence of the Skeptics on Hegel has now been ably studied by M.N. Forster (*Hegel and Scepticism* [Cambridge: Harvard Univ. Press, 1989]).

27 Duesing-Troxler, p. 63; compare *Difference* (*G.W.* IV, 31: Harris and Cerf, pp. 113–14). M. Baum has studied the "Origin of the Dialectic" (Bonn: Bouvier, 1987). But the only study that traces the evolution of Hegel's logical method from the very beginning is that of R. Pozzo (*Hegel: 'Introductio in Philosophiam'* [Florence: La Nuova Italia, 1989]).

28 Slavery and serfdom have no place at this level, so the natural order (or "real concept") here is neither Greek nor medieval. Laurence Dickey (*Hegel*, Cambridge, 1987) has given us a convincing analysis of how Hellenism and civic Protestantism came together in the *System of Ethical Life*.

29 Rosenkranz gave us both the system-outline (1844, p. 179; cf. Harris and Knox, p. 6) and a summary of the "biography of God" (1844, pp. 132–41; Harris and Knox, pp. 178–86). The lecture fragment from which the outline came will be published in *G.W.* V.

30 Thus the fragment called the "Divine Triangle" (*Hegel-Studien* X, 1975, 133–35; *Night Thoughts*, pp. 184–88) is certainly early and may possibly be a sketch of Hegel's "Metaphysics" in a theological mode. But in the four-part system, the content would have to be repeated in the "Resumption of the Whole."

31 See *Night Thoughts*, pp. 200–25.

32 Rosenkranz (1844), p. 201.

33 Compare note 28. For the text itself, see *G.W.* VII; translated by J. Burbidge et al. (Montreal-Kingston, 1986). J. Heinrichs (Bonn: Bouvier, 1974) has tried to use this manuscript as a logical ground plan for the *Phenomenology*. The hypothesis was worth trying, but I think it soon becomes implausible.

34 *T.W-A.* II, 55; *Independent Journal of Philosophy*, III, 1979, 4.

35 The attack on academic language, and on the "formalism of Schelling's School," began in October 1804 (Rosenkranz, 1844, pp. 181–85; Harris and Knox, pp. 256–59). But the new Logic, and the "history of consciousness," were conceived only in the early months of 1805. The letter to Voss (Letter 55 [May 1805], *Briefe* I, 95–101; Butler and Seiler,

pp. 104–8) is where the ambition "to teach philosophy to speak German" is announced.

36 See the "Selbstanzeige der Phänomenologie," G.W. IX, 446–47 (translated in Kaufmann, Hegel, Texts and Commentary [Anchor, 1966], pp. 4–5).

37 See Hegel's notes for a new preface, G.W. IX, 448. The necessary presence of a stage properly called "Phänomenologie" in the encyclopaedic "Philosophy of Spirit" has no bearing whatever on the question of the continued validity of the Phenomenology of 1807 as a "science of experience." "Phenomenology" in the system is the mediating phase of "subjective spirit" (i.e., it embraces nothing beyond Chapter V in the work of 1807); and we can recognize this necessary phase in the 1805 "Philosophy of Spirit" (see note 39). Hegel wrote "the science of experience" to introduce precisely that system. It would be surprising, in fact, if we did not find the logical ground for the "science of experience" in a fairly explicit shape within the system itself.

38 See, especially, the reminiscences of Gabler (Nicolin, report 92, p. 66).

39 All of this is available only in German (G.W. VIII, 3–184). We have an English translation of the following Philosophy of Spirit (G.W. VIII, 185–287) by Leo Rauch (Detroit: Wayne State, 1983).

40 See G.W. VIII, 217, 17–231, 22; Rauch, pp. 114–27.

41 Kimmerle has even used "Natural Law" as an organizing category for the practical philosophy of the Jena period, and his interpretations seem to me to be correct. See the summary of his views in D.P. Verene, ed., Hegel's Social and Political Thought (Atlantic Highland, N.J.: Humanities Press, 1980), pp. 53–57.

42 This is a marginal addition, and although Rauch was probably right to take it as a heading, there is no warrant for the insertion of "B" here (or for "A" before "Die Stände" at VIII, 266, 1). The articulation intended when Hegel writes "C. Kunst, Religion und Wissenschaft" is uncertain. But it may refer to the "A" of "Gestaltung" (VIII, 34, 15), and the "Philosophy of [finite] Spirit" itself may have begun with the "B" heading.

43 See Hegel-Studien VII, 1972, 11–22; translated by C. Butler in Clio XIII, 1983/4, 369–76.

44 Leutwein, in 1838, consciously intended to "correct" the "Kantian" claim in this article. But as we have seen, Leutwein's concept of a "proper Kantian" was too rigorous to embrace Hölderlin either, and Hölderlin got his "Kantian" expertise recorded in his Tübingen graduation testimonial.

45 Compare p. 4 above. We do hear something of various scientific studies at Jena: colour experiments, a geological expedition, even an expressed readiness – under extreme economic pressure – to give lectures on bot-

any (see Letter 87, *Briefe* I, 141–42; Butler and Seiler, pp. 686–87; Nicolin, report 98; Rosenkranz, p. 220). But it is only a biographical recollection of this kind that tells us how important these concerns were.

46 Zwilling's philosophical theory has now been reconstructed as well as the surviving record will allow by P. Henrich and C. Jamme in *Hegel-Studien*, Beiheft 28, 1986.

2   You Can't Get There from Here: Transition problems in Hegel's *Phenomenology of Spirit*

I. WHAT IS A PHENOMENOLOGY OF SPIRIT?

Beginning around the summer of 1802, Hegel began to prepare his friends and students for the immanent publication of his own "system," or at least a part of it. For a young professor out to make his mark, this was apparently the thing to do in those heady days in the university city of Jena, which had already seen several of Fichte's "Doctrines of Knowledge" and Schelling's influential "System of Transcendental Idealism." But no such work appeared, since Hegel began to change his mind rapidly about a number of important elements in such a system, especially, after the lectures given in the 1803–4 academic year, about the relation between his category theory, or logic, and his metaphysics, and even more deeply, about many of Schelling's ideas.[1] These changes also prompted an interest, sometime around 1805, in a proper "Introduction" to such a system, a work that was to be a "Science of the Experience of Consciousness," and that would be published, together with his "Logic," in a single volume at Eastertime 1806.

That combined work also never appeared. By October of 1806, Hegel for some reason had ended up with something very different from these original intentions. He had hastily written and decided to publish not the originally planned 150 page introduction within a systematic study, but a very long, independent Introduction to his system, again called a "Science of the Experience of Consciousness" (a designation that still appears at the end of the work's ultimately published "Introduction").[2] Finally, by the time he had corrected the proofs and written its new "Preface" and the work itself had appeared in early 1807, another crucial change had occurred. The old

52

title had been discarded and a new one appended. The book was now *The Phenomenology of Spirit* and it was itself an independent "first part" of the "System of Science." (The original publisher, understandably, appears to have been very confused by all this, and he simply published the work under, in effect, both titles.)[3]

Thus began a long controversy about the intention of the work, its internal organization, its relation to the rest of Hegel's mature project, and the extent to which Hegel changed his mind about its importance. There are to this day, as Hans Friederich Fulda points out, philosophers and scholars seriously interested in Hegel who would prefer to read and study only the 1807 *Phenomenology*.[4] (Many of these are among the most influential in the twentieth century, like Kojève, Lukács, Sartre, and Bloch, who read the work as a philosophical anthropology demonstrating the essentially historical, self-made nature of human being). And there are those who insist on the mature or Encyclopedic Hegel as the real Hegel, and therewith on the complete dispensability of what they regard as a mere piece of unsystematic juvenalia.[5]

This controversy about just what a "phenomenology of spirit" is supposed to be concerns both Hegel's original and his later understanding of the work. The original structure or architectonic of the work, the organization of its headings and chapters, is itself puzzling and raises many questions.

The book is organized this way. There are eight distinct chapters, each marked by roman numeral designations (I–VIII). But superimposed on these chapters is a puzzling, additional structure. There is a Preface, an Introduction, and then:

A. Consciousness
  I. Sense-Certainty
  II. Perception
  III. The Understanding
B. Self-consciousness
  IV. The Truth of Self-Certainty

and then a final lettered section, "C," which itself has no title, only subdivisions:

C.
AA. Reason

A first glance at this structure would appear to justify Otto Pöggeler's suggestion: that in actually writing the work Hegel seems to have simply lost control of its structure as he wrote the later sections, and had neither the time nor the inclination to revise the whole work in the light of those later discussions.[6] For one thing, the individual chapters do not appear to have been well planned or thought out in advance. In the original edition, chapter lengths look like this: Chapter One – 16 pages, Chapter Two – 21 pages, Chapter Three – 42 pages, Chapter Four – 61 pages; and then Chapter Five balloons to 214 pages! For another, the chapters on Spirit and Religion introduce a reference to actual historical chronology in a puzzling way, or at least in a way that seems difficult to integrate with the earlier chapters and their more-systematic, idealized presentation of various possible "shapes of spirit," possible stances toward the world, and others that bear no obvious (or at least no necessary) relation to actual historical institutions or societies, or even to individual philosophers.[7]

For some scholars, doubts about these historical sections and so about the overall coherence of the work are intensified by other pieces of evidence that purportedly show that Hegel himself adopted a radically revisionist stance toward his own work very soon after completing it. These include his own summary of the *Phenomenology* (as a "propadeutic") for his students at Nürnberg, which summary included only the material up to the chapter on "Reason."[8] This suggested to some that he always preferred a direct transition from "Reason" to his "Logic" and so to his whole system, and so that the historical chapters in the 1807 version were digressions or in some other way dispensable. Also, and perhaps most significant for all the deflationary approaches to the *Phenomenology,* when Hegel published versions of his full *Encyclopedia* system at Heidelberg and later at Berlin, there was indeed a "Phenomenology of Spirit" included, but not as a free-standing, introductory work, but as the middle section in the "Philosophy of Subjective Spirit." And, adding to suspicions about the real core of the work, he included in the *Encyclopedia* only general summaries of the sections on "Consciousness," "Self-Consciousness" and "Reason." It would appear that that additional material on "Spirit" and "Religion" in the 1807 version was simply reworked in lectures on the philosophies of history and religion, and that the original phenomenological project, itself ambiguous and never thoroughly worked out, had been abandoned. (This suspicion has been accepted in some quarters even though Hegel was preparing a new edition of the *Phenomenology* toward the end of his life. He certainly never abandoned the work, and continued to refer to it frequently. In the Introduction to the final edition of his most important work, his *Science of Logic,* he continued to insist on the *Phenomenology* as a necessary "presupposition," even "deduction" of the *Logic.*)⁹

Considerations like the above have led to several famous scholarly deconstructions of the work. For many years Rudolf Haym's, in his 1857 *Hegel und seine Zeit,* was the best known.¹⁰ He argued that the work was a "palimpsest": two texts, one overlaid on the other with no internal principal of order. It was, supposedly, originally planned as an account of the consciousness/self-consciousness/reason relation, a "psychology" in the tradition of Kant's transcendental psychology, or an account of the subjective faculties and activities necessarily involved in any representation of an object or intentional action. But Hegel supposedly shifted interests frequently in writing the book, adding on gratuitously a rational reconstruction of human history and an ambitious historical theodicy. "Put all at once, the *Phenomenology* is a psychology brought into confusion and disorder through a history, and a history brought to ruin through a psychology."¹¹

There are other such palimpsest interpretations more sympathetic to the internal, philosophical motivations that led Hegel away from any putative original plan. Theodor Haering also proposed that Hegel originally intended to end the book with the discussion of "Reason," but that, motivated by a desire actually to produce the first part of his long-promised system and to justify a claim that both he (Hegel) and human history had achieved the standpoint of absolute knowledge, he tried, clumsily and without much success, to work into the text various reflections on the development of historical spirit.[12]

The contemporary scholar Otto Pöggeler has convincingly attacked the philological evidence used by Haering, and has proposed his own more philosophically motivated version of the work's composition history.[13] In Pöggeler's account, it was when actually writing the chapter on Reason that Hegel realized the implications of his own earlier argument that the whole position or stance of "Consciousness" had been overcome or superseded. Once Hegel had demonstrated that our cognitive relation to the world could not be wholly passive or dependent, that the ways we take up the world were at least partly due to us as well as to the world (in Hegel's language once a "relation to an object" was understood to be a "self-relation in relation to an object"), the earlier planned "science of the experience of *consciousness*" was in effect already over.[14] The subject of such a "relation to an other" was now already "spirit," determining collectively *"for itself"* its relation to others and objects. This suggestion by Pöggeler is one of the most philosophically valuable to come out of the long scholarly controversy, and we shall return to it below.[15]

Finally, all such palimpsest, or anti-unity, interpretations have been challenged by scholars who believe that Hegel actually had a relatively clear idea of the structure of the book throughout, from beginning to end. Many of these commentators rely on Hegel's Jena lectures on Logic and his general ideas about immanent logical development and the architectonic of this development, as these were presented later in his Jena years. Fulda, one of the most persuasive of this group, does not deny that Hegel experienced a great deal of difficulty in carrying out such a "logically grounded phenomenology," both because of the incomplete state of the 1805 *Logic* and Hegel's own confusions about the *Phenomenology*.[16] But, he argues (together with J. Heinrichs and others), the overall architectonic of the *whole Phenomenology* is clearly derived from that earlier source.[17]

So much for the scholarly disputes. Have they brought us any closer to an answer to the question What is the *Phenomenology of Spirit*?

It will not be possible here or, in this limited context, very helpful to pursue these issues as philological or historical problems. But the long dispute about Hegel's intentions and the work's unity at least brings into focus a basic philosophical dispute about the book. Clearly, those who cannot see any overall unity in the work often make a broad philosophical as well as a textual criticism. They are really claiming that there is no good internal argument supporting Hegel's most revolutionary claim in the *Phenomenology of Spirit:* his rejection of both an empirical or naturalistic as well as a transcendental notion of subjectivity in favor of a notion of a subject of experience and action as necessarily *self-transforming in time* and necessarily *social,* in favor, that is, of the thinking and acting subject as *Geist,* Spirit. If, on the contrary, there is such an internal argument, then, as Pöggeler has suggested, we should at least be able to see in the work itself the philosophical reasons for Hegel's reconception of the problem of the "experience of consciousness" as a "phenomenology of spirit," why he would claim that the problem of consciousness's possible relation to objects and to others is really the problem of spirit's (basically social) relation to itself and why that relation must be accounted for in historical terms. Hegel's expansion of the work from an introductory indictment of various realist and Cartesian epistemologies into a fuller, more positive account of social subjectivity, and his reliance on the details of human history, literature, and religion to establish what seem to be philosophical conclusions about such a subject would thus represent far more than a hasty presentation of several separate ideas, loosely and clumsily thrown together.

In fact, the general problem of the work as a whole, and its most important transitions, bring into focus theses quite famously, even if often only vaguely, associated with Hegel. These concern (a) his critique of *individualist* models of the mind-world relation, a problem that includes the possibility of determinate representation at all as well as possible truth claims about the world, and (b) his critique of *individualist* models of agency, especially self-conscious, rational agency.

Understanding how Hegel would defend these sorts of claims will not resolve all the major controversies about the structure and implications of the work. In this context, raising the question this way will focus our attention mostly on limited questions: Why, according to Hegel, must the problem of "consciousness of objects" or human intentionality be reconceived as the problem of a mutually recognizing, social self-consciousness? and Why must reason become spirit; why is the attempt to base beliefs and deeds on universal criteria, on what any thinker or agent would believe or do, to be reconceived as some sort of participation in a socio-historical practice? I am suggesting that understanding Hegel's answers to these questions can clarify the larger philosophical and methodological issues at stake in the work's overall movement, what general goal Hegel is after, how he proposes to pursue it, and that it is the most interesting issue raised by the scholarly controversies.

II. THE PROBLEM OF THE ABSOLUTE

I want to consider first Hegel's famous presentation of self-consciousness as itself a social struggle for recognition between independent and dependent subjects. Hegel calls this chapter the very "turning point" of the whole *Phenomenology* and in it first introduces the idea of an " 'I' that is a 'we,' and a 'we' that is an 'I.' " It is puzzling that such a theme also appears to be introduced as a resolution, in some sense, of various aporiai that developed in the course of an assessment of "object-dependent" and essentially passive theories of human consciousness. This apparent shift of interest from accounts of how we could take up and have or represent a world, to what appears to be an independent interest in purposive agency, social identity, prestige, and religious accounts of human worth, presents us with probably the most serious of the transition problems, the "you can't get there from here" problems in the *Phenomenology*, so serious that even those with a minimalist reading of the real or original core of the *Phenomenology* have no satisfactory account of it.

To make matters worse, such a problem cannot even be addressed without taking some stand on a host of other interpretive controversies already at issue in the infamous transition. To get to the issues I am interested in, I shall simply have to set out the details of these controversies and briefly sketch what seem to me the most reasonable interpretations.

(i) In both his Preface and Introduction, Hegel introduces the central problem of the *Phenomenology* as if he were referring to a common philosophical term of art, as common as "truth of reason," or "innate idea," or "natural law." Without preparation or explanation, Hegel assumes that, in one way or another, philosophy is about *"the Absolute."* Such a term immediately suggests that the book's final chapter, on "absolute knowing," will defend a claim to have discovered something like absolute reality, the truly, not apparently real, or the highest degree of reality as opposed to some finite or imperfect realm. If this is so, then a defense of *"spirit" as "absolute,"*[18] our central interest here, would seem to involve some claim about the immaterial, spiritual nature of what truly is, and thus, ultimately, quite an implausible metaphysical model of the work's unity.

Yet, especially in the Preface, Hegel works hard to distinguish his position from any traditional claim about "what is in-itself," which he calls a knowledge of "substance." In a famous claim, "everything depends on grasping and expressing the true, not just as substance, but just as much as subject" (18; 10). To describe such a subject as yet again another sort of substance, this time an immaterial or mental one, would be to miss the whole point of the quoted phrase. Rather the "Absolute . . . is essentially a result, . . . it is first at the end what it truly is; and . . . precisely in this consists its nature, viz. to be actual, subject, the becoming of itself" (19; 11). This self-transforming *process*, or self-determining *activity*, is later glossed as a "self-moving selfsameness, or is a reflection into self, the moment of the 'I', for itself, pure negativity, or, simple becoming" (19; 11).

This emphasis on understanding the "Absolute" as "the I's" self-reflection and self-determination has a number of important implications. Since, Hegel tries to show, any possible cognitive relation to objects must involve the "I's" taking up the world "for itself," and so some sort of self-relation, or apperception, understanding theoretically how a subject could come to know itself in its relation to all otherness (and understanding this finally and without sceptical doubt) is how Hegel wants to understand "the Absolute as Spirit"; and how he wants to be understood when he claims that "the Spirit that, so developed, knows itself as Spirit, is Science; Science is its actuality and the realm which it builds for itself in its own element" (22; 14).[19]

This language of subjectivity and self-reflection is so prominent (and so tied to what Hegel regards as the problem of his own, or "the new" age), that there is little evidence to support the first impression that Hegel takes the task of "knowledge of the Absolute" to be the achievement of some first-order truth about what there is. The problem is rather our self-conscious justification of the *possibility* of any first-order truths about the world, the warranting principles or justificatory criteria by appeal to which the possibility of a world "for us," what counts as a world and evidence about it, could be established.[20]

(ii) Hegel accepts the claim (due to Kant) that all sorts of knowledge claims are "conditioned" and rely on *a priori* presuppositions that cannot be confirmed by any relation to objects (because such assumptions determine or constitute what counts as relations to objects). But he rejects Kant's transcendental account of necessary conditions for any possible relation to objects as well as his regulative idea theory, and he proposes a different approach. In fact he rejects any attempt simply to propose and defend a philosophic claim about what knowledge is or its conditions, or what it is for thoughts to have content, or how one could be said to know who one is, or what concepts are, and so on. All such claims, in his special sense of the term, "scientific" claims, can themselves always be shown to carry with them their own baggage of conditions, presuppositions impossible to discharge all at once in a pure philosophical account. (In a famous phrase, the "Absolute" cannot be "shot from a pistol.")[21] In a move that would virtually inaugurate what we now call "Continental philosophy," Hegel claimed that "Science, just because 'it *comes* on the scene (*auftritt*) is itself an *appearance*; in coming on the scene it is not yet developed and unfolded in its truth" (55;48). That is, there is no external or autonomous philosophic standpoint from which a critical assessment of possible claims to know could go on, no "bar of reason," above the fray, to which candidate accounts could be brought for a hearing. Any such standpoint is itself a mere appearance, by which Hegel means itself conditioned, or ultimately unable to account for its own possibility. As a consequence, "science must free itself from this semblance (*Scheine*) and it can do so only by turning against it" (55;48). It is this internally self-correcting progression of possible claims about the absolute possibility of knowledge that will comprise the narrative of the *Phenomenology* (where it is understood that the "problem of what knowing is" is quite wide-ranging, includes the possibility of representing a world, establishing truth-conditions, understanding others, recognizing the good, and so on). The book will be an "exposition of how knowledge makes its appearance," how the collective human "soul journeys through the series of its own shapes as though they were the stations set for it by its own nature, so that it may purify itself for existence as Spirit, and achieve, through a completed experience of itself, the awareness of what it is in itself" (55;49).

In the Preface, this sort of final telos is described in quite explicit terms: "the goal" of this self-negating process is simply *"Spirit's insight into what knowing is"* (25; 17), even though Hegel's language already makes very clear that such an insight will not conform to standard expectations about such an account. The fact that Hegel has inherited and affirms much of the Kantian account of the apperceptive nature of experience, the Kantian critique of empiricism, the general problem of "unconditioned conditions," and that he seems to adopt the goals of the critical philosophy itself (e.g., "what knowing is") all should not lead one to think that the project of the *Phenomenology* is epistemological. There is, again, no autonomous standpoint from which a purely epistemological critique could operate. Or: in recognizing the Kantian turn, that any claim about a correct discriminating or evaluating must be understood to amount to a claim that *"we take* such an activity to be a correct discriminating or evaluating," we must not thereby assume that we have any methodologically pure way of identifying *who* such a "we" is (as in a transcendental account of subjectivity), or any independent criteria for resolving the issue of when such a "we" ought to be satisfied that the ways in which the world and others are taken up and assessed are well grounded or "absolute." (Any such account would simply reflect "us.")[22] The whole point of Hegel's book is to counter any epistemological view of these tasks for critical philosophy and to develop a new account of such a "we" and such reassurance. Of course, to many this now looks like a recipe for relativism, historicism, sociologism, and so forth, but we ought to allow Hegel to launch his vessel properly before we worry about whether he has pushed it onto that slippery slope.

(iii) In the first three chapters of the *Phenomenology*, Hegel attempts a radically "internal" critique of very broadly described positions on the Absolute, or the possibility of knowledge. It is supposed to be internal in that no assumptions are made other than those shared by the positions in questions, and any inadequacies revealed are thus the result of inconsistencies and incompleteness internal to the position. The first three chapters all share the common assumption that "what is true for consciousness is something other than itself" (103;104). Commonsensically, this does not seem to be a position one ought to be eager to attack, but, by the start of Chapter Four on Self-Consciousness, Hegel thinks himself entitled to claim that he has shown "this whole Notion vanishes in the experience of it" (103; 104), presumably meaning what is now realized is that "what is true for consciousness" is *not* "something other than itself," that what we appeal to, what *makes* knowledge-claims true or false, is internal too, not other than consciousness itself.

This all suggests a metaphysical idealism that maintains that consciousness knows only itself, its own thoughts, and seems both extravagant and unsupported by any results established in the first three chapters. There Hegel had explored various "direct realist" accounts of the possibility of objects of consciousness, what we today might call the problem of intentionality or the possible content of representations. If the question is how we account for the directedness of conscious experience, for the fact that we think this, not that, thought and thereby successfully refer to this, not that, fragment of the world, Hegel tries to show the incompleteness and inadequacies of any account that maintains that the answer to such a question is: it is the world itself which, by impinging on our senses or mind, draws our attention to it in this or that way, given this or that feature of the object. Along the way in this account, he also tries to show why not much is gained by postulating different, non-sensible, sorts of external entities by apprehension of which a discriminating reference to the sensible world is possible: universals, abstract objects (in a later tradition, senses, thoughts, etc.), forces, and so on. Any relation to objects, even nonsensory objects, is, it is argued, inexplicable, or at least radically underdetermined, by any direct apprehension or causal influence of the object itself. Such a possibility is said already to presuppose some way of *comporting oneself toward* the world, some active attending and discriminating that cannot be a simple result of our encounter with the world, since the world offers up too many different ways for such a taking up and holding together. If this is true, then in experiencing the world any consciousness is also experiencing the world *as* discriminated and taken up in terms of such a comporting, or such a consciousness is not simply directly attending to some "other than consciousness," but, at least indirectly or implicitly, to itself, its own mode of comportment, a mode at least relatively empirically independent.

And none of this has anything to do with Hegel shifting the focus from the what's "Out There" as the guarantor of truth claims to what's all "In Here." In the first place, he maintains explicitly in the compressed opening passages of Chapter Four, that the "knowing of an other" has been "preserved" in the expanded account of knowledge as self-consciousness knowledge; that, for any self-consciousness, "the whole expanse of the sensuous world is preserved for it, but at the same time, only as related to the second moment, the unity of self-consciousness with itself" (104; 105). In the second place, he proceeds immediately to show that any account of the self "in the form of consciousness," supposedly simply grasping or apprehending its own thoughts or ideas, will simply replay the realist aporiai of the earlier chapters.

III. CHANGING THE SUBJECT: FROM CONSCIOUSNESS TO SPIRIT.

So far, perhaps, so good. But in the second full paragraph of Chapter Four, Hegel seems to shift topics abruptly, with little transition or even preparation. In discussing the stage now reached, he notes that the "sensuous world" is still understood as an "enduring existence," but in itself is merely an "appearance," discriminated as it is, possessing the sense or significance it has, only as a result of a subject's comporting itself toward it in a certain way.[23] He realizes that he has thus introduced the problem of how to account for these modes of comportment, or active, empirically undetermined ways of taking up and rendering intelligible the "sensuous world." In his language, this involves the "unity of self-consciousness with itself," and he simply states that "this unity must become essential to self-consciousness; *i.e., self-consciousness is desire in general*" (104; 105).

This claim about desire introduces a discussion of maintaining and reproducing life, eating, struggling with others to the death, and the social institution of mastery and slavery, all of which would seem to have little to do with the problem of adequately understanding how we might come to know more and more about the sensuous world.

One clue to why Hegel thinks such practical issues are relevant to the earlier topics is evident in his early, increasingly frequent use of the language of independence and dependence in accounting for the relation between a self-conscious subject and an external world.

True to dialectical form, we shall eventually learn that an abstract opposition between an independent, self-legislating subject ("commanding" rather than "begging" nature in Kant's phrase) and some wholly dependent other or other subject is an illusion. But at the present stage, Hegel believes he has just revealed the equally abstract one-sidedness of an independent, subject-determining sensible world, and that there must be some considerable measure of independence involved in how the subject takes up and orders its world. Since he is assuming that such independence means that such a contribution by the subject is *actively* contributed, and is not causally, even if remotely, dependent on its interaction with the world, he now assumes such activity is genuinely or internally self-directed, *purposive* in some sense. Or: if he has made his case that any coherent, unified experience of, or representation of, objects requires some truly independent activity on the part of a subject, then such independence can be realized only if the subject is purposively *self*-directing, if self-consciousness is desire or purposive activity in general.

Another important factor derives from the relation between phenomenology and epistemology cited earlier. He believes he has shown, by an internal critique, the insufficiencies of various realist or dependent accounts of consciousness. This means that any successful intending requires that a subject actively comport itself toward the world in some way, introducing the problem of the nature of this self-relation, how we should account for it. Here Hegel tries, not to purpose various theories and to test their adequacy, but to begin with a description of an "experience" of such a "self-relation in relation to an other" with minimal theoretical presuppositions, one putatively the most immediate or uncontroversial form of such a self-relation. Thus he proposes we consider the "sentiment of self" involved in leading or maintaining one's *life*, and so discriminations of experience that, while "objective," tied to the real properties of the world, are also necessarily relational and presuppose such a minimally self-directing, living being (e.g., categories like "food," "dangerous," "inedible," etc.).[24] Hegel has no illusions about this being an adequate classificatory scheme for our experience or an adequate account of the self-relation in question, but he wants to develop these inadequacies, and their resolutions, from within the framework of such an immediate form of self-consciousness.[25]

This can still, of course, smack of paradox. The world's being a possible, determinate world for me now seems somehow *dependent* on it "mattering" for me in a determinate way (it being an object of desire), given some general purposive agency in the world. And while there might be some very interesting link between possible modes of representing and such mattering (or desire), obvious care must be exercised lest the world seem to be too quickly "lost," lest its own constraints on what could matter, and, perhaps, its own role in what comes to matter, drop out.

But Hegel is just beginning, and, as indicated, he *is* careful, introducing what are self-evidently too crude, too simple examples of a "living" relation to the world, all the while making the general point that such a relation must be conceived in *some* way as such a living or purposive one, about the dependence of the determinacy of objects of experience on *some* form of self-directed comportment toward the world. Having introduced this demand for the subject's empirical independence and linked it with self-directed or purposive activity, he then proceeds to move from immediate versions of such self-relation to progressively more adequate accounts not only of such desiring activity but of such activity in relation to another, to externality or to other selves.

This involves him first, as indicated, in a dense account of life as the end or purpose of desire and finally to the most important internal transition in this transitional chapter, one effected in two very compressed sentences.

We need first to note the following. Hegel explains that even though a living subject could be said to be relatively independent in relation to objects by virtue of being in what he calls a "negative" relation to them, overcoming their resistance to its pursuit of life, ingesting them, etc.,[26] it is still the fact that "something other than self-consciousness" is the "essence of desire" (107; 109). That is, this immediate experience of a minimally self-directing comportment toward the world (what, putatively, the first three chapters had established as a condition of determinate experience) turns out to be only a relative independence, still tied as it is to given biological imperatives and to the kinds of objects contingently experienced to be capable of satisfying such imperatives.

Such a living subject still understands itself, its own relation to self, on the model of a dependent or passive consciousness, and so we are about to introduce all the problems hitherto demonstrated for such a model. How we come to understand our own desires, how we interpret such issues as intensity or priority, how we come to categorize the various objects or kinds of objects we think best satisfy such desires, will depend on, as it were, the conceptual arsenal we can deploy; and this again is not something, Hegel argues, we can understand as simply fixed or determined by our natures or by our direct interchange with the external world. As he will make clearer in the Introduction to the *Philosophy of Right*, our desires must be *rendered* determinate to be determinate, and they must be connected to various kinds of objects by us, something not explicable if our self-relation is understood as a sentiment of life or an experience of indeterminate wants and urges.[27]

It is not fully explicable for reasons Hegel thinks have already been established in the *Phenomenology*. That is, we should certainly admit, for example, that many animals could be said to act on the basis of a sentiment of and great attachment to life, and any cat owner knows that animals can be said to have preferences in the satisfactions of their desires. But Hegel is interested in the cognitive discriminatory capacities now taken to have something to do with a desiring, living relation to the world and, especially, in the origins of the determinate discriminations experienced as such by a subject and maintained as such over time. He thinks he has shown that no direct or immediate relation to objects could account for (or "radically underdetermines") such determinacy, nor for the way such a subject could be said to experience the confirmations or disconfirmations of such discriminations in experience. This is so whether such a relation is conceived in causal-sensory terms or as simply established by the various pulls and pushes, desires and aversions, of "life." To understand this possibility again means understanding the nature of the subject's "independence" in its relation to the world.

Such an independence in this context means that any such rendering determinate is not simply arbitrary but is always based on some general self-conception. This in turn cannot be understood as the result of any simple self-inspection, for all the reasons (the objections to "Consciousness") already cited. It is, to come to the term used to describe the major section in the chapter, a "free" self-determination. But just because of that, it is by no means *self-certifying*. In other words, Hegel is proposing an account of self-reflection that would be rendered simpler and much more dramatic by Sartre a century later. The self is not and cannot be an internal object of self-inspection, but a "project," a way of projecting oneself forward into the world; a "promise to oneself to act" in a certain way or, in Hegel's account, a kind of practical resolution that fundamentally orients one to a world and is of crucial importance in any basic categorization of the world. When viewed this way, a great possible gap opens up between the putative "certainty" of such a self-understanding and its "truth," what, in the world, could be said to confirm or reject, render adequate or false, or render, phenomenologically, finally "satisfying" about such a self-understanding.

One threat to such a defeasible self-projection is, according to Hegel, unique. Hence the transitional passage spoken of earlier.

> But at the same time it [self-consciousness] is just as much absolutely for itself, and it is so only through the sublating of the object; and it must, for itself, become satisfied in this, for it is the truth. Because of the independence of the object, therefore, it can achieve satisfaction only when the object itself completes this negation in itself, and it must itself complete this negation in itself, for it is in itself the negative, and must be for the other what it is. (108; 109)

The *problem* is how such a self-determining self-consciousness could be said to "satisfy" itself such that its own negative relation to objects and to itself, or its independence of such objects, has been genuinely realized. The *premise* is that a matter of fact negation of passive objects cannot accomplish such satisfaction. As we saw, such activities can occur under various possible self-interpretations and world-categorizations, and mere success (staying alive, leading a life with success against obstacles) establishes nothing about such conceptions. The *solution* suggested is that such a satisfaction can occur only by means of another free, self-determining being (the "object" which achieves "negation within itself"), or which is likewise self-determining with respect to its desires and ends. Or: "self-consciousness finds its satisfaction only in another self-consciousness" (108; 109).

Hegel is implying that the kind of resistance offered by another self-consciousness to the realization of my desires in the world (and so the kind of test or challenge to my self- and world-conception raised by such a subject) is of a qualitatively different sort than that posed by normal objects. Given a finite universe, it is inevitable that two such independent self-consciousnesses will conflict in their struggle for resources or attempts to satisfy their desires. Implicit in this sort of struggle, however, is the realization that each rejects the other ("negates" the other) *as subject* by opposing each other; each implicitly rejects the subjective self-determination that would have led each to this contested object. In the most immediate form of such a struggle, each is rendered object by the other, a means for a subject's negative independence. Alternatively, such a situation also provides the opportunity for a kind of confirmation of my subjectivity in the possibility of a genuinely "mutual recognition" of such subjectivity.

Thus Hegel is denying that we can presume any common ground between such struggling subjects, at least not without begging all the interesting questions. There is no way to assume that each fears most passionately a violent death, that each values a rational or mutually acceptable secure satisfaction of as many of her projects as possible, that each will adopt a "live and let live" attitude. All of these cannot be explained naturally or metaphysically as uncontestable facts of the matter, once the whole structure of "Consciousness" has been abandoned. Each sort of possible resolution thus represents a self-determined, or negative, relation to objects and others which we have no reason to expect will be simultaneously determined or affirmed by any other.

Now, admittedly, Hegel is not as precise as he might be in stating exactly what he means to claim about such subjects. For the most part, he remains true to the above gloss and to his famous claim that a self-consciousness finds *satisfaction* in another self-consciousness, that the very independence from the world established thus far makes possible only one way of realizing or confirming such a projecting, self-determining subjectivity: in mutual recognition, something that will eventually introduce the Hegelian notion of universally binding institutions, and so the necessity (the lived or experienced necessity) of a common commitment to rationality. Occasionally, however, he says such things as, "There is a self-consciousness for a self-consciousness; it is first of all by means of this fact that there really is a self-consciousness" ("*ist es in der Tat*") (108; 110). Or he claims that "self-consciousness exists only in being recognized" (109; 111). Such claims have led many commentators directly to the theory of social identity at stake in these sections, and so to the controversial claim, apparently, that such a form of identity is the only possible one. This in turn suggests some sort of Robinson Crusoe thought experiment, the attempt to imagine the kind of self-awareness possible for a radically isolated subject, all as if the claim is supposed to be that such a subject could not use the first-person pronoun or be self-conscious in any sense.

But Hegel's own gloss on such passages suggests no such argument. In fact he sets up the discussion by positing that "there is a self-consciousness for a self-consciousness," presuming some conflict of independently self-relating beings. What *is* claimed is that it is only in such a relation that a self-consciousness can be realized or confirmed in its self-understanding, only therein can it be *"in der Tat,"* actually, a self-consciousness. Or, when he says that self-consciousness "is only in being recognized," he means a self-consciousness that is "in and for itself," or a finally realized, completed, or reassured self-consciousness. Again, "self-consciousness achieves its *satisfaction* only in another self-consciousness."

Such claims will loom large in Hegel's ethical theory, later in the book and later in his career. They introduce Hegel's insistence that the modern idea of freedom as self-determination and the modern demand that I be able to recognize myself in my deeds as their originator must also take account of the fact that I am not my own origin; I am free even though a socially dependent being (in his unique terms, I am "an absolute substance which in the complete freedom and independence of its oppositions, namely different self-consciousnessness existing for themselves, is a unity with itself" (108;110). Or, I am "spirit."[28]

Here, however, he continues to make reference to the problematic begun in the Consciousness chapters; he continues to search for ways in which reflective beings might *reassure themselves* about the independent ways they take up and categorize the world as well as each other. If this reassurance cannot be provided directly or immediately, say, by truths of reason (the faith that the order of knowing and the order of being are the same), a rigorous, narrow, universal method, or by some reliance on an immediate, direct experience of the sensible world, then, he has argued, the problem of a *"self*-relation in relation to the world" can only be understood as the purposive self-relation within which the world is immediately lived. The relevance of another self-consciousness for me is said to be that "only in this way" (through my opposition to and struggle with such a subject) "does the unity of itself in its otherness come to be for it" (108; 110). I take this reference to a "unity of itself in its *otherness*" to be quite a general claim and, I have been suggesting, to signal Hegel's shift away from the modern problem of epistemology, away from an individual subject reassuring itself about its mode of repre-senting, to a realization that any such mode of representing should be understood as already a social product, requiring some account of the possibility of such social origins and a possible social resolution of conflicting modes.[29]

There are still miles to go before Hegel can try to demonstrate why such mutuality should be relevant to a genuine "relation to otherness" (why we should not have simply introduced here the prospect of mutual self-delusion or a proposal to turn the problem of knowledge wholly into an issue of "socially sanctioned beliefs"), but Hegel himself explicitly introduces these problems when he returns to philosophic expressions of the independence-dependence problems here introduced. His own introduction of his crucial term of art, spirit, is couched in the language of the rejected *cognitive* alternatives hitherto discussed. "In Self-consciousness, in the con-cept of Spirit, consciousness first has its turning point, from which it leaves behind the colorful appearance of the sensible immediacy [*Diesseits*] and the empty night of the supersensible beyond [*Jen-seits*] and steps out into the spiritual daylight of the present" (108–9; 110–1).

This putative "spiritual daylight" illuminates what Hegel de-scribes as a "many sided" phenomenon with "many meanings" (109; 111). His famous account of a "struggle to the death for recogni-tion," the resulting Master-Slave dialectic, and moments reactive to such social power, the slave's work, the reconciling philosophies of Stoicism and Skepticism, and finally the unusual account of the social significance of the Jewish and early Christian experiences of God, "the unhappy consciousness," are all said to be consequences of the attempt by self-conscious subjects to find their "satisfaction" through each other and *thereby* establish a relation to objects secure from the *Phenomenology's* "pathway of doubt" and "highway of despair."

We can now summarize the results of this reading this way: how we come to understand each other as purposive, self-directing subjects should not be understood as exclusively a problem concerning some unique metaphysical object or domain, or one with its own "logic" that must be respected for some metaphysical or practical reason.[30] It is not that there are simply special, irreducible categories for the "human sciences" or purposive beings. Rather, Hegel is suggesting that how we come to understand or make judgments *about anything* must be a function of some sort of mutually sanctioning process *among* such subjects, and that this process can be understood only by considering such subjects as practical, purposive, or living beings. Hegel has thus tied the possibility of some epistemic reassurance about our representational strategies and conceptual schemes to some form of social or mutual reassurance, and so to a general claim that the possibility of judgment always requires such independent, mutually related subjects.

IV. WHY REASON MUST BECOME SPIRIT.

In Hegel's presentation of the remaining sections of the Self-Consciousness chapter, the attempt to secure or confirm such a necessary form of independence in the face of the obvious experience of a dependence on an other ("the Master") and the biological necessities of life is a constant theme. Or at least this is the way Hegel interprets what Nietzsche would call the fundamentally "ascetic" character of much of the history of Western culture. Stoic dualism, the negative activity of skepticism, and the "unhappy" displacement of real worth and subjectivity in a relation to a beyond and an afterlife are all said to represent strategies by which laboring, dependent subjects could still nevertheless affirm, collectively, without engendering a new struggle for recognition, what cannot be denied even if not yet realized: their independence or freedom.

In the course of this narrative, Hegel presents a highly idealized account of a transition between elements of the Christian, ascetic, otherworldly self-understanding and a very different sort of assertion of independence with respect to this world, one not so abstractly negative, and so not so empty and dissatisfying. This more successful realization of what, controversially, Hegel identifies as the real Christian intention (to secure or realize the independence of a self-

consciousness now conceived collectively, in the light of each other)
is identified as the standpoint of "Reason."

"Up to now," Hegel argues,

self-consciousness has only been concerned with its independence and freedom, concerned for itself to save and preserve itself at the cost of the world
or its own actuality, both of which seemed to it as the negative of its own
essence. But as Reason, assured of itself, is at peace with them, and can
endure them, for it is certain of itself as reality, or that all actuality is
nothing other than it; its thinking is immediately, actuality, and so it relates
to it as idealism. (132; 139)

Initially, such a notion of idealism seems quite general and, since
Parmenides, quite familiar: what reason cannot determine to be is
not, and not-being cannot be. Or, to be is to be intelligible, where
intelligibility is understood in terms of some procedure or method or
intuition which can ensure the universal assent of anyone who "relies on reason alone." But Hegel goes on to suggest how such an
idealism must develop "for itself" and from itself the categories by
means of which its "identity with being" is concretely realized, and
he very quickly begins to develop this problem in the explicit terms
of post-Kantian and post-Fichtean idealism, the I's self-relation and
the "outrage on Science" left by Kant, that the Understanding
should not be able to demonstrate its own categories, "demonstrate
a necessity . . . in its own self, which is purely necessity" (135; 143).

This leads Hegel into an account of what a subject that understands
its "self-relation in relation to an other" as wholly based on reason,
universal criteria of evidence and inference, would look like. That is,
both the social origins of such an appeal to the authority of reason,
and the social implications of such an appeal for the subjects who
bind themselves to it, are kept in view as Hegel examines the nature
of such a criterion. Or he treats reason as everywhere also a social
sanction; he continues to keep in view the general problem of realizing some form of a self-determining subjectivity in a mutually self-
reassuring way. And he again tries to develop this account by beginning with the most straightforward sort of appeal to reason, one
wherein what counts as an acceptable claim about anything should be
confirmable by strict, methodologically rigorous *observation*.

Given the way Hegel has set up the problem, this issue leads to a
discussion of *who* the subjects of such an inquiry are, or at least what

they would look like within such a methodologically rigorous procedure, and so what sorts of claims they would or could have on each
other, how their relation to each other would look if defined by an
appeal to "observing reason." His question is whether that relation
could be consistent with the canons of observing reason itself. His
argument, too complex and too involved with various nineteenth-
century sciences to summarize here, is that such a narrow view of a
rational basis for mutual reassurance ends up inconsistently reducing
such subjects to observable things, and thereby is unable to account
for the authority or even the determinate character of the procedures
by virtue of which that reduction is accomplished.[31]

In a way that parallels his earlier treatment, Hegel again argues that
such an epistemic warrant ("Reason") must be consistent with the
conditions under which it could be a mutually imposed sanction and
could be authorized *by* self-authorizing, ultimately mutually recognizing subjects. Since this cannot happen under "observing reason,"
subjects must then be explicitly reconceived as *rationally acting* or
self-realizing subjects, agents whose claims on each other must be
based somehow on their recognition of each other as subjects who
mutually commit themselves to a common, rational standard. And
this development, the introduction of "The Actualization of Rational
Self-Consciousness Through Its Own Activity," brings us close to
another famous transition problem. For in exploring what could
count as a reason in action or for a genuine *subject*, and why such an
appeal would be necessary if any agent were to be a successfully self-
determining subject, Hegel again criticizes an individualist notion of
such agency, again introduces the explicit theme of sociality, or *Geist*,
this time in a way that will lead to an extensive, detailed historical
narrative, involving well-known accounts of Greek tragedy, Roman
law, court culture, and the French Revolution.

There is one section in particular where Hegel's intentions in this
transition can be most economically discussed, the section intrigu-
ingly titled "The Spiritual Realm of Animals and Deception; Or, the
Real Thing."[32] The section is preceded by Hegel's attempt to detail
the insufficiencies of various accounts of a rational realization of
one's individuality: a simple hedonism (the most rational assumption we can make about everyone is that they seek pleasure), a
romantic individualism (what is rational is the recognition that
there is no legitimate constraint on the each becoming who he or

she truly is), and a moralistic, sentimental individualism, locked in a perpetual fight to preserve an individual, self-certifying purity against the inevitably corrupt "way of the world."

The inadequacies of all of these as standards for what is individually rational bring us to the section in question. In these "immediate" forms of rational agency, where the assumption is that rationality is measured by one's success in realizing or satisfying one's individual "true nature" (or "heart"), the common problem concerns how an individual would come to identify some content as his own nature or true individuality. And at one point Hegel comes to consider a form of individuality that rejects any potentially alienating conception of "true" individuality (measured against some "law" or ideal requiring that I *become* a "true" individual) and which instead simply "takes itself *to be* real in and for itself," and so for which "action changes nothing and opposes nothing. It is the pure form of a transition from a state of not being seen to a state of being seen" (215; 237). Individuals view each other as naturally and/or historically endowed with particular and unique talents and capacities, and the public space or social world, now conceived as, at least minimally, rationally ruled and structured, is to be the arena wherein these capacities and talents are mutually displayed, where each is, as much as mutually possible, "who he is."

Predictably, Hegel again asks, "Let us see whether this concept is confirmed for it by experience and whether its reality corresponds to it" (220; 242). This examination takes up yet again an individualist notion of agency and again suggests a reason for Hegel's dissatisfactions, a kind of reason we have been seeing throughout the *Phenomenology*. Here the general problem is Hegel's dissatisfactions with what a contemporary audience would most easily recognize as an individualist, *prudential* notion of rationality. It is in this context that he describes the liberal notion of social space as an arena of mutual self-realization, something he calls a "spiritual animal kingdom."[33]

The target of Hegel's concerns could be termed a prudential notion of rationality because "Hegel's spiritual animal is an acting consciousness that knows of no demands opposing it. It determines itself strictly in accordance with its own nature."[34] It appears that Hegel is trying to show that no such conception of reason, in which a course of action is rational for me simply if it fits into and helps realize my overall life plan and interests, could count as a reason, that "good reasons for action, to qualify as such, must fit into a supra-individual context of meaning,"[35] or, in other words, could be reasons only if tied to the development or realization of a supra-individual subject, *Geist*. The idea would be that nothing could conceivably count as a reason for *me* unless *I* can understand myself as also counting for something larger or of more general significance than just "little old me."[36]

The question is how Hegel would argue for such a claim or effect such a transition to spirit. Of crucial importance in that argument is what Hegel calls the experience of "the antithesis of doing (*Tun*) and Being (*Sein*)" (221; 244) that results from my prudential action, my attempt simply to act for, to exhibit, myself. The argument turns on this issue, and it appears to refer to the fact that, no matter what I intend and plan, once I act, the results and implications of my action, most of which could not have been foreseen, determine on their own, contingently, what it is "I did," and so the *act* "vanishes" in the doing of it, is swallowed up by these implications and consequences. A gap opens up between what I *do* and, contingently, what the act *is*. I act, prudently, to secure my reputation for honesty, because that is important to me; but what I end up doing is insulting a friend, ruining a marriage, and become known as a mindless busybody. So, as the argument apparently proceeds, I come to experience this "vanishing" of my work as itself something that "vanishes," or is not real, does not really count, does not affect the true significance of my work, now called "die Sache selbst," or *the real thing* I am trying to effect, some supra-individual context not tied to me as an individual or to the contingent effects of my deeds in the world.

Reading Hegel this way (as committed to a kind of question-begging claim that such contingency alone deprives prudential reasoning of its possible worth)[37] will not get us very far into his argument. The problem is not that Hegel is looking for a kind of significance for my deeds that can console me about the variable interpretations, confusions, ambiguities, unforeseen effects, and general contingency that attach to any deed of mine. For one thing, Hegel is clearly by no means satisfied with the abstract "Real Thing Idealism" by which acting subjects do try to console themselves, by appeal to which they insist that there is a "real thing" or "heart of the matter" that transcends their particular fate. He admits that while this sort of resistance to my losing control over the significance of my deeds and work introduces the idea of an ethical "substance," it does so only "immediately" and has not yet progressed into a "truly real substance" (224; 247). In this limited social context, the attempt by subjects to preserve a kind of integrity or "honesty" about the true significance of their deeds turns out to be a difficult, ambiguous attempt. "The truth about this honesty, however, is that it is not as honest as it seems" (225; 248–49). What I "remain true to" as the "real thing" in my deed has exactly as much self-certifying authority as the immediate presumption of a self-determining subjectivity in the original struggle for recognition, that is, no self-certifying authority. What I hold back as "real" in the act and what the other takes up as real cannot be independently measured or confirmed either by me or the other. "Since, in this alternation, consciousness holds one moment as essential, for itself, and considers another moment as only externally in the deed, or for others, there occurs a play of individualities with one another, wherein everyone finds themselves everywhere deceiving and deceived" (226; 250).

At this stage of the narrative, no subject could presume simply to master another subject, to demand that such a subject's "Sache selbst" be recognized as such. All are committed to a universally affirmable standard recognizing individually self-determining agency. But the result of such an invocation of an individualistically and prudentially conceived "Reason" as a standard of mutual recognition is, as it has been before, an unsatisfying and uncertain *self-relation*.

That is, the problem at stake for Hegel goes much deeper than worries about contingency and still concerns what it is for any deed *to be mine* in the first place, or whether I can reassure myself that my "life plan" is *mine*. What is important to him from the start about the "being" (*Sein*) of a work or deed is that it "is, i.e. exists for other individualities," and these others confront the work as an "alien" or "strange" actuality which they, in their own "work" must "make their own in order to secure through their work their consciousness of a unity with the actual" (221, 243).

This situation is nicely summarized by the claim that,

It is just as much a *deception of oneself* and others to be concerned with some pure "real thing." Any consciousness that takes up such a real thing finds rather that others hurry along to such a thing, like flies to freshly poured milk, and want to busy themselves with it. One discovers that others treat one's affair not as an object, but as their own affair. (227; 251; my emphasis)

Hegel goes on in this section to point out that even what I regard as my own powers and capacities, my very individuality, is always something that is just as much for others and so never, even for me, can result in a pure "doing."

Thus for Hegel the heart of the on-going, often implicit social negotiations within modernity (when the notion of mutually free, self-determining subjects has been introduced and the realization of which has become an inevitable demand) cannot concern only the mutually secured, efficient satisfaction of interests, preferences, or life-plans. Even under the assumptions of such a project, a course of action could count as a prudential or instrumental reason for me to act only given some sort of reassurance that the interests or preferences are mine, are not the socially manufactured results of someone else's (or some other group or class's) "Sache selbst." But it is then obviously hard to see such a social struggle, about something so elusive and hard to confirm as, in essence, one's identity as a free agent, as some explicit issue that could be addressed *by* individual subjects (however free and unconstrained their communicative situation might be, to note a contemporary resolution of this issue). Action, the reality (*Sache*) of which is now conceived as "of each and everyone," requires an analysis of "the essence which is the essence of all beings, spiritual essence" (227; 252), or what Hegel had earlier introduced as the historical community, the *Volk*, within which reason is sustained and realized. And all of this is said to be necessary even if we assume that reasons can count as reasons only if they can count for me. That "me" can function no more successfully as "the real thing" as any other candidate, or at least not without some attempt to locate it within, to see its dependence on, "the spiritual essence."

But how to account for such a spiritual essence, now argued to have such explanatory priority in any account of mind-world relations or human agency? At this point Hegel notes that it might still be possible to account for the bonds of such a spiritual community in terms of what he calls "thought" as "distinguished from actual self-consciousness" (228; 252). Or subjection to very general practical "laws of reason" might be sufficient to realize at least some minimal form of mutual agency in some publicly confirmable, "testable" way. These laws, however, without the connection to "actual self-consciousness" that Hegel will now introduce, mostly have a vague "don't make yourself an exception" character or "be rational" form which, Hegel argues, ensures that they cannot be concretely action-guiding. He will of course return to this theme when he considers the "actual" historical institution of "morality," but for now he turns quickly to the narrative of such actual self-consciousness itself. The extraordinarily rich details of that narrative cannot be followed here.

V. CONCLUSION

Hegel's *Phenomenology of Spirit* is a book that had no predecessors and, with the possible exceptions of works such as Nietzsche's *Genealogy of Morals*, Proust's *Remembrance of Things Past*, Lukács *History and Class Consciousness*, or Pound's *Cantos* (and perhaps Wittgenstein's *Investigations*), no true successors. Many parts of it will doubtless always seem mysterious and unconnected to other parts. But it is not a hopeless gallimaufry of insights, suggestions, and stories. There certainly is a common theme running through its turns and transitions, and a common goal Hegel thinks he much reach: a mutually recognizing and so mutually reassured social subjectivity. Or the book is about what Hegel finally decided it was about – *Geist*.

The preceding discussion is only an introductory account of how Hegel thought he could reach that goal, but it does, I think, allow some generalizations about the work's form. First and most obviously, even those most skeptical about the work have to try to take into account the fact that Hegel intended a transition from "Consciousness" to "Self-Consciousness." There is no evidence that he simply regarded himself as changing topics, and there is good evidence that he explicitly did not regard himself as doing that. This meant that he wanted to connect the problem of the "mind-world" relation to the "subject-subject" relation, an argument summarized, or at least sketched, above. Moreover, since he wanted to avoid thinking of such subjects as understanding themselves and each other on the discarded "Consciousness" model, he tried to reconceive such subject-subject relations in a way that avoided any suggestion of fully formed, self-inspecting rational agents confronting each other in social space. Such relations were to be understood as mutually self-forming in time.

This aspect of Hegel's case is introduced in as general and schematic a way as possible. He is not trying to talk about historical forms of such relations but about what must be the case for any sort of historical relation to be understood as relations of free subjects. (Of course he uses identifiable examples of such general possibilities, but it is very important that he avoids names, designations, or references to actuality, something he does do freely later.) He tries then to show that with the problem of a self-determining subjectivity understood this way, as a problem of mutual recognition or mutual reassurance, some common subjection to a universal criterion of thought and action, "Reason," one that would make possible a much more determinate (less "abstractly negative") relation to the world, would serve as the most likely resolution of this problem.

As noted above, from the very beginning of this discussion, still an idealized and theoretical account of what could accommodate subjects to each other in their relations to the world, Hegel already promises a completion or realization of such a hope in an account of actual historical communities and their histories, something he repeats at the end of the chapter. Again, as with the first transition, there is no great shifting of gears or leap to another topic. No account, no internal account, of the rationality of prudential and legalistic candidates for such an integrating, reconciling absolute turns out to be possible, or at least not without some account of how I got to be me, came in real human time to identify with all others what has come to count as "the real things."

With this insistence on the relevance of "actuality" (*Wirklichkeit*), though, Hegel does not abandon the general possibility of a rational integration in a modern community in favor of some social anthropology or sociology of knowledge; he carries on with the argument that only a concrete historical narrative of what we have come to count as essential to our mutually recognized self-determining agency will be able to account for, and *rationally* reconcile us to, such a developed form.[38] Or, put a final way: once the mind-world problem is linked to the subject-subject problem, and such subjects are understood in the mutually dependent, self-transforming way they are, the problem of consciousness must become the problem of *Geist*, and *Geist* can only be accounted for by a "phenomenology" of its collective self-transformations. This, at any rate, is the argument (and the hope) of Hegel's *Phenomenology*.

NOTES

1 Cf. H.S. Harris, "Processional Interlude," *Hegel's Development: Night Thoughts (Jena 1801–1806)* (Oxford: Oxford University Press, 1983), ix–lxx, and the discussion and notes in my *Hegel's Idealism: The Satisfactions of Self-Consciousness* (Cambridge: Cambridge University Press, 1989), Chapter Four, 60–66.

2 G.W.F. Hegel, *Phänomenologie des Geistes*, ed. Wolfgang Bonsiepen and Reinhard Heede (Volume 9 of the *Gesammelte Werke*, published by the Rheinisch-Westfälischen Akademie der Wissenschaften) (Hamburg: Felix Meiner Verlag, 1980), 61. All translations in the text are my own and will be followed by the page number of this edition, then the page number of *Hegel's Phenomenology of Spirit*, transl. A.V. Miller (Oxford: Oxford University Press, 1979), 56.

3 Actually the situation is even more confused than this. See Friedhelm Nicolin, "Zum Titelproblem der Phänomenologie des Geistes," *Hegel-Studien* 4 (1967): 113–23. In what the best evidence indicates was Hegel's final intention, there is a "Hauptitel" page, announcing a "System der Wissenschaft: Erster Theil: die Phänomenologie des Geistes," and there is an additional so-called "Zwischentitel" page inserted after the new preface, proclaiming simply "I: Wissenschaft der Phänomenologie des Geistes." There is a good summary in Nicolin's article of attempts by editors over the years to resolve the problem, and of the latest efforts by researchers at the Hegel archives to come up with a definitive narrative of Hegel's intentions. To complicate matters, the most-used German edition for years was Hoffmeister's Philosophische Bibliothek version, which, while recognizing that Hegel changed his mind, confusingly and with no justification, still inserted the "Wissenschaft der Erfahrung" title immediately after the Preface.

4 Hans Friedrich Fulda, *Das Problem einer Einleitung in Hegels Wissenschaft der Logik* (Frankfurt: Klostermann, 1965), 1–13.

5 For a strong defense of the priority of the *Logic* in Hegel, but which nonetheless attempts to take account of the *Phenomenology*, see Stanley Rosen, *G.W.F. Hegel: An Introduction to the Science of Wisdom* (New Haven: Yale University Press, 1974).

6 Otto Pöggeler, "Die Komposition der Phänomenologie des Geistes," in *Materialen zu Hegels 'Phänomenologie des Geistes'*, ed. Hans Fulda and Dieter Henrich (Frankfurt: Suhrkamp, 1973), 334.

7 Rosenkranz claims that the idea of the rationality of historical actuality began to take shape in notes for 1805–6 winter semester, and therewith the problem of the historical possibility of Hegel's system. See Karl Rosenkranz, *Hegels Leben* (Darmstadt: Wissenschaftliche Buchgesellschaft, 1963), 201–6. The best summary of the twists and turns in the Hegel literature on this issue is provided by Pöggeler, "Zur Deutung der Phänomenologie des Geistes" in his *Hegels Idee einer Phänomenologie des Geistes* (Freiburg/Munich: Verlag Karl Alber, 1973), 170–230.

8 See Pöggeler, "Zur Deutung," op.cit., 176–/8.

9 "The Notion of pure science and its deduction is therefore presupposed in the present work in so far as the *Phenomenology of Spirit* is nothing other than the deduction of it." G.W.F. Hegel, *Wissenschaft der Logik*, Vol. I (Hamburg: Felix Meiner Verlag, 1969), 30; *Science of Logic*, trans. A.V. Miller (London: George Allen & Unwin, 1969), 49. For an analysis of this claim, see my *Hegel's Idealism*, 94–99.

10 Rudolf Haym, *Hegel und seine Zeit: Vorlesungen über Entstehung und Entwicklung, Wesen und Wert der Hegelschen Philosophie* (Berlin: R. Gaertner, 1857).

11 Ibid., 243.

12 T. Haering, "Die Entstehungsgeschichte der Phänomenologie des Geistes," in *Verhandlungen des dritten Hegelkongresses*, ed. B. Wigersma (Tübingen: J.C.B. Mohr, 1934), 118–38.

13 Pöggeler, "Zur Deutung," op.cit., 193ff, on Haering's "Sackgasse" or dead end.

14 Hegel defines the stance of "consciousness" as our natural or unreflective experience of a subject standing over against and trying to represent objects successfully, and of knowledge as a way of closing this subject-object gap, of grasping or picturing or intending the world as it is. By the chapter on self-consciousness, as we shall discuss below, that pre-theoretical attitude has already been undermined in various ways.

15 See Pöggeler, "Zur Deutung," op.cit., 221. See also his discussion in "Die Komposition," op.cit., 353–54.

16 H.F. Fulda, "Zur Logik der Phänomenologie," in Fulda and Henrich, eds., *Materialen zu Hegels Phänomenologie*, op.cit., 391–422.

17 Johannes Heinrichs, *Die Logik der Phänomenologie des Geistes* (Bonn: Bouvier, 1974).

18 "That the true is only actual as system, or that Substance is essentially subject, is expressed in the representation of the Absolute as Spirit – the

most sublime concept and the one which belongs to the new age and its religion" (22; 14).

19 This interpretation of the Hegelian Absolute is the central theme in my *Hegel's Idealism*. Kark Ameriks, in a review article to appear soon in *Philosophy and Phenomenological Research*, has raised a number of questions about the logical status of the claim that "all" human knowledge and agency is "self-reflexive." He suggests that if Hegel can help us out with an "analysis" of the conditions for any thought or agency which *is* self-reflexive, then we ought to be satisfied and ought not to extend the analysis into a suspect claim about what is necessary for *all* thought or agency (i.e., implying that there are plenty of relations to objects and others that are not reflexive in the Hegelian sense). But (a) Hegel has no reason to deny that there can be matter-of-fact relations between psychological subjects and the physical world, or between such subjects; his question is the same as Kant's: What makes such relations *cognitive*, directed toward objects by means of *possibly true or false* claims? and (b) there is always, in this and many other cases, some sense in which claims about the conditions necessary for such relations could be said to be "analytic," where that simply means "not based on any matter of fact" or "autonomously philosophical." But in Hegel the notion has nothing to do with any thesis about language, meaning, truths of reason, and so forth. Moreover, Hegel has his own reasons for denying that the traditional (Kantian) analytic/synthetic distinction presents well-formed alternatives. See *Hegel's Idealism*, 251–52.

20 Several other questions about such a reading of the Absolute naturally arise, many related to suspicions that Hegel's famous accounts of history, sociality, and religion would be incoherent without a "metaphysical" Absolute. For some suggestions about that issue and a denial that such suspicions are warranted, see Terry Pinkard, "The Successor to Metaphysics: Absolute Idea and Absolute Spirit," *The Monist* 74 (1991): 295–328.

21 In the *Phenomenology*, the phrase occurs in the Preface, 24; 16.

22 This is one of many reasons to be careful about any claim concerning Hegel's "transforming" epistemology into "social theory," a turn of phrase that implies that Hegel believes in the autonomy of social theory. Cf. the Preface to J. Habermas, *Knowledge and Human Interests*, trans. J. Shapiro (Boston: Beacon, 1971), and the discussion in G. Kortian, *Metacritique: The Philosophical Argument of Jürgen Habermas* (Cambridge: Cambridge University Press, 1980). See also my "The Idealism of Transcendental Arguments," *Idealistic Studies* XVIII (1988): 97–106. A number of important dimensions of this problem, many of great relevance to Hegel, are insightfully discussed in Jonathan Lear, "Transcen-

dental Anthropology," in *Subject, Thought and Context,* ed. P. Petit and J. McDowell (Oxford: Oxford University Press, 1986), 267–98.

23 More precisely, such a spontaneous activity is at least a necessary condition of any experienced determinacy, although certainly not sufficient. The sensuous world does not "vanish" what vanishes is its status as wholly independent ground of experience.

24 See Pöggeler's discussion on the Aristotelian issues introduced by the issue of life; "Die Komposition," op.cit., 363.

25 It is thus a mistake to ask in too narrow a way directly, as posed earlier, what arguments about possible objects of consciousness have to do with, e.g., practical strategies like eating, struggles for recognition, etc. Such an approach narrows a reader's focus too much and does not allow the full problem of a self-determining subjectivity to emerge, or Hegel's explicit account of the internal inadequacies of various pragmatic or social experiences of self-consciousness (or why subject-subject relations *themselves* require some resolution of mind-world problems). Looked at more broadly, I am suggesting, one can see how and why the more recognizable issue of a "self-relation in relation to objects" re-emerges with philosophies like Stoicism. See the discussion in *Hegel's Idealism,* op.cit., 143–71.

26 "Certain of the nothingness of the other, it posits this nothingness for itself as its truth; it destroys the independent object and thereby gives itself the certainty of itself as a true certainty, a certainty which has become explicit for it in an objective way" (107; 109).

27 See, especially, the Remarks to section 12 and 13 in *Grundlinien der Philosophie des Rechts* (Hamburg: Felix Meiner Verlag, 1955), 36–37; *Hegel's Philosophy of Right,* transl. T.M. Knox (Oxford: Clarendon Press, 1967), 26; and the discussion in my "Hegel, Ethical Reasons, Kantian Rejoinders," *Philosophical Topics* 19 (1991): 105.

28 There is a very good discussion of the implications of this theory of agency in the *Phenomenology* by Terry Pinkard in his forthcoming *History and Self-Identity: Hegel's Phenomenology of the Human Community.* I should also note here that I am concentrating on the neglected topic of the continuity between aspects of Hegel's account of theoretical and practical philosophy in the *Phenomenology,* and so am neglecting the very great, direct relevance of his account of recognition for his philosophy of religion and his social theory. Compared with his earlier Jena period theory, Hegel himself alters and narrows his early account of recognition in the *Phenomenology* in order to make this continuity issue easier to see. Cf. my account of this issue in *Hegel's Idealism,* 154–63, and the valuable discussions by H.S. Harris, "The Concept of Recognition in Hegel's Jena Manuscripts," *Hegel-Studien* 20 (1980):

229–48; Ludwig Siep, *Anerkennung als Prinzip der praktischen Philosophie* (Freiburg/Munich: Karl Alber, 1979); and Andreas Wildt, *Autonomie und Anerkennung, Hegels Moralitätskritik im Lichte seiner Fichte-
Rezeption* (Stuttgart: Klett-Cotta, 1982).

29 Putting the point this way naturally introduces the topic of the relation
between Hegel's project and Habermas's. For a more-extended discussion, especially of their differences, see my "Hegel, Habermas, and
Modernity," *The Monist* 74 (1991): 329–57. Also see one of the most-
suggestive Hegelian discussions of Habermas, Axel Honneth, *The Critique of Power: Reflective Stages in a Critical Social Theory*, trans. K.
Baynes (Cambridge: MIT Press, 1991).

30 He does of course believe that purposive beings require different sorts
of accounts than those limited to mechanistically conceived, or merely
organic, "growing" beings. But his reasons are complex and non-metaphysical. See my "Idealism and Agency in Kant and Hegel," *Journal of
Philosophy* LXXXVIII (October 1991): 532–41.

31 An exemplary account of Hegel's worries here can be found in Alisdair
MacIntyre, "Hegel on Faces and Skulls," in *Hegel: A Collection of Critical Essays* (Notre Dame: University of Notre Dame Press, 1976), 219–36.

32 "The real thing" is a translation of "die Sache selbst," which is in this
context, to put it mildly, difficult to translate. "The heart of the matter"
or "the matter at hand" seem too far from the original.

33 This odd phrase is meant to capture the irony of subjects who demand to
be taken "just as they are," as if simply displaying to each other natural
species-differences in the animal kingdom, but whose self-conscious
interaction creates an experience that undermines such an immediate
reconciliation with one's "nature" or "life interests," which reveals one
as, oddly, a "*spiritual* animal" (or no simple animal at all).

34 Rüdiger Bittner, *What Reason Demands* (Cambridge: Cambridge University Press, 1989), 146. Cf. *Phenomenology*, 220–21; 242–43.

35 Ibid., 144.

36 "Rational determination of action is conceivable only as taking place in
a context of meaning extending beyond the individual's actions" (ibid.,
143).

37 If this problem of contingency is what is worrying Hegel, it would always be possible to claim, as Bittner does, that there is no such disconso-
late experience, "not because the spiritual animal does not care about
the work" but "for the opposite reason." "As a rational being, the spiritual animal does not console itself on the transience of its works with
the ideals if the 'matter in hand', but surrenders itself and its work to
this transience" (ibid., 151).

38 All of which only introduces the greatest "transition" problem – to the

Logic and the system. Although the Encyclopedia system includes accounts of individual and collective subjectivity, Hegel (for the most part) understands himself to be presupposing that he has "introduced" and justified such notions as: the general idea of a historically self-determining subject, the kind of formation process by means of which such subjects could come to understand themselves, the whole problem of a "reconciliation" among subjects and with their world and why that is *the* problem, both for philosophy and for modern societies. No claim for the "self-grounding" character of the *Logic* and the system can, it seems to me, dispense with the way the *Phenomenology* introduces and legitimates such ideas, although, admittedly, Hegel could never seem to make up his mind finally about such issues. Cf. the discussion in my "Hegel and Category Theory," *Review of Metaphysics* XLIII (1990): 839–48.

I am much indebted to Terry Pinkard for many helpful discussions about the issues raised in this paper.

3 Hegel's conception of logic

Hegel has two books that are called *Science of Logic*, but neither of them resembles what normally serves as a logic text. Instead of beginning with symbols and rules, they start by talking about "being," "nothing," and "becoming." And the structures of formal inference appear only well into the third and final part, called the "Doctrine of Conceiving."

Because of this discrepancy between expectation and actuality, many interpreters discount the term "logic" in the title of the two works and discuss their content in terms of metaphysics or, if they are of a Kantian frame of mind, in terms of a transcendental system of categories. Yet Hegel seemed to be serious when he placed them under the rubric of the traditional discipline. The smaller of the two versions, the first part of his *Encyclopedia of the Philosophical Sciences* (1817), continued to develop through the two subsequent editions of that work in 1827 and 1830. And the larger version was being extensively revised when Hegel died in 1831. The question to be asked, then, is: What did Hegel mean by "logic"?

A first clue to answering that question can be found in what he said about the formal logic of his own day: the traditional categorical syllogisms, induction and analogy, hypothetical and disjunctive inference. The section begins with a discussion of the main sorts of elements involved: general concepts (now called propositional functions) and individuals (or singular objects of reference) as well as judgments (or propositions) that combine such terms into more-complex units.

The consideration of these forms constitutes the first third of the final volume of the larger *Science of Logic*. Various types of judgment and of inference become in sequence the topic for discussion.

Not only their structure and validity are described but also their limitations. In each case Hegel suggests that the form does not do full justice to what is to be expressed thereby – to the constraints on the terms used in the various propositions and to the inferences required to make the syllogisms valid. These limitations evoke their correctives, which turn out to be further types of judgments or syllogisms. In this way Hegel "derives" the various logical forms. They are not simply presented as a contingent list; rather, one leads to the next, the latter intended to correct the former's inadequacy.[1]

In this section of the *Science of Logic*, then, Hegel was writing something rather like a philosophy of formal logic, showing the basis for, as well as the limitations of, the various types of logical judgment and inference. Logic, for him, is not simply the abstract form of valid syllogisms, but rather the process of reasoning that both generates the forms and moves beyond them. It is reasoning about reasoning. Or, as Hegel himself said, it is thought thinking about itself.

Because logic is the only discipline that thinks about its own operations, it provides the appropriate starting point for philosophy. All other reflective disciplines begin with something given in nature, society, or the human person, and then use thought to get to the ultimate principles that explain why things are the way they are. They all presuppose thinking as something self-evident. Logic alone uses thinking to examine the way thinking itself works: how it moves from term to term; how it identifies what is essential in its subject matter; how it analyzes concepts into their component parts.

As one plunges more deeply into Hegel's analysis of the patterns of thought, one finds that he identifies and develops inferential moves that are so basic and elementary that most people never become aware of them. Where Hegel is spelling out a very small and insignificant detail, interpreters assume that he is talking about something mystical and profound – or more frequently something silly and inconsequential. Few people are prepared to work out in full detail the ways in which thinking actually works in logical reasoning.

Frege and Russell, two of the fathers of modern symbolic logic, have mounted significant challenges to this project of Hegel's. Frege, in identifying the forms of valid inference, wanted to avoid the "psychologizing" involved in the act of thinking; and Russell developed the theory of types because of the contradictions that arise when logical terms and propositions refer to themselves – when thought thinks about itself. Let us consider these objections in turn.

I. FREGE ON PSYCHOLOGISM

"Psychologism" is not clearly defined by Frege. It appears to mean any theory that tries to justify the standards of logical validity by appealing to the way people actually think. The contingency of empirical fact cannot establish a universal logic.

To avoid such contingency and to justify the forms of valid inference, Frege makes reference basic to all logic. The primary term in any proposition refers directly to something in the world; the secondary term is a description of that thing. The proposition as a whole refers to a state of affairs and can be either true or false. General words, or concepts, collect groups of things referred to in this way into classes.

Words, however, never refer or describe; people do so by means of words. And these actions are inevitably psychological. Nor is the act of reference immediate and direct. It always involves some measure of discrimination, of divorcing the thing referred to from its environment. This is particularly true for general words or concepts. Consider how we learn to use terms.

A cat is not the same as a dog. For a very young child, "dog" might serve to identify both, but it soon learns that there is a difference that must be expressed by different words. This sense of determinate difference develops and expands so that we come to use words for things that cannot be imaged. We differentiate, for example, between "the rate for changing pounds into dollars" and "the balance of trade between the United Kingdom and the United States." Thus our use of words is refined not by indicating new general classes, but by noticing a specific difference, by limiting the range of a general term.

So the concepts expressed by words are defined not only by reference to the world but also by differences that distinguish one term from another. The more complicated the concept, the more layers of differentiation. Differences, however, are not things we can simply refer to; they are not directly seen or heard. They must be thought: they result from an act of comparison.

So when Hegel talks about "thinking," he is not interested in contingent psychological processes. He is talking about the way thought takes account of differences inherent in the meanings of terms, and draws out from them what inevitably follows. One thought implies another. That relation of inference and implication does not depend on chance psychological connections, but on the differentiated content being thought.

Sometimes we recognize a limitation in the original concept and move beyond to its contrary. "Some," for example, leads to the thought of "other," since "some" is not the same as "all." At other times thought notices a basic similarity underlying two concepts (like "matter" and "form"), showing that they are not simply diverse, but contraries sharing a common ground. At still other times, thought takes a general concept and spells out its determinate components – the aspects of its meaning that need to be fully differentiated if the concept is to be defined properly.

Differentiated determinations enable thought to move from concept to concept in a way that does not depend on contingent psychological processes. This movement is the result of distinctions that have been discovered and developed as society, and the human race generally, have interacted with the natural and social environment.

Some of these logical processes of moving over from one concept to another Hegel identifies with the concepts "becoming," "alteration," "repulsion and attraction," and "relation" in the first book of the *Science of Logic*, "The Doctrine of Being."

Frege's attack on psychologism, then, fails to take account of its own subtle appeal to psychological operations. By appealing only to the act of reference, he misses a distinctive feature of logical thought: the act of differentiating. Hegel, in contrast, appeals to both operations; they are so basic to human thought that they ground its universality and the validity of its inferences. In this way his analysis of logic is more thorough-going than Frege's abstract formalism.

II. RUSSELL ON SELF-REFERENCE

Russell challenged the legitimacy of self-reference – of having thought think about itself. Examples of sentences that refer to themselves (where someone says he is currently lying, for example), lead to contradictions that should be avoided. So Russell jumps to a theory of types that decrees that no logical expression can ever refer to itself. There is no way of talking about everything, since such talk would have to include itself in its subject-matter.

The problem with this solution to the paradox is that it violates its own rubric. The theory of types applies to all logical expressions. Since it is itself a logical expression, it violates its own ban on self-reference.

Russell's reasoning for his thesis is instructive, for it illustrates the way logical thinking proceeds. Some acts of self-reference lead to paradox. Since contradictions cannot be consistently thought, logic proposes a solution to the problem. Russell's response is to declare that all acts of self-reference are illegitimate.

Yet if the argument is to succeed at all, some attempt has to be made to think the initial self-referential statements. At the very least, they have a passing and transitory legitimacy as hypothetical premises. In other words, they have some logical status despite the solution that ruled them out of court entirely. The argument violates its own conclusion.

The pattern of Russell's argument can be found elsewhere. A thought is applied to itself. That act of self-reference reveals an incongruity: its operation comes in conflict with what it says. Since any paradox demands resolution, we identify what the problems are, explain why they emerge, and suggest how to overcome them in a more adequate way. A legitimate solution does not jump to an arbitrary theory that rejects the legitimacy of anything like the original paradox, but probes into the grounds of the contradiction – why it arises in the first place – and so gets to the heart of the matter: the central, essential core that is involved in thinking such thoughts.[2]

This is the process of thinking that Hegel analyzes in the second book of the *Science of Logic:* "The Doctrine of Essence." The attempt to get at what is essential by identifying and differentiating leads to contradictions. These paradoxes are neither rejected absolutely nor allowed to remain unchallenged. They collapse ("fall to the ground"), and the task of thought is to discover the reason (or ground) that explains why they emerged in the first place and indicate appropriate resolutions to the conflict.

Russell's theory of types shows itself to be not sufficiently self-reflective, for it uses a kind of reasoning that belies its own content. Only a thinking that self-consciously thinks about its own reasoning can hope to be fully justified, so that it does not inadvertently fall into such anomalies.

III. UNDERSTANDING, DIALECTIC AND SPECULATION

For Hegel, thinking involves three distinct operations, which he calls understanding, dialectical reason, and speculative reason. When we understand, we determine or define a concept – fixing its meaning so that it can be correctly used. Dialectical reason is the movement of thought that responds to a limit defined by understanding by going on to what it implies: the contrary concept that lies beyond the limit – its opposite or counterpart. Speculative reason reflects on the total movement from original fixed concept to its opposite and establishes an overall perspective, or ground, that will explain how the two contraries fit within a single, complex thought.

It is tempting to think of these logical operations as distinctively Hegelian. But they can be found elsewhere. In the first place, understanding is the process of conceptual analysis – of getting concepts and their use appropriately defined. In the second place, Carnap and Ryle, in their discussion of category terms, identify the way in which the negation of a term refers to its contrary, not its contradictory; the opposites share a common perspective. In many of Plato's dialogues, as well, a thorough examination of a definition leads to the opposite of what was originally intended.[3] In the third place, theory construction responds to paradoxes and anomalies by developing explanations or grounds that can do justice to all the aspects involved.

In ordinary reflection, however, these operations function in isolation. Once understanding fixes its terms, it stops thinking and simply holds to the distinctions made. The paradoxes in Plato's dialogues are not ultimately resolved, and the modern theory of categories is simply a way of dispelling paradoxes. Theory construction, divorced from the discipline of understanding and the awareness that anomalies develop out of inherent limitations, becomes pure fantasy and loses its tie with reality.

For Hegel, rational thinking involves integrating all three operations into a single complex process of thinking. A category is fixed by understanding; that in itself leads over to thinking its opposite in

a dialectical transition; thought then reflects on the whole development to identify its essential dynamic and set it within a more
general context. But the process does not stop there. For the result of
speculative reflection is a complex thought, whose components
need to be fixed by understanding and whose internal dialectical
relations need to be defined. Once that is done, the complexity col-
lapses into a singular term that understanding must again determine
and fix. If understanding, consistently followed through, leads on to
dialectical reason, and if the paradoxes of dialectical reason require
speculative resolution, the syntheses of speculation must themselves be understood and fixed determinately in thought. Reason is
the process of thinking that moves on from one of its distinct operations to the next. It requires both the variety of their differences and
the integrity of their relation to be fully complete. It unites their
differences with their identity in a complex, but comprehensive,
pattern.

IV. IS THE LOGIC TRANSCENDENTAL?

The result of logical reasoning, then, is a series of fixed categories:
being, becoming, one, many, essence, existence, cause, effect, universal, mechanism, and life. Since these categories are the inevitable way
thought progresses, they mold the conceptions we have of the world.
It is tempting to see Hegel's logic as an elaboration of Kant's transcendental analytic – expanding the twelve categories into eighty-one or
more. Its concepts are forms, imposed on the matter presented by
sensation.

It is not just the categories, however, that structure our thinking
of the world. It is, as well, the ways in which concepts are related:
how one category is implied by another; how a second explains
paradoxical relations implicit in its predecessors; how a third is the
more-determinate definition of something more general. Those conceptual relations are as significant as the formal categories. If the
logic is transcendental in Kant's sense, dynamic relations as well as
categorical classifications are involved.

Yet it is misleading to see the *Science of Logic* as a realm of pure
thought, divorced from the actual world, and applied to it by an
independent and free self. It is not transcendental in this sense. For
Hegel points out that the thinking self is itself part of the world,

interacting with other selves and with nature. The thoughts it has are not pure forms appearing from some sort of Platonic heaven, but the distilled essence of that experience of the world – an experience that has accumulated over the centuries and that has acquired a sense of what is ultimately true and real.[4] This total realm of dynamic, self-conscious life Hegel calls "spirit," and the logic of pure thought is simply an abstract moment of that life, divorced from all the contingencies of experience and particularities of circumstance. It explores how the fixed determinate differences that characterize the universe are related to each other.

That is why the logic is true of the world, why it can be called a metaphysics: because it is the essential structure, now made self-conscious, of all that the world actually does. This explains as well why the logic is not static and formal: because it makes explicit the life and energy that characterize all existence. It comprehends all that is.

Since it is aware of itself as an abstraction, it can anticipate that there will be contingencies in nature and history not included in its pure forms; and with its own sense of difference, it is prepared to do justice to them. This openness to contingency is a necessary condition of being genuinely comprehensive. As a result, the logic provides the basis for a philosophy of nature and a philosophy of history, disciplines that identify what is necessary and systematic within the realm of contingency.

V. THE TWO *LOGICS*

The tendency of interpreters to overlook the dynamic inherent in Hegel's logic stems from their preference for the shorter *Science of Logic*, the first part of the *Encyclopedia of the Philosophical Sciences*. This work was written as a series of theses to be developed orally in lectures.[5] Hegel himself occasionally added written remarks. His editors have assembled student notes from courses on Logic that he gave over many years and appended them to the relevant paragraphs. The result is a sequence of stills, each one of which may become the basis for extended meditation. So the dynamic is lost.

Hegel himself recognized that this work did not present in full the process of thinking. He had already worked that out in the three volumes of the larger *Science of Logic*. There he attempted to display the movement of thought: what happens when we fix a certain concept, the anomalies that result, and the resolution of each paradox. That display of pure thinking makes difficult reading. For it does not work with images, illustrations, and analogies, except in added remarks. It concentrates on thinking determinate concepts in their purity: their definitions and their conceptual meaning. As a result it is highly abstract.

In addition, whereas we are prone to assume in reading that a paragraph dwells on one main point, spelling out what is involved, Hegel's paragraphs frequently describe a movement; they end up some place quite different from where they begin. They reproduce a dialectical transition to something other.

It takes discipline in thinking pure concepts to become adept in reading the larger *Logic*. It helps to be familiar with the logical terms he uses and how they are defined within the logic itself. But it is this larger *Science of Logic*, not the handbook published to help with his lectures, that displays in the most developed form what Hegel's conception of logic was.

VI. THE DIALECTIC OF BEING

For Hegel, logic is thought thinking itself. That is, we are to think about the process of thinking, to identify its distinctive components and the ways they are related. We are not interested in a casual, psychological dynamic, but rather in the kinds of thinking that are universal and binding, the kinds of thinking most reflective people share. Logic spells out these most-basic intellectual operations.

That cannot be done all at once. The most sensible way to proceed is to look at the most-elementary characteristics of thought and then to build in complications in an orderly way, so that we need only understand what has already been discussed to do justice to the new item being discussed.

The first problem with this program is that the reflective discipline that undertakes it is itself thought. It uses the whole battery of characteristics and features that are ultimately to be identified and distinguished. In talking about the earliest and simplest terms, we shall use technical terms to be defined later, even though we may be using them negatively ("What we are now thinking about is *not* reflection," ". . . is *not* differentiated," and so on). We shall have to distinguish the simplicity of what we are talking about from the complex way we talk about it.

The second problem with the program is deciding what is the most-elementary feature of all thought. Thinking is a process of determining, of getting things fixed in our minds. So we should begin from something (or rather some thought) that is completely *in*determinate.[6] What particular thought satisfies this requirement? Hegel suggests that it is the simple thought of "being." (Rather than expressing it as a gerund, we could use the infinitive "to be.") That thought can be used in all sorts of places. It does not restrict the context in which it is used, for it can be used with irrational numbers, figments of imagination, and even out-and-out contradictions ("this contradiction *is* unthinkable"), as well as with apple trees and interest rates and Marxist theories. When taken on its own, "being" is completely indeterminate, yet it is certainly something that can be thought.

It might seem that "nothing" would fill the bill equally well. But nothing, as privation, is in some sense determined by what is eliminated. It is somewhat mediated, not immediate, and so it is not completely indeterminate. Nonetheless, Hegel points out that when we really focus on "being" in its purity – apart from any context – we realize that we are thinking nothing. Without any determination, there is nothing there to think.

So we need to look in the second place at the concept "nothing." It too is completely indeterminate, like "being." As well, it is something that we are thinking about. In other words, its definition is no different from that of the concept from which we started. Getting "nothing" fixed in thought lands us back at "being."

All of this is pretty elementary, but there is nonetheless something peculiar about what has been going on. Thinking "being" seems to be the same as thinking "nothing" and vice versa. Yet "being" and "nothing" are quite different thoughts; they are radically opposed to each other. In other words, we are faced with a contradiction between their similarity or identity, on the one hand, and their radical opposition, on the other. Such a contradiction requires resolutions, so we need to reflect on how we got there.

We say the two thoughts are the same because when we tried to think one we found that our thoughts had passed over to thinking the other (or, if we want to highlight their opposition, one disappeared into the other.) To be thorough in our effort to get at thinking, we need to look at that "passing over/disappearing." The term we use to name such a movement is "becoming."

That is still a bit obscure, for "becoming" is complex. In the first place, "being" passed over to "nothing"; in the second place, "nothing" disappeared into "being." We call the first kind of becoming "passing away" and the second, "coming to be." In other words, there are two distinct kinds of becoming.

The next step is the most difficult in Hegel's logic, even though a similar move emerges again and again. In the same way that we identified "becoming" by thinking about "being," "nothing," and their relation in one complex thought, so we consider both "passing away" and "coming to be" together at the same time. So we get "being" to "nothing" to "being" again. We end up where we started in a kind of circle, which is complete in itself. That whole thought – of being becoming out of nothing, which in turn came out of being – is a single thought. But this time it is not the thought of "being" pure and simple. It is one being among several: "a being." (Most translators of Hegel's German word, *Daseyn*, use "determinate being," but we have not yet reached such a complex thought as "determination," although it will soon emerge.)

"A being" (or *Daseyn*) is the starting point for a new movement. It is "qualified" and becomes "something." "Some" leads to "other" by a process of "alteration," which involves a change of "determination" that goes beyond a "limit." A limited something is "finite," but the barrier implicit in "finite" always requires reference to a beyond, or "infinite," which could be considered as an infinite regress, an infinite other than, and hence limited by, the finite (and hence itself finite), or as an infinite that includes both finite and limited infinite as complementary components of a single perspective. When we think of that single perspective as a simple unity, rather than as complex, we have the thought of "being on its own account" or *Fürsichseyn*

VII. ESSENTIAL SPECULATION

There is no room here to sketch every stage of Hegel's logical development. In the first book, on Being, thought progressively identifies more discrete units (indeed "unit" is one of the terms that emerges) and isolates more abstract transitions or movements, until ratios measure qualities in terms of quantities. At this point each term of the relation acquires equal value and the comparative act of measuring is designed to get at what is essential: it distinguishes what is significant from what is simply there. So thought moves on to an even more complex kind of thinking – a thinking that looks behind what is present to what is essential. All such thoughts involve comparison, the combination of two distinctly different thoughts within a single perspective. This kind of thinking Hegel calls "reflection." Reflection starts from something but does not take it simply as given. Rather it is considered as not itself significant – a "nothing" – since what is important is to determine what is essential. This act of reflective thought stands outside that which it is thinking about, using its own principles to determine what is essential: the principles of identity, difference, non-contradiction, and sufficient reason.

The second book of the *Science of Logic*, then, looks at concepts that are related as contraries. In every case, the relation between the pairs alters on our careful examination. What starts out being the essential moment turns out to be inessential, altering the meaning involved. But that altered meaning itself will not stay fixed, and the earlier relation returns, although changed by the process thought has gone through. The resolution of the paradox that results requires a new pair of terms to distinguish what is essential from what is inessential. So, for example, "identity" cannot be clearly thought without "difference"; and "difference" requires reference to "identity." A difference and an identity that are indifferent to each other is a simple "diversity." In diversity there is a likeness (or equality) and unlikeness (or inequality). But "like" and "unlike" are not simply diverse; they are opposites, and we need to think through the nature of "opposition" as an exclusive relation that separates positive from negative. To have something that is both positive and negative at the same time and in the same respect is a contradiction. Since a contradiction cannot be consistently thought, it falls to the ground. In other words, "contradiction" requires the reflective investigation of "grounds" or "sufficient reasons."

Hegel progressively explores the many ways reflection differentiates between essential and inessential: form and content, essence and existence, thing and property, part and whole, inner and outer, actual and possible, cause and effect. Eventually it comes to a relation between two terms in which neither claims precedence over the other: the thought of pure "reciprocity." At that point the book on Essence draws to a close, and the third book, on Conceiving, begins.

VIII. CONCEPTUAL UNDERSTANDING

Reciprocity is a comprehensive thought in which a number of distinct items are contained in a relationship that involves no priority for any one of them. It is something general. Conceiving involves starting from such generals or universals and spelling out what is involved in them. Such universals need to be rendered determinate to be understood; their terms need to be defined. This involves particularizing them to the point that one can identify singulars that instantiate the universal.

So the third book involves the way in which general or universal thoughts determine themselves: the conceptual analysis of concepts. A universal is not simply distinguished from the singular that instantiates it, but the two – universal and singular – are related in judgments and propositions by way of predication, conditionals, or disjunctions. Such judgments are shown to be necessary when a middle term can be found to bridge the connection and justify the relation. The logical mediation that generates necessity finds expression in the different kinds of syllogisms and inferences.

This does not happen haphazardly. As I have already suggested, each type of judgment or inference implicitly presupposes a relation or a mediation that has not been expressed in its own form. This requires that the next type be identified and clarified.

In all of this, universal thought is determining and defining its own operations. But when it has finished its task, it realizes that thought is also used to refer to objects that can be distinguished from its own subjectivity. It even looks at its own operations objectively. Since this approach considers the objective realm as a whole, it involves a way of determining, or understanding universals. We could think of an object as made up of discrete items externally related, as in mechanism.[7] We could see the constituent items as each incomplete in itself, requiring reference to something else to be completely understood, as in chemism. Or we can think of the items integrated into a unity by some end, whether imposed from outside or intrinsic. In talking about this third kind of objectivity, or teleology, Hegel is building on Kant's analysis in the second part of the *Critique of Judgement*. There Kant recognizes that we reflectively understand some objects in the world (organisms, for example) as wholes that both determine how their constituent parts mutually determine each other and are themselves determined by that interaction.

Mechanism, chemism, and teleology presuppose a distinction between the act of thinking and the content being thought. But ultimately, if thought is to become fully self-referential, it must consider how its own operations integrate subjective activity and thought object. In its most basic form, this is the thought of "life," the dynamic that integrates diversity into a comprehensive teleological unity. Living thought determines itself, however, in two different kinds of acts: knowing (where the subject opens itself to the object) and willing (where the object is appropriated by the subject). Since each of these is one-sided and incomplete, they can only be integrated in a process that includes both, in which knowing passes over to willing, and willing disappears into knowing. In that kind of thinking, thought both distinguishes (or breaks up a unity) and unifies (or ties together distinct moments). Not only that, but the two moments of distinguishing and unifying are maintained as distinct within a comprehensive unity. This is pure thinking, fully determinate, or the absolute Idea. It is the inherent pattern, or method, of all thought, at once both analytic and synthetic. From more-limited perspectives, the two operations can fall apart into a simple diversity. But a thinking that thinks its own operations in the most comprehensive way possible maintains the two as reciprocal and distinct moments of a single comprehensive activity.

When thought does so, however, it becomes aware of its own limitations. In the logic it has already distinguished inner from outer, contingent from necessary, finite from infinite. It is now aware that its own dynamic is intrinsically necessary, internal to thought itself; and it can wonder what it would be like to have a realm that is characterized instead by externality and contingency. That is to say, it recognizes its own finitude in that, ultimately, it is not itself external and contingent. Although it can think about "externality" and "contingency," its own operations are not, in the last analysis, external and contingent.

But thought can anticipate something else. If there is a realm of external contingency, it can be characterized by terms that have already emerged in the logic. We have already mentioned "externality" and "contingency," and we could include "finitude," "diversity," "mechanical," and many others. In the *Science of Logic*, thought discovered that these thoughts required resolution in other, more-comprehensive thoughts. So it can anticipate that the realm of external contingency (or nature) will be comprehensible and thinkable.

That is the limit that pure thought can reach. To go further, it must abandon thinking altogether and let itself go, opening itself to that which is other than thought in pure receptivity. Only when it discovers what the external contingent world is like can it begin to think about it, reflectively identify what is essential, and understand the way it fits into the total picture. But first something must happen that involves no thinking at all. That could be pure willing (as God in the Christian tradition did when he created the world, or as we do when we choose to do something that has never been done before), or it could involve taking a radically empirical stance, and simply receive or take in what is there. Thought cannot describe this move by appealing to a further characteristic of thought, for the move "goes beyond" thought. Rather we must appeal to metaphor: thought "lets itself go"; it surrenders control.

IX. CONCLUSION

That, in outline, is what Hegel attempted to do in his *Science of Logic*. He tackles the puzzle, first identified by Plato, concerning the role of thought in knowledge. As Kant had shown, we do not simply receive the impressions of sense. We distinguish and compare; we organize and structure the rich panorama of sense experience into identifiable components. Kant's categories attempted to identify the basic principles of organization. But Hegel goes further. In the first place, he shows that there are many more concepts of pure thought than Kant's twelve. In the second place, the principles of organization include dynamic processes that relate concepts to each other: passing over or becoming, synthesizing, determining. But his most-radical claim is that these concepts and categories are not simply diverse. The dynamic of thought generates complex from simple in a systematic way.

The analysis of that total process identifies all kinds of basic inferences that are so familiar and "obvious" that they have never before been scrutinized by thought. It also justifies the belief that the world is itself rational. What is real can be fully comprehended by thought, since thought is a part of that world become self-conscious. At the same time, the relations inherent in thinking are so fundamental that they inevitably find expression in the world. For all the contingency and externality that might emerge, nature and history will not remain totally impervious to the categories of logic.

In other words, it is Hegel's *Science of Logic* that justifies his claim that the rational is real and the real is rational.

NOTES

1 In *On Hegel's Logic: Fragments of a Commentary* (Atlantic Highlands, N.J.: Humanities, 1981, pp 125–192), I suggest that Hegel's analysis could also be applied to the terms and formulae of modern symbolic logic, to the benefit of both sides.

2 For those knowledgeable about Hegelian terminology, I am here talking about *der Sache selbst.*

3 The best scholarly debate follows a similar tack, following through the implications of a position consistently to show that it leads to the opposite of what was intended.

4 Hegel makes this point, but not in the *Science of Logic* itself. It is the theme of his *Phenomenology of Spirit,* which he wrote as an introduction to pure philosophy.

5 See the three prefaces to the *Encyclopedia,* only now published in English in the edition of *The Encyclopedia Logic,* translated by T.F. Geraets, H.S. Harris, and W.A. Suchting (Indianapolis: Hackett, 1991).

6 Note the negative definition.

7 Hobbes's psychology is a mechanistic way of understanding thought.

4 Hegel's idealism: The logic of conceptuality*

The term "absolute idealism" is generally used to characterize the metaphysical view that Hegel presents in his philosophy. Although this phrase does not occur often in Hegel's work, he does use it to describe his own philosophy: "The position taken up by the concept is that of absoulte idealism" [EnL 160 Z; 8, 307].[1] Since Hegel uses the term "the concept" to signify a set of philosophic categories that contain an accurate description of the real, we can take this statement to indicate that the term "absolute idealism" is an appropriate means of characterizing his philosophy.

But what exactly is absolute idealism? Hegel provides us with some insight into his understanding of this phrase in a passage that describes the ontological status of the concept.

It is a mistake to imagine that the objects which form the content of our mental ideas come first and that our subjective agency then supervenes, and by the aforesaid operation of abstraction, and by colligating the points possessed in common by the objects, frames concepts of them. Rather the concept is the genuine first; and things are what they are through the action of the concept, immanent in them, and revealing itself in them.

(EnL 163 Z2; 8, 313)

The object of Hegel's criticism in this passage is the empiricist account of concept formation developed by John Locke.[2] Hegel takes issue with the priority that that account accords to things and our individual mental ideas of them. Hegel asserts that, contrary to the empiricist account, the concept has priority over objects and mental ideas. Although Hegel's unusual but characteristic use of the singular term "*the* concept" will require some explanation, it is clear that he holds that things are subordinate to it. Hegel claims that the concept is "immanent" in things and it causes them to have the character that they do.

This would seem to entail that Hegel's idealism is a form of conceptualism, a theory that holds that concepts are the most basic objects in reality and the things that there are have reality only insofar as they reflect the structure of these concepts. This impression is substantiated when Hegel claims, later in the same passage, that matter should not be thought of as external to thought:" Thus religion recognizes thought and (more exactly) the concept to be infinite form, or the free conscious activity, which can realize itself without the help of a matter that exists outside it" (*EnL* 163 Z; 8, 163) The claim that the concept does not require matter that exists independently of it suggests that Hegel's view is indeed a form of conceptual idealism.

Although there is a sense in which Hegel's philosophy is one in which matter is made subordinate to conceptuality, we need to be wary of attributing this thesis to Hegel without qualification. For although he claims that the concept is the inner principle of things, Hegel also claims that "The idea is truth *in itself and for itself, – the absolute unity of concept and objectivity*" (EnL 213; 8, 367). Here, Hegel places concept and object on a par and makes them both subordinate to the idea. The stated identity between concept and object seems to place Hegel in the realist camp, for it suggests that our concepts provide us with adequate knowledge of objects.[3]

All this suggests that achieving a clear and precise understanding of Hegel's idealism is difficult. Indeed, a recent commentator concludes a discussion of Hegel's idealism with the pessimistic conclusion that "we have yet to find a simultaneously accurate, substantive, and appealing sense in which Hegel should be regarded as an idealist."[4] In this essay, however, I will argue that there is a clear sense in which Hegel is an idealist, namely because he believes that concepts determine the structure of reality.

I shall begin be developing an interpretation of Hegel's idealism that is unabashedly metaphysical. The basic thesis of this idealism is that reality must conform to the conditions of a coherent categorial system. Having developed this account, I will consider a number of recent interpretations of Hegel's philosophy. I will show that the different types of interpretations of Hegel's philosophy result from different understandings of the project of interpretation on the part of his interpreters. I will argue that these interpretations, interesting as they may be on their own, do not do justice to Hegel's philosophy.

I. THE METAPHYSICS OF ABSOLUTE IDEALISM

All too often, Hegel's idealism is approached with a set of categories that were developed for understanding the idealism of modern European philosphy, that is, the idealism of both Berkeley and Kant. In such theories, the claim that a certain item is ideal is tantamount to the assertion that it is dependent for its existence upon the minds of conscious beings. Berkeley's metaphysics states that the being of things is their being perceived (*"Esse ist percipi"*), that is, that nothing is real that is not present to the consciousness of a subject.[5] Kant's more-sophisticated metaphysics of transcendental idealism rejects the claim that there cannot be unperceived objects of sense, but nonetheless claims that the nature of such objects is, in a transcendental sense, dependent on the characteristics of the minds of perceivers.[6]

In order to approach Hegel's idealism, we need to distinguish two different claims made by this modern form of idealism. The first is the negative claim that a given item is not fully real, that is, that its being is dependent on the being of something else.[7] Both Berkeley and Kant hold that material objects are ideal, that is, that they are not among the most basic entities in existence, but have only a "second-class" status since their being is dependent upon the existence of other, "first-class" entities.[8]

This thesis is supplemented in both Berkeley's and Kant's metaphysics with a philosophic account of the nature of this dependency, namely that the entity upon which material objects are dependent is the human being. Both Berkeley and Kant assert that material objects are, in a sense that needs to be specified, the result of the actions of the human mind, rather than independent existences that confront the perceiving human being, as is assumed by common sense.[9] The theory that the human mind constitutes the objective realm provides an explanation of the ideality or dependence of material objects.

The importance of these distinctions will emerge once we realize that Hegel rejects only the *second* of these two theses. That Hegel rejects the role attributed to the human mind in the constitution of objectivity by Berkeley and Kant emerges in his discussion of Plato's idealism, a form of idealism that Hegel thinks is superior to the modern versions.

> However, the idealism of Plato must not be thought of as being subjective idealism, and as that false idealism which had made its appearance in modern times, and which maintains that we do not learn anything, are not influenced from without, but that all conceptions are derived from out of the subject.   (LHP, II, 43; 19, 54)

Although Hegel's characterization of modern European idealism is clearly tendentious, there can be no doubt about his attitude toward it. He clearly rejects the claim characteristic of that type of idealism that the mind of the individual human subject is the source of ideality. That is, his rejection of subjective idealism is a rejection of the *second* of the two theses distinguished above, namely the account that modern European idealism develops of the ideal status of material objects. It is for this reason that Hegel characterizes this form of idealism as *subjective* idealism, in contrast to his own *absolute* form of idealism.

But Hegel's rejection of the modern European theory of the origin of dependency for items classified as ideal does not mean that he rejects their classification of those items as dependent. Indeed, when Hegel spells out his own view of what idealism is, he does so in a manner that suggests that he agrees with modern European idealism's classification of material objects as ideal, that is, as dependent, although he generalizes that classification to include all finite entities, not just material objects.

> The proposition that the *finite is ideal* [*ideell*] constitutes *idealism.* The idealism of philosophy consists in nothing else than in recognizing that the finite has no veritable being. Every philosophy is essentially an idealism or at least has idealism for its principle, and the only question then is how far this principle is actually carried out.   (SL, 154–5; 5, 172)

To understand this claim, we need to understand what Hegel means by "The finite." Hegel characterizes the finite in the following manner: "the finite not only alters, like something in general, but it *ceases to be*" (SL 129; 5, 139). All the physical objects that we encounter, as well as ourselves, are finite in this sense, for we all will cease to exist. Here we see that, unlike his predecessors, Hegel's concern is not limited to the status of the objects of normal perception. His understanding of idealism extends to the status of all finite things. His claim is that all finite beings are dependent beings and thus not fully real.[10]

But if finite beings are dependent, it follows that there must be some nonfinite being upon which they are dependent. In traditional Western theology, God was conceived of as the infinite being upon whom finite beings were dependent. Although Hegel's philosophy also posits an infinite being, his understanding of both the nature of that being and the manner in which to conceive of the dependence of finite things upon it is very different than that of the theological tradition.[11] "Every individual being is some aspect of the idea. . . . The individual by itself does not correspond to its concept. It is this limitation of its existence which constitutes the finitude and the ruin of the individual" (EnL 213; 8, 368).

This is an important passage, for in it Hegel not only gives us a key to understanding what he thinks the nature of the infinite is, viz. the idea, but he also provides an account of the ideality of finite or individual beings. His first claim is that the only "first class" existent is the idea itself. Although we are not yet in a position to develop a clear understanding of what Hegel means by the idea, we have seen that he holds individual or finite beings to be aspects of this one infinite entity.

In this passage, Hegel also puts forward a criterion for the reality of an entity, namely the correspondence of the entity with its concept. We have already seen Hegel claim that the idea is the unity of concept and object. Any lack of such a correspondence between concept and object is now seen by Hegel as a defect, one that explains the limited nature of finite beings. Correlatively, the idea is real and unlimited in virtue of the correspondence of concept and object in it.

The central claim of Hegel's idealism, then, is that finite things are dependent upon the idea for their being. The use of the term "idea" to characterize the infinite reality suggests the validity of characterizing Hegel's philosophy as a form of idealism, for it suggests that reality is fundamentally conceptual. But, as we have seen, we need to be very careful not to view Hegel's idealism through the lens of positions developed by previous philosophies. However we ultimately come to view the nature of this idealism, it is not a thesis that reduces one type of finite entity to another.

In his various writings, Hegel puts the basic claim of his own idealism in different ways. For example, in the *Phenomenology of Spirit*, Hegel presents his understanding of idealism within the context of a discussion of truth. As a result, he states his idealism in the following way: "The true is the whole. But the whole is nothing other than the essence consummating itself through its development" (PS 11/20; 3, 24). This manner of characterizing his idealism emphasizes that it is a form of holism. According to this view, individuals are mere parts and thus not fully real or independent. This characterization also emphasizes Hegel's belief that the whole exists in a process of development.

In a subsequent passage, Hegel discusses the notion of development in his own characteristic fashion.

What has just been said can also be expressed by saying that reason is *purposive activity*. . . . purpose is what is immediate and *at rest*, the unmoved which is also *self-moving*, and as such is subject. . . . in other words, the actual is the same as its concept only because the immediate, as purpose, contains the self or pure actuality within itself.   (PS 12/22; 3, 26)

In this characterization of his idealism, Hegel claims that the development that characterizes the idea is a self-development.

So far, then, we have seen that Hegel's idealism amounts to the claim that finite beings are ideal. We have seen that he also claims that what is real is the whole, which Hegel characterizes as the idea. This idea is portrayed as a developing whole. Hegel also adds that the manner in which this holistic idea develops is to be thought of as its own self-actualization.

II. THE LOGIC OF ABSOLUTE IDEALISM

Although we have begun to make some progress toward understanding Hegel's idealism, the previous section ended with Hegel's claim that the idea or concept was self-actualizing. In order to grasp the unique features of Hegel's idealist metaphysics, we need to achieve a more-precise understanding of what this means.

It will be useful if we begin by focusing on the nature of an organic entity such as a plant, an entity that is self-actualizing. That is, it is part of our understanding of such an entity that it has a tendency to grow and develop in accordance with a set process. It begins as a seed and, in the presence of the appropriate conditions, develops into a full-grown plant that produces fruit and seeds for a new generation of such plants before it dies.

How would we proceed in attempting to explain this process of the plant's development as one that is rational, that is, capable of explanation? If we take the production of fruit as the goal of the plant's existence, then we would see all the plant's other features as aspects of its nature that contribute to the realization of this goal.[12] For example, we would explain the plant's having colorful flowers by saying that such flowers attract bees to pollinate the plant and thus make the production of fruit possible.[13]

If we go on to ask how the plant "knows" to develop in this specified way, we might be tempted to claim that there must be some sense in which this "developmental plan" exists in the plant. Indeed, we might be tempted to say that the entire developmental plan of the plant's existence had to be "in" the seed in order for the seed to develop in the way that it did. If we follow this line of reasoning, we might even be willing to say that the seed had to have an idea of its own process of growth and development, even though we would be quick to add that we did not mean this in any conscious sense. The unconscious idea of the plant's development would nonetheless have to be present in the seed in some way.

The structure that we have just developed by considering the growth and development of the seed is one that is referred to by the concept of an *organic whole*. A whole is organic just in case its parts are dependent upon the whole for their existence. A plant is an organic whole because each of its parts – whether it is a temporal stage such as the seed or an element of the plant's structure such as the flower – has a nature that depends on the entire plant. We have just seen this in both the case of the seed and the flower. The existence of these parts is dependent on the developmental plan of the plant as a whole, what I have called the idea of the plant. In this sense, we can say that a plant is a self-actualizing being, a being whose existence is made intelligible via its idea.

We now need to see how this analogy with an organic whole such as a plant provides us with a way of understanding Hegel's metaphysics. The question that Hegel's metaphysics attempts to answer is whether it is possible to understand the nature of all that exists, the real, as having a rational structure, that is, as something whose existence is intelligible.[14] This is the same question that we asked in regard to the plant. And, just as in the case of the plant, Hegel claims that reality does have an intelligible structure, one that involves the notion of self-actualization.

As a first approximation, we can put Hegel's view as the claim that the real has a rational structure, one that exhibits a process of development, and that what is developing is simply the idea itself. Hegel is claiming that reality must contain the developmental plan of its own existence just as the seed does. In this sense, Hegel claims that reality is an organic whole. What he means by "the idea" is simply the developmental plan for all that exists, something that we can think of on analogy with the developmental plan of a plant.

We have now arrived at a deeper understanding of Hegel's idealism. Previously, we saw that Hegel asserted that all finite entities were aspects of the one existing reality, the idea. We now see that he thinks of this idea as containing the developmental plan for reality as such. On analogy with organic wholes, the idea is thought of as the plan the conformity with which makes out the self-actualizing nature of reality as such.

This way of thinking about Hegel's philosophy allows us to see why it is so problematic to think of it through the categories of modern European philosophy. Although Hegel's idealism involves the attribution of priority to the idea, this is not simply the reduction of all that exists to its concept. To see this, we need only reflect on the plant analogy. To attribute priority to the idea of the plant is simply to assert that the process of growth and development is that which constitutes the being of the plant. But this priority does not deny that the idea must be embodied in an actual set of material elements that are the realization of the idea itself. Similarly, when Hegel claims that the idea is what is real, he is not denying that there is more in reality than the idea itself. All that he is asserting is that whatever it is that there is must conform to the idea's structure.

While the analogy with the explanation of the growth of the plant has helped us get a better sense of Hegel's metaphysics, we need to consider one element of the analogy in more detail. Although it makes sense to say that the plant "contains" the concept of its own development, we need to consider what sense it makes to say that reality contains the concept of *its* own development. Is there a way of understanding reality such that it might plausibly contain the concept of its own structure and development?

In fact, this question provides us with an important perspective for considering Hegel's philosophical writings. From the perspective that we have just developed, we can see that Hegel's philosophic system will have to provide us with the developmental plan for reality as such. That is, the task of his own philosophy, and of his logic in particular, is to provide us with the idea of a self-actualizing reality, just as our idea of a plant allows us to see it as a self-actualizing entity.

Hegel's most-complete presentation of his philosophy is in a work entitled *The Encyclopedia of the Philosophical Sciences*. This work presents Hegel's understanding of the developmental plan of the world. The philosophic system it contains consists of three parts: a logic, a philosophy of nature, and a philosophy of spirit. The logic is intended to describe the categorial structure that is necessary if anything is to exist at all. As such, it abstracts from the specific nature of that which exists and considers the structure of existence only in general. It is this that Hegel calls "the idea." The latter two parts of Hegel's system are his descriptions of the more-specific conceptual structures that are realized in nature and spirit, the two concrete realms in which the idea exists. Each of these concrete realms exhibits the systematic structure that is necessary for anything to exist, but does so in a determinate manner that accords with its own specific nature. So, for example, Hegel treats the state or government as a means of placing individual human beings into the sorts of systematic relationships with one another that are necessary for spirit to be an existent entity.

Our exploration of the concept of an organic whole has brought us a long way toward understanding Hegel's idealist metaphysics by allowing us to see what it means to claim that reality is a self-actualizing whole. The idea, as Hegel uses the term, stands for the categorial structure of the development of a systematic whole. But we have not, so far, directed our attention to the concept of development itself. If we look more closely at what exactly development means, we will understand some of the more-perplexing aspects of Hegel's philosophy.

To begin with, we need to see how difficult it is to form an adequate definition of what development is. One thing that is clear is that our usual understanding of development is of a specifically temporal process. As soon as we try to characterize what occurs in a developmental process, however, we find ourselves speaking in rather bizarre ways. For example, one might be tempted to say that a developmental process is one in which a thing becomes what it is or what it should be. It is important to notice the self-referential nature of such statements. In them, a thing is characterized as remaining the same even as it undergoes a process that, in some sense, makes it what it is, which implies that it previously was not that which it now is.

One of the central problems of ancient Greek philosophy was that of developing a conceptual framework with which to describe such processes in which things are both what they are and not what they are. Aristotle's distinction between potentiality and actuality is, among other things, a metaphysical scheme that attempts to provide a way of describing such processes. According to this scheme, a developmental process is one in which the potentialities of an entity become actualized, thereby *becoming* that which it was not.

Before looking at Hegel's own solution to this problem, we need to see that Hegel's problem is more complex than that faced by Aristotle. Aristotle was trying to find a coherent means of description for developmental processes as they are perceived by us. For Hegel, however, this specific goal is insufficient, for there are non-temporal processes that he thinks of as developmental for which he needs to have a means of description.

Consider, for example, Kant's argument in the transcendental deduction of the categories. Kant begins with the accepted metaphysical understanding of the concept of an object as something that exists independent of us. By analyzing, however the nature of our knowledge, Kant argues that an object is something whose concept keeps our knowledge from being arbitrary. Let us put this claim in the following way: our concept of an object is that of a unifier of sensory input. If we accept this aspect of Kant's transcendental deduction, then we have enriched our understanding of the concept of an object.

Hegel's manner of conceptualizing this would be to say that Kant's deduction involves the development of the concept of an object. Although following the steps in such an argument is itself a temporal process, the reasoning is logical rather than temporal. Hegel takes this to entail that conceptuality itself has a developmental structure. Since this developmental structure is not temporal, he needs to have a set of conceptual distinctions that allow him to describe development per se.[15]

The first set of concepts that Hegel uses for conceptualizing development are those of the "in itself" and the "for itself." Whereas Kant had spoken of objects in themselves as things (*noumena*) that really existed as opposed to those of which we have knowledge (*phenomena*), Hegel rejects this bifurcated metaphysics. He therefore reinterprets the concept of the "in itself" to mean that which a thing is implicitly. Development is then the transition from the "in itself" to the "for itself":

> Though the embryo is indeed *in itself* a human being, it is not so *for itself*; this it only is as cultivated reason, which has *made* itself into what it is *in itself.* And that is when it for the first time is actual. But this result is itself a simple immediacy, for it is self-conscious freedom at peace with itself, which has not set the antithesis on one side and left it lying there, but has been reconciled with it.   (PS 12/21; 3, 25–26)

The distinction between the *in itself* and the *for itself* is thus one means that Hegel uses to conceptualize development. By itself, however, this conceptual distinction does not provide any account of how such transformation from the *in itself* to the *for itself* takes place.

In order to specify the mechanics of this process of development, Hegal adopts probably the most peculiar and difficult set of terms in his entire philosophy. Hegel conceptualizes development by means of a conceptual system based upon the concepts of negation and contradiction. Hegel actually introduces this system with the very analogy of the development of a plant that we have been discussing:

> The bud disappears in the bursting-forth of the blossom, and one might say that the former is refuted by the latter; similarly, when the fruit appears, the blossom is shown up in its turn as a false manifestation of the plant, and the fruit now emerges as the truth of it instead. These forms are not just distinguished from one another, they also supplant one another as mutually incompatible. Yet at the same time their fluid nature makes them moments of an organic unity in which they not only do not conflict, but in which each is as necessary as the other; and this mutual necessity alone constitutes the life of the whole.   (PS 2/2; 3, 12)

In describing this development process, Hegel invokes such terms as "false," "refutation," and "incompatibility" in unusual senses. To say that the bud and the flower are refutations of one another is highly peculiar, to say the least. This usage is not, however, simply the result of an arbitrary decision on Hegel's part to put his philosophical arguments in perplexing terms, as it sometimes might seem from reading the claims of his commentators. The conceptual system of negation and contradiction is Hegel's solution to the problem of describing the mechanism by means of which developmental processes in general take place.

But how exactly does this solution work? To begin, we need to see that Hegel's use of a conceptual framework based on the concepts of negation and contradiction involves a departure from our normal way of thinking about development. In the previous quotation, Hegel rejected the usual manner of describing the development of an organic whole in favor of a description that employs the theoretical vocabulary involving negation and contradiction. Rather than simply saying that the bud and the blossom are two distinct temporal stages in the life of a plant, with the former preceeding the latter in its goal-oriented development, Hegel here talks about two "mutually incompatible" manifestations of the plant, although he goes on to say that such mutual incompatability is necessary to the existence of an organic whole.

Hegel's reconceptualization of development thus involves the replacement of the temporal terms with which we normally describe developmental processes with a set of logical terms based upon the concept of negation. The idea of the teleological development of the plant is then conceptualized as describable by means of the concept of negation and its associated concepts. Hegel holds that the plant, in order to develop, has to embody a series of incompatible aspects as necessary for its development. In so doing, Hegel conceives of negation and its associated concepts as explicating the logic by means of which developmental processes take place.

If this strategy of reconceptualization is successful,[16] Hegel will have found a way to abstract from our specifically temporal understanding of development and to provide a logical, rather than a temporal, characterization of development. The kernel of this logical understanding of development is the use of "negation" to conceptualize the mechanism by means of which development takes place.

Relying on the somewhat paradoxical formulations we saw before, according to which developing entities become other than they were, Hegel adopts a system of theoretical terms based upon that of negation to characterize the logical structure of development.

Hegel's use of the conceptual framework of negation is thus his means of specifying the mechanism by means of which the movement from the in itself to the for itself takes place. The significance of this practice is that the logical structure of negation can be used by Hegel to characterize developments that are not specifically temporal. Since, as we saw, the goal of Hegel's metaphysics was to characterize all of reality – and this has to include the idea as well as its manifestations – as a developing whole, his use of this framework of negation is a key step in the articulation of his unique idealist philosophy.

III. SPECULATIVE AND TRANSCENDENTAL LOGIC

So far, I have made sense of Hegel's idealist metaphysics by considering it as an attempt to show that reality has a rational structure. But this view of Hegel's philosophic system makes it seem unconnected to the philosophic developments that preceded him. In particular, it makes it seem that Hegel simply decided to pick up the project of Western metaphysics without any consideration of Kant's criticism of its viability. Since this has been a worry of some of the interpretations that I will discuss in the following section of this chapter, I will now show that Hegel's project of developing a speculative logic results from his own reflections on the strengths and weaknesses of Kant's project of a transcendental logic.

Transcendental logic was intended by Kant to specify, in the most general way possible, what it is for something to be an object of knowledge.

In the expectation, therefore, that there may perhaps be concepts which relate *a priori* to objects, not as pure or sensible intuitions, but solely as acts of pure thought ... we form for ourselves by anticipation the idea of a science of the knowlege which belongs to pure understanding and reason, whereby we think objects entirely *a priori*. Such a science, which should determine the origin, the scope, and the objective validity of such knowledge, would have to be called *transcendental logic*.   (*CPuR* A57/B81)

Kant divided the project of transcendental logic into two parts: a constructive part that determined the concepts that had a legitimate use in determining the nature of objects in an *a priori* fashion, and a critical part that established the illegitimacy of attempting to determine the nature of certain other objects – God, the self, and the world – without reference to experience.

For our purposes, we can focus on the constructive part of Kant's project.[17] Kant argued that it was possible to show the validity of certain specific metaphysical concepts – those that he called "categories" – because these concepts were necessary conditions for the possibility of experience. The central aspect of the constructive part of his transcendental logic thus included the "transcendental deduction of the categories," that is, the argument that these non-empirical concepts had a necessary role to play in the articulation of experience. Specifically, Kant argued that the twelve categories together specify what it is to be an object of empirical knowledge, that they articulate the meaning of objectivity in Kant's new and critical sense.

Hegel conceived of speculative logic as the successor discipline to Kant's transcendental logic. That is, from Hegel's point of view, the goal of speculative logic is the same as the goal of transcendental logic, namely the determination of the concepts by means of which objects are determined in an *a priori* manner. The difference is that Hegel rejects many specific aspects of Kant's attempt to realize this project.

Hegel is not critical of the goal of Kant's transcendental logic; rather, his problem is with the manner in which Kant carries out his project. Hegel argues that Kant places his own logical terms in the conceptual space of subjectivity, that is, within the realm of mental or spiritual existence. Although the idea of such a logic requires that it be conceived of as analogous to what we now call formal logic (a discipline that both Kant and Hegel thought of as general logic), Hegel claims that Kant fails to maintain this level of generality in his exposition of transcendental logic.

Hegel frames his complaint by focusing on Kant's use of the term "concept." Hegel claims that Kant treats concepts as mental entities rather than as entities within "logical space." We can see the validity of Hegel's criticism if we examine a passage in which Kant seeks to justify his use of the term "idea." Kant's concern in the passage is to show that the term "idea" should not be used "to indicate any and every species of representation, in a happy-go-lucky confusion, to the detriment of science" [CPuR A320/B376].[18] He continues by listing the various terms in their proper order:

The genus is *representation* in general (*repraesentatio*). Subordinate to it stands representation with consciousness (*perceptio*). A *perception* which relates solely to the subject as the modification of its state is *sensation* (*sensatio*), an objective perception is *cognition* (*cognitio*). This is either *intuition* or *concept* (*intuitus vel conceptus*).   [CPuR A320/B376–77]

Although the list continues, this part is sufficient for understanding Hegel's point. Kant's list differentiates types of *mental states*. The distinctions he draws therefore belong to a theory of philosophic psychology or, as Hegel calls it, the philosophy of subjective spirit. As a result, Kant is not operating at a general enough level for the project he has framed. Although he intends to develop a transcendental logic, his actual terminology is too psychological for that purpose.

But this means that an adequate version of a transcendental logic would have to develop a different account of the status of its own terms, an account that is not located within the conceptual space of psychology but of logic itself. As Hegel says: "Similarly here, too, the concept is to be regarded not as the act of self-conscious understanding, not as the *subjective understanding*, but as the concept in its own absolute character which constitutes a *stage of nature* as well as of *spirit*" [SL 586; 6, 257]. Hegel's claim is that the logical structures of the concept need to be seen as realized in both nature and spirit and therefore cannot be treated in a specifically psychological manner, for that would limit them to the realm of spirit alone.

The specific point of Hegel's criticism, then, is that Kant's characterization of his own philosophic terminology is located in too specific a domain, that of the psychological. This seemingly specific complaint about Kant's terminology has important implications. For this complaint means that an adequate theory of "conceptual determination" cannot be "located" within the conceptual space of philosophical psychology.

One of the significant characteristics of most seventeenth- and eighteenth-century philosophy, however, was its location of conceptual determination within the sphere of the mental. This is one of the results of Descartes's philosophical innovations that is equally valid for Locke and the empiricist tradition. Even Kant, as Hegel points out, was not free of it.

This means that the theory of conceptuality that Hegel develops in his speculative logic will reject the subjective, psychological orientation of the modern European philosophic tradition. This is an important "break" with that tradition, one of the ways in which Hegel moves to a position that acknowledges a trans-subjective basis. Although many interpretations of Hegel see the metaphysics of *Geist* as his means of avoiding the subjectivism of this tradition, his theory of conceptuality is itself an important and more-fundamental departure from it.

Understanding this aspect of Hegel's departure from the tradition of modern European philosophy allows us to gain more insight into how Hegel distinguishes his own idealist philosophy from Kant's. We have already seen that the central difference between Hegelian and Kantian idealism is Hegel's rejection of the psychological understanding of idealism according to which objectivity is the creation of a mind. In place of this "psychological idealism" (SL 589; 6, 261), Hegel presents a conceptual idealism according to which conceptuality itself determines the nature of objectivity. This conceptuality then is applied to two domains – nature and spirit. Hegel sees Kant as failing to distinguish the specific application of the concept to the realm of spirit from a general discussion of its nature.

Hegel's speculative logic can, therefore, be seen as attempting to free Kant's transcendental logic of its mentalistic framework. Although Kant's framing of the question of transcendental logic should have led him to reject the mentalistic terminology that he actually employs, Hegel sees him as being inconsistent on this point and seeks to develop a philosophic theory that is adequate to the project that Kant himself inaugurated.

IV. INTERPRETATIONS OF HEGEL'S IDEALISM

Having explored the nature and significance of Hegel's idealism, I shall now turn to some recent interpretations of Hegel's philosophy. First, I will look at one traditional interpretation of Hegel, that of Charles Taylor, in which Hegel is viewed as developing a monistic metaphysics. I will show that this interpretation of his idealism is flawed. I will then turn to a number of different non-metaphysical interpretations of Hegel, attempting to explore the reasons for the growth of this mode of interpretation.

The most significant reason for the great amount of disagreement about what Hegel's idealism consists in has to do with differences among his interpreters' aims. As we shall see, one will arrive at a different interpretation of Hegel's idealism depending on what one's aim is. For example, if one wishes to understand how Hegel was understood by his contemporaries, one will be likely to adopt a metaphysical interpretation of his idealism, for this interpretation was the one that provoked intense discussion among his followers and critics. On the other hand, if one is a contemporary philosopher interested in defending certain of Hegel's insights, one might opt for an interpretation of Hegel's idealism that makes it a more plausible candidate within contemporary philosophic theory. Although a great deal more could be said about such different orientations, my concern is to see how they have functioned in interpretations of Hegel's philosophy. In considering a number of recent interpretations of Hegel's idealism, I do not mean to be exhaustive but to consider some of the different positions that contemporary interpreters have taken on the issue of Hegel's idealism.

A. Spirit Monism

This is the traditional, and still very influential, interpretation of Hegel. According to this interpretation, Hegel's idealism amounts to the assertion that there is a single supra-individual entity, *Geist*, and that all that exists is to be thought of as part of the development of this single, supra-human individual.

According to this interpretation, Hegel is an idealist because he thinks that reality is composed of an entity, *Geist*, that has the structure of a subject, something that has consciousness. Hegel is interpreted as denying that the objects of normal perceptual awareness are basic and then asserting that what is basic has the structure of a subject rather than an object. Furthermore, since *Geist* is a trans-individual subject, this interpretation shows how Hegel rejects the subjectivist tendencies of earlier European philosophy by developing a metaphysics that goes beyond the individual subject.

An important and influential adherent to this mode of interpretation of Hegel's idealism is Charles Taylor. In his lengthy study, *Hegel*, Taylor asserts that Hegel adopts this form of metaphysical idealism. "For *Geist* can be thought to have as its basic aim simply that spirit, or rational subjectivity, be. . . . the design of the universe could be shown to flow of necessity from the single basic goal: that rational subjectivity be."[19]

As Taylor explains it, Hegel thinks that the supposition that reality is constituted of *Geist* alone provides a means of understanding the nature of existence. *Geist*, in order to exist, winds up creating all the other aspects of reality as part of th necessary process of its own realization. In this sense, *Geist* is a process of creation that allows all other things to exist. "But for *Geist* [as opposed to human beings] nothing is given in this sense, i.e. as a brute fact. The only starting point is the *requirement* that subjectivity be; and the only 'positive' content attached to this subjectivity is that of rationality, and this belongs to its very essence."[20] *Geist* is subjectivity freed from the limitations of human existence. Taylor claims that Hegel's metaphysics shows that all of reality can be understood as the result of the attempt of '*Geist* to exist.

This allows Taylor to characterize Hegel's idealism in the following manner.

Absolute idealism means that nothing exists which is not a manifestation of the Idea, that is, of rational necessity. Everything exists for a purpose, that of the coming to be of rational self-consciousness, and this requires that all that exists be the manifestation of rational necessity. Thus absolute idealism is related to the Platonic notion of the ontological priority of the rational order, which underlies external existence, and which external existence strives to realize, rather than to the modern post-Cartesian notion of dependence on knowing mind.[21]

Taylor is here pointing out that Hegel's idealism cannot be assimilated to the subjective idealism that asserts that things are dependent upon the individual mind of the human knower. In place of that understanding of idealism, Taylor opts for an understanding of idealism according to which all that exists is simply a result of the existence of rational self-consciousness itself.

There is a general consensus among interpreters that there is something to this interpretation of Hegel. That is, most interpreters agree that elements of Hegel's texts do provide evidence for this view. For example, there is the oft-quoted statement from the Preface to the *Phenomenology of Spirit* in which Hegel asserts that an adequate account of reality requires that reality be viewed as having the structure of subjectivity. "In my view, which can be justified only by the exposition of the system itself, everything turns on grasping and expressing the true, not only as *substance,* but equally as *subject"* [PhS 18/10; 3, 22–23]. If one understands Hegel's invocation of the concept of substance as a reference to Spinoza, then one will easily see the use of the concept of subject to be Hegel's attempt to argue that the one existent entity must be grasped not, as Spinoza did, as a substance, but as a subject, that is, as something that has the structure of self-consciousness. In the following paragraph, Hegel goes on to speak of "the living substance" in "the process of its own becoming," phrases that support this interpretation.

Nor does Hegel make such assertions only in his early work. For example, in the introduction to his lectures on world history, Hegel asserts that world history is the result of spirit's actions:

It is only an inference from the history of the world, that its development has been a rational process; that the history in question has constituted the rational necessary course of the world-spirit – that spirit whose nature is always one and the same, but which unfolds this its one nature in the phenomena of the world's existence.   [PH 10; 12, 22]

Here, again, we see Hegel asserting that spirit is the essential being whose unfolding constitutes the reality of the world as we know it.

The central problem with the spirit monist interpretation of Hegel's idealism is that it assumes that assertions that Hegel makes in the context of his philosophy of spirit are adequate characterizations of his overall metaphysics. As we have seen, however, the philosophy of spirit is only one of the two branches of Hegel's philosophy of the real *(Realphilosophie)*. The idealism of Hegel's philosophy cannot be reduced to a claim about spirit alone. Rather, it is based upon Hegel's more-general assertion that anything that exists must exhibit the logical structure of the idea.

B. Non-Metaphysical Interpretations

The dominant tendency among contemporary interpretations of Hegel is away from the spirit monist interpretation. Although this may be partially the result of the inadequacy of that interpretation, there are other important reasons for this trend.

The first has to do with the understanding of the history of philosophy that has become predominant among interpreters influenced by analytic philosophy. For them, the point of pursuing the history of philosophy is not so much to understand what a given philosopher might actually have thought about their own system of thought, but to analyze the position of the philosopher from the standpoint of its legitimacy. That is, such interpreters privilege the argumentative structure of a text and ask what conclusions, if any, can be legitimately maintained by the text in question.

The guiding principle of their interpretations is therefore to isolate the argumentative structure that will allow the name "Hegel" to stand for an intelligible position on contemporary philosophic issues. For this reason they seek to unveil the "rational core" behind the "mystifying shell" of Hegel's idealism. Often, however, they fail to acknowledge the specific thrust of their own interpretation.

This manner of interpreting the writings of a philosopher is guided by a desire to make those writings into objects of respect in the contemporary philosophic landscape inhabited by the interpreter. Since philosophic texts are not immediately understandable as making a contribution to contemporary debates, the central aim of this form of philosophic interrogation is to precipitate out from the confused solution of the philosopher's texts the one core philosophic position that is of contemporary interest.

Once this standpoint is articulated, it becomes clear why so many contemporary interpreters of Hegel's idealism reject the spirit monist reading. From the standpoinnt of the contemporary analytic philosopher, the idea that all of reality – both physical nature and human social existence – is the product of the actions of *Geist* is simply unpalatable. If Hegel's idealism is understood in this manner, then it will simply not wash as a position of relevance to contemporary philosophy. Even if this interpretation has historical relevance, it does not meet contemporary standards of philosophic intelligibility.

It should be remembered that at least part of the reason that interpreters adopt this standpoint is that they think that Hegel does have philosophic insights and positions that are of contemporary relevance. Since they wish to defend or, at least, articulate these, they feel compelled to reject those elements of Hegel's texts that obscure these insights. Thus, for example, we find J. N. Findlay claiming "that Hegel is worth restating and reassessing" – these are the goals of Findlay's interpretation – "on account of the great contemporary relevance of many aspects of his thought."[22]

As the name indicates, the central trend in these analytically influenced interpretations is to deny that Hegel was a metaphysician in the traditional sense. That is, this line of interpretation simply claims that Hegel's project – or at least its defensible core – did not include an attempt to provide an inventory of the basic items in reality, the traditional understanding of the project of metaphysics.

Findlay, one of the first proponents of such an interpretive strategy, states that Hegel is not a metaphysical idealist in either of the senses that he, Findlay, recognizes as applicable:

Hegel, we may maintain, is no idealist in the sense of holding that to be is to be perceived, or that to be is to be conceived, or that objects exist only if there are conscious minds to consider them or to refer to them. Even less is he an idealist in the sense of thinking that the mind *imposes* its forms on the material of sense, or that is "constructs" the world in its activities of imagination or thought.[23]

In this passage, Findlay distinguishes Hegel from the two prominent forms of idealism in the modern philosophic tradition that we have also discussed: Berkeleyan and Kantian. Berkeleyan idealism asserts that physical objects are ideal, that is, that physical objects are not among the basic objects in the world. They have being only because they are perceived. Kantian idealism, on the other hand, holds that physical objects are empirically real, even though they are transcendentally ideal.

Although Findlay does not explicitly state his assumption that metaphysical idealism exists only in two forms, Berkeleyan and Kantian, it is clear that assumption guides his argument. For this reason, he rejects the idea that Hegel is a metaphysical idealist. And, as we have seen, Hegel views both of these forms of idealism as subjective and clearly rejects the viability of such subjective idealism.

However, the rejection of subjective idealism does not entail that there is no sense in which Hegel is a metaphysical idealist. Findlay clearly thinks that this is the case and that we have to introduce a new sense of "idealist" in order to understand what Hegel means by idealism.

Hegel, in fact, must be recognized to be an "idealist" in a thoroughly new sense of the word: he employs throughout the Aristotelian notion of teleology or final causation, and he holds mind or spirit to be the final form, the goal or "truth" of all our notions and the world.[24]

Ironically, this particular statement of Findlay's sounds nearly identical to the metaphysical interpretation of Taylor. If Hegel is an idealist in that spirit is the goal of all existence, it would seem to accord well with Taylor's interpretation even if the specific metaphysical reduction of things to spirit is rejected.[25] Nevertheless, it is possible to recast Findlay's point in a non-metaphysical way. From that point of view, Hegel's idealism would amount to a claim about the nature of the explanations that are necessary for our understanding. This idealism would entail that we accept teleological explanations whose goal or end is the existence of *Geist*. Although we would not thereby endorse the claim that all of existence is the product of *Geist*, we would accept such teleological explanations.

One of the elements of Hegel's system that Findlay rejected was Hegel's claim to be proceeding in a logical manner.

Though Hegel frequently speaks of the "necessity" of his moves, he is clear, too, that this is not like the necessity of deductive inferences. And as regards the application of Hegel's peculiar method to the facts of nature and history, it is plain that the fit is loose, and intended to be loose.[26]

This is the assumption of Findlay's that is most troubling to subsequent interpreters. If anything about Hegel is clear, it is that he did not intend his logical arguments to be loose. Findlay's interpretation, then, has generally been seen to depart too much from the structure of Hegel's texts. One aim of subsequent non-metaphysical interpreters is to find a means of understanding Hegel that does not jettison this important aspect of Hegel's philosophy.

C. Category Theory

An important line of interpretation of Hegel simply rejects the idea that there is any philosophically defensible sense in which Hegel is an idealist. This form of the non-metaphysical reading of Hegel sees his philosophic importance to be in his *ontology* rather than his *metaphysics.*

The distinction made by this interpretation between a metaphysics and an ontology needs to be explicated. What this interpretation means by a metaphysics is a theory that makes an assertion about the nature of the basic entities in the world. So, if Hegel did assert that the only ultimate entity in existence was *Geist*, that would be an example of a metaphysical assertion. An ontology, on the other hand, delimits a set of categories that are used to characterize the nature of reality. As Klaus Hartmann, the originator of the categorial interpretation puts it:

[W]hat Hegel wishes to give is an account of the determinations of the real, or what is. . . . Thus, Hegel's philosophy is a *theory of categories* or of such determinations of the real as permit of reconstruction and are thus borne out as categories. . . . A category is "understood," explained, or justified in terms of its function with respect to making ontology – the satisfaction of reason – possible.[27]

To say that Hegel is an ontologist in the sense of a category theorist is to say that he is concerned with developing the categorial framework that must be employed in meaningful discourse about reality.

Over against the metaphysical reading, Hegel's philosophy appears to us as categorial theory, i.e. as non-metaphysical philosophy, or as a philosophy devoid of existence claims and innocent of a reductionism opting for certain existences to the detriment of others. The only claim is that the categories granted for reconstruction be not empty or without instantiation.[28]

Like Findlay, Hartmann is clear that he is not developing an interpretation of all that Hegel claims, but only of that central aspect of his position that is defensible. "We feel free to single out that systematic core of Hegel's philosophy which exhibits strictness. In that sense, the interpretation . . . can stand for a 'minimal interpretation, or for a non-metaphysical interpretation' of Hegel."[29]

This interpretation of Hegel's philosophy has become popular in recent years.[30] One reason for its popularity, no doubt, is the fact that it renders Hegel's complex and obscure texts quite intelligible. But as in the case of Findlay, the question remains as to whether this particular "core" of Hegel's thought does not reject too much that is significant in his philosophic project.

D. Transcendental Idealism

One of the most complex and interesting recent interpretations of Hegel's idealism is that developed by Robert Pippin in his book

Hegel's Idealism. Pippin shares with other non-metaphysical readings of Hegel the rejection of spirit monism. Unlike those readings, however, he thinks that there is an important sense in which Hegel is an idealist.

> Hegel is not heading toward any neo-Platonic theory of conceptual emanation, with some "cosmic spirit" ejecting the world in its becoming self-conscious. . . . He is committing himself to the necessity of nonempirically derived and so (for Hegel) "self-determined" conditions for the intelligible experience of any object; to an eventual claim that these conditions can be derived by showing how even the most general conceptual function (e.g., the notion, "being") requires a much more complicated conceptual structure just for its own application; and to a strategy that can show why this idealist program is not subject to the standard realist attack – that even if *our* best criteria for "knowledge of X" are fulfilled, we still have no way of knowing whether such fulfillment does tell us anything about X.[31]

This quotation shows that Pippin's project fits squarely into the interpretive tendency that we have been surveying. He rejects any interpretation that attributes a metaphysical thesis to Hegel. In place of that, he attributes to Hegel a philosophic program that has a clear relation to contemporary analytic philosophic issues, such as that of realism as a theory of meaning.

But what exactly is Pippin claiming Hegel's idealism consists in? Pippin is arguing that Hegel's philosophic project has much more in common with Kant's than has previously been recognized. Specifically, Pippin thinks that Hegel is attempting to solve the general philosophic problem raised by Kant in the *Critique of Pure Reason:* how knowledge of objects is possible. Although Hegel rejects much in Kant's solution, there is a core that he accepts: a theory of categories, albeit with a different orientation than that of the categorical interpretation we have just explored.

> Whatever else Hegel intends by asserting an "Absolute Idealism," it is clear . . . that such a claim at the very least involves Hegel in a theory about pure concepts, and about the role of such concepts in human experience, particularly in any possible knowledge of objects, but also in various kinds of self-conscious, intentional activities. Moreover, his account of this role is clearly committed to the priority of such a conceptual element.[32]

While Pippin's interpretation has the virtue of placing Hegel's idealism in clear relationship to Kant's philosophy, it fails to accord sufficient importance to Hegel's epistemological break from Kant:

his critique of Kant's subjectivism. Although Pippin acknowledges the importance of this break in the innovative discussion of the Self-Consciousness chapter of the *Phenomenology,* it is not integrated into Pippin's understanding of Hegel's idealism itself. That is, as the previous quotation makes clear, Pippin still sees Hegel as attempting to answer a Kantian question. As I have tried to argue, however, Hegel rejects the subjectivist philosophic stance from which this question is asked. An adequate account of Hegel's idealism needs to recognize this fact.

V. CONCLUSION.

In this chapter, I have presented an interpretation of Hegel's idealism that is metaphysical. It is an interpretation that diverges both from the spirit monism and non-metaphysical interpretations. In developing this interpretation, I have not claimed that this form of idealism is valid, only that it marks an important development of the modern European tradition of philosophy. That development is grounded in a rejection of the subjectism of that tradition in favor of a logic of conceptuality. It is the reorientation of philosophy that prepares the ground for the most influential of Hegel's philosophic innovations: his attempt to theorize human social existence in a systematic manner.

An assessment of Hegel's philosophic system is beyond the scope of this chapter. The interpretation of Hegel's idealism that I have presented, however, makes Hegel's idealism an interesting and creative solution to issues in metaphysics that were raised by his predecessors. As a result, we can understand the interest that his philosophy has generated, even as we remain suspicious of its ultimate validity.

NOTES

*References to Hegel's texts are given parenthetically. The volume and page of the German edition – *Werke in zwanzig Bänden,* ed. by Eva Moldenhauer and Karl Markus Michel (Frankfurt: Suhrkamp, 1969) – follows the pagination of the English translation according to the following abbreviations:

EnL   *The Logic of Hegel translated from the Encyclopedia of the Philosophical Sciences,* trans. William Wallace (Oxford: Oxford University Press, 1873).

LHP *Hegel's Lectures on the History of Philosophy*, trans. E. S. Haldane and Frances H. Simson (Atlantic Highlands, N.J.: Humanities Press, 1982).

PH   *The Philosophy of History*, trans. J. Sibree (New York: Dover, 1956).

PS   *Phenomenology of Spirit*, trans. A. V. Miller (Oxford: Oxford University Press, 1977). Paragraph numbers are followed by page references.

SL   *Hegel's Science of Logic*, trans. A. V. Miller (London: George Allen & Unwin, 1969).

A "Z" indicates the additions to Hegel's texts. I have removed the capitalization of Hegel's philosophic terms in all quotations. References to Kant's *Critique of Pure Reason* are to the Kemp Smith translation (New York: St. Martin's, 1929) and are cited parenthetically as CPuR.

1 For another self-attribution of absolute idealism, see *EnL* 45 Z; 8, 123. Tom Rockmore claims that Hegel does not characterize his own philosophy as absolute idealism in his "On Hegel's Absolute Idealism," *Dialogue and Humanism* Vol. 1 No. 1 (1991): 99–108. I shall translate *"der Begriff"* as "the concept" in order to render Hegel's relationship with Kant more visible, and will alter all translations to accord with this usage.

2 See Locke, *Essay Concerning Human Understanding*, Book II, Chap. xi, Para. 9. Care should be taken not to confuse Locke's use of the term "idea" to refer to all the contents of our minds, including sensations and concepts, and Hegel's own use of that term to refer to the highest conceptual content, i.e., the idea. Hegel here refers to the subjective status of such mental contents and distinguishes them from concepts that he views as intersubjective.

3 That Hegel is, in fact, a realist has been argued most extensively by Kenneth Westphal in *Hegel's Epistemological Realism* (Dordrecht: Kluwer Academic Publishers, 1989).

4 Karl Americks, "Hegel and Idealism," *The Monist* 74:3, p. 22 (of typescript).

5 See, for example, his *Principles of Human Knowledge*, Part I, Para. 3.

6 See the second edition of "Refutation of Idealism," *The Critique of Pure Reason*, B 274 ff.

7 We should note the assumption that independence is what constitutes the reality of an entity.

8 This formulation obscures the differences between Berkeley and Kant. In particular, the latter clearly argues that it is not individual material objects, but the framework in which such objects exist that is dependent.

9 The role of God in Berkeley's philosophy suggests that not only finite minds constitute the existence of material objects. I leave this complication out of consideration. It is worth noting that the emphasis on the constructive role that the mind plays in human knowledge was originally articulated by Locke, albeit in service of the realism that both Berkeley and Kant criticize.

10 The importance of this point is that it means that Hegel's idealism, unlike modern European idealism, is not simply a program that seeks to reduce one category of commonsense entity to another category of commonsense entity. Hegel is concerned with the validity of common sense in general. For this reason, his form of idealism can be consistent with a version of realism.

11 Only Spinoza's view of *Deus sive Natura* as composed of both thought and extension has a clear resemblance to this aspect of Hegel's philosophy.

12 It is not clear whether the fruit or the seed should be considered the end of the plant's existence. I use the fruit since that is what Hegel does in a subsequent quotation.

13 On such a view, there will be certain aspects of the plant's existence that are fully contingent, that is, not able to be explained by the posited goal of the plant's existence. For example, the yellow color of the flower of this plant cannot be explained in the same way that its being colorful can. There is thus room for contingency in this explanation, as in Hegel's metaphysics.

14 Hegel's attempt to answer this question places him in explicit confrontation with Kant's attempt to limit the questions that metaphysics is capable of answering. I shall take up the question of whether this means that Hegel returns to the standpoint of pre-Critical metaphysics in a moment.

15 In a sense, Hegel is following Kant's theory of concepts, according to which there are pure concepts (the categories) that gain an empirical meaning for us by being schematized. We can think of our temporal notion of development as one schematized version of the pure concept of development that Hegel seeks to articulate. Thus, although the pure concept of development is not specifically temporal, it can be given a temporal schematism.

16 This brief characterization of Hegel's use of the concepts based upon negation needs a more-complete articulation and explanation. It has been the subject of much critical discussion. See, for example, Dieter Henrich's various attempts to explicate the role of negation in Hegel's philosophy, in among other places, *Hegel im Kontext* (Frankfurt: Suhrkamp, 1971), 95–156.

17 Although there are also many connections between the critical part of Kant's project and Hegel's, I cannot go into them here.

18 Presumably, the object of Kant's attack is Locke's use of the term "idea" for all species of mental contents.

19 Charles Taylor, *Hegel* (Cambridge: Cambridge University Press, 1975), 93.

20 Ibid., 94.

21 Ibid., 110.

22 J. N. Findlay, *Hegel: A Re-examination* (Oxford: Oxford University Press, 1958), 26.

23 Ibid., 22.

24 Ibid., 22–23.

25 Robert Pippin mentions the tendency of non-metaphysical views to wind up employing a set of terms that is even more metaphysically problematic than Hegel's own. See Robert B. Pippin, *Hegel's Idealism: The Satisfactions of Self-Consciousness* (Cambridge: Cambridge University Press, 1989), 298, fn. 27.

26 Ibid., 23.

27 Klaus Hartmann, "Hegel: A Non-Metaphysical View" in Alasdair MacIntyre, ed., *Hegel* (New York: Doubleday Anchor, 1972), 103, 104, 107.

28 Ibid., 110.

29 Ibid., 123.

30 Two examples are Alan White, *Absolute Knowledge: Hegel and the Problem of Metaphysics* (Athens: Ohio University Press, 1983), and Terry Pinkard, *Hegel's Dialectic: The Explanation of Possibility* (Philadelphia: Temple University Press, 1988).

31 Pippin, ibid., 39.

32 Ibid., 91.

5   Hegel's dialectical method

The dialectical method is pervasive in Hegel's mature philosophy. It governs all three parts of his system proper: the Logic, the Philosophy of Nature, and the Philosophy of Spirit. And it also governs the discipline that he developed as an introduction to this system, the Phenomenology of Spirit (expounded in the book of that name).

Few aspects of Hegel's thought have exerted as much influence or occasioned as much controversy as this method. Yet, paradoxically, it remains one of his least well understood philosophical contributions. The aim of this essay is to cast a little light where there remains much darkness.

It seems to me that three main shortcomings in the secondary literature have hindered a clear understanding of the method. First, most interpreters, if not actually denying that there is such a thing as the dialectical method, have at least characterized it in terms that remain too vague. Second, interpreters have generally made too little effort to explain the method's philosophical motivation. Third, many critics have been too hasty in dismissing the method as guilty of one or more of a variety of original sins that would render it useless *in principle,* such as violating the law of contradiction.

The main task of this essay will therefore be to overcome in turn each of these obstacles to understanding. Part I will attempt to give a reasonably precise characterization of the method. Part II will offer an account of its philosophical motivation. Part III will give it a qualified defense against the allegations of original sin.

Finally, in Part IV, I shall append a few notes concerning the origins of the method for those readers who may be interested in this question.

130

I. THE GENERAL CHARACTER OF THE METHOD

Sometimes commentators go as far as to deny that Hegel has or aspires to a dialectical method at all. For example, Solomon writes: "Hegel *has no method* as such . . . Hegel himself argues vehemently against the very idea of a philosophical 'method.' "[1] To see how deeply mistaken this view must be, one need go no further than the first edition preface of the *Science of Logic,* where Hegel gives a description of what he calls his "absolute method of knowing" and says that it is only by way of this method that philosophy is able to be "an objective, demonstrated science."[2]

Many more interpreters characterize Hegel's method in terms that simply remain too vague. For example, according to Acton, it is "a method in which oppositions, conflicts, tensions, and refutations [are] courted rather than avoided or evaded."[3] And according to Popper, it is the theory that something, such as human thought, develops in accordance with the pattern "thesis, anti-thesis, synthesis."[4] The problem with these characterizations is not that they are false. In particular, the 'thesis, anti-thesis, synthesis' model does capture the intended general structure of the method reasonably well; Hegel does not, as Kaufmann claims, "deliberately spurn" and "deride" this model in the preface of the *Phenomenology of Spirit* (or anywhere else).[5] The problem is just that such characterizations remain too vague to be of much help.

A first step toward eliminating this vagueness is to recognize that the dialectic of the Logic enjoys a certain primacy over the dialectics of the Philosophies of Nature and Spirit and the Phenomenology of Spirit. Hegel understands the dialectics of the latter three disciplines to be just *the dialectic of the Logic as it appears through the media of natural phenomena, spiritual phenomena and consciousness* (respectively). For the pure thought, which is the subject matter of the Logic, "encompasses [everything natural and everything spiritual] and is the foundation of everything"; and the development of consciousness, "like the development of all natural and spiritual life, rests solely on the nature of the pure essentialities which constitute the content of Logic."[6] If we wish to determine the character of Hegel's dialectic, then, we will do well to focus on the form it takes in his Logic.

In the Logic, the dialectic is essentially a method of expounding our fundamental categories (understood in a broad sense to include not only our fundamental concepts but also our forms of judgment and forms of syllogism). It is a method of exposition in which each category in turn is shown to be implicitly self-contradictory and to develop necessarily into the next (thus forming a continuously connected hierarchical series culminating in an all-embracing category that Hegel calls the Absolute Idea).[7]

In order to form a more precise picture of the intended structure of the method, we must look to Hegel's general accounts of it in the *Science of Logic* and Logic of the *Encyclopaedia*. Consider, for example, the following general account from the Logic of the *Encyclopaedia*: "The logical has in point of form three sides . . . These three sides do not constitute three *parts* of the Logic, but are moments of each logical reality, that is, of each concept . . . a) Thought, as the Understanding, sticks to finite determinacies and their distinctness from one another . . . b) The dialectical moment is the self-sublation of such finite determinations and their transition into their opposites . . . c) The speculative moment, or that of positive Reason, apprehends the unity of the determinations in their opposition – the affirmative that is contained in their dissolution and transition."[8] (Note that Hegel affirms this pattern for *each* logical reality or concept.)

If one takes these general accounts of the method together, the following emerges as its intended general structure. Beginning from a category A, Hegel seeks to show that upon conceptual analysis, category A proves to contain a *contrary* category, B, and conversely that category B proves to contain category A, thus showing both categories to be self-contradictory.[9] He then seeks to show that this negative result has a positive outcome, a new category, C (sometimes referred to as the "negative of the negative" or the "determinate negation"). This new category unites – as Hegel puts it – the preceding categories A and B.[10] That is to say, when analyzed the new category is found to contain them both.[11] But it unites them in such a way that they are not only preserved but also abolished (to use Hegel's term of art for this paradoxical-sounding process, they are *aufgehoben*).[12] That is to say, they are preserved or contained in the new category only with their original senses modified. This modification of their senses renders them no longer self-contradictory (and not a source of self-contradiction in the new category that contains them both).[13] That is because it renders them no longer contraries, and therefore no longer self-contradictory in virtue of their reciprocal containment. At this point, one level of the dialectic has been completed, and we pass to a new level where category C plays the role that was formerly played by category A.[14] And so on. Hegel understand each step of this whole process to be necessary.[15]

We may illustrate this general model of the Logic's dialectic by means of the textbook example from the beginning of the Logic. Hegel starts from the category Being, and first tries to show that this contains its contrary, Nothing: "*Being, pure being*, without any further determination . . . It is pure indeterminateness and emptiness. There is *nothing* to be intuited in it . . . Just as little is anything to be thought in it . . . Being, the indeterminate immediate, is in fact *nothing*, and neither more nor less than *nothing*."[16] Hegel than undertakes to demonstrate the converse containment of the concept of Being in that of Nothing in a similar way. Having thus reached the negative result that these two categories are self-contradictory, Hegel finally tries to show that there is a positive outcome that unites them but in a manner that avoids their self-contradictoriness, because it not only preserves them but also modifies their senses: the category Becoming. (To see what he is getting at here, one should reflect on the fact that what is simply in a state of becoming *in a sense* is or *has being* and also *in a sense* is not or *is nothing*.) Becoming then forms the starting point for a new round of the dialectic – going on to develop a self-contradiction that leads to subsumption under the category of Determinate Being (Dasein).[17]

Having in this manner expounded our categories as a dialectical hierarchy in the Logic, Hegel then in the Philosophies of Nature and Spirit attempts to interpret natural and spiritual phenomena as embodiments of this same dialectical hierarchy (essentially interpreting natural phenomena as embodiments of its lower stages and spiritual phenomena as embodiments of its higher stages).

Now, certain aspects of Hegel's method call for further explanation (some of these will be addressed later). But it should at least be clear that he intends this method to have a considerably more definite character than Acton's courting of "oppositions, conflicts, tensions and refutations" or Popper's "thesis, anti-thesis, synthesis."

II. THE PHILOSOPHICAL FUNCTIONS OF THE METHOD

Interpreters have not made sufficiently clear the philosophical *motivation* behind the method, its philosophical *point*. It is no doubt evident that the method is supposed to capture the single underlying structure common to both our thought and the world of natural and spiritual phenomena that we think about (thereby verifying Hegel's monistic vision of reality). In addition to this descriptive function, it is designed to serve a number of more easily overlooked but equally important philosophical functions.

These further functions may be divided into three main classes: *pedagogical* functions – functions concerning the teaching of Hegel's system to a modern audience; *epistemological* functions – functions concerning the justification of his system; and *scientific* functions – functions concerning standards that his system must meet in order to have a truly scientific character. The pedagogical and epistemological functions of the method are most prominent in Hegel's introductory discipline, the Phenomenology of Spirit, where the method is applied to very general viewpoints referred to as "shapes of consciousness."[18] The method's scientific functions, on the other hand, are performed within the system proper: Logic, Philosophy of Nature, and Philosophy of Spirit. (Since I have discussed elsewhere the pedagogical and epistemological functions served by the method in detail, I shall explain these only briefly and dogmatically in what follows.)[19]

Consider first the pedagogical functions of the method. The Phenomenology of Spirit is supposed to perform "the task of leading the individual from his uneducated standpoint to knowledge."[20] This process has both a negative and a positive side. Negatively, it involves (1) discrediting, by demonstrating the self-contradictoriness of, viewpoints other than that of Hegel's system – hence Hegel refers to the course of his discipline as "a pathway of *doubt*, or more precisely, . . . of despair" for the individual educated.[21] Positively it involves simultaneously (2) leading the individual from his initial viewpoint by way of a series of compelling steps up to the viewpoint of the system and (3) in the meantime giving him a compelling provisional exposition of the contents of the system.

The dialectical method of the Phenomenology of Spirit is the means by which both the negative and the positive sides of this pedagogical project are to be accomplished. The method runs through a series of non-Hegelian viewpoints or "shapes of consciousness." As it does so, it shows that each of these in turn is self-contradictory – thus realizing the negative side of the project, (1).[22] Moreover, it shows that each necessarily develops into the next until the series culminates in Hegel's system. And in running through them, it also generates a sort of provisional exposition of the contents of Hegel's system.[23] So that in these two ways it realizes parts (2) and (3) of the positive side of the pedagogical project as well.

Consider next the epistemological or justificatory functions of the method. In the *Phenomenology of Spirit* Hegel strives to meet three justificatory standards on behalf of his system: (1) the standard of showing his system to be immune to the skeptical objection that equally strong contrary positions might be adopted; (2) the standard of showing that his system does not fall victim to skeptical doubts about the instantiation of its concepts, doubts about whether or not these have instances in reality; (3) the standard of showing his system to be *provable for every other viewpoint,* in the sense that it be provable to each other viewpoint, purely on the basis of that viewpoint's own views and criteria, that the system is invulnerable to the skeptical problems just mentioned and is true.

Hegel's strategies for meeting these three justificatory standards in the *Phenomenology of Spirit* again make essential use of the dialectical method. His strategy for meeting standard (1) – immunity to the skeptical problem of equally strong contrary positions – is to show that his system in fact faces no such competition from contrary positions because *these all turn out to be implicitly self-contradictory.* In order to show this, he tries to prove that all viewpoints within which other positions could be articulated, all "shapes of consciousness," are self-contradictory. The dialectical method serves two essential functions in this proof. First, it shows the *self-contradictoriness* of each shape of consciousness considered. Second and less obvious, it shows the *completeness* of the collection of shapes of consciousness thus discredited.[24] How does it accomplish this demonstration of completeness? In two ways. On the one hand, it shows that all the shapes of consciousness that we know about develop into one another in a continuous series that eventually forms a kind of circle, hence demonstrating that they constitute a single entire system.[25] That they constitute a single entire system is already a strong indication that they include not only all the shapes of consciousness we happen to know about but all there are. On the other hand, the dialectical method's demonstration that these self-contradictory shapes of consciousness develop into one another in a necessary fashion and eventually culminate in Hegel's self-consistent system provides Hegel with a key for the interpretation of the whole course of human history. For the dialectical sequence turns out to be the same as the historical sequence – spanning the whole course of human history up to the present – in which the various shapes of consciousness and, eventually, Hegel's system have appeared. Hence Hegel is able to interpret human history as a teleological process aimed at unfolding, in order, this very dialectical sequence of shapes of consciousness with the purpose of escaping earlier self-contradictions and eventually reaching the self-consistent position of his own system. And that human history admits of this interpretation provides further proof that the collection of shapes of consciousness considered by the *Phenomenology of Spirit* is complete. For it is thereby seen that this collection of shapes constitutes not only an entire system but also an entire system the genesis of which has been the very purpose of human history. And this lends strong support to the view that this is the *one and only* system of these items – that there are unlikely to be further systems of them or additional ones lacking systematic connections.

In order to meet standard (2) – the standard of defending his system against skeptical doubts concerning the instantiation of its concepts – Hegel seeks to demonstrate the impropriety of an assumption that underpins any such skepticism, namely the assumption that the relevant concepts could exist without there being anything in reality to instantiate them. His way of doing this is to prove that all viewpoints that regard a concept as distinct from its object or instance are self-contradictory. These viewpoints are once again the "shapes of consciousness" treated in the work. Hence, this proof coincides with that used in order to meet epistemological standard (1), and the dialectical method plays the same essential roles here as there.

In order to meet standard (3) – proving the invulnerability to skepticism and the truth of his system for each other viewpoint in the light of that viewpoint's own views and criteria – Hegel does two things. First, he constructs the dialectical response to skepticism (sketched above) in such a way that this response is compelling for each non-Hegelian viewpoint in the light of its own resources. This dialectical response to skepticism thus takes the form of a "ladder," as Hegel calls it, on which each viewpoint finds a rung corresponding to itself, starting from which it can be compelled, simply by having its existing commitments pointed out to it, to develop the dialectical response to skepticism sketched above in its entirety. Second, he constructs this dialectical "ladder" in such a way that, having run through and discredited all non-Hegelian viewpoints, it eventually reaches the stable, self-consistent viewpoint of the Hegelian system. Hence each viewpoint can, by climbing onto the ladder and seeing where its own commitments lead, come to recognize its own (and indeed every viewpoint's) implicit commitment to the truth of Hegel's system. Clearly, the dialectical method is fundamental to this whole strategy for meeting epistemological standard (3).

Finally, we should consider the scientific functions of the dialectical method, the functions through which it is supposed to give Hegel's system a truly scientific character (as we saw earlier, Hegel says that through this method alone philosophy is able to be "an objective, demonstrated science"). In Hegel's view, a philosophy, if it is to be truly scientific, must meet, in addition to the sorts of standards of justification described above, several further demanding standards. (1) It must have a genuine method: In a letter from 1810, Hegel rejects unmethodical philosophizing, says that philosophy must become an "ordered structure (regelmaessiges Gebaeude)" like geometry, and proclaims that his task is "to invent the scientific form or to work on its development."[26] (2) It must constitute an entire system: "Without a system, philosophizing cannot be something scientific."[27] (3) Its account must demonstrably cover everything, for, "The true is the whole"; "The true . . . exists only . . . as *totality*."[28] (4) It must in a certain sense demonstrate the necessity of everything: "Reason demands its . . . satisfaction with respect to form; this form is necessity in general" and is undermined if certain facts are left "external and accidental to each other."[29] (5) It must give to the subject matter of the existing empirical sciences – understood in a broad sense, including both the sciences of nature and those of man – "an *a priori* character".[30]

The dialectical method is essential to Hegel's satisfaction of all five of these scientific standards in his philosophical system. Obviously, since it is the method of his philosophy, it is essential to his satisfaction of standard (1), the standard requiring that philosophy be methodical.

The dialectical method is also essential to Hegel's satisfaction of scientific standard (2) – entire systematicity. For that his philosophy is a genuine *system* is established by the fact that the dialectical method shows its parts to form a connected series – "The method itself expands itself . . . into a *system*."[31] And that it is an *entire* system is shown by the fact that this dialectical series has a circular structure.[32]

The dialectical method is also essential in several ways to Hegel's satisfaction of scientific standard (3) – giving an account that demonstrably covers everything. This standard proves to be less outrageously demanding than it might sound at first hearing. It turns out that Hegel will be satisfied if certain aspects of reality are accounted for only in the modest sense that it is shown necessary that there be aspects of reality, such as these, that *cannot really be further accounted for* – what he describes as a sphere of mere *existence* (*Existenz*) as opposed to *actuality* (*Wirklichkeit*).[33] Hence the challenge is to have his philosophy demonstrably cover the merely existent in this modest way and also, in a more full-blooded way, everything actual. The demonstrable modest coverage of the merely existent is a relatively straightforward matter: the general category of Existence is dialectically deduced in the Logic. The demonstrable full-blooded coverage of everything actual is a bit more complicated. First, Hegel seeks to derive all known actuality – whether actual categories or actual natural or spiritual phenomena – by means of his philosophy's dialectic. Second, he again uses a strategy that we encountered earlier in a different context in order to show that he has thereby in fact covered not only all *known* actuality but *all* actuality: he attempts to show that his philosophy's dialectical course, in addition to covering all known actuality, forms an *entire system*. The essential roles that the dialectical method played in satisfying scientific standard (2) – entire systematicity – are hence also roles that it must play in order for Hegel to meet scientific standard (3), demonstrable coverage of everything.

The dialectical method is also essential to Hegel's satisfaction of scientific standard (4) – showing that everything is necessary. As Bergmann points out, the necessity Hegel has in mind here is *teleo-*

logical necessity, necessity for a purpose.[34] More precisely, he has in mind the model of teleological explanation developed by Kant for organic life in the *Critique of Judgment:* an organism is understood as the sum of its parts, and the parts are explained in terms of the contribution they make to the whole organism as their end, so that each part is viewed as reciprocally both end and means.[35] One sees this, for example, from the fact that immediately after pointing out that "Reason demands ... necessity in general," Hegel goes on to give as grounds for empirical science's inadequacy to this demand the circumstances that "the universal contained in it is ... not in itself connected with the particular, but both are external and accidental to one another, and likewise the collected particularities are in themselves external and accidental to each other."[36] In order to give a demonstration that everything has the relevant sort of necessity, then, Hegel will seek to show that each thing is interconnected and interdependent with each other thing, so that each thing can be seen as contributing to a whole that they collectively constitute as its end; he will seek to demonstrate an "essential or necessary connection [of facts]."[37] The dialectical method is supposed to achieve this: "The dialectical principle ... is the principle which alone gives immanent connection and necessity to the body of science."[38] If we bear in mind the distinction between *actuality* and mere *existence*, Hegel's strategy is, more precisely, as follows. He will seek to demonstrate necessity in a full-blooded sense for each aspect of actuality, showing it to be interconnected and interdependent with every other aspect of actuality, by deriving it from the others, and vice versa, in the course of a circular dialectic. At the same time, he will seek to demonstrate the necessity of the merely existent in an appropriately more-modest sense by showing that the general category of Existence participates in the same system of dialectical interconnection and interdependence.

Finally, the dialectical method is essential to Hegel's accomplishment of scientific standard (5): giving the subject-matter of the existing empirical sciences an *a priori* character. It turns out, once again, that this standard is less implausibly ambitious than one might suppose at first hearing. First, it demands *a priori* explanation only of what is *actual* in the empirical sciences, not of what is merely *existent;* it does not require *a priori* explanation of such states of affairs as, for example, that there are so and so many varieties of orchids.[39] Second, the *a priori* explanation required even for actual features of nature, human society, history, etc., is not envisaged as a knowledge of them wholly independent of experience. Rather, it is envisaged as an explanation of these features *once they are empirically known* in terms of something that can be known independent of experience, namely the structure of the Absolute Idea expounded in Hegel's Logic. The Logic provides us with knowledge of a dialectically ascending series of categories culminating in the Absolute Idea, which embraces the whole series, and it provides us with this knowledge independent of experience. We, then, in the Philosophies of Nature and Spirit, use this *a priori* principle to interpret and explain the empirically known contents of the empirical sciences (interpreting natural phenomena as embodiments of the lower steps of the logical hierarchy and spiritual phenomena as embodiments of its higher steps).[40] As Hegel puts it:

If . . . we consider Logic to be the system of the pure types of thought, we find that the other philosophical sciences, the Philosophy of Nature and the Philosophy of Spirit, take the place, as it were, of an Applied Logic, and that Logic is the soul which animates them both. Their problem in that case is only to recognize the logical forms under the shapes they assume in Nature and Spirit – shapes which are only a particular mode of expression for the forms of pure thought.[41]

Clearly, the dialectical method is fundamental to Hegel's attempt to confer an *a priori* character on the empirical sciences in this way.

These, then, are the main functions that the dialectical method is supposed to serve in Hegel's philosophy, in addition to the descriptive function of capturing what he believes to be the single underlying structure common to both our thought and the world of natural and spiritual phenomena (which we think about, and thereby verify his monistic vision of reality). It should now be clear that, far from being short of philosophical motivation, as most of the secondary literature would lead one to suspect, the method has a very complex and rather sophisticated philosophical point.

If one is looking for a general way of thinking about the method, I suggest that one should understand it as the core of a grand hypothesis – concerning the structure of our shapes of consciousness, our categories, and natural and spiritual phenomena – whose fascination for Hegel lies in the fact that, if true, it promises a sweeping solution to a host of pressing philosophical challenges. These include not only the challenge of giving a monistic description of the world but also the challenge of meeting the sorts of pedagogical, epistemological, and scientific demands described above.

III. THE METHOD'S ALLEGED ORIGINAL SINS

Many interpreters of the dialectical method have suggested that it suffers from one or more of a variety of original sins that render it useless *in principle*. In this part of the paper I will offer a qualified defense of the method against the most important of these criticisms.

One common charge, leveled by Popper, is that the method involves Hegel in the affirmation of contradictions.[42] This is by no means a foolish objection. We have seen that Hegel regards the dialectical, self-contradictory categories of the Logic as constituting the underlying essence of all natural and spiritual phenomena. In consequence of this view, he not infrequently makes alarming statements such as "Everything is inherently contradictory."[43]

The most obvious and familiar strategies for defending Hegel against this objection do not work. Many commentators suggest that when Hegel talks about contradictions and self-contradictions, he really means something more innocuous. For example, he means the kind of vacillation in judgment that flows from a *vagueness* in our concepts.[44] Or he means the application of logically incompatible predicates *at different times*. Or he means "opposed tendencies."[45] Or he means a failure of something to realize its *telos*.[46] Each of these suggestions corresponds to *something* in the texts.[47] Yet it is clear that they do not get to the bottom of Hegel's conception of his contradictions. Certain of these suggestions quickly succumb to specific problems. For example, Hegel's complaint with the categories dealt with in the *Logic* is not, in general, that they are vague; on the contrary, the Understanding, from which they come, is conceived by him as a faculty of sharp distinctions.[48] And Hegel pointedly rejects the suggestion that the incompatible predicates involved in his contradictions concern different times.[49] More important, general problems of the following sort rule out *any* such extenuating interpretation. If Hegel does not mean *contradictions* when he uses the word, but something more innocuous, then why are so many of his specific examples of contradictions – especially in the fundamental Logic –

clearly meant to be just that? Why does he repeatedly present himself as taking issue with the logical law of contradiction?[50] Why does he place his dialectic in the tradition of Socrates, Plato's *Parmenides*, and Kant's Antinomies, that is, a tradition concerned with contradiction in the usual sense?[51] How could he expect his method to do justice to the negative side of the pedagogical and epistemological projects that were explained in Part II (and which – see Part IV – were predominant among his earliest motives for developing the method)? And so forth.

Another superficially attractive strategy of defense runs as follows: There are two quite different ways in which one might be said to "affirm contradictions," one objectionable, the other perfectly respectable. It is objectionable to affirm (self-)contradictory propositions about reality, but quite respectable to affirm that certain propositions or concepts are self-contradictory. Since Hegel is talking about *categories* or concepts in his Logic, he is only affirming contradictions in the latter, respectable way. And when he tells us that "everything is inherently contradictory," it is his colorful way of saying that our usual conception of reality is self-contradictory through and through.

This strategy of defense does not work for the following reasons. First, Hegel makes it quite clear that he would reject such an interpretation of his dialectic when he criticizes Kant for showing in his treatment of the Antinomies "an excess of tenderness for the things of the world" by locating the contradictions of the Antinomies in thought rather then in the world.[52] And second, it is fundamental to Hegel's conception of what he is doing in the *Logic* that its categories are *not distinct* from the reality they represent; they are thus quite unlike the sort of concept that Hegel's would-be defender has in mind.

A further, and complementary, strategy of defense, suggested by Oakeshott, for example, claims that for Hegel, self-contradiction is merely an "element . . . inherent in all abstraction," not something that afflicts his own all-embracing viewpoint.[53] There is a grain of truth in this interpretation, but not a sufficiently large grain to solve the problem. The grain of truth is that the all-embracing viewpoint in which the Logic culminates – the Absolute Idea – does not, like the partial categories that lead up to it, succumb to any *new* contradiction. (Hence Hegel denies that in moving beyond it to Being or Nature, we make a genuine transition of the kind that occurred earlier in the Logic.)[54] The snag, however, is that the Absolute Idea just *is* all these partial categories and their development through self-contradiction (together with the stable recognition of them *as* itself).[55] Hence Hegel speaks of "the absolute dialectic which is its nature."[56] And since it thus essentially includes within itself (as well as supersedes) the self-contradictions of the partial categories, it seems that if those self-contradictions were objectionable in themselves, then the Absolute Idea must be objectionable as well.

If we are to defend Hegel against the charge of endorsing contradictions, then, we must look elsewhere. A first and reassuring point to note is that it would be very surprising if Hegel were himself deliberately endorsing contradictions, given that his epistemological strategies, as explained in Part II, rested so squarely on an assumption of the *unacceptability* of doing so. Because all non-Hegelian viewpoints proved to be self-contradictory, they did not constitute genuine alternatives to Hegel's system; because all viewpoints that distinguished a concept from its object proved to be self-contradictory, a skepticism that assumed such a distinction in the case of Hegel's concepts was unacceptable.

Hegel's true situation is, I think, as follows. On the one hand, he recognizes with the rest of us that it is unacceptable to make contradictory claims about reality (hence his epistemological strategies). On the other hand, his own philosophical viewpoint is inextricably involved in affirming contradictions, *but it does not affirm them of reality and so does not fall foul of his and our proscription of this.* His viewpoint avoids affirming contradictions of reality because it does not use or recognize the validity of the concept of reality. It renounces the distinction between reality and thought (being and thought, object and thought, object and subject, object and concept, etc.). And consequently, in Hegel's view, it renounces these concepts themselves, since the distinction is, in his view, an essential part of their very definition. Thus he writes that "Pure science presupposes liberation from the opposition of consciousness. It contains *thought insofar as this is just as much the object in its own self, or the object in its own self insofar as it is equally pure thought.*"[57] However, strictly, "to talk of the *unity* of subject and object, . . . of being and thought, etc. is inept, since object and subject, etc. signify what they are *outside* of their unity."[58] Hegel's philosophical viewpoint thus officially makes no claims whatsoever about reality, and *a fortiori* no contradictory claims about it.

Of what, then, if not of reality, *does* Hegel wish to affirm contradictions? As we noted earlier, he does not merely wish to affirm them of thoughts or concepts (the preceding paragraph indicates one reason why not). Rather, he wishes to affirm them of whatever is left once the essentially oppositional concepts of reality or object, on the one hand, and thought or concept, on the other, have been overcome and synthesized. Hegel variously calls this Reason, the Logos, the Absolute Idea, the Concept, Absolute Spirit. It may not be entirely clear what this position amounts to positively. But it is clear, first, that Hegel intends it to be neither the (evidently objectionable) activity of affirming contradictions of reality nor the (evidently unobjectionable) activity of affirming them of thoughts or concepts. And it is also clear, second, that he understands it to be *more* like the latter (evidently unobjectionable) activity than the former (evidently objectionable) one. For, as one would already anticipate from the names he gives it – Reason, Absolute Idea, Concept, etc. – Hegel understands the outcome of his synthesis of the concepts of reality or object, on the one hand, and thought or concept, on the other, to be more like the latter than the former.[59]

Of course, it is possible that Hegel is simply *deluded* in thinking that he possesses a genuine concept of something that is neither reality nor thought but somehow a synthesis of the two, of which to make his dialectical affirmations. Perhaps he has no genuine concept at all here, or perhaps he is lapsing unwittingly into the use of one or both of the supposedly superseded concepts (in a manner involving him in various kinds of incoherence). Doubts of this kind concerning the intelligibility of the position that Hegel wishes to occupy arise repeatedly in connection with his philosopy.[60] They are both pertinent and pressing. Nonetheless, I would point out, first, that this is a different sort of worry from the charge that Hegel endorses contradictions in his dialectical method. And second, it is unclear whether this new worry will prove to be well founded, not primarily because of any unclarity about the nature of Hegel's texts, but because of deep unclarities in our own criteria for distinguishing sense from nonsense and sameness of sense from difference of sense in hard cases. (Perhaps not the least of the benefits to be drawn from reading Hegel is that he forces us to address this sort of unclarity in our own semantical concepts.)

Another alleged original sin of the dialectical method concerns its purportedly necessary derivation of a new category, the "negative of the negative," from the demonstrated self-contradictoriness of two preceding contrary categories: in our earlier example, the purportedly necessary derivation of Becoming from the demonstrated self-contradictoriness of Being and Nothing. As Inwood points out, it is particularly difficult to make sense of this aspect of the method; and many of Hegel's critics have denied that one can.[61]

The problem here lies not so much in Hegel's idea that, having discovered two contrary categories to be mutually implying and therefore self-contradictory, one might find some new category that eliminated the self-contradiction by unifying them in a manner that in a sense preserved while in a sense abolishing them (we were able to interpret this idea in a reasonably unmysterious way in Part I). The problem lies rather in the suggestion that the transition to this new category might be a *necessary* one.

Some commentators, for example, Findlay and Fulda, take this claim of necessity rather lightly, suggesting that the transitions in question could in fact have followed a variety of routes, but that this does no great harm to Hegel's overall project.[62] This position seems to me untenable, in view of the functions described in Part II that the dialectical method was designed to serve. Dispensing with the claim of necessity would, for example, wholly undermine the method's ability to demonstrate entire systematicity and thence completeness (whether within the *Phenomenology of Spirit* or within Hegel's system proper) and also its ability to demonstrate the kind of interconnection and interdependence in the subject matter of the system proper needed to ground a claim that this subject matter is teleologically necessary. We can only jettison Hegel's claim of the necessity of the transition to the "negative of the negative" at the cost of abandoning a very large part of his philosophical project.

I want to suggest that, in fact, reasonably good sense can be made, at least at a general level, of the idea that these transitions are necessary, as long as we take care to determine the kind of "necessity" that Hegel is interested in.

A first point to be made is the following. If one considers the nature of the necessity governing the transitions between the initial contrary categories (in our example, Being and Nothing), it seems that this is supposed to be basically the necessity of analytic implication – the kind of necessity that allows one to infer "Unmarried" from "Bachelor" (or "X is unmarried" from "X is a bachelor").[63] To be more exact, Hegel's idea is that the first category that the dialectic treats (in our example, Being) analytically implies one, and only one, contrary category (in our example, Nothing), and that this contrary category in turn analytically implies it and only it. Hegel hardly ever suggests that the necessity governing the subsequent transition to the "negative of the negative" (in our example, Becoming) is precisely the same kind of necessity.[64] Rather, he sometimes seems at pains to distinguish it by suggesting that whereas the transitions between the initial contrary categories are "analytic," the subsequent transition to the "negative of the negative" is "synthetic."[65] This fact, together with the intrinsic implausibility of understanding the necessity of the transition to the "negative of the negative" to be the necessity of analytic implication (or still worse, logical implication), rules this out as Hegel's considered position.

What sort of "necessity" *does* Hegel have in mind here? The first clue lies in the fact that many of the passages in which he discusses the transitions in question tend to suggest that his conception of them and their necessity simply *reduces to* the idea that the "negative of the negative" stands in that relation to the initial contrary categories which we have already explained: the relation of eliminating their self-contradictoriness by unifying them in a way which in a sense preserves while in a sense abolishes them. Thus he sometimes seems to imply that these transitions *consist in* the unification of the two preceding contrary categories: "The speculative moment, or that of positive Reason, apprehends the unity of the determinations in their opposition."[66] And he sometimes states that the necessity of these transitions *consists in* the drive to escape the self-contradictoriness of the two preceding categories: "The *drive* to find a stable meaning in Being or in both [Being and Nothing] is this *necessity* itself, which leads Being and Nothing to develop and gives them a true . . . meaning."[67]

A provisional account of the necessity of these transitions might, then, be the following: Hegel thinks that for each pair of mutually implying contrary categories, there will be one and only one new category that can be said to unify them in a way that in a sense preserves while in a sense abolishes them, thereby avoiding their self-contradictoriness. In application to the transition from Being and Nothing to Becoming, for example, the thought would be as follows: Unlike other categories that we might consider, such as Substance, the category of Becoming can be said to preserve in a way the categories of Being and Nothing while simultaneously modifying their senses and to this extent abolishing them – what is simply becoming *in a sense* has *being*, while *in a sense* it is nevertheless *nothing* – and it can be said thereby to render these two categories no longer contraries and hence no longer afflicted with their original self-contradictoriness. Now the necessity of the transition from Being and Nothing to Becoming just *consists in* the fact that Becoming is the only known category that can be characterized in this way.

This provisional explanation of the idea of the necessity of the transition to the "negative of the negative" requires modification, however. One reason is that Hegel in fact believes that there will generally be *more* than one known new category that stands in this relation to a given pair of mutually implying contrary categories. For example, he points out that in the case of the pair Being and Nothing, not only the category of Becoming but also that of Beginning stands in this relation to them: "Another . . . example is Beginning. In its beginning, the thing is not yet, but it is more than merely nothing, for its being is already in the beginning."[68] Again, one sees from his characterization of Determinate Being as "Being with negation" that he understands it too to stand in this relation to Being and Nothing.[69] Indeed, Hegel's official view seems to be that *every* higher category in the Logic stands in this relation to *every* lower pair of contraries, for he envisages the categories of the Logic becoming richer in a cumulative fashion as they develop out of each other.[70]

A clue to how we should modify the definition of the necessity of the transition to the "negative of the negative" in order to avoid this difficulty may be found in the ground Hegel gives for preferring Becoming over Beginning as the "negative of the negative" of Being and Nothing: "Beginning is itself a case of Becoming, but it already expresses the idea of further advance."[71] This strongly suggests that Hegel has in mind *greater proximity in conceptual content* to the two contrary categories being unified as his criterion for identifying one potential unifying category as the "negative of the negative" in preference to another. A more satisfactory definition of the necessity of the transition to the "negative of the negative" would, then, be that it consists in this category's unifying a given pair of mutually implying contrary categories by, in a sense, preserving while, in a sense, abolishing them, thereby eliminating their self-contradictoriness, *and being the one known category that does so while remaining closest to them in conceptual content.*[72]

There may still seem to be a problem with this account as it stands. If the maximal proximity in conceptual content in question is only maximal proximity relative to all *known* categories, then this appears to leave the necessity of the transition disturbingly weak and provisional: at any time, a previously unknown category might be found or invented whose conceptual content was closer, and then *this* would become the necessary "negative or the negative." And this threatens to undermine the method's ability to perform several of the functions it was designed to serve, which were indicated in Part II. If, on the other hand, we try to avoid this weakness by reinterpreting the maximal proximity in conceptual content in question not as maximal proximity relative to all *known* categories, but as maximal proximity *simpliciter*, then it becomes unclear if this condition is genuinely meaningful and, even if it were, how one could ever tell that it obtained.[73]

It seems to me that Hegel in fact has a way of sailing between this particular Scylla and Charybdis, although he nowhere explicitly makes the point. The necessity of the transition to the "negative of the negative" that we have defined must indeed be weak and provisional as long as particular transitions are considered *in isolation*. Hegel believes, however, that these transition will eventually produce a *system* comprising all known categories, and it is not at all clear that, when viewed in the light of such a system, the necessity in question must *remain* weak and provisional. Once a system has been exhibited through a necessity as yet weak and provisional, the hypothesis that some new category might come along and dislodge a given "negative of the negative" could come to look very implausible indeed. The realization of such an hypothesis would require the present "negative of the negative" either to be evicted from the system altogether or to be reintegrated into the system at some later stage, in which case it would have to perform the function of unifying some *new* pair of preceding contrary categories with minimal addition of conceptual content. And it would also require either that the new "negative of the negative" break up the existing system or that it be such that it mutually implies a contrary and finds a free category within the system that unifies itself and its contrary with minimal addition of conceptual content (or, if a sequence of new categories were added, that each stand in this relation to another and that the last of them finds a free category within the system to which it stands in this relation). If one had a system comprising all known categories exhibited before one, these possibilities might all look very remote indeed.[74]

I may now adduce one last, important ground for thinking that our definition faithfully reflects Hegel's considered conception of the necessity of the transition to the "negative of the negative." The necessity of our definition seems to be all the necessity Hegel requires in this transition in order for his dialectical method to accomplish the philosophical functions it was designed to serve – the functions outlined in Part II. (I shall leave it to the reader to verify this by reviewing those functions.)

It does seem possible, then, to make reasonably good sense, at least at a general level, of Hegel's idea of a necessary transition to the "negative of the negative," as long as one takes care to determine the kind of "necessity" he is interested in.

A third alleged original sin of the method concerns its negative side, its demonstration of the self-contradictoriness of our fundamental categories. Readers frequently find the whole idea that our thought is entangled in fundamental self-contradictions quite implausible, and consequently this aspect of the method tends to be regarded as another original sin. Findlay, for example, suggests the criticism of Hegel that "It seems hard . . . to believe that contradictions infect our most ordinary notions and categories."[75]

Hegel sees the negative side of his method as placing him within a long tradition of philosophers who have sought to show that thought was in fundamental ways self-contradictory. In this connection he mentions the Eleatics, Socrates, Plato (particularly his *Parmenides*), and Kant (the Antinomies).[76] Hegel is right to emphasize the continuity between the negative side of his own dialectic and this long tradition in philosophy. And the negative side of this method is, I think, best appreciated by keeping in mind that it is representative of this tradition.

A first point to be made in response to those who see the negative side of Hegel's method as a source of weakness in principle is that philosophers in this tradition arguably *have* succeeded in uncovering fundamental self-contradictions in thought. Consider Parmenides, for example, whose argument for the incoherence of the notion of not-being is of special interest to us because it provided the inspiration for Hegel's own argument in the Logic for the incoherence of the category Nothing.

Parmenides expressed the paradox of not-being in the pithy argument: "What is there to be said and thought must needs be: for it is there for being, but nothing is not."[77] Interpretation of this is of course a difficult and much-disputed matter, but the idea seems to be somewhat as follows: "Saying" and "thinking" are, like "seeing" and "beating" but unlike "sleeping" and "walking," essentially relational activities; they are essentially performed *on something*. There can no more be an act of saying or thinking that is not an act of saying or thinking *something* than there can be an act of seeing or beating that is not an act of seeing or beating *something*. Now when we speak or think of existent objects, or existent conditions of objects, and say or think that they exist, this seems unproblematic: we speak or think of *the object* or *the condition of the object*; this is the *relatum*. But what if we say or think (i) that an object or condition of an object exists when in fact it does not or (ii) that an object or condition of an object does not exist? In case (i), it looks as though there is no *relatum*, and hence after all no speaking or thinking either. In case (ii), it seems that if (per impossibile, as it turns out) the speaking or thinking were true, then again it would lack a *relatum* and so again not really be a speaking or thinking after all; at best it could be a speaking or thinking only if it were false. To claim that somebody says or thinks that some object or condition of an object exists when it does not, or that somebody truly says or thinks that some object or condition of an object does not exist is hence implicitly self-contradictory. To say or think that some object or condition of an object does not exist is to commit a sort of pragmatic self-contradiction.

There is perhaps an inclination to respond that the solution to this paradox is obvious: *thoughts* constitute the missing *relata* in each case. The problem with this suggestion is that, arguably, it does not provide the kind of genuine *relata* to whose existence Parmenides' contemporaries actually committed themselves when they ascribed meaningful speech or thought to people. Indeed, if one had offered this solution to them, they would probably have regarded it as no more than a bit of linguistic sophistry. To be sure, one can speak of "thinking a thought," but – even more commonly in our Greek than in your English – one can also speak of, for example, "fighting a fight"; it looks as though the thought, like the fight, is merely a cognate accusative, not a genuine *relatum*.[78] If a skeptical Ariadne had questioned whether there had really been anything in the labyrinth for Theseus to fight and whether, therefore, he had really fought, his response that, notwithstanding the absence of animate opponents, he had been able to fight a fight would not have impressed her. Why should we be any more impressed with the suggestion that thinkers, lacking *relata* of other kinds, may yet think thoughts?

Of course, there is a way of *avoiding* this paradox, namely by adding to one's ontology a domain of concepts and propositions to serve as *relata* in the problematic (and also the unproblematic) cases, and using terms like "say" and "think" in a way that implies no more than that there be *relata* of these kinds. But this is a solution which the best philosophical minds of Greece needed three generations to achieve (the Stoics were perhaps the first to approach such a position with the inclusion in their ontology of fictional "somethings" and incorporeal *lekta*).[79] Until then, men arguably were guilty of just the fundamental self-contradictions and pragmatic self-contradictions to which Parmenides drew their attention.

A second point to be made is that how one evaluates the idea common to Hegel and the dialectical tradition that our thought is in fundamental ways self-contradictory will depend very much on one's *semantical* intuitions and assumptions, one's intuitions and assumptions concerning *meaning*. Hegel and this tradition tend to semantical intuitions and assumptions that diverge from those typical of modern philosophers in two respects: (a) they tend to treat the boundary between what we now know as analytic and synthetic statements as though it included a good deal more on the analytic side than the modern philosopher would locate there, and (b) they tend to have stricter standards than the modern philosopher for saying of someone that he used a word or expression in more than one sense.[80]

These semantical intuitions and assumptions translate directly into a readiness to perceive widespread self-contradiction in thought, as follows. To determine that a proposition or concept is self-contradictory, one must show that its analytic implications contain a logical inconsistency; the larger the sphere of analytic implications one recognizes, the easier this will be to accomplish; and so if one adopts attitude (a) one will be more inclined to detect self-contradiction in people's thoughts. Moreover, the most common and effective technique for exculpating someone from a charge of self-contradiction is to impute to him a distinction between different senses of a key word or expression on two or more occasions of its use (or between the senses of two or more key words or expressions which at first sight appear to be synonyms); but the stricter one's standards for imputing distinct senses to someone, the less likely one will be to accept such an exculpation; and so if one adopts attitude (b) one will be more inclined to believe that people really are guilty of self-contradiction in their thoughts.

Let me illustrate Hegel's adoption of attitudes (a) and (b) in his dialectic. Consider first attitude (a), the expansion of the class of the analytic at the expense of the synthetic. Hegel adopts this attitude in one of his earliest dialectical arguments, where he tries to demonstrate the self-contradictoriness of the concepts of attraction and repulsion. His demonstration rests on the assumption that Newton's third law of motion, the law that to every action there is an equal and opposite reaction, is internal to the meaning of these concepts. He writes:

If the increased density or specific weight of a body is explained as an increase in the force of attraction, the same phenomenon can be explained with equal ease as an increase in the force of repulsion, for *there can only be as much attraction as there is repulsion . . . the one has meaning only with reference to the other. To the extent to which one were greater than the other, to that same extent it would not exist at all.*[81]

Consider next attitude (b), the adoption of strict standards for saying that someone used a word or expression in more than one sense. Hegel adopts this attitude in defending the genuineness of a self-contradiction when he criticizes Kant's solution to the (Dynamical) Antinomies. In his solution to the Third Antinomy, Kant, assuming the truth of incompatibilism, purports to show that the contradiction between our commitment to universal causation and our commitment to human freedom is illusory because, while universal causation may be and indeed is true of *appearances*, this yet leaves room for spontaneity in the sphere of *things in themselves*. Hegel rejects this solution to the Antinomy, in part on the ground that allowing us the truth of our belief in universal causation only in the sphere of *appearances* is like "attributing to someone a correct perception, with the rider that nevertheless he is incapable of perceiving what is true but only what is false."[82] One might put the point this way: Our belief in universal causation was simply a belief in *universal causation*, not a belief in universal causation *within the restricted sphere of appearances* or *within some subsphere of reality*. Allowing the truth of the latter claims, or showing their compatibility with our belief in human freedom, is therefore not at all the same as allowing the truth or our original belief in universal causation or showing this original belief compatible with our belief in human freedom. Kant has found a way of enabling us to *avoid* holding our original contradictory beliefs while continuing to talk much as before – namely, by distinguishing two different senses that we can assign to a claim that causation is universal, one of which is consistent with a belief in spontaneity. But he has not shown that the contradictoriness of our original beliefs was *illusory*, as he seems to think. For we originally did *not* assign both of these senses to the claim, and did not embrace the sense consistent with a belief in spontaneity.

These observations are intended to suggest that we should take more seriously than we may initially be inclined to the view shared by Hegel and the rest of the dialectical tradition that thought is in fundamental ways self-contradictory. For once we recognize the bearing of semantical intuitions and assumptions on the plausibility of this tradition, we should be prompted to ask questions like the following. Might it not be that semantical intuitions and assumptions of the type expressed in attitudes (a) and (b), which make the imputation of self-contradictions plausible, are – in some version, at least – philosophically defensible against the contrary semantical intuitions and assumptions typical of the modern philosopher? Might it not turn out that our ready hostility toward the dialectical tradition rests on the shaky foundation of semantical intuitions and assumptions which, even if today widespread and deeply engrained, are ultimately idiosyncratic and questionable? These difficult issues cannot be pursued here. But the very fact that they arise and *are* difficult should, I suggest, make us hesitate before dismissing the position shared by Hegel and the rest of the dialectical tradition.

It seems, then, that Hegel's method can be defended against at least the most-common forms of the objection that it is guilty of original sins that render it useless *in principle*. This defense must now be qualified with some more-critical observations concerning Hegel's application of the method *in practice*.

Even if it is wrong to dismiss the negative side of the method as flawed in principle, it may yet be right to say that it is flawed in practice; Hegel may fail to identify particular self-contradictions in our thought. Addressing this question properly would, of course, require a detailed treatment of the Logic. But my strong inclination is to think that Hegel is indeed less successful here than some of the earlier representatives of the dialectical tradition. And I would like to give one instructive example of this.

It was suggested earlier that a case could be made for seeing Parmenides's argument for the incoherence of the notion of not-being as a successful exposure of deep self-contradictions in the thought of his contemporaries. As I mentioned, Hegel, in his argument for the incoherence of the category Nothing in the Logic, attempts to revive a form of the Parmenidean paradox. This is perhaps clearest from the formulation of the argument in the 1808/1809 Logic: "[Being] is . . . the same thing as Nothing, which in thought is likewise and thus has the same being as Being itself."[83] Now, the problem with this is that by the time Hegel's era has arrived, an ontology of concepts and propositions (or judgments) has been established and a corresponding adjustment in the kind of *relata* implied when terms like "say" and "think" are used has taken place (especially, thought not exclusively, among philosophers), so that Hegel's contemporaries are no longer generally vulnerable to the paradox. Far from falling victim to Hegel's paradox, they are in a position readily to diagnose the error of raising it against them: In order for someone to think of Nothing there must *be* a *concept* of Nothing, to be sure, this is the *relatum* which thought requires in order to take place; but that does not commit us to the paradoxical admission that Nothing *itself exists*. Hegel often points out the futility of attempting to revive superseded forms of social life; it is equally futile to attempt to revive superseded paradoxes.

There is a great irony in the fact that Hegel should have rendered himself vulnerable to this particular criticism, an irony that enables us to make another point in his favor. The irony is that the history of the Parmenidean paradox that I have been suggesting as a ground for criticizing Hegel's treatment of the category Nothing is, after all, only Hegel's own general account of the historical development of thought writ small. For of course Hegel himself – particularly in the *Phenomenology of Spirit* and the *Lectures on the History of Philosophy* – is the great exponent of the idea that the history of thought is a process in which genuine self-contradictions arise and act as motors driving us to escape them by enriching our conceptual resources in ways that then enable us to avoid them. If my comments have done anything to call into question Hegel's paradox of Nothing, then, this is only by simultaneously providing some evidence to support his general picture of the historical development of thought.

One can generalize the above criticism of Hegel's treatment of the category Nothing and the negative side of his dialectical method: however defensible the method as a whole may be in principle, Hegel's applications of it in practice tend to be unconvincing, for two distinguishable sorts of reasons. First, Hegel, over large stretches of his texts, deviates from the intended general structure of the method in more or less extreme ways. In the Logic, for example, we find some slippage in the second round of the dialectic, the transition from Becoming to Determinate Being, where, instead of showing Becoming and a contrary category to be mutually implying and then showing them to be unified in Determinate Being, Hegel tries to find a contradiction between two component concepts contained in the category Becoming and then argues that these two component concepts are unified in Determinate Being.[85] This deviation may be relatively modest and harmless, but by the time we reach the Logic's treatment of the forms of judgment and syllogism, there is hardly even a trace of the official method, and it is difficult to see how this method, which was formulated primarily with concepts in mind, *could* be applied to forms of judgment and syllogism. Second, even at points where Hegel is seriously striving to realize the intended general structure of the method, this realization falls victim to specific problems. We have just seen reason to criticize his supposed demonstration of the self-contradictoriness of the category Nothing. We can criticize the transition from Quality and Negation to Boundary

(*Grenze*), on the ground that Boundary, instead of unifying Quality and Negation in the method's official sense of containing them both in its conceptual analysis, seems to do so only in the sense that a boundary can serve as a kind of metaphor for the relation between a quality and its negation.[86] We can criticize the transition from Being and Nothing to Becoming on the ground that it is not at all clear that the temporal, dynamic idea that the concept Becoming adds to the concepts Being and Nothing is really a smaller conceptual addition than the idea of qualitative determinacy added by the concept Determinate Being, as the method would require. And so forth.

No doubt a few hard-boiled Hegelians will try to defuse this general criticism by responding that what the features of the texts to which it points really show is that my account of the dialectic's structure has been too one-dimensional, that the dialectic is instead, to use Fulda's expression, "an extremely multi-structured formation."[87] My answer is that if they could succeed in describing and delimiting the alleged multiple forms of the method clearly enough to distinguish this from a non-method and could show them to be consistent with Hegel's general accounts of the structure of the method as exlained in Part I, and could show them to have at least a reasonable prospect of realizing the functions for which Hegel designed the method (and which were discussed in Part II), then their suggestion would be worth pursuing. Otherwise it must have the appearance of obfuscation. It may in fact be possible to come at least close to meeting these conditions for a very few of the deviations from the intended general structure of the method alluded to in the preceding paragraph, the structure of the transition from Becoming to Determinate Being. But it seems clear that this will not be possible in the great majority of cases where deviations and problems arise.

I would, though, enter a more modest qualification of the indicated general criticism: when we read Hegel's texts, we should always keep in mind the possibility of *reconstructing* their application of the dialectical method, or even of modifying the method itself in ways consistent with its performance of the philosophical functions for which it was designed. Neither his particular applications of the method nor even the method itself are ends in themselves for Hegel. Rather, they are means to meeting the sorts of philosophical challenges that were described in Part II. Hegel sometimes deters readers from approaching his texts in this spirit, by speaking in the tones of a sort of infallible discoverer of ultimate truths. But we should set against such passages the voice of a more modest and sympathetic Hegel – a Hegel working on the task of inventing or helping to develop a scientific philosophy and aware of his own fallibility as he does so. This is the Hegel who, in a letter quoted earlier, emphasizes the need for philosophy to become methodical and scientific and says, "My task is to invent that scientific form or to work on its development." And it is the Hegel who opens the preface to the second edition of the *Science of Logic* with the plea, "Earnestly as I have tried after many years of further occupation with this science to remedy its imperfection, I feel I still have enough reason to claim the indulgence of the reader."[88] There is, of course, no *a priori* guarantee that a reconstruction of Hegel's project could be appreciably more satisfactory than his own execution of it. But this part of our paper has suggested that there is also no *a priori* guarantee that it could not.

In conclusion, we recall the suggestion in Part II that we might usefully think of the dialectical method as the core of a sort of grand hypothesis that promises a sweeping solution to a host of pressing philosophical challenges. The results of Part III now suggest that if Hegel's dialectical hypothesis fails at all, it will probably be more in the manner of an hypothesis that is eventually proven false when tested against the facts (at the point where it becomes clear that no amount of reconstruction of its details is going to make it convincing) than in the manner of an hypothesis that is incoherent or otherwise patently false from the start.

IV. THE ORIGINS OF THE METHOD

This paper has considered the dialectical method as it appears in Hegel's mature philosophy – the philosophy he propounds in the 1807 *Phenomenology of Spirit* and later. The method has an even earlier history, and it is appropriate that a few notes be appended concerning this (these will of necessity be somewhat brief and dogmatic).[89]

1. Hegel's mature philosophy comprises an introductory Phenomenology of Spirit followed by the system proper in the form of Logic, Philosophy of Nature, and Philosophy of Spirit. By contrast, his ear-

lier Jena system (approximately 1801–1806) comprised an introductory Logic followed by Metaphysics, Philosophy of Nature, and Philosophy of Spirit. Duesing's judgment on the origin and development of the dialectic is broadly correct (a qualification will be entered later): "The dialectic as a method . . . arose in Hegel's early Logic, which as yet had the limited function of a systematic introduction to the system, and . . . only later spread as a general method to other parts of the system."[90]

2. The method's career in the early Logic takes a somewhat peculiar course. It seems fairly clear that Hegel was already in possession of something very like his mature method at the time when he wrote the essay *The Difference between the Fichtean and Schellingian Systems of Philosophy* in 1801. That is: a method which demonstrated both the self-contradictoriness of determinations and their constitution of a self-developing series, by repeated steps of showing a determination to involve a contrary determination and then showing these two determinations to be synthesized in a higher determination (in Hegel's later terminology, the "negative of the negative"). Consider the following two passages from the essay, in which Hegel describes in general terms the course of his envisaged introductory Logic:

Each being is, because posited, an op-posited, a conditioned and conditioning; the Understanding completes these its limitations by positing the opposite limitations as their conditions; these require the same completion, and the Understanding's task develops into an infinite one . . . Reason . . . completes [a relative identity] through its opposite and produces through the synthesis of the two a new identity, which is again itself an inadequate identity in the eyes of Reason, which again likewise completes itself.[91]

After this 1801 essay, we hear of nothing equally like Hegel's mature dialectic until the 1804–5 *Logic, Metaphysics and Nature Philosophy*. In the meantime, the evidence we have of the Logic's dialectic suggests a disappearance of continuous development through determinations by means of the transition to the "negative of the negative" and instead an exclusive focus on the demonstration of self-contradictions.[92] The dialectic then reappears in something much like its mature form in the Logic of the 1804–5 *Logic, Metaphysics and Nature Philosophy*. In particular, the transition to the "negative of the negative" is again at work.[93]

3. It seems clear that Hegel's dialectical method was a fairly direct descendant of the method used by Fichte in his *Science of Knowledge* and later adopted by Schelling in his *System of Transcendental Idealism* from 1800.[94] The striking similarity of the two methods in itself makes this highly probable. Hegel's method advances by demonstrating the self-contradictoriness of a determination through showing it to involve a contrary determination, and vice versa, and then overcoming these self-contradictions by unifying the two determinations in a third determination that preserves them in a modified form, finally repeating this whole process at the new level thereby reached. Fichte's method does essentially the same.[95] For example, the *Science of Knowledge* begins with the principle of the absolute self. Fichte first shows that this both requires and is required by a not-self and that the not-self *nullifies* the self, thus apparently showing both the principle of the self and that of the not-self to be self-contradictory.[96] These apparent self-contradictions are then resolved by a unifying principle that both preserves and modifies the self and the not-self: the principle that a *divisible* self faces a *divisible* not-self.[97] The same process is then repeated at this new level. (Note in particular how Hegel's idea of a transition from self-contradiction to the "negative of the negative" is anticipated here.) One may also compare to Hegel's method the version of Fichte's method that Schelling uses in his *System of Transcendental Idealism*, which he characterizes schematically as follows: "Two opposites a and b . . . are united by the act x, but x contains a new opposition, c and d . . . , and so the act x itself again becomes an object; it is itself explicable only through a new act = z, which . . . again contains an opposition, and so on."[98] The similarity of Hegel's method to that developed by Fichte and adopted by Schelling would, then, by itself make the hypothesis of its descent from the latter highly probable. But when one recognizes the occurrence of something already very like Hegel's mature dialectical method in his 1801 essay *The Difference between the Fichtean and Schellingian Systems of Philosophy* (see point 2 above), this debt to Fichte and Schelling becomes a virtual certainty. For Hegel in this essay praises Fichte for realizing the Kantian principle of a deduction of the categories "in a pure and strict form," referring to the procedure for "deducing" determinations that Fichte employs in the *Science of Knowledge*.[99] And he envisages his own method being used in an introductory Logic which is directly modeled on or even identical

with Schelling's *System of Transcendental Idealism* (together perhaps with his Philosophy of Nature).[100] (In this connection, one should also note the following remark from one of Hegel's introductions to Logic and Metaphysics in the Jena period: "Fichte's Science of Knowledge and Schelling's Transcendental Idealism are both nothing other than attempts to present Logic . . . in its pure independence."[101]

4. In the passage quoted earlier, Duesing described Hegel's dialectic as originally restricted to his early Logic alone, and he described the early Logic, and by implication the dialectic that arose within it, as serving the limited function of providing a "systematic introduction to the system." This is a little too vague and in certain respects inaccurate. What then, more precisely, was the function of the dialectic of the early Logic? Disregarding differences between the several versions of this discipline, we can identify the following main functions. First, it served pedagogical functions similar to those later served by the dialectic of the *Phenomenology of Spirit* – functions of teaching Hegel's system by discrediting other viewpoints, providing an approach to the system, and giving a sort of provisional articulation of the contents of the system.[102] Second, it served the same range of epistemological or justificatory functions vis-à-vis Hegel's system as the dialectic of the *Phenomenology of Spirit* later served, responding in ways similar to those indicated in Part II to the skeptical difficulties that the system appears to face competition from equally plausible contrary viewpoints and that its concepts might lack instantiation, and to the ideal of showing that the system can be proved to all other viewpoints purely on the basis of their own views and criteria.[103] Third – and here we encounter a function that, unlike those already mentioned, *cannot* properly be termed a "systematic introduction to the system," and which shows that the early dialectic already had a limited role beyond the confines of the early Logic – the dialectic of at least some versions of the early Logic already, though in a restricted way, served as an *a priori* key to the interpretation of natural and spiritual phenomena; it already in a restricted way served this function so characteristic of the dialectic of the Logic of Hegel's mature philosophy. One sees this, for example, in the 1801–2 fragment "The Idea of the Absolute Being," which sketches symmetrical Philosophies of Nature and Spirit, each of which divides into two parts: a lower part corresponding to and based on the Logic and a higher, subsuming part corresponding to

and based on the Metaphysics.[104] One sees it also in the 1802–3 *System of Ethical Life.*[105] The first half of this version of the Philosophy of Spirit corresponds to the Logic. This half begins by covering lower spiritual phenomena under the heading "Absolute Ethical Life *according to Relation*" – the roughly contemporary essay *Natural Law* assigns dialectic, and hence the Logic, the task of showing the nothingness of *relation.*[106] It then enters a negative phase, "The Negative or Freedom or Crime" that, as Trede argues, corresponds to the culminating dialectical stage of the version of the early Logic sketched in the fragment "Logica et Metaphysica."[107] In its second half, the work moves to a higher, subsuming spiritual sphere, that of "Ethical Life" simpliciter, which corresponds to Metaphysics.

5. With the inception of the *Phenomenology of Spirit* and the mature system associated with it that is, by 1807, the confinement of dialectic to the early Logic (and lower parts of the Philosophies of Nature and Spirit) came to an end. Dialectic became the method of Hegel's whole philosophy and added to its primarily pedagogical and epistemological functions the full complement of further functions described in Part II.

NOTES

1 R.C. Solomon, *In the Spirit of Hegel* (Oxford, 1983), 21–22.

2 G.W.F. Hegel, *Science of Logic* (London/New York, 1976), 28, cf. pp. 53 ff. / *Wissenschaft der Logik* I (Frankfurt am Main, 1969) – henceforth abbreviated as WdL – pp. 17, 48 ff.. (Translations are sometimes my own and sometimes borrowed from the cited English language editions, with modifications where necessary.)

3 *The Encyclopaedia of Philosophy*, ed. P. Edwards (London/New York, 1972), vol. 3, 444.

4 K.R. Popper, "What Is Dialectic?" in *Mind* 49 (1940): 404.

5 W. Kaufmann, *Hegel – A Reinterpretation* (Notre Dame, 1978), 154. G.W.F. Hegel, *Phenomenology of Spirit* (Oxford, 1979), pars. 50–52 / *Phänomenologie des Geistes* (Frankfurt am Main, 1970) – henceforth abbreviated as PdG – pp. 48–51. Hegel certainly criticizes the manner in which this model has been utilized by previous philosophers, especially Schelling's reduction of it to a "lifeless schema" externally applied to a subject-matter (instead of being allowed to emerge therefrom). But he does not criticize the model itself; on the contrary, he quite clearly assumes its *correctness*, saying, for example, that since Kant it has

"been raised to its absolute significance and with it the true form in its true content has been presented, so that the Concept of Science has emerged." (Similarly, in *Science of Logic*, pp. 836–37 / WdL II, pp. 564–65, Hegel resists undue emphasis on the *numerical* aspect of the model, its triplicity, suggesting that the method may, if desired, be divided up into more than three steps. But this does not imply any rejection of the "thesis, anti-thesis, synthesis" model itself; on the contrary, Hegel's comments occur in the context of an explanation of the method that accords it this structure.)

6 G.W.F. Hegel, *Encyclopaedia* (*Logic*, Oxford, 1975); *Philosophy of Nature*, Oxford, 1970; *Philosophy of Mind*, Oxford, 1971) / *Enzyklopädie der philosophischen Wissenschaften* I, II, III, Frankfurt am Main, 1970), par. 24, Zusatz 1; *Science of Logic*, p. 28 / WdL I, p. 17.

7 As Hegel puts it, dialectic is a principle that "alike engenders and dissolves" categories. See G.W.F. Hegel, *Philosophy of Right* (Oxford, 1976) / *Grundlinien der Philosophie des Rechts* (Frankfurt am Main, 1971), par. 31.

8 *Encyclopaedia*, pars. 79–82. Hegel's most-extended general accounts of the method occur in *Science of Logic*, pp. 53–59, 431–43, 830–38 / WdL I, pp. 48–56; WdL II, pp. 64–80, 556–67.

9 *Science of Logic*, p. 431 / WdL II, p. 56: "The self-subsistent determination . . . that contains the opposite determination . . . at the same time also excludes it . . . It is thus *contradiction*." Ibid., p. 433 / WdL II, p. 67: "Positive and negative, each in its self-subsistence, sublates itself; each is simply the transition or rather the self-transposition of itself into its opposite"; cf. the discussion of the behavior of pairs of contraries cited in illustration at ibid., p. 437 / WdL II, pp. 71–72; and *Encyclopaedia*, par. 214: while the Understanding claims that subjective and objective, finite and infinite etc. are quite opposed and different from one another, "the Logic shows instead the opposite, namely that the subjective which is supposed to be only subjective, the finite which is supposed to be only finite, the infinite which is supposed to be only infinite and so forth has no truth, contradicts itself and passes over into its opposite." On the role of conceptual analysis here, see, for example, ibid., par. 88: "The deduction of the unity [of Being and Nothing] is completely analytical."

10 It is "the unity [of the first concept] and its opposite" (*Science of Logic*, p. 54 / WdL I, p. 49).

11 Thus Hegel writes of the category Becoming, which unifies Being and Nothing, that it is "one idea" and that "when it is analyzed, the determination of Being, but also that of its straightforwardly other, Nothing, are contained therein" [*Encyclopaedia*, par. 88, (3)].

12 On these two aspects of the unification, and Hegel's use of the verb

aufheben to convey them both, see *Science of Logic,* pp. 106–8 / WdL I, pp. 113–15.

13 "The *drive* to find a stable meaning in Being or in both [Being and Nothing] is [the] *necessity* . . . which leads Being and Nothing to develop and gives them a true . . . meaning" (*Encyclopaedia,* par. 87).

14 "On the new foundation constituted by the result as the fresh subject matter, the method remains the same as with the previous subject matter" (*Science of Logic,* p. 838 / WdL II, pp. 566–67). Compare Fulda, "Hegel's Dialektik als Begriffsbewegung und Darstellungsweise," in *Seminar: Dialektik in der Philosophie Hegels,* ed. R.P. Horstmann (Frankfurt am Main, 1978), 159–60, who places too much weight on the superficial ordering in Hegel's table of contents.

15 Logic has the task of exhibiting thought "in its own immanent activity or what is the same, in its necessary development"; it shows "the *immanent coming-to-be* of the distinctions and the *necessity* of their connection with each other (*Science of Logic,* pp. 31, 55 / WdL I, pp. 19, 51).

16 *Science of Logic,* p. 82 / WdL I, pp. 82–83. Strictly speaking, since Being as the first category of the Logic is supposed to be unanalyzable and simple (*Science of Logic,* p. 75 / WdL I, p. 75), we should not, in this particular case, talk about "containment." What Hegel aims to show is rather the literal identity of the concept of Being with the concept of Nothing. Hence the formulation "Being . . . is in fact *nothing,* and neither more nor less than *nothing.*" (Hegel fails to address the obvious difficulty that if Being and Nothing are in fact the very same concept, then they can hardly also be contraries, as the method requires if it is to demonstrate a self-contradiction.)

17 *Science of Logic,* p. 106 / WdL, p. 113; *Encyclopaedia,* par. 89.

18 For the purposes of this essay, I shall not go into the distinctive form taken by the dialectical method in the *Phenomenology of Spirit,* which Hegel describes at pars. 84–87 / PdG, pp. 76–80. Nor shall I discuss the exact relation of this work's dialectic to that of the underlying Logic. These matters are dealt with in my *Hegel's Idea of a "Phenomenology of Spirit"* (Cambridge, Mass., forthcoming).

19 On both sets of functions, see my *Hegel's Idea of a "Phenomenology of Spirit";* on the epistemological functions, see my *Hegel and Skepticism* (Cambridge, Mass., 1989), chs. 6, 8, 9, 10.

20 *Phenomenology,* par. 28 / PdG, 31.

21 *Phenomenology,* par. 78 / PdG, p. 72.

22 As Hegel puts it at *Science of Logic,* p. 54 / WdL I, p. 49, each shape of consciousness "has for its result its own negation." Cf. *Phenomenology of Spirit,* pars. 84–85 / PdG, pp. 76–78.

23 For example, Hegel understands the series of shapes of consciousness

generated to be the Logic's series of categories seen through a glass darkly (*Phenomenology of Spirit*, pars. 89, 805 / PdG, pp. 80, 589).

24 As Hegel puts it, "The *completeness* of the forms of the unreal consciousness will result from the necessity of the progression and interconnection itself" (*Phenomenology*, par. 79 / PdG, p. 73).

25 On the circularity of the discipline's course, see *Phenomenology*, pars. 806–7 / PdG, pp. 589–90).

26 Draft of a letter to Sinclair, mid-October 1810, in *Briefe von und an Hegel*, ed. J. Hoffmeister (Hamburg, 1969), vol. 1, 332.

27 *Encyclopaedia*, par. 14.

28 *Phenomenology of Spirit*, par. 20 / PdG, p. 24; *Encyclopaedia*, par. 14.

29 *Phenomenology*, par. 9.

30 Ibid., par. 12.

31 *Science of Logic*, p. 838 / WdL II, p. 567.

32 *Science of Logic*, pp. 838–42 / WdL II, pp. 567–72; *Encyclopaedia*, pars. 14–15.

33 *Encyclopaedia*, pars. 6; 123, Zusatz. On this see further D. Henrich, "Hegels Theorie ueber den Zufall," in his *Hegel im Kontext* (Frankfurt, 1967), 157–86.

34 F.H. Bergmann, "The Purpose of Hegel's System," in *Journal of the History of Philosophy* (1964), p. 191: "The sense of 'necessity' that is crucial for Hegel is . . . that of Fichte's 'necessity for a purpose.' " (Bergmann's claim requires qualification: the word "necessity" and its cognates also bear other important senses in Hegel. For example, at *Encyclopaedia*, pars. 1, 9, 25, Hegel is concerned with the "necessity" of his philosophy in the epistemological sense of its possession of a justification or proof; and elsewhere he speaks of the "necessity" that governs his dialectical transitions, and which – see Part III – is different in nature again.)

35 Hegel is much less ambivalent than Kant himself about embracing this model of explanation. For example, when he discusses organic life he writes, "Life must be grasped as self-end, as an end which possesses its means within itself, as a totality in which each distinct moment is alike end and means" (*Encyclopaedia*, par. 423).

36 Ibid., par. 9; cf. par. 14: "A moment has its justification only as moment of the whole."

37 Ibid., par. 12.

38 Ibid., par. 81.

39 Thus Hegel remarks on the "positive" element that makes up the whole of some sciences, such as heraldry, and part even of those sciences that have a rational basis, and which element philosophy shuns (ibid., par. 16).

40 This fundamental difference between the Logic, on the one hand, and

the Philosophies of Nature and Spirit, on the other, is the key to understanding the "free self-release" of the Absolute Idea into Nature, which Hegel talks about when he makes the transition from the Logic to the Philosophy of Nature (and thence the Philosophy of Spirit). See *Science of Logic*, p. 843 / WdL II, p. 573.

41 *Encyclopaedia*, par. 24, Zusatz 2. Cf. pars. 6, 9, 12; *Science of Logic*, pp. 58–59 / WdL, pp. 54–56. Hegel repeatedly emphasizes the indispensability and the authority of the empirical element in this whole process: philosophy necessarily agrees with actuality and experience, and this agreement "can be seen as at least an external criterion of the truth of a philosophy"(*Encyclopaedia*, par. 6); "Not only must philosophy be in agreement with our empirical knowledge of Nature, but the *origin* and *formation* of the Philosophy of Nature presupposes and is conditioned by empirical physics" (ibid., par. 246). Earlier critics, for example, Trendellenburg and Mc'Taggart, who *criticized* Hegel for allowing empirical information into his Philosophies of Nature and Spirit, failed to realize that this was an essential part of his official method.

42 Popper, "What Is Dialectic?" pp. 416–19.

43 *Science of Logic*, p. 439 / WdL II, p. 74.

44 H. F. Fulda, "Unzulängliche Bemerkungen zur Dialektik," in *Seminar: Dialektik in der Philosophie Hegels*, p. 64, cf. p. 48.

45 J.N. Findlay, *Hegel – A Re-examination* (New York, 1976), 77–78.

46 Ibid., p. 66; M. Theunissen, "Begriff und Realität. Hegels Aufhebung des metaphysischen Wahrheitsbegriffs," in *Seminar: Dialektik in der Philosophie Hegels*, p. 348.

47 For example, "vagueness": see *Science of Logic*, p. 82 / WdL I, p. 82 on the indeterminacy of the category of Being; "different times": *Encyclopaedia*, par. 81, Zusatz 1 says, "We know that everything finite, instead of being something firm and final, is instead changeable and transient, and this is nothing other than the dialectic of the finite"; "opposed tendencies": ibid., par. 81, Zusatz 1 gives as examples of dialectic the facts that "the extremes of anarchy and despotism naturally bring each other about" and that "the extremes of pain and happiness pass into one another"; "failure to realize a *telos*": ibid., par. 24, Zusatz 2 notes that we may call something untrue in this sense and that "In this sense a bad state is an untrue state, and badness and untruth in general consists in the contradiction which occurs between the telos [*Bestimmung*] or concept of an object and its existence," cf. ibid., par. 213, Zusatz.

48 The Understanding contributes "fixity and determinacy" to thought; it is what ensures that in philosophy "one does not rest content with what is vague and indeterminate" (ibid., par. 80, Zusatz.

49 "Something moves, not because at one moment it is here and at another

there, but because at one and the same moment it is here and not here"
(*Science of Logic*, p. 440, cf. p. 835 / WdL II, pp. 76, 562–63).

50 Such as ibid., pp. 439–43 / WdL II, pp. 74–80.

51 *Encyclopaedia*, par. 81, Zusatz.

52 Ibid., par. 48.

53 M. Oakeshott, *Experience and Its Modes* (Cambridge, 1933), 328.

54 *Science of Logic*, p. 843 / WdL II, p. 573.

55 *Science of Logic*, p. 843/ WdL II, p. 572; cf. *Phenomenology of Spirit*, pars. 39, 47 / PdG, pp. 40–41, 46.

56 *Science of Logic*, p. 841 / WdL II, p. 570; cf. *Encyclopaedia*, par. 214.

57 *Science of Logic*, p. 49 / WdL I, p. 43.

58 *Phenomenology of Spirit*, par. 39 / PdG, p. 41.

59 Hence Hegel writes that one reason why it is wrong to characterize the Absolute as the "unity of thought and being" is that in the Idea, "thought [encompasses] being, subjectivity [encompasses] objectivity," although this "*encompassing* subjectivity, thought . . . is to be distinguished from *onesided* subjectivity, onesided thought" (*Encyclopaedia*, par. 215).

60 For example, E. Tugendhat raises a doubt about whether Hegel's categories of Being and Nothing are genuinely meaningful. See "Das Sein und das Nichts," in *Durchblicke: Martin Heidegger zum 80. Geburtstag*, ed. V. Klostermann (Frankfurt, 1976), 151–53.

61 M. Inwood, *Hegel* (London/Boston, 1983), p. 130; compare Findlay, *Hegel*, p. 81.

62 Findlay, *Hegel*, pp. 74, 81–82; Fulda, "Unzulängliche Bemerkungen zur Dialektik", pp. 42–43.

63 *Encyclopaedia*, par. 88: "The deduction of the unity [of Being and Nothing] is completely analytical."

64 One of the rare exceptions: ibid., where Hegel continues the above remark with the comment, "Similarly, the whole development of philosophy, as a *necessary* development, is nothing other than the *positing* of that which is already contained in a concept."

65 *Science of Logic*, pp. 835–36 / WdL II, p. 563.

66 *Encyclopaedia*, par. 82; cf. *Science of Logic*, p. 56 / WdL I, p. 52.

67 *Encyclopaedia*, par. 87.

68 Ibid., par. 88.

69 Ibid., par. 89.

70 *Science of Logic*, p. 840 / WdL II, p. 569.

71 *Encyclopaedia*, par. 88.

72 A problem might seem to arise for the underlined criterion in the fact that there are cases where it is unclear which of two concepts sharing a common core adds more conceptual content to it than the other. This fact may indeed cause difficulties for some of Hegel's particular exam-

ples of the transition to the "negative of the negative." For example, it is not really clear that the temporal, dynamic idea added to Being and Nothing by Becoming is a smaller conceptual addition than the idea of qualitative determinacy added by Determinate Being – or, for that matter, vice versa. But it does not show that there is anything intrinsically wrong with the criterion. There would be if we could *never* identify a concept as the one among a set of concepts having a common core which added least conceptual content to it. But such a strong claim appears implausible.

73 Both problems, the meaninglessness of the condition and impossibility of ascertaining whether it obtains, would be avoided if among the possible unifiers were ones that added *no* new conceptual content. But neither Hegel's general remarks nor his particular examples suggest that he believes this, and it has little intrinsic plausibility.

74 This account may qualify, but it boes not, I think, compromise Hegel's insistence that his dialectical transitions be *immanent* in character. See *Science of Logic*, pp. 40, 582, 829, 830 / WdL I, p. 30–31; WdL II, pp. 252, 555–56, 556–57.

75 Ibid., p. 76.

76 Hegel praises the historical Parmenides's argument for the incoherence of the notion of not-being (G.W.F. Hegel, *Lectures on the History of Philosophy* [London/New York, 1968], vol. 1, p. 252 / *Vorlesungen ueber die Geschichte der Philosophie* I [Frankfurt am Main, 1971], p. 288) and bases his own argument in the Logic for the self-contradictoriness of the category Nothing upon it. He asserts that dialectic proper begins with the Eleatic Zeno (ibid., vol. 1, p. 261 / *Vorlesungen ueber die Geschichte der Philosophie* I, p. 295). In the *Encyclopaedia*, he points out that "dialectic . . . is no novelty in philosophy" and refers to Socrates, Plato (his *Parmenides*), and Kant (the Antinomies) as earlier examples. See *Encyclopaedia*, par. 81, Zusatz; cf. *Science of Logic*, , pp. 55–56, 831–32/ WdL I, pp. 51–52; WdL II, pp. 557–59. Hegel sees it as a particular merit of Kant's (mathematical) Antinomies to have drawn attention, as his own dialectic does, to the circumstance that our fundamental categories or concepts are themselves a locus of self-contradiction (ibid., pp. 56, 832–33 / WdL I, p. 52; WdL II, pp. 559–60).

77 G.S. Kirk, J.E. Raven, and M. Schofield, *The Presocratic Philosophers* (Cambridge, 1983), 247.

78 On cognate accusatives in Greek, see, for example, H. W. Smyth, *Greek Grammar* (Cambridge, Mass., 1984), 355–57.

79 For the Stoic position, see A.A. Long and D.N. Sedley, *The Hellenistic Philosophers* (Cambridge, 1987), 162–65.

80 I focus on Hegel in what follows, but these matters are discussed in

detail for another representative of the dialectical tradition, Socrates, in my essay "Socratic Refutation" (unpublished).

81 G.W.F. Hegel, *Natural Law* (Philadelphia: University of Pennsylvania Press, 1975), p. 119 / *Ueber die wissenschaftlichen Behandlungsarten des Naturrechts*, in G.W.F. Hegel, *Jenaer Schriften 1801–1807* (Frankfurt am Main, 1970), 512–my emphasis.

82 *Science of Logic*, p. 46 / WdL I, p. 39.

83 G.W.F. Hegel, *Nürnberger und Heidelberger Schriften 1808–1817* (Frankfurt am Main, 1970), 91.

84 In fairness to Hegel, it *may* be that he is here relying on a principle that he supposes himself to have established in his Phenomenology of Spirit, namely that one cannot coherently distinguish between concept and object, so that one cannot appeal to such a distinction in order to avoid the paradox of Nothing. If so, then my skepticism about the cogency of this paradox must include skepticism about the proof of the incoherence of that distinction in the Phenomenology of Spirit.

85 *Science of Logic*, p. 106 / WdL I, p. 113; *Encyclopaedia*, par. 89.

86 Ibid., pars. 91–92.

87 Fulda, "Hegels Dialektik als Begriffsbewegung und Darstellungsweise," p. 162.

88 *Science of Logic*, p. 31; cf. pp. 27, 42, 54 / WdL I, pp. 19, 16, 33–34, 50.

89 For a fuller treatment – from which the following diverges in certain respects – see M. Baum, *Die Entstehung der Hegelschen Dialektik* (Bonn, 1986).

90 K. Duesing, "Spekulation und Reflexion," *Hegel-Studien* 5 (1969), 128. Hegel's earliest known use of the term "dialectical" occurs in his 1801–2 lectures on Logic, where it refers to the Logic's technique of demonstrating self-contradictions in finite concepts; see *Schellings und Hegels erste absolute Metaphysik (1801–1802)*, ed. K. Duesing (Cologne, 1988), 63–77. The method itself is visible in Hegel's various descriptions and drafts of the early Logic, especially the draft in the 1804–5 *Logik, Metaphysik und Naturphilosophie*, in G.W.F. Hegel, *Jenaer Systementwuerfe II* (Hamburg, 1982). On the other hand, the dialectic officially comes to an end when the transition is made from the early Logic to Metaphysics: "Cognition [that is, the transitional category] in that it makes the transition to Metaphysics is the sublation of the Logic itself, of dialectic" (*Logik, Metaphysik und Naturphilosophie*, p. 134).

91 *Differenz des Fichteschen und Schellingschen Systems der Philosophie*, in *Jenaer Schriften 1801–1807*, pp. 26, 46. A number of commentators have, for various reasons, denied that there is a real anticipation of Hegel's mature method here; see, for instance, Baum, op. cit., pp. 116–17; J.H. Trede, "Hegels frühe Logik," *Hegel-Studien* 7 (1972), 133; J.B.

Baillie, *Hegel's Logic* (London, 1901), 94. None of their reasons seems to me persuasive. In particular, Baillie is clearly wrong to claim that the method here "has not as such a positive side, it does not conserve the negated factors"; as we see, Hegel says that "Reason . . . produces through the synthesis of the two [opposites] a new identity."

92 See, in particular, the description of the Logic in the fragment from 1801–2 "Logica et Metaphysica," in G.W.F. Hegel, *Gesammelte Werke* (Hamburg, 1968 ff.), vol. 5, the notes from Hegel's 1801–2 lectures on Logic in *Schellings und Hegels erste absolute Metaphysik (1801–1802)*, and the examples of dialectic in the 1802–3 essay *Natural Law*.

93 Consider, for example, Hegel's description of the dialectic of Quality: "Quality . . . is the reality out of which it has become the opposite of itself, the negative, and out of this the opposite of the opposite of itself." (*Logik, Metaphysik und Naturphilosophie*, p. 6).

94 Here I agree with W. Hartkopf, *Der Durchbruch zur Dialektik in Hegels Denken* (Meisenheim, 1976), *Kontinuitaet und Diskontinuitaet in Hegels Jenaer Anfaengen* (Koenigstein, 1979). Baum takes a contrary view (op. cit., p. 5).

95 The most significant difference is that, unlike Hegel, Fichte understands the self-contradictions to be apparent rather than real. This is less a difference in their methods than a difference in their choice of criteria of identity for determinations. Fichte tends to think of these as including all the modifications or qualifications required to make a determination self-consistent; Hegel does not.

96 J.G. Fichte, *The Science of Knowledge* (Cambridge, 1982), 106.

97 Ibid., p. 109.

98 F.W.J. Schelling, *System of Transcendental Idealism (1800)* (Charlottesville, 1981), 61.

99 *Differenz des Fichteschen und Schellingschen Systems der Philosophie*, p. 9.

100 Ibid., pp. 26, 28, 115.

101 K. Rosenkranz, *Hegels Leben* (Darmstadt, 1977), 188.

102 For example, in the 1801–2 fragment "Logica et Metaphysica," Hegel advertises to his students that in the Logic he will "begin from what is finite . . . in order to proceed from there, namely in so far as it is first destroyed, to the infinite." For details on the pedagogical functions of the early Logic, see my *Hegel's Idea of a "Phenomenology of Spirit."*

103 For example, in the 1802 essay "Einleitung. Ueber das Wesen der philosophischen Kritik," in *Jenaer Schriften*, pp. 173–74, Hegel points out that his philosophy may find itself in the epistemological difficulty that it appears to be just "one of two subjectivities opposed to one another," and that "positions which have nothing in common come

forth for just that reason with equal right." As his solution to this epistemological problem he proposes – with the early Logic, on which he was currently working, in mind – to "recount how this negative side [that is, the views opposed to his philosophy] expresses its view and confesses its nothingness." For details on the various epistemological functions of the early Logic, see my *Hegel and Skepticism*, chs. 6, 8, 9.

104 In *Gesammelte Werke*, vol. 5.
105 G.W.F. Hegel, *System der Sittlichkeit* (Hamburg, 1967).
106 *Natural Law*, p. 88.
107 Trede, "Hegels frühe Logik," pp. 146–56.

6 Thought and being: Hegel's critique of Kant's theoretical philosophy

In Hegel's view, Kant made an indispensable contribution to the progress of philosophy by recognizing that the most basic principles of human thought reflect the structure of our own minds. But, like Moses who could see but not enter the Promised Land, he failed to grasp the ultimate truth, understood by Hegel himself, that the nature of our own thought and that of the reality to which Kant always contrasted it are in fact one and the same.[1] As he put it in the discussion of Kant in his *Encyclopedia of Philosophical Sciences,*[2]

> But after all, objectivity of thought, in Kant's sense, is again to a certain extent subjective. Thoughts, according to Kant, although universal and necessary categories, are *only our* thoughts – separated by an impassable gulf from the thing, as it exists apart from our knowledge. But the true objectivity of thinking means that the thoughts, far from being merely ours, must at the same time be the real essences of the things, and of whatever is an object to us.   (*Encyclopedia*, §41z, pp. 67–68).[3]

Hegel treats Kant's subjectivism, his insistence on an impassable gulf between thought and object, as mere dogma, indeed almost as a failure of nerve, and is confident that he can himself display knowledge of an absolute realm of being in which the merely apparently opposed poles of thought and object have the underlying identity that Kant failed to see.

Hegel does not engage in internal criticism in his response to Kant's theoretical philosophy: he does not proceed by demonstrating that Kant's own premises are unsound or that his conclusions do not follow validly from those premises. His arguments are external; he argues that Kant's conclusions fall short of his own philosophical expectations. In particular, Hegel does not examine Kant's own reasons for his subjectivism, and thus neither shows why Kant's sub-jectivist scruples are invalid nor how his own view can transcend them. And thus Hegel apparently fails to see that it was no mere accident that Kant thought that the universal and necessary catego-ries of our own thought were separated by an impassable gulf from reality itself, that he had instead argued that the universality and necessity of our thought could be gained *only* at the admittedly high cost of such a separation between thought and reality. Kant believed that any knowledge of universality and necessity had to be entirely *a priori*, or independent of experience, because, as Hume had taught, experience could deliver knowledge only of particular and contin-gent truths; but knowledge that is *a priori* could be knowledge only of the principles of our own thought and how things appear to us given those principles, not knowledge of how things really are in themselves. "For no determinations, whether absolute or relative, can be intuited prior to the existence of the things to which they belong, and none, therefore, can be intuited *a priori*" (*Critique of Pure Reason*, A 26/B 42);[4] "For this reason also, while much can be said *a priori* about the form of appearances, nothing whatsoever can be asserted of the thing in itself, which may underlie these appear-ances" (A 49/B 66). Hegel's critique of Kant reflects a profoundly different philosophical sensibility than Kant's, and it is by no means obvious that his work should be taken to be addressing the same issues as Kant's and thus be judged by the same standards. Neverthe-less, it would seem fair to require that a critic of Kant's subjectivism should have to explain how to justify claims to knowledge of neces-sary truth without accepting Kant's subjectivist explanation of the conditions of its possibility. At least within the confines of his ex-plicit discussions of Kant, Hegel offers no such explanation.

Hegel does not restrict himself to the criticism of Kant's insis-tence on this gulf between thought and being; it is only one of a list of Kantian dualisms to which he objects. As he puts it in his earliest but most detailed critique of Kant:

The fundamental principle common to the philosophies of Kant, Jacobi, and Fichte is, then, the absoluteness of finitude and, resulting from it, the abso-lute antithesis of finitude and infinity, reality and ideality, the sensuous and the supersensuous, and the beyondness of what is truly real and absolute.
(*Faith and Knowledge*, p. 62)

In good part, however, the various charges of unnecessary dualism that Hegel brings against the central theses of Kant's theoretical (and for that matter his practical) philosophy ultimately depend on his underlying objection to Kant's basic separation of thought and being. In that case they are all threatened by Hegel's failure to address explicitly Kant's basic thesis that claims to knowledge of necessary truth can be justified only at the cost of a severe restriction of their scope to the human representation of reality rather than reality considered without any such restriction. Thus, throughout his critique of Kant's philosophy, there is the danger that Hegel simply wants to buy Kant's claims to *a priori* knowledge without paying the high cost that Kant thought had to be charged for them.

Yet it should not be concluded that Hegel's critique of Kant simply misses the point. Beneath their surface, where they often appear superficial and sometimes simply false, there is an underlying germ of truth motivating Hegel's objections to Kant – the belief that those very principles which Kant holds to be necessary truths are in some respects also radically contingent. But while this point certainly deserves emphasis, it cannot be thought of as a outright refutation of Kant, for Kant himself recognizes that the necessities of our thought are connected with irremediable contingencies as well. For Kant, however, this element of contingency represents the inevitable limits of human cognition; for Hegel, merely the at-best historically inevitable limitations of Kant's philosophy.

I. KANT'S THEORETICAL PHILOSOPHY

To understand Hegel's critique of Kant, it is necessary to understand the main claims of Kant's own philosophy. The following outline will suffice for present purposes.

Kant divided his main exposition of his theoretical philosophy, the *Critique of Pure Reason* (first published in 1781, extensively revised in 1787), into two major divisions, a "Doctrine of Elements" and a "Doctrine of Method". He divided the former into a "Transcendental Aesthetic" and "Transcendental Logic," and the "Transcendental Logic" in turn into a "Transcendental Analytic" and "Transcendental Dialectic." The division between "Aesthetic" and "Logic" reflected his fundamental premise that all knowledge requires both the presentation of a particular subject-matter, through a singular representation or what he called an intuition (*Anschauung*), on the one hand, and the subsumption of this particular subject-matter under a general concept (*Begriff*) by means of a judgment (*Urteil*) on the other. The division between "Analytic" and "Dialectic" reflected Kant's distinction between the genuinely informative application of concepts constructed by the faculty of human understanding to intuitions furnished by the faculty of human sensibility, on the one hand, and the vain attempt on the other hand to construct knowledge out of ideas supplied by the faculty of reason alone, without any limitation by the possibilities of human sensibility. Althought Kant did recognize that there was a legitimate "logical" rather than "real" use of the faculty of reason to regiment judgments about intuitions made by the understanding, he argued that such logical regimentation of judgments was not itself knowledge of objects, and that any attempt to derive knowledge of objects, in particular the unconditional absolutes of traditional metaphysics, through ideas of reason alone would be natural but fallacious.

Each of these two main divisions, that between "Aesthetic" and "Logic," or intuition and concept, and that between "Analytic" and "Dialectic," or the legitimate use of understanding and the attempted but fallacious real use of reason, was motivated by a fundamental philosophical insight. Kant thought that a conflation between the separate roles of intuition and concept must lead to Leibniz's completely unjustifiable principle of the identity of indiscernibles, which asserts that what would otherwise be thought to be two distinct objects must in fact be numerically identical whenever their concepts are qualitatively indiscernible, and to the fanciful metaphysics of the monadology which was grounded upon this principle. And he held that the failure to distinguish properly between understanding and reason lay behind the traditional metaphysical assumption that the faculty of reason serves not merely to structure knowledge-claims produced by the cooperation of sensibility and understanding, our capacities to receive inputs about particular objects and subsume them under concepts, but also to provide unconditional knowledge of absolutes such as the soul, the cosmos as a whole, and God, which would be independent of any confirmation by sensory evidence and exceed all the limits of our sensibility. Kant's division of his *Critique* this reflected his division of our cognitive faculties, and his division of cognitive faculties was in turn required, as he saw it, to avoid some of the most pervasive errors of traditional metaphysics.

Kant's general division of the cognitive faculties thus reflects the main point of his critique of traditional metaphysics. Within his treatment of the several faculties, further distinctions are drawn that allow for his positive doctrine of synthetic *a priori* knowledge, that is, his explanation of the possibility of knowledge of propositions that are universal and necessary, and which must therefore be known independent of any particular experience, yet are genuinely informative or synthetic rather than merely definitional or analytic. First, Kant distinguishes between empirical and pure intuition, or the presentation of particular objects through sensory stimuli and the form in which such empirical intuition takes place. Kant argues that there are two pure forms of intuition through which all particulars are presented, namely space and time, and that the basic structure of space and time, as well as the mathematics that reflects this basic structure, particularly geometry as reflecting the structure of space, can be known *a priori*. But the only way in which these basic structures can be known independent of experience, he argues, is if they reflect the structure of our own capacity for sensibility, through which objects appear to us. In this case, space and time must be subjective forms of intuition, although it seems possible that they could at the same time also be forms inherent in the independent objects that we perceive. Kant further argues that if our claims about spatiality and temporality are to be *necessarily* true of *all* the objects of which they hold, then they cannot be true at all of things as they are in themselves, for we could never have grounds for supposing them to be anything more than *contingently* true of things existing independent of our necessarily spatial or temporal representations of them. Therefore, space and time are necessary features of all appearances of objects to us, but are true only of the appearances of those objects, not of the things as they may be in themselves (see especially A 47–8/V 65–6).[5] (Later, in the Transcendental Dialectic, Kant also argues that space and time must be regarded as features only of appearances but not of things in themselves, because otherwise we will be committed to incompatible but equally valid arguments that space and time are both finite and infinite in maximal and minimal extension, which is clearly impossible. See the Antinomy of Pure Reason, especially A 426–36/B 454–65).

Next, Kant argues that although empirical concepts of objects must always be based on empirical intuitions, we can have *a priori* knowledge of a set of pure categories of the understanding that determine the structure of empirical concepts just as the pure forms of intuition determine the structure of empirical intuitions. Kant begins by noting that any claim to knowledge is cast in the form of a judgment, and that the logical structure of all judgments can be characterized by means of a determinate set of functions. Specifically, all judgments possess logical quantity (they predicate a property of one, some, or all objects in a domain), quality (they affirm or deny a predicate of the subject),⁶ relation (they connect a predicate to a subject, an antecedent to a consequent, or several disjunctive alternatives to each other), and a modality (they are possibly, actually, or necessarily true or false, as the case may be) (A 70/B 95). Then Kant argues that *objects* must be conceptualized in such a way that *judgments* that are characterized in these terms can be asserted of them – thus, certain pure concepts of the understanding, commonly called the categories, must provide the form for all empirical concepts of the understanding so that judgments employing these logical functions can be asserted of objects of knowledge (see especially A 79/B104–5). The categories are thus known *a priori* as the conditions of the possible conceptualization of all objects.

Kant then attempts to connect this doctrine of categories with a conception of self-consciousness or "apperception" by means of an argument the purport of which is as obscure as it is important, the "Transcendental Deduction" of the categories.⁷ Here Kant tries to argue that the possibility of self-consciousness itself implies the use of judgment and therefore the possibility of knowledge of objects by means of the categories, and further that there is a unity among all the representations comprising one's self-consciousness that can be grounded only by means of judgments connecting them all as representations of a coherent realm of objects. Indeed, he goes so far as to suggest that the unity of objects in a coherent space and time is not given by the pure forms of intuition alone, but depends on the possibility of objectively valid judgments about objects in space and time structured by means of the categories (see B 160–61n.). Kant expands upon this hint in the discussion of the "System of the Principles of Pure Understanding," which follows the "Transcendental Deduction." Here he argues that certain principles applying the categories to spatio-temporal intuitions – the principles that all objects may be measured by means of extensive and intensive quantities, and then, most important, the principles of the conservation of substance and the universal validity of causation and interaction, which are central to his philosophical defense of Newtonian physics against the metaphysical and epistemological objections of Leibniz from one side and Hume from the other – are necessary conditions for the representation of a unitary and determinate realm of relationships among such intuitions understood as representations of both external objects and the states of one's own experience.

In the ensuing "Transcendental Dialectic," however, Kant argues that although it is natural for us to try to represent the traditional metaphysical absolutes of soul, (the absolutely simple), world (the absolutely all-inclusive), and God (the absolute necessary), by means of ideas of pure reason formed in analogy to the pure concepts of the understanding, especially the categories of relation (substance, causation, and interaction), we have no theoretical justification for so doing. We always need empirical intuitions given by sensibility to give content to the use of the categories, and empirical intuitions are given in a spatio-temporal framework that is unitary and determinate but indefinitely extendable. There can therefore never be completeness or closure in the use of the categories, although we can formulate the idea of completeness in their use, or in the use of reason to regiment empirical concepts formed in accordance with the categories into a classificatory and explanatory hierarchy. Thus Kant argues that the ideas of reason have a legitimate *regulative* but not *constitutive* employment – they properly describe our cognitive ambitions as well as presuppositions, but cannot be taken by themselves to furnish absolute knowledge of metaphysical reality (see A 642–704/B 670–732).[8]

In conclusion, then, Kant's position is that we can explain how we have *a priori* knowledge of the structure of appearance only by denying that we have knowledge of the ultimate nature of reality by means of sensibility, understanding, or pure reason. The pure forms of intuition provide knowledge of appearances, not things as they are in themselves, because they can be known to be necessarily true of appearances only by being denied to be true of things as they are in themselves at all. The pure concepts of understanding and the ideas of pure reason are not in themselves unfit for the *conception* of things as they are in themselves; on the contrary, they may be cogently used to *think* of such objects. But since both categories and ideas of reason yield *knowledge* only when applied to intuitions, and intuitions are restricted to the appearance rather than reality of things, the categories of the understanding and ideas of reason also provide actual knowledge only of appearances. In fact, Kant supposes that it is not only possible but necessary for us to use both the categories and ideas of reason to form concepts of things in themselves as contrasted to appearances, especially to form the concept of the freedom of things in themselves as contrasted to the determinism that reigns in the realm of appearances (see especially the third Antinomy, A 444–51/B 472–79); but as knowledge-claims always require instantiation in intuition, such speculations, even if necessary, do not amount to knowledge.

II. HEGEL'S CRITIQUE: THE UNDERLYING ASSUMPTIONS

In several places, not only the works already mentioned but also his *Lectures on the History of Philosophy*, Hegel offers a exposition of the several branches of Kant's philosophy and point-by-point criticism of it.[9] Here we consider only some of the most important of Hegel's objections to Kant's theoretical philosophy. In general, Hegel objected to what he indentified as both the subjectivism and the formalism of Kant's philosophy: "Because the essence of the Kantian philosophy consists in its being critical idealism, it plainly confesses that its principle is subjectivism and formal thinking"; thus, "It makes the identity of opposites into the absolute terminus of philosophy, the pure boundary which is nothing but the negation of philosophy" (*Faith and Knowledge*, p. 67). The opposition that Hegel objects to under the rubric of "subjectivism" is Kant's contrast between appearances and things in themselves, his claim that although we can and indeed must be able to coherently *think* of things in themselves, we can have both *a priori* and empirical *knowledge* only of appearances. The opposition that Hegel objects to under the rubric of "formal thinking" is Kant's insistence that, whether in the case of the pure intuitions of sensibility or the pure concepts of the understanding, we can have *a priori* knowledge only of the pure *forms* of representation, the abstract structures of intuition, judgment, and reasoning, and must always wait upon experience for completion of the knowledge of particulars – which is for that reason never entirely *a priori*. As we have seen, Kant thought that both of these contrasts, that between appearance and reality and that between the abstract form of knowledge and its particular matter, were necessary conditions for the explanation of the possibility of any *a priori* knowledge of universal and necessary truth at all. Hegel thought that these restrictions could be overcome.

Hegel's official position is that previous philosophical systems were incomplete but historically necessary stages in the self-expression of "spirit" or the intellectual core of reality. In the case of Kant, however, his comments suggest personal disappointment at a missed opportunity. Hegel seems to have been particularly disappointed with the dualisms of formalism and subjectivism in Kant's philosophy, because he thought that Kant had come very close to realizing the essential identity of thought and being at both the beginning and the end of his theoretical system – at the beginning in his conceptions of judgment and apperception, which are supposed to provide the foundations for much that follows, and at the end, in the idea of an intuitive intellect that Kant used to give graphic expression to the ideal of a completed empirical knowledge based on *a priori* foundations. The discussion of Hegel's critique of Kant should thus begin with his treatment of Kant's conceptions of judgement and apperception. In both cases, one may well conclude that Hegel read his own very different philosophical assumptions into Kant's system from the start, and thus ensured that his criticism could only be external rather than internal to Kant's own project.

Hegel's crucial reinterpretations of these fundamental Kantian concepts are evident in *Faith and Knowledge,* although they later disappear from view. Hegel forces Kant's conception of judgment into his own philosophical vision by interpreting the connection between subject and predicate as that between being and thought: "These heterogeneous elements, the subject which is the particular and in the form of being, and the predicate which is the universal and in the form of thought, are at the same time absolutely identical." Given this interpretation, Hegel thinks that Kant should have been led by the concept of judgment directly to his own conception of all rationality as the recognition of the fundamental identity of being and thought: "It is Reason alone that is the possibility of this positing [of identity in judgment], for Reason is nothing else but the identity of heterogeneous elements of this kind" (*Faith and Knowledge*, p. 69). In Hegel's view, in every judgment we get at least a partial glimpse of the fundamental identity between the structure of our thought and the structure of reality itself, and the function of the totality of our judgments is nothing less than to provide absolute knowledge of this identity, which is the culmination of philosophy itself. He therefore finds Kant's subjectivism and formalism to be a retreat from an insight that Kant himself reached in his own most basic conception of judgment.

Hegel's understanding of Kant's conception of judgment, however, is by no means Kant's own. First, note that Hegel offers "the Idea that subject and predicate of the synthetic judgment are identical in the *a priori* way" as Kant's answer to the question "How are synthetic judgments *a priori* possible?" (*loc. cit.*); but Kant does not explain the possibility of *synthetic a priori* judgments by means of identity – that is his explanation of *analytic* judgments. Analytic judgments give expression to a whole or partial identity between the concepts serving as subject and predicate; they can therefore be known to be true solely on the basis of the logical law that all identity statements are true, and for that reason are always *a priori*. Synthetic judgments are precisely those in which the predicate *adds* information to that conveyed by the concept of the subject, and therefore cannot be known to be true by means of merely logical principles about identity – that is why it is a problem how a judgment can be synthetic yet known *a priori*. Instead, Kant's account is that subject and predicate in synthetic *a priori* judgments are connected in virtue of the inherent structure of our capacities for intuition and judgment, and can be known *a priori* because of our *a priori* knowledge of these structures in spite of the absence of identity between subject and predicate concepts.

Second and even more important, Hegel's equation of a judgment's predication of a universal of a particular with the identity between thought and being is a far from obvious interpretation of Kant's own intention. Kant's account of judgment is far from clear,[10] but his basic idea seems to be that all judgments are composed of concepts, which are inherently general, yet ultimately relate to intuitions, which are representations of particulars (see A 19/B 33). Some judgments predicate one general concept of another concept that is also functioning in a general way, as in "All bachelors are males"; others predicate a general characteristic of a particular object not by incorporating an intuition directly into the judgment itself, but rather by using a general subject-concept to refer to a particular object in a certain context, as in a judgment like "This male is a bachelor." Here it is not the concept "male" by itself that succeeds in referring to a particular subject for the judgment, but rather the conjunction of the concept "male" with the indexical term "this" employed in an appropriate spatio-temporal context where both speaker and hearer understand which male is the object of reference. So on Kant's account, particular objects are always brought into judgments through a complex relationship between general concepts and the forms of intuition, and there is no question of any direct presence of real being in the judgment itself. Moreover, even if we were to ignore the contextual use of a general concept to refer to an object of intuition in Kant's conception of the subject of a judgment, and were to interpret Kant as supposing that intuitions themselves entered directly into judgments, Hegel's interpretation would still be problematic. For the Kantian intuition is not itself a particular real object outside the realm of thought, but rather a singular *representation* of an object. It may thus be contrasted to a concept in the particular Kantian sense of a universal, but in terms of the more-general contrast between thought and being, intuitions certainly remain on the side of thought. Indeed, as we saw, it is the most-basic claim of Kant's theory of knowledge that intuitions give us access to the appearances of things, not to those things as they are in themselves; so as long as judgments connect concepts to intuitions, whether indirectly or directly, it is difficult to see how they could be thought to express an identity between thought and being. For Kant, judgments are the fundamental structures of thought itself, although perhaps not purely *conceptual* thought. Hegel's interpretation of the relation between subject and predicate as that between being and thought reflects his own assumptions, not Kant's.

Something similar seems to occur in Hegel's interpretation of Kant's conception of the transcendental unity of apperception. For Kant, this kind of unity, like the unity of a judgment, remains within the realm of thought. Kant's idea of transcendental apperception is the idea of a synthesis or combination of all of my *representations* in a way that allows me to recognize that in spite of their diversity of content, they are all representations belonging to a single self that may say "I think" of each and all of them (see B 132–33). Kant tries to argue that it is necessary to interpret the representations comprised in such a unified set as representations of objects which are therefore governed by the categories as rules for conceiving of objects (B 137, 139); but this does not change the fact that the unity of apperception is itself a unity *among one's representations*. Hegel, however, interprets the concept of apperception differently, understanding it as a primordial recognition of unity out of which the more-limited conceptions of self and object are abstracted, but of course in such a way that they can ultimately be rejoined to make explicit the knowledge of the underlying identity of thought and being. Thus he writes:

In Kant the synthetic unity is undeniably the absolute and original identity of self-consciousness, which of itself posits the judgment absolutely and *a priori*. Or rather, as identity of subjective and objective, the original identity appears in consciousness as judgment. This original unity of apperception is called synthetic precisely because of its two-sidedness, the opposites being absolutely one in it. The absolute synthesis is absolute insofar as it is not an aggregate of manifolds which are first picked up, and then the synthesis supervenes upon them afterwards. . . . The true synthetic unity or rational identity is just that identity which is the connecting of the manifold with the empty identity, the Ego. It is from this connection, as original synthesis that the Ego as thinking subject, and the manifold as body and world first detach themselves.   (*Faith and Knowledge*, p. 72)

As he puts it on the next page, the unity of apperception is the "absolute identity of the heterogeneous." Hegel thus interprets the unity of apperception along the lines of what later came to be known as neutral monism.[11] Self or thought and object or being are not ultimately different but are represented as different by abstractions that it is the end of philosophy to overcome, thereby restoring the original recognition of unity implicit in apperception itself.

This is very far from Kant's own understanding of apperception. For Kant, again, the unity of apperception is a synthetic unity among one's own representations. The task of empirical judgment may be conceived of as that of placing a dual interpretation on these representations, using the forms of judgment to interpret them as both representations of the successive states in the history of the self and representations of the successive states in the history of the world of objects external to the self; but there is no hint of any identity between the self and its objects themselves. For Kant, apperception, like judgment, remains confined within the sphere of thought. It may require us to represent a unified world of objects, but it is by no means identical with such a world.

Hegel does not argue for his interpretation of these two basic concepts of Kant. The interpretation of Kant by intervening writers, especially Fichte, would no doubt contribute to an historical explanation of Hegel's reading of Kant. But from a purely philosophical point of view, Hegel is clearly reading his own profoundly different, one might almost say incommensurable, philosophical presuppositions into key points in Kant, points that Kant perhaps left undefended by stressing their centrality yet himself explaining only obscurely, but which would not have invited Hegel's interpretation of them except from someone already predisposed to Hegel's assumptions. But having read Kant's conceptions as pointing the way toward his own recognition of the identity between thought and being, Hegel could not conceal his disappointment that Kant refused to build upon it.

III. HEGEL'S CRITIQUE: THE BILL OF PARTICULARS

We can now turn to the details of Hegel's explicit criticisms of Kant. These criticisms can be classified under four headings.

(i) First, there are what we might think of as methodological objections to Kant's philosophy. Two of these are prominent. One is the charge that there is something incoherent about what Hegel takes to be Kant's proposal to scrutinize the faculties of knowledge before attempting to obtain knowledge itself. This project sounds plausible, Hegel says, for "Knowledge is thereby represented as an instrument," and it seems natural enought to suppose that we can examine an instrument before using it. In fact, he believes, it is as implausible as refusing to go into the water until one knows how to swim: you cannot learn to swim except in the water, nor can you determine limits on knowledge from some standpoint prior to knowledge (*Lectures on the History of Philosophy*, III, p. 428; *Encyclopedia*, §41z; p. 66). On the contrary, Hegel claims, "The forms of thought must be studied in their essential nature and complete development: they are at once the object of research and the action of that object. Hence they examine themselves: in their own action they must determine their limits, and point out their defects" (*Encyclopedia, loc. cit.*). This self-examination of forms of thought rather than external and antecedent scrutiny of cognitive capacities is what Hegel proposes to supply under the rubric of dialectic, which for him means not the external criticism of fallacious metaphysical theories, as in Kant, but rather the internal process of self-correcting development in both concepts and reality, which is reflected in philosophical theories whose incompleteness (prior to his own) is never a matter of mere fallacy but rather reflects the stages in the evolution of concepts and reality themselves.

Hegel's second methodological charge is that for all of Kant's differences with the empiricist school of Hume and his predecessors, there is something essentially empirical about Kant's method. According to Hegel, both Kant's enumeration of our cognitive capacities or "factors of consciousness" in general – thus, his tripartite distinction between sensibility, understanding, and reason – as well as his list of the twelve categories in particular are arrived at by merely empirical, historical, or psychological means. Hegel made this charge repeatedly over the years. In *Faith and Knowledge:* "Kant has simply no ground but experience and empirical psychology for holding that the human cognitive faculty essentially consists in the way it appears" (p. 89). In the *Encyclopedia:* "A further deficiency in the system is that it gives only a historical description of thought, and a mere enumeration of the factors of consciousness. The enumeration is in the main correct: but not a word touches upon the necessity of what is thus empirically colligated" (§60z; p. 94). And in his lectures: Kant "sets to work in a psychological manner, i.e., historically, inasmuch as he describes the main stages in theoretic consciousness" (*Lectures on the History of Philosophy*, III, pp. 432–33). Further, the same kind of claim is made more specificially about Kant's table of categories. Hegel claims that "Kant did not put himself to much trouble in discovering the categories" (*Encyclopedia*, §42, p. 68), and that "Kant thus accepts the categories in an empiric way, without thinking or developing of necessity these differences from unity" (*Lectures on the History of Philosophy*, III, p. 439). Indeed, in the latter place Hegel makes the same claim of merely empirical method about Kant's assertion of the unique status of space and time as forms of intuition: "Just as little did Kant attempt to deduce time and space, for he accepted them likewise from experience – a quite unphilosophical and unjustifiable procedure."

On their face, Hegel's methodological criticisms of Kant seem grossly unfair. His claim that Kant's attempt to scrutinize our cognitive capacities prior to actually using them is like trying to learn how to swin without actually getting into the water suggests that Kant supposes that we can somehow directly examine our cognitive faculties, perhaps by some form of introspection, as indeed Locke, with whom Hegel closely links Kant on this point, seems to have thought (see *Faith and Knowledge*, pp. 68–69). But although Kant does once suggest that the character of pure as contrasted to empirical intuition may be discovered by a Lockean process of abstraction (A 22/B 36), he does not suggest that the general distinction among sensibility, understanding, and reason, nor his claims about the transcendental rather than empirical principles and applications of these faculties, are reached by anything like an empirical, psychological method. Kant's fundamental distinction between sensibility and understanding, and between those two faculties and the further faculty of reason, are clearly, even if indirectly, argued for as necessary in order to avoid the major errors of previous metaphysics, both rationalist and empiricist. A serious criticism of Kant's distinction between sensibility and understanding, for instance, would therefore have to show that this distinction is not required in order to avoid the confusions of Leibnizian philosophy.

Nor does Kant attempt to describe the structure and operations of his cognitive faculties, especially at the transcendental level, that is, the level of necessary preconditions of knowledge, in abstraction from all application of these faculties. On the contrary, in many instances, at least in the case of what he calls his analytical or regressive method,[12] Kant makes inferences to the nature of our cognitive capacities as the only possible explanation of claims to *a priori* knowledge which he takes to be indubitable, whether these be specific, as in the case of our alleged *a priori* knowledge of geometry, or general, as in the case of our alleged *a priori* knowledge of the numerical unity of the self (see A 114). One might well object that these claims to *a priori* knowledge, which are the basis for inferences about the nature of our cognitive capacities, are themselves inadequately defended; but that is not the same as objecting, as Hegel does, that Kant tries to examine our cognitive capacities in complete abstraction from any actual knowledge-claims. In most cases, Kant's procedure is to begin with certain apparently indisputable claims to knowledge, make inferences to the cognitive capacities necessary to explain such claims, and only then make further determinations about the inevitable limitations of such cognitive capacities. This is not the same as examining an instrument before using it.[13]

Hegel's charge that Kant's list of categories is merely empirically derived is also peculiar. It is ironic that this is the same charge that Kant had brought against Aristotle's list of categories (A 81/B 107). Kant himself thought that his list of categories was systematically developed from the insight that all knowledge-claims must take the form of judgments and a rigorous logical analysis of the several aspects and therefore possible forms of judgment. To be sure, he may not have made the method of his logical derivation of the several aspects and forms of judgment terribly clear,[14] but there can be no doubt that Kant intended his derivation of the categories to proceed by entirely *a priori* means from the underlying insight into the judgmental nature of knowledge or even consciousness itself.

Hegel refers to Kant's link between the categories and the judgmental nature of thought once (*Encyclopedia*, §42, p. 68) but seems to find it unconvincing. Why? Part of the answer may be Kant's own fault. For all of his programmatic statements about the erroneous methods of previous philosophy, Kant was not very explicit about the nature of his own methods, and he sometimes made his most basic premises seem more mysterious than they actually are. One passage that might certainly have seemed objectionable to Hegel suggests that the origin of the list of categories as well as that of the forms of intuition is ultimately a mystery:

This peculiarity of our understanding, that it can produce *a priori* unity of apperception solely by means of the categories, and only by such and so many, is as little capable of further explanation as why we have just these and no other functions of judgment, or why space and time are the only forms of our possible intuition.   (B 145–6)

But this mystification is at least partially unnecessary. Although Kant may have had no further explanation to offer of the fact that we represent distinct external objects and their states as simultaneous and successive through the use of space and time, he did have a perfectly good explanation of why we use only "such and so many" categories: All thought takes the form of judgment, and the possible logical forms of judgment admit of an exhaustive analysis precisely in terms of his quite compact list of categories.[15] Moreover, Kant sometimes suggested that the categorical structure of judgment, or discursive thought, is by no means a peculiarity of human cognition in particular, but necessary for any form of judgment at all. Precisely for this reason Kant could argue that the categories, unlike space and time, could be used at least to *conceive* of things in themselves even if not to acquire actual *knowledge* of them.

A reader sufficiently impressed by Kant's connection of the categories to the fundamentally judgmental nature of thought would not be overly concerned with Kant's own mystification in the passage just cited. Why doesn't Hegel see past it? He believes that not Kant but only Fichte saw the "need of exhibiting the *necessity* of these categories and giving a genuine *deduction* of them," although no one before himself was capable of getting past "the classification of notions, judgments, and syllogisms . . . taken merely from observation and so only empirically treated" and instead deducing the forms of thought "from thought itself" (*Encyclopedia*, §42, p. 69). But why doesn't Kant's derivation of the list of categories from the essentially judgmental or discursive nature of thought itself fulfill Hegel's requirement of a deduction "from thought itself"? Part of the answer here would seem to be that Kant appeals to two premises, to the discursive nature of thought and to a separate logical analysis of the possible structures of judgment, whereas Hegel seems to suppose that genuine philosophy requires dialectical advance from a single premise, or not just from "thought itself" but from some *single* thought. This is a view entertained by some of Kant's predecessors, such as the middle-period Leibniz,[16] and revived by some of Kant's immediate successors, such as K.L. Reinhold and Fichte, but decidedly rejected by Kant himself, beginning with his 1762 prize essay *Enquiry into the Clarity of the Principles of Natural Theology and Ethics* and continuing throughout his life. On the assumptions that Hegel accepted from his immediate predecessors, only a derivation of all the categories from some single concept could justify a claim to necessity; Kant's conjunction of principles for the derivation of the categories must for that reason alone have seemed to him to doom Kant's categories to contingency.

(ii) Pervading Hegel's comments about Kant, and in the *Encyclopedia* directly linked to his complaint about Kant's merely empirical discovery of the categories, is his criticism that Kant unnecessarily takes the inherent forms of thought to be *no more than* forms of thought, not forms of real being as well. In the *Encyclopedia*'s opening comments on Kant's theoretical philosophy, Hegel makes it sound as if it is just one of Kant's quirks that he regards the categories as merely subjective: "To regard the categories as subjective only, i.e. as a part of ourselves, must seem very odd to the natural mind: and no doubt there is something queer about it." Hegel concedes that Kant is quite right not to try to find the categories in mere sensation, or to simply conflate thought and sensation – this was Hume's mistake, for instance, in looking for an *impression* of necessary connection – but wrong to think that because the categories must be added to sensation by thought, they are therefore merely valid for our own representation of the world, and not descriptive of genuine reality as well. Thus he continues:

Still, though the categories, such as unity, or cause and effect, are strictly the property of thought, it by no means follows that they must be ours merely and not also characteristics of the objects. Kant however confines them to the subject-mind, and his philosophy may be styled subjective idealism: for the holds that both the form and the matter of knowledge are supplied by the Ego – or knowing subject – the form by our intellectual, the matter by our sentient ego.   (*Encyclopedia*, §42z, p. 70)

Hegel goes on to say that not a "word need be wasted" on the "content of this subjective idealism." In the immediate context, what he seems to mean is that it can be ignored because it does not really affect the content of our description of the proper conceptualization of objects, which remains the same whether we take it to be merely subjective or to characterize how objects really are. But at another level, he also seems to mean that Kant's doctrine is beneath contempt, so obviously false as not to need any detailed refutation. He just seems to assume that the real nature of thought and being are identical, thus that if one had discovered the genuine structure of thought in the guise of the categories (and he believes that Kant's own list of the categories falls far short of doing this), then one would also have discovered the genuine structure of reality as well.

In this criticism Hegel takes no notice of Kant's special connection between transcendental idealism and the forms of intuition, that is, his argument that the categories do not furnish us with knowledge of reality not because of any defect of their own, but because they always require application to sensible intuitions, which however are given in forms – space and time – that cannot be forms of things in themselves as well. In other words, Kant does not argue that there is any reason why the categories themselves should not be fit to represent the structure of reality; it is space and time which are not fit to do so. We must apply the categories to the intuitions we have, and thus in the only application of them that is available to us, they do not give knowledge of external reality as it is in itself (see especially B 158). But in fact Kant always assumes that the categories "constitute the thought of an *object in general,*" and transcendental idealism applies to the categories only because of the transcendental idealism of the forms of intuition to which they must be applied in order to yield actual knowledge as opposed to mere thought.

In some places Hegel does recognize that it is not because of any defect in his conception of the categories themselves, but rather because of his requirement of their application to empirical intuitions that Kant includes them in the scope of his transcendental idealism. Thus in the *Lectures on the History of Philosophy*, he states that:

The knowing subject does not with Kant really arrive at reason, for it remains still the individual self-consciousness as such, which is opposed to the universal. As a matter of fact there is described in what we have seen only the empirical finite self-consciousness which requires a material from the outside, or which is limited. We do not ask whether these facts of knowledge are in and for themselves true or untrue; the whole of knowledge remains within subjectivity, and on the other side there is the thing-in-itself as an external.   (*Lectures on the History of Philosophy,* III, p. 443)

Here Hegel suggests that the problem with the categories is that they are merely empty forms of thought that need to be filled, but that when they are filled with "material from the outside," they will be filled with empirical data that cannot reveal things in themselves.

In order to combat Kant's transcendental, or, as he calls it, subjective idealism, Hegel would therefore have to criticize Kant's argument for the transcendental idealism of space and time, not just appeal to an alleged identity between thought and being. Although he obviously objects to Kant's theory of the transcendental ideality of space and time, Hegel does not actually explain what he thinks is wrong with Kant's argument that knowledge of necessity presupposes subjectivity. Thus even when he recognizes that Kant does not insist on the subjectivity of the categories per se but only on the subjectivity of their application to empirical intuitions, Hegel still does not explain what he thinks Kant's error actually is.

One problem that he does have in mind is that on Kant's account the material to which the categories must be applied is "from the outside" or "external" to the categories; that is, the categories do not produce their own applications from within themselves but rather are dependent on material for which they are not themselves responsible. In this sense it may be said that it is contingent that the particular categories we must employ do apply to the particular empirical intuitions to which we do apply them. Since in many places Hegel makes this an independent point, stressing not the subjectivity of the categories on Kant's account but rather a contingency that infects their application, we may treat this as a separate objection.

(iii) This criticism of Kant is linked to Hegel's objection that Kant's philosophy is "formal thinking." This is the charge that Kant confines necessity to the level of general forms or concepts, and thus leaves the application of such general structures to determinate particulars contingent. Hegel frequently expresses his point by objecting to Kant's distinction between intuition and conceptualization, but what he objects to is not just the distinction between the pure categories and pure forms of intuition but also that between the categories of thought and the particular objects of experience furnished by sensation, that is, empirical intuition. Thus at least a key part of his objection is a complaint about the contingency of the application of the categories to any particular empirical data. That is, he objects to the fact that although our use of just "such and so many" categories might be necessary in itself – although as we have just seen he does not really think Kant is entitled even to that claim – there is no necessity that our categories apply to just these and no other particulars given by sensation; thus, in the last analysis, that these categories apply to just these particular empirical intuitions is something that Kant leaves quite contingent.

In *Faith and Knowledge*, Hegel connects this point to the previous criticism about the gap between the categories and things in themselves, arguing that in Kant's scheme, the origin of sensations must be left to the action of things in themselves on our sensibility, but that precisely because we cannot cognize things in themselves, the origin of sensations is therefore incomprehensible to us:

> Identity of this formal kind [that is, of the forms of thought] finds itself immediately confronted by or next to an infinite non-identity, with which it must coalesce in some incomprehensible way. On one side there is the Ego, with its productive imagination or rather with its synthetic unity which, taken thus in isolation, is formal unity of the manifold. But next to it there is an infinity of sensations and, if you like, of things in themselves. Once it is abandoned by the categories, this realm cannot be anything but a formless lump . . . In this way, then, the objectivity of the categories in experience and the necessity of these relations become once more something contingent and subjective. . . . A formal idealism which in this way sets an absolute Ego-point and its intellect on one side, and an absolute manifold, or sensation, on the other side, is a dualism.
>
> (*Faith and Knowledge*, pp. 76–78)

Kant conceives of the categories, necessitated by the structure of our own understanding, as being externally applied to whatever sensations happen to present themselves to us, which originate in things in themselves over which the structure of our own intellects exercises no influence whatever. These sensations are thus a formless lump, to which our own forms are externally applied, but apparently it remains contingent that we can succeed in so doing – it is certainly not necessitated by anything in the source of the sensations themselves.

In the *Lectures on the History of Philosophy*, Hegel does not express this objection by reference to things in themselves, but rather through a comment upon Kant's doctrine of schematism, that is, his view that the purely logical content of the categories has to be reinterpreted in sensible terms before the categories can be applied to particular empirical intuitions.[17] Here he says:

> The connection of these two is again one of the most attractive sides of the Kantian philosophy, whereby pure sensuousness and pure understanding,

which were formerly expressed as absolute opposites, are now united. There is thus here present a perceptive understanding, or an understanding perception; but Kant does not see this, he does not bring these thoughts together: he does not grasp the fact that he here brought both sides of knowledge into one, and has thereby expressed their implicitude. Knowledge itself is in fact the unity and truth of both moments; but with Kant the thinking understanding and sensuousness are both something particular, and they are only united in an external, superficial way, just as a piece of wood and a leg might be bound together by a cord.

(*Lectures on the History of Philosophy*, III, p. 441)

As with his complaint about trying to learn how to swim before getting into the water, Hegel's complaint that Kant ties concepts and perception together like a leg and a piece of wood is graphic, but needs scrutiny. His objection ultimately seems to move at two levels. In part, he seems to be complaining that there is no necessary connection between Kant's pure forms of intuition and pure concepts of the understanding, thus that we could have a different sort of perception without having to have a different sort of thought; in part, it seems to be that there is no necessary connection betweeen pure concepts of the understanding and particular empirical intuitions, thus that as far as the categories alone are concerned, they could apply to different empirical intuitions or even to none at all, in which case they might well lack all *use* but still preserve their own identity or sense.

To Kant both of these complaints, but especially the latter, would have seemed unintelligible. Because intuition as the presentation of particulars and conceptualization as the connection and classification of them are essentially different activities, the former at least occurring in animals without the latter even if not vice versa, and because it is possible to conceive of the forms of intuition being other than they are without that requiring that the judgmental forms of discursive thought differ from what they are, any claim that both sides of knowledge are one in the sense of there being some single ground for their different formal structures would, in his eyes, have taken on an enormous burden of proof. And for the same reason, because reception of data and the classification of data are two distinct activities, the idea that the categories should in any way necessitate the data to which they are to be applied, or that there is some common source that necessitates both what categories we have and what data we are to apply them to, would seem equally inexplicable to Kant. For Kant, it is indeed obvious that the human situation requires an effort of applying categories and principles that flow from within to perceptions that arise from without, and thus it is obvious that there is an irremediable element of contingency in the application of the categories to empirical intuitions. In the absence of any powerful argument to the contrary, any denial of such an obvious fact about the human condition would seem to him merely wishful thinking.

Kant did believe that the ideal of a system of knowledge, in which not particular facts but at least particular laws of nature would seem to be as necessary as the entirely formal laws of nature furnished by the categories, is a necessary ideal of human reason. He held this because he believed that causal reasoning requires not just that particular sequences of events appear to be necessitated by higher-order generalizations, but also that those generalizations themselves be lawlike and thus at least apparently necessarily true (see *Critique of Judgment*, Introduction, section V). But precisely because individual laws of nature must also remain inductively tied to the particular objects of our experience, which remain contingent, he held that their necessity could not be more than a regulative ideal, not more than an appearance lent to them by their inclusion in a system of laws, the completeness and uniqueness of which can never be more than asymptotically approached. Thus Kant accepted the ideal of a continuum of necessity reaching from the most-general to the most-particular laws of nature, but not the absolute reality of such a continuum, which Hegel supposed to be possible. But this leads directly to the larger issue of Hegel's critique of Kant's conception of the faculty of reason, so we will turn to that next before further discussion of the issue of regulative ideals.

(iv) The final charge then in Hegel's official brief against Kant's theoretical philosophy takes the form of a critique of Kant's treatment of the faculty of reason instead of sensibility or understanding. This charge can be broken down into two complaints. The first is the claim that in Kant's hands the faculty of reason, in this regard like the faculty of understanding, is *empty*, meaning that it does not supply its own content but is only an apparatus for the organization of information supplied to it from elsewhere. The other claim, which Hegel makes first but which can be considered as at least in part a consequence of the first, is that, for Kant, reason's ideas of completeness are never granted reality but always remain mere *postulates*. Of course, it is precisely by insisting on these two features of the employment of the faculty of reason that Kant proposed to differentiate his critical philosophy from the dogmatic rationalism that preceded it. In Kant's eyes, by rejecting these aspects of his account of reason, Hegel could not have advanced philosophy but only returned it to the *status quo ante*.

Hegel opens his discussion of Kant in *Faith and Knowledge* with the charge that Kantian reason furnishes only postulates and not knowledge of reality:

When the Kantian philosophy happens upon Ideas [of reason] in its normal course, it deals with them as mere possibilities of thought and as transcendental concepts lacking all reality ... Kant's philosophy establishes the highest idea as a postulate which is supposed to have a necessary subjectivity, but not that absolute objectivity which would get it recognized as the only starting point by philosophy and its sole content instead of being the point where philosophy terminates in faith. (p. 67)

For Kant, reason introduces ideas of the unconditional simplicity of the self, completeness of the world, and necessity of God. But these ideas themselves do not bring along with them any evidence that these objects have these properties or even, in the case of God, exist; evidence about what objects exist and what properties they have must come from sensibility. Yet human sensibility, shaped by the open-ended structure of space and time, cannot provide evidence of unconditional simplicity or completeness, or of the existence of anything with unconditional necessity. So the ideas of reason can function as regulative but not constitutive ideas, postulates to goad us on in the search for ever more simplicity, completeness, and necessity within our scientific knowledge of self and world (see A 672–4/B 700–2) but never direct evidence of absolutely unconditional simplicity, completeness, and necessity.

The fact that reason depends upon sensibility, judged by understanding, for evidence of the actual existence of any objects is what condemns its ideas to serving as mere postulates or regulative ideals. Hegel recognizes this, and for that reason complains that Kant's account of reason leaves it dependent upon external sources of content. This complaint is voiced later in *Faith and Knowledge*:

Because of this refusal nothing remains for Reason but the pure emptiness of identity . . . after abstracting both from the content that the linking activity has through its connection with the empirical, and from its immanent peculiarity as expressed in the dimensions [forms of intuition?], the empty unity [that remains] is Reason. The intellect is the unity of a possible experience whereas the unity of Reason relates to the intellect and its judgments. In this general determination Reason is raised above the sphere of the intellect's relative identity, to be sure, and this negative character would allow us to conceive of it as absolute identity. But it was raised above intellect only to let the speculative Idea . . . finally sink down completely to formal identity. Kant is quite correct in making this empty unity a merely regulative and not a constitutive principle – for how could something that is utterly without content constitute anything?   (*Faith and Knowledge*, p. 80)

Thus Hegel suggests that reason is confined to providing mere postulates or regulative ideals because it does not supply its own content, but is dependent upon an empirical source of content from without.

The claim of the emptiness of Kantian reason is, if anything, even more forcefully stated in the *Encyclopedia:*

In this way thought, at its highest pitch, has to go outside for any determinateness; and although it is continually termed Reason, is out-and-out abstract thinking. And the result of all is that Reason supplied nothing beyond the formal unity required to simplify and systematize experiences; it is a *canon*, not an *organon*, of truth, and can furnish only a *criticism* of knowledge, not a *doctrine* of the infinite. In its final analysis this criticism is summed up in the assertion that in strictness thought is only the indeterminate unity and the action of this indeterminate unity.

Kant undoubtedly held reason to be the faculty of the unconditioned; but if reason be reduced to abstract identity only, it by implication renounces its unconditionality and is in reality no better than empty understanding. For reason is unconditioned only insofar as its character and quality are not due to an extraneous and foreign content, only insofar as it is self-characterizing, and thus, in point of content, is its own master. Kant, however, expressly explains that the action of reason consists solely in applying the categories to systematize the matter given by perception.

(*Encyclopedia*, §52 and §52z, p. 86)

In this passage, Hegel uses Kant's own terminology to report his view precisely, but as it were in a tone of voice diametrically opposed to Kant's own. What Kant sees as the most important result of his account of pure reason Hegel sees as its deepest failure. For Kant, metaphysics had traditionally supposed that by reason alone we could gain insight into the existence of the soul, the world, and God as possessing, respectively, a kind of simplicity, completeness, and necessity that we can never encounter in the always indefinitely extendible sensible experience of psychological states, space and time, and causal sequences. But when we realize that reason is not itself a source of direct representations of objects but only a source of principles for the regimentation of judgments, and that judgments in turn always require intuitions to secure their reference to particular objects, we must realize that reason itself cannot be a source for the knowledge of any objects. It can only be the source for the systematization of knowledge of objects that is indeed external to itself, and is therefore subject to the limitations inherent in the other faculties that supply its subject-matter. On Kant's view, no account of knowledge can be complete without the specification for a source of information of objects. Any alternative to his own account of the limitation of the faculty of reason would have to show how reason itself furnishes such information. If the ideas of reason could furnish their own content, as Hegel seems to suppose that it ought to, then they could also be freed of their restriction to the status of more regulative ideals or postulates. But at least in his comments on Kant's conception of reason, Hegel gives no suggestion as to how reason is to furnish its own content, or even what that means, a fortiori no proof that the contents of reason are free of the indefiniteness of sensible intuitions, which for Kant so limits the status of reason.

There is no room in this essay for a detailed discussion of Hegel's critique of Kant's moral philosophy,[18] but it may be noted in passing that at its deepest level, Hegel's critique of Kant's conception of practical reason precisely mirrors his criticism of the Kantian model of theoretical reason. First, Hegel objects to the emptiness of Kant's conception of practical reason just as he has objected to the emptiness of his conceptions of the categories and the ideas of reason, meaning by this in both cases that reason or understanding does not generate its own content and is therefore dependent on external contingencies. Hegel often expresses his objection to the emptiness of Kant's categorical imperative by saying that it allows for the universalization of any proposed maxim of action, whether good or evil, as long as the agent is consistent in allowing all to act on this maxim; but his real objection seems to be that the categorical imperative as the fundamental principle of practical reason is empty in the sense of depending upon antecedent desires for proposed goals of action rather than itself furnishing not only a criterion of necessary or permissible actions but the candidates for consideration as well. Hegel hints at this position in *Faith and Knowledge:*

As freedom, Reason is supposed to be absolute, yet the essence of this freedom consists in being solely through an opposite. This contradiction, which remains insuperable in the system and destroys it, becomes a real inconsistency when this absolute emptiness is supposed to give itself content as practical Reason and to expand itself in the form of duties. (p. 81)

The nature of his complaint is made even clearer in the essay *Natural Law,* publication of which began later in the same year as *Faith and Knowledge.* Here he objects that Kant's practical philosophy does not get past the "empirical and popular" view:

(i) that the real, under the name of sensuousness, inclinations, lower appetites, etc. (moment of the multiplicity of the relation), and reason (moment of the pure unity of the relation) do not correspond, this non-correspondence being the moment of the opposition of unity and multiplicity; and (ii) that reason consists in willing out of its own absolute self-identity and autonomy, and in constricting and dominating that sensuousness . . . It must be maintained [however] that, since morality is something absolute, this is not the standpoint of morality and there is no morality in it. (p. 74)

The categorical imperative is liable to the charge of emptiness because it treats desires as something external to itself instead of flowing from some deeper unity of sensible and rational nature.

Second, Hegel thinks that Kant's notion of the highest good, or the conjunction of happiness with virtue as the worthiness to be happy, is doomed to remain a mere postulate of practical reason, which can at best be hoped for from a God who is himself a mere postulate rather than a reality brought about by practical reason itself, because he insists on separating practical reason from its empirical source of content, namely the desires that actually determine an individual's conception of happiness and its fulfillment. Hegel expresses this point by claiming that Kant, and following him Fichte, do nothing but give systematic philosophical expression to the pessimism of Voltaire. They do this by transforming a French *apercu* into "a universally valid truth it is incapable of":

Because of the absolute subjectivity of Reason and its being set against reality, the world is, then, absolutely opposed to Reason. Hence it is absolute finitude devoid of Reason, a sense-world lacking [internal] organization. It is supposed to become equal to Ego in the course of an infinite progress.

(*Faith and Knowledge*, p. 179)[19]

The Kantian idea that we cannot find harmony between happiness and virtue in our natural lives but can only postulate an approach to it in a postulated immortal afterlife ruled by a postulated God is required, Hegel suggests, only because Kant has separated reason and nature as one more instance of his separation between thought and being from the outset. In Hegel's view, this separation is entirely unnecessary.

The same themes thus run throughout Hegel's critique of Kant's practical philosophy and of Kant's theoretical philosophy. Kant leaves the formal principles of thought, whether theoretical understanding and reason or practical reason, dependent upon external sources for their content, and because their content is only externally provided, the character of that content must remain contingent relative to the necessity of the principles themselves. This dualism of form and content, necessity and contingency, is enforced upon Kant by his insistence on separating thought and being. If he did not see thought as a mere formalism dependent upon being external to it for its content, but recognized that thought and being and thus form and content were always identical, or at least flowed from the same source, Hegel thinks that Kant could have seen his way to the higher unity that Hegel supposed he had originally glimpsed in his conceptions of judgment and apperception, but then rejected. But what he does not see is that if Kant had not rigorously separated thought from being, form from content, category from empirical intuition, and rational principle from sensuous nature, then he could have drawn no separation between the necessary and contingent – and in this case necessity would not have flown into the contingent, but rather the contingency of the real and particular would have undermined any claims to necessary truth at more abstract levels of understanding and reason.[20]

IV. CONCLUSION: THE INTUITIVE INTELLECT AND
RADICAL CONTINGENCY

Hegel sums up his critique that Kant glimpsed but refused to admit the identity of thought and being in his discussion of Kant's idea of an "intuitive intellect." This concept, which Kant introduced late and briefly in the *Critique of Judgment* only to give graphic expression to the inevitable limitations of human cognition,[21] is treated by Hegel as if it were a glimpse of the deeper reality recognized in Hegel's own philosophy from which Kant had recoiled, virtually as a coward. What is this concept?

At key points in the *Critique of Judgment*, particularly in its Introduction and its second half, the "Critique of Teleological Judgment," Kant stresses several consequences of the most fundamental limitation on human knowledge as he understood it. The most elemental fact about human knowledge, that it always requires the application of a concept formed by understanding to intuitions or representations of particular objects furnished by sensibility – the fact that, as Kant puts it, "two entirely heterogeneous factors, understanding for conceptions and sensuous intuition for the corresponding objects, are required for the exercise" of our cognitive faculties (*Critique of Judgment*, §76, 5:401)[22] – is also the source of its most basic limitation, that since representations of particular objects do not derive from the same source as the general concepts we apply to them, the existence and complete determination of particulars cannot be derived from our general concepts of them. As Kant put it, "the particular cannot be derived from the universal alone" (§77, 5:407). The fact that the existence and complete characterizations of its instances can never be derived from any general concept alone means that "Human understanding cannot avoid the necessity of drawing a distinction between the possibility and actuality of things": concepts by themselves merely limn possible objects, and only empirical intuitions demonstrate the actual existence of any particular objects (§76, 5:401–2). And this also means that both the actual existence and detailed determination of its instances must always seem contingent relative to any general concept – since the concept alone cannot imply that it has any instances, let alone that what instances it may have fulfill the partial description of them that is all that any general concept can contain, the general concept itself cannot appear to necessitate the existence or nature of its instances. As Kant puts it, "the particular by its very nature contains something contingent in respect of the universal" (§76, 5:404), or since "the particular is not determined by the universal of *our* (human) understanding," as far as we are concerned, "Though different things may agree in a common characteristic, the variety of forms in which they may be presented to our perception is may be presented to our perception is contingent" (§77, 5:406). We may express our sense of this fundamental limit and its irremediable implication of an element of contingency in all of our knowledge of particulars by contrasting our own cognitive faculties to the idea of a subject whose intuition is active rather than passive, in particular whose concepts are themselves the source of particulars and all of their determinations. For such an understanding, it would not seem contingent that its general concepts were instantiated and realized by the particular objects that did so, for the particulars would somehow flow from the general concepts; "Such an understanding would not experience the above contingency in the way nature and understanding accord in natural products subjects to particular laws." But, Kant stresses, such an "intuitive understanding" is just an idea to which we can contrast the nature of our own understanding in order to bring out its limitations: "Thus we are also able to imagine an *intuitive* understanding – negatively, or simply as not discursive – which does not move, as ours does with its conceptions, from the universal to the particular and so to the individual" (§77, 5:406). Kant does not suggest that we possess a single shred of evidence that would entitle us to claim to know that such an intuitive understanding itself actually exists, let alone that *our own* understanding can ever take on this form, which if we are even to imagine it must be ascribed to some being other than ourselves.

Kant does describe two contexts in which we are tempted to use the idea of a cognitive agent that is not confined to searching for instantiation of its general concepts among independently given intuitions as more than just a contrast to our own understanding, but rather as a regulative ideal to guide and motivate our cognitive inquiry. First (especially in the Introduction and in §76 of the *Critique of Judgment*) he argues that despite our recognition of the ultimate contingency of the instantiation of our general concepts in particulars, "reason demands that there shall also be unity in the synthesis of the particular laws of nature" or systematicity among all of our empirical concepts. This demand for systematicity has several sources: in the *Critique of Pure Reason*, Kant treats it as a desideratum of reason itself; in the *Critique of Judgment*, Kant suggests that systematicity among particular laws of nature is needed both to give us some assurance that we can always find a law for any particular experience and also to lend an appearance of necessity to particular laws of nature, which they can to some degree derive from their position in a system (see especially *Critique of Judgment*, section V, 5:181–86).[23] Just as we conceive of our own intellect as the source of our most-general concepts of nature, we can think of such as a system of empirical laws as if it were the product of a intellect more powerful than our own that excogitated it for our cognitive convenience (*Critique of Judgment*, section IV, 5:180). But this thought gives us no evidence of the existence of such an intellect; it merely gives us guidance in "our reflection upon the objects of nature with a view to getting a thoroughly interconnected whole of experience" (section V, 5:184), that is to say, a regulative ideal for our practice of empirical judgment.

Second, Kant argues that the implications of our basic cognitive structure lead us to formulate the idea of an alternative kind of understanding in attempting to deal with knowledge of living organisms. Here what limits us is not just that we need intuitions to supplement any of our general concepts, but the more particular fact that our intuitions are always given in time and thus successively. This causes a problem because, in order to understand organisms, we need to conceive of them as if the parts were the antecedent causes of various aspects of the whole, which is compatible with the temporally successive nature of our empirical intuitions, but also as if the whole were itself the cause of various features of its temporally antecedent parts – which is not. In order to cope with this, we postulate the idea of a designer of organisms whose design or "*representation* of a whole may contain the source of the possibility of the form of that whole and of the nexus of the parts which that form involves" (§77, 5:408), and which would thus function as an antecedent cause of the parts of the whole in a way that can be represented compatibly with the sequential nature of our own empirical intuitions. Such a concept could also be taken to eliminate the contingency in the relations of the various parts to the concept of the whole (407). But again, Kant stresses, we have no ground to infer that such an intellect different from our own actually exists: "It is sufficient to show that we are led to this idea of an *intellectus archetypus* by contrasting with it our discursive understanding that has need of images (*intellectus ectypus*)" (408). We only use the idea to reconcile the conceptualization of organisms with the limits of our own understanding, which does not produce particulars but awaits intuitions for knowledge of them.[24]

Hegel begins his discussion of Kant's concept of an intuitive intellect with an accurate enough description of it, as an intellect "for which possibility and actuality are one" and for which the accord between universal and particular in nature is not contingent (*Faith and Knowledge*, p. 88). But when he goes on to say that "Kant also recognizes that we are necessarily driven to this Idea" of an intuitive intellect, he misstates the case. Kant argued that we can use the idea of such an intellect to bring out, by way of contrast, the limitations of our own, and also that in certain contexts we need to use the idea of such an intellect not actually to overcome the limitations of our own cognitive faculties but merely to guide us to the maximal use of them within their insuperable limitations. But he never argued that we have any basis on which to suppose that such an intellect actually exists, let alone that it exists in ourselves.

Hegel thought that, in the concept of an intuitive intellect, Kant had reached his own idea of the Idea, a mind-like source of concepts that is at the same time the source of reality and thereby makes the fit between concepts and reality necessary rather than contingent. As he puts it in the *Encyclopedia*,

> If we adopt this principle, the Idea, when all limitations were removed from it, would appear as follows. The universality molded by Reason, and described as the absolute and final end or the Good, would be realized in the world, and realized moreover by means of a third thing, the power which proposes this end as well as realizes it – tht is, God. Thus in him, who is the absolute truth, these oppositions of universal and individual, subjective and objective, are solved and explained to be neither self-subsistent nor true.
>
> (*Encyclopedia*, §59, p. 90)

For Hegel, the idea of an intuitive intellect overcomes not only the opposition between thought and being but also even that between theoretical and practical reason, for of course the thought which is necessarily realized by such a being would also be necessarily good. But Kant never conceded the rational necessity of positing the existence of such an understanding in ourselves for a moment, at least in any context of theoretical philosophy; he only employed the *idea* of such a form of understanding in a being greater than ourselves for contrastive and regulative purposes.[25]

Hegel was obviously upset by the fact that the "Idea occurs [to Kant] here only as thought" (*Faith and Knowledge*, p. 89): "This makes it all the harder to see the Rational being muddled up again, and not just that, but to see the highest Idea corrupted with full consciousness, while reflection and finite cognition are exalted above it" (p. 92). He attributed Kant's denial of the "actual realization of the ultimate end," his "clinging hard to the disjunction of the notion from reality" to mere "laziness of thought" (*Encyclopedia*, §55, p. 88), or claimed that "Kant has simply no ground except experience and empirical psychology" for denying the reality of the intuitive intellect as the ultimate truth about human thought itself (*Faith and Knowledge*, p. 89). But Kant's hard-fought conclusion that the fundamental distinction between intuition and concept was the only way to avoid the philosophical confusions of Leibniz and Wolff, on the one hand, and Locke and Hume, on the other, can hardly be attributed to laziness of thought, and it seems equally implausible to characterize Kant's insistence on the need for reception of information about the particulars of nature as well as conceptualization as mere "empirical psychology." It is far too basic a fact, and compatible with far too many particular cognitive psychologies, to be treated as if it were just some sort of empirically verifiable or, more to the point, falsifiable observation. On the contrary, it is virtually impossible to imagine what it would be like to produce evidence for particulars out of mere concepts – except perhaps in the case of pure mathematics, where we can construct formal objects in accord with our definitions of them. If Kant was guilty of any laziness, it may have been only in suggesting that it is easy for us to *imagine* an intuitive understanding; it may be easy for us to verbally *describe* such a thing, but impossible actually to *imagine* it.

In any case it seems safe to say that, at least in his explicit discussions of Kant, Hegel makes no attempt to explain how concepts could actually produce their own instances, which is what he would have to do in order to prove the existence of an intuitive intellect as defined by Kant. In fact, he makes no attempt to provide direct criticism of Kant's grounds for separating intuition from concept and thus particular from universal. Instead, he appeals to one of his typical metaphors. He claims that "No one knows, or even feels, that anything is a limit or defect, until he is at the same time above and beyond it," thus that "a limit or imperfection in knowledge comes to be termed a limit or imperfection, only when it is compared with the actually present Idea of the universal," and that "to call a thing finite or limited proves by implication the very presence of the infinite and unlimited" (*Encyclopedia*, §60, p. 92; see also *Faith and Knowledge*, p. 89). Thus he tries to suggest that Kant cannot merely appeal to the idea of an intuitive intellect to bring out the limits of our own discursive intellect, but must concede its reality in the very attempt to place any limits upon our own intellect. But this form of argument, which was introduced into modern philosophy in Descartes's *Third Meditation* but can be traced all the way back to Plato and Augustine,[26] is not only one of the oldest arguments in the philosophers' book, it is also one of the worst. It simply is not true that one must recognize the existence of something that does not have a certain property in order to conceive of that property as a defect or limit. I can treat being liable to doubt as a defect or limit simply because I can see how nice it would be not to have to doubt, without having the least reason to suppose that anything exists that is not liable to this limitation, or I can treat being mortal as a limit if I think it would be nice to live forever without having any reason to think there is any creature that is immortal. In the same way, I can treat being dependent upon intuitions which are independent of my concepts as a limitation because it introduces an ineliminable element of contingency into my knowledge-claims without having the least reason to believe that there actually exists any cognitive agent that is not liable to this limitation. Thus Hegel cannot prove that Kant is committed to the reality of an intuitive intellect by the use of the idea of it to give expression to his conception of the limitations of human knowledge. He could not prove that the contingency inherent in Kant's dual sources of knowledge is eliminable except by a positive explanation of how understanding and reason could lead to knowledge without empirical intuitions which are independent of thought and thus contingent relative to it.

Hegel wrote as if he had offered detailed refutations of some of Kant's central theses, but in fact he hardly engaged in internal criticism of Kant's arguments at all. Instead, he criticized Kant's conclusions from the point of view of his own suppositions about the bond between knowledge and reality. In Hegel's view, Kant was guilty of leaving unnecessary contingency both at the general level, in his account of the forms of intuitions and categories, and at the particular level, in his account of the instantiation of these general forms of nature in individual objects and laws of nature. Kant would not have denied these charges. On the contrary, he viewed the latter contingency as the inevitable outcome of the fundamental difference between concepts and intuitions itself, and the former as the inevitable price to pay for the fact that we can explain our *a priori* knowledge of both forms of intuitions and categories only as a product of their subjective validity, with no possibility of explaining just why our subjective faculties of cognition are constituted in just this and no other way. His objection would not be to Hegel's account of his system – except insofar as Hegel ascribes it to laziness or mere empirical psychology – but only to Hegel's suggestion that there is an alternative. Hegel's alternative would require the elimination of the contingency in the forms of intuition and categories by the deduction of them from some single underlying idea, and the elimination of the contingency in the realization of these abstract forms of thought by the identity of thought and being and thus the derivation of both universal and particulars from some single source. Kant would have been very surprised if Hegel could have made good on these promises.

NOTES

1 For reasons of space, this essay will be confined to the issue of thought and being rather than action and being, that is, to theoretical rather than practical philosophy (one brief digression on the latter will be treated more fully in the essay by Allen W. Wood in chapter 7, this collection). [Also see the article by Kenneth Westphal, chapter 8.] For a sense of the full scope of Hegel's critique of Kant, see the volume edited by Stephen Priest, *Hegel's Critique of Kant* (Oxford: Clarendon Press, 1987), which contains a general survey by the editor and twelve individual essays by eleven authors. The first six of these, by Michael Inwood, Graham Bird, Justus Harnack, John Llewellyn, Stephen Priest, and W. Walsh, are relevant to the topics of the present essay. The best single treatment of these issues is Karl Ameriks, "Hegel's Critique of Kant's Theoretical Philosophy," *Philosophy and Phenomenological Research* 45 (1985): 1–35. For literature on Hegel's critique of Kant's practical philosophy, see note 18 below. A volume devoted specifically to Hegel's interpretation of the aesthetic, teleological, and systematic themes of the *Critique of Judgment* is *Hegel und die "Kritik der Urteilskraft"*, ed. Hans-Friedrich Fulda and Rolf-Peter Horstmann (Stuttgart: Klett-Cotta, 1990). I have discussed Hegel's critique of Kant's aesthetics in the volume: "Hegel on

Kant's Aesthetics: Necessity and Contingency in Beauty and Art," pp. 81–99.

2 This work dates from relatively late in Hegel's career – it was first published in 1817 but was substantially revised in 1827 and 1830 – but does not differ in essentials from what he had already been arguing for several decades. The main elements of Hegel's critique of Kant, in both theoretical and practical philosophy, appear to have undergone little change after his first publications including explicit criticism of Kant, the essays "Faith and Knowledge" ("Faith and Knowledge: or the "Reflective Philosophy of Subjectivity" in the complete range of its forms as Kantian, Jacobian, and Fichtean Philosophy"), published in the *Critical Journal of Philosophy* edited by Hegel and Schelling in 1802, and "Natural Law" ("The Scientific Ways of Treating Natural Law, Its Place in Moral Philosophy, and Its Relation to the Positive Sciences of Law") published in the same journal in 1802–3. For that reason I will draw on both these earlier and the later works in this essay without any attempt to demonstrate an evolution in Hegel's views about Kant. "Faith and Knowledge" is cited from the translation by Walter Cerf and H.S. Harris (Albany: State University of New York Press, 1977), "Natural Law" in the translation by T.M. Knox (Philadelphia: University of Pennsylvania Press, 1975), and the *Encyclopedia* in the translation by William Wallace, *Hegel's Logic: Being Part One of the Enclyclopedia and Philosophical Sciences (1830)*, 3rd ed. (Oxford: Clarendon Press, 1975).

3 The "z" indicates that the passage is an addendum (*Zusatz*) drawn from Hegel's lectures on the *Encyclopedia* and originally published in the version (edited by Leopold Henning) included in the edition of Hegel's works published after his death by the *"Freunde des verewigten"* (1840). These passages are not included in all modern German editions, but are included in Wallace's translation. I do not believe that philological scruples should preclude their use, since this material, like Hegel's whole lecture series on history, history of philosophy, and aesthetics, was published soon after Hegel's death by a group of Hegel's students, using copious notes in both his own hand and those of others. There seems little reason to doubt that these materials accurately portray Hegel's intentions.

4 In this essay I will use the translation by Norman Kemp Smith, 2nd ed. (London: Macmillan, 1933), but will give only the pagination of Kant's first edition of 1781 ("A") and second edition of 1787 ("B"), which is reproduced in Kemp Smith's edition and therefore obviates the need to cite his own pagination.

5 The interpretation of both the meaning of and the argument for Kant's so-called transcendental idealism, which I have given here, is controver-

sial. For a fuller defense of it, as well as references to further literature, see my *Kant and the Claims of Knowledge* (Cambridge: Cambridge University Press, 1987), chap. 16, pp. 345–70.

6 To preserve symmetry with the other three sets of categories, each of which has three specific forms, Kant attempts to define a third category of quality by distinguishing between "negative" judgments, which simply deny a predicate of an object, and "infinite" judgments, which affirm that an object is characterized by one of the infinite predicates remaining after the exclusion of a specific one ("x is non-F" as opposed to "x is not F") (A 72–73/B 97–98). This distinction, needed to reach the canonical twelve functions of judgment rather than the eleven mentioned above, has found few friends. There are also further difficulties in Kant's move from twelve logical functions of judgments to twelve pure concepts of objects (A 80/B 106), but they will be ignored here.

7 For a consideration of some of the interpretative difficulties of this argument and references to further literature on it, see Paul Guyer, "The Transcendental Deduction of the Categories," in *The Cambridge Companion to Kant*, ed. Paul Guyer (Cambridge: Cambridge University Press, 1992), 123–60. For a discussion of Hegel's difficulties with the transcendental deduction, see Ameriks, "Hegel's Critique of Kant's Theoretical Philosophy," pp. 5–13.

8 Kant also argues that there is a *practical* justification for the formation of the idea of and postulation of the existence of God, a moral imperative to posit the existence of God in order to reconcile the apparent lack of harmony between virtue and happiness, but he always argues that this practical postulate never amounts to knowledge in any form.

9 See *Hegel's Lecture on the History of Philosophy*, trans. E.S. Haldane and Frances H. Simson (London: Routledge Kegan Paul, 1896), Vol. III, 423–78, and *Lectures on the History of Philosophy: The Lectures of 1825–1826*, ed. Robert F. Brown (Berkeley: University of California Press, 1990), Vol. III, 217–29).

10 See, for example, Moltke S. Gram, *Kant, Ontology and the A Priori* (Evanston: Northwestern University Press, 1968), chap. 3, which argues that Kant is actually committed to two different accounts of judgment, an explicit theory like that now to be described and also an implicit theory on which intuitions are literally parts of judgments.

11 For an interpretation of Hegel stressing this aspect, see Rolf-Peter Horstmann, *Ontologie und Relationen: Hegel, Bradley, Russel und die Kontroverse über interne und externe Beziehungen* (Königstein: Athenäum-Hain, 1984).

12 This conception of method is contrasted to the synthetical or progressive method supposedly employed in the *Critique of Pure Reason* in the

introduction to Kant's 1783 attempt at a clarification and popularization of the *Critique*, his *Prolegomena to Any Future Metaphysics* (4:264). The idea is supposed to be that the analytical method assumes the existence of certain synthetic *a priori* knowledge and shows that the possession of certain *a priori* forms of intuition or thought is the only possible explanation of such knowledge, whereas the synthetic method does not begin with such an outright assumption of synthetic *a priori* knowledge. In fact, much of Kant's argument in the *Critique* also begins with the assumption of synthetic *a priori* knowledge, and the only difference is the degree of generality of that which is assumed, with the *Critique* emphasizing arguments beginning with the extremely general idea of synthetic *a priori* knowledge of the unity and identity of self-consciousness (the transcendental unity of apperception) and the *Prolegomena* focusing on more-specific premises about synthetic *a priori* knowledge in mathematics and physical science.

13 For futher discussion of this issue, see Ameriks, "Hegel's Critique of Kant's Theoretical Philosophy," pp. 15–21.

14 There is a long history of discussion of the completeness of Kant's table of categories. For the most-recent discussion, and a very insightful one, see Reinhard Brandt, *Die Urteilstafel: Kritik der reinen Vernunft A 67–76; B 92–101*, Kant-Forschungen, Vol. 4 (Hamburg: Felix Meiner, 1991).

15 Twentieth-century logicians, especially those working in the first half of the century, have taken great pleasure in demonstrating that any exhaustive representation of the logically possibly structures of judgments can be characterized through an even more-austere set of functions than Kant employed. See, for example, W.V. Quine, *Methods of Logic*, rev. ed. (New York: Holt, Rinehart, and Winston, 1959), 7–12.

16 I am referring to the Leibniz of the mid-1680s, the period of works such as "The Discourse on Metaphysics" and "Primary Truths," where Leibniz suggests that the principle of sufficient reason is itself derivable from the principle that the predicate of a true proposition is always contained in its subject, as opposed to the later Leibniz of the period of "The Monadology," where Leibniz treats these as two equally fundamental principles.

17 Kant discusses the schematism at A 136–47/B 176–87. For this interpretation of it, see *Kant and the Claims of Knowledge*, chap. 6, 157–66.

18 For more detailed discussion of this issue, see the essay by Allen Wood in this volume. (Chapter 7). For further discussion, see Karl Ameriks, "The Hegelian Critique of Kantian Morality," *New Essays on Kant*, ed. Bernard den Ouden and Marcia Moen (New York: Peter Lang, 1987), 179–212; Sally S. Sedgwick, "Hegel's Critique of the Subjective Idealism of Kant's Ethics," *Journal of the History of Philosophy* 26 (1988): 89–

105, and "On the Relation of Pure Reason to Content: A Reply to Hegel's Critique of Formalism in Kant's Ethics," *Philosophy and Phenomenological Research* 49 (1988): 59–80; and Allen W. Wood, *Hegel's Ethical Thought* (Cambridge: Cambridge University Press, 1990), chap. 9,
154–73.

19 This passage occurs in Hegel's discussion of Fichte rather than Kant. But
he has earlier referred the reader to the discussion of Fichte for the
discussion of his criticism of the Kantian conception of practical reason
(p. 85)

20 In an important essay, Dieter Henrich tries to defend Hegel from the
charge that he attempted to find claims of necessary truth about particular objects by claiming that Hegel's concept of reality includes the requirement that necessity posit its own opposite and thus entails the
existence of contingency ("Hegels über den Zufall," in his *Hegel im
Kontext* (Frankfurt: Suhrkamp, 1971), 157–86). But this seems like a
merely verbal solution, and in any case does not address the charge that
Hegel fails to see that from the Kantian point of view the contingency of
particular facts is ineliminable because of the duality of sources of
knowledge (and, for that matter, motivation as well).

21 The term "intuitive intellect" (*intuitive* or *anschauliche Verstand*) is
used only in §§76–77 of the *Critique of Judgment* to characterize the
conceptual possibility of an understanding whose *particular objects*
would somehow – of course we cannnot say how – be derived from its
concepts. The inverted expression "intellectual intuition" is employed
several times in the *Critique of Pure Reason* (see B 72) to connote the
related but distinct idea of an understanding that would not need the
pure forms of intuition to relate to objects. In both cases, the idea is
clearly intended only to characterize the nature of our own cognition,
not to assert that such an alternative is actually instantiated in any real
being.

22 For present purposes I have followed the translation by J.C. Meredith
(Oxford: Clarendon Press, 1911 and 1928). Page citations are to volume
5 to *Kant's gesammelte Schriften* (Berlin: Georg Reimer [later Walter
de Gruyter], 1913), which are reproduced in the margins of Meredith's
translation.

23 I have discussed the grounds for Kant's conception of systematicity in
"Kant's Concept of Empirical Law," *Proceedings of the Aristotelian Society, Supplementary Volume* 67 (1990): 221–42).

24 Of course, since the time of Darwin we have been able to see that Kant's
problem with the conceptualization of organisms is not due to the temporally successive nature of our empirical knowledge of causation itself,
but rather to an overly restricted conception of the temporally succes-

sive causal mechanisms at work in nature, that is to say, to his ignorance of random mutation and natural selection as perfectly mechanical, temporally sequential causal processes.

25 For further discussion of Hegel's treatment of the "intuitive intellect," see Fulda and Horstmann, eds., *Hegel und die "Kritik der Urteilskraft"*, particularly the articles by Klaus Düsing, "Naturteleologie und Metaphysik bei Kant und Hegel," pp. 141–157, and Burkhard Tuschling, "Intuitiver Verstand, absolute Identität, Idee," pp. 174–88.

26 See Alasdair MacIntyre, *Three Rival Versions of Moral Enquiry: Encyclopaedia, Genealogy, and Tradition* (Notre Dame: University of Notre Dame Press, 1990), 95.

7 Hegel's ethics

I. BACKGROUND

Hegel's philosophy is an attempt to renew classical philosophy, especially the philosophy of Plato and Aristotle, within the modern philosophical tradition begun with Kant. Hegel's ethical thought is no different from the rest of his philosophy in this respect. Classical ethical theory, culminating for Hegel in the ethical theory of Aristotle, saw ethics as aiming at a single final end or human good, called "happiness" (*eudaimonia*). By nature, human beings have a characteristic function; to fulfill that function is to be happy. Aristotle defined happiness as the actualizing of the soul's capacities in accordance with the excellences appropriate to them, and most especially the actualization of its highest capacity, reason. Our rational excellences include both theory and practice; practical excellences include not only the intellectual virtue of practical wisdom but a range of distinct moral virtues of character. Moral virtues dispose the non-rational part of our soul, which includes desires and feelings, to be governed by the rational part, so that our wants, likes and dislikes, pleasures and pains, all harmonize with reason.

Kant. The moral theory of Immanuel Kant (1724–1804) was decisive for modern ethical thought. Kant laid a new foundation for moral philosophy. In place of theories founded on the divine will, or on moral feeling, or on ends, such as the classical eudamonistic theories, Kant founded ethics solely on the autonomy of reason. Against eudaimonism, Kant insisted that there is a sharp distinction between the theory of self-interest or rational prudence and the theory of what is morally right or virtuous. The only unqualified good, Kant famously asserted, is a good will. A good will is one that acts solely "from duty," that is, from respect for reason's moral law, even in spite of all our natural inclinations. Against all theories based on ends, Kant held that the value of any end depends upon its being set as an end by a rational will, which presupposes a process of rational deliberation from principles. The same point is brought to bear against all theories founded on feelings, since the value of all feelings, whether for sensual pleasure or morality, must be estimated according to rational principles. In opposition to divine will theories, Kant objected that we have no way of knowing what God wills except by deciding what a perfectly good being *would* will; that presupposes an autonomous theory of the good will.

From Rousseau, Kant drew the idea that it is possible to reconcile moral obligation with freedom only if in obeying the moral law we are obeying merely our own true will. Kant therefore founded ethics on an imperative, universally valid for all rational beings and self-legislated by each rational being. The imperative is not hypothetical, based on the desire for some end previously set by the rational will, but categorical or unconditional. Such an imperative, Kant argued, can command nothing but the adherence of a rational being to principles or maxims valid for all rational beings. Thus the first of Kant's several formulations of the categorical imperative was "So act that you can will the maxim of your action to be a universal law." According to Kantian ethical theory, happiness is valuable, but its value is only conditional. First, happiness is objectively valuable only because it is an end set by a *rational* will, and second, the value of any individual's happiness is conditional on that individual's possessing a *good* will, which conditions even the worthiness to be happy.

Because morality is founded on automony of the will, Kant regarded its validity as dependent on the freedom of the human will. If there were nothing more to the human will than our being affected by natural desires, then the whole of morality would be nothing but a pitiful illusion. Moreover, in Kant's view, freedom cannot be demonstrated theoretically. However, in taking the moral life seriously, we commit ourselves to the faith that our acts are the effects of a free, supersensible self whose dignity raises us above that of all merely natural beings.

Fichte. Kant's most influential and original follower was Johann Gottlieb Fichte (1762–1814). Fichte made our active awareness of moral freedom fundamental not only to ethical theory but even to theoretical philosophy. The first principle of philosophy is the "I", the awareness of our own freedom, which is active in constituting our knowledge of the world as well as in our practical action on it. Fichte's entire philosophy is in effect an exploration of the necessary conditions for being a free, active self. One of these conditions, as Fichte presents them, is mutual interaction between the self and an objective world resisting the self's action. Because it must interact with a world, the active self must also be a material thing, a body; and because the world always presents itself to the self as resistance to a prior striving on the part of the self, the self must come into being as reflective awareness of a pre-reflective state of desire, whose form is that of subordinating the world to itself, or bringing the world into harmony with the self. Fichte makes the I into the criterion of worth, and even identifies Kant's "reason" itself with the I; he makes the I's conscientious conviction the final criterion of moral rightness, regarding Kant's moral principle as merely formal, incapable by itself of distinguishing moral maxims from immoral ones.

However, Fichte also argues that an "I" is possible only through relationship to another sort of "not-I", through which the self's striving can be limited through responding to a demand or requirement, giving the self a determinate self-identity. This other sort of not-I is a "thou," another self, and the self's harmonious relationship to it is one not of subordination, but of co-ordination or mutuality. The foundation of this relationship is "recognition," the mutual awareness by all that each individual has a right to a portion of the external world, beginning with the body and extending to all the individual's property. Fichte's theory of intersubjectivity, however, goes well beyond this. The individual's vocation, of becoming a whole and determinate I, also includes unification with others, defining oneself within a harmonious social whole. This means that the I's free activity, and the fulfillment of its practical striving, can be fulfilled only in and through a certain form of society, involving mutual respect, equality, and cooperative striving toward ends shared mutually on the basis of rational communication. Moral duty and the moral law thus acquire an intersubjective meaning for Fichte.

For Fichte, the self's very identity is bound up with its moral vocation, and in his moral philosophy many of the moralistic characteristics of Kantian ethics are found in exaggerated forms. Next to the real world, the striving of the I produces an entire ideal world of the "ought to be." The self's whole identity consists in its service of the moral imperative; any action that is not a duty is morally wrong, and any action not done from duty is considered contrary to duty. Fichte's moral theory exercised a profound influence on Hegel – even the influence of Kantian ethics reached Hegel largely through this medium – but the influence was as much negative as positive. In the case of Fichte's exaggerated Kantian moralism, the negative influence was especially strong.

II. THE DEVELOPMENT OF HEGEL'S ETHICAL THOUGHT

Hegel's mature views on ethical topics are found principally in *The Philosophy of Right*. But from Hegel's earliest writings in the 1790s, ethical topics were a focus of his philosophical concern, and some of Hegel's earlier writings on ethics have exercised an important influence of their own.

Early Writings on Religion. Hegel began as a Kantian. The writings of Hegel's Tübingen and Bern periods (1793–1796, but not published until 1921) show the impact of Kant's *Religion Within the Bounds of Unaided Reason* (1793). These so-called *Early Theological Writings* take the form of reflections on the history of the Christian religion and its relation both to Judaism and to ancient pagan culture; their deeper purpose is to diagnose the moral and religious needs of the modern world (TJ, ETW, TE).[1] Hegel focuses on the need for reconciliation between the rational and sensuous aspects of human nature, and on the roles of religious sentiments and social institutions in shaping human nature. Along with Kant, Hegel attacks ceremonial or "positive" religion, but in place of Kant's austere deistic moral religion, Hegel advocates a "folk religion" modeled on his conception of the harmonious naturalism of ancient Greece.

In the writings of Hegel's Frankfurt period (1797–1799), the same concerns lead Hegel to a radical critique of the moral standpoint, especially as exemplified by Kant's moral philosophy, with its emphasis on the conflict between duty and inclination, and the good will as the will motivated by respect for the law. In these writings Hegel first articulates many of his best-known criticisms of the moral standpoint: as self-alienated, pharasaical, a standpoint which can only blame and condemn but never convert its "ought" into an "is."

In 1800, Hegel began his university career in Jena. In his Jena period (1800–1806) he is preoccupied with the task of developing a system of speculative philosophy, and his writings show a continuing interest in ethical issues and in the relation of the human personality to its social context. The focus of Hegel's critical reflections on the moral standpoint now shifts to the ethical writings of Fichte. Following Fichte, Hegel regards Kant's principle of morality as "empty," incapable of yielding determinate duties; but unlike Fichte, who thought the defect could be made good through an alternative moral epistemology, Hegel finds the emptiness to be endemic to the moral standpoint as such. It is in 1802 that Hegel first begins to contrast the standpoint of "morality" (*Moralität*) with that of "ethical life" (*Sittlichkeit*) (GW 426/183, NR 504–6/112–14). "Morality" refers to the viewpoint of the Kantian and Fichtean theories, which Hegel identifies with that of the modern bourgeoisie, alienated from public life and preoccupied only with private self-seeking and private moral virtue. Hegel attacks the formalism of this standpoint, as well as its hostile separation of reason from natural inclinations. In ethical life, by contrast, the gap between reason and sense is overcome, and duties are drawn not from abstract moral reflection but from the concrete relations of a living social order. For Hegel the paradigm of "ethical life" is his nostalgic image of ancient Greek culture; he realizes that such a social order is gone forever, that the principle of modern society is that of the free individual. Hegel's spiritual history of Western culture in Chapter 5 of the *Phenomenology* thus begins with Greek "ethical life" (PhG ¶¶ 444–76) and ends with the problems of modern individualist "morality" (PhG ¶¶ 599–671).

As we have already mentioned, Hegel also understands this individualism of the moral standpoint in a socio-economic sense. By 1804 Hegel was familiar with the writings of the Scottish political economists James Steuart (1712–1780), Adam Ferguson (1723–1816), and Adam Smith (1723–1790), and under their influence he sees modern society as distinguished from previous ones by the existence in it of an economic organization of independent persons, distinct from the political state – an organization to which some years later he was to give the name "civil society" (*bürgerliche Gesellschaft*). As members of civil society, individuals are *Bürger* in the sense of *bourgeois*, not in the sense of *citoyens*; their primary orientation is toward their private good, not toward "ethical" ends; but civil society nevertheless forms a determinate social system that determines individuals objectively as it frees them subjectively. In Hegel's lectures from his Jena period, he articulates the concept of the free person as participant in this system in terms of an innovative adaptation of Fichte's theory of "recognition."

In the Jena period, however, Hegel was unable to integrate his picture of modern society (with its independent economic organization and its orientation to *Moralität*) into his positive conception of ethical life. His primary philosophical efforts in the decade after he left Jena were directed not to moral or social philosophy but to *The Science of Logic*. The principal text in which we find evidence of a development in his ethical views is the *Nuremberg Propadeutic* (1810–1811) (NP), lecture notes at the Nuremberg gymnasium where he was headmaster from 1808 to 1816. Although it may be attributable in part to pedagogical considerations, the notes are surprisingly Kantian on many points.

In that respect, the Nuremberg lectures prefigure the more positive treatment of *Moralität* in the writings of Hegel's maturity, beginning with the Heidelberg *Encyclopedia* of 1817 (EH) (later revised and expanded (EL, EG)). Here Hegel's philosophy of objective spirit is structured around the three stages of "abstract right," "morality," and "ethical life." "Ethical life," moreover, no longer refers paradigmatically to a lost Greek ideal, but instead means a *modern* ethical life, characterized by the uniquely modern institution of "civil society" and into which are integrated positively the correspondingly modern spheres of abstract right and morality. It was this structure around which Hegel built his definitive ethical theory in *The Philosophy of Right*.

III. THE SELF-ACTUALIZATION OF FREEDOM

A Self-Actualization Theory. Hegel's mature ethical theory may be viewed as an attempt to reconcile traditional Aristotelian ethical theory with the Kantian and Fichtean emphasis on free selfhood. Hegel's *Philosophy of Right* begins with "spirit" (*Geist*) in the specific form of the practical subject or free will, and works out the systematic self-actualization of its freedom (PR § 33). From Aristotle, Hegel draws the idea that ethics must be founded on a conception of the human good, regarded as the actualization of the human essence. But from Kant, Hegel has learned the lesson that this good is not to be identified with human happiness, or with any other good answering to what is merely given in our nature. Following Fichte, he conceives the human self as free in the radical sense that its identity, and therefore the content of its self-realization, is the result of its own activity. The human *Bestimmung*, the fundamental human property and at the same time the human vocation, is freedom itself (PR § 4).

The resulting theory cannot be comfortably classified either as a *teleological* theory, like Aristotle's, based on an *end* or *good* to be pursued, or as a *deontical* theory, like Kant's, based on a *commandment* or *principle* to be followed. Instead, it is an *agent-oriented* or *self-actualization* theory, based on a conception of the human self to be exemplified or instantiated. The theory recommends principles when they are the principles such a self would follow, and ends when they are the ends it would pursue.

Actually, Hegel's theory is based not on one conception of the self, but on a *system* of such conceptions, which determines Hegel's "system of right" in the *Philosophy of Right*. Hegel sees these conceptions as the results of a long historical development, in which the human spirit collectively has successively deepened its knowledge of itself. In the sphere of "abstract right," the individual is conceived as a "person" (PR §§ 34–36), a free volitional agent, capable of abstracting completely from its desires and situation, and demanding recognition for an external sphere in which the dignity of its personality can be actualized (PR § 41). Within this sphere, including the person's body and life (but extending to all its property), the person's right of arbitrary freedom must be recognized by others.

A second but less abstract sphere is that of "morality" in which the individual is conceived as a subject, an agent possessing moral responsibility and a distinctive good or welfare of its own, which makes claims on the subjective will of others. Morality is concerned with our responsibility for actions and their consequences (PR §§ 115–20), with the value of subjective freedom, the right of individuals to determine the course of their own lives and to take satisfaction in their choices (PR §§ 121–24). Self-actualization in the moral sphere consists in the actualization of the subject through the conformity of its insight and intention to the good (PR § 131). For morality, the good is conceived simply as human welfare or happiness in the abstract, whose goodness is contingent upon its consistency with abstract right (PR § 130).

Hegel sees the conceptions of person and subject as applying universally to all human beings, and regards this vision as an achievement of post-Christian European modernity. Both conceptions, however, are *abstractions*, which cannot be actualized directly. Hegel blames the disastrous limitations of modern theories of the state, as well as all the shortcomings of the moral standpoint, on the failure to appreciate this point. Personhood and subjectivity can be actualized only by being given concrete embodiment in the roles of a harmonious social system or ethical life. Hegel's *Philosophy of Right* is an attempt to present modern society as an ethical life in which distinctively modern self-conceptions are made concrete and so actualized. The distinctively modern social institution in which this takes place is civil society.

Objective Freedom. The essence and vocation of spirit or the will is freedom. Thus far we have looked at freedom "subjectively," in terms of the self-images of the free being. But Hegel thinks it can be looked at from an "objective" standpoint too. In his technical usage, "right" is freedom made objective or actual (PR § 29). Thus *The Philosophy of Right* is a developing hierarchy of *objects* in which freedom is actualized. But Hegel insists that what most people mean by freedom, the unhindered capacity to act aribtrarily or do as you please, is not true freedom (PR § 15R). Genuine freedom, "absolute," "concrete," or "positive" freedom, consists not in a mere capacity or potentiality, but in that activity which fully actualizes reason (PR § 22R).

Hegel's conception of freedom is derived from Kant's conception of autonomy and Fichte's conception of absolute self-sufficiency, a kind of action that has its source solely in the self-activity of the agent and not at all in anything alien or foreign to the agent. Hegel, however, significantly revises this conception as it is found in Kant and Fichte. For them, autonomous action is that which has its source in the agent's pure reason and not in the agent's sensuous impulses, still less in the external (natural or social) world. For Hegel, however, this represents a false and rigid conception of the relation of the self to otherness. Spirit, Hegel insists, is "self-restoring sameness" (PhG ¶18); it stands in an essential relation to otherness, and its actualization consists not in a separation from its other, but in overcoming that otherness. Spirit's freedom, therefore, consists not in holding itself separate from what is other, but rather in mastering it and making it one's own. Freedom for Hegel therefore consists in "being with oneself in an other" (*Beisichselbstsein in einem Andern*) (PR § 23). When the other which I distinguish from myself does not limit but expresses my self, then it is not a hindrance on me, but is in fact the very actualization of my freedom.

One consequence of this is that autonomous action is not action that (as in Kant and Fichte) holds itself aloof from empirical motivation, but rather action in which the empirical motives are themselves the self-expression of the agent's reason. Another consequence is that social institutions and our duties within them are not hindrances on freedom but in fact actualizations of freedom, when the content of these institutions is rational and the performance of our duties is a vehicle for our self-actualization. In such cases, we are "with ourselves" in our duties and in the social order of which we are a part; far from setting limits to our freedom, they constitute its actualization (PR § 149).

From one point of view, *The Philosophy of Right* is a system of "objective freedom," presenting the hierarchy of different kinds of objects in which spirit or the self or reason is "with itself" (PR § 33). In "abstract right," a spiritual self is with itself in external things, which are its property. In "morality," the self is with itself in its own subjective willing and with the external consequences of that willing. In "ethical life," the self is with itself in a system of social institutions that actualize it by fulfilling its various needs for both subjective individuality and substantive community. The most complete actualization of the individual's freedom is found in the institutions of the state.

Hegel explicitly distinguishes his conception of positive freedom from the "superficial" everyday notion of freedom as the ability to do as you please (PR §§ 15R, 22R, 149A, EL § 145A). But he emphasizes that the distinguishing feature of the modern state is the way in which its institutions allow for what Hegel calls "subjective freedom," including personal arbitrariness and private self-satisfaction (PR §§ 124, 185R, 206R), the sanctity of individual moral and religious conscience (PR § 139), and the universal status for all individuals of personhood and abstract right (PR § 209).

IV. ABSTRACT RIGHT

Abstract right corresponds to the image of the self as a *person*. To be a person is to have a claim on an "external sphere" for the exercise of one's arbitrary choice (PR § 41). Following Fichte, Hegel derives a conception of persons with rights from a theory of "recognition," through which individuals become aware of themselves in relation to other free selves. (Hegel's version of this argument is presented in the famous "Master and Servant" section of *The Phenomenology of Spirit* (PhG ¶¶ 178–96; cf. EG §§ 433–36).) Hegel interprets a person's external sphere of arbitrary freedom as the sphere of that person's *property*, taking that term in a very broad sense. A person's right to life and free status, which Hegel regards as inalienable and imprescriptible, depend on the fact that a person's body and life are paradigmatically that person's property, constituting an external sphere that is inseparable from personality itself (PR § 66). It follows for Hegel that slavery is necessarily a violation of basic right, as is moreover a society in which there are individuals who altogether lack property (PR §§ 46,R, 57).

Punishment. "Abstract right" is treated by Hegel under three main headings: property, contract, and injustice or wrong (*Unrecht*). Under the first heading he treats of the relation of a person to external objects; under the second, of relations between persons, through which they constitute a "common will"; under the third heading, Hegel deals with the opposition between the "universal will" implied in the mutual recognition between persons and the "particular will" that may set itself against the universal and do wrong (PR § 81). When wrong takes the form of an intentional violation of the right of a person, it is *crime* (PR § 95).

Hegel's theory of punishment is retributive, in the sense that he believes that a criminal act deserves to be punished solely because it is a violation of right, and that the beneficial consequences of punishing a crime are incidental to the justification of punishment (PR §§ 99–100). One theme in Hegel's theory of punishment is the claim that a criminal act, although externally real, is inwardly "null" or self-contradictory, calling forth punishment, or an "injury of the injury" to manifest its true nature (PR § 98). Another less obscure and metaphorical theme in Hegel's treatment of punishment is the claim that through the criminal act, a criminal directly *wills* its punishment. In effect, this is a theory of the forfeiture of rights, based on the criminal's consent. By violating the right of another, I give my express consent that a like right of my own should be violated (PR § 100). Hegel's argument that I do so is founded on his theory of recognition, according to which each person implicitly demands from all others an external sphere of rightful freedom and simultaneously concedes a similar sphere to them. When I violate the right of another, the rational meaning of my act is that I renounce my own claim on the right I violate (or on an equivalent right). When I am punished, the state infringes on (what would otherwise be) my right, but it does me no injustice because I have forfeited this right through an act of my own will.

This theory of punishment is well grounded in Hegel's theory of abstract right, and it succeeds, without appealing in any way to consequentialist considerations, in showing how criminals may be punished without any violation of their right. Moreover, it sets (again on purely retributive grounds) upper limits to the punishment that may be rightfully inflicted on a criminal: the punishment, regarded as the infringement of a forfeited right, may not exceed in gravity the right that was violated by the criminal's own act.

Nevertheless, considered in relation to the conclusions Hegel wants to draw from it, the theory is subject to several important limitations. First, it is conceived solely in terms of crimes that violate the rights of persons. Hegel clearly intends his theory to provide a retributivist rationale for punishing all violations of law, even laws (such as those prohibiting forgery, counterfeiting, perjury, and treason) that do not have to do with the protection of individual rights (PR § 95R). Second, since the mechanism of forfeiture of a right is a voluntary renunciation of it, Hegel's theory appears to imply that inalienable rights are also immune to forfeiture. This means that if the right not to be killed is inalienable, then it also cannot be forfeited. That would entail that the death penalty is always wrong, a conclusion Hegel wants to deny (PR § 100A). Finally, Hegel's theory appears to provide a purely retributivist justification only of the claim that punishing a criminal is not contrary to right. It provides no retributivist reason why the state should actually inflict the punishments the theory says they have a right to inflict. Contrary to Hegel's intention, the theory seems to need supplementing by consequentialist considerations in order to furnish such reasons.

V. MORALITY

Perhaps the most prominent theme in Hegel's ethical thought is the contrast between "morality" (*Moralität*) and "ethical life" (*Sittlichkeit*). It is commonly supposed that Hegel is a partisan of "ethical life" and an opponent of "morality"; in the thought of his Jena period, where the contrast originated, this is largely true. But in Hegel's mature moral thought, "morality" is not merely a pejorative term, and the moral outlook is not simply contrasted with the attitude of ethical life. On the contrary, morality is an essential aspect of the ethical life characteristic of the modern state.

Morality is the sphere in which the self is regarded as a volitional "subject." In the subject, the opposition between universal and particular will (which we found in crime) has been internalized; the aim of the moral subject is to make his particular will conform to the universal will. As a subject, the self seeks to actualize itself through its own volition and action, and so a central focus of morality is on the moral responsibility of the subject for acts and their consequences. It is crucial to Hegel's conception of morality that we deserve credit or blame only for real acts and accomplishments, not for mere inner intentions and dispositions. Hegel is the originator of the view, perhaps more often associated with Sartre, that "What the subject is, is the series of its actions" (PR § 124).

On the other hand, Hegel insists that morality is concerned only with the inner or subjective side of these actions and consequences. Hegel contrasts the modern moral attitude toward responsibility with the "naive simplicity" (*Gediegenheit*) of ancient ethical life, which (for example) ignored Oedipus's intentions and held him responsible for the whole compass of his deeds (PR § 117A). From the modern or moral standpoint, we can be held responsible only for those consequences that fall within our "purpose" – what we represented to ourselves as the consequences of our actions (PR § 117); and in assessing our actions morally, they should be considered in relation to the subject's "intention" – the abstract conception of the action that gave the subject a reason to do it (PR § 119). Hegel does insist, however, that because the subject is a thinker, he/we can be held responsible for all those apsects and consequences of our actions that rational reflection might have anticipated – for what Hegel calls the "nature" of the action (PR § 118R).

Modern moral agents further demand of themselves not only that they do what is objectively good but also that they do it with insight into the reasons why it is good; the value and dignity of the moral will consist in an insight and an intention that accord with the good (PR §§ 129–32). Hegel thus agrees with Kant that duty should be done for duty's sake (PR § 133). But he disagrees with the Kantian view that our acts lack moral worth unless they are performed solely from duty. In Hegel's view, an agent's intention accords with the good if the dutifulness of the act is, under the circumstances, a sufficient reason for that agent to do that act; where this is the case, the presence and efficacy of sensuous or self-interested motives take nothing away from the act's moral worth.

Even in his mature thought Hegel emphasizes the limits of the moral standpoint. He repeats his criticism of the Kantian moral principle, that it is unable to provide any determinate moral guidance (PR § 135); further, he maintains that the standpoint of morality generally is incapable of yielding a determinate doctrine of duties (PR § 148R). Sometimes the charge that the moral standpoint is "formal" and "empty of content" is presented merely as a criticism of Kant's "formula of universal law": "So act that you can will the maxim of your action to be a universal law." Hegel's charge is that this formula fails to distinguish morally permissible maxims from impermissible ones.

This criticism of Kant, although prominent in Hegel's writings and long associated with his name, was in effect taken over from Fichte, who regarded all Kant's formulations of the moral law as of "merely heuristic" import. Fichte held that our moral duty must be recognized in each individual case by conscientious reflection on particular circumstances. His principle of morality was unashamedly formal: "Always act according to the best conviction of your duty, or: Act according to your conscience."[2] In the *Phenomenology of Spirit*, Hegel follows Fichte in regarding "conscience" as the final criterion of duty from the moral standpoint (PhG ¶¶ 632–71). In the *Philosophy of Right*, Hegel draws the true content of our moral duties from ethical life (our duties are specified by our concrete relationships to individuals and institutions within an ethical order). Even there, however, Hegel regards the subject's moral conscience as indispensable in dealing with inevitable cases of ethical indeterminacy and conflict (PR § 148R).

Hegel emphasizes the sanctity of individual conscience as part of the modern recognition of the value of subjectivity (PR § 138). At the same time, however, he sees conscience as subject to an unavoidable moral ambiguity. In its self-centeredness, even self-worship, the attitude of conscience, for all its pretended purity, is very close to the essence of moral evil (PR § 139). Considered as a genuine moral criterion, the appeal to conscience is not, as Fichte would have it, merely an affair of the subject's inwardness. Instead, Hegel insists, it essentially involves language, and the social institution of giving and accepting subjective assurances of the agent's conscientiousness (PhG ¶ 652). By themselves, moreover, these assurances are always ambiguous and open to interpretation by others. If, in deciding what is right for you, there is no appeal beyond your own subjective conscience, then when I judge the morality of your action, it is to the same degree up to me whether to take your appeal to conscience as honest or as hypocritical (PhG ¶¶ 644–60).

In the *Philosophy of Right*, Hegel strongly criticizes an extreme or aberrant form of subjectivism to which he thinks the morality of conscience is prone: the "ethics of conviction" that he associates with the moral philosophy of Jakob Friedrich Fries (1773–1843). This is the view that no act can be morally condemned as long as the agent followed his own conscience or moral convictions (no matter how wrong and misguided those convictions might be). Hegel regards this view as a reduction to absurdity of the inherent emptiness of the moral standpoint if it is considered in abstraction from ethical life (PR § 140R).

In effect, Hegel thinks, the ethics of conviction abolishes the distinction between moral good and evil, because for it any content counts as "good" as long as it is accompanied by the subject's conviction that it is "good." But this provides so little content to the good will that it can no longer be distinguished from a thoroughly evil will. Thus, just as the sphere of abstract right showed its limitations by eventuating in the category of wrong, so the limits of morality are shown by its culminating in the category of evil. As the sphere of abstract right passed over into that of morality, so the sphere of morality is transcended in the sphere of ethical life.

VI. ETHICAL LIFE

Hegel's use of the term *Sittlichkeit*, which might be translated from ordinary German as "customary morality," has often been inter-

preted as an endorsement of moral traditionalism, of the view that
to do what is morally right, all I need to do is act in conformity with
the accepted standards of my people and culture. It is true that Hegel
regards objective and determinate moral standards as founded on the
organization of a concrete social order, and that he regards some
enlightenment moral theories as shallow and overly individualistic.
But Hegel's conception of the ethical life of modern society (as presented in the *Philosophy of Right*) is not conservative or traditionalist in its orientation. Hegel insists that the institutions of the modern state have a claim on us only because they are *rational* (PR §
258R), and Hegel takes it to be the function of rational reflection to
confirm what we do by custom and habit through insight and scientific cognition (PR § 147R). The "ethical" standpoint in Hegel is
better interpreted as a certain type of critical reflection on existing
social institutions than as a rejection of such reflection.

The point of Hegel's emphasis on custom is not to endorse what is
old or traditional, but to stress the importance of freedom, that is,
self-harmony or being with oneself in one's social life, as the foundation of ethical norms. Hegel means to criticize both ethical and
political views that treat ethics entirely as a matter of *coercion* or
constraint, whether the external coercion of the state in matters of
abstract right, or the inner self-coercion characteristic of the moral
standpoint (especially as represented by Kant and Fichte).

Ethical subjectivity: virtue and duty. This issue is the focus of
Hegel's first use of the term *Sittlichkeit* in contrast to *Moralität*,
which occurs in 1802 (GW 426/183) and concerns issues in Fichte's
moral psychology. Hegel feels that the divorce of reason from sense
in Kant and Fichte, and insistence on the constraint of the empirical
self by the rational self, represents an unhealthy form of self-
alienation. The term "ethical life" is coined to describe a state of the
human will in which reason and sense are in harmony. Accordingly,
"ethical life" originally refers to an ethics of character, emphasizing
rational dispositions and practical judgment in concrete situations,
in contrast to a morality of norms, where the emphasis is on deriving particular actions from general rules.

Hegel associates the ethical attitude with virtue: "the ethical insofar as it is reflected in individual character determined through nature" (PR § 150). He intends this conception of virtue to be Aristotelian, involving natural dispositions so constituted that they follow a
rational principle (VGP 2:222–24/204–6). The virtuous person is

one whose desires and inclinations are so constituted by nature and education that they are in harmony with right reason. Virtuous people not only do what they ought but desire what they should, and are pleased and pained by the right things. Thus there are two ways of doing the right thing without exhibiting virtue. Kant is correct when he denies virtue to the person who does good to others because it happens to please him to spread joy around. Equally, however, there is no virtue in one of Kant's favorite examples of the good will: the cold-hearted man who thwarts his inclinations and behaves kindly toward others purely from a sense of moral duty.

From the standpoint of morality, Hegel insists, any act that accords with the good may be considered a duty (PR § 133). Moral duties are experienced as constraints on our will but have no specifiable content. Ethical duties, by contrast, are "duties of relationships" (PR § 150). They are the actions we perform in fulfillment of the social roles that constitute our concrete identity as individuals. The fulfillment of these social roles is also self-fulfillment. Moral duties tell me what I must do in order to go about my own personal business with a clear conscience; they constrain me, so that my proper life begins only when they have been discharged. Ethical duties, however, are "the substance of my own being" (PR § 148). They include the love I feel for my family and the self-satisfaction I get from my profession. Leaving them unfulfilled would not so much offend my conscience as empty my life of its meaning. For this reason, Hegel insists that ethical duties are not constraining but liberating (PR § 149).

This does not mean that ethical conduct maximizes the agent's self-interest, any more than it means that it conforms to some impartial universal law or that it maximizes the general tendency of pleasure over pain. We do not experience a fulfilling family or professional life as a sacrifice of personal happiness, even though we know we could often do better for our own interests if we ignored the duties they impose. Ethical conduct would not be fulfilling if it cut too deeply into our happiness, but it seldom maximizes our self-interest. Hegel takes ethical action to be the most-powerful, as well as the most-admirable, mode of human conduct. If he is right, then that means that most of social life can be explained neither by egoistic motives nor by adherence to a universalistic morality, nor by both together. Yet these are the only two forms of motivation officially acknowledged by most modern ethical, social, or economic theories.

Ethical objectivity: the rational social order. As we can see from his account of ethical duty, Hegel thinks that the opposition of reason and sense goes hand in hand with another opposition, between social norms and individual moral reflection. Where individuals do not feel themselves at one with their social being, they will regard what is particular to themselves, their inclinations or sensuous desires, as something to be overcome or suppressed if their life is to conform to rational or universal standards, whose true source (whether moralists realize it or not) is the social reason embodied in their culture.

Hegel developed the conception of ethical life at a time when he was strongly influenced by his idealized picture of ancient Greek society, with its beautiful harmony of reason and sense, nature and spirit, individual and community. Accordingly, his primary image of ethical life is that of a society in which these harmonies are immediate, unreflective. But in *The Philosophy of Right*, Hegel is attempting to describe an ethical life that is distinctively modern, hence reflective and subjective in a way that Greek ethical life could not have been. At times Hegel still uses the term *Sittlichkeit* with connotations of unreflective and immediate acceptance of social norms; in some of these uses, however, the term has for that reason a pejorative connotation, since it implies a lack of subjective freedom (PR § 26). In the modern world, Hegel thinks, the harmony of ethical life need no longer be an unreflective harmony, but may be a rational harmony won through philosophical understanding. And he explicitly distinguishes the unreflective attitudes of "identity" or "trust" toward the ethical order from the attitudes of "insight" and "philosophical cognition" that are more appropriate in the modern world (PR § 147R). It is the avowed purpose of *The Philosophy of Right* to provide us with such cognition of the ethical life of the modern state (PR Preface 14).

This of course presumes that philosophical reflection on the state will inevitably result in its rational acceptance; thus it gives the impression that Hegel's attitude toward social norms is in principle an uncritical one. We will understand that this impression is a misleading one if we come to appreciate the fact that the ethical life of the modern state of which Hegel writes is not so much a description of any existing state as it is a rational reconstruction or projection of the form of the state based on Hegel's theory of modern humanity's self-understanding. Hegel explicitly distinguishes the "actual" state with which his theory deals from the various "existing" states we see before us, all of which are, to be sure, actual to a degree, but whose actuality is disfigured by contingencies and human failures of various kinds (PR § 258A).

The ethical as a rational standard. At no time in his career does Hegel regard just any social order that happens to exist as "ethical." A social order, and especially a state, counts as ethical only in virtue of its rationality (PR §§ 145, 258). To the extent that a social order is not rational, it is also not ethical. The members of a social order will not be generally fulfilled by their ethical duties unless the social order as a whole is harmonious and well constituted. Further, reflective individuals will not be able to find their lives in society fulfilling unless their reflection reveals to them the rational structure of their society. The fundamental aim of the *Philosophy of Right* is to provide a theoretical understanding of this kind for a rational modern state: "to win for the rational content a rational form" (PR Preface 14). It follows that ethical virtue and ethical duty are possible for reflective individuals only in a society which is objectively rational. Only such a society is "ethical" in Hegel's sense of the term.

The whole of the *Philosophy of Right* is Hegel's attempt to articulate these standards of rationality for a modern state. But there are two general criteria of ethical rationality that Hegel applies to societies irrespective of their historical position. First, to be ethical, a social order must be "articulated": it must involve the differentiation of social institutions – the religious realm and the political, the family and the state. (Oriental despotism, for this reason, is considered a pre-ethical form of society [PR § 355, cf. PR § 270R].) Second, ethical life requires the acknowledgement of human individuality as a value. Hegel counts Greek society as the first form of ethical life only because it was among the Greeks that the value of individuality first developed; moreover, because modern society displays the higher flowering of individuality, in the form of persons with abstract rights and subjects with moral freedom, it is more fully ethical than ancient Greece (PR § 150R).

Thus the Hegelian standpoint of ethical life does not involve an uncritical acceptance of the existing order, but rather a certain type of critical reflection on it. This reflection is based on a comprehension of the rational form of the existing social order in the light of its cultural and historical origins and its embodiment of progressive cultural values, such as those associated with individuality. Hegel intends this kind of reflection to be contrasted with a (Kantian or Fichtean) moralistic reflection based on principles of *a priori* reason, or a critique of the existing order that is founded on an abstract (ahistorical) conception of human nature.

The ethical as a universal standard. One of the connotations of the term *Sittlichkeit* is the suggestion, found in the thought of Johann Gottfried Herder (1744–1803) and other critics of Enlightenment thought, that different societies and cultures may legitimately have different customs and different norms. This suggestion sometimes prompts Hegel's readers to interpret him as a sort of ethical relativist who regards the accepted norms of every society as valid for the members of that society. This interpretion cannot withstand even the most casual acquaintance with Hegel's actual views. He has no hesitation in condemning certain social practices, such as slavery, and certain provisions of Roman law and morality, such as those that permitted creditors to commit bodily mutilation on their debtors and those that made children the property of their parents (PR § 3). More generally, despite the connotations of the term *Sittlichkeit,* Hegel's conception of modern ethical life makes strikingly little provision for cultural diversity between modern states. Hegel's *Philosophy of Right* must be read as a powerful contribution to the argument – directed against the conservative Romanticism of Hegel's age – that the institutions of modern society must be held accountable before the bar of reason.

VII. ETHICS AND THE FREE SOCIETY

Hegelian ethics is founded on *freedom*. Hegel regards the state as the "actuality of the ethical idea" (PR § 257) only because the state is "the actuality of concrete freedom" (PR § 260). Hegel often makes his meaning obscure, but these statements are uncharacteristically lucid; their meaning is quite plain. Nevertheless, we tend to react to them either with puzzlement or outrage. His association of the state with freedom sounds absurd to us because we simply cannot get it through our heads that anyone could hold the view they express. We can interpret it only as an obscure philosopher's paradox, or else as some sort of preposterous Orwellian lie devised by a demented totalitarian who seeks to subvert our common sense.

Max Weber defined the state as the institution that claims a monopoly on the use of violence.³ Since Hobbes, the state has been conceived mainly as a *coercive* institution: for conservatives a preserver of peace and order, for liberals a protector of individual rights, for radicals a promoter of ruling class interests, but always at bottom an enforcer.

What distinguishes Hegel from virtually all other modern social theorists is his view that the state is fundamentally an *ethical* institution, hence founded not on coercion but on freedom (PR § 257). He sees the source of its strength not in force, but in the way its social structure organizes the rights, the subjective freedom, and the welfare of individuals into a harmonious whole, whose rational unity makes possible each individual's identity as a free person, a moral subject, and a fully self-actualized human being. In ethical action, individuals find their fulfillment, which includes a generous measure of subjective freedom and private welfare but is grounded more deeply on the universal, the state, which is an "unmoved end in itself" (PR § 258). Hegel's view is that individuals, as individuals, can be fully self-actualized and concretely free only if they are devoted to ends beyond their own individual welfare, indeed beyond anyone's individual welfare, to universal or collective ends, which are summed up in the rational organization of the state. The state for Hegel is not a mechanism for the keeping of peace, or the enforcement of rights, or the promotion of any interest beyond its own existence. Instead, it is most fundamentally the locus of the higher collective ends, which, by rationally harmonizing the rights and welfare of individuals, liberate them by providing their lives with meaning. As Hegel conceives of the state, its action on individuals is not the external coercion of policemen, but the internal, ethical disposition that fulfills their rational nature and so makes them free.

Hegel does not deny the coercive functions of the state, but he assigns them to the *Notstaat* or "civil society" – that is, to the economic realm, where persons need external protection for their abstract rights and the market needs regulation to keep it in harmony with the collective needs of the community (PR § 183R). In other words, the state appears as a coercive power only from the fragmented and self-interested perspective of individuals as members of civil society. This is simply because only civil society (the so-called "free market") makes the use of coercive force socially necessary on a large scale. The state's real power, however, always rests on a deeper ethical harmony; only through this can it retain the loyalty and support of individuals, which is the basis of all social life, including the unselfconscious co-operation of civil society, and even of the state's monopoly on violence.

Hegel's conception of ethical life thus underwrites a conception of modern social life that is unique among modern theories in its emphasis on spontaneous harmony and free community as a condition for the possibility of all social institutions and relationships. On this conception, a free society is not merely one that protects personal rights and provides for the subjective freedom and welfare of individuals. It is one in which the individual good of its members is brought into rational harmony and grounded in a collective end, which its members understand and pursue both spontaneously and rationally for its own sake.

Hegel thought he saw a free and rational community of this kind in the modern state as it actually exists. Most of us, however, cannot share this vision of our actual social life. For us, modern society remains a battlefield of interests and the state is simply an enforcer, either of some interests over others, or else of the rules of their combat. Thus Hegel's conception of the free society, if it refers to anything, can refer only to a nonexistent freedom, a radically anti-liberal and anti-individualistic ideal of liberation inspiring and haunting our social imagination. From the standpoint of the liberal status quo, however, the same ideal can appear only as a dangerous delusion, one that threatens to deprive us, in the name of freedom itself, of the only sort of freedom we know how to possess. Hegel's ethical thought remains vitally relevant to us because it is still the principal source of those troubled dreams that continue to torment our collective life.

NOTES

1 All translations from the works listed below are my own. The original German pagination will be cited first, separated by a slash (/) from the pagination of the standard English translation.

> Werke   Hegel: Werke: Theorie Werkausgabe. Frankfurt: Suhrkamp Verlag, 1970. Cited by volume.

EL   *Enzyklopädie der philosophischen Wissenschaften* I (1817, rev. 1827, 1830), *Werke* 8.
      Hegel's Logic, translated by William Wallace. Oxford: Oxford University Press, 1975. Cited by Paragraph (§) number. Additions are indicated by an "A".

EG   *Enzyklopädie der philosophischen Wissenschaften* III (1817, rev. 1827, 1830), *Werke* 10.
      Hegel's Philosophy of Mind, translated by William Wallace and A. V. Miller. Oxford: Oxford University Press, 1971. Cited by Paragraph (§) number. Additions are indicated by an "A".

EH   *Enzyklopädie der Philosophischen Wissenschaften* (1817 Heidelberg version). *Hegels Sämtliche Werke*, 4. Auflage der Jubiläumsausgabe, edited by Hermann Glockner. Stuttgart: Friedrich Frommann Verlag, 1968. Volume 6. Cited by paragraph (§) number.

GW   *Glauben und Wissen* (1802), *Werke* 2.
      Faith and Knowledge, translated by Walter Cerf and H. S. Harris. Albany: SUNY Press, 1977.

NP   *Nürnberger Propaedeutik* (1808–1811), *Werke* 4.

NR   *Ueber die wissenschaftliche Behandlungsarten des Naturrechts* (1802), *Werke* 2.
      Natural Law, translated by T. M. Knox. Philadelphia: University of Pennsylvania Press, 1975. Cited by page number.

PhG   *Phänomenologie des Geistes* (1807), *Werke* 3.
      Phenomenology of Spirit, translated by A. V. Miller Oxford: Oxford University Press, 1977. Cited by paragraph (¶) number.

PR   *Philosophie des Rechts* (1821), *Werke* 7.
      Elements of the Philosophy of Right, translated by H. B. Nisbet, edited by Allen W. Wood. Cambridge: Cambridge University Press, 1991. Cited by Paragraph (§) number. Remarks are indicated by an "R", additions by an "A". Preface and sometimes longer paragraphs cited by page number in German edition only.

TJ   *Theologische Jugendschriften* (1793–1800), *Werke* 1.

TE   *Hegel: Three Essays, 1793–1795*, translated by Peter Fuss and John Dobbins. Notre Dame: University of Notre Dame Press, 1984.

ETW   *Early Theological Writings*, translated by T. M. Knox. Philadelphia: University Of Pennsylvania Press, 1971. Cited by page number.

VGP   *Vorlesungen über die Geschichte der Philosophie*, Bd. 1–3, *Werke* 18–20.
Lectures on the History of Philosophy, translated by Elizabeth Haldane. New York: Humanities Press, 1968. Cited by volume and page.

In writings cited by paragraph (§), a comma used before "R" or "A" means "and". Thus. "PR § 33,A" means: "PR § 33 and the addition to § 33"; "PR § 270,R,A" means: "PR § 270 and the remark to § 270 and the addition to § 270".

2 Fichte, *System der Sittenlehre, Sämtliche Werke*, ed. I. H. Fichte (Berlin: deGruyter, 1971), 4,156.

3 Max Weber, "Politics as a Vocation," in *From Max Weber* ed. H.H. Gerth and C.W. Mills (New York: Oxford University Press, 1958), 78.

8 The basic context and structure of Hegel's *Philosophy of Right*

I

My aim in this essay is to sketch the political and philosophical context of Hegel's *Philosophy of Right* and to reconstruct the basic aim and structure of its main argument.[1] I argue that Hegel is a reform-minded liberal who based his political philosophy on the analysis and fulfillment of individual human freedom. Hegel gave this theme a profound twist through his social conception of human individuals. He argued that individual autonomy can be achieved only within a communal context.

II

To understand Hegel's political views, it is helpful to see how they stand with regard to conservatism, romanticism, and liberalism. Hegel has been accused of conservatism or worse. The most common basis for this charge is Hegel's claim that what is rational is actual and what is actual is rational (Preface 24/20). This claim has been taken as a blanket endorsement of the status quo, but in the paragraph headed by this statement, Hegel distinguished between phenomena that embody a rational structure and those that do not. The mere fact that a state exists, on Hegel's view, does not entail that it is either rational or, in Hegel's technical sense, "actual." Hegel's distinction between existence and actuality is tied to his metaphysics, according to which the universe's rational structure progressively actualizes itself. In the political sphere, this means that social institutions aspire and tend to achieve a fundamentally rational form. The basis of this view cannot be explored here. For present

I have published an Addendum to this essay under the title: "Hegel on Political Representation: Laborers, Corporations, and the Monarch," in *The Owl of Minerva* 25 No. 1 (1993), 111-116.

purposes it suffices to note that Hegel's slogan is not a blanket endorsement of extant institutions.[2] This does not, however, determine where Hegel's politics lie in the political spectrum. That requires determining what political institutions Hegel thought were rational and why.

Hegel has been branded a conservative by associating him with the historical school of jurisprudence, whose most prominent representative was Friedrich Karl von Savigny. In a phrase, the historical school of jurisprudence sought to justify (then) contemporary German law by tracing its roots back to Roman law. Hegel refuted this main principle of the historical school by charging it with the genetic fallacy – with a twist. Instead of justifying laws by determining their origins in specific historical circumstances, this effort *de*legitimizes laws because those circumstances no longer exist (§3R)![3] The historical school also opposed codification of civil law because they viewed law as an organic growth thoroughly rooted in a changing society. Codification appeared to them to be antithetical to an organic conception of law and society. Hegel opposed the historical school on this point, too, firmly insisting on the need for law codified and promulgated in the national language as a key element in achieving rational freedom (§§258R, 211R).

Hegel has also been styled the philosopher of the Prussian *Restauration*. This is incredible, in view of Hegel's merciless attack on the leading figure of the *Restauration*, Karl Ludwig von Haller, author of *Restauration der Staatswissenschaft* (1818). Haller appealed to a version of natural law and so is subject to Hegel's criticisms of natural law in general (see below). Haller's version of natural law equated natural law with divine law, and regarded the natural might of the stronger as the basis for their natural right to rule. Haller opposed any binding legal codification, regarding a code only as a way princes could choose to inform judges of their commands. Hegel condemned Haller's view that legal codes are optional and reiterated the irrelevance of historical origins for determining matters of legitimacy (§219R; *cf.* §258R). Hegel further condemned Haller's antirationalism and opposition to codification in a long paragraph and an even longer note appended to it (§258R & N). Hegel's tone in these passages is extremely sharp and makes plain his opposition to the main tenets of the *Restauration*.[4]

Hegel has also been taken as a conservative because he espouses an organic conception of individuals and society. Most organic theories at the time, such as Burke's, were conservative. Organicism opposes atomistic individualism by holding that people do not enter society fully formed in order to satisfy their pre- or non-social aims and interests. According to organic views, individuals are formed, together with their needs, aims, and ways of thinking, within the social group to which they belong. An organic view becomes specifically conservative if it additionally holds that individuals have no conception of themselves apart from their group, that individuals cannot escape their group because it has formed their identities and needs, that individuals thus are incapable of evaluating society by pre- or non-social standards, and that because individuals are formed by their society's cultural traditions and social and political institutions, their society also suits them.

Hegel did espouse an organic conception of individuals and society. However, it is crucial to understand how he recast the issue. Typically it is supposed that there are two positions on this issue. Either individuals are more fundamental than or are in principle independent of society, or vice versa: society is more basic than or "prior to" human individuals. Hegel realized that these two options form a false dichotomy. Briefly, Hegel held that individuals are fundamentally social practitioners. Everything one does, says, or thinks is formed in the context of social practices that provide material and conceptual resources, objects of desire, skills, procedures, and the like. No one acts on the general, merely biological needs for food, safety, companionship, or sex; and no one seeks food, safety, companionship, or sex in general. Rather, one acts on much more specific needs for much more specific kinds of objects that fulfill those needs, and one acts to achieve one's aims in quite specific ways; one's society deeply conditions one's ends because it provides specific objects that meet those ends, and it specifies procedures for obtaining them. Even so, Hegel realized that this fact does not render individuals subservient to society. First, what individuals do depends on their own response to their social context. In addition, Hegel argued that there are no individuals, no social practitioners, without social practices, and vice versa, there are no social practices without social practitioners – without individuals who learn, participate in, perpetuate, *and who modify* those social practices as needed to meet their changing needs, aims, and circumstances. The issue of the ontological priority of individuals or society is bogus.[5] Hegel's views have been widely misunderstood and castigated by critics who were beholden to a false dichotomy.

Conservatives of a certain stripe recognize that social institutions and practices are subject to change in the face of changing circumstances; Hegel's stress on the corrigibility of social practices alone does not absolve him of conservatism. Reform conservatives, as they may be called, do not believe in progress, but will adapt the status quo piecemeal to accommodate ineluctable social, economic, and political changes. Like conservatives in general, reform conservatives are skeptical about our ability to comprehend society rationally, much less to reconstruct it rationally. They place much more trust in customs, traditions, or even prejudice than in human reason, and they regard the non-rational components of human nature as the foundation of society and as a bulwark against the aspirations of rationalist reformers.[6] Conservatives thus stress the importance of a society's molding of individual character and sentiment to inculcate allegiance to one's society. In conservative political thought, feelings of patriotism are fundamental to political allegiance.

Hegel acknowledged the force of Romantic criticisms of the Enlightenment's a-historical, a-social, individualist account of reason, but he held strong Enlightenment ideals concerning human rationality. For Hegel, as for Kant, human rationality is the key to autonomy, to self-determination, and Hegel stressed this point as Kant's great contribution to practical philosophy (§135R). Hegel regarded the demand for rational understanding and justification of norms and institutions as the hallmark of modern times,[7] and he sought an account of society and government that met that demand (Preface 26/21). He also held that, although important, patriotism is too weak and insufficiently rational a basis for a modern state (§273R). In this regard, Hegel was a rationalist in principle, not out of rear-guard action, and so in this crucial regard Hegel was not a conservative, not even a reform conservative. He firmly believed in historical progress as a rational process (§§342, 343, 345). Finally, Hegel's organicism is not inherently conservative because he stressed that a society's practices are subject to rational criticism and revision. This point has been overlooked due to the assumption that rational criticism must be based on non-social standards. Hegel denied this assumption and developed subtle accounts of internal criticism, of self-criticism, and of the social bases for evaluating norms and principles. These views cannot be explored here,[8] but they are crucial for understanding the fundamental role assigned to social practices in Hegel's political philosophy.

Hegel is also reputed to be the philosopher of the reactionary Prussian state. In fact, Hegel's political philosophy became prominent during a fortunate break in conservative dominance. Conservative forces in Germany were in retreat after the Battle of Jena in 1806. The Prussian Restoration began reversing this political trend in 1815 and achieved dominance only after Hegel's death in 1831. Hegel's political philosophy is rightly associated with the core of an energetic liberal reform movement led by Prime Minister Baron Karl vom Stein, Prince Karl August von Hardenberg, Wilhelm von Humbolt, and Baron von Altenstein. The details of Stein's and Hegel's views converged significantly, and Altenstein and Hegel agreed on a number of fundamentals.[9] Among the reforms instituted by Stein were the abolition of trade barriers between provinces, the break-up of the ossified Guild system, and improvements of roads and canals for the sake of commerce. Hardenberg recognized the civil rights of Jews and championed the political interests of the middle class. Altenstein brought Hegel to Berlin in 1818 and fostered the Hegelian school at the University of Berlin, in part as a bulwark against Romantics and the Historical School. Hegel first published the *Philosophy of Right* while at Berlin in 1821.

There was a deep split between these ministers and both the conservative nobility and the superstitious and reactionary king, Friedrich Willhelm III. The king was suspicious and fearful of Stein, and the nobility regarded both Stein and Hardenberg as the worst of republicans. Although the king twice promised a constitution, he probably never intended to provide one. The king belonged to the Rosicrucians, an anti-scientific cabalistic Christian sect devoted to the occult,[10] and he was quite taken with Haller's *Restauration der Staatswissenschaft*. He showed his antipathy to sharing power with the middle class by suppressing Görres's newspaper and book, which advocated these policies, and by ordering his arrest.

Hegel distinguished between the old absolutist form of monarchy and the modern constitutional form, and he held that the constitutional form is the sole rational form worthy of the times (§273). Hegel thus took a decisive and progressive stand on a burning issue in Prussia at the time. Hegel also advocated a permanent representative assembly, although none was to exist in Prussia until 1848. In attacking Savigny and especially Haller, Hegel vociferously attacked views shared by the king. Moreover, his admonition near the end of the Preface to dance in the cross of the present was directed against other-worldliness, in particular, that of the Rosicrucians – including that of the king (Preface 26/22)![11]

Hegel's differences with the Prussian conservatives, the landed nobility or *Junkers*, deserve comment. The *Junkers* favored a monarchy that was independent of popular consent but was nevertheless limited by the nobility's positions in the military, in government, and as land owners. Haller was the political philosopher most closely associated with the *Junker* aspiration to reestablish a feudal state. Hegel opposed these conservative elements. He put the government bureaucracy in the hands of an educated middle class instead of the nobility (§297). He also placed the landed classes in the upper house of his representative assembly, where they would have to function under pressure from the crown above and from the commercial classes from below (§304; *cf.* §302 & R). This institutional arrangement would preclude a return to the feudal "dualistic state" (where power was shared between the king and landed nobility) and would thwart independent political action by the estates, including the landed nobility. In sum, Hegel opposed all the conservative forces of his day.

Hegel unquestionably shares some themes with Romanticism, for example, an organicism according to which things are essentially related by their contrasts, and a social conception of individuals. Romantics loved symbols and viewed the monarch as a symbol of political unity. Hegel's governmental arrangements vaguely resemble Novalis's proposal.[12] The Romantic Görres advocated a corporate constitution that shared political power with the provinces and the middle class. Even so, when one examines their respective treatments of these themes, the differences between Hegel and the Romantics strongly predominate.

In style, Romantics tended to be epigrammatic and intuitive or inspirational rather than rationally systematic or argumentative. They began as fanatic individualists, but they came to view individuals as lacking self-sufficiency, a defect to be corrected by membership in an organically organized society.[13] Romantics were suspicious of capitalism; they venerated the nobility and denigrated the bourgeois as an acquiescent philistine. They fled from their present dissatisfactions into an idealized feudal age. They held that individuals are related to the state through devotion and veneration. They based state authority on religion, and many Romantics reacted against rationalism by converting to Catholicism. Novalis even denounced Protestantism as an interruption of the organic development of humanity.

On all these counts, Hegel differed unequivocally with Romanticism. Hegel regarded the Reformation as an important contribution to the historical development of autonomous, morally reflective individuals who rightly require rational justification for acts and institutions (Preface 27/22).[14] He denied that religious authority is the basis of state authority (§270R), and in his lectures he castigated the Romantics' conversions to Catholicism as willful capitulation to intellectual servitude (§141Z).[15] When Hegel grandiloquently described the state as God standing in the world (§270R), his point was not to divinize the state. One main point of this remark is best understood against the backdrop of the Dialectic of Kant's Second *Critique*. According to Kant, happiness results from fulfilling one's inclinations. For moral agents, on Kant's view, happiness is a gift of divine grace, first, because it's luck that one's causally determined inclinations are morally permissible, and second, because God is required to ensure that one has the luck and ability to achieve one's morally permissible ends.[16] In ways indicated below, Hegel's state is designed to minister to both these allegedly divine tasks.

Although Hegel sought to incorporate many traditional elements, such as corporations, in his view of society, he did so because he thought that they could serve a current rational purpose. Hegel rejected any retreat to a prior age or circumstance. His detailed political studies of Württemberg taught him what the Romantics never realized, that reestablishing a feudal order could not provide a stable state.[17] He looked to the middle class as a crucial foundation of any modern state, both in commerce and in the civil service. Hegel qualified his approval of capitalism (§236), but he did not oppose it and indeed based his political philosophy on a careful rethinking of modern political economy.

Having distinguished Hegel's views from conservatism and Romanticism, I now turn to his stance toward liberalism, in particular to his views on political autonomy, natural law, the social contract tradition, and utilitarianism. Modern liberalism typically has upheld two important principles. One is the principle of individual autonomy, that each person is competent to and ought to participate in making law. The other principle is the rule of justice, the idea that there are standards any law must meet to be good or just. Providing for individual autonomy requires coordinating individual decisions in order to maintain a viable social unit, and conjoining these two principles requires explaining the relationship between autonomous individuals and objective standards of justice. There are three general strategies explaining this relationship. One strategy holds that the general will is an aggregate of individual wills. Another holds that correct policy is independent of individual wills and awaits their discovery. The third, collective strategy holds that there is a general or collective will that is not simply a function of individual wills and is not simply a reflection of some antecedent correct principle.[18] Hegel took a collective approach to reconciling the two liberal principles of individual autonomy and the rule of law. In his view, individuals do play a crucial role in determining the content of law, although it is not performed by plebiscite. Individuals play a role in forming the content of law by maintaining and modifying social practices as needed to secure their freedom and their individual ends. Those social practices necessary for achieving freedom are, in Hegel's view, the proper basis of and content for statutory law. (I return to this point below.)

Hegel's rejection of two standard liberal strategies for justifying normative principles may be considered together, since Hegel makes analogous criticisms of both. One strategy for justifying normative principles or claims, especially in morals, is to appeal to conscience. Another strategy, especially in politics, is to appeal to natural law or, analogously, to natural rights. In either case, one appeals to a kind of self-evidence to justify one's claim or principle. Hegel disputed such alleged "self-evidence" for two basic reasons. First, theories of self-evidence either conflate or fail properly to distinguish between being certain that something is true, and thus believing it, and something's being true, and thus being certain of it. Second, he knew that the claims allegedly justified by appeals to conscience or to natural law are diverse and even mutually incompatible. A main desideratum for any mode of justification is to sort justified from unjustified claims, in order to help sort true from false claims. This is especially important for the controversies in our collective moral and political life. Any mode of justification that can warrant a claim and its negation fails to meet this basic desideratum and is, as such, inadequate. Appeals to conscience or to natural law fail to meet this basic requirement.[19] Hegel also held that appeals to natural law or conscience tend to omit relevant principles or considerations. This produces incomplete accounts of an issue, what Hegel called one-sided or abstract accounts.[20] Although Hegel disagreed fundamentally with standard approaches to determining the *content* of natural law, he nevertheless upheld and revamped a basic principle of natural law, namely, that right is a function of freedom of the individual will. This principle is fundamental to his argument in the *Philosophy of Right.*

Hegel's objections to the social contract tradition are merely suggested in the *Philosophy of Right.* They may be summarized briefly. Hegel argued that the state of nature is arbitrarily contrived to obtain the theorist's desired outcomes, and that abstracting from any points that might be regarded as inessential, arbitrary, or controversial would empty the state of nature of all descriptive content.[21] The principles attributed to the state of nature often have the same sort of justification as natural laws and suffer the same deficiencies. Most important, the social contract misrepresents the nature of our membership in society. Our membership in society is inevitable, necessary, and constitutive of much of our character, whereas the social contract models our membership on an elective association of otherwise independent individuals (§§75R, 100R, 258R, 281R). Viewing membership in society in this way misrepresents ourselves as mutually independent parties to a fictitious contract whereby we agree to join society, or to form a government, in order to achieve some specified range of antecedent interests we independently choose to pursue. This thwarts recognizing and understanding the social dimensions of human life. On this basis, laws or principles of justice can only be seen as restricting individual freedom of action in return for security and peaceful coexistence (§29).[22] Hegel stressed instead the role of laws and principles of justice as enabling conditions for a wide range of aspects of character development and individual action. On this basis he claimed to sketch a far more detailed and accurate account of our social involvements and our political allegiance. Hegel agreed with the social contract tradition that membership in society and obedience to government are matters that require rational justification, but he sought this justification in rational insight into the nature of our involvement in actual institutions (Preface 24–26/20–22, §31R, *cf.* §189R). Taken together, Hegel's most-fundamental objection to the social contract tradition is that the abstractions used by social contract theories to describe the state of nature, and to describe persons in that state, evade a whole range of benefits and obligations we have as members of a politically organized society (including the obligation to defend the state [§§325, 326]). Consequently, social contract theory is implicitly skeptical about those benefits and obligations and is morally and politically irresponsible, since it precludes their proper recognition and analysis. Hegel's objections to the social contract tradition do not, however, preclude him from sharing many issues and points of doctrine with that tradition.

Hegel agreed with one of Kant's main criticisms of utilitarianism, that it cannot account or provide for human autonomy because it takes given desires as the basic locus of value and source of ends.[23] He believed that utilitarianism does not take proper account of the intellectual character of the will; that it involves too atomistic a view of individuals, too instrumental a view of the state and the government; and that it is incompatible with the proper basis of right, which rests on freedom and autonomy. He regarded the concept of utility as an important component of an intelligent grasp of one's alternative courses of action and of the coherence of one's long-range plans (§§20, 63, 77). He also regarded utility writ large, welfare, as a fundamental component of the aims of individuals and organizations and a basic responsibility of a number of civil institutions (§§123, 125, 128–30). However, he viewed freedom as a more-fundamental value than utility – considerations of utility cannot justify sacrificing freedom or individual rights (§§125, 126) – and he regarded securing freedom as the most-basic obligation of governmental institutions. Indeed, Hegel regarded happiness as beyond the competence of political arrangements. A rational state and its government are obliged to secure the conditions for the success of individual actions; they are not obliged to secure success itself, and so not the happiness it brings. These are Hegel's basic reasons for rejecting utilitarianism.

Hegel thus opposed the main forms of liberal thought in his day and in our own. I nevertheless maintain that Hegel is a progressive liberal. One basis for this claim has already been suggested, namely, that Hegel upheld the liberal principles of individual autonomy and the rule of law. There is in fact a deep point of continuity between Hegel and the social contract tradition: both Hegel and the social contract tradition take the analysis of the individual will and its freedom as the starting point for justifying basic political principles and institutions. Indeed, Hegel expressly credits Rousseau with contributing the fundamental idea that the state must be based on the will (§258R).

III

Hegel realized that to be relevant to modern life political philosophy must take economics into account (cf. §189R). This is especially important for a view like Hegel's that provides a social analysis of the origins and justification of normative principles. Early industrialization generated considerable personal and social fragmentation. Hegel recognized that personal and social fragmentation were two sides of the same coin and that the solution to either problem must solve both.[24] Hegel realized that the division of labor, which produces social fragmentation, is not simply an obstacle to an integrated social and political community. Rather, the relations and lifestyles engendered by the division of labor form a substantial set of practices and norms shared among the members of a modern society. Hegel discerned in the workings of modern society an increasing social interdependence that indicated the social, rather than the atomically individual, nature of human beings. He argued that achieving community and actualizing freedom are based on recognizing this common mutual interdependence. Effecting this recognition and its attendant freedom is the very point and purpose of the social and political institutions in Hegel's theory of the state.

Hegel's view of the liberating effects of modern economic developments enabled him to reinterpret Kantian autonomy. Hegel regarded autonomy of the will, our ability to legislate normative laws to ourselves, as Kant's most important contribution to practical philosophy (§135R). Autonomy requires avoiding two kinds of heteronomy, the heteronomy of determining how to act on the basis of naturally given inclinations, and the heteronomy of determining how to act on the basis of external authority. Kant's analysis and defense of autonomy rest on his transcendental idealism. Hegel criticized Kant's transcendental idealism, rejected Kant's metaphysics, and was very sensitive to ways in which Kant's metaphysics caused problems for his theory of action, and hence for his moral theory.[25]

Hegel shared Kant's aim of avoiding the heteronomy of acting on naturally given impulses or inclinations. Unlike Kant, Hegel did not view this as a problem of psychological determinism within the phenomenal realm. Instead, Hegel viewed this much more as a problem of self-knowledge and attitude. This is because no mature adult has inclinations that are causally given by nature; human motives are a joint product of biological nature, cultural inheritance, and individual response to circumstance. Hegel avoided the metaphysical issue of freedom of the will by focusing instead on the moral, social, and political issue of bringing people to understand how (in a well-ordered society) their needs, aspirations, and principles form a rationally acceptable system. This system enables them to lead integrated personal lives, where their individual lives are integrated into a network of social institutions.

Defending human autonomy requires showing how individuals are self-legislators, how they give themselves their own principles, aims, and objects of will. (Hegel called these the "content" of the will [§9].) The problem of heteronomy is serious because Hegel argued that the free, rational, spontaneous human will cannot generate or specify its own principles, aims, or objects *a priori* (§258R). The content of the will thus derives from nature, but it must be transformed into a self-given content: "the drives should become the rational system of the will's determination; to grasp them thus in terms of the concept [of the will] is the content of the [philosophical] science of right" (§19). This statement is crucial; it indicates that the issue of avoiding natural heteronomy by rationally integrating our needs, desires, ends, and actions is basic to Hegel's whole argument in the *Philosophy of Right*. One reason Hegel viewed human freedom as a social phenomenon is that through collective efforts to meet individual needs, natural needs are elaborated into more-specific needs for the kinds of goods communities make available to their members. The social elaboration of needs transforms those needs from a natural level of mere givenness to a social level, indicating that humans come to give themselves their own needs.

One of Hegel's most brilliant insights is how the development of commerce contributes to the development of human enculturation, a collective process whereby we liberate ourselves from our naturally given needs and desires. Political economy is thus crucial for overcoming natural heteronomy and to achieving autonomy. Achieving autonomy from nature is central to Hegel's account of the family and civil society.

IV

Analyzing the structure of Hegel's argument in the *Philosophy of Right* shows that achieving political autonomy is fundamental to Hegel's analysis of the state and government. Hegel divides his exposition into several distinct parts. His introduction sketches an account of the will, freedom, and the nature of right. Part One, "Abstract Right," treats principles governing property, its transfer, and wrongs against property. Part Two, "Morality," treats the rights of moral subjects, responsibility for one's actions, and *a priori* theories of right. Part Three, "Ethical Life" (*Sittlichkeit*), analyzes the principles and institutions governing central aspects of rational social life, including the family, civil society, and the state as a whole, including the government.

The *Philosophy of Right* analyzes the concept of the will (§§4–7, 279R); the main issue is what is required for a will to achieve its freedom.[26] Hegel's introduction indicates two basic requirements for achieving freedom: achieving one's ends and engaging in actions voluntarily. Hegel's sense of "voluntary" combines Aristotle's sense of not regretting one's act after the fact in full view of the actual consequences (§7 & R) with Kant's sense of autonomy, of obeying only laws one legislates for oneself. Acting freely, on Hegel's view, requires both achieving one's ends and matching one's intentions with the consequences of one's acts (*cf.* §§10 & R, 22, 23, 28, 39). Unintended consequences may give grounds for *post facto* regret, or for the sense of being bound by circumstances one did not foresee and would not desire or approve.

The main question of Hegel's analysis is, What sort of action, in what sort of context, constitutes this kind of free action? Hegel's dialectical arguments rely on indirect proof, critically analyzing alternative views that purport to solve this problem. When analyzing alternative accounts of freedom, Hegel's main critical question is, To what extent does the kind of act or intention in question succeed at its aim? Hegel argued that the conditions for successful free action are enormously rich and ultimately involve membership in a well-ordered state. His argument rests on an unspoken principle much like Kant's principle of rational willing: Whoever rationally wills an end is rationally committed to willing the requisite means or conditions for achieving that end.[27] On Hegel's analysis, the most basic end of the human will is to act freely (§27). Hegel held that obligations are generated by commitment to the basic end of willing to be free, and by the consequent commitment to the necessary legitimate means or conditions for achieving freedom (cf. §261R). Correlatively, rights are generated and justified by showing that a right secures some necessary legitimate means or condition for achieving freedom (§§4, 29, 30, 261R). Principles, practices, and institutions are justified by showing that they play a necessary and irreplaceable role in achieving freedom.

Hegel's discussion of "abstract right" concerns basic principles of property rights. It is abstract in three ways. First, actions and principles are (initially) abstracted from interpersonal relations; second, they are abstracted from moral reflection; third, they are abstracted from legal and political institutions. These abstractions are sequentially shed as Hegel's analysis develops. Hegel's argument begins by analyzing a standard liberal individualist proposal for the most-basic free act, taking something into possession. He holds that thoroughly analyzing the presuppositions and the inadequacies of this alleged basic free act ultimately leads to justifying membership in a specific kind of modern state.

According to most modern social contract theories, taking something into possession is the most-elementary free act, at least as regards political philosophy. For example, according to Locke, the rights that make such an act intelligible and possible are natural. In opposition to this view, Hegel expands upon Hume's and Rousseau's lesson that property rights are not natural, but are founded on conventions.[28] Hegel aimed to show that possession and other rights of property exist only on the basis of mutually recognizing the principles that constitute those rights. He defended this point through the internal criticism of the opposed natural law or "possessive individualist" view.

Although Hegel came close to Hume's view that rights are a matter of conventions, Hegel disagreed with Hume about the nature and philosophical import of conventions. Hume held that reason is primarily analytic and deductive, that given motives and desires set the ends of human action, and that custom was the great guide of human life. He therefore stressed the affective and habitual components in the customary basis of conventions. Most significant, while Hume justified conventions in terms of utility, Hegel justified conventions by their contribution to actualizing freedom. This standard follows directly from the concept of a rational will. Hegel stressed that the will is an intellectual and rational faculty (§21R, 258R), and he denied that reason only analyzes and deduces. Reason legislates the fundamental end of human action, achieving freedom, and rationality involves recognizing principles, acting on their basis, and critically assessing or revising them. Consequently, Hegel stressed the rational aspects of social conventions, especially in his discussion of the abstract principles governing property and its exchange (§§13R, 21R, 211R). Hegel highlighted the necessary role of mutual agreement to principles in any system of property rights and the intellectual achievement reflected in such agreement. Such agreement involves a common "object" among individual wills, where that object is a set of principles and their maintenance, since these are required for any successful individual act that is constituted by those principles.

Simply grasping and holding an object is not an adequate example of freedom, because it does not achieve its aim, which includes stability of holding (§45). Mere seizure of things doesn't prohibit others from making off with one's holdings. Possession (or ownership) is distinguished from mere holding by others' recognition that one possesses something (§51). Such recognition involves recognizing a set of principles that govern possession (§71). While such mutual recognition may be implicit in simple possession, it is quite explicit in contractual relations, because contractual relations involve agreeing to the principles of contractual exchange as well as agreeing to the particular exchange governed by a specific contract (§§72–74).

Hegel argued that these property rights are abstract, and that they do not constitute a self-sufficient system of actions and principles because they generate several problems that cannot be resolved within such an abstract system of rights. Hegel analyzed these problems under the heading of "wrong" (*Unrecht*). The first problem is that this system of principles enables agents to commit wrong acts in the form of theft, fraud, or extortion. Hegel noted that, within this system of rights as such, the agreement between contracting parties is merely contingent (§81); the express contractual agreement may be duplicitous (as in fraud) or the exchange may be forced (as in coercion or crime). This abstract system of rights cannot of itself train agents habitually and intentionally to uphold rather than to violate the system of rights. This problem, which is generated on principles internal to the abstract system of property rights (including the fact that people make contracts to advance their personal aims), cannot be solved within the abstract system of rights. It can be solved only within a system of education. This is one way in which an effective and stable system of property rights presupposes a social ethos as one of its conditions of success.

It is possible to define wrongs against property within this abstract system of property rights and to argue that wrong acts are incoherent expressions of freedom. Wrongs against property are defined as acts that violate specific rightful acts of others (§92; cf. §126). Wrongdoers, thieves, seek to own something that rightfully belongs to someone else. Successful theft thus presupposes a system of principles of ownership while also violating that system of principles of ownership. Therefore, thefts are incoherent expressions of freedom (§92).

It is not possible to distinguish between revenge and punishment within the abstract system of property rights. Revenge can be defined within the abstract system of property rights as the informal exchange of bads for (alleged) bads, instead of goods for goods. The principles that define violations are defined within the abstract system of property rights; they simply are the system of property rights. But in addition to principles that define violations, punishment requires impartial application of those principles, and it requires common recognition of the impartiality of judgment. The common recognition of impartial judges directly anticipates social institutions of courts. But courts without impartial judges are illegitimate. Impartial judgment requires individuals to ignore their individual circumstances and to judge according to universally valid and accepted norms (§103). This is much more stringent than can be defined within the abstract system of property rights. Within the abstract system of property rights, agents commit themselves to and act in accord with the system of property rights only insofar as doing so enables them to achieve their private wants and desires. This is an insufficient basis for impartiality, because impartiality may require judging to the disadvantage of one's personal interests. The concept of a particular agent who judges impartially thus transcends the realm of abstract property rights. Indeed, such an agent is fundamentally a moral agent (§104). This is the key to Hegel's transition from "Abstract Right" to "Morality." The abstract system of property rights is not self-sufficient because its maintenance and stability require impartial judges, but the capacity of impartial judgment cannot be defined or developed within the abstract system of property rights. For this reason, the abstract system of property rights must be augmented by moral agency and reflection.

The second part of Hegel's exposition, "Morality," has two basic aims. The first is to enumerate a set of rights that are fundamental to moral agency. The second is to argue that moral principles cannot be generated or justified *a priori*. I treat these in turn.

Hegel distinguished between mere proprietors and moral agents, referring to abstract proprietors as "persons" and moral agents as "subjects." Hegel identified a number of "rights of the subjective will." These rights are due to and required by moral subjects. These rights include the rights only to recognize something (such as a principle) insofar as one adopts it as one's own (§107), only to recognize as valid what one understands to be good (§132), only to be responsible for one's actions insofar as one anticipates their results (§117), and in general to be satisfied with one's acts (§121). These rights are due moral subjects because they are necessary to preserve and promote the autonomy of thought and action that are required to assess alternative courses of action, to justify and accept responsibility for one's acts and their consequences, to evaluate behavior, and to form impartial, well-reasoned judgments. Although the rights of subjectivity are abstract (they are too general to determine any specific injunctions or directives), they are crucial to Hegel's enterprise, and Hegel regarded them as crucial to humanity. The recognition of these rights marks the divide between antiquity and modernity (§124R); freedom simply isn't actual, it doesn't exist, without the free voluntary action of moral subjects (§106).[29]

One responsibility involved in moral reflection is to reflect adequately on the principles, circumstances, and consequences of action. Hegel was aware that the rights due moral subjects just enumerated, as such, allow a radical subjectivism or backsliding due to ignorance or irresponsibility (§132R). He insisted that moral reflection must be based on correct principles (*cf.* §140R), and he insisted on a "right of objectivity" to the effect that agents are responsible for the actual consequences of their acts, even if they were unintended (§§118 & R, 120, 132R). Furthermore, important as the rights and capacities of moral subjectivity are, Hegel held that moral reflection alone can neither generate nor justify a set of substantive moral principles (§258R). Having criticized natural law theory and utilitarianism elsewhere, Hegel focused his critical attention in *The Philosophy of Right* on the two strongest remaining contenders, Kant's ethics and the ethics of conscience. I treat these in turn.

Hegel's criticisms of Kant's moral theory are as brief and obscure as they are crucial to his whole undertaking; only their basic import may be indicated here. One basic issue between Hegel and Kant concerns moral motivation. Hegel agreed with Kant that duties ought to be done because they are duties (§133), but he disagreed with Kant that duties ought to be done *solely* because they are duties. Kant distinguished sharply between motives and ends of action, and he held that the cause of action, the motive, determines the moral worth of an action. Acting from duty is the sole morally worthy motive. Any other motive is an inclination. While acting on inclination may lead one to do the right act, it cannot give an act unconditional moral worth, because inclinations only contingently motivate right acts.[30] Kant devised a special motive, "respect," just for this case. According to Kant, respect for law is the sole rationally generated motive. Consequently it is the sole motive that reflects our transcendental freedom, and it is the sole motive that is entirely self-determined.[31] Thus it contrasts with all other "heteronomous" motives that may be caused by our (phenomenal) psychology, upbringing, environment, or other circumstance not chosen by us. (Kant allowed us to perform duties out of mixed motives, as long as the motive of respect predominates and as long as we strive to act solely on the basis of respect.)[32]

Hegel held that there can be no such pure rational motive as Kant's "respect for law." One of his reasons is straightforward: He held that Kant's arguments for transcendental idealism, and in particular for the distinction between phenomena and noumena, are inadequate.

Hence transcendental idealism provides no legitimate basis for distinguishing between the sole noumenally grounded motive of respect and all other phenomenally grounded motives (that is, inclinations) in the way Kant proposed. Furthermore, all else being equal, parsimony requires a uniform account of human motivation. This point underscores how Kant devised his account of "respect" to fit the narrow requirements of transcendental idealism.[33] Hegel also held that one cannot distinguish sharply between motives, as causes of action, and the ends of action. He held that humans act on the basis of the ends they seek to achieve, and that there are various ends sought in any action. In addition to any specific ends, Hegel believed that there is always a general end to any act, the end of enjoying one's abilities. This is reflected in successfully executing one's intended action, which results in what Hegel called "self-satisfaction" (§124 & R). If Hegel is right about this, then Kant's view that we must abstract from all ends, determine how to act solely on the formal requirement of the conformity of a maxim to universal lawfulness, and perform an act solely because it is a duty, is impossible (cf. §124). It is impossible because such an abstraction would leave us with no reason to act, because reasons for acting always concern ends. If we did nevertheless act, our action could not be specified on the basis of pure dutifulness. Since Kant's requirement of doing one's duty solely because it is a duty abstracts from all ends, it cannot have any content at all, since (Hegel held) actions are always conceived, intended, and performed in view of ends (§135R).[34]

Hegel also charged that Kant's Categorical Imperative cannot determine duties unless some other principle is antecedently presupposed. Hegel's charge appears to rest on some crude mistakes about Kant's test of the categorical imperative. Kant insisted, after all, that the categorical imperative requires "anthropology" to apply it to human circumstances.[35] Kant's categorical imperative takes into account a wide range of logically contingent information about our abilities, ends, and circumstances by using a principle of rational willing, that "who wills the end, wills (so far as reason has decisive influence on his [or her] action) also the means which are indispensably necessary and in his power."[36] Hegel seems to ignore this crucial aspect of Kant's view.

This Kantian rejoinder does not meet Hegel's fundamental contention. Roughly put, on Kant's theory, inclinations propose and the categorical imperative, as a test on maxims, disposes. The main way in which the categorical imperative disposes of maxims is by ruling out selfish maxims, maxims that allow one to make demands on others without allowing them to make similar demands on oneself. Because maxims are formed in specific circumstances, in view of an agent's desires, abilities, and available resources, Kant's test on maxims does presuppose a rich context of wants, ends, circumstances, practices, and institutions. Hegel argued that the categorical imperative cannot be the *fundamental* normative principle, because what needs evaluation is the normative status of precisely those antecedent wants, ends, social circumstances, practices, and institutions. The idea that ends are permissible insofar as they do not violate the categorical imperative must itself be justified by a normative analysis of ends and their permissibility. Perhaps, for example, theft does involve treating others as a mere means, but why is property legitimate to begin with? Kant of course offered grounds to suppose, for instance, that human life must be respected and that there must be property. Human life is to be respected because humans are rational agents and as such have an incommensurable value called "dignity."[37] Property must be possible (roughly) because to regard any object as, in principle, ownerless involves contradicting the principle that the will can and must be able to make use of anything it needs.[38] Hegel's point is that this is where the fundamental normative principles and justifications lie, not in subsequent tests of the categorical imperative about whether our maxims are consistent with such norms and institutions (§135R). I must leave aside for now issues between Kant and Hegel about the nature and adequacy of Kant's reasoning about these more fundamental matters.

Hegel continued his argument to show that moral reflection is not sufficient, of itself, to generate a substantive set of moral norms by criticizing the ethics of conscience. He distinguished two forms of conscience. One holds that conscience, of itself, is sufficient to generate a substantive set of moral norms. The other holds that conscience is an important aspect of moral reflection that is properly rooted in an ongoing system of social practices. Hegel called this latter type "true conscience," and he indicated that this type was not the object of his criticism (§137 & R). He criticized only the stronger type of conscience that claims normative self-sufficiency. To repeat, Hegel's basic objection to this type of theory of conscience is that it cannot reliably and adequately distinguish between subjective certainty, being convinced of something and thus concluding that it is right, and objective certainty, where the correctness of a principle forms the basis on which one is certain of its rightness (§137 & R). Subjective certainty is no guarantee of the correctness of moral principles, yet reasoning with correct moral principles is essential (§140R).

To recapitulate, one aim of Hegel's analysis of "Morality" was to show that moral reflection is essential to the individual integrity required for impartial judgment and for the stability of the system of property conventions, and yet that moral reflection *alone* cannot establish any principles of right. If Hegel was right that objective principles cannot be justified on the basis of natural law, utility, Kant's categorical imperative, or conscience, then he had very strong grounds for concluding, by elimination, that the relevant standards must be social. If Hegel substantiated these conclusions, then he established an important pair of biconditionals: first, principles of right can exist if and only if there is personal integrity and moral reflection; second, there are principles of right on which to reflect if and only if there are social practices. (Social practices were presented abstractly in "Abstract Right" as mutually recognized principles.) Such a system of integrated principles, practices, and morally developed agents is what Hegel called *Sittlichkeit* ("ethics" or "ethical life").

Hegel explicitly stated that his argument for introducing "Ethical Life" is regressive, since the communal phenomena analyzed in this Part provide the ground for the possibility of the phenomena analyzed in "Abstract Right" and "Morality" (§141R). "Ethical Life" analyzes a wide range of social practices that form the basis of legitimate normative principles. Social practices, however, cannot occur without social practitioners, agents who behave in accordance with social practices and who understand themselves and others as engaging in those practices. Thus these practices also include subjective awareness on the part of agents of their own actions and the actions of others. In "Abstract Right" Hegel argued that property rights cannot be understood adequately or established in abstraction from subjective reflection on the principles of action. In "Morality" Hegel argued that moral reflection on principles of action cannot be understood adequately or be effective apart from some set of objectively valid norms. In "Ethical Life" he argued that rational social life accounts both for the validity of objective norms and for the conscious knowledge and acceptance of those norms. His justification of ethical life is that the conditions for the possibility of abstract right and of morality are not given within the accounts of abstract right or of morality. The conditions for their possibility – their grounds – are provided only by ethical life.

Hegel held that normative moral, social, and political theory should focus on rational social life because so doing solves the related problems of the possibility, the principles, and the motivation of moral action. Since rational social life couldn't exist unless it were practiced and supported by individuals, action in accordance with its norms must be possible (§151), and transcendental idealism is not required to explain the possibility of moral action. Second, since rational social life consists of recognizable norms that guide the action of particular people, there can be no problem in principle about its being abstract or empty of content (§150R). Third, since individuals inevitably develop their aims, desires, skills, and knowledge by maturing within their particular society, they naturally tend to develop characters and a self-understanding that value what their rational social life promotes. Hence, by doing what their rational social life requires, they fulfill aims essential to their own characters, and their motivation for behaving ethically is quite understandable (§§152–55).

Even so, justifying *Sittlichkeit* as the proper locus for analyzing human freedom and its conditions does not, of itself, solve much. Hegel addressed several problems in his analysis of *Sittlichkeit*. First, how does rationally ordered social life enable agents to achieve their aims successfully? Second, how can the principle that one is responsible only for the anticipated consequences of one's acts be reconciled with the principle that one is responsible for all the consequences of one's acts? Hegel proposed to reconcile these principles by regularizing and making known the social context of individual action, so that individuals could act knowingly and reliably succeed. A third problem then is, how can the social context of action be regularized and made known? Fourth, how are natural needs and desires customized to make them rational self-given ends? Fifth, How can political autonomy, the right to obey only those laws and principles that one legislates for oneself, be preserved within a social context? finally, how do extant institutions perform the functions required by the points just indicated?

The usual objection to Hegel's emphasis on a community's practices and standards is that it simply endorses the status quo of any community. Two points should be made in advance. First, on Hegel's account, not just any communal structure will do; it must be a structure that in fact aids the achievement of individual freedom. This is central to his whole account of the justification of acts, norms, and institutions; they are justified only insofar as they make a definite and irreplaceable contribution to achieving individual freedom. Moreover, Hegel required that an adequate rational society make the civil, legal, and political structure of the community known to its members, along with how individual activities contribute to and benefit from this structure. This is crucial to preserving political autonomy within a social context. Ultimately, Hegel required that a society be so effective at providing this knowledge and at satisfying individual needs for objects, relations, culture, and for belonging, that once individuals understand all of these features of their community and their roles within it, individuals will affirm their community as fulfilling their aims, requirements, and needs. Only in this way can individuals freely engage in actions in their society. This requirement stems directly from Hegel's initial analysis of freedom (§7).

Because humans act collectively to promote their freedom, the primary question of modern political philosophy, on Hegel's view, is not *a priori* what institutions would fulfill these functions, but rather how and to what extent existing institutions do fulfill these functions. This is why Hegel analyzed the rationality of extant institutions.[39] Some of the institutions to which Hegel assigned basic functions are now long gone, while others never developed in the form he described. Although we may find neither merit nor likelihood in the specific institutions Hegel advocated, we may still learn much from his accounts of the functions he assigned to various institutions and how those institutions are supposed to fulfill those functions. I turn now to an overview of Hegel's interpretation of modern social and political life, of the roles he assigned to the family, civil society, and the government. (For a graphic illustration, see the organizational chart of Hegel's state following the notes at the end of this essay.)

Among other things, the family provides an institutional context for customizing and rationalizing sexual desire, and it affords a way of fulfilling the duty to raise the next generation. This involves not simply reproducing human organisms but raising human beings by introducing the child to the ways and means available in one's society for meeting basic needs and by educating the child in the principles and practices established in one's society for achieving various purposes and upholding various rights. Customizing whatever needs are due solely to biological and psychological nature occurs here, through upbringing and socialization (§§174, 175). Since in modern economies the vast majority of families do not produce for their own subsistence, the family must have dealings with the economic and civil life of society.

Civil society comprises the institutions and practices involved in the production, distribution, and consumption of products that meet a variety of needs and wants. Hegel called this the "system of needs" (§188). The system of needs transforms natural impulses, needs, and wants by providing socially specific goods that meet those needs and wants, by modifying and multiplying those needs and wants (§§185, 187R, 193, 194 & R), and by inculcating the social practices through which individuals can achieve their ends (§§182, 183, 187). Hegel saw what atomistic individualists overlook in the division of labor: specialization requires coordination, and coordination requires conformity to "the universal," to common practices (§§182, 198, 199). (Hegel indicated that the "universal" he analyzed just *are* those practices, since those practices are the relations among individuals in question [§182].) Furthermore, the collective development of social practices, based on the joint pursuit of individual aims, *is* the collective development of implicit principles of right (§187R; *cf.* §§260, 270). Hegel stressed the fact that these "universal" principles derive their content from the ends and activities of particular agents who determine for themselves what to do (§187R). This is the most-fundamental role individuals have in developing the content of principles of right, in Hegel's view. Legitimate law simply codifies those practices that require legal protection in order to remain effective (§§209–12). In this connection he refers back to his opening endorsement of Montesquieu's point that laws are justified on the basis of their systematic interconnection within present social circumstances (§§212, 3R).

Civil society and the economy must support the basic freedom of choosing one's vocation (§§206, 207). Everyone has equal civil (and later, political) rights, not on the basis of *recherché* grounds of the incommensurable value of rational agency (Kant's "dignity"), but because there is no legitimate reason to distinguish among persons to the disadvantage of some and the advantage of others (§§36, 38, 209R, 270N3). (Hegel explicitly repudiated the antisemitism of his conservative and liberal contemporaries [§209R; cf. §270N3].)

Civil society contains three distinct kinds of institution: the Administration of Justice, the Public Authority, and Corporations. The Administration of Justice codifies, promulgates, and administers statutory law. Codification makes explicit the normative principles implicit in social practices (§§209–12; cf. §§187R, 249). Promulgating codified law contributes to informing people about the structure of their social context of action (§§132R, 209, 211R, 215; cf. 228R). This is why law must be codified and promulgated in the national language (§216), and why judicial proceedings must be public (§§224, 228R). The enforcement of law regularizes the context of individual action and protects and preserves the social practices people have developed to exercise their freedom and achieve their individual aims (§§208, 210, 218, 219). Establishing recognized courts replaces revenge with punishment (§220).

The Public Authority is responsible for removing or remedying "accidental hindrances" to achieving individual ends; it minimizes and tends to the natural and social accidents that impair or disrupt successful free individual action (§§230–33, 235). Its responsibilities include crime prevention and penal justice (§233), price controls on basic commodities (§236), civil engineering, utilities, and public health (§236R), public education (§239), moderation of economic fluctuations (including unemployment) (§236), the eradication of the causes of poverty and poverty relief (§§240, 241, 242, 244),[40] and the authorization and regulation of corporations (§252). If these factors are not regulated, individuals cannot plan or conduct their lives reliably; their freedom is compromised.

The coordination among different economic agents, whether persons or businesses, entails that the economy consists of sectors or branches of industry or commerce (§201, 251). This results from the division of labor and the distribution of specialized manufacture across various regions of the country. In modern specialized production, individual jobs and businesses depend on a complex of far-flung economic factors (§183; *cf.* §§182, 187, 289R, 332). Hegel recognized this fact and sought to ensure that such factors would not hold uncomprehended sway over people's activities and lives. Such unknown influences limit freedom and autonomy. He addressed this need by advocating a certain kind of professional and commercial "corporation." These corporations are a kind of trade association, one for each significant branch of the economy, to which all people working in that sector belong. Membership in a corporation integrates one's gainful employment explicitly into a sector of the economy and provides information about how one's sector of the economy fits with and depends on the other sectors. Corporations also moderate the impact of business fluctuations on their members (§§252 & R, 253 & R). Corporations counteract the divisive tendencies of individual self-seeking in commerce by explicitly recognizing individual contributions to the corporate and social good and by bringing together people who would otherwise form two antagonistic groups, an underclass of rabble and a class of elite captains of industry who would wield inordinate social influence due to their disproportionate wealth (§§244, 253R).

The final institution in Hegel's state is a central goverment.[41] He distinguished between the government and the state as a whole. He called the government the "strictly political state" (§§273, 276) and reserved the term "state" for the whole of a civilly and politically well-organized society (§§257–71). He called civil society – *sans* representative government – "the state external" (§183). Civil society is an "external" state because it does not fulfill the requirements of political autonomy and because the state institutions in civil society, the Administration of Justice and the Public Authority, are viewed as mere instruments for achieving personal aims. The members of civil society are bourgeois but not (as such) citizens, since they must obey coercive laws without recognizing, and without having public and official recognition of, their role in constituting legitimate law. The Public Authority and the Administration of Justice act on their behalf, but not under their purview. Thus the political aspect of autonomy is not achieved within civil society (*cf.* §266). Achieving political autonomy and, with that, citizenship is the primary function of Hegel's government.

Hegel ascribed sovereignty to the state as a whole, and not simply to the monarch or even to "the princely power" (*die fürstliche Gewalt* or "crown") as a whole (§278). No element of the state holds sovereignty (although each has an institutionally defined role in sovereignty), and no office is a private, individual possession (§§277, 278R). Hegel treated the government under the general heading of the constitution. It is important to note that, although Hegel said that the constitution ought to be viewed as eternal (§273R), he recognized that the constitution is subject to change (§§273R, 298). What he said of law in general holds of constitutional law as well, namely, that to be executed, a law must be determinate. By being specific enough to be acted upon, a law must have what Hegel called an "empirical side," where this empirical side is subject to change in the process of implementing the law (§299R). Although this may seem to contravene the nature of law, it does not since, as Hegel stressed, following Montesquieu (§3R), a law is justified by the function it presently performs within an integrated society. As conditions change, so must laws change in order to remain legitimate and effective (§298). In this way, Hegel noted in his lectures, a country can gradually bring its constitution to a very different condition from where it began (§298Z).[42] Hegel regarded this not as an inevitable concession to historical contingency, but as a rational process of gradual collective revision of the legal conditions required to achieve and preserve freedom. He held that the constitution ought to be regarded as eternal to ensure that change results gradually from detailed knowledge of genuine need, rather than from insufficiently informed ratiocination. He equally held that reform must be a deliberate ongoing process, so that it does not require revolution.

Hegel's government comprises the "princely power" or Crown, the Executive, and the Legislature (§273). The Crown consists of a hereditary monarch and chief ministers of state (§275). The ministers formulate laws that articulate and protect the basic social practices necessary for individual free action (§283). Cabinet ministers must meet objective qualifications (§§291, 292) and are strictly accountable for their actions (§284). At their recommendation laws are enacted by the monarch (§§275, 283, 284). The Crown protects the interests of one's state and one's interests in the state through foreign policy, either by diplomacy or war (§329). The Executive administers the laws necessary for knowledgeable individual free action (§287). The Legislature consists of an advisory body, drawn from high-level servants with direct ties to the Crown and the Executive (§300), and the bicameral Estates Assembly.

Hegel assigned a quite restricted but very important role to the Estates Assembly. The Estates Assembly provides crucial popular insight into affairs of state (§§287, 301). In particular, the Assembly affords popular insight into the fact that the laws enacted by the Crown and administered by the Executive are laws that codify and protect the social practices in which one participates and through which one achieves one's ends (*cf.* §§314, 315). The Estates Assembly thus places the government under popular purview (§302). Corporate representatives to the lower house of the Estates Assembly are elected by their respective memberships (§§288, 311). Representatives from the agricultural sector, landed aristocrats (§306), inherit their right to enter the upper house (§307). Hegel based his system of representation on the Corporations and other branches of civil society, because doing otherwise would divide political from civil life and leave "political life hanging in the air" (§303R). It must be stressed again that citizens have a hand in developing and modifying social practices as needed, and the law, on Hegel's view, is to follow suit. The main function of Hegel's Estates Assembly is educative, to inform people systematically and thoroughly about the activities of their government and the principles, procedures, and resources for acting within their society, so that individuals can resolve to act in an informed and responsible manner, unencumbered insofar as possible by unexpected consequences. This education and information enables individuals to act voluntarily and autonomously within their society (§301 & R). Hegel expected that when people understood how their society meets their needs and facilitates their ends, they would affirm their membership in society and would act in it willingly. The fact that the institutions of government, especially the legislative assembly, are necessary for free, autonomous action is their primary political justification, according to Hegel.[43]

Hegel opposed rule by open democratic election. He held that democracy rests too much on political sentiment (§273R), that open elections encourage people to vote on the basis of their apparent particular interests at the expense of their interests in the community as a whole (§§281R, 301R), and that the tiny role each elector has in large general elections results in electoral indifference (§311R). Open elections also do not guarantee that each important economic and civil branch of society is represented (§§303R, 308R, 311R). Consequently, open elections threaten to allow what Hegel's corporate representative system was designed to avoid: the overbearing influence of factions, especially of monied interests, on the political process (§§253R, 303R). Hegel also recognized that legislation requires expert knowledge; he expected popular opinion to supply general ideas or feedback about matters of detail (§301R). Finally, Hegel was aware of the relative political inexperience of his contemporary Germans. His civil and political institutions were designed to provide regular, publicly acknowledged, institutionalized channels for political education so that people would not act in political ignorance. Hegel may have opposed standard democratic procedures, but he was a staunch republican, and he took the vital issue of an informed body politic and universal participation in political life much more seriously, and at a much deeper institutional level, than any modern democracy.

V

Perhaps the greatest internal weakness in Hegel's organizational scheme is his account of the monarch. Although the monarch's role is constitutionally narrowly defined, it is also unstable. Hegel defended an inherited monarchy in part because no talent is needed to sign legislation, since the cabinet ministers are experts and are accountable for the entire content of the law (§§283, 284). But he also counted on the monarch's watchful eye from above (in conjunction with scrutiny by the Estates Assembly from below) to hold the ministers responsible (§295). He can't have it both ways.

Hegel built a number of institutional guarantees into his governmental structure by insisting on a division of mutually interdependent powers (§§272R, 286 & R, 301R, 308, 310 & R), and he listed a number of fundamental civil rights (equal rights and freedoms of person, belief, property, profession, and trade [§§35, 36, 38, 41–49, 57, 62R, 66, 206, 207, 209R, 252, 270R]). Still, he placed the courts under the administration of justice (§219). This would make it difficult to accommodate a doctrine of judicial review of legislative or executive action. Hegel emphasized coordination and the cooperative aspects of civil and political institutions (for instance, §§272, 303 & R), although he insisted that cabinet ministers are strictly responsible and accountable for their actions (§284). He did not, however, describe precisely how ministers are to be held accountable. This may be because he published only the "elements" (*Grundlinien*) of the philosophy of right. Hegel may have used this excuse because insisting more explicitly on such institutions might have brought him under official censure – or worse. When agents of the state press for personal or factional interests, then politics becomes contestative, as Hegel knew, and strong constitutional structures are needed – stronger than he published – to deal with misappropriations of power.[44]

These sources of possible administrative recalcitrance or irresponsibility raise the political specter that concerned Weber, that independent interests generated within bureaucracies make them unresponsive to their official obligations and constituents. Hegel did not have the historical experience to share this concern, since in his day the state bureaucracy was relatively new and was in the forefront of reform. Although this problem is not unique to Hegel's institutions, it is a genuine and pressing problem, especially in view of the crucial contribution Hegel's government is to make to political freedom and autonomy.

The last problem I note concerns the actualization of Hegel's rationally structured institutions. Hegel designed his political institutions as a bulwark against the fragmenting tendencies of economic self-interest and the overbearing influence of economic factors on politics, especially the influence of an active and monied entrepreneurial class. Hegel's efforts thus bear witness to the tension between sectors of the economy and a political process aimed at universal freedom and autonomy. Historically, under pressure of economic interests and developments, few of Hegel's institutions developed at all, much less in the specific form he described. The extent to which modern political institutions serve the functions Hegel advocated cannot be explored here, but it is unlikely to be very great, since few of them are officially assigned those functions. By grounding legitimate law and institutions in social practices, including those practices that are part of the economy, Hegel came much closer to historical materialism than Marx recognized – without being an historical materialist.[45] Hegel's theory of historical change, cast in terms of the world-spirit actualizing itself by achieving deeper self-understanding (§§342–43, 345–46), may perhaps gloss the results or significance of some historical developments, but it does not explain the causes or process of historical change. In this regard, Hegel's philosophy is silent where we most need guidance: when facing the problems of achieving genuine political freedom and autonomy through institutional reform. Hegel outlined the basis and rationale of these ideals quite well, but his institutional program remains an idealized image of its age. Marx's political projections are little help, since they require transcending the relative scarcity of goods that makes principles of justice necessary.[46] The persistence of relative scarcity condemns us to politics and to the issues of bourgeois right. Hence Hegel's idealized model retains great political relevance: To what extent do contemporary political institutions secure and promote genuine freedom and political autonomy? To what extent ought or can they be reformed to achieve this basic aim?[47]

NOTES

1 I refer to Hegel's works, including *Grundlinien der Philosophie des Rechts*, in *Werke in Zwanzig Bänden* ed. Moldenhauer & Michel (Frankfurt: Suhrkamp, 1970; cited as *Werke*). I give my own translations. I cite *Elements of the Philosophy of Right* ed. A. W. Wood, tr. H. B. Nisbet (Cambridge: Cambridge University Press, 1991). References to Hegel's Preface are indicated as "Preface," followed by the German page number/ and the page number of Nisbet's translation. With the exception of Hegel's Preface, all references to Hegel's *Philosophy of Right* are given by section number, which are shared by the original and the translations. The "Remarks" Hegel wrote and appended to these sections are designated with an "R" suffix: "§138R." If a section and its remark are cited, they are cited as "§138 & R." Notes are indicated similarly with an "N" suffix; if there is more than one note to a section, its number follows: N3. Citations from lecture notes appended to the *Philosophy of Right* are indicated by a "Z" suffix.

2 See *Enzyklopädie der philosophischen Wissenschaften im Grundrisse I* (*Werke* 8; hereafter "*Enz.*"); *The Encyclopedia Logic* tr. T. F. Geraets, H. S. Harris, & W. A. Suchting (Indianapolis: Hackett, 1991), §6.

3 Reinhold Aris mistakenly attributes to Hegel the very principle of the historical school Hegel criticized (*History of Political Thought in Germany from 1789–1815* [rpt: New York: Kelly, 1968], 227). I have relied on Aris for historical details.

4 See Walter Jaeschke, "Die Vernünftigkeit des Gesetzes" in *Hegels Rechtsphilosophie im Zusammenhang der europäischen Verfassungsgeschichte*, ed. H.-C. Lucas & O. Pöggeler, (Stuttgart-Bad Cannstatt: Frommann-Holzboog, 1986), 221–56.

5 See my *Hegel's Epistemological Realism* (Dordrecht & Boston: Kluwer, 1989 [hereafter *"HER"*]), 166, 169–72. Hegel stated his view in easily misunderstood metaphysical terms. He stated that individuals are related to the ethical order and its powers "as accidents to substance" (§145). This certainly can sound like individuals are subservient to a social whole. Yet Hegel held that "substance is in essence the relation of accidents to itself" (§163R). This is to say that substance is essentially the relation among the "accidents" (properties or members) of something. More briefly, he stated that "substance is the totality of its accidents" (§67R). This doctrine is part of Hegel's holistic metaphysics, and it is stated in the section of the *Encyclopedia* to which Hegel refers in §163R, *Enz.* §150. On Hegel's holism, see *HER*, ch. 10.

6 This characterization of reform conservatism is adapted from Klaus Epstein, *The Genesis of German Conservatism* (Princeton: Princeton University Press, 1966), 13. I have relied much on this work for historical details.

7 This demand and its satisfaction are essential to what Hegel calls the modern "rights of subjectivity" (§§106, 107, 117, 121, 124R, 132) and to Hegel's effort in the *Philosophy of Right* to present and justify an integrated doctrine of rights and duties (§§148R, 149, 150).

8 See *HER*, chs. 1, 6–8.

9 Compare what is said below with Aris's account of Stein's views (*Political Thought*, ch. 13), and see Wood's editorial notes to §§271n2, 273n9, 277n1, 288, 289, 291, 303, and 312.

10 On Rosicrucianism, see John Passmore's entry on Robert Flood in *The Encyclopedia of Philosophy* ed. P. Edwards (New York & London: Macmillan, 1967), vol. 3, 207–8, and Epstein, *Genesis*, pp. 104–11.

11 See Adriaan Peperzak, *Philosophy and Politics: A Commentary on the Preface to Hegel's Philosophy of Right* (Dordrecht: Nijhoff, 1987), 108.

12 Compare Aris's citation from Novalis's 1798 *Athenäum* (*Political Thought* p. 279) with Hegel's account of the government, discussed below.

13 See Jacob Baxa's citation of Friedrich Schlegel in *Einführung in die romantische Staatswissenschaft*, 2nd ed., (Jena: Gustav Fischer, 1931), 68.

14 Also see *Vorlesungen über die Geschichte der Philosophie* III (*Werke* 20; hereafter *"VGP"*), p. 57; *Lectures on the History of Philosophy: The Lectures of 1825–1826* ed. & tr. R. F. Brown and tr. J. M. Stewart (Berkeley: University of California Press, 1990; hereafter *"LHP"*) III, 102–3. Also see *Vorlesungen über die Philosophie der Geschichte* (*Werke* 12; hereafter *"VPG"*), 496–97; *The Philosophy of History* tr. J. Sibree (New York: Dover, 1956; hereafter *"LPH"*), 416–17.

15 Lectures of 1822–23. See *G. W. F. Hegel: Vorlesungen über Rechtsphilosophie 1818–1831. Edition und Kommentar in sechs Bänden* ed. K-H

Ilting (Stuttgart-Bad Cannstatt: Frommann-Holzboog, 1974; hereafter "Ilting"), vol. III, 475.

16 See my "Hegel's Critique of Kant's Moral World View," *Philosophical Topics* 19, No. 2 (1991): 133–76, §IV.

17 "Die Verfassung Deutchlands" (*Werke* I), pp. 461–581, and "Verhandlungen in der Versammlung der Landstände des Königreichs Württemberg im Jahr 1815 und 1816" (*Werke* 4), pp. 462–597; "The German Constitution" and "Proceedings of the Estates Assembly in the Kingdom of Württemberg, 1815–1816" in *Hegel's Political Writings*, ed. Z. A. Pelczynski, tr. T. M. Knox (Oxford: Clarendon Press, 1964), 143–242 and 246–94.

18 I have adapted the formulation of this issue from C. Dyke, "Collective Decision Making in Rousseau, Kant, Hegel, and Mill," *Ethics* 80, No. 1 (1969): 22. Dyke misunderstands Hegel's approach to this issue.

19 Hegel makes this point against Jacobi's doctrine of "immediate knowledge." See my "Hegel's Attitude Toward Jacobi in the 'Third Attitude of Thought Toward Objectivity,'" *The Southern Journal of Philosophy* 27, No. 1 (1989): 135–56, §VII, 148–51.

20 "Wer Denkt Abstrakt?" (*Werke* 2, pp. 575–81); "Who Thinks Abstractly?" in *Hegel: Texts and Commentary* tr. W. Kaufmann (Garden City: Anchor, 1966), 113–18.

21 "Über die wissenschaftlichen Behandlung des Naturrechts, seine Stelle in der praktischen Philosophie und sein Verhältnis zu den positiven Rechtswissenschaften" (*Werke* II, pp. 434–530), p. 445; *Natural Law* tr. T. M. Knox (Philadelphia: University of Pennsylvania Press, 1975), 63–64.

22 See Joyce Beck Hoy, "Hegel's Critique of Rawls," *Clio* 10, No. 4 (1981): 407–22).

23 *VGP* III, p. 334; *LHP* III, pp. 244–45.

24 See Roy Pascal, " 'Bildung' and the Division of Labor" in *German Studies Presented to Walter Horace Bruford* (London: Harrap, 1962), 14–28, for discussion of this issue among Hegel's immediate predecessors.

25 See my "Hegel's Critique of Kant's Moral World View," cited above.

26 Hegel often speaks simply of "the concept" (see §§19, 106). One must recall that "the concept" at issue is the concept of the will.

27 *Grundlegung der Metaphysik der Sitten* (*Gesammelte Schriften*, Königliche Preussische Akadamie der Wissenschaft: Berlin and Leipzig: de Gruyter, 1904–; hereafter "Ak"]; *Groundwork of the Metaphysic of Morals* tr. Paton (New York: Harper, 1964), vol. IV, 412, (cited hereafter as "*Groundwork*"). I cite only the Akademie pagination, which appears in all recent translations of Kant's writings.

28 Hume, *A Treatise of Human Nature*, ed. Selby-Bigge (Oxford: Clarendon Press, 1888, 1965), 488–91; Rousseau, *On the Social Contract*, tr. Masters & Masters (New York: St. Martin's, 1978), 47.

29 Hegel's view that "individuals" develop historically has raised controversy. What was Thrasymachus, if not an individual? Two points need to
be noted. First, Thrasymachus was a product of the decline of Greek life,
a decline brought on, according to Hegel, in part by the development of
individualism. More important, the conception of "individual" of interest to Hegel is a conception of an individual who has the moral ability to
reflect on and evaluate normative principles, the kind of individual who
is capable of such acts as conscientious objection or civil disobedience.
Hegel finds the first clear precedents of that development in Antigone,
Socrates, and Jesus. This conception of the individual is not an historical
constant; even less are examples of it an historical constant. (Socrates
may have engaged in something approximating conscientious objection
when he openly refused to obey the command of the thirty tyrants to
arrest the general Leon in Salamis [*Apology* 32cd], but he nowhere considers civil disobedience; this is not a Greek notion.)

30 *Groundwork*, Ak IV, p. 398, *cf.* pp. 393–94.

31 Ibid., p. 401n.

32 *Kritik der praktischen Vernunft* (*Critique of Practical Reason*, tr. Beck
[Indianapolis: Bobbs-Merrill, 1956]), Ak V, 155–56.

33 *Phänomenoligie des Geistes* (*Werke* 3), p. 457; *Phenomenology of Spirit*
tr. Miller (Oxford: Clarendon, 1977), 377.

34 See Allen Wood, "The Emptiness of the Moral Will," *The Monist* 72, No.
3 (1989): 454–83).

35 *Groundwork*, Ak IV, p. 412.

36 Ibid., p. 417.

37 Ibid., pp. 428, 434–35.

38 *Metaphysische Anfangsgründe der Rechtslehre* (*Metaphysical Principles of Justice*, tr. J. Ladd [Indianapolis: Bobbs-Merrill, 1965]), Ak VI, 246.

39 More properly, extant modern institutions (§299R). Hegel thought, *e.g.*,
that the Roman and medieval epochs objectively lacked properly rational institutions and so were not amenable to such interpretation.
Roughly, the Roman world lacked sufficient community; the Middle
Ages lacked sufficient individuality. See *VPG*, pp. 340, 345–46, 349, 351,
358, 359, 441, 444–47, 455–60; *LPH*, pp. 279, 284, 287, 289, 295, 366,
369–72, 378–83.

40 Although the Public Authority is to deal with accidental events, and
Hegel here listed poverty relief under its authority, he did not think that
poverty was an accidental phenomenon. Rather, he recognized that it
results from the workings of civil society (§245), and in his lectures he
stated what his text clearly implies, that poverty is a wrong done by one
class to another (§244Z; lectures of 1824–25, Ilting IV, p. 609). He held it
to be an evil because it produces wretched living conditions and because
it systematically excludes the poor from participation in society (§244).

He was deeply concerned with this problem and was not satisfied with any solution to it he proposed.

41 Although Hegel advocated a centralized national government, he also held that regional and municipal concerns should be handled by regional or municipal government (§§288, 290).

42 Lectures of 1822–23 (Ilting III, pp. 788–90). *Cf.* Hegel's lectures of 1824–25 (Ilting IV, p. 698).

43 One might wonder about a situation like that described in *Brave New World*, or about a society that progressively reduced its needs and ends so that they were simpler to satisfy and required little political or social activity. Would either society meet Hegel's criteria of freedom by default? The "Brave New World" circumstance is ruled out by the fact that in it social harmony is produced by social engineering initiated and directed by the government. This directly contradicts the nature of legitimate law on Hegel's view, where the content and legitimacy of law flows from the free actions of individuals up through the legislative and executive apparatus. The prospect of social degeneracy is very real, on Hegel's view, but also fails his criteria for freedom. Hegel believed that part of the development of rationality and freedom through history involves an expansion of the understanding of the range of human possibilities, activities, and responsibilities, which, once achieved, serves as an historical benchmark for assessing how free a society is.

44 Karl-Heinz Ilting shows that Hegel's descriptions of these mechanisms were much more specific – and republican – in his lectures. See his introduction to his edition of *Die Philosophie des Rechts: Die Mitschriften Wannemann (Heidelberg 1817/18) und Homeyer (Berlin 1818/19)* (Stuttgart: Klett-Cotta, 1983), 25–27.

45 Marx credited Hegel with seeking the roots of government in civil society but claimed as his own insight that the roots of civil society are in political economy. See the 1859 "Preface to the Critique of Political Economy" in *The Marx-Engels Reader*, ed. Tucker (New York: Norton, 2nd ed. 1978), 4. This misrepresents Hegel and consequently misrepresents Marx's own originality. Hegel sought the roots of civil society in political economy; Marx's innovation was to seek the anatomy of civil society *and* its economy in the historical development of productive forces. This root idea of "historical materialism" did not occur to Hegel.

46 "Critique of the Gotha Program," in *Marx-Engels Reader*, p. 531. On relative scarcity as a condition for the relevance of principles of justice, see Hume, *Treatise on Human Nature*, pp. 485–95.

47 I wish to thank Allen Wood, Michael Hardimon, Fred Neuhouser, David Kettler, and my departmental colleagues, especially Bob Scharff and Bill DeVries, for comments on previous versions of this essay.

Organizational Diagram of Hegel's State

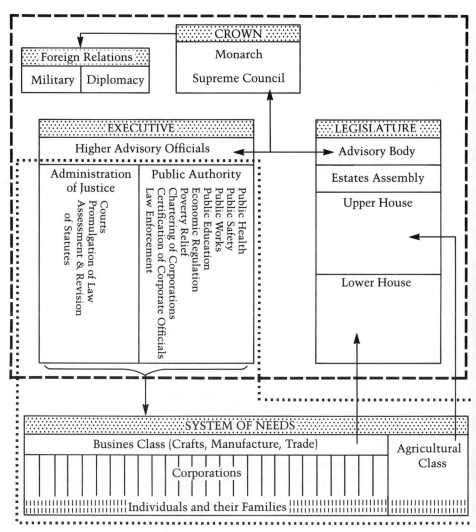

Civil Society (The "state external") • • • • • • • • • •

The Political State (the government)— — — —

The State Proper is the entire system.

9   Hegel's historicism

I. HEGEL'S HISTORICAL REVOLUTION

History cannot be consigned to a corner in Hegel's system, relegated to a few paragraphs near the end of the *Encyclopedia* or confined to his *Lectures on the Philosophy of History*. For, as many scholars have long since recognized,[1] history is central to Hegel's conception of philosophy. One of the most striking and characteristic features of Hegel's thought is that it *historicizes* philosophy, explaining its purpose, principles, and problems in historical terms. Rather than seeing philosophy as a timeless *a priori* reflection upon eternal forms, Hegel regards it as the self-consciousness of a specific culture, the articulation, defense, and criticism of its essential values and beliefs. This historical conception of philosophy is epitomized clearly by Hegel himself in the famous lines from the preface to his *Philosophy of Right:* "Philosophy is its own age comprehended in thought" (VII, 26).

Hegel's historicism amounted to nothing less than a revolution in the history of philosophy. It implied that philosophy is possible only if it is historical, only if the philosopher is aware of the origins, context, and development of his doctrines. Hegel thus threw into question the revolution with which Descartes began modern philosophy. It is not possible to create a presuppositionless system of philosophy à la Descartes, Hegel believes, by abstracting from the past and by simply relying upon one's individual reason. For if Descartes were a completely self-sufficient, self-enclosed mind, transcending the realm of history, he would not have been able to produce his philosophy. The aims of his system, and the ideas he defended in it, were typical products of the culture of seventeenth-century France.

So if philosophy is to be truly presuppositionless, Hegel maintains, then it must not abstract from, but incorporate history within itself.

Hegel's philosophical revolution consisted in not only subverting the Cartesian heritage, but also in historicizing the traditional objects of classical metaphysics, God, providence and immortality. Hegel argues that metaphysics is possible only if its central concepts are explicable in historical terms. He accepts Kant's critical teaching that metaphysics is not possible as speculation about a realm of transcendent entities, and that it is possible only if it does not transcend the limits of possible experience. He therefore attempts to provide a "schematism" of the central concepts of metaphysics, explaining them in empirical terms. To explain them in empirical terms means, however, defining them in historical terms, since for Hegel experience consists not only in present-sense perceptions but also in the totality of all forms of human experience, past, present and future.[2] Thus God is not an entity beyond the world, but the idea realized in history. Providence is not an "external end," a supernatural plan imposed by God upon nature, but an "internal end," the ultimate purpose of history itself. And immortality is not life in heaven, but the memory of someone's role in history. It is indeed noteworthy that, in Hegel, the philosophy of history usurps the traditional function of a theodicy: it explains the existence of evil by showing it to be necessary for the realization of the end of history.

If Hegel's historicism amounted to a revolution, it still was not a radical break with the past. For historicism, understood in a broad sense as the doctrine that emphasizes the importance of history for the understanding of human institutions and activities, must by definition also be the product of history. It was indeed anything but new in Hegel's day.[3] In his *Spirit of the Laws* (1749) Montesquieu saw the constitution of a nation as the product of its history, as the result of its changing economic, geographic, and climactic circumstances, and the evolving traditions, religion, and character of its people. In his *Inquiry concerning the Principles of Political Economy* (1767), James Steuart developed an evolutionary theory of the development of society, explaining how mankind grew from primitive simplicity to complicated refinement through the pressure of economic factors. In his *Ideas for a Philosophy of History of Humanity* (1784–88), Herder explained how such human activities as philosophy, religion, and literature are the product of the history of a people, the characteristic form of their national culture. And in his *System of Transcendental Idealism* (1799), Schelling explained how the intellectual intuition of the "I am," the first principle of philosophy, was the product of the ego's history. Some forms of historicism had indeed become a commonplace by the middle of the eighteenth century. It had become a popular pastime among radicals and free-thinkers, for example, to explain away the supernatural claims of religion by exposing its all-too-human origins. Thus Spinoza, and the English free-thinkers John Toland and Matthew Tindal, attempted to debunk the supernatural status of the Bible by considering the circumstances and culture of the ancient Jews. It is clear, then, that historicism was not born with Hegel. Indeed, from his early life and writings we can see how much he learned from the works of Montesquieu, Ferguson, Herder, and Spinoza.[4]

If historicism does not begin with Hegel, what, if anything, is new and distinctive about his historicism? With Hegel, historicism becomes the self-conscious and general method of philosophy, the weapon to be wielded against its own pretenses and illusions. This self-reflective, self-critical element is not found in the historicism of Hegel's predecessors or contemporaries. Hegel made historicism the self-critical method of philosophy because he believed that philosophy stood in the same need of historical explanation as politics, religion, or literature. In adopting a timeless and a-historical view of their discipline, philosophers had made the same kind of mistake as theologians, jurists, and aestheticians. Just as the theologians believed the Bible to be the record of a supernatural revelation, just as the jurists saw their constitutions as the embodiment of a natural law, and just as the aestheticians claimed that their taste was the canon of a universal beauty, so the philosophers regarded their doctrines as the product of an eternal reason. They too had failed to learn the simple lesson of history: that what appears to be given, eternal, or natural is in fact the product of human activity, and indeed of that activity in a specific cultural context. To expose this illusion, Hegel believed that he had no choice but to historicize philosophy itself.

This self-critical dimension of Hegel's historicism was his completion of Kant's project for a critique of pure reason. Like Kant, Hegel believed that philosophy should become self-critical, aware of its own methods, presuppositions, and limits. He too saw the source of

"transcendental illusion" in the self-hypostasis of reason, in its supposing that there are some eternal entities corresponding to its laws.
But, unlike Kant, Hegel held that such self-critical reflection demands that philosophy be aware of the genesis, context, and development of its own doctrines. Rather than claiming that they were the
product of pure reason, as Kant had done, the philosopher should see
them as the result of history. The problem of transcendental illusion
would become fully eradicated, Hegel thought, only when philosophy became fully historicized, for only then would the philosopher
see how his belief in supernatural or eternal entities arose from his
culture. The real source of transcendental illusion thus lay in amne-
sia, forgetting the origin, context, and development of our ideas.

To appreciate the point of Hegel's historical criticism, it is worth-
while to consider how deep-seated and widespread the illusion of
a-historicity has been in the history of philosophy. There have been
many forms of such a-historicity, and all of them became in one
form or another the subject of Hegelian criticism. (a) The belief that
certain laws, beliefs, or values are universal, eternal, or natural when
they are in fact the product of, and only appropriate to, a specific
culture. (b) The doctrine that certain ideas or principles are innate,
the inherent elements of a pure *a priori* reason, although they are
learned from experience, the product of a cultural tradition. (c) The
claim that certain institutions and forms of activity have a supernatural origin (for example language, religion, and the state) when
they in fact originate from all-too-human sources. (d) The reification
of certain activities and values, as if they were entities existing
independent of human consciousness, when they are in fact the
product of its subconscious activity. (e) The belief that certain intuitions and feelings are the product of innate genius, although they
are the result of education. (f) The attempt to create a presuppositionless philosophy by abstracting from all past philosophy
and by relying upon individual reason alone.

However central to his philosophy, Hegel's historicism is never
fully explained or defended in any single text. It is perhaps most
explicit in his *Lectures on the History of Philosophy* when he argues
that there is no distinction between philosophy and the history of
philosophy.[5] But here he does not explain the critical dimension of
his historicism. This is more the underlying message that we gain
from some of his early writings, in particular *The Positivity of the*

Christian Religion (1795), *The Spirit of Christianity* (1799), and especially *The Phenomenology of Spirit*.[6] Throughout these early writings we find Hegel criticizing a wide variety of philosophers for their
a-historical beliefs. Thus he castigates the romantics for their claims
to have eternal intellectual intuitions, which are in fact the product
of their education. He attacks the Kantian theologians for ignoring
the social and political factors behind the rise of early Christianity,
and for assuming instead that it has its source in the eternal demands of practical reason. He scolds the Kantians for thinking that
their categorical imperative is the demand of an eternal reason when
it is only appropriate to the ethic of modern individualism. And he
pours scorn upon those French *philosophes* who presume that they
can recreate all of society *ab initio* in abstraction from all the historical traditions and institutions of France. What all these philosophers
have in common, in Hegel's view, is a tendency to forget the past, to
ignore the social, political, and historical origins and context of their
own doctrines.

II. THE BASIS OF HEGEL'S HISTORICISM

What drove Hegel into his historical conception of philosophy? Why
did he think that philosophy is only its own time comprehended in
thought? One basic premise of Hegel's historicism is his doctrine
that each society is a unique whole, all of whose parts are inseparable from one another.[7] The art, religion, constitution, traditions,
manners, and language of a people form a systematic unity. We cannot separate one of these factors from the whole without changing
its nature and that of the whole. This organic whole is what Hegel,
following Montesquieu, calls "the spirit" of a nation, its characteristic manner of thinking and acting. Now philosophy, Hegel maintains, is simply one part of the social whole.[8] The philosopher cannot leap beyond his own age any more than he can jump outside his
own skin. His task is simply to make each nation self-conscious of
its underlying spirit, of its characteristic values and beliefs. The
organic nature of the social whole, and the role of philosophy within
it, then means that philosophy cannot be separated from its social
context. If the factors composing the social whole were to change,
then philosophy would be bound to change with them. It would
simply have a new spirit to express.

Another central premise behind Hegel's historicism is his general Herderian view of the role of tradition in the development of the arts and sciences.⁹ Citing Herder, Hegel refers to tradition as "the sacred chain" that links the present with the past. It is tradition that shows us that the past continues to live in the present. What we are now, Hegel says, is what we have become, and the process of our becoming is our history. The power of reason that mankind now possesses, he argues, is not given to it at birth, but has been acquired through centuries of effort. The arts and sciences have not been created immediately – shot from the pistol of absolute knowledge – but they are the product of all past achievements. Philosophy, Hegel reminds us, is no exception to this rule. The material or subject matter of philosophy is not given to the philosopher or created *a priori* by his individual reason. Rather, it is a legacy handed down to him from the past. Hegel does not mean, of course, that it is the role of the philosopher simply to transmit this tradition. He insists that it is his task to transform it, to assimilate it in his own individual and original manner. Only in this way, he says, does the tradition remain vital. Nevertheless, without a material handed down to him, the philosopher will have nothing to work upon or produce.

Hegel's historical conception of philosophy was not derived, however, simply from his general views about the nature of society and the arts and sciences. These considerations were important for his historicism, to be sure, but they do not account for the fundamental and characteristic conception that underlies it. There is a far more important argument at stake, one central to and distinctive of Hegel's philosophy as a whole. The arguments given so far show that philosophy is no more historical than other disciplines, such as art, science, and religion. But Hegel's central and characteristic argument for the historical nature of philosophy, which he expounds in his *Lectures on the History of Philosophy*,¹⁰ maintains that there is something special about the very subject matter of philosophy that makes it more historical than other disciplines. Whereas the subject matter of other disciplines is fixed, given, and eternal, that of philosophy undergoes constant development and transformation. Why is this?

According to Hegel, the distinctive subject matter of philosophy is thought, the ideas or concepts by which we think about the world. This conception of the subject matter of philosophy is perhaps banal, but Hegel immediately adds to it a striking thesis central to his philosophy as a whole: that thought is by its very nature historical. Thought is not a fixed state of being, he maintains, but a restless activity, a process of development from the indeterminate to the determinate, from the vague to the clear, from the abstract to the concrete. The fundamental premise behind his historical conception of thought is that it is not possible to separate the object of thought from the activity of thinking about it, for it is only through our thinking about an idea that it becomes clear, determinate, and concrete. Like all activity, though, the activity of thought takes place not in an instant but throughout time. Hence thought itself must be historical.

In making this point, Hegel was taking issue with the Platonic tradition of philosophy, which had been responsible for so much of the a-historicism of the history of philosophy. According to the Platonic tradition, the object of thought is an eternal form, complete in all its meaning prior to our reflection upon it; and the reflection upon it is an eternal contemplation, a passive intuition or timeless perception of these forms. The main problem with this Platonic conception of thought, in Hegel's view, is that the meaning of ideas is never complete and given to us, as if it were only a question of our perceiving their transparent essence. Rather, they become clear and distinct and take on a determinate meaning only through our activity of thinking about them. Thus we must analyze the idea into its elements, contrast it with other ideas, find its context, and so on. Since the idea acquires its determinate meaning only through our activity of thinking about it, we cannot make a sharp distinction between the object and the activity of thought. The object of thought is not given to, but created by our thinking about it. It is posited by the very act of discovering its meaning. This is a point upon which Hegel laid some stress in his *Lectures on the History of Philosophy:* "The history [of philosophy] that we have before us is the history of the self-discovery of thought; and with thought it is the case that it discovers itself, indeed it exists and is actualized only through its discovery" (XVIII, 23).

Prima facie it would seem that the activity of thought takes place only within the mind of the individual philosopher, so that it is historical only in a trivial sense. But Hegel insists that the full development of the main idea underlying a system of philosophy is not the work of a single philosopher but of a whole generation. He stresses the enormous length of time, and the collective effort, required before the meaning of an idea becomes fully determinate. No single philosopher is able to develop alone all the implications of his system. As Hegel puts the point in his inimitable German: "*Der Weg des Geistes ist der Umweg.*"[11] The path of the concept is not simple and easy, the day trip of a single individual, but involved and difficult, a detour negotiable only over many generations.

The epitome of Hegel's doctrine of the historicity of thought is his claim that we cannot separate philosophy from the history of philosophy. The discovery of the nature of thought in philosophy becomes the history of philosophy itself. Hegel's simplest and boldest formulation of this thesis is his statement that the temporal succession of ideas in the history of philosophy is the same as the logical succession of moments of the idea (cf. XVIII, 49 E XX 478). Each system of philosophy in the past stands for one stage or moment in the logical development of the idea, and the order in which these systems follow one another in time is the same as the order in which the moments of the idea follow one another in logic. In making such a bold equation, Hegel did not intend to equate temporal and logical succession *simpliciter.*[12] His point is only that the succession of these systems in time is primarily determined by the underlying logic of their main ideas. What compels system B to follow A in history, for example, is that B is more consistent or precise than A.

III. IN DEFENSE OF HEGEL'S HISTORICISM

It should not be surprising that the most revolutionary aspect of Hegel's thought has also been the most controversial. Hegel's historicism has been castigated as the chief source of his errors. Three kinds of objection have been hurled against it; each of them deserves careful consideration.

The first objection comes from the Marxist tradition, and in particular from Marx's attack upon Hegel in the *German Ideology.*[13] According to Marx, Hegel's historicism is vitiated by his metaphysics. Hegel did not go far enough in attempting to transform metaphysics; the point is to abolish it. Hegel's historicism involves a topsy-turvy picture of reality because it is infected with the metaphysics of absolute idealism. Rather than seeing the basic determining force of history as the concrete material needs of particular human beings, Hegel claims that they are found in the absolute idea. Allegedly, he holds that "the world is ruled by ideas, that ideas and concepts are its determining principles." To arrive at the true picture of reality, Marx argues, we should turn the Hegelian picture upside down: ideas and concepts are the product of human beings in a specific system of production. The Hegelian subject – the logic of the idea – has to be turned into the predicate of the real subject – the material needs of human beings. Thus Marx turned Hegel's historicism against itself: it too was simply the product of its age, the deification of the Prussian Restoration.

Yet Marx's critique is directed against a boogey-man. For there is nothing in Hegel's historicism that excludes in principle a naturalistic, indeed a materialistic, account of the origin of ideas.[14] Just as much as Marx, Hegel sees philosophy, religion, and literature as the product of social and political conditions; nor does he neglect the basic role of the economy in the formation of society.[15] Indeed, in his *Encyclopedia* Hegel explains human intelligence as the highest organization and development of all the powers in nature.[16] Of course Hegel, unlike Marx, assumes that social, political, and economic factors are ultimately manifestations of the absolute idea. But this still does not jeopardize any naturalistic or materialistic account of the origin of ideas. The point is that the idea realizes itself *only through* the workings of these social, political, and economic factors. It is important to avoid the vulgar error, sometimes suggested in Marx's critique, that Hegel thinks that ideas, as formulated in the minds of individual people, have a primary role in the development of history, a role prior to social and economic factors. Hegel not only holds that such ideas are the product of their social and political environment, but that it is naive for moral reformers to think that they can fashion all of society according to their moral ideals.[17] His scorn for the naivity of moral idealism is indeed equal to that of Marx. Ultimately, then, Hegel's historicism is much closer to Marx's historical materialism than Marx's tendentious caricature-filled polemic makes it appear. In tracing the genesis of ideas to their social, economic, and political context, in stressing the importance of economic factors in the formation of civil society, and in debunking the a-historical illusions of philosophers, Hegel anticipates much in Marx's own materi-

alist historicism. Marx's materialism is indeed little more than Hegel's historicism without the metaphysics of the absolute idea.

The second objection to Hegel's historicism is that it leads to a
complete relativism, the doctrine that all cultural values are incommensurable and not appraisable by any higher or absolute standard.[18]
In attempting to show that apparently universal values are only
those of a specific culture, and in stressing that philosophy is only
the self-consciousness of its age, Hegel allegedly goes too far and
undermines any basis for universal moral standards. Thus the only
advice that he gives to someone who asks "What should I do?" is
that he should follow the ethics of his own age. This is because
Hegel has no basis to discriminate between different cultures.

Yet this objection fails to come to grips with the central thesis of
Hegel's philosophy of history: that *the* end of history is the self-
awareness of freedom. This goal is not purely formal and abstract, as if
Hegel thinks that each culture achieves it in its own unique and
incommensurable manner. For in his *Philosophy of Right* he outlines
in very specific terms the necessary conditions for the realization of
freedom. A state that is to achieve this end must fulfill very definite
conditions, viz., it should provide for popular representation, it
should have a written constitution limiting the powers of the central
authority, it should permit liberty of press and freedom of conscience,
and so on. Clearly, not any constitution or culture fulfills these conditions. In general, it is important to see that Hegel did not reject the
tradition of natural law, which posited certain universal and necessary standards of right and wrong. Rather, he simply transformed and
reinterpreted this tradition. Instead of seeing natural law as an eternal
law above the process of history, Hegel historicizes it, so that it becomes the purpose of history itself. This then gives him an absolute
standard by which he can appraise all the different cultures and constitutions of world history. They are good or bad according to whether
they contribute toward the self-consciousness of freedom.

It might well be asked, then, how Hegel's absolute standpoint
jibes with his theory that each constitution is appropriate for its age
and circumstances.[19] Here it is necessary to recognize that Hegel's
philosophy of history operates on two levels, one horizontal and the
other vertical. The horizontal level comprises the specific circumstances of a nation, its economic, geographic, climactic, and demo-
graphic conditions. Since each nation must adapt to these circum-

stances, and since these circumstances are unique, each nation will have unique and incommensurable values. Its constitution and ethos will be appropriate to, and therefore justifiable in the light of, its circumstances. The vertical level consists in world-history as a whole and the contribution each nation has made toward the realization of its end. It is clear that, from this perspective, different cultures will have different degrees of good and evil according to how they promote progress toward the self-consciousness of freedom.

The third and final objection against Hegel's historicism is that it is guilty of a simple logical mistake, "the genetic fallacy," the assumption that to determine the origin of an idea is also to determine its truth or falsity.[20] It is a simply fallacy to argue, for example, that the dogmas of Christianity are false simply because they serve the interests of a priestly caste, or that Smith's economics is mistaken since it supports the domination of the bourgeoisie. To assess the truth of a proposition according to the laws of logic and the evidence for it is one thing, but to determine its origins (the motivations behind it, the purposes it serves) is another. Now in attempting to debunk the a-historical pretensions of philosophers by making them aware of the genesis and context of their doctrines, this objection goes, Hegel is confusing the appraisal of the truth of a belief with the assessment of its origins.

Once we admit that the genetic fallacy is a fallacy, is Hegel guilty of committing it? The answer to this question must be a clear and simple "No." Hegel himself was perfectly aware of the pitfalls of the genetic fallacy and explicitly warned against it. In his polemic against the German historical school in the introduction to the *Philosophy of Right*, for example, he criticized the attempt to justify an institution or practice simply by revealing its historical origins (VII, 35–36, §3). To show the origins of an institution or practice is not *ipso facto* to justify it according to the principles of right, Hegel argued, for we can establish the historical origins and necessity of practices and institutions that are completely unjust and irrational. So, if Hegel is guilty of the genetic fallacy, it can be only by ignoring his own explicit warnings.

This objection rests upon two misunderstandings. First, it assumes a vulgar conception of Hegel's intentions. It is not his aim to discredit ideas by revealing their reprehensible origins. For it is central to his historicism that the philosopher accept the origin of ideas for what they are without passing judgment upon them. After all, the purpose of philosophy, as Hegel tells us in the preface to the *Philosophy of Right* (VII, 26), is not to prescribe how the world ought to be, but only to comprehend why it must be as it is. Second, this objection also fails to note the precise target of Hegel's criticism. This is not the truth of a philosopher's doctrine itself, but the a-historical claims he makes in its behalf. It is just a fact that philosophers attempt to give extra authority to their doctrines by making claims about their a-historical origins. They assume, for example, that their system is the product of pure reason alone, that their intellectual intuitions are the insights of pure genius, or that their principles are revolutionary and a complete break with the past. The truth of such assumptions can be properly appraised only by examining their genesis and origins.

In general, it is important to see that Hegel does not argue that because a philosophy has arisen from a specific social and political context that it is true only for that context. If this were the case, then he would indeed have to accept a complete relativism. But Hegel is no more a relativist in the sphere of epistemology than in ethics. Rather, he explicitly says the direct contrary: that the truth is eternal, universal, and permanent. This is a point upon which he lays much emphasis in the Berlin version of his *Lectures on the History of Philosophy:*

The thought, the essential thought is, is in and for itself, is eternal. That which is true is contained in thought, is true not only today and tomorrow, but beyond all time; and insofar as it is in time it is always and at each time true. How is it then possible for the world of thought to have a history?

(XII, 23–24)

The question Hegel raises here is indeed crucial. If the subject matter of philosophy is the eternal and universal truth, then how can philosophy have a history where everything undergoes change? In other words, how can philosophy be knowledge of the universal and eternal truth *and* the self-consciousness of its age?

To resolve this problem, it is again necessary to make a distinction (analogous to that above) between two standards of truth in Hegel's philosophy of history. The first standard of truth determines whether a philosophy adequately expresses the spirit of its age, whether it is true in describing its characteristic values and beliefs. According to this standard, different, and even incompatible, philosophies can be true as long as they succeed in expressing the spirits of their cultures, which have different and incompatible beliefs and values. The second standard is the universal goal of world history, the self-consciousness of freedom. It is this standard that allows Hegel to speak of a universal truth amid all the change of world history. Since each culture strives to attain this ideal, and since, as we have already seen, it can be achieved only under very specific conditions, it follows that some cultures will be more adequate and successful than others in attaining it. The philosophies that express these cultures will therefore have different degrees of truth according to the degree to which their culture achieves or approximates the goal of universal history.

IV. HEGEL'S HISTORICAL METHOD

Given the role of history in Hegel's thought, his ideas on historical method are obviously of the first importance. On this central issue, however, Hegel has surprisingly little to say. There is only one place where he does explain his views on historical method, and that is in the introduction to his *Lectures on World History*.[21] And even here Hegel's exposition is, as usual, very brief, dense, and obscure. Nevertheless, his introduction deserves close attention if only because so much has been written about Hegel's historical method without consulting his own views upon it. Philosophers of history have been more concerned to impose their own methodological paradigms and classifications upon Hegel than to interpret his own difficult texts. Thus Hegel has been seen as the paradigm of a "speculative historian," as someone whose main purpose is to explain the ultimate purpose of history according to his metaphysics rather than to examine facts for their own sake.[22] He has also been castigated as the chief practitioner of *a priori* history, as someone who imposes his own *a priori* schematism upon the facts, compelling them to conform to his own metaphysical preconceptions.[23] Yet it is significant that Hegel rejects both these approaches. He insists that the philosopher of history examine facts for their own sake, and that he lay aside all metaphysical presuppositions. Indeed, he states explicitly: "We must take history as it is; we must proceed historically, empirically" (XII, 22). He is painfully aware of the problems of applying *a priori* schemes to history, and he is even critical of other German historians for doing just this. So, given Hegel's explicit rejection of the methodologies that have been foisted upon him, there is all the more reason to examine his own ideas about historical method.

In his introduction Hegel distinguishes between three different kinds of history: original, reflective, and philosophical. In original history the writer narrates events in which he has participated. The spirit of the writer and that of the events he narrates is one and the same. The writer's account of the events is itself, then, an historical document. What the author has written about the events is constitutive of them. The classical examples of such original history, in Hegel's view, are Thucydides and Herodotus. Although Hegel praises the identity of the writer and his subject in original history, he also thinks that it suffers from a serious weakness: it considers only the events that the author witnesses. It lacks a universal perspective. This defect is surmounted by reflective history. Its perspective is broader, an entire epoch or all of world history. The reflective historian applies general ideas or conceptions to history and attempts to make sense of it; he does not limit himself to narrating events, as does the original historian. Like original history, though, reflective history is also subject to a fatal flaw. Although it has a more universal perspective, it imposes the view of the author upon the past. The identity between the writer and the event, the subject and object, in original history is destroyed; there is a dualism between the object (history) and the subject (the perspective of the historian).

Hegel's philosophical history is meant to cancel the weakness, and preserve the strengths, of original and reflective history. The philosophical historian has a universal perspective; but he does not impose his own ideas upon his subject matter. He achieves the identity of subject and object of original history, yet he does so on a "mediated," universal, or reflective level. How is this feat possible? What precise form must philosophical history take if it is to cancel the weaknesses and preserve the strengths of original and reflective history? It is just at this point that Hegel's explanation becomes very sketchy and obscure.

If Hegel is very vague about the method of philosophical history, he is at least very clear about the basic problem confronting it. In his introduction he explains that there is a "contradiction" between the methods of philosophy and history (XII, 20, 557–58). Philosophy has an *a priori* method where thought is active, producing its own content from itself. History, however, has an empirical method, demanding that we examine the given for its own sake and cast aside all *a priori* preconceptions. It would appear, then, as if the very idea of a philosophy of history is a contradiction in terms. How does it resolve this contradiction? Here again Hegel's text becomes very vague.

If we are to understand Hegel's method in the philosophy of history, then we have to reconstruct his meaning by considering his general ideas about philosophical method. It is necessary to consult other texts beside the *Lectures on World History*, and in particular the *Phenomenology of Spirit*, which also has an historical subject matter. The contradiction between the methods of philosophy and history that Hegel presents in his introduction has a striking resemblance to the conflict between the standpoints of orinary consciousness and philosophy in the introduction to the *Phenomenology*. Ordinary consciousness says that its object is given, something external to itself. Philosophy, however, stands by its principle of subject-object identity, according to which the object is not given but produced by pure thought. How, then, is it possible to resolve the conflict between them? Hegel's solution is his phenomenological method. This demands that the philosopher bracket his own principles and presuppositions and permit consciousness to examine itself according to its own standards. The philosopher will then find that, through its self-examination, ordinary consciousness will be compelled to admit the truth of subject-object identity. Ordinary consciousness will discover through its own experience that the object is not given to it but essential to its own self-consciousness.

Now the method of the philosophy of history is, I suggest, analogous to that of the *Phenomenology*. Like the phenomenologist, the philosopher of history suspends his own *a priori* metaphysical principles and examines his subject matter according to its own internal standards. In more historical terms, this means that the philosopher of history will examine the cultures of the past in terms of *their own* beliefs, values, and ideals. As in ordinary consciousness, each culture is subject to a dialectic where it discovers through its own *self*-examination that its ideals and goals are in conflict with its experience. The only means of resolving this conflict will be through the higher ideals of a more-advanced culture. The end of this dialectic will also be similar to the *Phenomenology*. What the philosopher knows *a priori* through reflection – that the end of history is the self-consciousness of freedom – becomes the result of the inner dialectic of history itself.

The advantage of this phenomenological reading of Hegel's method is that it explains (a) how the conflict between the methods of history and philosophy is resolved and (b) how the method of philosophical history maintains the strengths and avoids the weaknesses of original and reflective history. The phenomenological method avoids the conflict between the historical and philosophical methods by combining aspects of them both. It is empirical insofar as it surrenders all preconceptions and examines its subject matter for its own sake, according to its own ideals and goals; and it is *a priori* insofar as there is an inner dialectic, a logical necessity, in history where the contradictions of a culture are discovered and resolved. The phenomenological method also unites the strengths of original and reflective history. It has the subject-object identity of original history since the historical subject examines itself according to its own ideals; but it has the universal perspective of reflective history since the dialectic ascends from the narrow perspective of one culture to the higher perspective of another. This method also avoids the chief problem of reflective history, since the philosopher's standpoint is that of his subject matter itself, given that he examines it only in the light of its own ideals and aspirations.

If this account of Hegel's method is correct, then the subject matter of his philosophy of history should be not historical events *simpliciter*, which can be described by some reflective historian or external observer, but the agent's *consciousness* of these events. In other words, the subject matter of history should be the *self-consciousness of a nation* or, more precisely, *the dialectic* by which it arrives at its self-consciousness. This assumption finds more than ample confirmation from Hegel's introduction when he tells us that the subject matter of philosophical history is "the spirits of those nations which have become conscious of their inherent principles, and have become aware of what they are and of what their actions signify" (XII, 12, 545). Hegel makes the same point from another angle when he says that the subject matter of history is "spirit" (XII, 31). One of the "main characteristics" of spirit, he says, is "its consciousness of its own ends and interests and the principles which underlie them" (VG 7; 13). He then goes on to make self-consciousness into the defining characteristic of spirit; it is its very nature to have itself as an object. "I am not just this, that, or the other, but what I know myself to be" (VG 54; 47). This conception of spirit or the self as self-explaining or self-interpreting, which Hegel derives from Fichte, is crucial to the method of the *Phenomenology* and *Philosophy of History*. For it means that the philosopher does not have to import his own abstractions and principles to explain his subject matter. Rather, his subject matter will explain itself. This is what Hegel means when he says that the philosopher only has to describe "the thing itself" (*die Sache selbst*) or "the immanent movement of the concept."

It becomes all the more plausible to ascribe a phenomenological method to Hegel once we recognize that such a method had become current in his day. This is the very method that Herder had prescribed in his influential 1774 tract *Another Philosophy of the History of Mankind*. Before Hegel, Herder had castigated those historians who judged the past in the light of their own contemporary standards of right and wrong. He demanded that the historian should examine each age according to its own standards and values. The fundamental precept of the historian became "empathy" (*Einfühlung*) with the past, a sympathetic reconstruction of its guiding ideals. Herder preached to the new generation of historians: "go into the age, into the region, into the whole of history, feel yourself into everything – only now are you on the path of understanding."[24] In following a phenomenological approach, then, Hegel was simply following Herder's advice.

The obvious question that arises is how the historian is able to follow such a method. Is there not a danger that he will subconsciously apply the attitudes and values of his own age in his attempt to understand the past? Will not his sympathetic reconstruction be simply a projection of his own ethnocentric imagination? This problem certainly did not escape Hegel. In his introduction he warned that it is not possible to immerse ourselves fully in the past because we, as historians, belong to our own age. We cannot understand the ancient Greeks, he says, any more than "the perceptions of a dog" (VG, 13–14; 18). This difficulty seems to undermine the phenomenological method, however, which presupposes that we can understand an age as it would have understood itself. Yet the problem here, while it is a very real and serious one, should not be exaggerated. Although we cannot ever *fully* understand a past culture as it would have understood itself, we can still do this to some degree. We can approach, even if we cannot attain, this goal. There is indeed all the difference in the world between the historian who criticizes a past culture according to his contemporary prejudices and one who attempts to reconstruct it sympathetically on the basis of the most painstaking and detailed investigations. This difficulty, then, does not amount to an impossibility. The problems of Hegel's phenomenological method are simply part and parcel of the general problem of doing history in general.

Once we recognize that Hegel's method is phenomenological, we can quickly see what is wrong with those who accuse Hegel of following a "speculative" or a priori method. The very opposite is the case, given that it was precisely Hegel's aim to avoid the problems of such methods. His own phenomenological method is more akin to the empirical method of the historian, who immerses himself into his subject matter. Rather than beginning his philosophy of history with a metaphysics, Hegel intended metaphysics to be only its result.

Yet a nagging doubt still remains. If Hegel's method is in principle phenomenological, is it also in practice? Does Hegel abide by the guidelines that he sets for himself? It is in this respect that some of the objections of Hegel's critics have their point. However wrong they are about Hegel's principles and intentions, they are still correct about much of his practice. It is necessary for even the most-loyal Hegelian to admit that Hegel violates his own ideals. Rather than allowing his metaphysics to emerge from his analysis of the subject matter, he classifies and examines his subject matter according to his metaphysics. The dialectic proceeds from China to India, for example, because the idea of an organism means that a moment of diversity (the differentiated caste society of India) should follow that of unity (the uniformity of Chinese society) (XII, 180). The division of history into the Oriental, Classical, and Germanic worlds according to the principle of one, some, or all being free derives from Hegel's treatment of the forms of judgment in his Logic. In general, Hegel does not hesitate to pass harsh judgments upon foreign cultures (the American Indians, the Chinese, the Indians) according to the standpoint of modern Western individualism,[25] falling prey to the very ethnocentrism from which historicism should liberate us. When we consider factors like these it is difficult not to say of

Hegel's historical method what Kierkegaard said of his philosophy as a whole: "Hegel is to be honored for having willed something great and having failed to accomplish it."[26]

V. THE METAPHYSICS OF HEGEL'S HISTORICISM

It seems obvious that Hegel employs metaphysics in his philosophy of history. His text literally teems with metaphysical terms, such as "spirit," "idea," "providence," and "God." It is this metaphysical dimension of Hegel's text that has given it such a bad name among historians, and that has provoked the criticism of Croce, Marx, and others. They can rightfully grumble that, however much Hegel preached against metaphysics, he certainly did practice it.

After we concede the metaphysical dimension of Hegel's philosophy of history, the next question to raise is whether its presence is necessarily fatal. We cannot provide here a general defense or criticism of Hegel's metaphysics. We can, however, answer a much more modest question: Does Hegel's metaphysics remain true to his own strictures about the limits of knowledge? Is it a strictly immanent metaphysics, remaining within the limits of experience? Or does it involve speculation about transcendent entities? Hegel's critics usually dismiss his metaphysics because it seems to them to be a transcendent metaphysics, describing obscure metaphysical entities not encountered in any possible experience. But is this attitude fair? I would like to argue here that it rests upon a misunderstanding.

The metaphysical dimension of Hegel's philosophy of history ultimately rests upon its teleology, its claim that world history is governed by a single dominating purpose. Rather than contenting himself with a piecemeal description of events, Hegel thinks that the philosophy of history should answer the question "What is the ultimate purpose of history?" No sooner has he raised this question, though, than he seems to plunge into the deeper end of metaphysics. He immediately refers to God's providence and the idea governing history (VG, 28–49; 27–44). Without any further explanation or justification, we seem to return to the old theology of the eighteenth century.

Read out of context, Hegel's language here can be extremely misleading. If, however, we consider Hegel's remarks in the light of his other works, it becomes clear that the kind of teleology in question

is not that commonplace in the eighteenth century. In his *Logic* and
Encyclopedia, Hegel rejects the idea that there is a supernatural
design imposed upon history and nature by a transcendent God.[27] It
is just such "external teleology," he argues, that has given metaphysics a bad name, because it involves illegitimate speculation about
entities beyond experience. To avoid such speculation, Hegel insists
that the end of history and nature must be *internal to* history and
nature themselves. In other words, any explanation in teleological
terms must not violate the principle that everything in nature is
explicable in its own terms without reference to the supernatural. So
rather than theologizing Hegel's account of history, as his initial
remarks would seem to suggest, it is more appropriate to naturalize
his theology. Providence will be determined by some end within
history and nature.

What, then, is the ultimate purpose of history? Hegel's answer to
this question involves no more metaphysics than his conception of
natural law, his idea about the "essence" or characteristic nature of
man. The nature or essence of man, Hegel tells us simply, is freedom
(XII, 30). Just as the essence of matter is gravity, so the essence of the
self is freedom. Freedom is not simply one quality of the self, he
argues, but the basic quality that all others serve. To say that man is
free "by nature" does not mean, Hegel explains (XII, 58), that he is
born free or that he *exists* in some state of nature as a free being.
Rather, it signifies only that the *purpose* or *end* of man is to realize
his freedom. The essence or nature of man is of necessity, then, a
goal that he must achieve, not a reality that is given to him. The
realization of this goal therefore demands human activity. In other
words, it can be achieved only in history.

This concept of the essence of man determines Hegel's view of the
purpose of history itself. The end of history is nothing more nor less
than the realization of human freedom. It is, as Hegel puts it, "the
self-awareness of freedom," the knowledge that man as such is free
(VG, 62–63; 54–55). Since Hegel thinks that the essence of freedom
is realized only in the state, it follows that the purpose of history
will be to achieve the perfect state, that in which human freedom is
realized. It is for this reason, and not because of any Prussian authori-
tarianism, that Hegel believes that the state is the primary subject of
history.

The dialectic of Hegel's philosophy of history is also structured by his account of the end or purpose of man. The dialectic consists in the conflict between the end of man and his actual political conditions, and the attempt by man to change these conditions so that they are more in accord with his nature. Since man is not from the beginning fully or clearly aware of his goal, and since he does not know the necessary conditions to realize it, the process of achieving his end will be a journey of self-discovery.

This non-metaphysical account of Hegel's philosophy of history is implausible, someone might say, because it assumes that the main agents of history are finite human beings. But such a reading seems to fly in the face of Hegel's texts. For he tells us time and again that the main subject of history is "spirit" (*Geist*):

the history of the world is a rational process, the rational and necessary evolution of the world spirit. This spirit is the substance of history; its nature is always one and the same; and it discloses this nature in the existence of the world. The world spirit is the absolute spirit.   (VG, 30; 29)

If this absolute spirit is anything at all, this objection continues, then it is not this or that finite individual, nor even the mere sum of them. Rather, it is a suprapersonal substance of which all finite persons are only modes. This reading of spirit as a supernatural substance appears further strengthened by Hegel's famous concept of the "cunning of reason." According to this concept, all individual actions, though apparently directed by private ends, conform to a rational pattern or goal, the self-realization of spirit. Spirit, it would seem, is the super puppetmaster directing all individual actions.

This metaphysical reading of Hegel's concept of spirit is not, however, consistent with his general principles. Spirit by itself, apart from any of the finite individuals in which it appears, would be only a general term or universal. But Hegel insists that no universal can exist on its own apart from, and prior to, particular things. By itself it is simply an abstraction. Hegel's insistence on this point comes from his adherence to the Aristotelian dictum that universals exist only *in re*. Using a simple example, he clearly states this doctrine in his *Encyclopedia*:

The animal is not to be found, but it is always something determinate. The animal does not exist, but it is always the universal nature of the individual animals; and every individual animal is something much more concretely determinate, a particular.   (VIII, 82; §24, Zusatz 1)

It is this Aristotelian doctrine that Hegel applies to his concept of spirit in the *Philosophy of History* when he tells us most emphatically that spirit by itself is only an abstraction and comes into existence only through the activity of finite agents. In this passage Hegel explicitly warns us against any hypostasis of spirit:

> The first thing we have to notice is this: that what we have hitherto called the principle, or ultimate end, or destiny of the nature and concept of spirit in itself, is purely universal and abstract. A principle, fundamental rule, or law is something universal and implicit, and as such, it has not attained complete reality, however true it may be in itself. Aims, principles, and the like are present at first in our thoughts and inner intentions, or even in books, but not yet in reality itself. In other words, that which exists only in itself is a possibility or potentiality which has not yet emerged into existence. A second moment is necessary because it can attain reality – that of actualization or realization; and its principle is the will, the activity of mankind in the world at large. It is only by means of this activity that the original concepts or implicit determinations are realized and actualized.
>
> (VG, 81; 69–70)

Elsewhere in the *Philosophy of History*, Hegel further prohibits hypostasizing his concept of spirit by telling us that he does not mean by it some self-conscious being (VG, 37; 34).

It might be asked how the concept of spirit has any explanatory value at all if it exists only in finite agents. If spirit by itself is only an abstraction, how does it explain the rational plan behind the chaos of individual actions? If it exists only in individuals, it would seem to amount to nothing more than the sum of their disparate actions. The rational plan behind history, the cunning of reason, still seems to give some reason, then, for thinking of spirit as some suprapersonal substance acting behind the scenes. But such hypostasis is completely unwarranted, and indeed for good Hegelian reasons. Here it is important to invoke another Aristotelian doctrine, one that Hegel incorporates into his teleology. This is Aristotle's distinction between what is first in order of explanation and what is first in order of existence. A particular is first *in order of existence,* since to know *that* a thing exists we must know something about particular or determinate things. This is because a universal, if it exists, exists only in particulars. A universal, however, is first *in order of explanation* because to know *what* a thing is we must be able to specify some properties of it, some features that it shares in common with other things. We identify a thing, for example, by saying that it is red and round, or blue and square. Similarly, to know *why* a thing acts, for what purpose or end, we must also be able to state some universal. The final cause of a thing is, for Aristotle, some universal specifying its essence or characteristic nature. Now this Aristotelian distinction is crucial for Hegel's account of historical explanation. It means that the universal, in this case spirit, has an explanatory value even though it exists only in particular persons. It has an explanatory value because it is first in order of explanation, if not first in order of existence. Without the concept of spirit we cannot explain what all finite agents are trying to achieve throughout history (the realization of their freedom). Nevertheless, because it is first in order of explanation does not mean that it is first in order of existence; in other words, the concept of spirit still does not come into existence except through the activity of all finite agents. Hence, thanks to this Aristotelian distinction, the concept of spirit should have some explanatory value without the need to make some commitment to an abstract or transcendent entity.

If we further examine Hegel's concept of spirit, we find that it conforms perfectly to our non-metaphysical reading of the purpose of history. The concept of spirit is indeed simply a more-specific account of what Hegel means by the end of history, the self-awareness of freedom. If we closely consider those chapters of the *Phenomenology* where Hegel first deduces the concept of spirit, chapters IV and IV.A, then we find that it is indeed the self-awareness of freedom. It tells us precisely what form this self-awareness should take. More specifically, spirit is the mutual recognition between free and equal persons, their intersubjective self-awareness of their freedom. It is, as Hegel puts it, "the I that is a We and the We that is an I." In these chapters Hegel argues that my self-awareness as a free being must be social or intersubjective. It demands the recognition of others as equal and independent beings because only by this means do I achieve the recognition necessary to confirm to myself that I too am an independent being. The mutual self-awareness of spirit is of course not reducible to the self-awareness of particular persons. It is possible only through their abandoning their sense of themselves as separate individuals and by their identifying themselves with the social whole. But at the same time, neither is spirit a substance or entity that exists apart from the persons who become *mutually* self-aware. By itself it is simply mutual self-awareness, intersubjective self-consciousness, and hence an abstraction. It is the task of the *Philosophy of Right* to specify the political conditions necessary for the realization of spirit, for the development of the self-awareness of freedom. To say that the end of history is the realization of spirit *and* a state where there is a community between free and equal individuals is one and the same thing.

VI. THE POLITICS OF HEGEL'S HISTORICISM

What were the political intentions and implications behind Hegel's historicism? This question has been the subject of a famous dispute, a controversy that has lasted more than a century. Some commentators have argued that Hegel's aims were fundamentally conservative, indeed reactionary.[28] They regard Hegel as the spokesman for the Restoration in Prussia, as the defender of the reactionary policies of the government of Friedrich Wilhelm III. Hegel's philosophy of history was, in their view, no less reactionary than his philosophy of the state. They argue that it was Hegel's purpose, in giving such importance to history, to defend the value of established institutions and traditions against those radicals who would model all of society according to abstract principles. Nowhere are Hegel's reactionary views more apparent, they contend, than in his making the present Prussian state into the apotheosis of world history. Other commentators, however, especially the left-wing Hegelian school, have acknowledged Hegel's philosophy of history as the inspiration for their own radical doctrines.[29] They stress the revolutionary implications, if not intentions, of his dialectic. In saying that history is a process of dialectical development, of ceaseless conflict, destruction, and regeneration, Hegel allegedly passed the death sentence upon any status quo.

If we carefully examine all the passages from Hegel's writings in which he draws some political point from history, we find that neither of these interpretations is correct. The truth lies somewhere in between. For Hegel appealed to history to justify the middle path of reform, to criticize both radicals and reactionaries alike. In his view, both the radicals and reactionaries had failed to understand history. The radicals could not see that their ideals have to be adapted to the history of a nation, while the reactionaries were blind to the fact that history undergoes ceaseless change. If history made it impossible to create a totally new society according to some abstract plan, it also prohibited attempts to return to the past.

In the spectrum of political belief in Germany after the French Revolution, Hegel reveals himself to be a progressive moderate. Unlike the reactionaries, he approved of the fundamental ideals of the French Revolution, such as equality of opportunity, constitutional government, individual liberty, and representative assemblies; and he insisted that it was impossible to return to the older institutions of the *ancien régime*. Unlike the radicals, however, Hegel did not believe that these ideals could be achieved through popular agitation, still less through sweeping away all the historical traditions and institutions of Germany. The ideals of the Revolution would have to be established through piecemeal reform from above, through gradually adapting them to the historical conditions prevalent in Germany.

There can be no doubt that there is a conservative side to Hegel's historicism. In many of his writings Hegel appealed to history to criticize the attempts by radicals to remodel all of society according to their abstract ideals.[30] The lesson to be drawn from the failure of the Revolution in France, in Hegel's view, was that it is not possible to change the constitution and institutions of a society in complete abstraction from its history, from such given circumstances as its religion, economy, traditions, and national character. When the French radicals discovered that their ideals could not be easily imposed upon these circumstances, Hegel maintains, they engaged in a "fury of destruction," destroying all the historical institutions and traditions of France. The result was that there was nothing for them to build upon, so that the country lapsed into anarchy and terror.

The conservative element of Hegel's historicism largely lay in his naturalism, his belief that the constitution and institutions of a nation are the product of its environment, and in particular its climate, geography, economy, religion, and traditions. Hegel acquired this doctrine from Montesquieu in his youth, and he adhered to it all his life. No less than his illustrious predecessor, he drew a conservative conclusion from it: that the constitution and institutions of a nation are adapted to its circumstances and are therefore appropriate to them. As Hegel put the point succinctly in his *Philosophy of Right:* "Every nation has the constitution appropriate to it and suitable for it" (VII, 440, §274). It was largely for this reason that Hegel sharply attacked utopian and radical reformers. In prescribing how the state ought to be, they failed to take into account its natural causes, the circumstances that make it of necessity as it is. The state cannot be created according to an arbitrary plan, but arises from historical causes, from the force of environment acting upon it.

It is no less clear, however, that there is a progressive side to Hegel's historicism. In seeing the end of history as the self-awareness of freedom, as the recognition that all are free, Hegel made the ideals of liberty and equality of the French Revolution into the very end of history itself. He thus bestowed the iron law of necessity upon these ideals. They were goals that people not only *ought to* strive for but *must* strive for through the inherent laws of history itself. Since these ideals were inherent in the natural development of history, Hegel argued that it was impossible in the post-revolutionary era to return to the old *status quo ante* of the *ancien régime*. This would be to fail to recognize the fate of the modern world, the fundamental spirit of modern life since the French Revolution. This was the principle of subjectivity, the idea that nothing could be accepted as valid until it accorded with the reason of the individual.

This progressive side of Hegel's historicism becomes especially plain from two of his political articles, his 1799 "On the German Constitution" and his 1814 "Proceedings of the Estates of Württemberg."[34] Although they were written on separate occasions and for different reasons, these articles shared a common critical orientation. Both attacked those jurists and aristocrats who were bent on returning to the political structure of the *ancien régime*. The jurists continued to write as if the Holy Roman Empire still existed and as if nothing had changed since Charlemagne, while the aristocrats insisted upon the return of all their old privileges and powers as if Napoleon had never revamped the entire structure of Germany. The trend of history since the revolution, Hegel argued, had been against restoring the old feudal constitution of the Holy Roman Empire, which had not been able to adapt to the new situation in Europe. If the princes' attempt to restore this constitution, ignoring all recent history, then they would revive only "empty forms without a substance." The spirit of the times demands, Hegel insisted, the creation of a completely new constitution for Germany, a constitution providing for a strong central government, representative institutions, the role of law, and popular influence on legislation.

The progressive and conservative sides of Hegel's historicism are succinctly captured by his famous dictum in the preface to the *Philosophy of Right:* "What is rational is actual, and what is actual is rational" (VII, 24). The first phrase expresses Hegel's progressive beliefs. To say that the rational is actual means that the ideals of liberty and equality, which have been sanctioned by reason, will become realized of necessity in history itself. The second phrase states Hegel's more-conservative convictions. Here he means that the present constitution and institutions of a nation are rational in the sense that they arise of necessity from their environment, and are therefore appropriate to it. These two phrases appear to conflict with one another, however, for what if the present constitution violates, or at least does not recognize, the principles of liberty and equality? Hegel's reply to this question is that each constitution is appropriate not only to its circumstances but also to its stage in the world-historical development of freedom and equality. The cunning of reason means that even if a nation does not recognize these ideals, it is still a necessary stage in their dialectical development.

What allows Hegel to unite the progressive and conservative sides of his historicism – to reconcile the ideals of the Revolution with the demand of historical continuity – is his belief that these ideals were already present within, and central to, the Middle Ages. They do not involve a complete break with feudalism, he believes, but they are simply the final coming to self-consciousness of its underlying spirit. In his essay on the German constitution, for example, Hegel ridicules those who think that the modern principle of representative government arose only with the French Revolution. This principle was in fact basic to government during the feudal period, he contends. According to the medieval ideal of government, each vassal should have a direct personal share in the shaping of common policy. The representation of the individual in the government was direct and immediate, since each vassal personally stood for his own territory in the assemblies. The fundamental challenge to government in the modern age, Hegel maintains, is to unite the medieval ideal of participation in government with the need for a strong central authority. The modern state has simply grown too large and complex for direct participation. If, under these conditions, the principle of direct participation is not relinquished, as in the Holy Roman Empire, then the state will simply dissolve into anarchy, a jumble of separate territories.

Both the radicals and reactionaries, Hegel believed, had failed to see that there is reason in history, that the realization of freedom and equality is the inherent law of its development since the Middle Ages. The radicals recognized the authority of reason, to be sure, but they did not understand that it is the law of history itself. It was for this reason that they mistakenly believed that they had *to impose* reason upon history and to break with the past. On the other hand, the reactionaries fully recognized the value of historical continuity and development, but they did not comprehend that it has an underlying end or reason, the realization of freedom and equality.

In considering the politics of Hegel's historicism, it is illuminating to compare Hegel with Burke.[32] Both stressed the value of historical continuity and tradition. Both appealed to history to undermine the claims of French radicals to change all of society according to some abstract plan. Nevertheless Hegel, unlike Burke, saw history as an argument *for* rather than against a new constitution based upon reason. Burke argues against the attempt to create a new constitution on the grounds that it is *incompatible with* historical development. Hegel, however, argues in favor of such a constitution on the grounds that it is *necessary to* historical development. In general, Hegel affirmed the fundamental legal principle of the Revolution, that laws are legitimate only if they accord with a critical reason.[33] He criticized traditionalists like Burke on the grounds that historical precedent by itself could never be the source of law. Age, Hegel argued, has nothing to do with justice or rights. Even the abrogation of slavery, despotism, and human sacrifice was a violation of old rights and privileges. Turning the principle of positive law against the traditionalists, he argues that if the basis of law is history, then law must change with history.

NOTES

All references in the text are to the *Werkausgabe* of Hegel's works edited by E. Moldenhauer and K. Michel, *Werke in Zwanzig Bänden* (Frankfurt, 1970). Roman numerals refer to volume numbers, Arabic numerals to page numbers. All translations of Hegel's works are my own (with the exception of the Nisbet translation of the *Philosophy of World History*). Page numbers cited after a semicolon are to the appropriate English translations cited below.

The following works and abbreviations have been used:

Die Vernunft in der Geschichte, ed. J. Hoffmeister (Hamburg, 1970), volume
    I of *Vorlesungen über die Philosophie der Weltgeschichte*. Cited as VG.
Lectures on the Philosophy of World History, trans. H.B. Nisbet (Cambridge
    England, 1975).
History of Philosophy, trans. E.S. Haldane (London, 1892–95). Cited as HP.
Hegel's Political Writings, trans. T.M. Knox (Oxford, 1964). Cited as HPW.
Philosophy of History, trans. T. Sibree (New York, 1956).

1 See, for example, Rudolf Haym, *Hegel und seine Zeit* (Leipzig, 1927),
    45–46; Georg Lukács, *Der junge Hegel* (Frankfurt, 1973), I, 62, 135–36;
    and Jean Hyppolite, *Genesis and Structure of the Phenomenology of
    Spirit* (Evanston, 1974), 27–34.
2 See, for example, Hegel's critique of Kant's concept in his Lectures on
    the *History of Philosophy* XX, 352; HP III, 444–45. Also see Hegel's
    critique of empiricism, *Werke* XX, 79; HP III, 303.
3 The definitive study of the origins of historicism is Friedrich Meinecke's
    Die Entstehung des Historismus (Munich, 1959). Unfortunately, Mein-
    ecke does not discuss Hegel. For a briefer discussion of Hegel's predeces-
    sors and Hegel himself, see R.G. Collingwood, *The Idea of History* (Ox-
    ford, 1980), 86–113.
4 On the influence of Montesquieu, see *Werke* I, 60, 206, 263, 440; on the
    influence of Herder, see *Werke* I, 201, 215; XIII, 349; and XVIII, 21; and
    on the influence of Ferguson, see Rosenkranz, *G.W.F. Hegels Leben* (Ber-
    lin, 1844) 87.
5 See *Werke* XVIII, 18–19, 49; and XX, 478–79; HP I, 29.
6 See especially the new introduction to Hegel's *Positivity* essay, *Werke* I,
    227–29; ETW, 167–81. For a study of the critical historical themes in
    Hegel's *Phenomenology*, see Judith Shklar, *Freedom and Independence:
    A Study of the Political Ideas of Hegel's Phenomenology of Mind* (Cam-
    bridge, England, 1976).
7 Hegel stresses this doctrine in his *Lectures on the Philosophy of History*,
    Werke XII, 65–66; PH, 46. *Cf.* 52.
8 See Hegel's *Lectures on the History of Philosophy*, *Werke* XVIII, 73–75;
    HP I, 53–54.
9 See Hegel's *Lectures on the History of Philosophy*, *Werke* XVIII, 20–28;
    HP I, 2–3.
10 *Werke* XVIII, 25–27; HP I, 29–32.

11 *Werke* XVIII, 54–55; cf. *Werke* XX, 506–9.

12 Cf. *Werke* XVIII, 49, and XX, 478–79.

13 See *Die deutsche Ideologie, Marx-Engels Gesamtausgabe* (Berlin: Dietz, 1973) III, 26–27, 39. Cf. Ergänzungsband I, 568–88.

14 Here I disagree with Collingwood, *Idea of History*, p. 125, who sees Marx's fundamental difference with Hegel as his naturalism.

15 On the importance of economics for the young Hegel, see Shlomo Avineri, *Hegel's Theory of the Modern State* (Cambridge, England, 1972), 132–54.

16 *Werke* X, 43–199, §388–411.

17 See the *Philosophy of History, Werke* XII, 52–53; PH, 45–46.

18 This objection is made by Haym, *Hegel und seine Zeit*, 375–76, and by Meinecke, *Die Idee der Staatsräson in der Geschichte* (Munich & Berlin, 1929), 451–52. The same objection is implicit in the critique of those who accuse Hegel of legal positivism. This is the objection of Popper, *The Open Society and its Enemies* (London, 1945), 39, 62–63.

19 See below, section VI, 294–95.

20 The term "genetic fallacy" has received various definitions. The one I follow here is that of Morris Cohen and Ernest Nagel, *An Introduction to Logic and Scientific Method* (London, 1978), 388–90. For a criticism of the Hegelian and Marxist tradition on this score, see H.B. Acton, *The Illusion of the Epoch* (London, 1955), 108–9.

21 See *Werke* XII, 11–20, 543–58. Also *Die Vernunft in der Geschichte*, pp. 3–27, and particularly 11–24.

22 See W.H. Walsh, *An Introduction to the Philosophy of History* (London, 1967), 143–50.

23 The *locus classicus* for this view is Benedetto Croce's *What is Living and What is Dead in the Philosophy of Hegel*, trans. Douglas Ainslie (London, 1915), 134–49.

24 Herder, *Sämtliche Werke*, ed. B. Suphan (Berlin, 1877–1913), V, 503.

25 This point has been argued in detail by W.H. Walsh, "Principle and Prejudice in Hegel's Philosophy of History," in *Hegel's Political Philosophy*, ed. Z.A. Pelczynski (Cambridge, England, 1971), 181–98.

26 See *Concluding Unscientific Postscript* (Princeton, New Jersey, 1969), 100n.

27 Cf. *Werke* VIII, 362–63, §205–6; and *Werke* VI, 458.

28 The *locus classicus* for this criticism of Hegel is Haym's *Hegel und seine Zeit*, pp. 357–91. For a more-recent criticism of Hegel as a reactionary, see Popper, *The Open Society*, II, 27, 57–75.

29 The *locus classicus* for the left-wing interpretation of Hegel's historicism is Engel's *Ludwig Feuerbach und der Ausgang der klassischen Philosophie*, MEGA XXI, 266–68.

30 See, for example, the *Phenomenology, Werke* III, 431–41; *Philosophy of History, Werke* XII, 64–65; and the *Philosophy of Right, Werke* VII, 400–401, §258.

31 See *Werke* I, 470–71; HPW, 152–53; *Werke* XI, HPW, 250–51, 273–74.

32 For a more-detailed comparison of Burke and Hegel, see J-F Suter, "Burke, Hegel and the French Revolution," in *Hegel's Political Philosophy*, pp. 52–72.

33 *Werke* IV, 506; HPW, 281–82.

10 Hegel on religion and philosophy

This essay addresses some of the themes that modern scholarship has identified as central to an understanding of Hegel's thoughts on religion. For a variety of pedagogic reasons, which will become evident over the course of this essay, I have chosen to approach these themes historically and contextually rather than philosophically and abstractly. To that end, my discussion of Hegel's thoughts on religion focuses primarily on the religious, philosophical, and political circumstances that conditioned, and were conditioned by, his writings during his so-called Berlin period (1818–1831).[1]

During these years – from his appointment to the prestigious chair in philosophy at the University of Berlin in 1818 until his death in 1831–Hegel's philosophy came to public prominence.[2] Indeed, it was in Berlin that Hegel's philosophy became an ideological factor in public debate. As we shall see, that was especially true in the realm of religion, for from about 1821 on Hegel's views on Christianity in general and on Protestantism in particular were not only publicly debated but fiercely contested as well. Thus, Hegel's Berlin period provides an important context both for measuring the ideological impact his views on religion had on public consciousness and for determining the ways in which the public opposition to his views shaped his private as well as public pronouncements on religion.

To friend and foe alike, then, Hegel was someone to be ideologically reckoned with between 1818 and 1831. It is the religious views of that Hegel, the Hegel whom modern scholarship has made familiar to us as the philosopher of the Prussian state, that I have chosen to examine here.

I. THE IMPORTANCE OF CONTEXT

That Hegel was deeply interested in religious issues all his life is evident from even a cursory glance at just about any of his major writings. From the 1790s, through his years in Jena, Nuremberg, and Heidelberg (1801–1818), to his Berlin period, Hegel's published and unpublished writings (including his personal correspondence) testify to his abiding concern with the world's great religions in general and with the history of Christianity in particular.[3] As a young man, the so-called "young Hegel" chose to write a life of Jesus as well as several other essays on Christian themes.[4] And as letters to and from his friends during the 1790s indicate, Hegel saw himself and was regarded by others as a thinker whose main concern was to take up "religious concepts" in order to make them philosophically understandable.[5] Similarly, during the Berlin years, Hegel continued to exhibit unflagging interest in the religious issues that had exercised him in the 1790s. Not for nothing did the always astute Karl Löwith identify Hegel as the "last Christian philosopher".[6]

If Hegel's writings manifest a life-long involvement with Christian themes, it was not until after his appointment to the chair in Berlin in 1818 that his ideas on what it meant to be a Christian in general and a Protestant in particular drew public attention.[7] We know, of course, that with the publication of The Philosophy of Right in 1821, Hegel's political views became subject to public scrutiny. Often overlooked by scholars is the fact that Hegel began his lectures on the philosophy of religion in the same year. As it happened, these lectures proved to be, and perhaps were intended to be, controversial, for in substance they challenged the religious views then being expounded in lectures by the famous University of Berlin theologian F. Schleiermacher.[8] Thus, whereas before 1821 Hegel's philosophy could be (and was) described as one "without a label,"[9] after that date it entered the realm of public discourse – which is to say, it became an ideological factor in the religious and political controversies of the day.[10] For that reason, it is quite impossible to make any *historical* sense of the importance of Hegel's views on religion without paying proper attention to the ideological context in which those views were developed and expressed.

It is regrettable but nonetheless true that twentieth-century schol-arship's understanding of Hegel's religious views has never taken proper account of this context.[11] Consequently, most of the scholar-ship on Hegel's views of religion has been governed by themes that, while certainly pertinent to the ideological debates of the 1820s, do not accurately represent Hegel's position in those debates or his view of them. Indeed, it would be no exaggeration to say that mod-ern scholarship has taken more heed of what Hegel's opponents said about his religious views than of what he himself wrote about religion.[12]

This uncritical acquiescence in the say-so of Hegel's opponents has fostered much confusion about him both as a thinker and as a public figure in Berlin during his years there. And nowhere is the confusion more evident than in the claim that Hegel was the philoso-pher of the reactionary Prussian government during these years.[13] In this essay, I will avoid confusions of that sort by discussing Hegel's views on religion in their proper historical context.

II. THE SOURCES: HEGEL'S VIEWS ON RELIGION AND PHILOSOPHY DURING THE BERLIN PERIOD

One of the reasons scholars have failed to develop a proper historical perspective on Hegel's religious views during the Berlin period is because Hegel published no books on religious subjects during those years. Yet, during his Berlin period Hegel pronounced himself on religious subjects repeatedly and in a variety of different sources.

Between 1821 and 1831 Hegel lectured four times on the philoso-phy of religion. At the same time, from 1822 on, he used the format of his lectures on the philosophy of history to develop an historical framework within which many of his most-important religious views were advanced (for example, the role of Protestantism in the modern world). These lectures, and especially the latter, were ex-tremely popular within and without the university, circulating in notebook form among students and interested parties throughout the city.[14] Hegel even received requests for copies of these notebooks from foreigners who wished to gain access to his thinking.[15]

In addition to these lectures, Hegel had several opportunities in Berlin to deliver public addresses in which he spoke to the religious issues of his day. Thus, in his Berlin inaugural of 1818, he not only commended governmental authorities for "the moral and religious seriousness" with which they were seeking to put philosophy at the service of the reformation of all spheres of cultural and spiritual life in Prussia, but also offered some critical remarks about the religious teachings of those who, like Schleiermacher, mistakenly thought a theology of "feeling" expressed what was most dignified about religious life.[16] Likewise, in 1830, in a speech Hegel gave in his capacity as rector of the university to commemorate the three hundreth anniversary of the Augsburg Confession, he expounded on why he dated the beginning of modernity from the Reformation rather than from the French Revolution.[17]

Furthermore, between 1827 and 1831 Hegel used the occasion of bringing out new editions of The Encyclopedia (in 1827 and 1830) and The Logic (1831) to castigate the religious views of Protestant extremists in Berlin.[18] While positioning himself relative to theological rationalists on the one hand and to evangelicals on the other, Hegel made clear how his own "speculative philosophy" avoided the theological and socioethical pitfalls of the two extremes.[19]

From 1826 on, moreover, Hegel and his associates – particularly Gans in the law faculty and Daub and Marheinecke in the theological faculties of Heidelberg and Berlin – had at their disposal a journal, The Yearbook for Scientific Criticism, in which the theological and ethical implications of speculative philosophy were explicated.[20] It was also in this journal that Hegel defended himself against recurrent charges of atheism and panlogism, charges that intensified after 1827.[21]

Finally, and above all else, Hegel's letters to friends and opponents of speculative philosophy during the Berlin period are spectacularly clear where Hegel thought he stood relative to the competing theological tendencies of his day. Indeed, it would not be too much to say that Hegel's letters contain the most precise formulations that we possess of his understanding of the relationship between speculative philosophy and religion.[22] What is more interesting still is that these letters are comprehensive in scope – which is to say, they often take full account of the exact theological points that are at issue between Hegel and his opponents. As such, the letters reflect Hegel's self-consciousness about the position of speculative philosophy in the polarized religio-political context of Restoration Prussia.

III. SPECULATIVE PHILOSOPHY: THE POLITICS OF BILDUNG IN THE 1820S

If we look closely at the sources in which Hegel expressed himself on religious matters during the Berlin period, it becomes obvious that even before arriving in Berlin in 1818 Hegel had inklings that any attempt on his part to apply the principles of speculative philosophy to Protestant religious issues would provoke instant opposition from religiously active groups in Berlin – from orthodox Lutherans, from theologians of feeling such as Schleiermacher, and from the neo-pietists whose dogmatic approach to questions of Protestant orthodoxy had found a receptive and enthusiastic audience among important aristocratic groups in Berlin and throughout Prussia.[23] And insofar as these religious minded groups could number among their allies romantics, conservatives, and Friesian subjectivists in philosophy, Hegel expected opposition from them, too.[24]

Yet, what worried Hegel in the early 1820s about the opposition of these Berlin "demagogues" was how much support they would receive from Prussian authorities.[25] In 1818, Hegel could be confident of Altenstein's support.[26] After all, as minister of culture, Altenstein (with Hardenberg's support) had arranged to bring Hegel to Berlin, where, it was thought, he would be an advocate of the principles of liberal reform that a key group in the Prussian bureaucracy was hoping would revitalize the Prussian state after the ravages of the Wars of Liberation.

But by 1821 a reactionary religio-political coalition of Protestants was forming around the figure of the crown prince, the future Frederick William IV of Prussia.[27] Over the next score of years, the crown prince proved to be highly sympathetic to the cause of Pietist-orthodoxy, with the result that as the decades of the '20s unfolded Hegel increasingly realized how precarious were the prospects of speculative philosophy both in the capital city and in the university. Indeed, with only Altenstein to protect him, Hegel knew there would be risks involved in trying to push the religious agenda of speculative philosophy too far. Thus, as early as 1819, after some of his students had been arrested for supposedly subversive political activity, Hegel confessed to Niethammer, a long-time friend, that his influence in Berlin was quite limited – by which he meant that it was confined to the rather narrow academic world of university teaching and noncontroversial faculty appointments. All the same, he confided to Niethammer that "as a professor I have only begun. Much still remains to be achieved for me and the Cause."[28] To that end, Hegel began immediately to recruit and train followers for the cause of speculative philosophy. As we shall see, it is in the context of the pedagogic need to gain an institutional base and audience for speculative philosophy that Hegel's views on religion must initially be understood.

IV. SPECULATIVE PHILOSOPHY: RELIGIOUS METAPHYSICS AND SCIENTIFIC METHOD

Once it is realized how circumscribed Hegel's influence in Berlin was from 1818 on, it becomes easier to understand why speculative philosophy in the Hegelian mode became an academic "school" of thought more than anything else.[29] Even so, it would be wrong to assume that the pedagogic thrust of Hegel's philosophy in the 1820s was merely a reflection of frustration and sublimated political ambitions. For Hegel's decision to give speculative philosophy a pedagogic turn dates from well before his invitation to Berlin. Thus, in 1819, when Hegel mentioned the "cause" of his philosophy to Niethammer, he was referring to the role he had set for himself early in his teaching career – at a time, in fact, when he and Niethammer were collaborators of sorts in an ambitious educational reform effort in Bavaria.[30]

In this regard, the thoughts Hegel developed between 1811 and 1816 on how to teach speculative philosophy to students in the Nuremberg Gymnasium (where he was employed as a teacher from 1808–1816) are especially revealing. And, for us, what makes these thoughts all the more important is the role religion (that is, Christian values in the key of liberal Protestant humanism) plays in them.

During these years – in his correspondence as well as in the prefaces he wrote for *The Logic* (1812) and *The Encyclopedia* (1817) – Hegel presented speculative philosophy as a "definite methodical procedure" for making "what is of substantive value" in a "spiritual" sense both "intelligible" and "communicable" in a pedagogic sense.[31] Embarrassed, he said, by the then-current tendency of German thinkers to organize philosophy around feeling and fantasy,

Hegel offered speculative philosophy as a method for teaching students how to think.

Hegel's strategy for attaining this end was threefold.[32] First, he recommended speculative philosophy as a "critical" method of thought. As an alternative to what he described as the "intensive" method of various philosophical subjectivists (such as Fries, F. Schlegel, and F. von Baader), Hegel proposed to use the critical method to raise philosophy to the level of science. Such an elevation, he argued, entailed two things: making philosophy "teachable," and giving it a regular structure with which to facilitate its teaching. Accordingly, Hegel associated speculative philosophy with a pedagogic procedure that militated against what in *The Encyclopedia* he called the "knight-errantry" of philosophical "willfulness," a willfulness that Hegel contended had led to "the mania" of "everyone [wanting] to have his own system" of philosophy.

Second, Hegel regarded the establishment of philosophy as science as a way of giving man back the dignity of a "philosophical consciousness."[34] As Hegel saw it, the upheavals of the French Revolution, which in his mind had disrupted things "in the realm of science no less than in the world of politics," had compromised philosophy, turning the discipline into little more than a forum for competing forms of philosophical subjectivism.[35] It was Hegel's view, moreover, that were philosophy to be rescued "from the cul-de-sac" into which it had been driven since 1789,[36] human dignity would have to be philosophically reborn within the world. Thus, from at least 1812 on, the aim of speculative philosophy was to instill in man a sense that the achievement of philosophical consciousness constituted a crucial step in the attainment of human dignity.

Finally, Hegel's pedagogic agenda emphasized that the aim of speculative philosophy was to remind men of the religious dimension of their nature.[37] For Hegel, grounding human nature in religion enabled him to show men that they were spiritual beings rather than "merely" natural ones.[38] As such beings, so went Hegel's argument, men could "consider and grasp" what was divine about themselves. And then, by rising "above the [petty] interests of the hour," they could "come to" themselves as selves, as "persons" who, according to Hegel, were now in a position to establish "the Kingdom of God" on earth. Since "man is spirit," Hegel declared, "he should and must deem himself worthy of the highest; he cannot think highly enough of the greatness and power of his spirit." For that reason, Hegel concluded, "faith in the power of the spirit is the first condition of philosophizing."

What Hegel is suggesting here, I think, is something that he makes clear in very abstract language in the preface to the second edition of *The Logic* (1831). There, shortly before his death, Hegel argued that man comes to himself, becomes truly free, when he knows himself as his own concept – as a person, that is. According to Hegel, teaching men to recognize and grasp themselves in those terms was a long, slow cultural process – a process of *Bildung* whereby philosophy gradually enabled "the mind" or man to come into contact with his "soul," with the deepest purpose, the *telos*, of his being.³⁹ In Hegel's speculative system, therefore, man realizes himself as *Geist* – in the double sense of mind and soul – when philosophy persuades him of both his religious nature (or potential) and his religious destiny.

From that perspective, the "methodical procedure" that raises philosophy to the level of science also triggers for Hegel a process whereby man becomes increasingly conscious of his religious *telos*. Given this convergence of religious, scientific, and philosophical considerations in Hegel's thinking, it can hardly be surprising that as early as 1811 Hegel ridiculed Fries for having attempted to ground "logic" in "anthropology."⁴⁰ As Hegel never tired of arguing, logic had to be grounded in religion – in Christian anthropology – if proper account were to be made of the spiritual dimension of human nature.⁴¹ Only on those terms, he counseled, could the dignity of man be reestablished in the post-Napoleonic world.

V. CHRISTIAN CONSCIOUSNESS: CONTENT AND FORM IN HEGEL'S PHILOSOPHY

Between 1811 and 1831, then, there is much evidence to show how and why Hegel proposed to run together religious and philosophical conceptions in his understanding of scientific procedure. He is perhaps clearest about all this in the preface he wrote for the second edition of *The Encyclopedia* that was issued in 1827. There, while discussing the religious dimension of speculative philosophy, Hegel took time to situate his religious thoughts relative to those of his rationalist and evangelical opponents.

What Hegel says in this preface is consistent with the religious convictions he had held all his life. He begins by defining religion as "a mode of consciousness" that seeks to establish the truth of the relationship between man and God.[42] That truth, Hegel implied, had expressed itself differently at different moments in human history. Speculative philosophy, he then conjectured, articulated a form of that truth that was appropriate to the advanced consciousness of the modern world. Given this conviction, he castigated Protestant demogogues in Berlin for stigmatizing speculative philosophy simply because it expressed its view of traditional religious values in nontraditional philosophical language.

Having made this general point, Hegel turned to the real issue at hand: the growing belligerence and intolerance of evangelical Protestants to every form of religion that deviated from their own dogmatic certainties.[43] Since at least 1821 a varied coalition of such orthodox Protestants had attacked speculative philosophy as atheistic.[44] To these Protestants, speculative philosophy had sanctioned the usurpation of the rank of God by men.[45] Rising to the challenge of the "inane priests in Berlin," Hegel assured his readers that speculative philosophy had no intention of replacing either God with man, Christianity with atheism, or Lutheranism with speculative philosophy.[46]

In amplifying this, Hegel claimed that "the substance" of the Christian religion and his philosophy were "the same." What the small-minded parsons had to understand, he continued, was that the truth of the relationship between man and God – the essence of religion, as it were – could now be expressed in two different "languages," which, while possessing the same "substantiality," assumed different cognitive forms in the modern world.

Elaborating still further, Hegel argued that one of these forms operated with the language of "feeling" and piety," and registered the deep need of mankind in general for religion. By contrast, the other language of religion – that of "scientific cognition" – manifested itself in speculative philosophy. As Hegel then explained, this language sought the "scientific ascertainment of [religious] truth." But because grasping this truth in this way involved "a labor which not all but only a few" could undertake, Hegel distinguished the one language from the other, implying, as he had written earlier, that the scientific language of speculative philosophy spoke to the "educated" consciousness of his age, that of faith addressed the needs of the "ordinary consciousness" of all men at all times.[47] To that end, Hegel wished to make speculative philosophy integral to Christianity so that it could then *participate* in the "intelligent expansion" of the "contents" of "modern religiosity."[48] In this, like many Christians before him, some of whom were Fathers of the Church, Hegel aimed at making philosophy the agent for expanding Christian *pistis* into Christian *gnosis*.[49]

While delineating this twofold conception of Christian cognition, Hegel criticized the evangelicals for having unnecessarily "contracted" the religious core of Christianity. By implying "that religion may well exist without philosophy," Hegel alleged, they had restricted Christianity to such a "narrow" sphere of existence that it enfeebled the spirit of man and militated against spiritually inspired efforts of self-transcendence.[50] In Hegel's view, such a religious attitude encouraged men to celebrate themselves as natural rather than spiritual beings. Propagation of speculative philosophy, Hegel confidently predicted, would prevent further development of that naturalizing and spiritually demeaning religious disposition.

Even though Hegel was under considerable pressure in the 1820s to bring speculative philosophy into line with the dogmas of Pietist-orthodoxy, it would be wrong to interpret the distinction he drew between the languages of faith and knowledge as anything other than a sincere expression of his personal religious convictions. Hegel, after all, articulated the same view of things in his personal correspondence of those years. For example, as early as 1822, in a letter in which he was responding to a request for an explanation of his religious views, Hegel explained the difference between religious and philosophical approaches to Christian truth in terms of a distinction between believing and knowing, respectively.[51] Similarly, two years later, in a letter to F. von Baader, he explained the distinction in terms of different forms of cognition.[52]

Hegel's public and private writings, therefore, make it clear that, although he distinguished between religion and philosophy, he meant for the distinction to promote rather than retard the expansion of Christian consciousness. The problem, of course, was that while Hegel posited speculative philosophy as the Christian-inspired synthesis of faith and knowledge, the synthesis itself could be viewed in alternative ways.[53]

For example, Hegel's acceptance of feeling as a core element in religion could be viewed an an attempted reconciliation with either neo-pietism, Schleiermacher, or both at once. Alternatively, the progression from the language of religion to that of philosophy could be interpreted as a movement from one discrete stage of Christian consciousness to another. If this were the case, two very different interpretations of Hegel's synthesis were possible. On the one hand, philosophy could be said to be preserving faith by raising it to the level of knowledge. On the other hand, in raising faith to knowledge, the latter could be viewed as superseding the former. Finally, speculative philosophy could be seen as trying to steer a *via media* between the subjectivity of an anti-philosophical dogmatism and the sterile abstractions of theological rationalism.

Among these various options, Hegel's writings between 1827 and 1831 indicate a marked preference for the last alternative. For as his correspondence and preface to the third edition of *The Encyclopedia* (1830) reveal, Hegel wished to free Christianity from both the subjectivity and intolerance of dogmatic evangelicals and the rational "pretensions" of " 'liberal' theology."[54] Between these extremes, between the views of groups he associated with reactionary German and revolutionary French principles of thought, Hegel expected to find an audience for his own views.[55] His problem, of course, was that the audience for such views was rapidly vanishing. And it was vanishing precisely because of the religio-political polarization that Hegel's philosophy was designed to arrest.[56] Thus, however much credit Hegel deserves for realistically addressing his philosophy to the crisis of his age, his idealism prevented him from associating his philosophy with either of the groups at the antipode. Small wonder that his philosophy remained only "a school" of thought until well into the 1830s.

VI. ATHEISM AND EGOCENTRIC RELIGION

If the religious polarization among Protestants in the 1820s illuminates why Hegel drew a conceptual line between the content and the form of Christian thought, it also helps to place the question of Hegel's (alleged) atheism in proper context. For some time, of course, it has been conventional wisdom to explain the polarization of the 1820s in terms of a conflict between theists and atheists.[57]

Just as conventional has been the equation scholars have drawn between these polarized religious groupings, on the one hand, and the emergence, respectively, of right and left political Hegelians, on the other.[58] But if the religious situation of the '20s is approached historically, it soon becomes obvious how little justice this overly simplistic view does to the complexities of the religious situation in Prussia during those years.

The matter of Hegel's atheism was a public issue throughout the '20s. More specifically, and as Hegel himself acknowledged, it was an issue raised by the "demagogues" in Berlin against speculative philosophy from about 1821 on.[59] As we have seen, Hegel had anticipated that Schleiermacher would oppose him were he to push the "cause" of speculative philosophy too far. Despite this expectation, Hegel seems to have made a point of challenging Fries and Schleiermacher on political and religious issues almost from the beginning of his years in Berlin.

The reaction to Hegel's provocations came early in 1821, when the king issued an edict that instructed Altenstein (who opposed it) to prohibit the teaching of speculative philosophy at the University of Berlin.[60] And this was only the beginning, for from about 1823 on a series of spokesmen (such as the neo-pietist Thorluck) registered their contempt for Hegel's thought on the grounds that it was atheistic.[61] Unintimidated, Hegel insisted, in a 1826 letter to his harsh critic Thorluck, that "I am a Lutheran, and through philosophy have been at once completely confirmed in Lutheranism."[62] Similarly, in the same year, when some Catholics complained to Altenstein about a discernible Protestant bias in Hegel's lectures, Hegel responded unapologetically: "I have . . . explained and expressed Luther's teaching as true, and as recognized by philosophy as true." Adding insult to injury, he then proclaimed he had done this in "the interest of science."[63]

Of equal interest in this context is a letter Hegel's ally, the theologian K. Daub, wrote him in 1827.[64] In that letter, Daub differentiates "dogmatic theology" – of the sort ennunciated by the neo-pietists – from what he proudly called "another theology" – the "fruit" that grew from applying the principles of speculative philosophy to Christian theology.[65] In his response to Daub's letter, Hegel concurred in the distinction and, while doing so, reminded Daub that the new preface for the second edition of The Encyclope-

dia (1827) – the preface in which we saw Hegel distinguish between the languages of faith and knowledge – made just this point.[66] Their mutual admiration notwithstanding, neither Daub's nor Hegel's distinctions appear to have appeased the opposition to speculative philosophy, which explains why Hegel continued to be dogged by the atheism charge until his death in 1831.

Students of the history of Christianity will find much that is familiar in the general outlines of the debate between dogmatic theology and speculative philosophy in the 1820s. For, as was noted earlier, Fathers of the Church such as Clement and Origen had developed views of the relationship between faith and knowledge that were quite similar to those later propounded by Hegel. In terms of the history of Christianity, therefore, Hegel's discussion of the relationship between religion and philosophy is anything but novel. Recognizing this, of course, does not entail impugning Hegel's originality as a thinker. But acknowledgment of the perennial character of Hegel's religious views does raise an important scholarly issue for us: what standards are scholars to use to determine whether Hegel was or was not an atheist in the 1820s?

There are several ways to answer this question. First, scholars who identify Hegel as an atheist can simply acquiesce in the claim of Hegel's Pietist-orthodox opponents that he was indeed an atheist. Needless to say, there are normative grounds both for making such a charge and for several generations of scholars to have endorsed it; but since the grounds for such acquiescence are so obviously normative, it has been difficult for scholars who ascribe to this view to make a compelling case for their position without recourse to special pleading.

A more-convincing way to portray Hegel as an atheist would be to proceed along the lines A. Nygren used in *Agape and Eros* to raise questions about the orthodoxy of all those Christian thinkers who, before Hegel, had sought to turn Christianity into an ethical religion (religion of *Sittlichkeit*, as it were).[67] As Nygren argues, Christians from the Alexandrian Fathers, through Pelagius, and on to the Christian Platonists of the Renaissance, had been convinced that the teachings of Jesus Christ turned on two assumptions: that following the Incarnation men were capable of living an ethical life, and that the measure of a Christian life hinged on men voluntarily accepting responsibility for living such a life among their fellows.[68] Against this view, which he said derived from a Hellenistic scheme of eros salvation, Nygren insisted on viewing Christianity exclusively from a theistic perspective.[69]

Although Nygren's intention in *Agape and Eros* was to affirm theism – theocentric religion – as the *normative* measure of Christian orthodoxy, it is ironic that his overall argument shows why it is *historically* inappropriate to discuss Hegel's religious views in a theism-versus-atheism conceptual framework.[70] For while discussing the pervasiveness of the Hellenistic scheme of salvation in Christian theology, Nygren makes it clear that what he calls "egocentric religion" was as much a part of the history of Christianity as "theocentric religion."[71]

According to Nygren, egocentric religion is not Christian because it is not theistic. Rather, for him, it is a pagan-inspired religious doctrine that had been concocted in Alexandria by Clement and Origen, among recognized Church Fathers, and by Plotinus, a pagan philosopher. Under the auspices of these Alexandrian thinkers, egocentric religion was given sophisticated theological form and then, through their various works, was passed on to posterity where it frequently assumed the form of Christian Neo-platonism. Since, therefore, Nygren detects a Hellenistic scheme of salvation in all forms of egocentric religion, he has no reservations about labeling as atheistic any Christian doctrine that appears to operate with that motif. Hence, his sustained diatribe against Christian Neo-platonism in whatever form it assumed in the history of Christianity.

Any number of scholars have recently drawn attention to the pervasiveness of Christian Neo-platonism in German religious thought after 1770.[72] Thus, there are good reasons for associating Hegel's speculative philosophy with egocentric religious motifs in general and with Christian Neo-platonism in particular. (Not for nothing was Hegel's discussion of the relationship between faith and knowledge cast in the form of what Nygren calls the Alexandrian world-scheme.) By the same token, it is not hard to see how Nygren's conceptualization of the history of Christianity might be enlisted in the effort to portray Hegel as an atheistic thinker.[73]

The problem with this approach, however, is that, like the previous one, it too is normative. Moreover, it asks us to purge Christian thought of many of the motifs that governed its development as a religious tradition in the West. As such, Nygren's approach forces us to choose sides in a dispute in which normative rather than historical considerations have been used to set the terms of our choices.[74]

By refusing the terms of choice, however, we can historicize the problem, can allow egocentric as well as theocentric religious motifs to exist as legitimate impulses in the history of Christian thought. Peter Brown has used this kind of historicizing approach in his magnificent discussion of the relationship between Pelagianism and Augustinianism in Christian thought.[75] The same procedure, I think, should be used to assess the dispute between Hegel and his orthodox critics in the 1820s. In Brown's terms, that would mean treating speculative philosophy as a legitimate tendency within the intellectual history of Protestantism rather than as an atheistic expression of an anti-Christian tendency in German philosophy.

VII. HEGEL AND PANLOGISM: CHRISTIANITY AND THE ACTIVISM AND PROGRESSIVISM OF OLD-LEFT HEGELIANISM

If the distinction between normative and historical approaches to problems in the intellectual history of Christianity raises methodological questions about evaluating Hegel as an atheist, it also helps us to differentiate between the groups of thinkers that John Toews had identified as old-left and new-left Hegelians.[76]

The place to begin such an investigation is with the allegation that Hegel's philosophy was, at bottom, panlogist. Throughout the 1820s, Hegel was hounded by the claim that the application of speculative philosophy to matters of religion led to panlogism.[77] That is to say, Hegel was constantly criticized for having cut the core – literally, the heart – out of Christianity.[78] He did this, it was alleged, by creating a religio-philosophical system in which knowledge and the mind were given priority over faith and the heart. This, Hegel's critics charged, meant that he had forsaken the real world of Christian feeling for an abstract world of concepts that had been shaped in his own, rather than God's, image and likeness.[79] To this criticism, which in the history of Christianity has been invariably leveled at thinkers of "gnostic" persuasion, Hegel had a pat reply: by raising the truth of Christianity to the level of philosophical consciousness, and by putting Christian values in a more-teachable form, he had made that truth and those values more, rather than less, accessible to Christians in the modern world.[80]

More specifically, Hegel said – and this is quite clear in two letters he wrote to Edouard-Casimir Duboc in 1822 and 1823 – that he had set two religious tasks for speculative philosophy.[81] First, and as has previously been noted, Hegel wished to present Christians with scientific proof that "the Idea in the highest sense [is] God." To do that, he argued, God had to be conceptualized so that He was "in no way entangled in the finite." In this form, Hegel conceded, God could be viewed as an abstract truth lacking in substance. Hegel observed, however, that what his concept of God lacked in the way of historical specificity it gained in the way of philosophical comprehensiveness. As such, he declared, philosophy was now free to discuss God as a logical concept rather than just a reflection of the way people at certain times and places chose to represent God to themselves.

And yet, despite the philosophical benefits Hegel saw in an abstract conception of God, it is highly instructive that, after distinguishing between God as concept and representation, he acknowledged that his concept of God was "one-sided." As he proceeded to admit, that conception could indeed be construed as an expression of "abstract indifference" to life and to "the content of living, actual faith." To correct this one-sidedness – that is, to demonstrate that his philosophy was not in the final analysis panlogist – Hegel introduced the second religious task of speculative philosophy: to show how Christian truth, after having been given conceptual form in speculative philosophy, had to then be made concrete for human beings in their everyday lives.[82]

To clarify what he termed the all-important "progression from the abstract to the concrete," Hegel made two points.[83] First, he noted that in speculative philosophy "the truth is not defined as stationary or immobile . . . but rather as movement, as life itself." Second, he held that the truth of the Idea (or concept of God) would become concrete only if it were recognized and consciously grasped by human beings who then proceeded to make that truth the measure of their lives.[84] For speculative philosophy, in short, the truth of Christianity revealed itself in a complicated twofold process of development. Christian truth first had to be given abstract form – which is to say, believing had to be translated into knowing.[85] After this was achieved, speculative philosophy had to become the pedagogic agent through which Christian knowledge became not only the conscious possession of human beings but also the guiding principle of action in their lives.[86] As Hegel argued in *The Philosophy of Religion*, believing, knowing, and doing were the cornerstones of Christianity.[87] That this trinity of concerns also governed the movement of speculative philosophy is hardly accidental.

Given what Hegel tells us about the way the truth of Christianity is formulated first into abstract and then into concrete terms, it is easy to see why he identified human history as the framework within which Christian truth progressively manifested itself to human beings.[88] Moreover, Hegel's conception of this process explains why he deemed it necessary for this truth to register itself in human self-consciousness – in man's increasingly sophisticated conception of his relationship to God and to the role freedom played in that relationship.[89]

Hegel's decision to ground the religious interplay between God and man in history also explains why he chose to invest so much intellectual capital in the conceptual distinction between the representation and conception of God. In his scheme, of course, the former was time bound in a way the latter was not. On those terms, Hegel could argue that, while God had been variously represented at different moments in Christian history, none of the particular forms of representation had ever completely expressed the nature of man's relationship to God. To that end, he separated representation and conception and, in the process, underlined the fact that the Christian God was a God of historical becoming as well as a God of abstract philosophical being.[90]

Hegel's careful explanation to Duboc of why speculative philosophy should not be viewed as panlogist is of the sort that can be found in Lessing's *Education of the Human Race*, in Kant's *Religion Within the Limits of Reason Alone*, and in the work of thinkers who had created the accommodationist tradition of Christian theology.[91] As a time-honored tradition of Christian discourse, in which believing, knowing, and doing were identified as the governing principles, respectively, of three successive ages in the history of Christianity, Hegel's recourse to accommodationism had the effect of alleviating the doubts that some of his critics in the 1820s had had about his religious beliefs.[92]

In 1829, for example, K. Windischmann, who had corresponded

with Hegel for years and who had early on publicly appreciated the connection between Lessing's *Education* and Hegel's philosophy, used the occasion of a letter to congratulate Hegel for having recently shown himself to be "so definitely Christian" in his thinking.[93] As it happened, Windischmann's remark about Hegel's Christianity was written with specific reference to a complimentary review Hegel had written in 1829 of a book by K. F. Goschel.[94] In Goschel's book, the aim of which was to reconcile speculative philosophy with orthodox piety, some attention had been given to the possibility of a panlogist reading of Hegel's philosophy. Like Goschel, Windischmann had also been worried about the prevalence of this tendency in his friend's philosophy.[95] Thus, when Hegel assured readers in the Goschel review that speculative philosophy was not panlogist in inspiration, Windischmann's worries were relieved as well.

More specifically, what particularly moved Windischmann to congratulate Hegel for being so definitely Christian was Hegel's assurance – the same assurance he had given Duboc several years earlier – that speculative philosophy intended to sanction the kind of Christian activism that aimed more at re-divinizing the world in an ethical sense than at escaping from it in an other-worldly theological sense.[96] In the 1820s, Windischmann had committed himself to – and written to Hegel about – a program of Christian activism in which Jesus Christ was not only "the Divine Actualizer of the Idea of eternal truth" but also the substantive inspiration for Christian progressivism.[97] Windischmann's 1829 letter indicates that he thought Hegel concurred in both those judgments.

Unlike the atheism charge, which distorts rather than clarifies our understanding of the relation between philosophy and religion in Hegel's thought, the panlogism issue allows us to penetrate deeply into the religious context of the late 1820s. For while someone like Windischmann could detect an implicit theory of Christian activism and Christian progressivism in Hegel's explanation of the "progression from the abstract to the concrete," some of Hegel's other followers were drawing very different conclusions from the same progression.

Two extraordinary letters written to Hegel in 1828 and 1829 by two of his students reveals what is at issue here very well. One of these letters was written by C. H. Weisse; the other, by L. Feuerbach. The former's letter I take to be representative of the concerns of old-left Hegelianism;[98] that of the latter, which will be discussed in the next section of this essay, as representative of the outlook of new left Hegelianism.[99]

Weisse's letter to Hegel in July 1829 was prompted by the latter's review of Goschel.[100] Referrring to Hegel as "honored teacher," Weisse focused his attention on the panlogism issue.

In terms that pre-figure much of the ideological debate among the young Hegelians in the 1830s about the meaning of Hegel's philosophy, Weisse framed the panlogism theme in terms of a tension between Hegel's method and his system – in Weisse's words, between the "fundamental principle of [Hegel's] entire philosophy" (that is, what Weisse called the principle of "unlimited dialectical progress") and Hegel's "systematic teachings." The dialectics of the former, Weisse argued, held out the promise of an "endless progress in the deepening, enrichment, and perfection" of "the logical idea." According to him, that meant that there would be "new progress and new forms of the universal spirit beyond the form of science achieved" in Hegel's system. As Weisse saw it, however, the "logical idea," as it was expressed in Hegel's system, "definitely" excluded "such a progress of the world spirit." The reason for this, he thought, was that Hegel's elevation of philosophy to the level of science made it seem as if recognition of "the abstractly logical concept" was the "highest of all conceivable forms of spiritual activity." On those terms, Weisse felt, Hegel's "science of pure thought" was panlogist, for in that abstract form philosophy not only was closed off to the world of flesh-and-blood human beings but also seemed to exempt the world from further religious reform. In the reactionary context of the 1820s, Weisse obviously thought that was an unconscionable position for a progressively minded Christian to take.[101]

To give his plea for Christian activism and progressivism more of a personal touch, Weisse recalled a conversation he and Hegel had had a few years earlier on that very subject. Weisse reminded his teacher that on that occasion Hegel had agreed that once philosophy had been given "absolute logical formation" as science, its task was to then apply itself to life, to "domains of spiritual activity" other than science. On the basis of his recollection of that conversation, Weisse then advised Hegel that "I seek to interpret your system [dialectically] so that it does not . . . exclude the possibility of such progress." As he explained, "if the science of pure thought is truly the unconditionally highest of all conceivable forms of spiritual activity, then the creation brought forth by such thought is the final goal of every development not only of the human but also of the divine spirit." Or to put it another way, Weisse thought he was rescuing Hegel's system from the charge of panlogism by using the principle of dialectical progression to shift the focus of speculative philosophy from questions of abstract "science" to those of ethical "life."[102]

Weisse's interpretation of the activistic implications of the relationship between system and method (or principle) in Hegel's thinking may be taken as an expression of Hegel's own understanding of the progression from the abstract to the concrete. Indeed, as we have seen, there is much in his writings as well as in the testimony of others that confirms the view that Hegel expected the gains of philosophy to be extended through the long, slow process of Bildung to "all spheres of life."[103]

Evidence that this was in fact Hegel's view can be found in a letter written to him by K. Daub in April 1829. There Daub expressed dismay about insinuations Weisse had made in a recently published book about the panlogist tendency in Hegel's philosophy. As Daub interpreted it, Weisse's book contained a "great misunderstanding" of speculative philosophy because it implied that Hegel's philosophy discouraged ethical activism in the world.[104]

Be that as it may, what is remarkable about Daub's letter to Hegel is that its defense of Hegel was self-consciously framed in terms of Weisse's own self-proclaimed dialectical critique of Hegel's system. As Clark Butler has shrewdly observed, Daub's letter "represents endorsement by a committed Hegelian of Weisse's belief in further progress of the world spirit."[105] On those grounds, then, and in light of Weisse's own recollection of Hegel's position on the matter, it is plausible to argue that Hegel and Daub both regarded the purely theoretical aspect of Hegel's work – his system – as a step in a larger process that would eventually entail the translation of scientific theory into the ethical practice of everyday life.

In 1829, then, various thinkers, all of whom were close to Hegel, sought to vitiate the charge of panlogism by emphasizing how the ultimate end of speculative philosophy was, in Weisse's words, to translate the "abstractly logical concept" into a "demand for an unbounded progress of the world spirit in general and of the historical spirit of man in particular."[106] That is to say, speculative philosophy as system stood to itself as method both as science stood to life and as theory stood to practice. On those terms, on the historical terms of the late 1820s, it is easy to understand in what sense Hegel and his students thought ethical activism and Christian progressivism were implicit in speculative philosophy. And insofar as speculative philosophy's program of *Bildung* was designed to encourage both developments, the distinction between Hegel's system and his method testifies to the activism and progressivism of his and his followers thought in the late 1820s. Or to adapt Toews's terms to our purposes here, Hegelianism seems to have evolved into old-left Hegelianism as it was forced to explain why it was not a panlogist system of thought.

VIII. HEGEL AND FEUERBACH: FROM RELIGION TO ANTHROPOLOGY

From the perspective of the debate about Hegel's panlogism, the pivotal historico-ideological issues that lie behind the emerging distinction between system and method in Hegel's thought become clear. Indeed, Weisse's interpretation of Hegel's philosophy shows that as the emphasis moves from system to method, the focus of speculative philosophy not only moves from the abstract to the concrete but begins to be ideologically associated with historically progressive Christian positions as well.

At this point, what is not exactly clear is how the philosophical discussion of "the progression from the abstract to the concrete" relates to particular aspects of Hegel's understanding of Christianity. In Windischmann and Weisse, men who were not timid about their Christian convictions, the progression is interpreted in a Christian key of endless striving for ethical perfectionism (for Nygren, such striving constitutes the stuff of egocentric religion).[107] And Hegel, especially in his capacity as a philosopher of *Sittlichkeit*, seems to have philosophically made provisions for that kind of striving too.[108]

But in the late 1820s, as theocentric religion re-asserted itself in Germany under the auspices of Pietist-orthodoxy, Christianity was increasingly viewed by many as a reactionary rather than a progressive historical force. For thinkers who perceived the world this way, a new reference point for progressivism had to be found, one that would not be compromised by any association with Christianity. That many of Hegel's students – Carove, Gans, and Heine – found such a reference point in the emancipatory priciples of the French Revolution is the single most important reason why new-left Hegelianism needs to be separated from old-left Hegelianism.[109]

To make sense of this crucial development in German intellectual history, we need to look closely at L. Feuerbach, especially at the monumentally important letter he wrote to Hegel in 1828 in which he proudly announced to his former teacher that he had just completed his doctoral thesis.[110] For in that letter Feuerbach developed a perspective on Hegel's philosophy that led directly to the atheistic values of new-left Hegelianism – to what Nygren would call an "anthropocentric" conception of religion.[111]

As is well known, Feuerbach had experienced a Hegelian conversion in the early 1820s. Indeed, during those years Feuerbach had studied under Hegel in Berlin and, apparently, had some social contact with his teacher outside the classroom. It is not surprising, therefore, that in 1828, just after completing his dissertation, Feuerbach wrote to Hegel in order to explain what that work, a copy of which accompanied the letter, was all about.

Feuerbach's letter begins by expressing "veneration" and "high esteem" for Hegel as a teacher.[113] Describing himself as a "disciple," Feuerbach goes on to say that his dissertation was "executed in the spirit of [his] teacher" – by which Feuerbach meant his work breathed "a speculative spirit." Then, in what surely had to be a calculated attempt to distance himself from his teacher, Feuerbach says that what he had learned from Hegel had been rather freely assimilated. As Feuerbach proceeds to explain, what was "free" about this assimilation was that it aimed at giving real "living" rather than merely "formal" expression of Hegel's ideas.[114] In that respect, Feuerbach says in an astonishing sentence, my philosophy "could be called the actualization and secularization of the *idea*, the *ensarkosis* or incarnation of the pure logos."[115] Feuerbach, in short, proposed to translate the spirit of "abstract ideas" (in their "colorless purity," he bluntly and boldly said) into a "world-determining intuition" that would give rise in the "immediate" present to "a new period of world history."

As Feuerbach elaborates this view, it becomes evident that the relationship between student and teacher goes well beyond self-proclaimed discipleship. True, Feuerbach depicted himself as one who would make the teachings of Hegel's "school" available to "humanity"; and, according to Feuerbach this entailed the "translation" of "a higher literary activity" (that is, Hegel's science of the concept) into an historical force – a "universal spirit" – that would realize itself "in actuality." When this translation was achieved, Feuerbach intimated, Hegel's notion of "the Idea" of "world spirit" would "burst the bounds of a single school [and] become a general world-historical and public intuition."[116] In that context, Feuerbach saw his work as involving the "founding of . . . the Kingdom of the Idea" on earth rather than in the "heaven" of Hegel's abstract philosophy.[117] Thus, from Feuerbach's perspective, teacher stood to pupil as theory stood to practice and as the science of the concept stood to the new philosphy of the living intuition.

Now insofar as the latter set of terms expressed the substance of the former, Feuerbach's understanding of the "progression from the abstract to the concrete" could be interpreted as Hegelianism in the activistic key of old-left Hegelianism.[118] By that measure, Feuerbach's reference to "the actualization and secularization of the idea" would have to be understood as the realization of Christian values on earth instead of in heaven. And, as Windischmann had argued, this commitment could be expressed in terms of "faith in [Jesus Christ] as the Divine Actualizer of the Idea of eternal truth."[119] Through secularization of "the idea," in other words, the Kingdom of God would be established on earth at the same time as the Kingdom of the Idea, which had been manifest in Christ's ministry, became progressively more realized in human life. For Hegel and old-left Hegelians, then, secularization and actualization of the idea entailed Christianization of the world in a down-to-earth ethical sense of *Sittlichkeit*. "Secular life," as Hegel said in the lectures on the philosophy of history, "is the positive and definite embodiment of the Spiritual Kingdom . . . manifesting itself in outward existence."[120]

The historical importance of Feuerbach's 1828 letter arises at precisely this point. For, despite its allusions to *logos ensarkosis* and the Incarnation, Feuerbach's letter gives the "secularization of the idea" argument a completely different turn, one that is signaled by Feuerbach's phrase "pure logos" and by his conception of the new philosophy as marking the emergence of a new age in history in which Christian values would be abolished from, rather than realized in, human consciousness.[121] Indeed, as Feuerbach portrays it, his philosophy is post-Christian. Conversely, he depicts Christianity, whether in its "orthodox" theocentric or "rationalistic" egoistic form, as an oppressive system of values that prevented humanity from realizing itself as the absolute. Because of this abridgement of human freedom, Feuerbach argued, Christianity had "to be driven from its tyrannical thone" so that "the idea" of humanity, man's true religion, would become the reference point for all discussions of divinity. When that shift of focus took place, when theology became anthropology, pure logos – rather than Christian logos – would become "actual and reign" on earth.

In this framework, Feuerbach goes on to say, Christianity could be conceived neither as "the perfect and absolute religion" nor as the culmination of history. Indeed, according to Feuerbach, Christianity was only an unhappy religious phase in the history of Western philosophy, a phase that Feuerbach's philosophy rather than Hegel's crypto-theology would bring to an end. Thus, instead of asking men to measure their spiritual progress against either Christianity's theistic conception of God or Hegel's Christian-inspired conception of the ideal self, Feuerbach urged men to ground his self-conception in the intuition he had of himself as a "sensuous" and "natural" being.[122] By so doing, Feuerbach thought, the unnatural (because dualistic) distinction Hegel had established between the natural and spiritual dimensions of the human personality would be dissolved, with the result that man would then be in a position to engage in what Feuerbach called "a second creation," a creation in which the infinite potential of natural man rather than the spiritually oppressive principles of Christian theology would determine the scope and substance of human fulfillment.[123]

We cannot, of course, discuss in great detail all that follows from Feuerbach's analysis of the negative role Christianity played in the development of Western philosophy. Yet, we can draw attention to the decisive issues that seem to divide Hegel and Feuerbach and, ultimately, old-left and new-left Hegelians.

First, Feuerbach obviously thought his free assimilation of Hegel's philosophy involved grounding the logic of Hegel's concept in human anthropology. As was indicated earlier, however, Hegel had vehemently argued against just this kind of reduction as early as 1811.[124] At that time, he called such reductionism "twaddle" and linked it with subjectivist philosophy.[125] Later, in *The Encyclopedia*,

Hegel added that this kind of reduction made religion appear to be little more than an anthropological projection.[126] Thus, even before Feuerbach's letter of 1828, Hegel was on record as having had committed himself to a view of religion that tried not to confuse the principles of Christian thought and action with those that Feuerbach singled out as characteristic of anthropocentric religion.

Second, Feuerbach's claim that he was preparing the way for Hegel's philosophy to become a world historical principle of human emancipation is belied by his divorce of Christianity from the new philosophy. As we have seen, the question of the relationship between Hegel's system and the principles of human emancipation arises when the logic of the concept is required to become the basis of human action. In Hegel's philosophy, this translation process – which is essentially pedagogic – never claimed to be producing a new religion. Rather, for Hegel, the whole point of this *Bildung* process was to cultivate and expand Christian consciousness and to promote the philosophical comprehension of the Christian religion. That is why in *The Encyclopedia* Hegel maintains that his philosophy reveals the truth of the Incarnation in the logical form of the concept.[127] Consequently, when that truth is translated back into the life of men through the progression from the abstract to the concrete, Christian values in an *axiological* sense are being offered to men as principles of life in a *teleological* sense.[128] On those terms, human emancipation involves an expansion of consciousness but not a change in mankind's understanding of the religious value of Christianity. And, as Feuerbach well understood, it is by way of the expansion of consciousness that Hegel meant to preserve Christian values in the modern world.[129]

Although Feuerbach was certainly correct to interpret Hegel as a Christian philosopher, his own conception of a world-determining intuition has nothing to do with the values of Hegel or of old-left Hegelianism. Indeed, Feuerbach's "founding . . . of the Kingdom of the Idea" on earth involves not only a rejection of Christianity and Hegelianism but also a revolution in the values that govern religious consciousness in general. That is what is meant by calling Feuerbach a post-Christian thinker whose religion of humanity promised to usher in a new age of history.

There is, to be sure, a promise of human emancipation in Feuerbach's thought. For in his mind man's finite nature included the infinite right of the human spirit to realize itself in whatever form it willed itself to be.[130] But by collapsing the difference between spirit and nature the way he did, Feuerbach made it possible for man in an anthropological sense to become his own creator in a religious sense. From Hegel's point of view, of course, such a conception of man entailed humanity's usurpation of the rank of God for itself; and from the beginning to the end of his life Hegel opposed that usurpation. Indeed, for Hegel as well as for many Christians before him, becoming god-like was one thing; becoming God quite another.[131] That means, of course, that atheism – in the form of anthropocentric religion or a post-Christian philosophy of the future – was what divided Hegel and Feuerbach in 1828. But because Hegel was not Feuerbach does not mean he was an orthodox theist. Careful use of the concept of egocentric religion allows us to avoid slipping into that either/or situation.

Finally, Feuerbach's decision to draw a sharp line between Christianity and philosophy enabled him to historicize and de-socialize Christianity in general and Hegel's Protestantism in particular.[132] To see how Feuerbach does this, we need only recall that in his 1828 letter to Hegel, Feuerbach had relegated Christianity to a second stage of history that lay between antiquity, on the one hand, and the emerging new age of history, on the other. The tripartite periodization of history that emerges here, of course, was a pervasive motif in the thought of French and German thinkers during the 1820s;[133] so it is not all unusual to find Feuerbach working with it. But the scheme was used very differently in French and German circles. In the work of Lessing, Kant, Schiller, and Hegel, and among the old-left Hegelians, the three-age scheme was meant to culminate in Protestant activism and in the realization of Christian values within the ethical life of Protestant communities.[134] On those terms, Hegel's commitment to *Sittlichkeit*, to the establishment of socio-religious community among men, expressed a desire to realize the Kingdom of God on earth in terms of the values of liberal Protestant humanism.

Throughout the 1820s, and especially in the lectures on the philosophy of history, Hegel reiterated this theme time and again, and each time he associated *Sittlichkeit* with Protestantism – the religion that, for him, had become the agent of Christian freedom in the modern world.[135] Hence, in his mind "the principle of Protestantism" was simultaneously the key to human emancipation, to the Christianization of social life, and to the socialization of Protestant-ism.[136] It is indeed that trinity of religiously grounded socio-ethical concerns that informs the criticism of orthodox Lutheranism that Hegel advanced in the lectures on the philosophy of history.[137] As those lectures make perfectly clear, there can be no doubt either about the social dimension of Hegel's Christianity or about his de-sire to offer *Sittlichkeit* as a socio-Protestant alternative to the vari-ous kinds of anti-social subjectivism that he thought had pervaded the modern world since 1789.[138]

Feuerbach surely knew this – surely knew that Hegel's concep-tion of Protestantism contained a sharp criticism of the kind of anti-social Protestantism that characterized orthodox Lutheranism in the 1820s and in the seventeenth and eighteenth centuries. But when Feuerbach historicized Christianity in his letter the way he did – making it the governing principle of the second stage of history in which anti-social egoism was alleged to be triumphant[139] – he made it impossible for liberal Protestant humanism's conception of *Sittlichkeit* to become an agent of emancipation and socio-religious recollectivation in the third age of history. Indeed, in Feuerbach's three-age view of history, which is modeled along the lines of an anti-Protestant conception of Christian history that had previously been developed in France among progressive as well as reactionary political groups, the social agenda of liberal Protestantism becomes indistinguishable from the anti-social agenda of Lutheran orthodoxy.

The ideological ramifications of Feuerbach's move here are of par-ticular importance for German intellectual history in the nineteenth century. For in Feuerbach's scheme, which later finds more concrete and comprehensive expression in the work of the new-left Hegelians, liberal German Protestants are confronted with a self-destructive choice: either embrace orthodox theism (and compromise their lib-eral Protestant values) or opt for Feuerbach's (French-inspired) reli-gion of the future (and abandon Christianity all together). As Feuer-bach defined the terms of ideological debate, in other words, there was no middle ground between the two positions. Once the debate between reaction and revolution was defined on those grounds – once Christianity in general and Protestantism in particular were ideologi-cally associated with egoism, with an anti-social conception of the self, and with reactionary institutions of political oppression – it was relatively easy for thinkers such as Heine, Cieszkowski, Hess, Engels, and Ruge (after 1840) to represent the thought of Kant and Hegel as inimical to human emancipation.[140] To this very day that view has dominated modern scholarship's conception of the relationship between religion and philosophy in Hegel's thinking. The germ of that mistaken conception can be found in Feuerbach's letter and in the anti-Christian conception of secularization that governs much of that letter's argument.

IX. HEGEL: THOUGHT AND ACTION IN THE CONTEXT OF SECULARIZATION

From what has just been said, it should be obvious that Feuerbach's letter to Hegel in 1828 constitutes something of a watershed in German intellectual history, for on the level of ideas it reveals exactly at what points and over what issues an emerging new-left Hegelianism can be distinguished both from Hegel's position and from that of the old-left Hegelians.

What makes Feuerbach's radical departure from Hegel so difficult to see, of course, is his self-proclaimed discipleship and the Hegelian terminology he uses to advance his case for human emancipation.[141] As was the case with Heine in the late 1820s, Feuerbach tended to use Hegel's concept of the "idea" to explain the emergence of "the people" as a political force in European history.[142] Implicit in Feuerbach's mixing of German and French discourses, of course, was the view that German philosophical and French traditions of revolutionary discourse had found an ideological point of mediation in his work.[143] If we take Feuerbach at his word, therefore, it would appear that his "secularization of the Idea" involved no more (or less) than the translation of Hegel's theory of the idea into democratic political practice.[144] And since other students of Hegel (for example, some of the old-left Hegelians) were engaged at roughly the same time in a very similar translation process – namely, in drawing out of Hegel's system a principle of action that promised emancipation for those who read history in the key of "progress" – it is tempting to read Feuerbach in the key of "prophetic activism" that marks the thought of the movement that, following Toews, we have identified as old-left Hegelianism.[145]

We have seen, however, that in Feuerbach's three-age scheme of history, the third age had nothing at all to do with the realization of

Christian values in history. To be sure, activism, progressivism, and human emancipation were signal features of Feuerbach's third age; but his conception of these interrelated processes was not informed by any consideration of Christian values – either transcendent or immanent. Rather, his conception of action was contentless – value free in a substantive sense.[146] That, to be sure, is why he was careful to use the phrase "pure logos" to characterize what would be emancipated if the idea were ever to become secularized.[147]

This, of course, is what made Feuerbach's activism so radical, for in the name of emancipation Feuerbach proceeded to demand the peoples' participation in the processes that governed their lives. Thus, for Feuerbach, the "actualization and secularization of the Idea" entailed liberation from, rather than the realization of Christian values.[148]

When Feuerbach began to operate in this conceptual framework, a framework in which secularization is anti-Christian rather than Christian in inspiration, his understanding of the thought/action problem becomes profoundly unHegelian. That is because in the final analysis, Feuerbach's notion of anthropological religion is governed by a procedural commitment in which the end of human action and the substance of human emancipation emerge out of the collective decision making process itself.[149] According to Toews, this is the starting point of the secular humanism of new-left Hegelianism.[150] It is also, as the writings of Heine, Feuerbach, Cieszkowski, Hess, and Ruge make clear, the point in time when the reference point for the context of "the Idea" shifts from a German religious to a French socio-political mode of discourse.[151] The continued use of Hegelian terminology by these thinkers conceals this radical shift of focus, but the illusion of continuity between Hegel and old-left Hegelianism, on the one hand, and new-left Hegelianism, on the other hand cannot hide the fact that the substance of the "idea" is completely different in the two cases.[152] There is, as it were, no substantive ideological continuity between the activism of the old-left Hegelians and that of the secular moralists.

There is, I think, a useful way to grasp more substantively what is at issue here. As was noted previously, C. Weisse had attempted to solicit support from Hegel for his own program of Christian progressivism by distinguishing between Hegel's system and his method. According to Weisse, the latter promised "unbound progress of the world spirit" in all domains of life. As Toews has shown, moreover, many of Hegel's other students (such as Carove and Richter) interpreted Hegel this way in the early 1830s.

At some point in the 1830s, however, the terms the old-left Hegelians used to orient themselves on the issue of the relationship between system and method in Hegel's thinking underwent a very subtle change. How this came about can be seen in the work of K. Michelet, one of Hegel's most well known and informed students of those years.[153]

As Michelet saw it, the main achievement of Hegel's philosophy had been to register on the level of "principle" – on the level of value, that is – the scientific and theoretical truth of Christianity. As early as 1831, Michelet saw himself using that principle as a reference point for criticizing institutions that either impeded or did not measure up to the liberal Protestant standards of value set by Hegel's philosophy. As Michelet noted later, one could expect Hegel's "system" to change as the scope of its various undertakings expanded from one cultural sphere of action to another; but the "principle" of Hegel's philosophy, so Michelet held, should never be changed. So, while using terms with which we are already familiar, Michelet sought, in his words, to translate "science" into "life" and, by so doing, to make what was real conform to what was deemed rational in Hegel's philosophy. Thus, in 1831, when Michelet wrote that he expected the "owl of Minerva" to give way to "the cockcrow that announces the dawn of a new day," he was seeking to promote an authentic Hegelian as well as old-left Hegelian program of action, one through which Christian values would be realized in human history.[154]

Despite the difference of terminology between what constituted principle and system in Hegel's philosophy, Weisse and Michelet seem to have agreed that Hegel's philosophy and the Christian values it embraced had to be the point of departure for progressive and rational action in the modern world. In this respect, Hegel stood to old-left Hegelianism not only as theory stood to practice but also as Christianity as axiology stood to Christianity as teleology. That is how liberal Protestant humanists from Lessing to Hegel understood mankinds' relationship to Jesus Christ; and, as Hegel's lectures on the philosophy of history make clear, that is how liberal Protestants interpreted their relationship to Luther. It is hardly a coincidence that that is how the thinkers who formed the core of old-left Hegelians interpreted their relationship to Hegel. All indeed are participants in one long continuum of Christian discourse on how to establish the Kingdom of God on earth.

By contrast, Feuerbach's conception of the relationship between theory and practice redefines action so that action – action that registered the self-creation process itself – precedes theory rather than follows from it. This explains, I think, why Feuerbach saw substantive values emerging from revolutionary action rather than from Hegel's theory. Like Michelet, Feuerbach saw such action as inaugurating a new day in the history of the world. But unlike Michelet, and like Heine, the cockcrow that announced the new day for Feuerbach was a radical French political one, not a reactionary German-Christian one.[155]

X. PROTESTANTISM AS A POLITICAL IDEOLOGY: HEGEL AS A PHILOSOPHER OF THE PRUSSIAN STATE

An understanding of the religious context in which Hegel worked during his years in Berlin enables us to make much better sense of how liberal Protestant religious values informed his philosophy. Specifically, it allows us to appreciate how the crucial system/method and thought/action conceptual distinctions figured in his very Christian and liberal Protestant conception of what the "progression from the abstract to the concrete" entailed in a value sense for human beings. As Löwith has observed, Hegel's understanding of that progression makes him a philosopher whose conception of secularization was fully Christian in character. That is why Hegel is, for Löwith, a Christian philosopher before he is anything else.

In addition to all this, the religious context tells us a great deal about how Protestantism functioned as a political ideology in Prussia during Hegel's Berlin period. For a variety of historiographical reasons, I wish to conclude this essay with a brief discussion of Hegel's Protestantism and its relationship to the Prussian state.

As we have seen, by 1829 Hegel's religious views had been challenged from at least four different vantage points. Pietist-orthodoxy inveighed against Hegel's rationalism; the theological rationalists castigated him for the provisions his philosophy made for faith in religious matters; the group that we have identified as old-left Hegelians urged him to declare himself more openly for Christian activism and progressivism; and Feuerbach broke with Hegel over the theological characteristics of speculative philosophy.

Between 1827 and 1831, we saw, Hegel responded in detail to this array of criticism and, while so doing, assumed the posture of an old-left Hegelian himself, a position, I would argue, that had been Hegel's since the 1790s when he became a liberal Protestant and a philosopher of *Sittlichkeit* at one and the same time.[156] In keeping with his liberal Protestant convictions, then, Hegel dismissed Pietist-orthodoxy for promoting a narrow, dogmatic, and anti-social form of Protestant religiosity; he derided theological rationalism for encouraging a "formal, abstract, [and] nerveless" approach to religion, an approach that made it impossible to organize Christian life around the principle of *Sittlichkeit*; and, as far as we know, he would have criticized Feuerbach for having reduced theology to anthropology.[157]

Now from Hegel's perspective – and this is fully developed in the concluding sections of his lectures on the philosophy of history – these three religious positions had reactionary and revolutionary political correlates. Accordingly, Hegel thought Pietist-orthodoxy provided religious sanction for the throne-and-altar alliance around which the Prussian state had begun to organize itself in the 1820s. Conversely, he located theological rationalism and Feuerbach's brand of secular moralism (or atheism) in the ideological camp of those who took their ideological cues from the abstractions of the French Revolution.[158]

Given this assessment of the situation, Hegel presented his own philosophy as the *via media* between the reactionary German and the revolutionary French political tendencies of his age.[159] And he saw things this way because to his mind what occupied the middle ground between the two political extremes was, as W. Jaeschke was well understood, the political principles of liberal Protestantism.[160] As we have noted, *Sittlichkeit* constitutes a core conviction in this kind of Protestantism. It is, to be sure, the religious value that explains why Hegel acquiesced neither in the anti-social individualism of Lutheran orthodoxy nor in the economic, social, and political atomism of the Enlightenment and French Revolution. Indeed, it is precisely because Hegel tried to preserve the cooperative nexus between divinity and humanity, religion and the state, Protestantism and Prussian politics, in his religion of *Sittlichkeit*, that his philosophy was anathema to an orthodox critic such as K E. Schubarth and to a radical critic such as Feuerbach in 1829.

And yet, because he refused either to accommodate himself to the throne-and-altar alliance or to associate himself ideologically with the revolutionary principles of 1789, his own view of the relationship between religion and politics was constantly misrepresented in public debate. To Schubarth, for example, there was little to choose between Hegel's position and that of someone like Feuerbach – both were atheists and, as such, were threats to the political stability of the Prussian state.[161] To someone like K. F. F. Sietze, who in 1829 had tried to explain why Hegel was not an anti-Prussian thinker, Hegel's philosophy, especially his philosophy of history, recognized and perhaps even celebrated the Prussian state as the agent of Protestant values in the modern world.[162] And to someone like Feuerbach, Hegel's reservations about the political trajectory of the French Revolution made him an apologist for the political status quo.[163]

The upshot of this is that as early as 1829, Hegel's thought was being used as a religio-philosophical foil for advancing the political agenda of the revolutionary and reactionary forces of his day. In the context of the ever-shifting contours of that debate, it proved quite difficult for Hegel's contemporaries to grasp exactly where he stood on any number of issues. Hence the great confusion about his relationship to Prussia, a Protestant state which, from Hegel's liberal perspective, was on the verge of forsaking Protestantism.

There was, to be sure, a moment in 1838 when A. Ruge tried to explain to the readers of the *Hallische Jahrbucher* how Hegel's understanding of the relationship between Protestantism and Prussianism fit together.[164] At the time Ruge, who was the spokesman for the young Hegelian movement, regarded himself as a "Hegelian Christian" and as political liberal who would support the Prussian state as long as it pursued the political ends of liberal Protestant humanism. In this, I would argue, Ruge was very much an old-left Hegelian in 1838, an advocate of Hegel's religion of *Sittlichkeit*, as it were.[165]

Ruge implied, however, that, if Prussian authorities chose to pursue an illiberal religio-political agenda, he would endeavor to create a Protestant political alternative to the throne-altar alliance. No more than Hegel, though, did Ruge find and audience for his political views. This explains why between 1838 and 1843 we see Ruge, under the direct ideological influence of Cieszkowski, Feuerbach, and Hess, gradually abandoning the position of old-left Hegelianism for the political radicalism of new-left Hegelianism.

Given this political trajectory, it is hardly surprising that during this five-year period Ruge played a crucial role in blurring the ideological differences between orthodox and liberal Protestantism as well as between political liberals and reactionaries. Not coincidentally, as Ruge did this the inspiration of his thinking and the focus of his discourse became increasingly French. And, as that happened, Protestantism and Prussianism become increasingly associated in his mind with a retrograde religio-political movement that aimed at thwarting the realization of the democratic political principles of the French Revolution. And so it was that between 1838 and 1843, the religio-political debate in Prussia was once again defined in either/or terms: either reactionary German religio-political ones or revolutionary socio-political French ones.[166]

For a complicated set of reasons, then, Ruge's development between 1838 and 1843 reflects the larger ideological shift in German intellectual history from old-left to new-left Hegelianism. Students of German intellectual history are just beginning to straighten out the role (or non-role) of Hegel's philosophy in that ideological movement. But the more we know about the religious context of the 1820s and about Hegel's position in it, the easier it will be to make progress in that vital research area.

NOTES

1   Some recent Hegel scholarship has made this sort of scholarly endeavor much easier to conduct. As my citations throughout reveal, I am deeply indebted to the work of C. Butler, P. Hodgson, and J. Toews for key aspects of what I have to say about Hegel during his Berlin period. After completing the text of this essay, I had the opportunity to read W. Jaeschke's *Reason in Religion* (henceforth *Reason*), trans. J. Steward and P. Hodgson (Berkeley, Calif: 1990). I was pleased to discover that several of the interpretations I advance here have been elaborated in Jaeschke's important book.

2   Throughout this essay, I take the view that Hegel's actual influence in Berlin – at least outside the small world of the university – has been greatly exaggerated. For example, to speak as K. Barth does in *Protestant Theology in the Nineteenth Century*, trans. B. Cozens and J. Bowden

(London, 1972), 387, of "the age of Hegel" is to misrepresent the influence as well as staying power of his thought. Being the focus of an ideological debate is not the same as exercising influence.

3 As Hegel's lectures on the philosophy of religion reveal, the range of his interest in religion expanded and deepened as he grew older.

4 On the religious thought of the young Hegel, see my *Hegel:Religion, Economics, and the Politics of Spirit, 1770–1807* (New York, 1987)

5 See, for example, Hölderlin's letter to Hegel (11/26/1795) in *Hegel: The Letters* (henceforth *Letters*), trans. C. Butler and C. Seiler (Bloomington, Ind., 1984), 33–34.

6 Karl Löwith, *From Hegel to Nietzsche* (henceforth *From Hegel*), trans. D. Green (Garden City, N.Y., 1964), 47.

7 In his editorial comments on Hegel's *Lectures on the Philosophy of Religion* (henceforth *Religion*), ed. P. Hodgson, (Berkeley, Calif., 1984), v. 1, 8 and 20, Hodgson downplays the public impact of all this. I do not quite understand that decision given the scope of the reaction against Hegel in the 1820s.

8 Consult ibid., pp. 4, 7, and 61, for P. Hodgson's editorial comments on Hegel's calculated move against Schleiermacher.

9 *Letters*, p. 463.

10 My sense of ideology here is simply that of contested thought. Such usage, I think, draws attention to the public nature of the debate in which Hegel was involved during his Berlin years.

11 In addition to the literature cited in n. 1 above, I would like to acknowledge the important (and neglected) book of N. Lobkowicz: *Theory and Practice: History of a Concept from Aristotle to Marx* (London, 1967).

12 A remarkable (and clever) example of this can be found in A. Kojeve, "Hegel, Marx, and Christianity," *Interpretation*, (1970): 1, 1.

13 Despite Toews's *Hegelianism* (New York, 1980), which confirmed in great detail views expressed earlier by S. Avineri in *Hegel's Political Philosophy*, ed. W. Kaufman (New York, 1970), 71–79, this mistaken claim still informs much that is written about Hegel and German idealism.

14 In the *Letters*, such as p. 543, Hegel expressed concern about the circulation of these unauthorized notebooks. P. Hodgson (*Religion*, v. 1, p. 5) argues that Hegel did, however, find these notebooks useful when revising his lectures in the 1820s.

15 See Hegel's letters to V. Cousin (7/1/1827 and 3/3/1828), *Letters*, pp. 640 and 665, respectively.

16 The Berlin inaugural reiterates the theme of the 1816 Heidelberg inaugural. A translation of the latter can be found in Hegel's *Introduction to the Lectures on the History of Philosophy*, trans. T. Knox and A. Miller (Oxford, 1895), 1–3. For the German original see *Sämtliche Werke*, ed.

H. Glockner (Stuttgart, 1958), v. 17, 19–22). Translated excerpts from the former can be found in *Hegel's Encyclopedia of Philosophy* (henceforth *Encyclopedia*), trans., G. Mueller (New York, 1959), 57–61.

17 For a discussion of the contents of Hegel's lecture (6/25/1830), see J. Ritter, *Hegel and the French Revolution*, trans. R. Winfield (Cambridge, Mass., 1982), 183–191. For the Latin original see *Sämtliche Werke*, ed. Glockner, v. 20, 532–44.

18 There is an excellent commentary on, and excerpted translations from, the prefaces of the 1817, 1827, and 1830 editions of Hegel's *Encyclopedia* in W. Wallace's "Bibliographical Notice," *Hegel's Logic* (Oxford, 1975), xxxi–xliii (henceforth "Notice"). These prefaces can be found in *Werke*, v. 8, pp. 11–38. A translation of the preface to the second (1831) edition of *The Logic* can be found in Hegel's *Science of Logic*, trans. W. Johnston and L. Struthers (London, 1929), v. 1, 39–51. See *Werke*, v. 5, pp. 19–34.

19 Modern scholarship, of course, has noted at least three divergent tendencies among the evangelical group: a neo-orthodox tendency under the leadership of E. Hengstenberg, a neo-pietist tendency under the leadership of A. Thorluck, and a theology of feeling movement that early on was associated with Schleiermacher. Toews, *Hegelianism*, p. 247, correctly identifies these tendencies as manifestations of theological anti-Hegelianism.

20 Few, if any of these writings have been translated. For them, see Hegel, *Werke* (Frankfurt am Main, 1970), v. 11, 131–204. C. Butler's commentary, *Letters*, pp. 503ff, is perceptive and important to this issue.

21 The year 1827 is an important date in the intellectual history of German Protestantism. For a full appreciation, see R. Bigler, *The Politics of German Protestantism* (henceforth *Protestantism*) (Berkeley, Calif., 1972), esp, 88ff.

22 In this context, C. Butler's careful and informed commentary in *Letters* deserves to be commended. Read in conjunction with Jaeschke's *Reason*, esp. Chap. IV, Butler's work on the religious context of Hegel's thought gives us access to issues of great importance to the intellectual history of the 1820s. Jaeschke does not seem to have relied on Hegel's letters for much of the information he uses in his study.

23 All of these groups have roots in the so-called "Awakening" (*Erwecksungbewegung*) of the 1810s. But as Toews, *Hegelianism*, and Bigler, *Protestantism*, point out, these groups begin to go their seperate ways after 1817.

24 The great legal scholar Savigny, for example, not only was a supporter of the neo-pietest movement (Toews, *Hegelianism*, p. 247) but also regarded Hegel's teachings as atheistic. See Savigny's letter of 1822 quoted in W. Brazill, *The Young Hegelians* (New Haven, Conn., 1970), 48.

25 Hegel, *Letters*, p. 467. Bigler, *Protestantism*, pp. 43ff, traces the origins of the *Demagogenverfolgen* back to 1819.

26 See *Letters*, p. 487, and Butler's comment, p. 441.

27 The importance of the crown prince in the establishment of a "throne-altar" alliance in Prussia in the 1820s has been noted by Bigler, *Protestantism*, pp. 81–84 and 137–38, as well as by many others.

28 Hegel to Niethammer (3/26/1819), *Letters*, p. 443.

29 Toews, *Hegelianism*, passim; and C. Butler, *Letters*, pp. 475ff, make the case for this quite well.

30 As H. S. Harris has shown in *Hegel's Development* (Oxford, 1972), xix–xxxi and 1–47, Hegel's commitment to educational reform, of the sort he would try to carry out with Niethammer later, dates from the 1790s. In *Letters*, p. 251, Hegel refers in an 1811 letter to "the cause" in the context of just this kind of educational reform.

31 For these quotations, see *Letters*, pp. 275–82 and 338–41.

32 Unless otherwise noted, all the quotations in this paragraph come from ibid., pp. 339–41.

33 Hegel, quoted in Wallace, "Notice," p. xxxv; compare. *Werke*, v. 8, p. 12.

34 Hegel, quoted in Wallace, "Notice," p. xxxvi; cf. *Werke*, v. 8, p. 13.

35 Hegel, quoted in Wallace, "Notice,"; cf. Hegel's preface to the first edition (1812) of *The Logic* (*Werke*, v. 5, pp. 13–18. In both instances, Hegel offers the long, slow process of *Bildung* as a corrective to the impatience of subjective enthusiasm.

36 Hegel, "Heidelberg Inaugural," p. 2; compare *Sämtliche Werke*, ed. Glockner, v. 17, p. 21.

37 Unless other wise noted, all the quotations in this paragraph come from the Knox and Miller translation, *Introduction to the Letters*, pp. 1–3.

38 Löwith, *From Hegel*, pp. 304–7 and 323–24, understands completely what is at issue in Hegel's separation of nature and spirit. Moreover, he quite correctly explains (pp. 15, 17, 33, 39) the separation in terms of Christian logos theology.

39 Hegel, *Science of Logic*, p. 45; compare pp. 40 and 44; *Werke*, v. 5, pp. 21–22.

40 Hegel, *Letters*, p. 257. As Löwith (*From Hegel*, p. 407n57) observes, the issue here is crucial to understanding Hegel's relationship to Feuerbach.

41 W. Wallace, "Notice," p. xlii, calls Hegel a "Christian philosopher." He does so because he understands the relationship between logic and religion in Hegel's thinking. Besides Löwith, Lobkowicz, *Theory and Practice*, p. 191, and Jaeschke, *Reason*, p. 419, also make this point.

42 Unless otherwise noted, the citations in this and the next four paragraphs come from the excerpted passages from this preface that can be found in Wallace, "Notice," pp. xxxvii–xl. Parallels to what Hegel says

in the 1830 preface can be found throughout the 1820s in his lecture on the philosophy of religion.

43 As noted in n. 21 above, the ideological aggressiveness of the evangelicals intensified after 1827.

44 In *Letters*, pp. 467 (to Creuzer; 5/1821) and 493 (to Duboc; 7/30/1822), Hegel offers this as an assessment of the contemporary situation.

45 In the preface to the 1830 edition of *The Encyclopedia*, Hegel specifically contested this interpretation of his thinking. For the authors of some of these criticisms of Hegel, consult Jaeschke, *Reason*, pp. 357–73. esp. 358 and 368.

46 Hegel, *Letters*, p. 663 (to his wife; 10/12/1827). Later V. Cousin, in his *Souvenirs d'Allemagne*, recalled that this was Hegel's stated position during their travels together in 1827. The full text of Cousin's recollection can be found in G. Nicolin. ed., *Hegel in Berichten seiner Zeitgenossen* (Homburg, 1970), 526–29). Butler provides an excerpt in *Letters*, pp. 663–64.

47 See Hegel's 1824 letter to F. van Baader: *Letters*, p. 572 (1/19/1824). P. Hodgson (*Religion*, v. 1, p. 61) notes that this view was articulated in the 1821 manuscript of Hegel's lectures on the philosophy of religion.

48 From at least Basil the Great on it was understood by many educated Christians that the teaching of Christian values by Christian gnostics was integral to the synergistic conception of Christian salvation.

49 The Alexandrian Fathers, Clement and Origen, are the key figures here. On their relation to Hegel, see my *Hegel*, pp. 12–17.

50 The nature versus spirit issue (n. 38 above) is important here, for it turns on important teased-out differences between transcendence as a form of self-conquest and as a form of self-expression.

51 Hegel, *Letters*, p. 492 (to Duboc; 7/30/1822).

52 Ibid., p. 572 (to van Baader; 1/19/1824).

53 Jaeschke, *Reason*, pp. 357–62, is most illuminating on this.

54 The indictment of liberalism here, or of what Hegel (*Letters*, p. 544) calls the concept of "formal liberty," is consistent with the view he develops of French abstractionism in the lectures on the philosophy of history, which also date from these years.

55 It is not insignificant that in the 1831 edition of the lectures on the philosophy of religion (see *Religion*, v. 1, pp. 451–60) Hegel grounds this kind of thinking in Catholicism.

56 E. Voegelin, *From Enlightenment to Revolution* (Durham, N.C., 1975), 180, has some interesting observations to make on the context of this polarization.

57 There is a fine paragraph on this in Löwith, *From Hegel*, p. 68.

58 See, for instance, E. Kamenka, *The Philosophy of Ludwig Feuerbach*

(London, 1970), p. 14. That this wisdom is incorrect has been ably demonstrated by Toews, *Hegelianism*, whose distinction between old-left
Hegelians and new-left Hegelians is extremely important. More recently, Jaeschke, *Reason*, has developed an equally important distinction between right Hegelianism and speculative theism in the 1830s.

59 Hegel, *Letters*, p. 467 (draft to Creuzer; 5/1821).

60 C. Butler's account of this is useful and informed. See *Letters*, pp. 441
    and 465.

61 Hodgson, *Religion*, v. 1, p. 8, and Jaeschke, *Reason*, pp. 362ff, discuss the
    situation. I discuss the pantheistic aspects of all this below n. 73.

62 Hegel, *Letters*, p. 520.

63 Ibid., p. 531.

64 On Daub, consult Toews, *Hegelianism*, pp. 141ff, and Butler's commen-
    tary on him in *Letters*, pp. 512ff.

65 Daub, in *Letters*, p. 517.

66 Hegel, ibid, pp. 518–19.

67 A. Nygren, *Agape and Eros*, trans. P. Watson, (New York, 1969).

68 I discuss much of this in my *Hegel*, pp. 12ff.

69 Jaeschke, *Reason*, pp. 365–73, makes an important distinction between
    naive and speculative theists.

70 The importance of this has been appreciated in ibid., pp. 357–73.

71 Nygren, *Agape*, p. 45.

72 See M. H. Abrams's still remarkable *Natural Supernaturalism*, (New
    York, 1971), esp. 143–95.

73 As a general rule, Hegel's relationship to pantheism has not been ade-
    quately dealt with by modern scholarship. W. Jaeschke (*Reason*, pp. 362–
    63) offers the best brief discussion of the issue (it is brief because
    Jaeschke regards much of the matter as "trivial"). His claim is that the
    charge of pantheism against Hegel has two very different dimensions:
    one involves the charge that Hegel's philosophy leads to the "deification
    of everything"; the other that it sanctions the view that "God is not God
    without the world". Jaeschke, I think, correctly shows that the first
    charge – in effect, that Hegel was a Spinozist – is historically false. The
    second charge, I would argue, is also false, and on two grounds. First, it
    confuses Hegel's concept of God with his discussion of the role of God in
    religion. As Hegel makes clear, while the former exists independent of
    the world, the latter, which by definition entails a relationship between
    man and God, encompasses God on the one hand and man and the world
    on the other. Second, and this follows from the first point, Hegel's discus-
    sion of God's role in religion assumes the possibility of His "extension"
    into the world through revelation and education. That, of course, is
    precisely where accommodationism and synergism become relevant to

Hegel's thoughts on religion. On those terms, God indeed becomes dependent on the world. The question, then, is this: On what grounds is it appropriate to call Hegel a pantheist because he is an accommodationist? The question is all the more important because, as several students of the early history of Christianity have shown, much of the inspiration for accommodationism, especially among the Alexandrians, grew out of an opposition to Stoic pantheistic materialism. In *God in Patristic Thought*, for example, G. L. Prestige notes the early Christian distinction between logos-immanent and logos-expressed. As he explains, while the former is Stoic and pantheistic, the latter is, among other things, accommodationist and spiritualist. As I have detailed in my *Hegel*, much of Hegel's religious thinking derives from the latter tradition. Feuerbach knew that, yet he insisted on calling Hegel a pantheist. The result: a century and a half of confused scholarship on the issue. Were it not for Fred Beiser's criticisms of an earlier version of this essay, I would never have thought to address the pantheism issue this way.

74 Among Hegel scholars, R. Haym was surely one of the first to define the issue in either-or terms. See Löwith's discussion, *From Hegel*, pp. 56–57, of Haym's "ruthless historicization" of Hegel's thought. Yet, as I try to show below, it is Feuerbach who philosophically lays the foundation for this radical critique of Hegel.

75 P. Brown, *Augustine of Hippo* (Berkeley, Calif., 1969), esp. 345–55.

76 Toews develops the distinction in *Hegelianism*, p. 242. He says there that the hallmark of new-left Hegelianism is a "totally immanent" conception of human nature. I agree with that; but following N. Lobkowicz (*Theory and Practice*, pp. 183–91), I would add that this "radical immanentization" was eschatological in a lay social, rather than Christian theological, sense. This "lay eschatology," as F. Furet has argued in *Interpreting the French Revolution*, trans. E. Forster (Cambridge, 1981), 52–53, is the driving force behind much of the democratic politics of the post-revolutionary period in European history. My claim in this essay is that Feuerbach is the theorist both of new-left Hegelianism and of lay eschatology. What this means, in short, is that, while the circumference of what is immanent for old-left Hegelianism is defined by the Christian values and eschatological concerns of logos theology, no such connection exists for new-left Hegelianism. From the perspective of the young Hegel, that is the difference between a philosophy of "good" and "bad" infinity."

77 The best discussion of this issue can be found scattered through C. Butler's commentary in *Letters*. I am indebted to his scholarship for drawing the matter to my attention.

78 Note the quotations in Jaeschke, *Reason*, p. 358.

79 Ibid.

80 Ibid., pp. 358–59, and Lobkowicz, *Theory and Practice*, pp. 188–89. Anyone who has read Clement's theological writings will find all this quite familiar.

81 Unless otherwise noted, all the quotations in this and the next two paragraphs come from the *Letters*, pp. 491–94 and 498–500.

82 Much of the discussion in Jaeschke, *Reason*, Chap. IV, focuses on Hegel's contemporaries' misunderstanding of this. C. Butler, *Letters*, p. 538, is helpful on this, too.

83 That this issue needs to be understood in the context of Hegel's understanding of the absolute as both a logical and theological concept goes far to explain the complications that develop when Hegel's thought begins to be discussed in a thought-to-action sequence.

84 A parallel to what Hegel says to Duboc can be found in P. Hodgson's discussion of the relationship between concept and purpose in Hegel's lectures on the philosophy of religion. See *Religion*, v. 2, pp. 26, 44, and 49–50.

85 This, of course, is after the essence of the concept, its truth, has been revealed in Jesus Christ. Needless to say, this is precisely why Hegel, in *Encyclopedia*, pp. 283–84, says: "The revelation of the Absolute [i.e., Jesus as the incarnate logos] is not confined to religion, but can and must also be thought in the logical form of truth."

86 In my *Hegel*, pp. 43ff, I discuss the shift from knowing to doing in terms of the distinction between eschatology as axiology and eschatology as teleology. On these terms, it makes sense to speak both of Christian immanentization and of Hegel's philosophy as "immanent theology." But as we noted in n. 76 above, this would not be true of the lay eschatology of new-left Hegelianism.

87 Hegel, *Religion*, v. 1, p. 456.

88 A major theme in my discussion of the theology of the divine economy in *Hegel*, passim.

89 Consult the passages in n. 84 above.

90 The idea goes back to at least to Irenaeus.

91 Accommodationism is an important but sadly neglected and misunderstood discourse in the history of Christianity. K. Gründer, *Figur und Geschichte* (Freiburg, 1958), Chap. II, discusses the tradition. For a more-recent appraisal, see the always reliable A. Funkenstein, *Theology and the Scientific Imagination from the Middle Ages to the Seventeenth Century* (Princeton, 1986), 213–71. Also consult my *Hegel*, pp. 12–17.

92 Hegel operated with a three-age view of Christian history from very early on. There is a good discussion of this in Jaeschke, *Reason*, pp. 159–65. Even then – as I have shown in my book and as Jaeschke has appreciated

in his book – Hegel approached the third age of Christianity from the perspective of *Sittlichkeit*. Consult K. Löwith, *Meaning in History* (Chicago, 1949), 209–10, for how Schelling arranged the three ages of Christian history. As I show below, the designation of this third age – either as the fulfillment of Christianity in ethical practice or as the moment when Christianity is superseded as a value system – is crucial to the differences between Hegel and Feuerbach as well as between old-left and new-left Hegelians.

93 Windischmann, in *Letters*, p. 566.

94 Consult C. Butler's commentary, *Letters*, pp. 537ff.

95 Windischmann's worries are articulated in a letter to Hegel. See *Letters*, p. 566.

96 Jaeschke's observation (*Reason*, p. 351) that Hegel was not seeking "refuge in the concept" is apposite here. Cf. Löwith, *From Hegel*, p. 327.

97 Windischmann, *Letters*, p. 566.

98 Jaeschke, *Reason*, p. 363n13 and pp. 401ff, offers an extremely useful discussion of Weisse. In that connection, and in the context of the 1830s, he interprets Weisse as a "speculative theist." At the time of the 1829 letter, however, Weisse was (as Jaeschke notes, pp. 358 and 401) still "close" to Hegel.

99 As I shall argue, Feuerbach's break with Hegel is clearly articulated in the 1828 letter.

100 Unless otherwise noted, all the quotations in this and the next three paragraphs come from *Letters*, pp. 539–40.

101 Both Weisse's misreading of Hegel and what follows from it have been discussed by Jaeschke, *Reason*, pp. 402ff. Of decisive importance here is Jaeschke's claim (p. 410) that in Weisse's misreading of Hegel we can see how the profound differences between Hegel's Protestantism and that of his orthodox Lutheran opponents came to be obscured.

102 As I show below, these terms became crucial to the discussion of the progress from the absolute to the concrete in the debates of the 1830s.

103 See, for example, the Berlin inaugural of 1818.

104 Daub, quoted by C. Butler, *Letters*, pp. 540–41. The implication of the error is precisely what Jaeschke delineates in *Reason*, pp. 402ff.

105 Butler, *Letters*, p. 541.

106 The terms are Weisse's. See *Letters*, p. 540. For contrasting views as to whether these efforts were internal to Hegel's school or responses to external pressures on the school, see, respectively, Jaeschke, *Reason*, p. 353, and Toews, *Hegelianism*, p. 342.

107 I have a good deal to say about the eschatological dimension of this kind of "striving" in my *Hegel*, pp. 40–76.

108 On this reading, striving for *Sittlichkeit* becomes synonymous with

establishing the kingdom of God on earth. Or to put it another way, Hegel regards *Sittlichkeit* as the foundation of the third age of Christian history.

109 See n. 76 above.

110 Although this letter has drawn the attention of many scholars, only Jaeschke, *Reason*, pp. 384–85 and 396, strikes me as having interpreted it correctly. M. Wartofsky, *Feuerbach* (New York, 1977), 46–47, offers an uncritical reading of the letter.

111 Nygren, *Agape and Eros*, pp. 672ff. There Nygren correctly links this kind of religion with Feuerbach.

112 Toews, *Hegelianism*, pp. 175–99, presents the best discussion of Feuerbach's thinking in the 1820s.

113 Unless otherwise noted, all the quotations in this and the next four paragraphs come from this letter. See *Letters*, pp. 547–50.

114 Here Feuerbach misreads Hegel in the same way Weisse does (n. 101 above). The parallels between Feuerbach's and Weisse's views between 1828 and 1843 deserve scholarly attention, for both thinkers delegitimized Hegel with the same kind of relativizing conceptual move.

115 The sentence is astonishing because, as I show below, it speaks directly to the issue of what separates Hegel's concept of secularization from that of Feuerbach. For a wide-ranging account of the implications of these two conceptions of secularization, see H. Blumenberg, *The Legitimacy of the Modern Age*, trans. R. Wallace (Cambridge, Mass., 1983).

116 Feuerbach will use this language again in 1843 in his famous essay "Provisional Theses for the Reformation of Philosophy." A convenient translation can be found in L. Stepelevich, ed., *The Young Hegelians* (New York, 1983).

117 Moses Hess as well as Feuerbach will later use the heaven-versus-earth language to de-legitimize Hegel.

118 I show that this is not the case below. In addition, I was delighted to discover in Jaeschke, *Reason*, pp. 4–5, that he too regards Feuerbach's so-called "transformatiom" of Hegel as less of a transformation than a "replacement" of one system with another.

119 Windischmann, *Letters*, p. 566.

120 Hegel, *The Philosophy of History*, trans. J. Sibree (New York, 1956), 442. Throughout Part IV Hegel reveals his penchant for viewing *Sittlichkeit* as the culmination of Christian history.

121 I take it here that Feuerbach's "pure logos" signals a break with logos theology in both its Christian and Hegelian forms. That is, it represents a break with a long tradition of "revelation-believing-rationalism" that starts with Philo and runs down through the ages to Lessing and Hegel.

122 In 1839, in his "Towards a Critique of Hegelian Philosophy," Feuerbach

urges a "return to nature" as the only way to salvation for modern man. Throughout this text, which is translated in L. Stepelevich (n. 116 above), Feuerbach opposes "sensuous being" to Hegel's "logical being."

123 This theme becomes important later when action rather than theory becomes the measure of life for many of the new-left Hegelians (for example, M. Hess and A. Cieszkowski).

124 See n. 40 above.

125 Hegel, *Letters*, p. 257

126 Hegel, *Encyclopedia*, p. 270.

127 Ibid., pp. 281–84. A suggestive parallel to what Hegel says here can be found in the writings of Meister Eckhart. See Eckhart in *Library of Christian Classics*, v. 13, ed. R. Petry (Philadelphia, 1957), 197.

128 Hegel, *Encyclopedia*, p. 278. On the importance of the distinction between axiology and teleology in Christian thought, see my *Hegel*, pp. 40–57. My claim in this essay is that the axiology-teleology distinction enables us to conceptualize the famous thought-action problem in German thought with much more sophistication than has hitherto been the case.

129 See Feuerbach's often-quoted remark in "Provisional Theses" as to Protestants becoming "de jure Hegelians in order to be able to combat atheism." I quote from Feuerbach, *The Young Hegelians*, ed. Stepelevich, p. 167. Needless to say, Feuerbach's statement can be challenged on historical grounds.

130 Ibid., p. 168.

131 I discuss the distinction in my *Hegel*, pp. 75, 170, and 279–80.

132 Although Feuerbach hints at this in his 1828 letter, it is not until 1839 that he develops a full argument for relativizing Hegel. See "Critique of Hegelian Philosophy" in *The Young Hegelians* (n. 129, above), pp. 97–9.

133 See M. Reeves and W. Gould, *Joachim of Fiore and the Myth of the Eternal Evangel in the Nineteenth Century* (Oxford, 1987), Chap. 2 and 3, for a recent discussion of the issue.

134 See notes 92 and 108 above.

135 Consult Jaeschke's interesting essay "Hegel's Last Year in Berlin" in *Hegel's Philosophy of Action*, ed. L. Stepelevich and D. Lamb (Atlantic Highlands, N.J., 1983), 31–48.

136 When Feuerbach relativizes Hegel, it is the social dimension of the latter's Protestantism that is obscured.

137 The best account of this triangular interplay can be found in Hegel's *Philosophy of History*, Part IV.

138 For Hegel's view in 1830, see the preface to the third edition of the *Encyclopedia*.

139 Although representing Protestantism as a form of anti-social egoism

can be found in the 1790s writings of J. de Maistre and Novalis, it was also a central motif of Saint-Simon's and Comte's writings in the early 1820s. It is from the latter, mediated through the writings of the Saint-Simonians in the late 1820s, that so many of the new-left Hegelians drew their inspiration.

140 See, for instance, Ruge's essays translated in *The Young Hegelians*, pp. 211–59.

141 As mentioned in n. 110 above, Wartofsky takes Feuerbach's claim of discipleship at face value. A. Cieszkowski was more candid, writing in 1838 that "we have described the transition [from thought to action] in Hegel's own terms and we have only altered the results thereof." See Cieszkowski in *The Young Hegelians*, p. 77.

142 See H. Heine, "English Fragments," in *The Works of Heinrich Heine*, trans. C. Leland (New York, 1906), v. 3, 439–40, where he claims that since the Revolution the people "sind selbst zur Idee geworden." Most of these fragments were written in 1828.

143 This is a common theme in the work of many new-left Hegelians.

144 The democratic implications of Feuerbach's philosophy (or anti-philosophy) are noted by Kamenka, *Feuerbach*, passim.

145 Michelet's comment (quoted in Löwith, *From Hegel*, p. 401n12), that "The goal of [Hegelian] history is the secularization of Christianity" is relevant here. For the "prophetic" activism argument, see Toews, *Hegelianism*, pp. 162–63 and 235–42.

146 This is precisely what Feuerbach means in 1843 when he says: the "essence" of a "human being" is "undetermined, but capable of infinite determinations." See Feuerbach, in *Young Hegelians*, p. 168. It is, of course, Feuerbach's cosmic sense of this lack of determination that makes him an atheist.

147 In ibid., pp. 164–65, Feuerbach equates "French sensualism" with a revolutionary tradition that "believes in nothing other than its own self, . . . its essence." Moreover, he associates this "French disposition" of "unbelieving" with the "atheistic principle." What he is doing here is making democracy and atheism the respective political and religious pre-conditions of "pure logos." And since the idea of pure logos is "undetermined," it is quite wrong to speak of Feuerbach in particular and new-left Hegelianism in general as an immanent form of anything. As was T. Paine before him, Feuerbach is quite serious about the relationship between his philosophy and the idea of a "second creation."

148 M. Hess, "The Philosophy of Act" (1843), pp. 259, 267, and 269, speaks of the "power of negation" in precisely these terms. As he says (p. 251), "Activity is . . . self-creation, the law of which is perceived by spirit through its own act of self-creation." The Hess essay can be

found in *Socialist Thought*, ed. A. Fried and R. Sanders (New York, 1964), 249–75.

149 Although Wartofsky (*Feuerbach*, p. 6) labels Feuerbach an "emergentist," he errs (p. 10) in trying Feuerbach's philosophy to some kind of "immanent dialectic." As I have already insisted, a philosophy of self-creation cannot be said to be immanent theology without many qualifications.

150 Toews, *Hegelianism*, p. 242.

151 As I have noted in n. 76 above, the shift in values entails a shift in eschatology as well.

152 For all too long we have allowed the continuity argument to stand unchallenged. A fine example of it can be found in an 1841 essay by Hess, who at that time wrote of the young Hegelians that "the more they move from idealism to the praxis of the idea, the more they move towards the positive construction of the future." See Hess, quoted in S. Avineri, *Moses Hess* (New York, 1985), 80–81.

153 Consult Toews, *Hegelianism*, pp. 230–33, for Michelet. We desperately need a modern study of him.

154 A. Liebich, *Between Ideology and Utopia* (London, 1979), 28–31 and 50–54, is very clear on Michelet's attitude toward Hegel. Although Liebich calls Michelet an old Hegelian (rather than an old-left Hegelian), it is clear from Liebich's remarks that in his view Michelet stands to his pupil Cieszkowski as I have positioned Hegel relative to Feuerbach.

155 See Heine's 1831 essay "Introduction to Kahldorf" in *The Romantic School and Other Essays*, ed. J. Hermand and R. Holub (New York, 1985), 245.

156 For this argument, see my *Hegel*, passim.

157 The themes in this paragraph are specifically addressed in the preface to the 1830 edition of the *Encyclopedia*. According to student notebooks, Hegel voiced the same concern in his discussion of the relationship between religion and the state in his 1831 lectures on the philosophy of religion. See Hegel, *Religion*, v. 1, pp. 451–60, esp. 454.

158 The common element in all this is Hegel's objections to "one-sidedness" of whatever subjective sort.

159 Of the utmost importance is the fact that as late as 1831, Hegel insisted on equating the two political extremes, respectively, with retrograde Protestant and Catholic forms of thought. See *Religion*, v. 1, pp. 454–56.

160 See n. 135 above.

161 Schubarth is discussed briefly by C. Butler, *Letters*, pp. 523–25.

162 For Sietze, consult Toews, *Hegelianism*, pp. 86 and 120–21, as well as Ritter, *Hegel and the French Revolution*, pp. 93 and 98.

163 See n. 132 above. Heine was making this claim publicly as early as 1832.

164 Consult Toews, *Hegelianism*, Chap. 7, for particulars.

165 Ruge in 1841 uses the phrase "die Religion der Sittlichkeit" to characterize Hegel's concept of religion.

166 Jaeschke, *Reason*, pp. 375–81, discusses the either-or context for the religio-political developments of the years 1835–38.

11 Hegel's aesthetics: An overview

When Hegel presented his lectures on aesthetics in the 1820s, he probably believed that his system of beauty and the fine arts was the most up-to-date and comprehensive of its time. And perhaps he was right. But Hegel himself would have been the first to admit that only in retrospect would a proper assessment of his theory emerge. As we now look back, Hegel's aesthetic theory stands as the product of mutually influencing currents of inquiry within German intellectual life of the early 1800s, the most salient of which was the philosophical effort to comprehend the universe within the contours of an encyclopedic, organically structured thought-system. Under the spell of this hopeful enterprise, Hegel composed his theory of art and beauty as a movement within his comprehensive metaphysical theory. Following the interpretative conventions of the time, he tacitly assumed that his readers would view his aesthetic theory as part of this greater metaphysical symphony – as a reflection and extension of his conception of a dynamic but essentially rational and harmonious universe. Although systematic, Hegel's aesthetics is not self-contained, and it solidly depends upon the presuppositions of his idealistic outlook.

The systematic, metaphysically grounded aspect of Hegel's aesthetics is not its only key feature. Hegel was writing when romanticism inspired a younger generation, and when self-conscious questions concerning the relative merits of "modern" artworks in comparison to those of the "ancients" were at the center stage of aesthetic theory. Questions concerning the comparative values of individual arts such as architecture, sculpture, painting, music, and literature also filled the intellectual air. Hegel's comprehensive aesthetic theory – a theory expressed in a decade of classroom lectures

348

amounting to over 1000 pages – moves within the orbit of each of these debates and concerns. It stands, then, as far more than an essential component of a systematic metaphysics. It also embodies a specific historical era and style of reflection about beauty and the fine arts.

In this essay, I will locate Hegel's philosophy of art within his general theory of cultural development, and then examine four inter-dependent components of the theory: (1) his account of art history; (2) his hierarchical organization of the five fine arts; (3) his analysis of artistic beauty; and (4) his famous "end of art" thesis. During the course of this exposition, the architectonic shape of Hegel's aesthetic theory will be highlighted. Once the theory's overall configuration becomes clear, it will show itself to be surprisingly non-dialectical and non-exemplary of the kind of theoretical underpinnings one would ideally expect from a dialectical thinker such as Hegel. Having shown that the dialectical core of Hegel's philosophy of art does not reside within its architectonic skeleton, I will indicate how it lies implicit within Hegel's theory of beauty – the aspect of Hegel's phi-losophy of art that inspires his entire aesthetics.

I. ART AS THE EXPRESSION OF METAPHYSICAL KNOWLEDGE: HEGEL'S CONCEPTION OF ARTISTIC BEAUTY

Hegel's supremely positive assessment of philosophy is well-known, and his estimation of artistic beauty is hardly less Olympian. For him, artistic beauty reveals absolute *truth* through perception (*Werke*, XIII, 151/111).[1] He holds that the best art conveys metaphysical knowl-edge by revealing, through sense perception, what is unconditionally true. In accord with the religious overtones that often attend Hegel's own voice in his *Lectures on Aesthetics*, we may say that beautiful art, for Hegel, offers a perception of "the divine" or "what is godlike." Simply and broadly stated, beauty is God's appearance.

Hegel's conception of "God" or "the divine" is rather non-traditional, however, and is fully understandable only in reference to his metaphysics of self-consciousness. Upon further reflection, He-gel's assertion that beauty perceptually presents "what is divine" or "God" amounts to an expression in religious terms of what is more aptly described philosophically: beauty, according to Hegel, is the perceptual presentation of what his metaphysical theory affirms to be unconditional or absolute – that "what is conceptual" (that is, what is rational) is the driving force intrinsic to a self-conscious universe.[2] Since Hegel maintains, moreover, that the self-conscious human being most clearly embodies this conceptual, rational principle, he concludes that the highest beauty resides in the artistically perfected appearances and actions of the rational human being.

Insofar as Hegel asserts that art conveys metaphysical knowledge, he agrees with other major art theorists of the time. Schelling and Schopenhauer, for instance, were of similar mind. A distinguishing feature of Hegel's thinking on artistic matters, however, is his pervasive philosophical impulse to elevate purely conceptual modes of expression above sensory ones. Since artistic expression is, as a rule, achieved by modifying the appearance of objects in sense-experience, Hegel's preference for what is purely conceptual ultimately compels him to locate art in a position of mild disrepute. He ennobles art insofar as it conveys metaphysical knowledge, but he tempers his assessment in view of his belief that art's sensory media can never adequately convey what completely transcends the contingency of sensation. With this, one uncovers a crucial ambivalence in Hegel's attitude toward art – an ambivalence that permeates many of his analyses.

Finally, to the aforementioned general characterizarion of artistic beauty as the appearance of "the divine," Hegel adds a further dimension which, in contrast to the standpoints of earlier theorists, renders his view quite innovative for the times: Hegel introduces an indispensable reference to the concrete context in which art is produced, and claims that artistic beauty must be understood in historical terms.

In light of his central belief that humans seek to surpass their finitude by increasing their degree of self-consciousness – that is, all humans strive for what is absolutely true – Hegel's more-comprehensive understanding of artistic beauty assumes the following form: artistic beauty, as a vehicle for the expression of absolute truth, perceptually presents the deepest values – what counts as "divine" or "godlike" – of each passing civilization. As human history is transformed by the replacement of outmoded civilizations with new ones, the profile of artistic beauty itself transforms as each new stage in the global development of self-consciousness arrives upon the scene.

II. THE SOCIAL CONTEXT OF ARTISTIC EXPRESSION: ART, RELIGION, AND PHILOSOPHY

Artistic, religious, and philosophic expression serve the same end on Hegel's view: they give form to a civilization's constellation of intrinsic values. Depending upon the time period, one of these three modes of "absolute" expression will prevail as the preferred mode. Whatever the choice, however, art, religion, and philosophy will together constitute a people's cultural fabric by variously articulating a particular, historically conditioned expression of the general human aspiration for perfection and ultimate truth.

Although art, religion, and philosophy share the same universal content, their respective media differ. Speaking most broadly, the medium of art is *sensation*. Art presents its content sensuously by means of human fabrications which, in ideal cases, exemplify a limited kind of perfection. These are artworks which, through their beauty, present perfection through sensation. The medium of religion is *mental imagery*, and its empirical content is given shape through internal pictures of "what is godlike." Last, the native realm of philosophy is *pure conception*, and its content is logically patterned in the dialectical form of "what is conceptual," or what Hegel calls "the concept." In art, religion, and philosophy, then, a constant universal human aspiration – the goal of complete self-development – is variously expressed in the form of perceivable external objects, empirically constituted mental images, and pure concepts.

As one moves from art to religion to philosophy within Hegel's theory of human culture, one follows a progression from "sensation" to "conception" – a progression that is part of Hegel's intellectual inheritance from Plato. Just as Plato characterized the spiritual passage from ignorance to truth as a movement from a realm of sensation to the realm of pure conception, Hegel traces the passage of cultural expression from art, to religion, to philosophy as a movement that begins with the confusion and contingency of sense-perception and concludes with the clear precision and necessity of pure thought. Inspired by Plato, Hegel devalues sensation in favor of

pure conception, and inevitably allows the spirit of Plato's own notorious devaluation of art to haunt his own theory.[3]

In addition to his clear preference for purely conceptual modes of
apprehension as opposed to sensory modes, a second feature of Hegel's general outlook deeply influences the structure of his aesthetics. This is his belief that the purely conceptual relationships discovered through logical inquiry unfold themselves once again at the
level of human history. That is, Hegel believes that the logic of pure
thought determines the course of history. Given Hegel's idealistic
metaphysics – one that regards the entire universe as the concrete
realization of what is conceptual – this is not a remarkable claim.

On Hegel's view, then, the "sensation to conception" ordering
characteristic of the logical relationship between art, religion, and
philosophy specifies the actual structure of artistic, religious, and
philosophic history. As modes of expression that share the identical
purpose of expressing what is unconditional, the historical divisions of art, religion, and philosophy at bottom coincide: each begins with an initial "pre-Greek" period, advances on to a classical
"Greek" period, and finally reaches a "Christian" period. In accordance with their "sensation to conception" logical order, however,
art is always the first to assume cultural supremacy as a civilization's predominant mode of cultural expression. Religion and philosophy then historically follow. According to Hegel, art embodied
the deepest interests of civilization during the Greek period, and
religion and philosophy successively did the same during the Christian period.

Through the lens of Hegel's tripartite division of history into "pre-
Greek," "Greek," and "Christian" periods, we can discern one of the
pivotal dichotomies in Hegel's thought: classical Greek polytheism
as opposed to Christian monotheism. This division – "Athens versus Jerusalem" or "the ancient versus the modern" – defines the two
foci around which Hegel's vision of human cultural history revolves,
if not his philosophical horizon. Indeed, Hegel's system of thought
can be condensed into a celebration of Christianity's surpassing of
Greek polytheism tempered by a nostalgia for the classic. For the
purposes of highlighting the structure of Hegel's philosophy of art, I
will presume that Hegel's magnification of Christianity is the nu-
cleus of his mature thought, and will allow this interpretation to
govern the present exposition.

III. HEGEL'S THEORY OF ART HISTORY:
SYMBOLIC, CLASSIC, AND ROMANTIC ART

Art, religion, and philosophy, as mentioned above, are "absolute" modes of cultural expression that express a society's intrinsic values. Broadly stated, these modes of cultural expression articulate what society regards as "godlike." Of the three, art and religion are especially linked for Hegel, for unlike philosophy, these two spheres of expression are both grounded in sensation. On the basis of this sibling-like relationship between art and religion, Hegel constructs his theory of art history. Specifically, he surveys the various conceptions of "what is godlike" within the history of religion and estimates the degree to which these conceptions are individually compatible with a sensuous, perceivable artistic expression. In view of the purpose of art to provide an expression of "what is godlike" that has a *sensory* content, Hegel observes that certain construals of the divine are better suited for artistic expression than others. This observation forms the template for his threefold, stylistic division of art history into the "symbolic," "classic," and "romantic" periods.

After reviewing the various conceptions of the divine within human history, Hegel concludes that during the time of ancient Egypt and before, the prevailing conceptions of "what is godlike" were too generic and indeterminate in comparison to what would later historically emerge as a truer, more specific concrete conception. On his interpretation, such early conceptions were characteristic of "nature-religions" that took as divine *not* the human being in particular, but either *natural forces* or *life in general.* Although the art of that time, as does all art, sought to express adequately what is divine, it had only a vague and indeterminate conception with which to work. As a consequence, it could, on Hegel's view, express the yet-to-be-realized determinate conception implicit in its striving only indirectly, by means of *symbolism* – a mode of expression that grasps its subject matter only indirectly and approximately. For example, the Egyptians represented their beliefs that life in general is divine through animal symbols. Hegel, accordingly, describes this style of art as "symbolic"[4]

The ancient Greeks, as Hegel frequently notes, "solved the riddle of the sphinx" and transformed the generic Egyptian conception of absolute being into a specifically human-centered one, developing for themselves a truer, more accurate and more determinate conception of what is divine. Since they deified the human being as a creature distinct from all other living things, human self-consciousness emerged as a primary artistic subject matter in Greek culture. Moreover, since the *entire* human being was idealized, the Greek concept of absolute being retained a *sensuous* aspect, namely, the physical human form. This sensuous aspect made it possible for the theoretically more accurate and specific Greek conception of absolute being to be presentable in a perceivable, artistic form: the mathematically proportioned, idealized, three-dimensional human figure. With respect to the course of art history, this transformation from the Egyptian to the Greek understanding of what is divine indicated to Hegel that art itself transformed from a "symbolic" period to a "classical" one – a period where artistic expression attained a harmony and consistency between its subject matter and its sensuous mode of expression.

The rise of Christianity transformed the classical Greek understanding of what is godlike into a more personal, inward, ideally nonempirical conception. No longer was the cultural object of admiration an athletic, well-proportioned, self-consciously animated creature. Christianity (and Roman Stoicism, one might add) concentrated and contracted the living presence of the human being into an intangible entity alien to the physical body, and idealized this entity as the immortal soul or inner character. The body was cast aside as a mere worldly shell, and it, along with its sensuous appearance, became an object of contempt.

According to Hegel, this Christian rendition of what is godlike set distinct limits upon what art could now express. Since this new religious conception devalued the body and its appearances, it proposed to cast out the sensuous, material dimension from its conception of the divine – the very dimension that made it possible for the previous Greek religious outlook to harmonize with the sensuous media of artistic expression. Hegel judged that at this point art history transformed from a "classical" into a "romantic" phase – a phase where artistic expression tried to reach deeper and deeper into the interior of human subjectivity. In an important sense (to be examined below) this transition marked the culmination, or "end," of ideal artistic expression.

IV. THE FIVE FINE ARTS: ARCHITECTURE,
SCULPTURE, PAINTING, MUSIC, AND POETRY

With the above in view, we may now attend more specifically to
Hegel's hierarchy of the five fine arts of architecture, sculpture,
painting, music, and poetry.[5] His hierarchy rests upon three theses,
of which the first two are familiar: (1) that art's prime subject
matter – that which is "godlike," or that which is taken to have
intrinsic value – historically develops from sensuous conceptions to
non-sensuous conceptions; (2) that *art in general* grows, flourishes,
and declines in accord with this historical development from sensuous to non-sensuous conceptions; and (3) that *each individual art*
grows, flourishes, and declines in accord with the historical development from sensuous to non-sensuous conceptions of the divine.

The last thesis above yields five overlapping patterns of growth
and decline – one for each art – that cumulatively constitute the
historical growth and decline of art in general. Hegel claims that of
these five patterns, only one (that of sculpture) is synchronized with
the development of art in general, while the remaining four introduce and conclude art's overall development. The latter four arts
reach their highest excellence either before or after the fulfillment of
artistic expression in general, and appear in art history as either
primitive, symbolic foreshadowings of the ideal of classical art (viz.,
architecture as the precursor to sculpture) or as post-classical, romantic efforts to surpass the very limits of artistic expression (viz., painting, music, and poetry as the successors to sculpture).

Hegel further structures his account of the individual rise and fall
of architecture, sculpture, painting, music, and poetry in terms of
his threefold stylistic division of art history into the "symbolic,"
"classic," and "romantic" periods. For Hegel, each individual art
attains its ideal form during one of the three periods. Architecture is
most charcteristic during the symbolic period; sculpture (as does art
itself) reaches perfection during the classical period; and painting,
music, and poetry all blossom during the romatic period.[6]

Hegel's mapping of the five individual arts onto the three art-
historical periods is an attempt to provide the (traditionally non-
historically defined) individual arts with a historical interpretation
and organization. Following the "sensation to conception" progres-

sion characteristic of the historical movement from symbolic, to classical, to romantic art, Hegel systematically ranks the five arts according to the "materiality" of their respective media, beginning with three-dimensional artistic media (architecture and sculpture), continuing to two-dimensional media (painting), and concluding with non-spatial media (music and poetry). With this, Hegel molds the five fine arts into a historical progression that serves as the spiritual foundation for the development of the more-advanced religious and philosophic forms of cultural expression.

Hegel positions architecture as the first and most inadequate of the arts, claiming that both its heavy natural materials and its restricted purposes preclude it from adequately expressing the mature conception of the divine – rational human subjectivity – even in a perceivable form. He judges that gravity and solidity, the principles of its artistic materials, are too mechanical and rudimentary to reflect the nature of self-consciousness in any explicit manner. Moreover, he asserts that architectural works do not themselves exemplify what is physically godlike, but only serve to protect or enhance such exemplifications, namely, humans and human-shaped artifacts. On these (controversial, if not dubious) grounds Hegel concludes that architecture remains external and distanced from the proper subject matter of art – human subjectivity – and that the limited purposes of architecture do not correspond to art's primary task.

Sculpture is the second art in Hegel's hierarchy. It is comparable to architecture in its three-dimensionality, but its purpose significantly differs. The purpose of sculpture – to make the human form express something spiritual (*Werke*, XIV, 382–83/727) – necessitates that sculptures themselves ought to *embody* spirituality and stand as that which architecture can only indicate. Yet the sculptural embodiment of what is essentially human must remain quite limited: with its similar architectural materials, sculpture can provide only a static, material, three-dimensional vision of humanity – a vision embodied within a form quite foreign to the dynamic rationality of the human subject. As we shall see, this natural, three-dimensional aspect of sculpture marks both its ascendancy within the sphere of art and its descent beneath the spiritual horizon.

Since sculpture's mode of expression is three-dimensional, Hegel maintains that it ideally *reconciles* humanity with nature: it expresses what is essentially human with the greatest degree of physicality. Owing to this reconciliation, the purpose of sculpture – to embody what is essentially human (viz., rationality) in three-dimensional material – matches the general purpose of *art* – to embody what is divine (i.e., rationality) in a natural, perceivable form. Sculpture thus becomes the art *par excellence* for Hegel. Its medium is the most "natural" or "physical" in its three-dimensionality, and yet it has the capacity to express what is essentially human. In this respect it is perfectly balanced; neither its medium nor its message upstages the other.

Sculpture may be *artistically* perfect, but it cannot contain the inner complexity of human experience. With respect to this task, the romantic arts of painting, music, and poetry far exceed sculpture's capacities. Hegel notes, however, that these romantic arts, in surpassing sculpture in this regard, must sacrifice the classical balance between the natural medium and the subject matter and lose a measure of sensuous beauty in the process.

The two-dimensional art of painting is both the first romantic art and the third art in Hegel's overall hierarchy. Through the use of shading and linear perspective, painting represents three spatial dimensions within the constraints of a two-dimensional surface, and transports the third dimension of space into the perceiver's visual imagination. Owing to this diminished "materiality," painting crosses the midpoint where natural medium and the human subject-matter remain in balance. Now, with a dimension of the physical medium eliminated, the artistic subject matter attains a greater freedom to show itself in its own form. This line of reasoning may seem peculiar at first, but Hegel's general thought is this: as successive material dimensions of the artistic medium dissolve, so are lifted the veils that obscure our comprehension of the ideal artistic subject matter, namely, human self-consciousness as it is in itself. As the ideal subject-matter of art slowly presents itself in its truest form, the very form of art itself gradually fades away.

Hegel maintains that painting, owing to its partial withdrawal into an illusory space, can delve deeper into human subjectivity than either architecture or sculpture and can capture feeling that neither art can approach. Accordingly, he asserts that the proper task of painting is to portray, in a two-dimensional form, the inner life of human feeling. As the ideal content of painting, Hegel specifies a feeling less complex than those especially suited to music and poetry and yet more personal than those that can be expressed by either architecture or sculpture. This is the feeling of "love reconciled and at peace with itself" – an artistic content that reiterates, at a more introspective level, the content of ideal sculpture (viz., "self-satisfied" gods at peace with themselves). From these reflections stem Hegel's high regard for Raphael's Madonna and Child depictions.

The fourth member of the hierarchy – the romantic art of music – eliminates spatial dimensions altogether and represents feeling through a temporal sequence of sound which, as Hegel describes it, "remains subjective in its objectivity" (Werke, XV, 133/889). By this, he means that musical sound patterns are indeed material, but that they "remain subjective" insofar as they represent the flow of human subjectivity more faithfully than either architecture, sculpture, or painting. Since music and feeling share a temporal structure, Hegel judges that moving sound patterns are superior modes of exhibiting the structure of human feeling than either static two-dimensional illuminated surfaces or static three-dimensional arrangements of stone or other materials.[7] Since music is simply temporal and non-spatial, the materiality of its medium dissolves even further into the background as its subject-matter – the dynamic flow of human feeling – projects itself into the immediate foreground of aesthetic experience.

Despite its remarkable capacity to display the forms of human feeling, music fails to convey what Hegel believes is essential to human subjectivity: self-consciousness and its associated interplay of *conceptual* forms. Although music is far more transparent than architecture, sculpture, or painting, Hegel believes that music is restricted to the representation of *feeling* – an aspect of consciousness that humans share with other sentient creatures. In this, Hegel notes the grave deficiency of music in comparison to poetry.

Throughout his mature philosophical writings, Hegel constantly condemns feeling in general as a mode of knowledge, associating it with a superficial, unreflective immediacy of apprehension that can never articulate the inner complexity of things.[8] Hegel's attitude toward music is thus mixed, just as is his attitude toward art in general.[9] Acknowledging its non-spatiality, he accords music a high value. But because of its confinement to the generic realm of feeling, he refuses to locate it at the highest spiritual level. To convey artistically what is truly human *in a particularly human form*, a nonspatial, conceptual medium is necessary. Hegel thus turns his attention to poetry and ranks it as the most-profound art.[10]

What strikes Hegel positively about poetry is the almost arbitrary relation between its material medium and its subject matter, a relationship that he sees as a corollary of a generally arbitrary relationship between language and thought. With regard to the latter, he notices that verbal sounds or written inscriptions usually bear a merely conventional relationship to the thought contents they convey. The words "dog," "Hund," "chien," "cane," and "perro," for instance, all represent the same thought, and one word may easily be substituted for another in translation. From this common observation, Hegel (problematically) concludes that language is merely a vehicle for the externalization of thought, and is not itself a necessary condition for, nor a constitutive aspect of, thought.[11] Since we tend to overlook the particular sounds or shapes of words in ordinary discourse and simply focus upon the sets of meanings they invoke, Hegel assumes that much the same happens when we attend to poetry. This leads him to conclude that of the five fine arts, poetry transports us most directly into the interiority of human subjectivity. The verbal form of poetry serves merely as a transparent skin through which we apprehend its distinctly thoughtful nature.

Hegel's hierarchy of the five fine arts ends in poetry, and with it, artistic expression reaches its limit. As one moves from architecture, to sculpture, to painting, to music, to poetry, the sensuous medium becomes less and less conspicuous within the aesthetic experience. In poetry, finally, the relation between word and thought becomes a mere convention. In view of the implicit tendency here – a tendency to dissolve the sensuous artistic medium altogether in an effort to express perfectly a non-empirical content – Hegel locates poetry at the very edge of art. Poetry approaches this ideal form of expression, but it remains tied to the specificity of language through its use of figurative expression. The deepest aim of poetry, the very aim of the human spirit in general, thus conflicts with the very conditions for artistic expression. Poetry ultimately strives to become philosophy, but it remains bonded to its literary mode of expression. For this reason, poetry contains overtones that immediately point in the direction of the more-advanced modes of cultural expression, namely, religion and philosophy.

Hegel defines the nature of beauty from the standpoint of a teleological metaphysics specifically grounded on the principle of self-consciousness. Since self-consciousness is the model for all other universal principles, on Hegel's view, we should expect that his principles of aesthetic evaluation issue from the content and/or structure of self-consciousness. Within Hegel's *Lectures*, though, there is no explicit articulation of evaluative principles; they need to be extracted from his discourse. From a survey of Hegel's numerous aesthetic judgments, I offer two summary principles. These are what I entitle the principles of "humanity" and "perfection." In accord with what appear to have been Hegel's intentions, the principle of humanity will prescribe the ideal *content* of the most beautiful artworks; the principle or perfection – a principle that I will further explicate in reference to the notions of "self-correspondence," "idealization," and "organic unity" – will account for the ideal *structure* of the most beautiful artworks. The realization of both main principles in an artwork will correspond to Hegel's conception of ideal beauty.

A. The Principle of Humanity

Hegel defines beauty in general as "the sensory *appearance* of the idea" (*Werke*, XIII, 151/111). To this global definition, he adds that "what is human constitutes the center and content of true beauty and art" (*Werke*, XIV, 19/432). This latter specification follows from Hegel's view that the essence of humanity, with its attendant principle of self-consciousness, best expresses and embodies the metaphysical core of things, and that the task of beauty is to display to sense this "divine" aspect of the cosmos. Hegel's theory of beauty thus glorifies human appearances and actions far above either the inanimate natural beauty of sunsets and rainbows or the sentient beauty of creatures such as butterflies and swans. On this view, degrees of beauty correspond to the degrees to which self-consciousness is made perceptible.

Given that the ideal artistic subject matter is human self-consciousness in its diverse modes, a link is forged between art and freedom – that mode of being which Hegel often equates with a developed social or spiritual self-consciousness. The best artworks, consequently, express perceptible human freedom. Moreover, since freedom and morality themselves interpenetrate within Hegel's outlook, aesthetic and moral values also intertwine at the highest level of aesthetic value. Humanity, with its characteristic moral freedom, defines the realm of ideal beauty and demands that the best art contain a necessary *moral* content. On Hegel's view, beauty and goodness walk hand-in-hand. Since Hegel's conception of ideal art also involves the notion of *truth* as self-correspondence (see below), his aesthetic theory revitalizes the famous Platonic triad of truth, goodness, and beauty.

B. The Principle of Perfection

Two decades before Hegel lectured on the philosophy of art, Kant formulated a distinction within his own aesthetic theory that served the purpose of attacking A. G. Baumgarten's assertion that beauty is "perfection perceived."[12] That was Kant's distinction between *judgments of beauty* and *judgments of perfection*. Contrary to Baumgarten, Kant maintained that (pure) judgments of beauty are "quite independent of the concept of perfection" and do not involve any reference to "what sort of thing [the thing judged] ought to be."[13] Judged from Kant's perspective, Baumgarten's aesthetics disastrously confused perfection and beauty.

For Kant, a pure judgment of beauty issues solely from a harmonious accord between an object's organized structure and a person's capacity to understand that object through a projected set of organized, and organizing, concepts. Upon perceiving a systematically structured object, Kant claims that an immediate pleasure arises in apprehending the conformity between the object's organization and the organized/organizing structure of one's own intellect. An immediate pleasure, in short, results from perceiving rational structures external to oneself. It is a pleasure to know that one can know; it is a pleasure to apprehend another rational presence in the world beside one's own.

The experience of this reflective pleasure, however, does not depend upon categorizing the object and comprehending it as a thing of some specific sort. For Kant, the pleasure in beauty is merely the general pleasure of grasping the harmony between self and world, a harmony that is a precondition for both empirical categorization and moral achievement. Kant concludes, accordingly, that judgments of beauty cannot be cognitive judgments and cannot therefore involve an estimation of whether a thing is what it ought to be. Judgments of beauty are independent of the concept of perfection.

If Kant's distinction between (pure) judgments of taste and judgments of perfection is well grounded, then Hegel simply appears to have repeated the same confusion that Kant attributed to Baumgarten.[14] How was this possible? What a follower of Kant might have construed within Hegel's view as a "Baumgartian confusion" stems from several deeply rooted features within Hegel's dialectical, reconciliatory, holistic perspective. First is Hegel's wholesale rejection of Kant's theory of knowledge owing to the latter's dependence upon the hypothesis of an unknowable thing-in-itself, and with this, an ultimate rejection of Kant's radical segmentation of the human mind into the difficult-to-bridge spheres of "cognition," "pleasure/displeasure," and "judgment." Second is Hegel's anti-romantic reluctance to acknowledge a foundational role for non-conceptual mental processes such as feeling or pleasure, whether it be reflective or sensory. Third is Hegel's commitment to a teleological metaphysics that demands that everything is construed in terms of the idea of perfection as the completion of a goal. Fourth is Hegel's further commitment to the view that the teleological structure of things is modeled upon the goal-oriented nature of self-awareness – a phenomenon that Hegel judged to be fundamentally conceptual. When taken together, all these factors coalesce into a holistic theory that demands a "fusion" or organic unity between the sharp divisions in things necessitated by the Kantian view, and that calls for a theory of value judgment that comprehends all such judgments as variants upon a single, fundamental structure of judgment, a structure that itself reiterates the dialectical structure of self-consciousness.

In the section of his *Logic* where Hegel examines what he takes to be the most advanced form of judgment, namely, the evaluative judgment or "the rationally explicit judgment" (*Das Urteil des Begriffs*), he claims that every such judgment involves estimating whether or not something *is* what it *ought* to be (*Werke*, VI, 344–51). That is, Hegel maintains that all evaluative judgments, whether they are judgments of goodness, beauty, truth, or some other value, are judgments of perfection. This implies that every evaluation involves a comparison between two aspects of a thing – its actual condition and its ideal condition – in an effort to determine the degree to which the two aspects converge. Insofar as there is a coincidence or harmony, a positive evaluation results, and the judgment is "true"; insofar as there is a discrepancy, a negative evaluation follows. Evaluative judgments, on Hegel's view,[15] are thus a species of identity judgments.

Hegel distinguishes judgments of beauty from other kinds of value judgments in reference to the specific *purpose* of beauty in contrast to other purposes. A judgment of beauty in general, then, involves estimating whether the purpose of a beautiful thing, viz., to perceivably express "what is godlike," is concretely realized in an artwork or natural object. In more specific artistic contexts, Hegel narrows his general conception of a beautiful thing's purpose and formulates it in further reference to either the artistic style, the individual art, or the subclass of art which the artwork represents. Regardless of the particular purpose, Hegel always judges whether the object in question "is" what it "ought" to be and invokes the concept of perfection.

Perfection as Self-Correspondence

If something is in a state of "self-correspondence," it is in a state of perfection. It has fulfilled its intrinsic purpose and is "complete" in that its existence and its essence are no longer sharply distinguishable. In such a condition, something becomes a "true" one of its sort. This style of teleological evaluation – one which has its historical sources in Aristotle[16] – defines the core of Hegel's conception of truth and is at the heart of Hegel's philosophical system. Within Hegel's thought, this teleological mode of evaluation logically derives from his analysis of human consciousness. For him, consciousness is itself goal-directed: it aims to recognize itself through what is other to it, and to reconcile itself with this otherness which, in a trans-individual sense, is its own projection to begin with. This point of recognition and reconciliation in an act of reflection generates a condition of "self-correspondence" – a state of *truth* as perfection. From this dialectical structure of self-realization flows the pervasive discourse of "perfection" within Hegel's theory, a discourse that involves the teleological notions of truth as self-correspondence, beauty as perfection in sensation, and the good as perfection in social practice. In each instance, the idea of perfection takes its specific form from the very thought of becoming self-aware.

Hegel's teleological style of evaluation operates within his aesthetic theory at four distinct levels and defines the shape of the theory's architectonic. It appears at the level of (1) evaluating art itself in relation to religion and philosophy; (2) evaluating the symbolic, classic, and romantic art-historical styles; (3) evaluating the individual arts of architecture, sculpture, painting, music, and poetry; and (4) evaluating individual artworks themselves. At each of these levels, Hegel defines a general *purpose* for that which is to be judged and grounds his evaluation upon whether the object of judgment successfully embodies, or can embody, the defined purpose.

At the level of art in general, we have already encountered Hegel's ambivalent evaluation of artistic expression. To recall, he asks most generally whether artistic expression can achieve the most central human purpose of expressing what is unconditionally true, that is, metaphysical knowledge, and he compares artistic expression to the other alternative modes of conveying such knowledge – religion and philosophy. Owing to art's restriction to sensory media, Hegel judges that although art numbers among the three "absolute" forms of cultural expression, it nonetheless remains the least adequate. This conclusion is familiar, but we can now note how Hegel's teleological mode of evaluation prescribes the structure of this assessment.

At the level of art history, we find the same mode of evaluation. Here Hegel asks two questions: whether each of the three art-historical styles – symbolic, classic, and romantic – can (a) achieve the general purpose of the human spirit to express metaphysical knowledge in a form proper to metaphysical knowledge itself (that is, through *conception*), and (b) achieve the specific purpose of *art* to express metaphysical knowledge through *perception*. From the above discussion, it is clear that romantic art, owing to its almost non-empirical Christian content, comes closest to achieving the first task. It is also clear that only classical art, owing to its humanly sensuous "ancient" content, fulfills the second task on Hegel's view. Both of these conclusions are familiar, but we now see how Hegel's systematic application of a particular style of evaluation is beginning to show itself at every major level of the theory.

With respect to the five fine arts, Hegel again asks the same two questions as above, tailored to fit this more specific level of inquiry:

(a) whether the respective artistic media are each capable of express-ing metaphysical knowledge in a form adequate to that of metaphysi-cal knowledge itself (that is, a non-sensory form), and (b) whether the media peculiar to each art are capable of expressing metaphysi-cal knowledge in a *sensory* form. As the most-advanced romantic art, poetry is judged to be the most-"spiritual" art owing to its high degree of subjective interiority; as the representative classical art, sculpture is judged to be the best art owing to its balance between medium and subject matter. Once again, we can note Hegel's perva-sive teleological style of evaluation.

At the level of evaluating specific artworks, Hegel's art critical procedure follows the same route. It also, for this reason, seems disturbingly simplistic: Hegel *prima facie* evaluates an individual artwork in reference to whether it embodies the specific purpose of the *artform* of which it is an example.[17] This procedure may seem simple, but artworks exemplify many categories and purposes, and this quickly complicates the evaluation procedure. Within Hegel's framework, a work may be good as painting, but not the best as art (with respect to its medium) if compared with a sculpture having a similar theme; a work may be bad as painting, but good as art (with respect to its content) owing to its classical theme; a sculpture may be good as art, simply owing to its medium, but fail because it tries to portray a subject matter that lies beyond its expressive capacities, and so forth.

An art critic in the Hegelian style, then, must decide (a) which of an artwork's many categories and associated purposes are essential to it, (b) whether the artwork realizes these respective purposes, and (c) how to weigh the comparative importance of the (often conflicting) purposes themselves. The basic structure of Hegel's art criticism is indeed simple: evaluations are carried out within a fairly well defined genus-species hierarchy of purposes that the artwork may or may not embody. At the same time, however, the actual process of art-critical judgment is neither straightforward nor mechanical.

Where does such an art criticism lead? One distinctive feature of Hegel's approach is that it authorizes an artwork's subject matter to significantly determine the artwork's aesthetic value. As an example, consider two portraits that appear to be duplicates of each other, but that are actually depictions of one member of a pair of identical twins. Suppose that the twins are of opposing characters – one is good; one is evil – and that the two portraits depict each twin as having a good character. On many accounts of aesthetic value, the perceptual indistinguishability of the two portraits will necessitate, at least provisionally, identical attributions of aesthetic value to each work.

Within Hegel's teleological mode of evaluation, the perceptual indistinguishability of the two portraits does not legitimate even a suspicion of an equivalence in aesthetic value. If the *purpose* of portraiture is to display faithfully a person's character, then an estimation of whether this purpose has been achieved is essential to the portrait's aesthetic evaluation. Since one of the above-mentioned portraits fails to achieve its purpose, Hegel will judge that, despite its perceptual equivalence to another portrait (which does achieve its purpose), this former portrait must be inferior to the latter. It is inferior because it is a misrepresentation. This is a clear case of Hegel's insistence upon a close connection between beauty and truth. Hegel does not restrict his art-critical judgments to the mere "aesthetic surface" of the artwork, but considers the artwork's subject matter in relation to the artwork's purpose. The portrait as such can only reach a state of "self-correspondence" or "artistic truth" when it fulfills its purpose as a portrait.

In sum, Hegel refuses to detach what *is* perceived from what *ought* to be perceived in his evaluative procedure, whether the evaluation concerns art in general, art historical style, individual arts, or individual works of art. In every case, the concept of perfection underlies the evaluative judgment.

The Artistic Means to Achieve Perfection as Self-Correspondence: Idealization and Organic Unification

Hegel sometimes attributes perfection to an artwork as a consequence of its *idealization* of a given subject matter. References to this sort of perfection are scattered throughout Hegel's lectures and appear in his accounts of Greek sculpture, heroic action in epic poetry, and portraiture in painting. With respect to portraiture, Hegel's expression of perfection as idealization is quite direct:

[the artist] must omit little hairs, pores, little scars, blemishes, and grasp and represent the subject in its universal character and in its steadfast individuality. It makes a great difference whether the artist merely reproduces a person's physiognomy, as it quietly presents itself to him in its surface and external configuration, or whether the artist insightfully represents the true features which express the subject's own soul. For the Ideal necessitates, without exception, that the external form accord with the soul.

(*Werke*, XIII, 206/155–56)

Similar to his principle of truth as self-correspondence, Hegel's demand for idealization in artistic representation is also inspired by his account of the structure of self-consciousness. In an act of self-conscious reflection, one first "posits" oneself as an object other than oneself – one stands beside oneself – and then recognizes this "other" as that which is identical to oneself. One says, in short, "that is me." In the pictorial idealization of a face, this process occurs at the level of perception. One perceives an object external to oneself that represents what one is *ideally*, and identifies with that appearance insofar as it perceptually displays one's essence.

This experience of self-recognition is obviously not unique to portraiture, for the same reflective awareness can arise, for instance, upon apprehending an inscription of one's name, or upon looking in a mirror. The difference between the idealized portrait and these other instances resides in the comparative faithfulness of the portrait. Since Hegel describes a person's inner character as a "universal content," he believes that if this content is to be displayed accurately in a perceptual form, then all contingencies in appearance must be eliminated to the greatest extent such as to allow the universality of this content to exhibit itself through the image. A properly *artistic* portrait intensifies and condenses one's physical appearance into a perceptual representation of one's unchanging character. Within Hegel's view, this discloses a general principle of artistic representation, for he calls for such idealization in all artistic portrayals that aim to be beautiful.[18] With respect to human action, for instance, he demands that artistic representation elevate human actions to a godlike, heroic status, one that of necessity must be serious and devoid of comic contingencies. For Hegel, the contingencies upon which comedy depends are beauty's ruination.

The principle of *organic unity* – a principle that historically originates in Aristotle's theory of tragedy – also determines beauty as a mode of perfection. According to this well-known principle, the beauty of an artwork or natural object corresponds to its degree of organization or integration. In the ideal case, no elements of an artwork or natural object appear arbitrary, unplanned, accidental, or irrational. The best artworks have no "dead spots." Beauty thus becomes identified with systematicity, or an intense "unity in diversity" in the field of appearance.

The principles of idealization and organic unity both serve to eliminate contingency or accidentality in the artwork, and both have the purpose of illuminating what is universal in the given subject matter. The principle of organic unity, however, more clearly exemplifies how a beautiful artwork renders perceivable Hegel's metaphysical vision of the total systematicity of the universe: the organic unity of the artwork visually represents the metaphysical interconnectedness of all things, perceptual and non-perceptual. The beautiful artwork is a microcosm and perceptually reveals one aspect of "the divine" through its perceivable exemplification of organic structure. The most-beautiful artworks offer us a vision of what is perfect, what is unconditional, what is true, what is "divine," by means of their perfected, idealized, systematically unified appearance. The perception of systematicity is a necessary condition of the appearance of "what is godlike."[19]

When Hegel expresses his view that the structure of self-consciousness most explicitly illustrates the structural core of what is, he usually emphasizes one of the following: the inner dynamic of self-consciousness, its organically related "moments" wherein what initially appears as alien is later recognized to be selfsame, or the intrinsic directedness of self-consciousness that makes such recognition possible. In the realm of aesthetic value, the principle of organic unity reflects the second, most explicitly dialectical of these aspects of self-consciousness. Here the perceptually interdependent elements of the artwork mirror the ontologically interdependent aspects of self-consciousness. Just as Hegel claims that the entire universe articulates the dialectical structure of self-consciousness, he claims that the organically structured artwork is a tiny reflection of the total system in which it is embedded.

VI. HEGEL'S "END OF ART" THESIS

Hegel's "end of art" thesis flows from his interpretation of the way Greek antiquity transformed into Christianity. In recognizing a fun-

damental difference between the Classical and the Christian outlooks, Hegel was far from alone. Schiller, for instance, used this
historical division to distinguish between two contrasting attitudes
toward the world – the "naive" and the "sentimental" – and to characterize two corresponding poetic temperaments – the "natural"
and the "reflective."[20] Schelling also invoked this historical parti-
tion in his division of mythologies into the "natural" or "Greek"
style, as opposed to the "historical" or "Christian" style.[21]

Although Hegel accepted the general division of history into the
Classical and the Christian periods, he did not unreservedly favor
the Classical over the Christian outlooks, as did many of his intellectual contemporaries. Hegel shared the view that the Christianity of
the then established Church was ossified, rule-bound, and mechanical, but he did not agree that invoking the classical Greek spirit
could alone generate a true, living religion.[22] Hegel felt a nostalgia
for the classic, but he was too historically sensitive and realistic to
believe in its contemporary resurrection. This down-to-earth historical attitude led inevitably to his "end of art" thesis.

Hegel's claim that art has reached its "end" is indeed one of the
most provocative implications of his aesthetic theory. In brief, the
thesis is as follows: there comes a time when art no longer expresses
the deepest interests of humanity at large, and that time has come.
Hegel is quite blunt about this and states that "for us, art belongs to
the past" (*Werke*, XIII, 25/11). He also adds the hope that "art will
someday reach its perfection" (*Werke*, XIII, 142). In one sense art has
reached its perfection, and in another sense it has not. It remains to
specify these senses.

As Hegel construes matters, art was the central mode of cultural
expression in ancient Greece but was eclipsed by the rise of Christianity. Since Hegel believed that he still lived in the long-enduring
Christian era, this historical transition is certainly what he had in
mind when he remarked that "for us, art belongs to the past." Such
statements could easily suggest, as they did to Benedetto Croce, that
Hegel's aesthetic theory is a "funeral oration" for art.[23] Many have
since disputed Croce's claim, but none, as far as I am aware, has
construed Hegel's end-of-art thesis in reference to the following
brief, but very telling, remark – one that indicates how Hegel envi-
sions the broader historical landscape within which he situates the
transformation of the Greek outlook into the Christian outlook, and

the subsequent deemphasis upon artistic expression as the central mode of grasping what is divine.[24] He writes: "With the advance of culture, there generally comes a time for *every people* [emphasis added] when art points beyond itself" (*Werke*, XIII, 142/103).

In view of the above statement, it cannot be Hegel's view that artistic production will totally cease at some point within the progressive development of human history. Nor can it be Hegel's view that, as we presently stand, art will never again serve to express the deepest interests of humanity. On the contrary, he states that art will be produced in *every* civilization, past, present, and future, and that in every instance, art will eventually point "beyond itself" to a new form of cultural expression. In what respect, then, does art reach its end? Hegel's "sensation to conception" account of cultural development provides an answer. Within this model, every civilization follows an "art-religion-philosophy" progression in its cultural development: art initially expresses the culture's intrinsic values and is later abandoned in favor of religious and philosophical modes of expression. If there were only one human civilization, then art would indeed have no resurrection. But there are many civilizations, each of which has its own rise and fall.

Hegel's "end of art" thesis thus indicates a perennial, or timeless, "end" of art. If we combine this with Hegel's more well known claim that successive epochs always stand at higher levels of self-consciousness than the previous ones, we uncover within history two distinct rhythms of change, one progressive and the other cyclical. Along the progressive dimension, self-consciousness gradually increases as humanity approaches the perfect rational state. Along the cyclical dimension, the "art-religion-philosophy" pattern constantly reiterates itself as whole epochs rise and fall. At the interface between epochs, there is a transformation from philosophy at a lower level of self-consciousness to art at a higher level of self-consciousness. Within this cyclical dimension of historical change, Hegel's "end of art" thesis arises and leads to the emergence of romantic art, and with this, the inevitable transition from artistic expression to religious and philosophic expression as the preferred cultural modes.

Since art will always point away from itself toward a more inwardly grounded mode of cultural expression, one can ask generally: At what point within a civilization's development will the transition from artistic to non-artistic (that is, sense-grounded to conceptual) modes of expression occur? If one takes the movement from Greek to Christian/Stoic outlooks as paradigmatic, it appears that the transition occurs when the prevailing self-conception of the human being moves from an integrated "person" conception of the individual, which emphasizes the fusion, or harmony, of "psyche" and "body," to a divided "body/soul" conception, which emphasizes the absolute separation of matter and mind. The question of where our present epoch stands remains open for speculation. Whatever the judgment, it appears that within Hegel's framework, the historically prevailing self-conception of the human being indicates where a culture stands in its level of spiritual expression.

VII. CRITICISM AND CONCLUSION

Hegel's philosophy of art and beauty is certainly open to criticism. First, the present-day understanding of the individual arts includes far more than "the five fine arts." If Hegel's theory of the arts is to remain plausible, it must be flexible enough to sustain an expression to accommodate new and previously undervalued arts. Second, Hegel's aesthetics is primarily a philosophy of artistic beauty, and it stands in need of elaboration with respect to other aesthetic values. Third, Hegel's assertions that sculpture displays beauty most perfectly and that poetry is the most profound art are controversial, at best. Both evaluations issue from Hegel's metaphysical definition of beauty, which, in turn, rests on the truth of his metaphysics. So, fourth, there is the fundamental question of whether Hegel's metaphysics of self-consciousness is itself true, and hence there are doubts abouts his reasons for believing that the purpose of beautiful art is to convey metaphysical knowledge, let alone metaphysical knowledge in the form he prescribes. Fifth, there are problems in Hegel's theory of art history. Dividing the entire history of art into only three periods, each of radically different temporal length, seems to ignore the vast complexity of the subject matter. And last, there remain those who would claim, contrary to Hegel, that the subject matter of an artwork remains independent of an artwork's aesthetic value. Choosing the "right" subject does not guarantee an iota of aesthetic value. All these criticisms are available, and many are plausible. Hegel's philosophy of art is not without its problems.

In contrast to the above difficulties, which issue from standpoints external to Hegel's theory, I would like to put forward the following internal criticism and ask whether the architectonic structure of Hegel's philosophy of art is, as it ought to be, exemplary of the dialectical structure of self-consciousness. Ideally, this structure should involve a series of tripartite structures of opposition and subsequent reconciliation that together constitute the theory's conceptual scaffolding. This, however, is far from the case.

The movement of inquiry from "sensation" to "conception," as we have seen, defines a central (and to a significant extent) Platonic dimension of Hegel's thought. From the above exposition, it is also evident that this pattern of thought generates the architectonic structure of Hegel's aesthetic theory: it inspires the "art-religion-philosophy" sequence, the "symbolic-classic-romantic" sequence, and the "architecture-sculpture-painting-music-poetry" sequence. Now this general movement from sensory-based modes of expression to non-empirical modes is indeed progressive, but it is not *dialectically* progressive. Rather, it is linear and not intrinsically oppositional.

At each main level of the theory, the linearity of Hegel's account is manifest. With respect to the purpose of the *human spirit*, (a) cultural expression undergoes a smooth transition from sensory, to imagistic, to purely conceptual modes of expression; (b) art history begins with a style hardly suitable to express the depths of human personality, and gradually arrives at one that is at home in the complexity of subjectivity; (c) the materials of the individual arts transform by degrees from three-dimensional, to two-dimensional, to non-spatial types.

Moreover, with respect to the purpose of *art* itself, art history and the five fine arts assume a different pattern, namely, a "growth and decline" model that peaks at the middle stage. Along this second dimension of evaluation, the classical style reigns over the symbolic and romantic styles, and scripture surpasses the other four arts in beauty. The "growth and decline" pattern underlying these evaluations, however, is *neither* linear, *nor* purely developmental, *nor* dialectical. It is a biologically inspired, partly teleological model, and is the model, one might add, that underlies Hegel's thesis regarding the "end" or "death" of art.

The conceptual shell of Hegel's theory of art history and his theory of the five fine arts, then, is defined by two structural patterns, neither of which is manifestly dialectical and oppositional. One of these prescribes the path of the human spirit through artistic expression – a straight, linear, developmental pattern; the other is that of art itself as a means of cultural expression – a pattern of "growth and decline" that is partially developmental and partially retrogressive. We find, in short, that the skeletal structure of Hegel's philosophy of art – a structure that aims to express the ascension from "sensation" to "conception" – belongs to a rather non-Hegelian species.[25] The basic thought patterns of Hegel's philosophy of art are broadly teleological, but they are not dialectically teleological.[26]

To uncover Hegel's dialectical spirit within his aesthetic theory, one must look elsewhere than at the central theories of art history and of the individual arts. I offer the concluding thought that the dialectical core of Hegel's philosophy of art resides in his theory of beauty.[27] We have noted how the principles of humanity and perfection straightforwardly derive from the structure of self-consciousness. In reference to these two principles, we have also seen how the structure of self-consciousness displays itself to perception as beauty – as an organically unified, perfected presentation of humanity. In a Hegelian theory of beauty, this is what one should expect. Still, it remains regrettable that Hegel's theory of art history and his theory of the fine arts do not, in any obvious manner, uphold the same level of perfection.[28]

NOTES

1 All excerpts from Hegel's lectures on aesthetics are from *G.W.F. Hegel, Werke in zwanzig Bänden* (Suhrkamp Verlag, 1970), Volumes XIII, XIV, and XV. The translations are my own. For convenience and comparison, the page references to T.M. Knox's translation of Hegel's lectures on aesthetics (Oxford, 1975) will follow the page references to Hegel's original text.

2 I refer here to Hegel's general doctrine that the human power of self-consciousness is the highest development, and implicit principle, of all the powers of nature, and that the powers of nature are, in turn, the rudimentary realization of the purely conceptual essence of all that is. Hegel describes this fundamentally and unconditionality of "what is conceptual" in his *Science of Logic:* "the pure concept is the absolutely infinite, unconditioned, and free" (*Werke,* XI, 274).

3 I presently emphasize Plato's influence upon Hegel. To fully appreciate

Hegel's standpoint, however, it is essential not to ignore Aristotle's influence. Although Hegel was of one mind with Plato in his unambiguous preference for purely conceptual modes of expression as opposed to sensory modes, he did not accept – as an ultimate expression – Plato's particular conception of pure thought as constituted by (what Hegel termed) "abstract universals." In this regard, Hegel was more Aristotelian. Hegel insisted that *the actual thinking* of pure concepts (that is, the concrete, philosophic embodiment of such concepts in an actively thinking subject of experience) *constitutes* these pure concepts in their highest, concrete, spiritual realization. This actual embodiment of pure concepts in a thinker marks the difference between pure concepts as they appear in *logical* thought (pure concepts as they are "in themselves," a more Platonic conception) and pure concepts as they appear in *philosophical* thought (pure concepts as they are "in *and* for themselves," a more Aristotelian conception). The present comparison between sensory vs. non-sensory modes of expression in relation to art and philosophy – two forms of concrete, spiritual existence – assumes that the universal content in question is necessarily "embodied" in an Aristotelian fashion. Given this context, Hegel's preference for philosophical expression, in comparison to artistic expression, amounts to a preference for concrete embodiments of universal content that *lack* a sensory component (viz., philosophic thought), as opposed to those that necessarily contain a sensory content (viz., artistic expression). The present reference to Plato serves to highlight the historical source of Hegel's overall quest for thoughts of a non-empirical sort.

4   The term "symbolic" undergoes a change of meaning (in a negative direction) from its appearance in Schelling's philosophy of art to its presence in Hegel's aesthetics. What Schelling honors as "symbolic" art in his own lectures on the philosophy of art (1802–3) more closely corresponds to what Hegel terms "classic" art.

5   Hegel's assumption that there are only five major arts is an artifact of his own time. As Paul Kristeller observes, the "system of the five major arts . . . is of comparatively recent origin and did not assume definite historical shape before the eighteenth century." See Paul Oskar Kristeller, "The Modern System of the Arts," *Journal of the History of Ideas* 12 (1951): 465–527. Since the eighteenth century, "the system of the arts" has undergone a clear expansion.

6   In this systematization, Hegel inelegantly compresses five arts into a framework that supplies only three places. This is a clear case where the empirical structure of the subject matter clashes with the structural demands of Hegel's tripartite theoretical framework. Schelling's systematization of the arts suffered from similar headaches.

7   Hegel's account of musical expression prefigures Susanne Langer's

theory of music as expressed in her *Philosophy in a New Key* (Harvard University Press, 1942).

8 See, for example, Hegel's *Encyclopedia of the Philosophical Sciences,* Sect. 405 (*Werke*, X, 124–32).

9 Hegel's Platonistic aversion to sensation (an aversion that is not to be construed as a retreat from "concreteness") shows itself here in his critique of feeling as opposed to conceptual thought.

10 Music conveys its subject matter non-spatially, but its subject matter remains non-conceptual; painting conveys conceptual content, but it does so spatially. In its ability to convey conceptual content in a non-spatial manner, poetry combines the virtues of both painting and music.

11 The idea that language and thought are inextricably interwoven has slowly but steadily gained currency within this century. In recent decades, this view has crystallized into the widely discussed hypothesis of a "mental language" that underlies thought processes. Of the many writers who might be mentioned in this context, the most prominent is perhaps Jerry Fodor. For a recent work on this subject, see J. Christopher Maloney, *The Mundane Matter of the Mental Language* (Cambridge University Press, 1989).

12 Baumgarten expressed this view in his *Aesthetica* (Frankfurt an der Oder, 1750–1758), two vols. Shortly thereafter, G.F. Meier transmitted Baumgarten's ideas to a wider audience in his *Anfangsgründe aller schönen Wissenschaften,* (Halle: C. Hemmerde, 1754–1755), 2 vols. Kant, it is worth adding, used Meier's logic text – *Auszug aus der Vernunftlehre* (Halle: 1752) – as a guide for his own lectures on the subject.

13 *Kritik der urtheilskraft*, Sect. 15.

14 Hegel's aesthetic theory was initially received as a revival of Baumgarten's aesthetics. See, for example, Robert Zimmerman, *Geschichte der Aesthetik als philosophischer Wissenschaft* (Vienna, 1858), 693–97. The present essay, by showing how the concept of "perfection" permeates Hegel's aesthetic discourse, aims to give further voice to that original, and now largely forgotten, reception.

15 In the standard logic of Hegel's time, the word "is" signified the relation of identity. See, for example, E. M. Barth, *The Logic of the Articles in Traditional Philosophy* (D. Reidel Publishing Company, 1974), Chap. VII, 204–35.

16 See Aristotle's *Metaphysics*, 1021b.

17 Hegel defines the specific purposes of the individual arts in reference to the capacity of the respective media to express human subjectivity. They are defined in reference to the "sensation to conception" ordering of artistic media. This ordering is independent of whether one judges in reference to the purposes of the human spirit in general, or in reference to the purpose of art. Upon such an ordering, one can project either an

"ascending linear" model in reference to the goal of human spirit in general, or a "growth and decline" model in reference to the goal of art.

18 Artistic truth as the faithful representation of an "inner" essence sometimes calls for a divergence from classical idealization. Expressionist portraits, which employ distortion and non-natural coloration in order to faithfully represent a complex personality, make this clear. Similarly, a faithful portrait of an evil character (such as Oscar Wilde's Dorian Gray) would demand a similar divergence from classical idealization in order to preserve artistic truth.

19 Since organic unity and idealization are only formal principles, the proper subject matter – humanity – is further necessary for ideal beauty.

20 See Schiller's essay *"Ueber naive und sentimentalische Dichtung"* in *Schillers Werke, Nationalausgabe*, ed. Julius Petersen et al. (Weimar 1943–), XX, 413–503.

21 See Schelling's lectures on aesthetics in *Schellings Werke*, ed. Otto Weiss (Leipzig: Eckhardt, 1907; Leipzig: Meiner, 1911, III, 1–384).

22 The hope to recapture a lost classical past persisted after Hegel's time. For example, Nietzsche's *Birth of Tragedy* (1872) aimed to resurrect, via music and theater, a classical artistic culture in the face of what was perceived as a deteriorating Christian culture.

23 Benedetto Croce, *Aesthetic* (1901), trans. Douglas Ainslie (New York: Noonday Press, 1958), 302.

24 For a comprehensive survey of alternative interpretations of Hegel's "end of art" thesis, see Steven Bungay, *Beauty and Truth* (Oxford University Press, 1986), 71–89.

25 In his *Phenomenology of Spirit* and his *Encyclopedia of the Philosophical Sciences*, Hegel describes the movement from "sensation" to "conception" in a clearly dialectical fashion. Specifically, he initially uncovers the conflicts within the thought of an immediate, sensory "this," resolves these conflicts in notion of a complex "thing with properties" of perception, and continues the movement of consciousness through a reaction to emerging conflicts within the complex thing with properties. What appears, then, from the macroscopic perspective as a smooth, linear progression is more precisely constituted by a series of oppositions and reconciliations taking place at the microscopic level.

   This observation, at first sight, tends to soften the present thesis that the architectonic of Hegel's aesthetic theory deeply conflicts with his dialectic of self-consciousness. One could say, for example, that the linear structure of his aesthetic theory's architectonic is merely the non-dialectical, macroscopic appearance of fine-grain dialectical patterns of opposition and reconciliation. This interpretation is indeed what reasonably suggests itself in light of Hegel's paradigmatic discussions in his

Phenomenology and *Encyclopedia* regarding the "sense to conception" progression.

When the macro-level, non-dialectical linear progressions are interpreted as epiphenomenal structures, there are further complications. First, since dialectical structures of opposition and reconciliation purportedly constitute the essential structure of things, non-dialectical developmental structures should legitimately appear only at the relatively abstract, undeveloped level of natural objects and relationships. And this is exactly what one witnesses in construals of natural relationships in terms of causality. But linear, non-dialectical structures of this type are, in principle, out of place within the highly developed levels of spiritual existence (viz., art, religion, and philosophy). At these more mature developmental levels, the oppositional structure of self-consciousness ought be manifest. Second, Hegel's philosophical style is distinctly macroscopic in nature, and he often neglects specific detail in order to paint in broad strokes. So one would expect quite the opposite than what one actually finds: one would expect the *macrostructures* to be, as a rule, uniformly dialectical (i.e., more in keeping with Hegel's grand "logic-nature-spirit" triad) and the microstructures to be of other structural types upon occasion.

The internal criticism of Hegel's view offered here, then, extends beyond Hegel's aesthetic theory. It concerns the problem of how, or if, one can favorably interpret the substantial presence of smooth, linear developmental progressions within an outlook that maintains that dialectically structured progressions thoroughly saturate every subject matter.

26 Within the theory's architectonic, one encounters properly dialectical phases only infrequently, such as in the division of poetry into the "objective" epic, the "subjective" lyric, and the combinatory style of dramatic poetry. This is the exception, however, rather than the rule.

27 For example, if one applies the dialectical principles of Hegel's theory of beauty to the general theory of art history that Hegel provides, a "symbolic-*romantic*-classic" sequence would replace the "symbolic-*classic*-romantic" sequence that Hegel actually offers. This more dialectically structured construal situates classical art as the culminating, synthetic artform that reconciles the "externality" of symbolic art with the "interiority" of romantic art.

28 I would like to thank the scholars at the Hegel-Archiv in Bochum, Germany, and especially Helmut Schneider and Christoph Jamme, whose exceptional friendliness and encouragement greatly expanded my understanding of Hegel and made my studies of Hegel's aesthetics in their company most rewarding. I would also like to thank the Fulbright-Kommission, who supported my residence in Germany for those studies.

12 Transformations of Hegelianism, 1805–1846

The relationship between Hegel and Hegelianism will be approached in this essay in terms of the creative appropriation, reproduction, and transformation of the philosophical position articulated in Hegel's lectures and published texts. The term "Hegelianism" is not meant to designate appropriation or use of specific Hegelian arguments or judgments, but commitment to a general theoretical perspective or framework, to a specific way of prefiguring the field of knowledge and construing the relations of elements within that field. Switching to a linguistic metaphor, one could describe "Hegelianism" as a semiotic system, a distinctive "language" that defined the meaning of individual "signs" and within which all specific questions were addressed and problems resolved. For the intellectual historian, the history of Hegelianism is the story of the temporal connections between texts that define and order the totality of beings in the world told in Hegelian language.

My reconstruction of the evolution of this perspective or language in German intellectual life between 1805 and 1846 will be organized around two sets of differentiations. The first set might be described as "inner" differentiations, that is, the construction of divergent judgments about specific relations within a common perspective or shared language, the emergence of accommodationist, reformist, and radical positions (Right, Center, and Left) within a recognizable theoretical "school." The second and more problematic set of differentiations refers to transformations or translations of the Hegelian language itself, to critical reformulations of the Hegelian perspective in new terms that still retained a recognizably Hegelian structure of relations. The inclusion of the processes of transformative transla-

378

tion within a history of Hegelianism is problematic, since they inevitably involved a critique and occasionally articulated an explicit rejection of what was considered to be the Hegelian perspective, thus placing the boundaries of "Hegelianism" itself in question. The analysis will proceed historically, tracing the emergence of divergent positions, especially concerning the relationship between reason and reality, within a shared Hegelian language, and also the transformation of the original metaphysical Hegelian language of absolute spirit, first into the language of Hegelian humanism between 1835 and 1843, and finally into the paradoxically anti-Hegelian "Hegelian" language of contingent natural and historical existence between 1843 and 1846. Although the transformative translations of Hegelianism emerged in temporal succession, they never fully displaced each other. The descriptions that follow need not, therefore, be read in a teleological sense, but might also be interpreted as a contextual reconstruction of three possible, historical, contingent forms of Hegelianism.

In order to gain a grasp of the problematic relationship between Hegel's own philosophical project and the various academic schools, intellectual movements, and individual redescriptions of experience it inspired or justified, some preliminary working definition of the particularity or distinctiveness of Hegel's project and language is essential. As an intellectual historian I approach this problem not as a search for some essential core of doctrine in all positions that have defined themselves or been defined by others as Hegelian over the last two centuries, but in historical, contextual terms. A philosophical perspective self-consciously presented and publicly recognized as uniquely Hegelian emerged in Hegel's lectures and writings (particularly the *Phenomenology of the Spirit*) in the first decade of the nineteenth century as a variant of the Romantic philosophy of identity, and more specifically as an alternative to the version of absolute or speculative idealism espoused by Hegel's younger friend and colleague Friedrich W. J. Schelling. In the forty years between 1805 and the confrontation between the elder Schelling and the Hegelian academic school in Berlin in the 1840s, Hegelianism was defined in its most general form in terms of opposition to Schelling's philosophical perspective and what were conceived as explicit or implicit embodiments of this position in the academic discourses of Romantic theology, history, law, and politics.

I. HEGELIANISM AS A FORM OF SPECULATIVE IDEALISM

The polemical differentiations through which Hegel defined his own perspective vis-à-vis Schelling (and especially Schelling's disciples) during his years at Jena (1802–1806) tended to obscure the extent to which he and Schelling continued to share a common perspective and a common vocabulary. Their positions had evolved together beyond the critical and subjective idealisms of Kant and Fichte to an adoption and philosophical articulation of the early Romantic vision of the ultimate integration of all the polarities or bifurcations of reality in the concrete, dynamic totality of the "absolute" (the identity of identity and non-identity), and both used the language of self-generating process and relational totality in describing both the inner structure of the absolute Idea and its embodiment in nature and history. Where Hegel veered from Schelling was in his insistence that the concrete totality of the absolute could be completely comprehended as the structure of discursive Reason, that reality could be conceptually mediated into full transparency as a system of logic, that ultimately subject and substance, thought and being, logic and metaphysics were identical. For Hegel this variation or revision of the philosophy of the absolute was momentous in its consequences. It fulfilled the Romantic hopes for a total, immanent, present reconciliation of the autonomous human subject with nature, society, and God, transforming an ecstatic vision into a systematic knowledge that was "capable of being appropriated by all self-conscious Reason" (Phänomenologie, Werkausgabe, III, 14–18, 65). Moreover, knowledge of the absolute as a rational science could be taught and learned as a form of exoteric public knowledge, and communicated in a public universal language. In Schelling's philosophy, Hegel claimed, the absolute ultimately remained in the "beyond," as an unmediated otherness that could be encountered only in the subjective experiences of intellectual intuition, aesthetic contemplation, or religious feeling and thus communicated only in the private, esoteric, "edifying" discourse of metaphor and symbol or the authoritarian discourse of dogma and catechism. It could not produce a uniform public consciousness, but only small coteries or exclusive sects grouped around the special revelations of a charismatic visionary or philosophical "genius" (Aphorismen, Werkausgabe, II, 542, 551). Hegel was convinced that Schelling's philosophical failure to rationally penetrate and conceptually mediate the ultimate form of otherness implicitly restricted human autonomy and sustained the alienation of human spirit from its divine essence and ground. This theoretical failure entailed a practical therapeutic failure to produce the promised state of reconciliation and identity (Aphorismen, *Werkausgabe*, II, 548). Schelling's version of the philosophy of absolute identity simply could not fulfill the legitimate demands of the modern autonomous subject for universal, objective, systematic, fully mediated, transparent knowledge of the absolute. In contrast, Hegel believed his own perspective would be validated as objective, universal truth through its inevitable, practical, historical success, its transformation from a subjective perspective into "the property of all" (Phänomenologie, *Werkausgabe*, III, 20).

For more than a decade these claims in the preface to the *Phenomenology* must have seemed rather empty. During the heady years of internal reform and national liberation between 1807 and 1815, it was Schelling's truth rather than Hegel's that seemed to have approached something like the historical validation Hegel envisioned, at least among the younger generation of the German university-educated classes.[1] It was not until the decade after 1816, with Hegel's appointment to influential academic posts in Heidelberg (1816–1818) and Berlin (1818–1831), the publication of major texts that provided a systematic explication of Hegel's position and some of its implications (the third volume of the *Logic* in 1816, the *Encyclopedia of the philosophical Sciences* in 1817, and the *Philosophy of Right* in 1820), and above all the pervasive public disillusionment with the hopes for a spontaneously generated and religiously sustained national cultural regeneration and political unity produced by the euphoric years of inner reconstruction and national liberation, that a recognizable Hegelian perspective began to make significant inroads into academic and more broad public discourse in the primarily Protestant areas of central, northern, and western Germany. The first signs of this process were at the fringes of established academic institutions among young intellectuals seeking for an alternative to the dominant discourse of Romantic German nationalism and traditionalist historicism – the formation of a minority Hegelian faction in the student politics of the national fraternities (*Burschenschaften*) at German universities, and the creation of two short-lived journals of cultural criticism edited by small groups of institutionally marginal intellectuals in the early 1820s.[2] By the mid-1820s, however, such scattered and marginalized expressions of an Hegelian viewpoint within the cultural debates of the postwar period were absorbed into or replaced by the formation of Hegelianism into a consolidated and organized academic school centered at the University of Berlin, with close ties to the Prussian administration. In 1826 the Berlin Hegelians created a Society for Scientific Criticism and began to publish a state-subsidized academic journal, the *Jahrbücher für wissenschaftliche Kritik*, which remained the most visible public organ of Hegelianism until the late 1830s.[3]

During the years of consolidation and expansion, especially in the decade between 1827 and 1837, members of the Hegelian school as well as some of their opponents may have believed that Hegel's earlier claim that his perspective would eventually become the "universal" public consciousness, that his vocabulary would become "true" by being recognized and employed as simply the language of "scientific" knowledge, was being historically confirmed. But significant limitations on this Hegelian dominance must be noted. First, "dominance" was limited to Berlin. The further one moved from the Prussian capital and its university, the more Hegelianism appeared as a struggling, oppositional, minority perspective, even within academic life. Outside the universities, in the sphere of journalistic cultural criticism and popular religious and political writing, the influence of Hegelian vocabulary was even more tenuous, if present at all. Everywhere, however, the distinctiveness of Hegelianism was defined in terms of its relations to the major academic variants of the Romantic position that informed the three central academic disciplines of philosophy, theology, and law; Schelling's metaphysics, Schleiermacher's theology, and the social and historical theories of the "Historical School." Individuals revealed and articulated their Hegelian commitments by criticizing the inadequacy of the Romantic standpoint, by reorganizing the materials and issues in their discipline according to Hegelian categories, and by redescribing in detail some segment of the field of knowledge in Hegelian terms.

By the late 1830s the energy that fueled this attempt to translate descriptions of all dimensions of human experience into "Hegelese" appeared to have exhausted itself. Schelling and the remaining older

Romantics (Friedrich Carl von Savigny, Ludwig Tieck, and August Schlegel) saw this as a sign that the historical tables had been turned on Hegel, even in Prussia. When Schelling was called to Berlin in 1841 to expunge the "dragon's seed of Hegelian pantheism"[4] from the minds of Prussian youth, he insisted that the task of refuting Hegel's perspective had already been accomplished by "life."[5] Hegelese had failed to accomplish its goal of making human experience meaningful. A language not of total conceptual mediation but of relation to an unmediated, "transcendent" other, to a preconceptual ground of being (*Unvordenkliches Sein*), was required to sustain the finite individual's sense of meaningful integration into the ethical and religious substance of the historical human community.

During the 1820s and 1830s the belief in an accomplished elevation above the Schellingian dependence on some form of otherness, the attainment of the "standpoint of the concept" from which the world appeared as totally transparent, as the fully penetrable object of rational thought, remained the most-obvious distinguishing factor that separated Hegelianism from the various Romantic academic discourses. This movement beyond the perspective of Schelling was experienced and articulated as a "conversion" to the perspective of absolute knowledge. To become a Hegelian, to experience and think the world from the perspective of the identity of logic and metaphysics, involved a philosophical "rebirth." The language that individual Hegelians used to describe the shedding of their old, merely finite, "egoistic" selves, and the attainment of the "blessedness" of identity with the infinite spirit through the "labor of the concept," indicated the extent to which Hegelians experienced the appropriation of the Hegelian perspective and language as an existential transformation equivalent to "redemption" or "salvation."[6] For Hegelians to comprehend the world in the language of the concept was to experience the world as vessels of absolute reason, to have the language of the absolute spirit speak through them, and thus to have the text of the phenomenal world reveal its truth through them, from the "inside," from the perspective of its divine author.

Within the historical context of the post-Reform, postwar debates about the reconstruction of German politics and culture, the Hegelian perspective seemed to imply or justify specific stances concerning the ethical or socio-political relations between human beings, the relations between the human and the divine as articulated in aesthetic and especially traditional Chinese religious language, and the historical relations between communal ethics and religious faith. Against Romantic conceptions of ethical fulfillment as the merger of the finite ego into the prereflective communal substance of national existence (the *Volk*), traditional legal and political institutions, and customary religious rituals and beliefs, Hegelians insisted that the identity of individual and community attained its perfected form in the rational consensus of wills made possible by the systematically articulated "universalist," "rational" legal structure and participatory institutions of the modern post-revolutionary, or post-reform state. What distinguished the ethico-political perspective of Hegelianism in its original historical context was its focus on the rational articulation of universal norms in the public administrative and constitutional structures of the state, which allowed the self-conscious, autonomous individual subject to will the general will of the community as his/her own rational will. This stance presupposed an emancipatory transcendence of the particularist representations of the communal substance in national feeling and traditional custom (that is, it affirmed the emancipation of the individual in civil society). The peculiar German nationalism and/or Prussianism of Hegelianism was not tied to a defence of the pre-reflective core of ethnic particularity against foreign corruption (as in the various Roman idioms), but to the belief that historical developments in Germany and especially Prussia represented an actualization of the identity of the autonomous subject and the universal communal substance, which had been inaugurated by the epochal (in a pan-European, Western, and ultimately universal sense) legal changes of the French Revolution and the Napoleonic Era.[7] In the context of the political conflicts of Restoration Germany, these positions implied a clear affinity with those groups of bureaucratic reformers who favored a continuation of the transformation of a traditional order of legally differentiated, incorporated estates, communes, and regions from "above," through administrative centralization and legal rationalization, even if such "modernization" involved the repression of the expressed will of popular nationalist movements or traditionalist social elites.

A similar emphasis on universality and rational form distinguished the Hegelian perspective on the question of the adequacy of the symbolic language of aesthetic imagination or the representational language of religious faith in articulating the dynamic dialectical structures joining together the absolute subject and the natural and historical predicates of its self-determination, the transcendent and the immanent spheres of reality, the divine and human spirit. For Hegelians the subjective particularity and thus allegorical nature of these linguistic embodiments of absolute identity ultimately contradicted their content. The claim that the content of art and religion could be fully translated, without any loss of content, into the conceptual language of reason, that the absolute ultimately found a language adequate to its content in the conceptual terms of Hegelian logic, and that when God became self-conscious he spoke Hegelese was, for many contemporaries, the most striking and irritatingly pretentious manifestation of the Hegelian position.

Finally, conversion to Hegelianism seemed to imply a distinctive perspective on the historical relations between the ethical integration of individual self in the communal substance and the redemptive identity of individual and absolute in art, religion, and philosophy, in Hegelian terms, between "objective" and "absolute" spirit. For Hegel the absolute was philosophically comprehensible because its inner determinations were fully embodied in the natural and historical phenomena that were the object of rational reflection. The philosopher was the exegete of the texts of history, grasping the objectification of the will in historical actions and communal institutions as a dialectical structure of reason and translating it into conceptual terms. But the philosophical claim of absolute knowledge, the conviction that the absolute in the concrete expansiveness of its relations as a systematic totality could be made fully transparent in rational thought, that no mysterious otherness remained beyond the power of rational reflection, also implied something like the "end of history," or at least the transformation of history from a story of the (implicitly rational) progressive self-making of the absolute spirit to a story of the (explicitly rational) repetitive self-revelation of absolute spirit come to full self-consciousness. Yet the rational comprehension of reality as embodied reason was not synonymous with the manifestation or embodiment of reason in reality. The form of rational knowledge that translated the implicit into the explicit, the unconscious into the conscious, completed the reconciliation between the individual thinking subject and absolute reason. Without conceptual comprehension of the rational structure of will in the modern state, the individual subject would not actually experi-

ence that state as his/her "home," as the universal substance of his/
her rational will as an autonomous subject. Philosophical education
completed, and thus ultimately sustained and grounded, the "practical" ethical integration of self and society. In a sense philosophical
self-consciousness produced the ethical life it claimed merely to
comprehend. In the actualized ethical community of the modern
state, Hegelian philosophy displaced (as it absorbed their content)
art and religion as the collective articulation, the universal language,
of communal solidarity.[8]

In all major areas of cultural theory and the academic disciplinary
discourses attached to them – in philosophy, politics and law, art
and aesthetic criticism, religion and theology – a recognizable Hegelian position emerged and found polemical and systematic articulation in the 1820s and early 1830s. The Hegelian claim to have
accomplished a fully mediated, transparent sublation (Aufhebung)
of phenomenal existence into the "reality of reason" aroused intense
and persistent opposition and rejection from major disciplinary representatives of the various Romantic discourses it hoped to displace.
Although the connection between this opposition and Schelling's
perspective was not always explicitly drawn, the major dividing line
between the Hegelian discourse and its major competitors in German intellectual life remained generally consistent with the line
Hegel himself had drawn between himself and Schelling in the first
decade of the century, a line that remained internal to the broader
framework of speculative or absolute idealism. Before 1835, judgments as to who was an Hegelian insider, who was a renegade guilty
of betraying the central Hegelian doctrines, or who had never fully
achieved the final breakthrough to an Hegelian perspective inevitably centered around attitudes toward the relationship between
Schelling's and Hegel's systems. But there was also room for variation, disagreement, and conflict within the Hegelian language itself,
and, as developments in the late 1830s made clear, this language also
contained the possibility of transformative translation into new
terms or a new vocabulary. When Schelling came to Berlin in 1841
he interpreted the conflict, discontent, and disillusionment among
various current and former Hegelians within the terms of the project
and the language of speculative idealism he had shared with Hegel.[9]
By 1841, however, the general forms of a language that ordered the
world into transcendent and immanent dimensions, that structured

its inner relations in terms of the connective processes that produced a systematic totality out of this division, and that construed the meaning of the integrative process in terms of the derivation of human freedom and unity from the self-determination of the freedom and unity of the divine spirit were no longer able to function as an adequate framework for comprehending the whole spectrum of Hegelian positions.

II. DIVERSITY WITHIN HEGELIANISM AS A FORM OF SPECULATIVE IDEALISM

During the exhilirating period of conversion and early discipleship, most Hegelians were convinced that assimilation of the Hegelian perspective provided a resolution of all the major conflicts of human existence, a reconciling recognition of the identity of reason and reality, self and community, man and God. It soon became evident, however, that the Hegelian perspective contained its own problematic, capable of inspiring a discourse that was not merely reproductive but productive, and that individual Hegelians using the same vocabulary might disagree on the interpretation of significant and specific issues. The problematic around which diversity within the unity of Hegelianism emerged in the first, "metaphysical" stage of its history was the historical relationship between the universal structures of reason and the phenomenal reality in which reason articulated its self-determinations. In what sense should the existing cultural order, its political institutions and communal ethos, its artistic creations, and its religious language, rituals, and doctrines be regarded as the perfected embodiment of reason in the world, as the historical actuality of absolute spirit? Did Hegel's claim to have achieved systematic knowledge of the totality imply that the embodiment of reason in reality had been completed? Answers to such questions seemed particularly dependent on individual experiences of the phenomenal reality of the historical present.

In the decade after 1826, three general interpretations of the relationship between reason and reality emerged within Hegelianism. The position that came to be considered orthodox was articulated by the elder statesmen of the academic school at the University of Berlin, especially the theologian K. P. Marheineke, the administrative aide for higher education in the Prussian ministry of culture

Johannes Schulze, and the editor of the Hegelian *Jahrbuecher* Leopold von Henning, and might best be described as a stance of historical accommodation. This wing of Hegelianism (the core of what came to be called the Hegelian "Right" or "Old Hegelianism") confidently asserted that the legal, administrative, and political institutions of the post-reform German states, especially Prussia, constituted the perfected or complete objectification of reason in the world, the actuality of the absolute spirit as fully present. The only political tasks remaining for the present generation were educational and philosophical, that is, the production of a public recognition and collective subjective internalization of actualized reason. Moreover, this transformation of consciousness simply required a translation of the existing language of Protestant religious culture, a language of "representation" (*Vorstellung*), into the language of self-conscious knowledge, the language of the "concept" (*Begriff*). The overwhelming emphasis in this self-consciously epigonal stance was on the historical completion of the progressive actualization of reason in history, a process brought to self-consciousness in Hegelian philosophy.

As the reactionary political and religious groups who resisted and opposed many of the institutions and policies of the modernizing Prussian reformers increased their power and influence within the Prussian administration after 1830, the accommodationist stance became more problematic. Some accommodationists, unwilling to recognize the changed historical situation as the actuality of reason, became more sympathetic to the critical reformist interpretation (the view of the Hegelian "Center") of the reason/reality relationship that had developed simultaneously with the orthodox position in the late 1820s. At the level of ethico-political theory, the reformist position was most forcefully presented by the legal philosopher Eduard Gans. For Gans the reality of the perfected ethical community, which Hegel had grasped as the embodiment of reason in ethical practice, had attained historical objectification in the principles that animated the programs, policies, and political actions of the French revolutionaries, Napoleon, and the Prussian reformers, but this "essential" reality remained in dynamic, critical relation to the unreconstructed, irrational "appearances" still so obviously evident in the experienced reality of contemporary politics. For Gans, therefore, the tasks of the current generation were not restricted to comprehending a completed process, to translating phenomenal reality into conceptual form. Instead, philosophical comprehension provided the general principles for reformist activity and a concrete language of political activism directed toward the tasks of making appearances conform to the "essential" reality of actualized reason.[10]

By the mid-1830s a future-oriented, dynamic, critical-reformist version of the reason/reality relationship had become dominant among younger, academically insecure, and non-Prussian Hegelians. In 1838 two larger synthetic works that concluded histories of philosophy with histories of Hegelianism,[11] and the creation of two new Hegelian journals, Arnold Ruge's *Hallische Jahrbücher* and Eduard Meyen's *Literarische Zeitung*, gave indication of this shift in the center of gravity of Hegelianism. The reformist view was especially evident in the debate over the relationship between the religious language of representation and the language of self-conscious philosophical knowledge within the actualized presence of absolute spirit in Protestant Christian culture. Hegelian redescriptions of the progressive embodiment of absolute spirit in the historical development of the Christian language of representation were increasingly subjected to a critical analysis that attempted to separate the essential reality (that which could be *aufgehoben* in thought) from the arbitrary appearance (that which resisted conceptualization and demanded a contingent historical explanation) and thus to provide a convincing mediation between representation and concept. An increasing number of Hegelians seemed convinced that the language of religious representation could not be translated into philosophical terms as easily as Marheineke had suggested, and that the language of representation would have to be reformed in order to speak the truth of the actualized absolute spirit. In the early 1830s this debate was focused on problems of translating Christian doctrines about the immortality of the individual soul and the historical incarnation of Christ into conceptual terms.[12]

A third, utopian/revolutionary version of the reason/reality relationship also developed on the fringes of the Hegelian school during the 1820s (in the texts of Friedrich Wilhelm Carové and Ludwig Feuerbach)[13] and 1830s (in the works of Friedrich Richter, August Cieszkowski, and Moses Hess).[14] What distinguished this stance (we might call it the "old" Hegelian Left) was a consciousness of radical opposition between the theoretical, conceptual articulation of the accomplished unity of the divine and the human in the language of philosophy, and an experienced historical reality of fragmentation and bifurcation in every dimension of existence. In the texts of this wing of the school, the contemporary communal relations and religious ethos of Christian culture did not appear as the place where human redemption was finally grasped as actual but as a pathological situation of radical separation and contradiction from which humanity had to be redeemed. From this perspective Hegel's conceptual structures were transformed from a history comprehended into a program for future action; the actuality of the absolute in self-conscious freedom became not a presupposition of knowledge but the object of constructive historical practice. As such a program, moreover, the "abstract" truths of philosophy were perceived as requiring translation into a new "concrete" religious language, a new "myth of reason" that might articulate future hopes, and a new language of the will that could give form to ethical practice directed toward the fulfillment of these hopes among the philosophically uninitiated (the "people"). It was in practice, in communally directed will, in love and faith, that the long-sought reconciliation of the human and the divine could actually be achieved. One might argue that reading Hegel as a text for such utopian prophecies exceeded the bounds of legitimate exegesis, that this radical fringe of Hegelianism should not be regarded as Hegelian at all. And it is true that in the writings of Carové, Richter, Ciezskowski, the young Hess, and the young Feuerbach, few attempts, of the type that were standard among reformist and orthodox Hegelians, were made to authorize positions through exclusive citation of Hegelian texts. This radical variant of Hegelian interpretation, however, was a reminder of Hegel's and the original Hegelians' general participation in the eschatological language of speculative idealism and of the roots of this language in Protestant conceptions of redemptive community and personal salvation. The actualization of reason in reality was not conceived by any of the original Hegelians of the 1820s and early 1830s as the self-realization of humanity's essential powers, as humanity's self-making, but as the objectification and thus self-determination of absolute spirit in and through human action, human expression, and human self-consciousness, as a "sacred" process in which the divine became incarnate in human culture, the transcendent actualized itself in the immanent. Until the publication of Strauss's *Life of Jesus* in 1835–1836, all Hegelians shared this quasi-theological, metaphysical vocabulary and its figuration of the relationship between the depth and surface dimensions of experience as a relation between the transcendent and the immanent.

III. HEGELIAN HUMANISM

A metaphysically framed Hegelian perspective centered around the actualization of absolute spirit in nature and history did not suddenly disappear in 1840. Some Hegelians continued to speak this language well into the second half of the nineteenth century. Nonetheless, in the years between 1835 and 1840 there emerged, at first implicitly, a new version of the Hegelian perspective in which the attributes formerly attached to the absolute spirit were displaced on to "the idea of humanity," "human species-being," or "human self-consciousness," and the tasks of comprehending the concrete totality of experienced reality were displaced from philosophy as a form of metaphysical knowledge, to the human sciences as forms of immanent historical interpretation and cultural critique.[15] This secularization or humanization of the Hegelian perspective has usually been defined as the foundation of the Hegelian Left or the radical Young Hegelian movement. But it should be noted that there were no logical or historically obvious ties between the utopian, prophetic views of the old Hegelian Left and the new framework. Although Hegelian Humanism did of course imply opposition to political and cultural forms based on belief in a transcendent absolute, different political positions and views of the historical process were possible within it. As was true within the older metaphysical language, Hegelian humanist discourse allowed for differential judgments not only on the definition and comprehensibility of the deep structures of the essential (now "human") subject but also on the present historical status of the relationship between this essence and historical human existence. In fact, the language of Hegelian humanism was first articulated in three rather different idioms tied to different historical and critical contexts.

Strauss's inauguration of the humanist Hegelian perspective was indirect and almost inadvertent as he struggled to construct a convincing, and thus more critical, dialectical and historical reconciliation between the content of traditional Christianity and philosophical knowledge than that offered by orthodox Hegelians like Marheineke. By the early 1830s Strauss was convinced that if the language of religion were really to be translated into philosophical terms without loss of content, its claim to present a literal description of historical truth would have to be abandoned. More specifically, Strauss addressed the question of whether the narrative of the incarnation of the divine in the human spirit in the specific historical individuality of Jesus Christ was simply a formal aspect of religious expression or an essential part of its content. Strauss finally concluded that the historicity of Christ as incarnate God was tied to the mythical form in which universal truths were expressed by the collective human unconscious in a primitive state of cultural development. Only if the historical claims of the Bible were dismissed could its narrative accounts be comprehended as figural projections of the truth of the ultimate identity of infinite and finite spirit, of "divine" human essence and individual human existence. By interpreting Biblical history as myth, Strauss thought he had saved the true content, the significance or the "idea" of Christian religion for modern knowledge.[16] However, his contemporary critics, including those Hegelian scholars and philosophers he considered his mentors and colleagues, interpreted his position as a reductive, immanent interpretation of the content of both Christian faith and Hegelian philosophy. The historicity of the incarnation, whatever mythical accretions may have surrounded its description in the accounts of the gospels, was the basis for the Hegelian claim of the identity of absolute and finite spirit in the act of rational comprehension of the real. The historicity of Christ sustained the belief in the historical reality of the Hegelians' present consciousness of being the vessels of absolute reason.[17]

The apparently universal opposition to the principles informing the *Life of Jesus* induced a brief period of hesitation and doubt in Strauss, but by 1839 he was ready to accept and draw out the implications of his position. In a critical history of Christian doctrine, published in 1840–1841, he boldly asserted that the content of religious representation was the objectification of human essence defined as the spiritual unity of free, rational beings. Since this "idea of humanity" was presented in religious language as a particular divine being with transcendent authority and supernatural powers, however, religious consciousness also constituted an alienation or estrangement of human beings from their own essential nature, and a diversion from their historical duty to actualize the idea of humanity within the immanent realm of human relations. The hidden meaning of the history of religious consciousness was not the actualization in existence of the identity of God and man, but the progressive realization of the essence of man; not a relationship between transcendence and immanence, but a self-relationship within immanence. Once the false transcendence of the religious relationship, and thus the human content of the religious representation, was recognized, religion became superfluous, and history could be freely affirmed as a secular process of cultural spiritualization, a progressive assertion of humankind's collective control over the determinations of nature and the mutual recognition among human individuals of their common spiritual identity. Sacred history disappeared into secular history, and the former tasks of theology were transformed into the tasks of cultural history and of cultural education, since the actualization of the idea of humanity as a real, collective historical subject was displaced into the future as a goal of educational practice.[18]

By the time Strauss had clarified the principles of his new humanist Hegelianism in 1840–1841, Bruno Bauer, one of his earliest and severest critics from the standpoint of orthodox Hegelianism, had developed a different variant of the transformative humanist translation of the Hegelian language of absolute spirit. Like Strauss, Bauer constructed his humanist perspective through a critical analysis of the historical claims of Christian religion. Bauer, however, discerned a residue of transcendence in Strauss's attempts to translate Christian representations of the identity of infinite and finite spirit into the language of the idea of humanity. This "idea," Bauer claimed, still retained an aspect of the enigmatic and transcendent divine being, derived from its ultimately opaque historical origins in the prereflective myth-making activity of a collective "oriental" folk consciousness. Strauss was disloyal to his original Hegelian text by ignoring the claim that the substantial universal became real only as "subject" or, in the new secular humanist terminology, that the "idea of humanity" became actual in human history only through its internalization in the free activity of human self-consciousness. Belief in the suprapersonal substantiality of human "essence" was merely another version of the self-alienating form of religious consciousness.[19] In a series of books and articles produced in 1840–1842, Bauer tried to demonstrate that the language of objectification, alienation, and self-recognition of human self-consciousness could make transparent the true meaning of human cultural history and Hegelian philosophy. Terms like "God," "absolute spirit," "world-spirit," and so forth, were misleading and deceptive because they implied the actual existence of some suprahuman transcendent power that actualized itself in human self-consciousness. For Bauer, however, an honest Hegelian language would have to make obvious that "God is dead for philosophy and only the I as self-consciousness . . . lives, creates, works and is everything," that "self-consciousness is the only power in the world and history, and history has no other meaning than the becoming and development of self-consciousness."[20]

Unveiling the truth of theology and metaphysics in the humanist terminology of "self-consciousness" and its historical self-production clearly had momentous consequences for Bauer. The alleged objective content of religious experience and metaphysical knowledge, the absolute "substance," was revealed as an illusion that dissolved as soon as it was recognized as a temporary, limiting objectification of the ceaseless activity of self-consciousness: philosophy as the critical theory of human self-consciousness was a system of atheism and a practice of liberation rather than reconciliation. The various "positive," historically extant, cultural forms – social, political, religious, artistic, philosophical – had no universal content beyond the free activity of the human spirit articulated through them. Humanist Hegelianism was thus "revolutionary" and even "terroristic" as a critical practice of ceaseless emancipation from fixated cultural forms or structures of domination.[21]

Both Bauer and Strauss continued to use the terminology of embodied reason or spirit – now defined in immanent human terms as the dialectic of finite spirit and essential, "infinite" human spirit – in their "anthropological" translations of Hegelian metaphysics. Both continued to assume that the actualization of the human essence as spirit implied the rational control of spirit over matter, the domination of culture over inner and outer "nature." A third version of the humanist translation of Hegelianism constructed around 1840–that proposed by Ludwig Feuerbach – placed this assumption under critical scrutiny.

Feuerbach's thinking during the 1830s, like that of Strauss and Bauer, evolved toward a humanist inversion of Hegelian metaphysics through a concerted attempt to rethink and reconstruct the Hegelian reconciliation of reason and reality in a convincing fashion. For Feuerbach, however, the particular "reality" that needed to be "vindicated" or mediated into the self-transparency of absolute spirit was not only or primarily the reality of particular historical existence but the reality of nature, both nature external to man and the corporeality of man as a part of nature.

By 1838 Feuerbach was convinced that the reconciliation between reason and natural reality could not be accomplished within the framework of the Hegelian system of speculative idealism. Hegelian philosophy, Feuerbach claimed, had never taken the reality of natural, corporeal existence seriously. In the dialectical structure of absolute reason, the being that was "other" to thought, that which required sublation or "translation" into the concept in order to confirm the autonomy of spirit, was never the reality of existing beings, but simply the "abstract" concept of being, the thought of the otherness of thought. The *Aufhebung* of reality in reason was thus presupposed and predetermined in Hegel's system. In fact, Feuerbach claimed that the whole metaphysical structure of absolute spirit was a transcendent mystification, an objectification and self-alienation of human reflective processes, which denied the limitation of human thinking by the conditions of actual human existence in space and time. The historically relative form and the human content of Hegel's thought was veiled by a language that made this thought appear as the transparent representation of a metaphysical reality.[22]

The general implications of Feuerbach's critique of speculative idealism entered the realm of public controversy and debate through his reformulation of the relationship between religion and philosophy from the new humanist perspective in *The Essence of Christianity* (1840–1841). Religious consciousness and language, Feuerbach claimed, constituted "a projection of humanity's essential nature as an emotional and sensuous being, governed and made happy only by images," on to a transcendent being or God.[23] The Hegelian translation of the figural language of religion into the rational language of the concept had not only continued the mystifying, pathological process of attributing essential human qualities to a transcendent, suprahuman power but had impoverished the religious content through this translation by restricting it to mankind's rational, spiritual qualities, thus ignoring the essential reality of a human being in space and time as a sensuous, emotional existence.

Like Bauer and Strauss, Feuerbach affirmed that humanity was defined and differentiated from the rest of nature by the ability to make its own essential nature an object of thought, its capacity to attain self-consciousness of its species-being, and thus to pursue critically and self-consciously the realization of its essence in historical practice. The true content of the Hegelian metaphysics of self-conscious absolute spirit was thus affirmed as self-consciousness of human species-being or human essence. "Man" was the authentic and real "subject/object" of history. At the same time, however, Feuerbach was clearly unhappy with the Bauerian translation of Hegelian metaphysics into the language of human "self-consciousness," a language that seemed to repeat the Hegelian limitation of species-being to man's reflective rational capacities.[24] The essential human content, the universal human nature that was grasped in the self-conscious knowledge of human sciences like anthropology, psychology, and cultural history, Feuerbach claimed, was a sensuous and emotional "essence." Self-consciousness was a predicate of man in nature, not a universal subject that somehow manifested itself in nature and history. Furthermore, Feuerbach did not believe that religious consciousness *per se*, the emotional, imaginative identification of the individual with his/her species-being, would cease with the destruction of its self-alienating Christian form. If the new humanist principles produced in the demystifying translation of the language of Christian religion, theology, and speculative metaphysics into the language of anthropology were to function practically as the ordering principles of a new humanist culture and inspire the immanent, active pursuit of human self-realization, they would have to be couched in terms that affirmed the sensuous, emotional, imaginative essence of mankind and thus take on a "religious" form.[25]

Between 1841 and 1843 the general similarities in the variant forms of translating Hegelian metaphysics into humanist terminology that had emerged in the critical writings of Strauss, Bauer, and Feuerbach between 1835 and 1841 were publicly recognized as the foundation of a distinctive theoretical perspective that articulated the consciousness of a radical oppositional wing of the Hegelian school – the Left Hegelian movement. Strauss, however, refused to recognize his own version of philosophical humanism in this Left Hegelian perspective, and he and his fellow Württemberg Hegelian humanists (like Friedrich Vischer) continued to use the language of the progressive incarnation of the "idea of humanity" in historical institutions and consciousness, in separation from and opposition to the radicalization process fueled by Bauer's and Feuerbach's conceptualizations of Hegelian humanism.[26] Bauer and Feuerbach willingly accepted the role of intellectual mentors to the radical Hegelians and participated actively in the tasks of clarifying the principles of their humanist reductions: developing, applying, and thus demonstrating the validity of these principles in a comprehensive and "positive" redescription of major areas of human experience and relating the new perspective to issues of contemporary political and cultural transformation.

Bauer seemed supremely confident that simply replacing the terminology of absolute spirit with that of human self-consciousness would retain the essential human content of the Hegelian metaphysical concept of history as a meaningful unified progress toward full autonomy and community, and that his own humanist terminology simply unveiled the genuine meaning of Hegel's quasi-theological terminology. The theory of the absolute as human self-consciousness was not a mere subjective ideal imposed on the world, but a comprehension, a bringing to self-consciousness of the actual historical process of human self-production. This bringing to self-consciousness was clearly, in Bauer's view, an epochal act, marking a world-historical break with the epoch of mankind's subordination to the illusions of a projected transcendent authority. Even though human beings had always been self-creators, their previous inability to appropriate this freedom self-consciously, to grasp and take full responsibility for their own historical actions involved a denial and self-alienation of their essential nature. But the ability to live without illusions, to affirm the truth of atheism, was a historical product of the development of human power and self-confidence. God could finally be negated only when this negation implied and assumed the affirmation of man.[27]

Bauer did not believe, therefore, that the critical destruction of transcendent illusions somehow robbed history of its collective meaning or severed the links between the finite individual and the universal community of humanity. Yet the mediating connections between individual freedom and responsibility for self-making on the one hand, and the collective process of the progressive actualization of self-conscious freedom on the other, was not clear in Bauer's writings. Before 1843 Bauer did not seem to notice this problem and simply assumed that he had spoken the "decisive" word that brought the collective historical practice and implicit consciousness of his age to articulate, self-conscious fulfillment, thus allowing his contemporaries, the "public" or the "people," to comprehend themselves and discard the self-deceptions of religious and metaphysical illusions.[28] Human "self-consciousness" retained the functions of Hegel's "absolute spirit" as a term that described the convergence of the finite individual's actualization and recognition of his/her essential nature, on the one hand, and the historical actualization of a universal collective historical subject that found its actualization in the "infinite," free process of criticism and self-production, on the other. Bringing man back to himself as free self-consciousness, Bauer insisted, also united human beings with each other.[29]

Feuerbach's attempts to construct a "positive" articulation of the new humanism between 1841 and 1843 were more self-consciously anti-Hegelian than Bauer's, but he also insisted that his critical reduction of theology and metaphysics to anthropology was a "positive negation" that retained the genuine human content of Hegelian philosophy. His "new" philosophy actualized the content of the old philosophy in the act of critical negation. In Hegel's speculative idealism, the absolute was the "subject" that was at the same time "object and principle," and the particular and finite, the world of natural and historical existence, was relegated to the status of a "predicate" in which the absolute manifested, or actualized, its essential attributes. In Feuerbach's new humanism, however, the inverted perspective of metaphysics was set back on its feet, as "man" or human species-being was recognized as the actual existing subject and the absolute or infinite defined as its predicate, as the determination, self-actualization, and self-recognition of the essence of the finite.[30] As Feuerbach struggled to give clear and positive form to his humanist principle, however, his transformative inversion of Hegelian categories became increasingly problematical and complex. The problem centered on the ability of the term "man" to fulfill the function of the central god-term of a totalizing discourse in the same manner as Hegel's absolute spirit, to function as the subject/object identity "who is and knows himself to be the real (not imaginary), absolute identity of all oppositions and contradictions."[31] The problem with Feuerbach's reductive translation was that it had two distinct aspects: an inversion of the relation between the infinite and the finite, and an inversion of the relation between thought and being, or spirit and nature within finite existence. Feuerbach's humanism was a naturalistic humanism: his notion of human essence or species-being conceived man's spirituality, or self-consciousness, as "the self-conscious essence of nature."[32] During 1841–1843, Feuerbach seemed to think that his naturalist inversion of speculative idealism was a corollary of the anthropological reduction of metaphysics. He did not really attempt to create a language that would describe how the whole cultural world of self-conscious spirit emerged as a self-differentiation of natural being. Thus "man" often appeared in Feuerbach's text as an abstraction uniting the contradictory determinations of nature and historical culture.

In its most general articulations, evident not only in the writings of Bauer and Feuerbach but also during the early 1840s in those of their Left Hegelian "comrades" like Karl Marx, Friedrich Engels, Max Stirner, Moses Hess, and Arnold Ruge, the anthropological translation of Hegelian humanism retained the formal structures of the Hegelian conception of the relation between theory and reality. The language of philosophical humanism was understood as the coming to self-consciousness of an actual historical process, as the realization of human species-being in an ethical community in which individuals achieved autonomy and fulfillment of their human potentialities not through separation from, but through identity with, others. Of course, the radical Hegelians described this ethical state as a "human," "free," "true," "genuine" state, not as the incarnation of the absolute in the world, but as the self-revelation and self-construction of the human essence in communal relations. The modern, post-revolutionary liberal-democratic movement to establish a secular, democratic republic was the immanent, contemporary historical reality comprehended in Hegelian humanism, and the historical self-confidence of Left Hegelians in 1841–1842 was tied to a belief that their theoretical practice gave the decisive, self-revealing voice or "word" to this movement and its agents – the "people" or the "public." It was the collapse of this sense of historical connection, a disillusionment with the political public as the agent of liberation after the uncontested repression in Prussia of its self-styled representatives in the winter and spring of 1843, that produced a reconsideration and self-criticism of the principles of Hegelian humanism, which had sustained the false hopes, the "illusions" of 1841–1842.

IV. FROM HEGELIAN HUMANISM TO THE ANALYTIC OF EXISTENCE

In the period 1843–1846, all of the major theorists and journalistic publicists of the Left Hegelian movement engaged in a divisive process of mutual criticism whose indirect object was the humanist theoretical perspective and language they had previously shared and which had sustained their collective historical hopes and sense of collective identity. The translations of the language of the Hegelian absolute spirit into the language of "man" increasingly appeared woefully inadequate for comprehending and mastering the actual historical conditions and relations of real, existing human beings. In fact the heaven-storming critical assault on the old language of transcendence in theology and metaphysics seemed to have produced a new language of self-deception and self-alienation, and it simply displaced the old pathological structures of egoistic fragmentation and surrender to self-forged domination into secular, humanist terms. Each of the former Left Hegelians accused his former comrades of remaining caught in the "theological" illusions of a language essence. Each also in his own way struggled with the implicitly shared dilemmas and tasks of constructing a convincing and metaphysically disabused description of natural and historical existence that could sustain and justify both the emancipatory and integrating dimensions of the Hegelian historical project. The common element in the competing array of perspectives that emerged from this process was the claim that "reality" must be comprehended and described as contingent, concrete, finite "existence," and that the "reason" or "meaning" of reality must emerge from or be produced by the actions of, and relations among, individual existing beings. Each of the former Left Hegelians perceived their own resolution of this task as a final liberation from the illusions of Christian culture as well as from the Hegelian translations of the terms of this culture into metaphysical or "philosophical" language. The post-humanist language of existence was self-consciously presented as a transcendence of Hegelianism, not merely its translation into new terms. Yet in the process of developing an historical and systematic theory on the basis of a description of existing reality, of creating a language that could both describe existence as a historical and systematic "totality" and explain the "failures" of earlier theological and metaphysical descriptions, the structural relations of Hegelian language often appeared in a new guise.

For Bauer and Feuerbach, who had been the public theoretical mentors of the Left Hegelian movement, the revisionist move "beyond" humanism was formulated not so much as a radical break with their recent past as a clarification of the differences that had characterized their conceptions of human essence in 1841–1842, that is, in a development of the principles of sensuality and self-consciousness as descriptions of existence rather than definitions of universal human essence. Both felt they had been too hasty in relating their principles to contemporary political practice and the emancipatory journalistic campaigns of 1842, and their process of taking stock began as they distanced themselves from the overemphasis in political practice they discerned among other Left Hegelians in the winter of 1842–1843. As they engaged in these tasks of revision, however, they encountered the criticism of former disciples and comrades (Stirner and Marx especially) who proposed a more-radical break with past positions and the language that had justified them.

Bruno Bauer's theoretical revisionism was articulated as a purifying clarification of "self-consciousness" that would demonstrate that it was not a name for a spiritual abstraction or metaphysical entity that somehow "actualized" itself in the concrete relations of existence, but a description of human existence as produced in culture. Bauer's clarifications tended to focus on three issues. First, he vehemently denied that the language of self-consciousness implied a denial of the sensuous, corporeal existence of man in nature. Human existence to be sure was not determined by, or a product of, natural existence; instead, human existence was defined by an overcoming of natural determination through rational knowledge that transformed corporeal existence and "external" nature into the material or content for self-mastery and self-determination. But self-consciousness existed only as a mastered, self-consciously controlled or determined nature, never in isolation from nature. Human culture, the communal organization of work and knowledge, produced this initial definition of human existence as an overcoming and mastery of natural determination. But until recent times this cultural transcendence of nature had been consciously articulated only in religious or metaphysical form. The creative activity of mastering nature was objectified as a transcendent principle, a suprapersonal power that was perceived as determining individual human existence and set in principled opposition to nature.[33]

The second issue addressed in Bauer's critical self-clarification was precisely the "religious" subordination of human existence to the self-produced objectifications of its "spiritual" activity, and the organization of human practice in social and political institutions in accordance with this principle of heteronomy. Bauer interpreted the history of religiously structured culture as a "necessary" (in the context of its ultimate purpose) collective discipline that made possible eventual recognition of the human freedom of self-production. Within the present historical conditions and the possibilities for self-mastery that they allowed, however, the subordination to such self-forged domination had become pathological, a denial of and retreat from human autonomy and responsibility.[34] Bauer's theory was meant to provide a recognition of cultural determination as self-determination, to introduce the era in which human beings would take full responsibility for the process of self-making, in which man would become "the work of his own freedom."[35]

Bauer's language of self-consciousness articulated a vision of human existence as a process of self-overcoming, self-making, and self-recognition. This process and its "laws," Bauer insisted, were not imposed on existence from the outside, but were produced by historical events and struggles. They brought to self-consciousness the actual concrete processes that transformed the natural and historico-cultural determinations of human existence into the conditions and opportunities of self-determination.[36]

Self-mastery, and the power, courage, and responsibility it entailed, were at the center of Bauer's perspective. But he insisted that this self-mastery must always be individual and rejected any collective projections of historical agency, even in the secular form of national peoples, social classes, political parties, or ruling elites. All conceptions of collective self-making (and he viewed most of his old Left Hegelian friends as guilty of such acts of theoretical error and moral irresponsibility) were denials of historical self-determination as a process of self-overcoming, which assumed individual responsibility for self-making.[37] But Bauer also interpreted "egoism," the pursuit of individual interest in competition with other individuals, as a denial of autonomy, since it accepted a naturally or culturally determined, a fixed and stable, definition of the self as its foundation.[38] Self-determination was a continuous process of self-abandonment, a fluid process in which all stable identities were recognized as temporary experiments and subjected to criticism and in which human existence was constantly redefined and produced in new ways. The vigilant resistance to being determined, the constant struggle for self-overcoming and self-mastery that characterized authentic individual existence, however, were also for Bauer clearly social and universally "human" acts. The practice of critical theory confronted others with the ephemerality and self-constructed nature of their perceived natural or cultural determinations; experiments in self-making presented possibilities for emulation, resistance, and overcoming for other individual existences. In Bauer's writing, therefore, "self-consciousness," although only actual in the acts of finite, contingent human existences, also provided a perspective on the totality of existence as an interactive process of critical resistance and active self-making. A description of human existence as the constant fluid process of self-overcoming through the mastery of natural and cultural determination thus eventually reproduced for Bauer the Hegelian view of the totality as a realm or world of self-conscious freedom and rational self-transparency, even though Bauer saw this totality as a possible, contingent, historical construction emerging from individual acts rather than a self-revelation of an absolute subject.[39] Even as an isolated, lonely critic, rejected and ignored by his contemporaries, Bauer believed that he somehow spoke for a universal truth that gathered all contingent existences into a general historical project.[40]

Bauer's close associate and friend during the early 1840s, Max Stirner (alias for Johann Casper Schmidt), noted these residues of the attempt to merge autonomy with historical and communal totality in Bauer's revisions of the theory of self-consciousness and defined them as central to Bauer's continuing residence in the "old" world of theological consciousness and essentialist language. Bauer, he claimed, had abstracted the pure, free activity of constant self-overcoming from the always particular, ineffable, and unutterable "thisness" of individual existence, objectified this abstraction as a universal self-consciousness, and demanded that every particular self-determination subordinate itself to the demand to be free. For Stirner this was the ultimate, final form of the domination of real human existence by culturally produced "objective," "universal" values, the dissolution of profane existence into sacred essence. Once the "spooks" of the sacred were dissolved, however, human existence revealed itself as always and only "this" existence or "my" existence.

Stirner's personal, unique "I" affirmed and asserted its reality through specific acts of insurrection or rebellion against the threats of definition, categorization, determination, or possession by powers outside of itself, and by taking "possession," by asserting "ownership" over itself and its relations to others. Any and all forms of socialization or universalization, of conformity to general cultural standards, objective moral laws, and so on, were forms of self-abnegation and self-alienation. The concrete, actually existing self was not a stable, durable entity that could somehow be grasped in reflection, but a fluid, contingent existence, actual only in its specific acts, its ephemeral determinations, its currently existing "property." Language could not penetrate to this ground of existence, but it could describe the shifting world of relations organized around it. The actually existing world, the "real" world, was always my world, the network of relationships that could be characterized as my relations, my property, my values, my knowledge.[41]

The creative self-defining power of the individual self was of course not "absolute," just as its world was not *the* world in the sense of an absolute, objective totality. "It would be foolish to assert that there is no power beyond mine," Stirner contended, and constantly reiterated that the freedom and power of individual egos was limited by the freedom and power of others.[42] His point was that the only "real" or positive freedom, power, and value of the individual was that which it made and grasped for itself, which it actually possessed. Stirner articulated his position most clearly in his response to those critics – Hess, Feuerbach, and Szeliga (a disciple of Bauer) – who had accused him of falling back into the delusions of an abstract absolute egoism à la Fichte:

Does Feuerbach live in any world other than *his* world? Does he live for example in Hess's, Szeliga's or Stirner's world? Is not the world experienced, perceived and thought in a Feuerbachian way? He does not simply live in the midst of it, but is its center, is the central point of *his* world. And like Feuerbach everyone is the center of his own world. For "world" is simply that which he himself is not, but which belongs to him, which stands in relation to him, which is for him. Around you everything turns. You are the center of the external world and the center of the inner world of thought and perception. Your world reaches as far as your grasp, and what you encompass in your grasp, that is, through this mere grasping, your own. You the unique one are "unique" only *together with your property.*[43]

Stirner thus repudiated the notion of "one" world structured and controlled by some universal power. There were only individual worlds, structured and owned by individual, unique egos. Positive freedom emerged from the recognition and assertion of the self's creative responsibility for its world of experience, from the affirmation that the individual existing self was the center of the world, the source of truth, value, and meaning. This "real" world was of course never fixed or stable. Its boundaries and inner structure fluctuated in correspondence with the actions, feelings, and thoughts of its fluid, contingent center.

Despite the apparent nihilism in Stirner's sweeping dismissal of the objectivity and universality of value, truth, and meaning, he presented his description of individual-centered existence as the final positive appropriation of the true content of his cultural and philosophical inheritance. The attributes formerly attached to the sacred "spooks" of God – absolute spirit, man, self-consciousness, and so on – were revealed and possessed as the forms of existence of the concrete, contingent human individual. The critical negation of the powers of God, absolute spirit, and human essence was also a positive appropriation of the richness, creativity, self-sufficiency, and innocent self-expressiveness of contingent human existence. Stirner's language thus also continued in the mode of a transformative translation of Hegelian terms. The historico-cultural narrative of the self-actualization of the spirit was rewritten in existential terms with the liberated, self-expressive, contingent, existing individual as the "laughing heir" of a dialectical development from immediacy, through self-division, to self-conscious freedom and transparency.[44] Ethical and communal relations were not repudiated, but reaffirmed in the "authentic" mode of direct (that is, not mediated through a third, "sacred" power), constantly renegotiated, voluntary "unions" or alliances among free, self-affirming "self-owners." Even the Hegelian description of redemption found an "existential" form in the "eternal now" of self-actualization and self-dissolution, the "living oneself out" of contingent existence in the manifold of its natural and cultural relations.[45]

Although Bauer and Stirner constantly set their own existential perspectives against the essentialism of Feuerbach and his alleged socialist "disciples," like Marx and Hess, Feuerbach's own development after 1843 moved toward a transformative translation of Hegelian humanism that paralleled their own. Feuerbach's reconsiderations and critical revisions of his earlier formulations of naturalistic humanism took the form of an amplification and intense rethinking of the relationship between thought and being, essence and existence. He was determined to expunge the remaining elements of philosophical essentialism from his conceptions of human species-being (*Gattungswesen*) and thus fill up the "cavities in the human head in which divine ghosts have always nested."[46] Only contingent sensuous being, "*Dasein*," he now insisted, was real. The real being of human existence was that which was unutterable (*Das Unsagbare*):

Where words cease life begins and being reveals its secret. If unutterability is equivalent to irrationality than all existence is irrational because it is always and forever *this* existence. But irrational it is not. Existence has meaning and reason in itself, without being verbalized.[47]

After 1843 Feuerbach set out to prove this last claim, to demonstrate that somehow the hidden, real content of the metaphysical language of the Hegelian absolute spirit could be derived from the contingent, sensuous "thisness" of existence.

Feuerbach began this reconstruction by describing sensuous existence as necessarily existence in relation to another existence, as being both for-itself, as subject, and a being-for-others, or object. The reality of *Dasein* was always a reality within active and passive relationships, a relation of sensitivity (suffering) and active desire. Human existence as self, as subject or as I, emerged only in relationship to a "thou": the I became real, objective, in relation to another I. The center that created or made possible a "world" of subjects and objects was thus not unique individual existence, but the relationship between at least two existing beings. Human existence as sensuous existence was also social existence, an existence for and with others. The self-consciousness of human existence as a subject/object identity, as being in totality, or as divine, "absolute" being, could not emerge from the self-reflections of an abstracted individual ego, but found its reality in the sensuous interaction of concrete individual beings. The history of human culture was not so much an actualization of spirit in the world as an education and development of the senses into refined, differentiated, "cultivated," distinctively "human" senses. Thinking could merely bring this rich content of human self-creation, the manifold of sensuous relations, to awareness and thus break the self-deceptive belief in the autonomy of the spirit and definitively dissolve the justifications for spiritual domination of sensuous existence. Like Stirner, Feuerbach defined the self or the I as contingent, particular, and present only in its acts and relationships; but for Feuerbach the most significant forms of the relations that defined specifically human existence were reciprocal or social. Existing as a sensuous concrete being entailed sharing a world of relations with others, living in a totality that was not limited by the grasp or power of the contingent individual I. The historical production of these proliferating relations and interactions and the diversity and refinements of sensuous existence they entailed constituted the human "essence." "Man" was a product of his own historical practice as a needy and desiring being, not a given "essence," but a continually redefined network of relationships.[48]

For Feuerbach after 1843, the descriptive language of sensuous *Dasein* thus recuperated the full content of the Hegelian absolute spirit; it defined both that which was real and the knowledge of the real; it was "being" as both substance and subject, as "concrete totality." Like Stirner's and Bauer's existential formulations, Feuerbach's description or analytic of existence could still be read as a translation of Hegel rather than as an erasure of Hegel and a radically new creation. This was of course also Marx's opinion as expressed in the *German Ideology*, but as Stirner, Bauer, other former Left Hegelians, and countless later scholars have been quick to point out, Marx's and Engels' historical materialism, despite all their disclaimers, also retained much of the structure of the Hegelian language in which they had begun their intellectual careers. The same might be said of that other historically influential transformative critic of Hegelianism in the mid 1840s, Søren Kierkegaard. I will conclude this brief survey of early nineteenth-century transformations of He-gelianism with a comment on the ways in which those two seminal texts of 1846, *The German Ideology* and *Concluding Unscientific Postscript*, recreated at least some of the characteristic structures of the Hegelian perspective within their sweeping critiques of Hegelian philosophy and language.

Both Marx and Kierkegaard declared their independence from He-gel by grounding their own perspective on what they believed had been invisible from the Hegelian perspective and silent in the He-gelian language: the concrete actuality of contingent individual exis-tence. They perceived their critiques as external rather than inter-nal, as critiques of premises rather than tactics or results. In their common conviction that the Hegelian perspective could not illumi-nate reality because it remained in a closed circle of abstract thought, and that Hegelian language could make no persuasive sense of experience because it never really confronted the actuality of lived experience, Kierkegaard and Marx shared a widespread con-sciousness among their intellectual contemporaries. But the "exis-tential" realities Kierkegaard and Marx dug out from behind the Hegelian mystifications and the languages they used to describe these realities were distinctive enough to eventually inaugurate their own discursive traditions.

For Marx the reality "from which abstraction could only be made in the imagination" was the sensuous reality of individuals whose physi-cal qualities were set into motion in relation to the natural world in order to produce their means of susbsistence.[49] Kierkegaard on the other hand defined the "thisness" of existing being as the passionate inwardness of personal ethical determination of the will, as the sub-jective choosing of values and purposes that gave distinctive, personal shape and direction to the always-unique life of the individual self.[50] Still, these contrasting "material" and "spiritual" conceptions of exis-tence possessed a common shape. Both Marx and Kierkegaard viewed existence as act or "practice," as a constant transcending movement relating the sheer contingency of individual existence to supra-individual structures and powers. For Marx, existence as productive labor inevitably became a social practice, connecting the individual to, and reshaping the individual within, systems of production and their historical transformations. For Kierkegaard passionate commit-ment to the subjective actualization of certain ethical possibilities in free acts of self-determination ultimately brought the individual self face to face with the absolute self (the historical God-man of Christian faith) in a religious relationship. In both cases the "truth" or significance of individual historical existence was ultimately tied to integration into an absolute subject/object, but in both cases this truth was affirmed as a result of transformative practice and as having its being or reality *as* transformative practice (rather than within theoretical knowledge), whether as the collective proletarian subject of revolutionary social practice or as the identification with the God-Man in the free, self-surrendering, personal act of religious faith.

In a distinctive and indirect fashion, therefore, Kierkegaard and Marx respectively restored, although in a mutually exclusionary and reductive fashion, the religious (transcendent) and socio-historical (immanent) substance of the Hegelian absolute subject that had eluded, or been consciously rejected by, the other anti-Hegelian Hegelian critics of the 1840s. And despite their own denial of the priority of language over existence, consciousness over being, and thought over reality, they created two languages and theoretical perspectives that allowed at least fragments of the Hegelian project to continue to shape the Marxist/Existentialist and Structuralist/Poststructuralist debates of our own century.

NOTES

1 For the formation and fate of the original small group of Hegelian disciples that emerged in Jena in 1805–1807, see Heinz Kimmerle, "Dokumente zu Hegels Jenaer Dozententätigkeit (1801–1807)", *Hegel-Studien* 4(1967): 21–99, and my *Hegelianism: The Path Toward Dialectical Humanism, 1805–1841* (Cambridge/New York, 1980), 77–83.

2 The leader of the Hegelian faction in the Burschenschaft was Friedrich Wilhelm Carove. See esp. his *Entwurf einer Burschenschaftsordnung* (Eisenach, 1818) and *Ueber die Ermordung Kotzebues* (Eisenach, 1819). The first two Hegelian journals were *Neue Berliner Monatschrift für Philosophie, Geschichte, Literatur und Kunst* ed. Friedrich Förster and Leopold von Henning (1821), and *Zeitschrift für die Wissenschaft des Judenthums* ed. Eduard Gans, Moses Moser, and Immanuel Wohlwill (1822–23).

3 Fritz Schlawe, "Die Berliner Jahrbücher für wissenschaftliche Kritik: Ein Beitrag zur Geschichte des Hegelianismus," *Zeitschrift für Religions- und Geistesgeschichte* 11(1959): 240–58.

4 Allegedly used by the Prussian monarch Frederick William IV, this phrase was cited in the letter from the Prussian Ministry of Culture offering Schelling the position in Berlin. The letter is printed in *Schellings Philosophie der Offenbarung 1841/2* ed. Manfred Frank (Frankfurt am Main, 1977), 408–9.

5 F.W.J. Schelling, "Erste Vorlesung in Berlin, 15 November, 1841," ibid., 92–93.

6 Detailed descriptions of Hegelian conversion experiences can be found in Juergen Gebhardt, *Politik und Eschatologie: Studien zur Geschichte der Hegelschen Schule in den Jahren 1830–1840* (Munich, 1963), and in Toews, *Hegelianism*, pp. 88–94.

7 These positions were polemically clarified in the controversies between Hegelians and the academic representatives of the Historical School like Savigny and Ranke. See Ernst Simon, *Ranke und Hegel* (Munich/Berlin, 1928), and Kurt Mautz, "Leo und Ranke," *Deutsche Vierteljahrsschrift für Literaturwissenschaft und Geistesgeschichte* 27(1953): 207–35.

8 Hegel formulated these reciprocal relations between ethical life and rational self-consciousness most succinctly in the 1830 edition of the Enzyklopädie (*Werkausgabe*, X, 353–65).

9 Schelling's emphasis on the priority of pre-reflective being in the 1840s, however, produced some confusion regarding the relationship between his positions and the new focus on the priority of contingent existence among some of the Left Hegelians, Marx and Kierkegaard. See Karl Löwith, *From Hegel to Nietzsche: The Revolution in Nineteenth-Century Thought*, trans. David Green (Garden City, N.Y., 1967), 113–19, and especially Manfred Frank, *Der unendliche Mangel an Sein: Schellings Hegelkritik und die Anfänge der Marxischen Dialektik* (Frankfurt 1975).

10 Gan's reformist stance, already evident in his lectures during the late 1820s, was displayed in a number of publications of the early 1830s: *Beiträge zur Revision der preussischen Gesetzgebung* (Berlin, 1830–32), and "Vorlesungen über die Geschichte der letzten fünfzig Jahren," *Historisches Taschenbuch* 4(1833), 285–326.

11 Karl Theodor Bayrhoffer, *Die Idee und Geschichte der Philosophie* (Marburg, 1838); Karl Ludwig Michelet, *Geschichte der letzten Systeme der Philosophie in Deutschland von Kant bis Hegel*, 2 vols. (Berlin, 1837–38).

12 The various positions in this debate are chronicled in Johann Eduard Erdmann, *A History of Philosophy*, trans. W.S. Hough, (London, 1890–92), III, 54–83.

13 [Feuerbach], *Gedanken über Tod und Unsterblichkeit, aus den Papieren eines Denkers*, in Feuerbach, *Sämtliche Werke*, ed. Hans-Martin

Sass, 13 vols., (Stuttgart, 1964), XI; Friedrich Wilhelm Carové, *Ueber das Recht, die Weise und die wichtigsten gegenstände der öffentlichen Beurtheilung, mit stäter Beziehung auf die neueste Zeit* (Trier, 1825).

14 Friedrich Richter, *Die Lehre von den letzten Dingen* I (Breslau, 1833); [Moses Hess], *Die heilige Geschichte der Menschheit* (Stuttgart, 1837); August Cieszkowski, *Prolegomena zur Historiosophie* (Berlin, 1838). See also Horst Stuke, *Philosophie der Tat: Studien zur "Verwirklichung der Philosophie" bei den Junghegelianern und wahren Sozialisten* (Stuttgart, 1963).

15 The themes of secularization and the "end of philosophy" have been taken up in two recent studies of the Hegelian movement: Robert Gascoigne, *Religion, Rationality and Community: Sacred and Secular in the Thought of Hegel and His Critics* (Dordrecvht/Boston, 1985), and Harold Mah, *The End of Philosophy, The Origin of "Ideology": Karl Marx and the Crisis of the Young Hegelians* (Berkeley/Los Angeles, 1987).

16 David Friedrich Strauss, *Das Leben Jesu kritisch bearbeitet*, 2 vols. (Tuebingen, 1835–36), II, 686, 729–40.

17 Even Arnold Ruge defended this position as late as 1837. See his "Strauss und seine Gegner," *Blätter für literarische Unterhaltung*, June 12, 1837, p. 657.

18 David Friedrich Strauss, *Die christliche Glaubenslehre in ihrer geschichtlichen Entwicklung und im Kampfe mit der modernen Wissenschaft*, 2 vols. (Tuebingen, 1840–41), I:68,355, and II, 75,495–96,737.

19 Bruno Bauer, *Kritik der evangelischen Geschichte der Synoptiker*, 3 vols. (Leipzig/Braunschweig, 1841–42), I, v–vi.

20 [Bruno Bauer], *Die Posaune des jüngsten Gerichts über Hegel den Atheisten und Antichristen:Ein Ultimatum* (Leipzig, 1841), 77,70.

21 Ibid, pp. 81–83.

22 Ludwig Feuerbach, "Zur Kritik der Hegelschen Philosophie," in Feuerbach, *Gesammelte Werke*, ed. Werner Schuffenhauer, 10 vols. (Berlin, 1967–), IX, 16–62.

23 *Das Wesen des Christentums*, in *Werke* (Schuffenhauer), V, 153–54; *The Essence of Christianity*, trans. George Eliot (New York, 1957), 75.

24 "Vorläufige Thesen zur Reformation der Philosophie," in *Werke* (Schuffenhauer), IX, 261.

25 Ibid, p. 256.

26 Fritz Schlawe, "Die junghegelsche Publizistik," *Die Welt als Geschichte*, 20 (1960): 40; Friedrich Vischer to Arnold Ruge, June 8, 1842, in Adolph B. Benson, "Eleven Unpublished Letters by Friedrich Theodor Vischer," *Philosophical Quarterly*, III (1924): 47. The Swabian Hegelians developed

their Straussian position in an independent journal, the *Jahrbücher der Gegenwart,* which began publication in 1843.

27 The positive side of Bauer's critique was extensively developed in the anonymous work *Das Entdeckte Christentum. Eine Erinnerung an das achtzehnte Jahrhundert und ein Beitrag zur Krisis des Neunzehnten* (Zurich/Winterthur, 1843), repr. Ernst Barnikol, ed. *Das Entdeckte Christenthum im Vormärz* (Jena, 1927).

28 This position was most forcefully stated in reviews of theological works published in Ruge's *Hallische Jahrbuecher* in July 1842 (col. 667), and in Ruge's *Anekdota zur neusten deutschen Philosophie und Publizistik,* 2 vols. (Zurich/Winterthur, 1843), II, 185.

29 Bruno Bauer, *Die Gute Sache der Freiheit und meine eigene Angelegenheit* (Zurich/Winterthur, 1842), 113

30 "Vorläufige Thesen," p. 244.

31 Ibid, p. 259.

32 Ibid.

33 *Das entdeckte Christenthum,* pp. 90–93.

34 The pathology of servility to anchronistic cultural forms is the central theme of Bauer's main works of 1842–43: *Die Gute Sache, Das entdeckte Christenthum,* and *Die Judenfrage* (Braunschweig, 1843).

35 *Das Entdeckte Christenthum,* pp. 96, 112. See also Bauer, *Die Judenfrage,* p. 81.

36 *Das entdeckte Christenthum,* p. 139.

37 "Die Gattung und die Masse," (1844) and "Was is jetzt Gegenstand der Kritik?" (1844) in Bruno Bauer, *Feldzüge der reinen Kritik,* ed. Hans-Martin Sass (Frankfurt, 1968), 213–23, 200–12.

38 *Die Judenfrage,* pp. 8, 12–13, 48, 87–89, 95–96; *Das entdeckte Christenthum,* pp. 90–93.

39 Bruno Bauer, "Charakteristik Ludwig Feuerbachs," *Wigands Vierteljahresschrift* 3 (1845): 87.

40 On the "social" dimension in Bauer's concept of criticism, see Lothar Koch, *Humanistischer Atheismus und gesellschaftliches Engagement: Bruno Bauers kritische Kritik* (Stuttgart, 1971).

41 Max Stirner, *Der Einzige und sein Eigenthum* (Leipzig, 1845), 237, 239.

42 Ibid., pp. 240–42, 410.

43 Max Stirner, "Rezensenten Stirners," in Max Stirner, *Kleinere Schriften,* 2nd ed., ed. John Henry Mackay (Berlin, 1914), 354–55 (Stirner's italics).

44 *Der Einzige und sein Eigenthum,* p. 286.

45 Ibid., pp. 427–28, 435–37.

46 Feuerbach to Georg Herwegh, November 25, 1845, in Marcel Herwegh and Victor Fleury, "Briefwechsel Georg und Emma Herweghs und Lud-

wig Feuerbach," *Nord und Süd. Eine deutsche Monatsschrift,* CXXVIII (1909): 31.

47 Feuerbach, "Gruendsätze der Philosophie der Zukunft," *Werke* (Schuffenhauer), IX, 308.

48 Ibid., pp. 304, 315, 317, 323, 338–39.

49 Karl Marx, "The German Ideology," in *The Marx-Engels Reader* 2nd ed., ed. Robert Tucker (New York, 1978), 149–50.

50 Søren Kierkegaard, *Concluding Unscientific Postscript,* trans. David Swenson and Walter Lowrie (Princeton, 1941), esp. pp. 169–224.

13 Hegel and Marxism

BACKGROUND

Shortly after Hegel's death, the influence of his philosophy began to wane. Part of this process involved the division of Hegel's followers into what David Friedrich Strauss (1808–1874) called "right," "center," and "left" Hegelians. Strauss himself may be regarded as the founder of the "left" Hegelian school with his book *The Life of Jesus* (1835). At first the battleground was theological. "Right" Hegelians, such as H. F. W. Hinrichs (1794–1861) and Johann Erdmann (1805–1892), employed Hegel's philosophy in defense of traditional Christianity; "center" Hegelians, such as Karl Rosenkranz (1805–1879) and Karl Ludwig Michelet (1801–1893), subjected religious dogma to Hegelian reinterpretation; and "left" Hegelians, such as Strauss, Ludwig Feuerbach (1804–1872), and Bruno Bauer (1809–1882), derived theologically radical (even atheistic and humanistic) conclusions from Hegelianism. Yet Strauss borrowed the terminology of "left" and "right" from French politics, and from the beginning the division was implicitly over social and political as well as theological issues. Left Hegelianism was explicitly linked to political radicalism and the communist worker's movement by Moses Hess (1812–1875) in *The European Triarchy* (1841).

Like most of the Left Hegelians, Karl Marx was a critic of Hegel as well as a disciple; some of his earliest theoretical reflections consist in a critique, along the lines marked out by Feuerbach, of Hegel's philosophy of the state. But Marx still avowed himself a "pupil of that mighty thinker" in later years, when it was highly unfashionable to do so (C 1:27/97).[1] Marx and Engels always paid homage to the Hegelian dialectic, although they qualified their allegiance by limiting it to the dialectical "method" (or "method of presentation"), as distinct from the Hegelian "system," which they rejected (MEW 21:269–70/ SW 599–600). Marxists of the Second International (1889–1914) in general continued to pay lip service to the "dialectical method," but tended to distance themselves from the philosophical roots of Marxism, and the philosophical side of their thought usually shows the influence of neo-Kantianism and positivism rather than of Hegel.[2] The importance of Hegelian thinking for Marxism was reasserted against the tendencies of the Second International by two important books, both appearing in 1923: Karl Korsch's *Marxism and Philosophy* and Georg Lukacs's *History and Class Consciousness*. Russian Marxism always retained a more Hegelian cast, and this was especially true of the Bolsheviks. Lenin had already criticized Marxists of the Second International on similar grounds,[3] and his *Philosophical Notebooks* (written during World War I, published posthumously in 1929) contain lavish praise for Hegel's system of speculative logic, together with meditations on how to effect the materialist transformation of the Hegelian dialectic. Most twentieth-century Marxism, even that operating well beyond the confines of Leninist orthodoxy, has continued to acknowledge its philosophical debt to Hegel chiefly by insisting on the importance of dialectical thinking (see, for example, Jean-Paul Sartre, *A Critique of Dialectical Reason*, 1961, and Theodor Adorno, *Negative Dialectics*, 1966.

DIALECTIC

As the above remarks indicate, the tradition of Marxist thought tended to treat the topic of "Marxism and Hegel" mainly in terms of the Marxian appropriation of Hegel's dialectical method. It is questionable, however, whether this shows any great insight on the part of the tradition regarding the nature of Hegel's real contribution to it. For Hegel, dialectic or dialectical reason constituted part of an ambitious program to canonize his system of speculative logic both as a replacement for traditional Aristotelian logical theory and as the metaphysical basis for philosophical thinking in general. There are strong indications that Marx, and especially Engels, continued to defend something like these pretensions for the Hegelian logic even after it had long become clear to almost everyone else that Hegelian logic was a non-subject, an attempted theoretical revolution that had simply failed. If it is true that Marx's social theory follows patterns laid down in Hegel's speculative logic, that will not account for anything of interest in the theory. For instance, Engels provides us with no interesting information when he portrays the transition from commodity to capital in Marx's theory as governed by Hegel's transition from being to essence (SC 439).

When Marxists themselves formulate "dialectic" in general terms – whether to separate it from Hegel's "idealism" or to save it from the shipwreck of speculative logic – the point they usually emphasize is that dialectic treats the world as a complex of processes rather than things, reveals everything to be shot through with tensions and contradictions demanding resolution and hence to be transitory, and involved in an inevitably progressive process of development.[4] This point sometimes carries in its train a number of other general ideas or philosophical theses. For example, it is often combined with the use of organic metaphors for societies and social change, usually implying a commitment to methodological holism and a willingness to employ functional or teleological forms of explanation. "Dialectic" connotes reciprocity or mutual interaction between opposed or contrasting aspects of something. This sometimes leads to the notion, especially emphasized by Korsch, that what is essentially "dialectical" in the thought of both Marx and Hegel is the comprehension of their own theoretical activity in its relationship to an ongoing social process: "The relation between philosophy and reality, theory and practice [is] the original meaning of the dialectical principle."[5] Dialectic as a kind of thinking entangled inevitably in contradictions is also interpreted by Adorno as a symptom of the fact that we are still entangled in social relations that are radically unfree and irrational: dialectic is "the ontology of the wrong state of things."[6] This, however, seems to involve the fundamentally un-Hegelian idea that truly free and rational thought would surmount dialectic altogether.

If there is nothing to dialectic except a vaguely optimistic spirit of Heracliteanism, then this tells us nothing deep about the thought of either Hegel or Marx. A commitment to organicism in a theory of society and history, although certainly controversial, does not identify anything unique to Hegelian or Marxian thinking. Among the wide variety of other ideas associated with "dialectic" by various

Marxian thinkers, some are admittedly original and suggestive, but none can be plausibly regarded as what either Hegel or Marx regarded as essential to dialectical thinking.

Clearly what is living and lasting in the thought of both Hegel and Marx has to do not with speculative logic or metaphysics, but with their theories of society and history and their insight into the spiritual predicament of human beings in modern society. In this area Hegel taught Marx a great deal that has yet to be comprehended by our liberal political theories and our orthodox social sciences, no doubt because it is still foreign to the alienated liberal society whose reflection they are. The most-productive approach to the theme of "Hegel and Marxism" will thus be one that ignores the overworked and fruitless theme of "dialectical method" and concentrates on concrete points of social theory and philosophy of history.

Of course Marx was a powerfully original social thinker in his own right, and it would be absurd to represent him as a mere epigone of Hegel. Marx was a trenchant critic of Hegel, just as Hegel's social theory, especially in recent years, has often been turned critically against Marxism. But I am inclined to think that much of what has lasting value in both is best appreciated when we focus more on the points where they agree than on the issues that separate them.

CIVIL SOCIETY

Let us begin with Hegel's conception of his own age. It is an age, he thinks, characterized by a new self-conception on the part of individual human beings. People think of themselves as *persons*, free choosers who are capable of abstracting from all their desires and qualities, and who demand for themselves an external sphere for the exercise of their arbitrary choice (PR § 41). This sphere begins with a person's body and extends to all of what we call the person's property (PR §§ 45–47). For Hegel, the only legitimate form of property recognized by modern society is private property (PR § 46).

Not only do individuals in modern society claim the right as persons to an external sphere in which their arbitrary choice is sovereign but they also see themselves as *subjects* who give meaning to their lives through the choices they make. Subjects require a self-dependent mode of life, so that their actions are seen by them as the results of their own reflective choice, not the results of habit or external compulsion. This requires that social arrangements provide them with what Hegel calls "subjective freedom" (PR § 124).

All this must remind us of modern liberal orthodoxy, whose conception of the nature and aims of social life is founded on the rights of persons and the dignity and freedom of moral subjects. It might look as though Hegel's main addition is merely to emphasize the historical specificity of the human self-conceptions on which modern society is founded. But the real difference is that for Hegel, "person" and "subject" are only abstractions; by themselves they are insufficient to provide a content either for human rights or moral duties. In the form of abstractions, Hegel thinks they tend to foster a "spirit of atomicity" that separates individuals from each other and from their common social life. When the political state is conceived solely in terms of the protection of the right of persons (as it is in Fichte's early political theory), then the state is inevitably turned into an abstract power in opposition to individuals whose sole function is to supervise and coerce them. The state, since it is viewed solely as a police power, tends to be reduced simply to a police state (NR 519/124). Instead of protecting the rights of persons, it becomes their deadly enemy. The abstractions of "person" and "subject" can count for something only when they are given content, through social institutions in which each individual achieves a completed social identity by being integrated into an organic system of social interdependence and mutual recognition. Right and morality can flourish only in a system that guarantees the freedom and happiness of individuals in determinate and recognized social roles, and simultaneously constitutes itself consciously for them as a shared or communal end. To such a system, Hegel gives the name "ethical life" (*Sittlichkeit*).

What is fundamental to modern ethical life is a new and distinctive institutional setting for the lives of individuals. Pre-modern societies were distinguished between the "natural" and "private" society of the family and the "artificial" and "public" society of the political state. In a social order partitioned in this way, there is no room for individuals to thrive as persons and subjects, employing their arbitrary freedom to pursue their private ends and develop their unique individuality in the larger public arena of social life. In the modern world, however, the individual's right and welfare have achieved a legitimate status independent of the good of the social whole. The pursuit of this good demands a new kind of social institution in which each individual's participation in the larger life of society must be mediated through that individual's arbitrary will and must express that individual's subjective opinion (PR § 206).

Hegel calls this distinctively modern social institution "civil society" (*bürgerliche Gesellschaft*) because it is a society composed of *Bürger*. But that German word has a twofold sense: it can mean the same as the French word *citoyen*, referring to the citizen of the political state, or it can mean the same as the French word *bourgeois*. Hegel emphasizes that by the term "civil society" he means the term in the latter sense (PR § 190R).

ESTATES

It is sometimes thought that "civil society" for Hegel refers only to the market economy, protected by a system of legal justice; the individual as bourgeois is simply the rationally self-interested *homo oeconomicus*. This might provide a quick connection with Marx's unflattering image of the bourgeois mentality of capitalism. But that connection would be entirely too quick. It would warp our understanding of both Hegel and Marx by imposing on them an image derived essentially from orthodox liberal theory.

Hegel's conception of the modern individual as bourgeois does *begin* with the conception of self-interested private persons who use the market as a means to their own ends (PR § 187). But the main point he wants to make is that in civil society such individuals are drawn by an apparently external necessity into connection with others, and this connection brings about changes in the individuals and their ends. Because of this, Hegel's civil society is not conceived as a sort of natural realm resulting from individuals pursuing their private desires through unconstrained participation in the open market. This liberal or purely economic conception of civil society is what Hegel ridicules under the name of the "spiritual animal kingdom" (PhG 1397).

The function of civil society for individuals is not simply to satisfy their contingent wants but to give actuality to their abstract self-images as person and subject. In other words, the point of living in civil society is not only desire-satisfaction but self-actualization. From the outset, Hegel emphasizes that the "concrete person" is only one principle of civil society, which is complemented by a second principle, "the form of universality" (PR § 182). Hegel's analysis of civil society thus concludes by considering the forms of social solidarity in which these systems terminate, and through which individuals relate themselves to the universal ends of the state (PR §§ 230–56). Civil society is a true *society*, in which individuals acquire definite social identities, develop determinate ethical interests in the right well-being of others, and are driven to relate themselves to shared or collective ends.

The deeper function of work in civil society is not need-satisfaction, but education. Work develops not only the specific practical capacities they need to do their job, but also lays the foundation for theoretical culture, and gives their life the ethical character of discipline and regularity needed for participation in the complexities of modern social life (PR § 197). The deeper function of the division of labor is not greater efficiency, but providing each individual with a definite mode of life, recognized by civil society in general for the contribution it makes to the common good. "The individual gives himself actuality only insofar as he steps into *existence* and hence *determinate particularity*, which he does only by limiting himself *exclusively* to one of the particular spheres of need" (PR § 207). Individuals are self-actualized when they acquire a definite *Stand* ("estate," "social position," "social "status," or "standing"). By belonging to a definite estate an individual acquires a determinate mode of life, a dignity recognized by others, and determinate standards for measuring subjective self-worth. Without this, my only identity in civil society is that of a free-lance hustler of whatever commodities (including myself) I have to offer in the market. The individual "will accordingly try to gain recognition through the external manifestations of success in his trade, and these are unbounded, because it is impossible to for him to live in a way appropriate to his estate if his estate does not exist" (PR § 253R).

For this reason, Hegel recommends that civil society be organized into "corporations" or professional guilds, which provide their members with a "corporation spirit," a sense of solidarity with others who ply the same trade or profession (*Gewerbe*), and a sense of collective responsibility to civil society at large for performing its distinctive function. This not only provides an ethical connection between the individuals who share a common estate, but it also directs them toward common or ethical ends, and provides a mediating link between the individual's particular life as person and subject, and the individual's common life as member of a universal society (PR § 255A). In this way "the sphere of civil society passes over into the *state*" (PR § 256R).

BOURGEOIS SOCIETY

The estates of civil society for Hegel include not only the "formal" or "professional" (*Gewerbe*) estate but also the "substantial estate," the landed nobility and rural peasantry, and also the "universal estate" or government civil service (PR § 202). Thus Hegel's conception of the bourgeois, or member of civil society, is meant to include much more than the urban middle class. Nevertheless, Hegel makes it plain that it is solely the "formal" or "professional" estate, which includes the trades belonging to handicraft, manufacture, and commerce, that truly partakes in the distinctive self-actualizing features of modern civil society. Only there, for instance, is corporation membership appropriate (PR § 250); only there does Hegel find a place for elected representation in the political process (PR § 308). Civil society for Hegel is "bourgeois" society in the sense that its dominant ethical principles are those arising from the urban middle class.

In this way, Hegel's theory already contains several crucial features of the Marxian analysis of modern capitalism. Hegel was the first to distinguish "civil society" or the economic realm from the family and the state as a distinctive type of social organization. Marx tells us that this conception that provided the key to his own materialist conception of history, which views the structures and changes of civil society as decisive for historical change in general (MEW 13:9/CW 29:263). Hegel also anticipated this use of the notion of civil society by viewing the distinctive institution of modern civil society as determinative of the modern family and the modern state.[7] Thus Hegel's theory of modern civil society also contains a version of the Marxian thesis that the urban bourgeoisie dominates modern social life. Just as important, Hegel anticipates Marx's view that the market is only a surface appearance of deeper social structures whose fundamental goals were collective rather than individual. Of course, for Hegel the deeper structure was a harmonious economic organism consisting of estates, whereas for Marx it was an explosive struggle between the conflicting interests of hostile social classes. But Hegel was also aware of the conflicts inherent in modern civil society, and he too used the concept of class to describe them.

POVERTY IN CIVIL SOCIETY

Hegel holds that subjective freedom can blossom only in a civil society founded on the institution of private property (PR § 46), where individuals achieve their social estate or status not by birth or the decision of political rulers, but through their own choice, effort, and good fortune (PR § 185R, 206R). At the same time, every member of civil society has a right to hold some property (PR § 49A) and a right to occupy an estate. Just as civil society may demand of its members that they provide for themselves by laboring in its behalf (PR § 240,A), so each member has a right against civil society to an estate in which labor is rewarded with a decent livelihood and an honorable and fulfilling life. Anyone who is excluded from such an estate, for whatever cause, suffers a wrong at civil society's hands (PR § 236,A).

Hegel thinks, however, that a sizeable majority are in effect excluded from these benefits without any perceptible loss to themselves. This is because not everyone's ethical disposition is such that they really require the active and reflective life of the bourgeois. The entire female sex, in Hegel's view, has an ethical disposition attuned to family piety, and its whole vocation lies in devoting itself to family life (PR § 166). The rural population, too, both the landowning nobility and the peasantry, are attuned to an unreflective life, which relies on trust in its unchanging relation with nature rather than on its own reflection and intelligence (PR § 203A).

There is another systematic exclusion of people from the subjective freedoms of civil society that Hegel cannot justify. This is the condition of the urban poor. Hegel sees poverty in civil society as a widespread problem, one produced by the workings of civil society itself. "The complications of civil society itself produce poverty" (VPR17 138); "the emergence of poverty is in general a consequence of civil society, and on the whole poverty results necessarily from it" (VPR19 193). In civil society, Hegel argues, the accumulation of wealth is facilitated by the "universalization" of both human needs and the means of their satisfaction (in other words, by mass production and mass marketing). Mass production, however, leads to the "individualization and limitation" of detail labor. This sort of labor yields the greatest profits precisely because it is unskilled and therefore it can command only a low wage. Wealth in civil society tends to accumulate in a few hands (PR § 244), and much of the growth of urban populations takes the form of people who are in a condition of "dependency and want" (PR § 243), because they have few saleable skills and are under the constant threat of unemployment and starvation. Although Hegel favors the displacement of the wider kinship group by the nuclear family, he also realizes that this tends to destroy one of the main protections individuals have against the contingencies of the market system (PR § 241). Moreover, there is little incentive for the wealthy to prevent poverty, because they actually benefit from its existence: "When there is great poverty, the capitalist finds many people who work for small wages, which increases his earnings; and this has the further consequence that the smaller capitalists fall into poverty" (VPR 4: 610).

Hegel describes the poor as a "class" (*Klasse*) rather than an "estate" (*Stand*). Estates rest on "concrete distinctions" between functionally complementary social positions and economic roles, but class distinctions rest on "*inequalities* of wealth, upbringing and education . . . through which some individuals receive a kind of activity more useful to the state than others" (NP 63). The poor are marked off from others because the activities open to them in civil society are of only marginal worth. As a consequence, the poor are "more or less deprived of all the advantages of civil society" (PR § 241). Unskilled labor commands only a starvation wage and does not qualify for corporation membership. Because they command little purchasing power, the poor cannot satisfy any of the new and varying needs and desires that are the constant products of civil society's life and one of its chief means for developing human nature and liberating the principle of subjectivity (PR § 185). Because they are uneducated, the poor are excluded from the higher cultural benefits of civil society, such as law, medicine, art, science, and religion (VPR 4: 606; PR § 241; VPR 4:606, VPR19 195). Hegel's view of the plight of the poor in civil society might be accurately summed up by use of one of Marx's earliest descriptions of the proletariat: "a class in civil society that is not of civil society" (MEW 1:191/CW 3:186).

In Hegel's view, the condition of poverty is always a wrong or injustice done by society to the impoverished: "Against nature no human being can assert any right, but in the condition of society want directly assumes the form of an injustice perpetrated against this or that class" (PR § 244A). Hegel regards the state (in its "police" function) as responsible for preventing or remedying such wrongs. (Private charity is by its nature unreliable, and even tends to make matters worse, because it degrades and humiliates those who receive it [PR §§ 242, 253R]).

Hegel is pessimistic, however, about the state's capacity to discharge its responsibility. If the state itself provides directly for the poor or requires the wealthy to provide for them, the fundamental problem is not addressed at all, since the poor still lack the dignity and self-respect that goes along with not being able to depend on one's own labor for a decent and honorable livelihood. On the other hand, if the state tries to provide them with the opportunity to work, then this only aggravates the original problem, which was an excess of production in relation to effective demand: "This shows that despite an *excess of wealth*, civil society is *not wealthy enough* – i.e., its own distinct resources are not sufficient to prevent [poverty]" (PR § 245). Hegel's final remarks on the problem of poverty are in effect a sober and hard-hearted counsel of despair: in England, he says, it has been found that the best way to deal with poverty is "to leave the poor to their fate and direct them to beg from the public" (PR § 245R, cf. VPR 4: 612).

THE RABBLE

Hegel and Marx agree that modern civil society tends to produce an impoverished class, whose existence violates its fundamental principles, but whose condition cannot be successfully remedied within the parameters of its economic institutions. They apparently differ concerning the seriousness of the threat poverty poses to civil society. Hegel is troubled by the insolubility of the problem, but he apparently does not think that it threatens the survival of modern society. Marx, on the other hand, sees the working poor as a powerful revolutionary class, destined to revolutionize civil society, to overthrow its basic institutions of private property, and to replace its limited bourgeois freedom with a genuine freedom for all.

Like Marx, Hegel thinks the condition of poverty gives rise to a distinctive disposition or mind-set on the part of the poor, which is hostile to the ethical principles of civil society. But whereas Marx sees the mission of the impoverished class as positive and its (at least incipient) mentality as creative and progressive, Hegel sees this mentality, despite the fundamental rationality embodied in it, as entirely corruptive and destructive, harboring no potentiality of abolishing or redeeming the evils that have produced it.

Poverty, Hegel says, turns the poor into a "rabble" (*Pöbel*). The mark of the rabble is not poverty itself, but "a disposition coupled with poverty, an inner indignation against the rich, against society, the government, etc." (PR § 244A). The poor turn into a rabble not through want alone, but through a certain corrupted attitude of mind that want tends inevitably to bring with it under the ethical conditions of modern civil society. The separation of the poor class from civil society's cultural benefits leads to a deeper separation, a separation of "mind" or "emotion" (*Gemüt*): "The poor man feels himself excluded and mocked by everyone, and this necessarily gives rise to an inner indignation. He is conscious of himself as an infinite, free being, and thus arises the demand that his external existence should correspond to his consciousness" (VPR19 195).

Poverty is a wrong, an injustice; but the poor do not suffer merely some contingent denial of a right, which might leave intact their dignity and their will to defend their rights generally. Instead, poverty destroys the sense of self that for Hegel is the necessary vehicle of ethical attitudes in modern society. (As Marx was later to put it, the poor can "claim no *particular* right because no *particular* wrong but *unqualified* wrong is perpetrated on it" [MEW 1:191/CW 3:186].) The rabble retain the sense that they are infinite and free beings with rights, but for them this abstract sense of self can never reach as far as the affirmation of an ethical life of duties done with self-satisfaction. They experience themselves as objects of wrong, but not as subjects of an independent life sustained by honorable labor. Hence their self-awareness sustains only feelings of indignation and hatred, but not a sense of honor, dignity or self-respect. In fact, it is precisely the possession of modern ethical values, especially a sense of personal right, that transforms "ingenuous poverty" (*unbefangene Armut*) into the "rabble mentality" (*Pöbelhaftigkeit*):

When individuals have not progressed to a self-consciousness of their right, then they remain in ingenuous poverty. But then this ingenuous poverty progresses at least as far as the condition of the idle and the unemployed, who are in the habit of just loafing around. With that, the modifications of self-feeling are totally lost. In the poor there arises an envy and hatred against all those who have something. (VPR19 195–96)

This involves further the destruction of the very ideas of right and personhood. To live under conditions of poverty is to experience in myself that the ideas of freedom, personhood, and right are a mere sham, that they are empty notions lacking any real existence. Since I experience no recognition of my personhood by anyone else, I cease in turn to recognize the personhood of others: "Self-consciousness appears driven to the point where it no longer has any rights, freedom has no existence. [Consequently,] the recognition of universal freedom disappears. From this condition arises that shamelessness that we find in the rabble" (VPR19 195). The rabble perceive, as *The Communist Manifesto* was to put it, that "laws, morality, religion, are only so many bourgeois prejudices, behind which lurk just as many bourgeois interests" (MEW 4:472/CW 6:494–95).

Hegel does not approve of the rabble mentality, but he acknowledges that its sense of wrong is entirely correct, even that its inversion and destruction of the fundamental ethical values of civil society is fundamentally sound. In civil society "everyone has the right to find his subsistence"; because the poor "have a right to subsistence, poverty is a wrong, an offense against right" (VPR 4:609). Further, Hegel holds that when the rights of others threaten my well-being as a whole, my violation of their right ceases to be a wrong; I act by a "right of necessity" (PR § 128). Normally, this right applies only under extraordinary circumstances of momentary danger or distress. But Hegel argues that when you are poor, the right of necessity comes to apply generally to you, because your whole life is carried on beneath the minimum level recognized as necessary for a member of civil society (PR § 244). Thus the right of necessity becomes universal for you; against you, no one has rights any longer: "Earlier we considered the right of necessity as referring to a momentary need. [In the case of poverty, however], necessity no longer has this momentary character." Poverty thus gives rise to "the non-recognition of right" (VPR19 196). The poor thus fall outside the ethical life of civil society; their way of life is beyond its standards of right and wrong. "The rabble is a dangerous ill, because they have neither rights nor duties" (VPR 1:322).

HISTORY AND SPIRIT

Probably the most-extreme and striking difference between Marx's "proletariat" and Hegel's "rabble" has to do with the capacity for collective agency. For Marx, the proletariat is taken to have a fundamental drive toward class solidarity, through which it will eventually accomplish its world-historical mission of revolutionizing society and achieving universal human emancipation. Hegel, however, regards all collective agency as a function of ethical life. Because the rabble is excluded from the ethical principles of its society, Hegel deems it incapable of any meaningful collective action. Even here, however, the views of Marx and Hegel tend to converge as we look more deeply into their theories of history.

Hegel holds that the world in general is an embodiment of the categories or "thought-determinations" of speculative logic. Thus Marx criticizes him and his followers for believing in the "dominion of thought," the idea that "the world is ruled by ideas, that ideas and concepts are the determining principles" (MEW 3:14/CW 5:24). The view Marx attributes to Hegel is not merely metaphysical but historical: that the course of human history is determined by human ideas and concepts, especially philosophical and religious ones. That is a serious distortion of Hegel's theory of history. Hegel does hold that human history is the history of mind or spirit (*Geist*). But Hegel does not understand spirit as something distinct from human activity in the objective world. On the contrary, spirit for Hegel is a certain kind of conscious activity, one that makes or actualizes itself by doing something outside itself, and then by coming to understand itself in light of an interpretation of what it has done (PhG ¶ 18). "The history of spirit is its own deed; for spirit is only what it does, and its deed is to make itself – in this case, as spirit – the object of its own consciousness, and to comprehend itself in its interpretation of itself to itself" (PR § 343). This means that the foundation of spirit's history for Hegel is the history of "objective" spirit – the history of the objective social forms that spirit successively gives itself.

Consider the following picture of how an individual personality might develop itself through its action. I begin with a certain conception of myself, involving not only an image of my own traits but also a concernful evaluation of what I am, and – inseparable from this – a set of goals and aspirations for myself. On the basis of this self-conception, I then take action aimed at actualizing myself according to that conception. As I act I alter myself, not only in the ways I intended, but also in other ways I did not intend or foresee. This will even be inevitable, if the imperfections I perceive in myself involve or imply defects in my self-image and in my conception of my goals and aspirations. Thus it is only to be expected that as I actualize myself, I will develop the knowleddge of the self I am actualizing, and thus also alter my conception of the ends I am seeking. "Spirit produces and actualizes itself in the light of its self-knowledge; it acts in such a way that its knowledge of itself is also actualized" (VG 56/48). Spiritual activity is this dialectical interplay between self-knowledge, self-actualization, and practical striving, in which the striving for a given set of goals, founded on a given knowledge of oneself, leads in time to a new self-knowledge, new goals, and so to an altered striving.

Spirit is this kind of self-transformative activity considered socially or collectively. Hegel thinks that the knowledge and purposive activity of human individuals can be regarded as contributing to a collective activity (by societies, nations, cultures, even by the human race as a whole) aiming at self-understanding and self-actualization, continually self-transformed through an ever-deepening understanding of people's cultural identity and common human nature. Collective activity becomes conscious of itself insofar as individuals articulate and communicate it, so that it becomes the shared consciousness of a culture and a tradition.

Hegel's philosophy of history does involve "consciousness," because spirit's activity is essentially conscious, dependent at each stage on a determinate self-conception and determinate ends and goals derived from that conception. But history for Hegel is not dictated by a series of changes in people's philosophical or religious conceptions, as though these lofty spheres of people's mental life followed an autonomous course, and the forms of their social and economic life were simply dictated by developments on the level of pure thought. On the contrary, Hegel thinks that the higher spheres of "absolute" spirit – art, religion, and philosophy – considered in themselves, fall outside history altogether, because their proper object, which is absolute truth or the divine Idea, is timeless and unchangeable. They have a history only because in each age they take a form that corresponds to the level of self-awareness attained by spirit through its objective striving for self-actualization. Hegel identifies the actual history of spirit with "objective spirit," that is, in the development of human social structures, paradigmatically, the political constitutions of states (PR § 349, VG 138/116). Philosophy and religion have a role to play in history only insofar as people employ philosophical or religious ideas to articulate their conception of themselves as social beings and their aspirations for the constitution of their social life.

NATIONAL PRINCIPLES AND WORLD HISTORY

World-history, for Hegel, is the history of nation-states. Each historical epoch is characterized by a determinate self-conception on the part of the human spirit, and each self-conception takes the form of a national principle put into practice in the social structure – most explicitly, in the political constitution – of a determinate world-historical people (PR § 344). Each historical epoch has its dominant people, in the sense that this people's principle corresponds to the truest conception that spirit has yet formed of itself. "The timely nation, the one which rules, is the one which has grasped the highest concept of spirit" (VG 69/60). Nor is Hegel disposed to the picture of a single nation-state exercising hegemony, even culturally, over many others. Especially in the modern world, he regards the dominant principle as embodied simultaneously in the constitution of a number of different nation-states, who share a common cultural heritage (PR §§ 339A, 358).

A people becomes a state in the course of a regular life cycle, during which it "blossoms, grows strong, then fades away and dies" (VG 67–68/58; compare PR § 349). After its time is past, a nation may die a "natural death" by continuing to subsist in a senescent condition of mere habit, or it may die a different kind of death, which is more like suicide (VG 68–70/59–60). The latter fate is suffered precisely by the most reflective nations, who develop their principle to a rational political constitution and thus become most fully conscious of it. "This spiritual self-consciousness of a nation is its highest point" (VG 177/146) but also its downfall. For in reflecting on its ethical life, the nation ceases to follow its principle spontaneously; it begins to demand rational grounds for doing so, and the demand can be answered only by a deeper reflective awareness of its principle. But this awareness inevitably shows it the limitations of the principle, which now appears as valid only conditionally, not universally. "This lies inevitably in any demand for grounds" (VG 179/146). Reflection thus leads inevitably to demoralization (VG 178/146) whose root for Hegel is not a failure of ethical motivation, but a greater insight into the rational basis of traditional ethical values. The result of reflection is that people are *justified* in turning away from ethical duty and virtue.

Widespread ethical decadence is the harbinger of a new age. The reflection that corrodes the old ethical principle also gives birth to a new one, still abstract and unactualized but invested with the universal validity the old principle has lost. The new principle cannot be grasped reflectively in its determinacy until much later in history, after it has been actualized. To actualize it is the mission of the next epoch.

Spirit, having cultivated itself inwardly, has outgrown its world and is about to pass beyond it; self-consciousness no longer finds satisfaction in this world, but this kind of dissatisfaction has not yet found what it wills – for this is not yet affirmatively at hand – and so it stands on the negative side. It is the world historical individuals who have then told people what it is that they will. (VG 98–99/84)

Hegel has a "great man" theory of history in the sense that he thinks that a new principle of spirit first shows itself through the action of individual political or military leaders, such as Alexander the Great, Julius Caesar, or Napoleon. World historical individuals serve a cause – that of "the higher universal" (VG 97/82) – but they do not serve it intentionally. They have no knowledge of "the Idea as such," and their immediate aim is self-interested ambition, personal glory, or even simply self-protection.

Hegel therefore does not have a "great man" theory in Carlyle's sense. He does not think that the peculiarities of extraordinary individuals determine the course of history, or that things go better if people find heroes to worship. World historical individuals for him are rather the unconscious tools or means through which spirit advances itself. They arise when the times call for them. World historical individuals are heroes and benefactors of humanity, but they are typically bad men from a moral standpoint. They achieve "undying fame" but not happiness, and their renown, both in their own time and for posterity, includes neither gratitude nor genuine honor (PR § 348). Nor does Hegel ever suggest that there is any injustice in this arrangement. On the contrary, he extols the "cunning of reason," that it "sets passions to work in its service, so that the agents by which it gives itself existence must pay the penalty and suffer the loss" (VG 105/89).

Hegel warns us against judging world historical individuals in moral categories not because he thinks we may do them an injustice, but rather because our moralistic prejudices may prevent us from appreciating the historical significance of deeds whose meaning lies beyond the bounds of ethics or morality. Hegel insists that such things as "justice and virtue, wrongdoing, violence and vice, guilt and innocence" have first place in the sphere of "conscious actuality," that is, within the scope of an existing ethical order. But world history, whose higher right renders transitory the principle of every ethical order, "falls outside these points of view" (PR § 345). The foundation of both ethical principles and world historical deeds is spirit's restless quest for freedom. Ethical principles represent freedom in the form of the ordered life of an age; but world historical individuals possess the "higher right" of world history, which overturns the ethical in order that spirit's freedom may advance further (VG 96–97/82). This is how it must be, since the cause they serve ranks higher on the scale of spirit's freedom than the claims of right, morality, or ethics that they violate (VG 171/141).

HISTORICAL MATERIALISM

The profound originality of Marx's theory of history lies in the fact that it ceases to present the Hegelian scheme in terms of human activity in general, and focuses instead on *productive* activity, or labor directed at satisfying people's material needs, with the further consequence that it sees the history of society fundamentally as a history of economic structures or "modes of production" rather than of political constitutions. Marx maintains that the "real basis" of all social life is the "social relations of production" into which human beings enter in their co-operative production. At any given time, these relations form a whole, which Marx calls the "economic structure of society" – the same structure to which, he says, Hegel gave the name "civil society." Other forms of social life, in particular the political state, belong to a "superstructure" erected on the basis of economic relations (MEW 13:9/CW 29:263).

Even this "real basis" of society, however, depends on the natural and historical conditions of human production. At any given stage of history, human beings have determinate "productive powers", whose employment requires determinate modes of co-operation between people. A given mode of co-operation is facilitated by determinate social relationships, such as those of property and authority, assigning effective control of the process and fruits of production to some individuals at the expense of others. Human productive powers tend to grow over time. Periodically, their growth requires a reorganization of co-operative labor, and with it a basic change in social relations of production, in the economic structure of society. Marx calls a periodic change of this kind a "social revolution"; he maintains that important political changes, as well as changes in people's philosophical or religious ideas, can be explained as a function of these fundamental revolutions in the economic structure of society.

The mechanism of social revolutions is the *class struggle*. Social relations of production divide people into groups with a common situation and common interests. These groups are not immediately classes, but they become classes when they organize to promote their class interests through political movements and class ideologies. Class interests are also not directly identical with the interests of the class's individual members, but rather with the interests of class movements. Marx's historical materialism does not hold that people pursue only their individual economic interests. Instead, it holds that they band together to pursue these interests, and in the course of so doing they acquire new desires and interests, collective interests that are not reducible to their individual good, and that sometimes require the sacrifice of individual good. In this respect the model for the Marxian class might just as well have been the Hegelian conception of ethical life. That, too, is a collective activity promoting the good of its participants, and also simultaneously proposing to them a larger collective good, by and large harmonious with their individual good but also sometimes requiring its sacrifice.

As long as class society persists, each mode of production will be characterized by a dominant class, the class whose members are empowered and benefited by the prevailing production relations. Conversely, because the historic mission of a revolutionary class is ultimately the overthrow of one set of production relations and the establishment of another, its class interests can also be identified with a determinate set of production relations, those which empower and benefit its members. Thus, for example, production relations founded on private property and the marketplace benefit the bourgeoisie. It has risen to dominance in the modern world because at this stage in the development of society's productive powers, private property and the marketplace are best suited to utilize and further develop those powers. Because Marx is convinced that this era is about to pass away, he looks to a new and rising class, the proletariat, to become the dominant class in the coming age, bringing with it a new socialist or communist mode of production.

ANALOGIES AND ANTICIPATIONS

There is a greater affinity between the Hegelian and Marxian theories of history than Marx usually acknowledges. G. A. Cohen speaks correctly when he says that "Marx's conception of history preserves the structure of Hegel's but endows it with fresh content."[8] Like Hegel, Marx regards human history as the history of human activity. Both Hegel and Marx identify human history with the development of objective social practice. Through practice, they hold, people develop new capacities and new needs (MEW 3:28/CW 5:42). The liberation of humanity in history consists in progressively altering social forms in order that the capacities may grow and the needs may be satisfied.

Like Hegel, Marx periodizes history according to social stages of development. Each stage exists only as long as the social form can contain the human activities that go on within it. Spirit, Hegel tells us, always imparts to every form as much of its content as that form is capable of holding, and then dissolves the old form in order to create a new one (PhG ¶ 11). Likewise for Marx: "No social formation ever perishes before all the productive powers for which there is room in it have developed; and new, higher relations of production never appear before the material conditions of their existence have matured in the womb of the old society itself" (MEW 13:10/CW 29:264). For both philosophers, the development of human capacities within a given social stage leads to changes in human nature and human goals. Humanity then feels constrained by the inherited social forms and throws them over in order to make way for new and liberating ones. As Marx puts it, in describing the rise of capitalism: "New forces and new passions spring up in the bosom of society, forces and passions which feel themselves to be fettered by that society. It has to be annihilated; it is annihilated" (C 1: 789/867).

In many respects, social classes play the same role in Marx's theory of history as nations play in Hegel's. Nations are bearers and actualizers of a spiritual principle in the form of a political constitution; classes are creators of a new mode of production, founded on new relations representing new human powers of production. The torch of history is passed from one world historical nation to another in an epoch of change; in a period of social revolution, the revolutionary class wrests social dominance from the ruling class. The religion and philosophy of each dominant nation display the timeless truth as it is apprehended from the standpoint of that nation's spiritual principle; the ruling ideas of every age are the ideas of its ruling class.

The two philosophers have similar attitudes to the role of right, morality, and ethical values in periods of radical change. Valid ethical principles depend on actual social structures. The ethical life of a nation and an age is the embodiment of its principle, and its rational validity is limited by the historical validity of that principle. World historical deeds of human liberation typically violate and destroy the prevailing principles of ethical life. But when the time comes to burst the bonds of an old social order, the claims of freedom are higher than the claims of right, morality, or ethics.

Marx's conception of revolutionary practice is similarly amoral or even anti-moral. He regularly uses the terms "morality" and "moralizing criticism" as epithets of abuse against socialists who base working-class demands on standards of right and justice, calling such appeals "outdated verbiage" and "ideological trash" (MEW 19:22/SW 325). When others prevail upon Marx to include bland moral rhetoric in the Rules for the First International, he apologizes for it to Engels: "I was obliged to insert two phrases about 'duty' and 'right'. . . ditto about 'truth, morality and justice,' but these are placed in such a way that they can do no harm" (CW 42:18). Like Hegel, Marx insists that in history "it is always the bad side which finally triumphs over the good side. For the bad side is the one which brings movement to life, which makes history by bringing the struggle to fruition" (MEW 4:140/CW 6:174).[9]

Hegel comes very close to seeing the "rabble" in modern civil society as a sign of incipient radical change. In the Preface to *The Philosophy of Right*, Hegel insists that "the owl of Minerva begins its flight only with the falling of dusk" and even implies that that the modern state, with its bourgeois economic system, is open to philosophical comprehension only because it is "a shape of life grown old" (PR Preface 28). Given Hegel's philosophy of history, it might be expected that the symptoms of its final illness would be easiest to detect in a class with neither rights nor duties whose outlook involves a fundamental alienation from civil society's ethical principles. Hegel and Marx are so close at this point, in fact, that what really needs to be explained is why Hegel did *not* see things this way.

THE FUNDAMENTAL ISSUES

On one level, the obvious answer is that Hegel saw the rabble only as a corrupter of social order, whereas Marx saw the proletariat as a potent revolutionary class, capable of building a new society. It is easy enough to find various explanations for this difference in social perceptions, explanations that are condescending to one or both thinkers. It is equally easy to miss the fact that their respective social perceptions are grounded in their respective theories of history. Hegel's theory of history is political, a history of peoples and the constitutions in which they actualize their national principle, while Marx's is economic, a history of classes and the modes of production in which they achieve social dominance. But is this the basic difference between the two thinkers, a rock-bottom difference between their visions of humanity and history? Or is it in turn the result of differences over something even more fundamental?

In his early critique of Hegel's philosophy of the state, Marx attempts to trace Hegel's state-oriented social theory to the mystifications of Hegelian speculative logic. Following Feuerbach, Marx claims that Hegel's method is to reverse "subject" and "predicate," making the actual subject, the true and active factor, into a mere predicate of the imaginary speculative Idea. Marx finds an instance of this in Hegel's treatment of the state's relation to family and civil society. Hegel treats the state, the merely imaginary community, as the active factor, while the real spheres of social life are held to be its results. "The *actual* relationship of family and civil society to the state is grasped as their *inner imaginary* activity. Family and civil society are the presuppositions of the state; they are really the active forms. But in speculation this is reversed" (MEW 1:206/CW 3:8; PR § 262).

This explanation is question-begging, since it takes for granted not only the metaphysical point that the world does not result from the Idea's activity, but also the point of social theory: that the family and civil society are the active factors, while the state is only their result. Moreover, it provides no explanation why the first error should lead to the second, unless we take seriously the purely polemical suggestion that since the principle of Hegel's method is perversity itself, it is bound to get things exactly backward wherever it is applied.

I want to conclude this essay with an alternative suggestion, beginning from a point that Hegel and Marx have in common. For both, the chief human good is freedom, and freedom in the social sphere consists above all in what I will call "self-transparency." We are free in our social life when we are fully conscious of the meaning of what we do, and do it in light of that consciousness. The aim of *The Philosophy of Right* is to give self-transparency to our participation in the modern state by displaying the state's rational meaning. Marx takes historical materialism to be a liberating doctrine because it removes the ideological veil that covers most social practice; the proletarian revolution will achieve universal human emancipation because it will abolish the class differences that make ideological distortions necessary to social life. Communism, as Marx and Engels put it in *The German Ideology*, is a liberating movement because only under it will individuals consciously "produce the form of intercourse" in which their social life consists (MEW 3:70; cf. CW 5:82). Neither Hegel nor Marx believe that self-transparency is available to people under all historical conditions. Both, in fact, seem to regard humankind as doomed to social self-opacity through much of its history. The basic differences that separate the two thinkers, I want to suggest, arise from their differing conceptions of how and when self-transparency becomes historically possible.

Hegel's theory treats the political state as the focus of social life because it is chiefly there that people attempt to deliberate rationally and collectively about how they will live together. The family, as Hegel understands it, is largely a natural affair, based on feelings and habits; participation in civil society is conscious and rational but oriented more to each person's individual life than to the life of society as a whole. The goal of a nation, in Hegel's view, is to give conscious actuality to its historical principle by turning that principle into a political constitution, in which the collective life of the nation may become self-transparent. Full self-transparency is achieved when a people has matured, so that its constitution is fully formed and the meaning of its national principle is fully available to both practical and philosophical understanding.

For Hegel, however, self-transparency is ephemeral. As a nation achieves knowledge of its principle, it also becomes aware of that principle in its determinacy, its limitations. The process of spirit's self-knowledge then becomes one of self-alienation, giving birth to a new principle that can become self-transparent only after it too has been actualized and reflected on. Hegel's conception of historical agency therefore entails that fundamental historical change, such as world historical individuals achieve, can never be self-transparent, since self-transparency is possible only for social forms that have reached maturity. True freedom is not possible for the agent who creates history; it is achievable mainly by the philosopher who reflects on a finished product of history whose process of formation is over (PR Preface 28).

Marx, on the other hand, thinks that up to now self-transparency has been largely an illusion. Human beings have never yet united to produce the social forms their activities inhabit, and class divisions between them have made it necessary for their consciousness of these forms to be systematically distorted and mystified by one class illusion or another. Political consciousness is only the most abstract and most persistent of these illusions, just as the political state is only the illusory form given to people's true common life in civil society. In the state "there is the illusion that right is based on will, that is, on will divorce from its real basis, on *free* will" (MEW 3:62/ CW 5:91). People will achieve genuine freedom only when their true common life, in civil society, is the object of "the will of united individuals" who are no longer subject to class divisions (MEW 3:70, CW 5:81). Human freedom, once won, will be lasting, not self-undermining. The communist revolution will not be the end of history, but only the end of human "pre-history" (MEW 13:10/CW 29:264). Communism, although "not as such the goal of human development" (MEW Erg.1:546/CW 3:306), is nevertheless "the riddle of history solved, and knowing itself as this solution" (MEW Erg.1: 536/CW 3:297).

Marx is further convinced that the action by which humanity is liberated will itself be free action, in other words, that its revolutionary practice will be self-transparent. The proletarian movement is distinguished from earlier movements of the oppressed by its clear perception of the nature of itself as a class and of the class struggle. They show this, Marx thinks, in their disillusionment with traditional ideological forms: religion, politics, right, morality. Communist revolutionaries are the revolutionary vanguard of the proletariat because they "clearly understand the line of march, the conditions, and the ultimate general results of the proletarian movement" (MEW 4:475/CW 6:497).

THE LIMITS OF SELF-TRANSPARENCY

Hegel's views about the nature and limits of self-transparency are derived directly from his conception of mind or spirit as "self-restoring sameness," making itself by making objects in accordance with its own self-conception, and then learning what it truly is only through an interpretation of what it has already made. On this view, self-transparency is possible for a social order only after the process of its formation is complete, for only through that process does spirit give itself the capacity to comprehend itself by interpreting its own deeds. The main idea here was articulated by Karl Popper, who confusedly thought it refuted "historicist" theories in the Hegelian tradition. Popper argues that we cannot predict the course of human history to the extent that it depends on the further growth of human knowledge, since that growth is in principle unpredictable by us.[10] Since we cannot predict the historical future, he warns us to avoid all attempts at radical social change and to content ourselves with cautious, piecemeal social experimentation.[11]

Hegel thinks we cannot understand the meaning of our own world historical deeds because their meaning depends on what those deeds are destined to bring to birth, but the comprehension of that meaning in turn depends on the ways in which spirit's self-knowledge will grow in the process. Spirit's possible self-transparency thus extends to the historical past, and to the present insofar as the philosophical mind is capable of "comprehending its own time in thoughts." But we can no more see into the future than we can "jump over Rhodes"; self-transparency belongs only to the "grey in grey" of philosophy, not to the golden tree of life that sends forth its living branches (PR Preface 27–28).[12]

Both Hegel and Popper exaggerate the conclusion to which this line of argument entitles them. Popper admits that his argument forbids us only those predictions about the future that depend on the future growth of our knowledge.[13] Given that concession, Popper's argument cannot rule out the possibility of radical social action, combined with rational predictions of its success, based on what we *already* know. Since Popper gives us no ground for thinking that the growth of our knowledge will decisively determine the course of social change, his attempt at a quick, decisive refutation of every form of "historicism" falls far short of its aim.

Hegel is in a much better position in this regard, since his theory implies that it is spirit's nature continually to transform its nature in fundamental ways by deepening its self-knowledge, and it locates this self-transformation mainly in social structures. That means that his theory does imply that radical social change will occur, and that the nature of this change will decisively depend on the growth of human knowledge. More specifically, it implies that rational knowledge of the ethical principles of a social order is available only after the order has reached maturity. This means that Hegel's theory does imply that those who take the first steps in creating a new social order cannot have a rational comprehension of the nature of what they are creating. They cannot predict what future society will be like, because they lack the knowledge of spirit necessary to understand how the new society will actualize spirit's nature.

It does not follow, however, that world historical action cannot be self-transparent, or that people cannot undertake radical social change with a rational knowledge of the fact that they are creating a new and higher social order. People might do this, consistently with Hegel's theory, if their action is rationally transparent to itself, in its revolutionary character, but in a way that does not depend on a determinate conception of the social order they are creating. Processes involving the growth of our knowledge are in principle unpredictable in some ways, but they need not be unpredictable in every way. A team of researchers looking for a cure for AIDS cannot in principle predict exactly what the cure will turn out to be. But after some preliminary research, they might be in a position to make justified predictions about whether the cure will be found at all, the general relation of the cure to the etiology of the disease, the type of research that will lead to the cure, and approximately how long it will take to find it. In a similar way, even if Hegel's theory is correct and we cannot predict the determinate nature of the next social order in which spirit will actualize itself, we still might be able to say some things about the present social action that will lead to this social order. We might be able to identify, for instance, the main social problems in the present order that the new social order will have to solve, and the social movement that will bring the new order into being. To this extent, at least, members of that movement might achieve self-transparency about their historical agency.

In this regard, Marx's own conception of proletarian revolutionary practice is entirely consistent with the strictures of a Hegelian theory of history. Marx pretends to no clear conception of what post-capitalist society will be like. (To that extent, he is simply not a "historicist" at all in Popper's sense.) Marx declines to write "recipes for the cookshops of the future" (C 1:25/99) because he insists that the nature of future society will depend on "a series of historic processes, transforming circumstances and men" (CW 22:335). Marx does think that the downfall of capitalism, and the victory of the working class, are both inevitable (C 1:12/91; cf. MEW 4:474/CW 6:496). That is because he thinks he can identify certain irrationalities in present-day capitalist society, which that society is incapable of solving, and also the class in present-day society that has both the greatest capacity to solve these problems and the strongest interest in solving them. The self-transparency of the proletariat's agency for Marx consists not in predicting the nature of the society the proletariat will produce, but in knowing what the proletarian movement itself is. That is just what Marx and Engels are telling us when they say that "communism is not for us a state of affairs to be brought about, an ideal to which reality will have to adjust itself. We call communism the actual movement which is abolishing the present state of affairs" (MEW 3:35/CW 5:49). As communists, in this sense, we can engage in what Hegel would call "world historical" action, and we can do so with self-transparency.

Of course Marx may have been mistaken about the working-class movement, or even about capitalism. Perhaps no world historical agent has ever been self-transparent or ever will be. The issue between Hegel and Marx is whether Hegel was right in thinking that his theory of history precluded the possibility of self-transparent world historical agency. I have tried to show that he was not; and that Marx's conception of proletarian revolutionary practice, whatever truth or falsity it may contain in other respects, is a conception of self-transparent world historical agency that is consistent with the strictures of a Hegelian philosophy of history. Whether self-transparent world historical practice has ever been or will ever be actually achieved, Hegel's theory does not rule it out. Hence there is no reason to give priority from the standpoint of self-transparency to politically oriented self-reflection, as Hegel did, and as he thought we must do. If, as I have suggested, this is the fundamental issue between Hegel and Marx, then we should conclude that on that issue Marx was right.

NOTES

1 All translations from the works of Hegel, Marx, and Engels are my own. Standard English translations will normally be cited along with the original, with English pagination following German pagination, separated by a slash (/).

Writing of G. W. F. Hegel (1770–1831)

Werke   *Hegel: Werke: Theorie Werkausgabe.* Frankfurt: Suhrkamp Verlag, 1970. Cited by volume.

NP   *Nürnberger Propaedeutik* (1808–1811), *Werke* 4.

NR   *Ueber die wissenschaftliche Behandlungsarten des Naturrechts* (1802), *Werke* 2.
       Natural Law, trans. T. M. Knox. Philadelphia: University of Pennsylvania Press, 1975. Cited by page number.

PhG   *Phänomenologie des Geistes* (1807), *Werke* 3.
        Phenomenology of Spirit, trans. A. V. Miller Oxford: Oxford
        University Press, 1977. Cited by paragraph (¶) number.

PR   *Philosophie des Rechts* (1821), *Werke* 7.
        Hegel's Philosophy of Right, trans. H. B. Nisbet, ed. Allen
        W. Wood. Cambridge: Cambridge University Press, 1992.
        Cited by paragraph (§) number. Remarks are indicated by an
        "R", additions by an "A". Preface and sometimes longer
        paragraphs cited by page number in German edition only.

VG   *Die Vernunft in der Geschichte*, ed. J. Hoffmeister.
        Hambrug, 1955.
        Lectures on the Philosophy of World History: Introduction,
        trans. H. B. Nisbet. Cambridge: Cambridge University Press,
        1975. Cited by page number.

VPR   *Vorlesungen über Rechtsphilosophie*, ed. K.-H. Ilting.
        Stuttgart: Frommann Verlag, 1974. Including notes and tran-
        scriptions from Hegel's lectures of 1818–1819 (transcription
        by C. G. Homeyer), 1821–1822, 1822–1823 (transcription by
        H. G. Hotho), 1824–1825 (transcription by K. G. von
        Griesheim), 1831 (transcription by D. F. Strauss). Cited by
        volume and page number.

VPR17   *Die Philosophie des Rechts: Die Mitschriften Wannenmann
        (Heidelberg 1817–1818) und Homeyer (Berlin 1818/19)*, ed.
        von K.-H. Ilting. Stuttgart: Klett-Cotta Verlag, 1983. Cited
        by page number.

VPR19   *Philosophie des Rechts: Die Vorlesung von 1819/1820*,
        anonymous transcription or transcriptions, ed. Dieter
        Henrich. Frankfurt: Suhrkamp Verlag, 1983. Cited by page
        number.

In writings cited by paragraph (§), a comma used before "R" or "A" means
"and". Thus: "PR § 33,A" means: "PR § 33 and the additional to § 33"; "PR
§ 270,R,A" means: "PR § 270 and the remark to § 270 and the addition to §
270."

Writings of Karl Marx (1818–1883) and Friedrich Engels (1821–1895)

MEW   *Marx Engels Werke*. Berlin: Dietz Verlag, 1961–1966. Cited
        by volume and page number.

CW   *Marx Engels Collected Works*. New York: International Pub-
        lishers, 1975–. Cited by volume and page number.

C   *Das Kapital*, MEW 23–25. Cited by volume (of *Das Kapital*,
        not of MEW) and page number.

Capital, Volume 1. Trans. Ben Fowkes. New York: Random House, 1977. Cited by page number.

SC   *Selected Correspondence.* New York: International Publishers, 1965. Cited by page number.

SW   *Selected Works* in one volume. New York: International Publishers, 1968.

2 The leading Marxist theorist of this period, Karl Kautsky (1854–1938), was so little acquainted with Hegel that his few perfunctory references to "dialectics" are generally couched in the utterly un-Hegelian jargon of "thesis-antithesis-synthesis," taken over from Hegel's vulgar expositors. See Karl Kautsky, *The Materialist Conception of History,* ed. John Kautsky (New Haven: Yale University Press, 1988), 34–37, 217–19.

3 Lenin, *Selected Works* (New York: International Publishers, 1971), 579–80.

4 Engels, SW 598; Lenin, *Selected Works,* pp. 21–22.

5 Karl Korsch, *Marxism and Philosophy* (1923), trans. Fred Halliday (New York: Monthly Review, 1970), 35.

6 Theodor Adorno, *Negative Dialectics,* trans. E. B. Ashton (New York: Continuum Press, 1973), 11.

7 Even modern society as a whole might be called "bourgeois" for Hegel in the sense that it is the distinctively modern institution of civil society that determines the modern form of the more traditional social institutions of the family and the political state. Because individuals must participate in the economic sphere as bourgeois, as concrete persons and subjects, there is no longer any legitimacy to the "clan" (*Stamm*), the extended family or wider kinship group, around which feudal and older agricultural economic institutions were often organized (PR § 172). The only legitimate family is the patriarchal bourgeois nuclear family, represented in the public realm by the father (PR § 177). Modern civil society, as distinct from feudal social organization, also distinguishes the modern state, whose sovereignty consists in the rational unity and public responsibility of political functions, from the feudal state, in which political offices were the hereditary property of noble families (PR § 278). The principle of subjective freedom also requires that the modern state include representative institutions, so that public business may be open to general public concern and influence (PR § 301). Hegel even traces the political form of constitutional monarchy, which he thinks most appropriate to the modern state, to the principle of individual subjectivity. To accord with this principle, the state's sovereignty must take the form of an individual subject, in whom the objectively rational content of state policies, as determined by a professional civil service

under the watchful guidance of representative institutions, is given the "moment of final decision" on the subjective side (PR § 279).

8 G. A. Cohen, *Karl Marx's Theory of History: A Defence* (Princeton: Princeton University Press, 1978), 26.

9 See my book, *Karl Marx* (London: Routledge, 1981), Chap. IX–X; "Marx's Immoralism," in *Marx en perspective* ed. *Chavance (Paris: Editions de l'Ecole des Hautes Etudes en Sciences Sociales, 1985); "Marx Against Morality," in A Companion to Ethics* ed. Singer (Oxford: Blackwell, 1990).

10 Karl Popper, *The Poverty of Historicism* (Boston: Beacon Press, 1957), ix–x.

11 Ibid., pp. 83–88.

12 Compare Goethe, *Faust* I: lines 2038–2039:

Grey, dear friend, is all theory,
And green alone life's golden tree.

13 Popper, *The Poverty of Historicism*, p. x.

14 Hegel and analytic philosophy

What I think, namely *that* something is true, is always quite distinct from the fact that I think it. . . . That "to be true" *means* to be thought in a certain way is, therefore, certainly false. Yet this assertion plays the most essential part in Kant's 'Copernican Revolution' of philosophy, and renders worthless the whole mass of modern literature, to which that revolution has given rise, and which is called Epistemology.[1]

It is often thought that analytic philosophy arises, at least in part, from a reaction against Hegel, or against philosophy inspired by Hegel. To some extent this is correct. The philosophy of Bertrand Russell and G.E. Moore in the first decade or so of this century, which was enormously influential for subsequent analytic philosophy, was developed in conscious reaction to idealist views that owed much to Hegel.[2] This fact, however, does not settle the question of the influence of Hegel, either on Russell and Moore or on analytic philosophy more generally; all that it does is to give us a way of posing the question. And the question is a complex one. Besides the general difficulties involved in tracing the influence of a view as complex as Hegel's, there is also a particular problem arising from the relation between Kant and Hegel. The philosophical views against which Russell and Moore were reacting, and which they grouped under the rubric "Idealism," were both Hegelian and Kantian. The contrast between Kantianism and Hegelianism, moreover, cannot be pressed too far: Kantian themes survive in Hegel's work, although modified or transposed to some extent, and Kant himself

445

can be interpreted as being, to a greater or lesser extent, a precursor of Hegelian ideas.

We might summarise the contention of this essay by saying that while Russell and Moore are to some extent reacting against the specifically Hegelian elements in Idealism, it is the Kantian elements that are the most important to understanding their reaction against Idealism. To put the point another way: the aspects of post-Kantian Idealism that are most important to understanding the early work of Russell and Moore are already present in Kant, at least if Kant is himself interpreted as a precursor of Idealism. The issue of the interpretation of Kant that this formulation raises is crucial. Both Russell and Moore interpreted Kant unequivocally as an Idealist. In this they followed the post-Kantian Idealist tradition in which they were educated, so the reading of Kant is an important way in which the Hegelians influenced Russell and Moore, and influenced them positively, rather than by way of reaction. If we are correct in saying that the most-influential work of Russell and Moore is best understood as a reaction against Kant (or Kant as interpreted by Hegel), then we are faced with the relevance of this fact to later analytic philosophy. Here it is even clearer than in the case of Russell and Moore that our focus should be on Kantian ideas, or on ideas common to Kant and Hegel, rather than on specifically Hegelian ideas. We shall attempt to illustrate this point by putting forward a schematic interpretation of the development of analytic philosophy that emphasises its relationship to, and rejection of, some crucial Kantian ideas.

Two significant limitations of our discussion should be noted at the outset. First, we discuss only theoretical philosophy, not practical philosophy. The crucial figures in the early period of analytic philosophy – say, Frege, Russell, Moore, Wittgenstein (in his early work), and Carnap – are, with one exception, noted for their work in theoretical philosophy – logic, metaphysics, epistemology, philosophy of language, and so on – rather than practical philosophy – ethics, political philosophy, and so on. The one exception is Moore, and it is arguable that his work in ethics involves conceiving of it as theoretical rather than practical (see note 33, below). This emphasis on the theoretical represents an important bias of analytic philosophy, at least until comparatively recently. In this respect there is a marked contrast between analytic philosophy and that of Kant (the situation with regard to Hegel is more complex: he did not accept Kant's doctrine of the primacy of the practical, and aimed to reinstate the idea of *theoretical* knowledge of the unconditioned; he did, however, place great weight on the practical, and aimed to incorporate it into his philosophy rather than simply leave it aside). In what follows we shall in general simply confine ourselves to theoretical philosophy; we shall, however, make some remarks on the reasons for the contrast, in this respect, between analytic philosophy and Kantianism (and, with qualifications, Hegelianism).

The second limitation is that we more or less confine ourselves to discussing the influence of Kant and Hegel on analytic philosophy as that influence is transmitted via the work of Russell and Moore. That is to say, we do not consider whether other formative influences on analytic philosophy may also have transmitted the influence of Kant and of Hegel. In particular, we do not discuss the influence of Kant on Frege, and we largely ignore the influence of Kant on Carnap and other members of the Vienna Circle. The reasons for this are in part purely practical: even as limited, our task is large for a single essay. There is also, however, the fact that the Kant who influenced Frege and Carnap was much more distant from Hegel than was the Kant who influenced Russell and Moore. As Sluga points out, "Hegelian idealism had in fact completely collapsed in Germany" by the middle of the nineteenth century.[3] Revivals of Kant later in the century emphasized the role of natural science in Kantianism. The more speculative elements of the view, which indicate its kinship with Hegelianism, were largely downplayed. In addition, it is also important that the Kantian elements in Frege's thought were largely ignored or unrecognized, at least in English-speaking countries, until the 1970s.[4]

Let us begin with a brief discussion of the main philosophical trends in Britain in the nineteenth century. Since these trends are the background to the early work of Russell and Moore, our discussion will enable us to bring the task of this essay into better focus. The initial reception of Kant, especially in literary circles, led to developments that to some extent parallel Hegel's thought.[5] These developments did not issue in sustained philosophical treatment. They did, however, provoke, by way of reaction, the resurgence of an empiricist view that based itself chiefly in psychology; the work of J.S. Mill, in particular, was very influential. This psychologistic empiricism also provoked a reaction, which took the form of a re-discovery and adaptation of Kant and, especially, of Hegel. Beginning with the publication of Stirling's *The Secret of Hegel* in 1865,[6] Idealism gradually became the orthodox view among most active philosophers in Britain. William Wallace's *The Logic of Hegel*[7] was an important translation of a portion of Hegel's encyclopedia. Edward Caird, like Wallace a Scot at Oxford, wrote influential books on Kant and Hegel.[8] But the most systematic, and deservedly the most influential, of this first generation of British Idealists was T.H. Green. It is significant that one of Green's major works was a sustained attack on Empiricism, in particular on the works of Locke and Hume. F.H. Bradley, also at Oxford, articulated a metaphysical view that owes much to Idealism, even though it balks at many idealist conclusions. (We shall discuss the views of Green and Bradley later.) At Cambridge perhaps the most important figure was McTaggart, who worked out his own version of Idealism by means of critical commentaries on Hegel.[9]

Under the influence of McTaggart and others at Cambridge, Russell and Moore became idealists in their student days, more indebted to Hegel, as they interpreted him, than to any other dominant figure. This allegiance lasted until the late 1890s. Russell's first philosophical book, *An Essay on the Foundations of Geometry*,[10] clearly shows him to be an Idealist of a broadly Hegelian kind. He says, for example, that he has learned most in logic "from Mr. Bradley, and next to him, from Sigwart and Mr. Bosanquet" (*Foundations of Geometry*, Preface). What he means by logic here is something clearly derived from Kant's conception of transcendental logic, as laying down the necessary conditions of experience (see below, pp. 451–54). Thus his test of being *a priori*, which he describes as being "purely logical," is "Would experience be impossible if a certain axiom or postulate were denied?" (*Foundations of Geometry*, p. 3). Russell gives an Hegelian twist to this Kantian idea, saying: "All knowledge involves a recognition of diversity in relation, or, if we prefer, identity in difference" (*Foundations of Geometry*, p. 82). While the details of the book owe most to Kant, the overall conclusion is Hegelian: that there are unavoidable contradictions in the conception of space, and therefore also in Geometry, and that these contradictions can be overcome by transition to a more-comprehensive subject (see *Foun-*

dations of Geometry, pp. 188, 201). In general, the book bears out the account he later gave of his philosophical views in the 1890s:[11]

I was at this time a full-fledged Hegelian, and I aimed at constructing a complete dialectic of the sciences. . . . I accepted the Hegelian view that none of the sciences is quite true, since all depend upon some abstraction, and every abstraction leads, sooner or later, to contradiction. Wherever Kant and Hegel were in conflict, I sided with Hegel.

Moore's idealist period was shorter, and perhaps less deep, but there is no doubt that he too was for a while an adherent of Idealism. His first published philosophical work was "In What Sense, if Any, Do Past and Future Time Exist?".[12] In that essay he resoundingly claims that the past and the future, and indeed the present, do *not* exist in the full sense: "neither Past, Present, nor Future exists, if by existence we are to mean the ascription of full Reality, not merely existence as Appearance" (p. 240).

Beginning in 1898, both Russell and Moore rejected the Idealism which they previously accepted, and rapidly evolved a rival realist view, which we shall call Platonic Atomism. In this initial step it was Moore who led and Russell who followed.[13] Much of the force of the view, however, and its appeal, came from the fact that in Russell's hands it became interwoven with the new logic that he constructed, following Peano (and, later, Frege). In the period, say, 1900 to 1914, Russell began to articulate themes that were of enormous significance for the subsequent development of analytic philosophy: the use of mathematical logic as a tool or method in philosophy; the use of this tool to argue not only (as Frege had) for the reducibility of mathematics to logic, but also for the reducibility of empirical knowlege in general to knowledge of sense-data and abstract entities; a concern with propositions and meaning, and with analysis of propositions as an explicit philosophical method; and an increasingly conscious attention to symbols. Moore too began to develop views that later became influential, especially his conception of philosophical analysis and his appeal to commonsense, both by extension of, and by reaction to, the views that he held in the initial rejection of Idealism.

Platonic Atomism, the early philosophy of Russell and Moore, is not merely anti-Hegelian, but is quite generally opposed to all forms of Idealism, including, as Russell and Moore held, Kantianism. It is in fact Kant, far more than Hegel, more even than contemporary British Idealists, whom both of them discuss and attack in their rejection of Idealism. (To give a crude measure, Kant has twenty entries in the index to Russell's *Principles of Mathematics*,[14] some of which are extended discussions of several pages; Hegel has five, three of which are passing references; Bradley has ten.) We shall focus on the thoroughgoing rejection, by Russell and Moore, of Kant's Copernican Revolution, and on the related ideas of necessary conditions of possible experience and of the transcendental. This emphasis on Kant, however, by no means eliminates Hegel from our consideration. In attacking Kant's Copernican Revolution, Russell and Moore took themselves – with good reason – also to be attacking a fundamental assumption not only of Kant but of Hegel and all the post-Kantian Idealists.[15] So their opposition to Hegelianism, as well as to Kant himself, is expressed in their rejection of Kant. It is also relevant that the interpretation of Kant that Russell and Moore assume is largely that of Hegel and his followers; even their criticisms of Kant can be seen as Hegelian criticisms pressed to an extreme degree. So, paradoxical as it may sound, part of Hegel's influence on Russell and Moore shows up precisely in their opposition to Kant, even though this opposition is extended to include Hegel himself. (The paradox here is only apparent. There is nothing inconsistent in the idea that reading a certain author may inspire one to adopt certain standards, which one then finds the author himself does not fully live up to. One might, for example, be inspired by the comparative rigor of Frege's presentation of logic to adopt standards of rigor that Frege himself does not meet.) We shall also see that some of the details of Platonic Atomism, the particular shape that the reaction to Kant's Copernican Revolution takes in Russell and Moore, are to be partly explained in terms of their reaction also against particular doctrines of Hegel. The overall picture, however, is distorted if we see those Hegelian doctrines as central to the rejection of Idealism.

In the remainder of this essay we shall proceed as follows. First, we shall explain salient features of Kant's Copernican Revolution, and the related ideas of the necessary conditions of knowledge and of the transcendental. Second, we shall examine the role that those ideas play in the sort of Hegelianism that Russell and Moore were reacting to by discussing the philosophy of T.H. Green; this will also enable us to consider the Hegelian interpretation and criticism of Kant (here too we shall at least mention the views of F.H. Bradley, who had considerable direct influence on Russell and Moore). Third, we shall argue that Platonic Atomism can be seen in large measure as based on a rejection of those Kantian ideas. This rejection can itself be understood against the background of the Hegelian interpretation and criticism of those Kantian ideas. Finally, we shall attempt to show that it is a significant fact about analytic philosophy in general that it follows Russell and Moore in rejecting those ideas. Obviously we cannot carry out any of these tasks in detail; the last, in particular, would require nothing less than a complete interpretation of analytic philosophy, which could hardly be presented and defended in a single essay. Nevertheless, we can perhaps do enough to make plausible a certain picture of the relation of analytic philosophy to Kant and to Hegel.

Let us begin, then, with Kant's fundamental revolution in theoretical philosophy, what has come to be known as Kant's "Copernican Revolution." In the Preface to the second edition of the *Critique of Pure Reason*,[16] Kant describes the revolution as follows:

Hitherto it has been assumed that all our knowledge must conform to objects. But all attempts to extend our knowledge of objects by establishing something in regard to them *a priori*, by means of concepts, have, on this assumption, ended in failure. We must therefore make trial whether we may not have more success in the tasks of metaphysics, if we suppose that objects must conform to our knowledge. (B, xvi)

What is the basis for these ideas? How can we legitimately suppose that objects must "conform to our knowledge"? The answer is that we are to focus not on objects themselves, considered apart from our possible knowledge, but on "the *intuition* of objects," on objects considered "as object[s] of the senses" (B, xvii). This shift of focus to experience, or to objects insofar as they are experienceable, makes the crucial difference:

experience is itself a species of knowledge which involves understanding; and understanding has rules which I must presuppose as being in me prior to objects being given to me, and therefore as being *a priori*. They find expression in *a priori* concepts to which all objects of experience necessarily conform. (B, xvii–xviii)

Here we see the crucial idea that experience – and therefore any-thing of which we can have experience – has necessary conditions. In a similar vein Kant describes the crucial issue for the transcenden-tal deduction of *a priori* concepts as being whether those concepts "must be recognised as *a priori* conditions of the possibility of experi-ence" (A 94–B 126).

Kant's "Copernican Revolution" – the shift of focus from objects as they are in themselves to the possibility of our experience of objects, and the introduction of the idea of the necessary conditions of the possibility of experience – is fundamental to his thought as a whole. Most obviously, perhaps, it gives rise to questions about what the conditions of possible experience are. Kant calls questions of this sort "transcendental," by which he means that they "concern the *a priori* possibility of knowledge" (A 55–B 80; cf., for example, B 25). The fundamental question of theoretical philosophy, which the *Cri-tique of Pure Reason* attempts to answer, now becomes: What are the conditions of the possibility of experience? The answer to this question will also show us to what extent we can have *a priori* knowledge of objects which is more than trivial or tautologous; knowledge of this sort, which Kant called synthetic *a priori* knowl-edge, is to be based on the conditions of the possibility of experience. An immediate consequence of this is that synthetic *a priori* princi-ples are valid only of objects of possible experience. The attempt to use such principles to gain knowledge of what is beyond possible experience is illegitimate; hence traditional metaphysics, purport-ing to give us knowledge of the supersensible, is also illegitimate. Kant argues, further, that the assumption that synthetic *a priori* principles are valid of things as they are in themselves, independent of our possible knowledge, is not only unjustified but actually leads to contradictions. Such contradictions can be avoided only by the doctrine that the objects that we seek to know are not things in themselves.

The "Copernican Revolution," and the consequences of it indi-cated above, are crucial for the distinction between the theoretical and the practical, as Kant draws it. The most obvious point concerns the limitation of our knowledge to objects of possible experience. This is a negative result, which denies the possibility of speculative metaphysical inquiry of the usual (and always dubious) kind. For Kant, however, it is precisely this limit on knowledge, on the theoretical, that leaves room for the practical. The belief in freedom, in the strict sense, the belief in God, and the belief in personal immortality are for Kant properly based on the practical demands of human life. If such matters were possible objects of theoretical knowledge, however, then it would be quite unjustified to hold those beliefs on that sort of basis. It is a paradox, perhaps, that Kant thus sees his exclusion of those matters from the realm of possible theoretical knowledge as rescuing them; rather than being the subject of endless and inconclusive metaphysical debate, they can be securely established on the basis of our practical needs. Another point, less clear but perhaps no less important, is Kant's emphasis on the importance of the *activity* of the mind in constituting the knowable world. This undermines the idea that what is due to us and our actions must be merely subjective, and that objectivity must be located in a realm of objects distinct from us. Thus it opens the way for the idea that there may be a viewpoint that is based in practice but is nonetheless objective.

While our account of Kant's views must remain very schematic, it is worth supplementing the above sketch with some points that will be particularly significant in what follows. To begin, Kant distinguishes two sources of human knowledge: sensibility, which is the source of intuitions, and understanding, which is the source of concepts. Kant sometimes writes as if sensibility presented us with *data*, with raw sensory experience, and understanding subsequently conceptualized it. But this view of the distinction, and the very idea of the distinction, has often been found problematic. First, we cannot be conscious of, cannot really experience, the "raw sensory experience" with which sensibility is alleged to present us; the alleged experience, as we shall see, does not conform to the conditions of the possibility of experience. And Kant himself seems to undermine the very idea of the distinction by saying, in a footnote, that intuition in fact presupposes the operations of the understanding (see B 160, note 17). Of the two faculties, Kant identifies sensibility with receptivity and understanding with spontaneity; both faculties are necessary for knowledge (A 50–51–B 74–75). Understanding is also identified as the faculty of judgment, as the source of concepts (A 68–69–B 93–94). (The only use for concepts is in judgment, so that the faculty of judgment is also the faculty of concepts; judgments do not simply exist but are the results of acts of the mind, of spontaneity.) One might suppose, from this account, that facts about understanding might give rise to conditions on the possibility of judgment, and thus of discursive knowledge, but not to conditions on the possibility of experience. Such, however, is not Kant's view. He argues, by means we shall discuss shortly, that the sort of fundamental unity that is manifest in a judgment is required for any kind of experience. For there to be any kind of experience, on this account, there must be a unifying act, a *synthesis;* and this act is at bottom the same as that required for judgment: "The same function which gives unity to the various representations *in a judgment* also gives unity to the mere synthesis of various representations *in an intuition*" (A 79–B104–5). Because of this identification Kant holds – notoriously – that the various conditions for the possibility of experience can more or less be read off from the various possible forms of judgment, where these latter are adapted from standard accounts of judgment, which have their antecedents in Aristotle's logic.

The basis for Kant's arguments for the conclusions indicated above is that any experience that is possible for me must be an experience that I can become aware of myself as having: "It must be possible for the 'I think' to accompany all of my representations" (B 132). The fundamental *a priori* condition, to which all of our possible knowledge is subject, is that our knowledge is the knowledge of a self-conscious, persisting and unified subject:

There can be in us no cognitive states [*Erkenntnisse*], no connection of one [cognitive state] with another, without that unity of consciousness which precedes all data of intuitions, and by relation to which representation of objects is alone possible. This pure original unchangeable consciousness I shall name *transcendental apperception*. (A 107)

This unity of consciousness cannot be *given;* it is possible only as the result of an *act* of synthesis. All our experience is thus mediated by such acts and thus by whatever conditions make those acts possible. Hence those conditions are also the conditions for the possibility of experience, and conditions that must apply to objects insofar as they are possible objects of experience.

We now turn to a discussion of T.H. Green, perhaps the most prominent of the British neo-Hegelians. One aim here is to examine the sort of Idealism that would have been familiar to Russell and Moore. A second aim is to see how that form of Idealism makes crucial use of the Kantian nexus of ideas sketched above, while also criticising Kant from a broadly Hegelian perspective. We should note that although Green is dubious about the dialectical method, he enthusiastically endorses what he takes to be Hegel's most important conclusions:[18]

> That there is one spiritual self-conscious being, of which all that is real is the activity or expression; that we are related to this spritual being, not merely as parts of the world which is its expression, but as partakers in some inchoate measure of the self-consciousness through which it at once constitutes and distinguishes itself from the world; that this participation is the source of morality and religion; this we take to be the vital truth which Hegel had to teach.

Green wrote in a context in which Empiricism was widely accepted, especially in the form of the views of J.S. Mill.[19] It is not surprising, therefore, that his own views were worked out and presented in the course of a criticism of Empiricism.[20] This criticism was explicitly Kantian in character, relying absolutely on the nexus of Kantian ideas discussed above. Green begins his discussion of the empiricists by focusing on a central concept in their thought, that of an "idea" or "impression." In this central concept, however, he finds a crucial ambiguity: Is it to be taken as the mere physiological occurrence of sensation, or as the simplest kind of knowledge? (see *Works* I, p. 13). The use of a single concept to span both ideas assumes that the simplest sort of knowledge, at least, has no presuppositions beyond mere receptivity. In contrast to this view, Green insists that there is no knowledge that is directly and immediately *given*. Like Kant and Hegel, Green holds that all knowledge is mediated. Even sensation, or "feeling," which the empiricists had taken as paradigmatic of the "merely given," in fact presupposes more than mere receptivity. The focus of the argument for this conclusion is on *relations*; experience, Green claims, requires not merely feelings but also relations among feelings. Strictly speaking, indeed, Green's view is that without relations, feelings are not even possible objects of thought; without relations, "the sensations would be nothing" (*Works*, I, p. 175; see also *Works*, I, p. 36). Hence he claims that knowledge cannot arise merely from the occurrence of feeling, but presupposes at least relations among feelings. And since these relations, he insists, cannot themselves be feelings, they must be imposed by the self-conscious mind to which the feelings are presented. This view, Green says, implies

> that the single impression in its singleness is what it is through relation to another, which must therefore be present along with it; and that thus, though they may occur in a perpetual flux of succession . . . yet, just so far as they are qualified by likeness or unlikeness to each other, they must be taken out of that succession by something which is not itself in it, but is indivisibly present to every moment of it. This we may call soul, or mind, or what we will. (*Works,* I, p. 176)

Hence experience, even of the simplest sort, presupposes a unifying agency, a self-conscious subject of experience; and this presupposition makes the crucial difference. Thus he says of "feeling" that "we cannot know it except under those conditions of self-consciousness, the logical categories" (*Works,* I, p. 198).

A similar point of view is presented in what is perhaps Green's most systematic statement of his views, *Prolegomena to Ethics.*[21] The reliance on Kantian ideas is even more explicit: "We have to return once more to that analysis of the conditions of knowledge, which forms the basis of all Critical Philosophy whether called by the name of Kant or no" (p. 12). Green summarizes the first thirty pages of the book by saying: "So far we have been following Kant in enquiring what is necessary to constitute, what is implied in there being, a world of experience – an objective world, if by that is meant a world of ascertainable laws, as distinguished from an unknowable world of things-in-themselves"; and by saying that the answer, as well as the question, is Kantian: "We have followed him [Kant] also . . . in maintaining that a single active self-conscious principle . . . is necessary to constitute such a world" (*Prolegomena to Ethics,* p. 45). Green explicitly identifies the "unifying principle" that he takes to be necessary for the possibility of experience with Kant's synthetic unity of apperception (*Prolegomena to Ethics,* pp. 39–40).

The nexus of ideas that I have grouped under the heading "Kant's Copernican Revolution" is thus fundamental to Green's philosophy. But Green also criticises Kant. He sees Kant's philosophy as containing tensions or contradictions that, when resolved, lead to a rather different view closer to that of Hegel; this view of Kant and his significance is itself Hegelian. Some, at least, of the contradictions that Green found in Kant were also the focus of Hegel's criticism of Kant,[22] and, as we have seen, Green holds that the view to which he led is, at least in outline, Hegel's.

We can divide Green's criticisms of Kant into two broad categories. First, Green, like Hegel, criticizes two related Kantian dualisms: the distinction between the knowable world of appearance and the unknowable world of things as they are in themselves, and the distinction between intuitions and concepts, between the material that is given to the understanding and the form that is imposed by the understanding.[23] Green's argument against these dualisms is intricate, but the point that underlies it can be briefly encapsulated. If we take the Kantian view seriously, he holds, then it is inconsistent to claim that we have knowledge about – or even that we can think of – things that are not subject to the necessary conditions of knowledge.[24] But on the Kantian view, both things as they are in themselves and the raw material of experience would fall into this category. The idea that there are such things, on Green's view, is thus absurd. The rejection of a raw material of experience is important, for Green concludes from it that the only true given is conscious experience. The Kantian attempt to analyze experience into the given matter, on the one hand, and the imposed form, on the other, fails; while we can of course talk of the form and the matter of experience, our ability to do so itself depends upon experience – so that form and matter are each intelligible only as abstractions that presuppose experience. Each aspect of experience presupposes the other and the whole; experience is ultimate and unanalyzable.

The other general issue on which Green thinks it necessary to go beyond Kant can be approached by asking: *Whose* experience is unanalyzable? Or again: *Whose* mind is to be identified with the unifying principle that constitutes the world? Clearly, Green thinks, not the mind of any finite individual human being; there is no justification for my thinking that the world ceases to exist if I cease to be conscious. The only way to avoid such absurd subjectivism, according to Green, is to accept that there is an eternal self-conscious mind. It is in virtue of the unifying actions of this eternal mind that there is a world. The eternal mind cannot simply be separate from our finite minds, for it must explain the possibility of our knowledge and experience; it was the possibility of our experience that was the starting point for the argument. So, Green says, a finite consciousness is the "vehicle" of the eternal consciousness, which realizes itself through finite minds. What we may think of as the history of consciousness is in reality the history of the process whereby "an animal organism, which has its history in time, gradually becomes the vehicle of an eternally complete consciousness" (*Prolegomena to Ethics*, p. 81).

The above criticism of Kant could be phrased by saying that Kant's view is too *subjective*, that Kant's unmodified view seems to make the constituting of experience, and thus of the experienceable world, simply a matter of the subjective psychological acts of the individual mind. Understood in that way, Green's criticism corresponds to Hegel's most-frequent line of attack against the Kantian philosophy. Hegel often refers to Kant's Transcendental Idealism as "subjective idealism"[25] and says that Kant "remained constricted and confined by his psychological point of view."[26] This sort of criticism is of particular importance from our point of view because, as we shall see, it is also a fundamental criticism that Russell and Moore make against Kant.

Before we leave the subject of British Idealism, let us touch on the philosophy of F.H. Bradley, who is, next after Kant, the most-common explicit target of the anti-Idealist criticism of Russell and of Moore. We may think of Bradley as accepting much of the line of argument that we have attributed to Green, but as reacting skeptically to its conclusion. He accepts that without relations there would be no knowledge and no experience of the ordinary kind. He does not, however, accept that relations are ultimately real. On the contrary, he insists that ultimate reality is to be found rather in something like a mystical experience of the world as a unified whole, with a unity that is given rather than relational. Relations are to be understood as an abstraction from this reality, an abstraction that is necessary but that nonetheless fails to preserve the crucial unity or oneness of reality. He draws the conclusion that what passes for ordinary knowledge and experience is, because relational, not fully real. It is, however, a misunderstanding – which Russell certainly appears to commit – to think that this view arises from some special animus against relations, and that it might be defeated by showing that relations are in fact presupposed by our ordinary knowledge. Just as the view of Kant and Green is that *all* of our knowledge, and the knowable world, presupposes the synthesizing activity of the mind (in some sense of mind) but is nevertheless real, so Bradley's view is that all our knowledge, and the knowable world, presupposes the synthesizing activity of the mind (in some sense of mind) and so is *not* ultimately real. Bradley's emphasis on relations must thus be understood within context of the general kind of argument that we have seen in Green.

We now turn Russell and Moore's opposition to Kant's Copernican Revolution. Our claim is that this opposition was fundamental to their early philosophy. Encouragement for this claim comes from the fact that such opposition is manifested, perhaps most explicitly, in the earliest anti-Idealist work of either Russell or Moore. This work is the second version of Moore's Research Fellowship Dissertation, entitled "The Metaphysical Basis of Ethics," written in 1898.[27] Discussing the idea of the necessary conditions or presuppositions of knowledge, Moore finds an ambiguity in both "knowledge" and "condition":[28]

By "knowledge" what is meant? If "truth", then it is difficult to see that there can be any other condition for a true proposition than some other true proposition. If empirical cognition, then does not empirical psychology investigate the conditions for the possibility of this? A similar ambiguity is involved in the word 'condition'.

Moore complains here of an ambiguity, but the form of the complaint perhaps conceals its basis. Kant's conditions of the possibility of knowledge or experience are neither straightforwardly empirical, in the sense of empirical psychology or physiology, nor are they logical, in the sense of the dependence of one truth upon another. If I am to know anything or have any experience, then no doubt there must be a certain level of hemoglobin in my bloodstream. So in one sense a certain level of hemoglobin in my bloodstream is a necessary condition of knowledge or experience, but clearly that sort of empirical condition is not the sort of thing that Kant means by a necessary condition of knowledge or experience. Similarly, a certain period of concentrated attention may be necessary if I am to know some complex fact. So in another sense a certain period of concentrated attention may be a necessary condition of my knowledge, but again this is clearly not what Kant means. The same point holds also of logical conditions: if I am to know that 2 plus 2 equals 4, then, since knowledge requires truth, it is no doubt a necessary condition of my knowledge that it is false that 2 plus 2 does *not* equal 4. But, again, this cannot be what Kant means. His concern is not simply with the logical conditions of the truth which is known, but with something like the conditions of its knowability, that is, the conditions that must be satisfied if it is to be known by a self-conscious subject.[29] Moore's accusation of ambiguity is thus implicitly a refusal to accept the sort of idea of a necessary condition that Kant needs – a *transcendental* condition of knowledge or of experience. He simply insists that any "condition" is either empirical or logical.

If one denies that there is any sense to the idea of a *transcendental* condition, then Kant's conditions of possible experience are bound to seem empirical, and, in particular, psychological. Hence the *a priori* knowledge that Kant claims arises from such conditions will seem to be an absurd delusion, like thinking that a house is dark if you enter it still wearing sunglasses, or thinking that if you cannot help believing something, then it is true in virtue of that fact. Thus Russell, in his *Philosophy of Leibniz*,[30] speaks of "The view . . . constituting a large part of Kant's Copernican Revolution, that propositions may acquire truth by being believed" (p. 14), and repeatedly represents Kant as holding that the *a priori* is "subjective" (for instance, pp. 74, 163). In *The Principles of Mathematics* Russell similarly describes Kantianism as "the belief . . . that propositions which are believed solely because the mind is so made that we cannot but believe them may yet be true in virtue of our belief" (p. 450). Concerning the nature of space and Kant's view that it is necessary rather than mere fact, Russell is openly scornful:

the Kantian theory seems to lead to the curious result that whatever we cannot help believing must be false. . . . the explanation offered [for the necessity of space] is, that there is no space outside our minds; whence it is to be inferred that our unavoidable beliefs are all mistaken. Moreover we only push one stage further back the region of 'mere fact', for the constitution of our minds remains still such a mere fact. (p. 454)

We have already seen, in the passage taken as epigraph to this essay, a similar attitude on Moore's part: he claims that the "certainly false" assertion that " 'to be true' *means* to be thought in a certain way" plays "a most essential part in Kant's "Copernican Revolution" ' (see above).

It would be easy to dismiss this reading of Kant as arising from the reaction by Russell and Moore against Idealism – as if, in the first flush of their anti-idealist enthusiasm, they supported their position by a tendentious interpretation of an opponent. Indeed, the interpretation, and the criticism that it inevitably suggests, may seem to presuppose realism. Certainly it presupposes standards of objectivity by which Kant's synthetic *a priori* counts as subjective. It is worth emphasizing again, therefore, that the view of Kant as allowing us access only to the subjective is an interpretation also to be found in Hegel and his followers, and to be found in Russell before his rejection of Idealism.[31] In this interpretation of Kant, then, and in the associated line of criticism, we have a crucial line of *positive* influence of Hegel on Russell and Moore (and thus, or so we shall claim, on analytic philosophy more generally). Of course the reaction of the Hegelians to Kant as thus interpreted is diametrically opposed to the reaction of Russell and Moore. Very roughly, we may say that the former reacted by attempting to conceive of the mind in a more objective manner, so that the role of the mind in knowledge would not cast the objectivity of knowledge in doubt; the latter reacted, both to Kant and to the attempts of the Hegelians, by attempting to disengage the mind from knowledge entirely, so that its role in knowledge becomes purely passive. The Russell-Moore reaction to Kant is thus diametrically opposed to that of Hegel and other Absolute Idealists. We can, nevertheless, see the same sort of dissatisfaction underlying each reaction.

The fundamental anti-Kantianism of Russell and Moore can be articulated into a number of interrelated doctrines that played a fundamental role in Platonic Atomism. The first is perhaps the most directly related to the Kantian issues discussed: the idea that the objects at which our knowledge aims are wholly independent of the knowing subject. Without the idea of transcendental conditions of knowledge, which are constitutive of the object to be known, there is no justification for denying that we aim to know objects that are wholly and in every sense independent of us. Hence Russell, writing in the *Principles of Mathematics*, says: "all knowledge must be recognition, on the pain of being mere delusion; Arithmetic must be discovered in just the same sense in which Columbus discovered the West Indies, and we no more create the numbers than he created the Indians."[32] More or less as a corollary of the sharp distinction between the object of knowledge and the knowing subject, Russell and Moore also make a sharp distinction between the mental act (of, for example, knowledge) and its object the known object). They frequently invoke this act/object distinction, especially to argue that rival views arise only from its neglect. The influence of this conception of the objects of knowledge on later analytic philosophy can be seen not so much in the prevalent realism of much analytic philosophy as in the standards by which a view is judged to be realistic or not realistic (either in general or about a particular subject-matter).

Second, since Russell and Moore denied that there are necessary conditions or presuppositions to knowledge, they see the fundamental epistemic relation as presuppositionless. Knowledge, at least of the fundamental sort, is direct and unmediated. Both Russell and Moore take our knowledge of simply sensory qualities as the paradigm and the model of this kind of knowledge (the Idealists would have denied that even that sort of knowledge is in fact unmediated). Thus Russell, in the Preface to the *Principles of Mathematics* says:

The discussion of indefinables – which forms the chief part of philosophical logic – is the endeavour to see clearly, and to make others see clearly, the entities concerned, in order that the mind may have *that kind of acquaintance with them which it has with redness or with the taste of a pineapple.* (p. xv; my emphasis)

Similarly, Moore's famous comparison of "good" with "yellow" in *Principia Ethica*[33] is clearly meant to suggest not only that both are simple and indefinable qualities but also that our knowledge of both rests simply on direct perception.[34] This sort of direct and unmediated epistemic relation to objects plays a large role in Russell's philosophy after 1905, where it is standardly called "acquaintance"; its role before 1905 is less explicit, because Russell was far less concerned with knowledge than in the later period. But the idea of such a relation is of fundamental importance to Platonic Atomism from its inception – and clearly arises from a rejection of the Kantian view of our knowledge as mediated by the transcendental conditions of knowledge.[35]

It is worth pointing out that Platonic Atomism is not, in the usual sense, an empiricist view. It assumes a direct and unmediated epistemic relation to the objects of knowledge, but it does not confine those objects to the spatio-temporal, or to possible objects of sensory experience. On the contrary, Moore insists that *good* and *truth* are among such objects,[36] and we have seen that Russell includes the indefinables of logic among such objects (also, and crucially, as we shall see, propositions). Although they conceive of our relation to such objects as *analogous* to sense-perception, it is only analogous. In one sense, then, Platonic Atomism is diametrically opposed to empiricism, for its ontology is immensely profligate with abstract objects. Russell and Moore themselves looked on this ontological issue as the crucial aspect of empiricism, a doctrine they regarded as definitely refuted.[37] On the other hand, their picture of the mind and of its relation to objects is reminiscent of the most-naive form of empiricism. Most striking is the insistence on the passivity of the mind: its function is merely to "perceive" what is out there. Speaking of inference – where one might ordinarily suppose the mind to be active – Russell says: "It is plain that where we validly infer one proposition from another, we do so in virtue of a relation which holds between the two propositions whether we perceive it or not: the mind, in fact, is as purely receptive in inference as common-sense supposes it to be in perception of sensible objects" (*Principles of Mathematics*, p. 32).

The influence of this view of knowledge, as paradigmatically presuppositionless, on later analytic philosophy, is, again, not in doctrine. There is no general dogmatic assumption that we *do* have direct and unmediated acquaintance with the objects of our (putative) knowledge. Even Russell and Moore were unable to sustain this assumption for very long; hence their view that we are in direct contact with, for example, ordinary physical objects was replaced by the view that we are in direct contact with sense-data, and that what we take to be knowledge of ordinary physical objects is to be explained, or explained away, in terms of our knowledge of abstract objects and sense-data.[38] But in the evolution of this new view, the concept of acquaintance, of direct and unmediated knowledge, plays the crucial role: sense-data are defined as suitable *relata* for such a relation (as an answer to the question If the fundamental epistemic relation is that of direct and unmediated knowledge of objects, what are the *objects* of knowledge like?). For many subsequent analytic philosophers, something like Russell's notion of acquaintance is important as a paradigm of knowledge – the standard against which our ordinary knowledge is to be measured, or the pattern that it is to be forced to fit.

A third point, which can also be seen as arising directly from the rejection of the Kantian idea of the necessary conditions of knowledge, is that among the independent objects with which we may be acquainted are *propositions:* objective entities, capable of truth or falsehood, which may be very roughly identified with the content or meaning of a declarative sentence. Very quickly the idea arose that a crucial part of philosophical activity consists in giving the *analysis* of propositions – of saying what their real form is, as opposed to their apparent form, what entities they are really about, as opposed to what they appear to be about, and explaining why they have the implications that they have.[39] In this idea of the analysis of propositions, a crucial role is played by an issue that we have only touched on in passing: the use of elementary mathematical logic as a philosophical tool. It was logic that made it possible to give a concise and apparently explanatory representation of the inferential powers of a sentence. By making this possible, and by holding up an ideal of clarity and rigor, the use of elementary mathematical logic may be as definitive of analytic philosophy as any other feature.

Our interest, however, is in the role played by the reaction against Idealism in the formation of Platonic Atomism, and of analytic philosophy more generally. Seen in this perspective, one obvious contrast to the doctrine that there are objective propositions is the Kantian view of judgment as the result of an act of the mind, a synthesis. Given the idea that synthesis can take place only in accordance with certain rules, this idea immediately yields the result that the world, or at least the world insofar as it can be the subject of our judgments, must obey those rules. If we identify a judgmental element in experience, we get the further consequence that our experience must obey those rules – that there are necessary conditions for the possibility of experience. Russell and Moore block this line of thought at the first step by insisting that the act/object distinction applies to the case of judgment. An act of judgment may be an act, but its object is a *proposition*, which is wholly independent of that act. Propositions, on this view, are not the result of synthesis or any other act of the mind, but are independent self-subsistent entities. We may be in direct and unmediated epistemic contact with them, but in no sense do we make them. Again, the commitment to this view in its stongest form did not last long: Russell's so-called multiple relation theory of judgment, which he adopted sometime between 1906 and 1910,[40] is an abandonment of the idea that there are propositions or judgments – the objects of acts of belief – that are wholly independent of human minds. But, again, the abandoned view continues to have an influence, perhaps most obviously in the overwhelming concern of analytic philosophers with questions of meaning, of analysis, and of language. Underlying these concerns is a general assumption that each of our utterances and beliefs has a perfectly definite "content," which may be abstracted from its content and "analyzed."[41] This procedure is perhaps theoretically unclear; in practice it usually amounts to the very familiar activity of re-formulating a sentence using logical constants, together with the claim that this sentence is a more precise version of, or a better representation of the content of, the original. Under the pressure of the general underlying assumption mentioned above, something very like the Platonic Atomism conception of a proposition has been revived and has come to play a significant role for some analytic philosophers.

To this point we have articulated ways in which Platonic Atomism can be seen as a reaction to Kantian ideas. Many of the most-characteristic features of the view, its extreme realism and anti-psychologism, and its free acceptance of propositions and other abstract entities, for example, fall into this category. In these cases, the reaction against post-Kantian Idealism is equally, or more significantly, a reaction against the Kantian ideas that underlie it. In addition, there are other features of Platonic Atomism that should be understood more specifically in terms of the opposition to Hegelianism (that is, that do not have to do with overtly Kantian ideas). Of these, the most notable, and perhaps the only one of fundamental importance, is atomism. In the work of Russell and Moore from the period of Platonic Atomism there is an explicit assumption that each thing exists, and can be understood, in isolation from all other things; the insistence on the externality of relations – that a thing's relations to other things make no difference to it – is a symptom of this atomism. This atomism is an explicit reaction to the holism, or even monism, that is characteristic of post-Kantian Idealism, which is expressed in an extreme form in the work of Bradley. The atomism of Russell and Moore, however, also connects with their other doctrines that we have examined. This is clearest in the case of the doctrine that knowledge, paradigmatically, is direct and unmediated, a simple relation of mind to object. If I can know an object completely by being in this relation to it (i.e. by being acquainted with it), then that piece of knowledge is independent of all others. If that is what knowledge is like, then one could know a single object completely while being ignorant of everything else. This sort of epistemological atomism makes ontological atomism almost inevitable, even if there is no logical implication between the two doctrines. Without ontological atomism, the epistemological atomist would be left without suitable objects of acquaintance. The view that knowledge is mediated, by contrast, leaves room for epistemological (and hence also ontological) holism, although without making it inevitable. Like the other doctrines of Platonic Atomism that we have articulated, its extreme atomism has been influential in later analytic philosophy; at the least it has functioned as the "natural" position, the position to be held unless there is positive reason to hold a different one. (Both for Platonic Atomism and for later analytic philosophy, atomism of propositions, or of meanings, has been particularly important.)

Our discussion of Platonic Atomism has alluded to subsequent analytic philosophy; now we must give more explicit consideration to this subject and to its relation to our guiding theme of the rejection of Kant's Copernican Revolution. We are not, of course, setting out to argue that the rejection of Kant provides the explanation for the development of analytic philosophy, nor even that it is the most-important theme for an interpretation of that development (as I have already indicated, I suspect that the use of elementary mathematical logic may be at least as important, and other factors could also be cited). Our task is, rather, to offer something like an overview of analytic philosophy from the perspective afforded by Kant's Copernican Revolution. The significance of that theme may then be gauged by seeing how useful that overview of analytic philosophy is.

To achieve this end, we shall articulate two themes and one subtheme, which are related to the rejection of Kantianism. These are, first, the relation of philosophy to other sorts of knowledge, especially what is called "commonsense"; second, the nature of the *a priori* (the sub-theme being the nature of philosophy – a sub-theme because we shall touch on it only in the context of discussing the *a priori*). In the case of the first, we shall simply state the theme and indicate where it is important; in the case of the second we shall quickly sketch its significance in various developments of analytic philosophy. (There are, of course, relations among our themes, which we shall indicate as we proceed.) It is important to note that much will be omitted, and not only details. We aim to discuss what has been most influential and what seems likely to be influential in the near future. Revivals of Kant, for example, have not greatly influenced the general course of analytic philosophy (if they had, our theme of the rejection of Kant would be inappropriate). Much of our emphasis will be on Logical Positivism and on what might be thought of as the American reaction (or reactions) to the failure of Logical Positivism. We do not discuss the later work of Wittgenstein at all, not because we take it to be unimportant nor because the work is too complex to treat in summary fashion. Rather, the relation of this body of work to the analytic tradition is too ambivalent for us to discuss it within the space available here. On the one hand, Wittgenstein's later work clearly is to be seen against the context of the tradition of analytic philosophy – including Wittgenstein's early work. On the other hand, to consider his later work as a further development within that tradition does scant justice to his thought.

Our first theme, stated briefly, is the relation of philosophy to other kinds of knowledge. In reading Kant, and even more in reading Hegel, one gets a sense of a conception of philosophy according to which that subject is able to place or limit other kinds of supposed knowledge. Philosophy is not answerable to other kinds of knowledge and does not compete with them. Rather, it is philosophy that lays down the sphere within which those other kinds of knowledge are valid. In Kant this point shows itself most clearly in the Antinomies. Kant argues that certain concepts that we use in everyday and scientific thought lead to contradictions if we take them to be unrestrictedly valid. The conclusion that Kant draws is that those concepts, although necessary for ordinary thought, are not universally valid: they apply only to phenomena, not to things in themselves. Such concepts are valid – indeed necessary – for our ordinary (empirical) thought, but not for philosophical thought. More generally, on Kant's view we must distinguish between empirical claims, which are made within the conditions of ordinary thought, and philosophical or transcendental claims, which are made about such conditions or (absurdly, according to Kant) independent of them. Thus Kant, by his own account, is an empirical realist but a transcendental idealist (see, for instance, A369–70). A similar point can be made, on a rather different basis, about Hegel. From Hegel's perspective, it would be missing the point of his work to say that such-and-such a claim of his conflicts with such-and-such a well-established and widely believed claim of commonsense, or natural science. It is not that Hegel would simply say: so much the worse for commonsense (or science). Rather, his attitude would surely be that while the claims of commonsense or natural science may be valid and correct within their sphere, their sphere is limited. Philosophy is to show what the limits are; it will thus become clear that the appearance of conflict arises only because we take the claims of commonsense, say, as unlimited – as being philosophical claims.

The sort of attitude attributed above to Kant and to Hegel is no longer available after we have completely rejected Kantian ideas of the transcendental (as Russell and Moore do; we have seen them riding roughshod over the very distinctions indicated above). Thus, within analytic philosophy there is a recurrent tendency not merely to use and appeal to the ideas of commonsense or natural science (which perhaps philosophy must always do) but to take those ideas at their face value, without making a distinction in kind between them and the claims of philosophy. We are talking here, of course, about a very broad tendency. In particular, it makes all the difference whether a philosopher chiefly relies on the ideas and truisms of commonsense, or upon the results and procedures of natural science. We might think of this difference as marking a major difference between kinds of analytic philosophy. From our Kantian-Hegelian point of view, however, what the two have in common is precisely a failure to distinguish the claims of philosophy from all other sorts of claims.

A particularly dramatic manifestation of this tendency is to be seen in Moore's work, from after the period of Platonic Atomism. In "Four Forms of Scepticism,"[42] for example, Moore goes over a skeptical argument of Russell's. His example is that of knowing that there is a pencil in front of him. The Russellian claim that Moore does not know that there is a pencil in front of him rests, Moore says, on four assumptions. Without arguing against any of these assumptions, Moore simply says that it is more certain that one or more of them is false than that he, Moore, does not in fact know that there is a pencil in front of him. Indeed, Moore says that he is inclined to agree with Russell about the truth of three of the assumptions, yet he says that even the truth of these three is less certain than that of his knowing that there is a pencil in front of him. In other words, Moore confronts the philosophical argument not by refutation or counter-argument, but simply by insisting that it denies something that is more certain than the correctness of any philosophical argument; the position of commonsense is allowed to outweigh the philosophical argument. While there are of course important differences, our Kantian-Hegelian perspective is distant enough to assimilate to this move of Moore's the rather different appeal to ordinary language that was characteristic of J.L. Austin and others, especially in Oxford during the decade and a half after World War II; and the appeal to "intuition" that is characteristic of much subsequent analytic philosophy (we shall return to this last point). In each of these cases, ordinary knowledge that appears to conflict with the results of philosophical argument is used to show that the alleged results are mistaken. Ordinary (non-philosophical) knowledge is accepted as being on a par with, and as outweighing, philosophical claims. In many cases, indeed, such knowledge – and particularly intuition – is taken to be the source of the premises from which philosophical argument must proceed.[43]

Our second focus, within analytic philosophy, is the theme of *a priori* knowledge and, closely related to this, the status of philosophy; here our discussion will be somewhat more extended. The issue of *a priori* knowledge is significant for our purposes both because it has played, directly and indirectly, a large part in analytic philosophy, and because it is directly related to our general theme of Kant's Copernican Revolution. The Copernican Revolution opens up the possibility of *a priori* knowledge that is neither simply trivial and tautologous, nor dubiously based on some alleged insight into necessities in the nature of things. Knowledge based on the conditions of the possibility of experience need be of neither of these kinds; it is, in Kant's words, synthetic *a priori*.[44] The issue of *a priori* knowledge is related to the issue of the nature of philosophy because of the general (although not universal) assumption that philosophy must be conceived as an *a priori* subject.

In Platonic Atomism, as one might expect, the issue of *a priori* knowledge receives very little attention. In *Principles of Mathematics*, Russell claims that mathematics is synthetic *a priori*;[45] he takes the reduction of mathematics to logic to show not that mathematics is analytic but rather that logic is synthetic.[46] The concept of the synthetic *a priori* in Russell's hands, however, is purely negative. He claims that mathematics (and logic) is synthetic simply in order to deny that it follows from the Law of Identity, and because he is at best skeptical about the existence of any analytic propositions; he claims that it is *a priori* simply in order to deny that it is in any way based on sense-experience. But beyond these denials the concept of the synthetic *a priori* has no role to play in his thought; the concept is simply not discussed. He has, therefore, no explanation of how it is possible for a proposition to have that status, nor is it easy to see how such an explanation could be accommodated within Platonic Atomism. His view of knowledge, as we have seen, is that it all, in the end, rests on immediate perception. Empirical or *a posteriori* knowledge rests on sense-perception and is knowledge of temporal entities; non-empirical or *a priori* knowledge rests on non-sensuous perception of objects that are not in time or space, and of relations among such objects. The main task of philosophy, after the work of analysis is done, consists – oddly enough – in having such perceptions and in trying to get others to have them; Russell says that "the chief part of philosophical logic" is "the endeavour to see clearly, and to make others see clearly, the entities concerned."[47] Yet no evidence is put forward for the existence of such non-sensuous perception; since each person supposedly has such perceptions, they are presumed to be self-evident and undeniable. Nor is an explanation offered of the possibility of such perception.

This view of *a priori* knowledge, and of philosophy, is clearly vulnerable. The appeal to self-evidence, to the supposedly evident fact of non-sensuous perception, must seem weak, given that many philosophers have denied any such source of knowledge. Further, the highly complex and unobvious character of the logic Russell was forced to devise to avoid the problems raised by the paradox that bears his name makes it implausible to claim that our knowledge of logic is based on direct and immediate perception.[48] More subtly, the idea of direct perception of an abstract realm does not explain what some have seen as the *necessity* of logic, mathematics (and perhaps philosophy).[49] To say that we perceive, in some non-sensuous fashion, the entities of logic, and that the truths of logic are based on the configuration of those entities, does nothing to suggest that the entities *must* be configured in that way, so it does nothing to suggest that the truths of logic are necessary. Nor, indeed, does this approach give us any idea what might be the content of a claim that some truths are necessary.

Issues of the sort indicated above were among those that motivated Wittgenstein in the *Tractatus Logico-Philosophicus*.[50] He attacks Russell for his reliance on self-evidence (see 5.4731); he insists that any theory must be mistaken that makes it appear as if a proposition of logic has a content, that is, represents some fact (such as about Russell's atemporal entities) which might have been otherwise (see 6.111). Wittgenstein's early work is, I think, an exception to our general claim about the anti-Kantian nature of analytic philosophy. Although the book was enormously influential, those who were influenced by it ignored or rejected those elements that make it Kantian. Indeed, noting how those elements were rejected will throw the anti-Kantianism of other analytic philosophers into higher relief.

There is an obvious *prima facie* difficulty with the claim that the *Tractatus* is Kantian in its approach to *a priori* knowledge. We noted that a crucial result of Kant's Copernican Revolution was that it opened up the possibility of *a priori* knowledge that is neither simply trivial and tautologous nor dubiously based on some alleged insight into necessities in the nature of things. But in the *Tractatus* the only sort of knowledge that is allowed as *a priori is* said to be tautologous; the propositions of logic are said to say nothing, to stand in no representational relation to reality, and, therefore, not to be genuine propositions at all (see 4.4–4.464). How, in view of this, can we think of the *Tractatus* as putting forward a Kantian view of *a priori* truth? Does not the book precisely deny the existence of *a priori* knowledge that is *synthetic*, or that makes contentful claims on the world? The answer to this question is that the notion of content, and thus of contentlessness, is, on the face of it, language-relative. A claim that in one language appears as trivial or lacking in content or may in another language appear as significant or even absurd.[51] Classical truth-functional logic, say, may be trivial, given a language of a certain sort; what is not trivial is that it is a language that is given, rather than, say, a language in which intuitionistic logic would appear as inevitable. The transcendental, or Kantian, element in the *Tractatus*, then, is that it lays down the sort of language that we must use if there is to be any language or thought (representation of the world); it claims that given that sort of (inevitable) language, the truths of logic are indeed trivial. They are given with the language, so to speak, and the language is given because (so Wittgenstein claims) it is the only possible sort of language.

Seen from our perspective, then, the *Tractatus* may be thought of as laying down the necessary conditions for the possibility of language and thought. In particular, it claims that the possibility of language, of any system that can represent the world, requires that language have a certain structure – a structure by no means obvious on the surface of our language. The *a priori* truths of logic and arithmetic are then said to be true in virtue of this structure. Those truths therefore appear as special not in virtue of their subject-matter – because, for example, they are about atemporal objects which are non-sensuously perceived. What distinguishes them is rather that they *have* no subject-matter: they simply reflect the necessary structure of any possible language.[52]

When discussing Kant we mentioned that a claim about the necessary conditions of possible experience faces two closely connected dangers. One is that it may appear to undermine itself by transgressing those limits to thought that it lays down, so that if it is true it is nonsensical; in that case the claim that it is true becomes, at the least, problematic. The other is that it is far from clear what justifies, or could justify, the claim that such-and-such is indeed the correct account of the conditions of the possibility of experience. Even if the account of such conditions is intelligible to us, how can we, with any confidence, know it to be correct? The *Tractatus* too faces the analogue of these difficulties. In the case of the first, the book simply admits that it is indeed nonsensical by its own standards of sense; it ends with the paradoxical claim that the propositions of the book are to enable us to recognize them as nonsensical (*unsinnig*). But of course if they are indeed nonsensical, they are not propositions after all, and so how could they be used for that or any other end? There may be ways of mitigating this paradox, or even of using it to obtain a deeper understanding of the book, but for our purposes the most important fact is that those who were influenced by the *Tractatus* – in particular, the Vienna Circle – could not accept this aspect of the book, which they saw as mysticism.[53]

The second difficulty, about the problem of knowing that we have indeed got hold of the correct account of the conditions of the possibility of language or of knowledge, also played a significant role in the response of the Vienna Circle to the *Tractatus*. The fundamental issue here is whether there is, as Wittgenstein claimed in that book, a single *unique* set of conditions that make our knowledge possible (a unique framework, so to speak), and if so, how we know that our account of it is correct. Wittgenstein's framework included (what is now called) classical truth-functional and quantificational logic. Hence one important fact for the Vienna Circle was the existence of alternative logics – for example, intuitionistic logic. Perhaps more important was the fact that there are different scientific languages with no direct equivalences among them. The paradigm case was the contrast between the language of Newtonian physics and the language of Einsteinian physics. (The influence of this example is a sign of the significance that the findings of natural science had for the Vienna Circle.)

Although the Vienna Circle was greatly influenced both by Kant and by the *Tractatus*, they did not accept the crucial claim that a unique structure is common to all possible languages.[54] They thus gave up the Kantian or transcendental element in the *Tractatus*, that is, its claim to be talking about the necessary conditions of any possible language. Instead they drew from it the idea that any language has an implicit structure, and that for any language there will be truths that are true in virtue of the structure of that language. The result is a language-relative view of the *a priori*. If you choose to speak this language, you must accept these truths as *a priori;* if you choose to speak that language, you must accept those truths as *a priori.* But as for which language one should choose in the first place, they advocated tolerance: let us choose, for any given task, whichever language seems best for it, being sure only to say carefully which we are choosing.

Since complex discursive thought can be carried on only in language or some equivalent symbolic system, it follows from the above conception that at any given time there are some truths that are *a priori* relative to one's situation at that time. The Vienna Circle and other logical positivists followed Wittgenstein in claiming that the truths of logic and mathematics have a special status quite unlike that of the truths of natural science, or history, or everyday life. They attempted to explain this assumed special status in terms of the above conception of the *a priori*. More to the point of our present concerns, they also attempted to use that conception to explain the nature of philosophy and its distinction from natural science. Philosophy was conceived of not as a discipline with its own subject-matter, like one of the natural sciences, but as concerned with the analysis of language – especially of the language in which the natural sciences are carried on. An example of the task of philosophy, on this view, would be to analyze a scientific dispute to say how far the dispute was a genuine factual issue and how far it arose from different choices of language. The "results" of philosophy would thus have the status of being analytic truths of some favored language, and thus *a priori*, in the language-relative sense indicated.

The views of the logical positivists have come under attack, most famously by W.V.O. Quine. We can separate two strands in Quine's attack.[55] First, the claim that the category "language-relative *a priori*," as I have described it, is not an epistemologically significant one. Since we may change our mind about a truth of this sort by changing our mind about which language to use, the epistemological significance of the category depends on there being some epistemological significance to the distinction between changing one's mind about which are the truths of the given language, what the logical positivists called a factual question, and changing one's mind about which language to use, what they called a pragmatic question. Quine argues, however, that the logical positivists' distinction between the factual and the pragmatic is spurious. In actual language-use, there is simply no difference between what are alleged to be the two different kinds of change. Second, and perhaps more controversially, Quine claims that the idea of language as containing rules which give rise to *a priori* truths is not one that can be justified if we think realistically about actual languages and their use. A truth that might appear as *a priori* on one account of a language might not so appear on another account, and the two accounts may be equally good, if considered simply as accounts of the bare facts of the use of the language. Each of Quine's lines of attacks can be seen as based on the insistence that we must take a naturalistic view of language.

From our point of view, we can represent the debate as follows. The logical positivists attempted to retain at least something of Wittgenstein's explanation of the *a priori* without Wittgenstein's metaphysical or transcendental view of language and its concomitant problems. Quine insists that the result is an unstable mixture: the language-relative *a priori* only appears as an explanatory notion because elements of a metaphysical view of language are retained; once we purge these and settle for a fully naturalistic view, even the language-relative *a priori* disappears. We said above that the language-relative *a priori* functioned for the logical positivists, among other things, as an explanation of the possibility of philosophy itself. A sign of this is Carnap's incredulity in the face of Quine's rejection of that conception. He insists that, in spite of what Quine says, he (Quine) must in fact be presupposing the conception; his (Carnap's) view seems to be that all philosophy presupposes it.[56]

Despite Carnap's incredulity, Quine is consistent and rigorous in his rejection of any conception of the *a priori* or of necessity.[57] And he accepts the conclusion that had made Carnap think his rejection could not be fully meant: he accepts that the truths of logic and mathematics, and of philosophy itself, are not *a priori* or necessary. In each case, to be sure, the relation of the truths to empirical evidence is remote – often so remote as to be almost undetectable. But the same could be said, Quine holds, of the most-abstract and general laws of physics. The differences here, on his view, are of degree and not of kind. Each sentence that we hold true ultimately gets its justification in terms of the whole body of such sentences. The primary evidential relation is that of this body or system as a whole to our experience as a whole. The relation of a particular sentence to the evidence that appears to justify it is secondary, in the sense that it may be overridden by the needs of the whole; it is never more than part of the story, and may sometimes be missing entirely.[58]

We saw that the relative *a priori* of the logical positivists could be seen as an attempt to have some of the results of Wittgenstein's Kantianism in the *Tractatus* without paying the metaphysical price that Wittgenstein paid: to preserve a conception of the *a priori* without having to defend the idea that all languages are in essence the same. Seen in these terms, Quine's philosophy represents a total and unequivocal break with Kantianism. Unlike Russell and Moore, however, it does not break with Kant by appealing to direct intuition and unmediated knowledge. Our knowledge is mediated, but not by any structures that can be separated out from that knowledge or given a special status.[59] While Quine's view accepts that knowledge is mediated, there is no conception of a transcendental level on which this mediation takes place. There is simply our overall theory of the world, which is gradually modified from within over time. A philosophical view of this kind leaves no room for a special kind of knowledge of the conditions of possible experience. Nor, as we have seen, does it leave room for philosophy as a subject that is different in category from others.

Among the various developments since Quine's work, one is of particular interest. Partly in reaction to the austerity of Quine's philosophical vocabulary, some philosophers now make free use of some conceptions that Quine rejected – in particular, necessity and the *a priori*. These ideas are freely employed in the discussion of philosophical issues, which they in turn modify; the use of such ideas also gives rise to further questions and problems. In most authors, the resurgence of these ideas does *not* represent a revival of anything like a Kantian conception of the necessary conditions of experience. In fact those ideas seem to have two bases. One is a return to the conception of the relative *a priori*, that is, a reliance on certain conceptual structures, without any attempt to argue that those structures are themselves necessary or inevitable. (It seems clear that a conception of the *a priori* obtained in such a way cannot be more than relative, but this point is often less clearly acknowledged in recent authors than it is in Carnap). The other basis is particularly striking from our point of view. It is a claim to have direct insight into the necessity of certain truths. In its reliance on supposed direct insight, this view is reminiscent of Platonic Atomism; its assumption of *necessity* as the subject of such insight, however, is a distinguishing feature. These bases are not always clearly separated, perhaps in part because both result in great weight being put on what are called "intuitions." In the case of the first basis, the intuition is into the structure of our language; in the case of the second, into the nature of things, taken as independent of language. (This distinction is too simple: often a claim about "into the nature of things" is grounded on the supposed intuition that a certain statement is commonsensical, or what most people would ordinarily say.) It would be absurd to seize too readily on the word "intuition" and on the fact that it is the standard translation of Kant's *Anschauung*, and to say that we are dealing with a revival of the idea of intellectual intuition. Nevertheless, the contrast with Kantianism is clear and, especially in the case of supposed insight into necessities in the nature of things, quite direct.

Our discussion of analytic philosophy has, of course, been both summary and highly selective. We have attempted to convey some idea of the way in which analytic philosophy appears when examined with Kant's Copernican Revolution in mind. We have suggested that analytic philosophy grapples with issues to which that nexus of Kantian ideas is directly relevant. Also, despite the diversity within analytic philosophy, it is in general opposed to those ideas. Our discussion of Platonic Atomism suggests that this anti-Kantianism can to some extent be traced back to the influence, on Russell and Moore, of Hegel's reading of Kant, and to their wholesale rejection of any form of Idealism.

NOTES

1 G. E. Moore, *Principia Ethica* (Cambridge; Cambridge University Press, 1903), 132–33.
2 See below, pp. 459–66; see also Nicholas Griffin, *Russell's Idealist Apprenticeship* (Oxford: Clarendon Press, 1991), and the present author's *Russell, Idealism, and the Emergence of Analytic Philosophy* (Oxford: Clarendon Press, 1990).
3 Hans D. Sluga, "Frege as a Rationalist" in *Studies on Frege*, vol. I ed. M. Schirn (Froman-Holzborg: Stuttgart-Bad, Cannstatt, 1976); the passage quoted is on 28.
4 The work of Sluga has played a large role in bringing those elements to the fore. As well as the essay already cited, see his book *Gottlob Frege* (London: Routledge & Kegan Paul, 1980). The lack of recognition of Kantian elements in Frege's thought is surely due, at least in part, to the fact that Frege never articulates in any systematic way the Kantian metaphysical and epistemological views that he seems to assume.
5 An important figure here is Coleridge. See Jean Pucelle, *L'Idealisme en Angleterre* (Neuchatel: Editions de la Baconniere, 1955).
6 James Hutchinson Stirling, *The Secret of Hegel* (London: Longmans, Roberts, and Green, 1865).
7 First published 1874; reissued with a foreword and minor revisions by J.N. Findlay as *Hegel's Logic: Being Part One of the Encyclopedia of the Philosophical Sciences (1830)* (Oxford: Clarendon Press, 1975).
8 Edward Caird, *The Critical Philosophy of Immanuel Kant*, 2 vols. (Glas-

gow: James MacLehose & Sons, 1877; 2nd ed. 1909); and *Hegel* (Edinburgh and London: W. Blackwood & Sons, 1883).

9 John M.E. McTaggart, *A Commentary on Hegel's Logic* (Cambridge: Cambridge University Press, 1910); and *Studies in the Hegelian Dialectic* (Cambridge: Cambridge University Press, 1921). Besides McTaggart, the influence of James Ward should be mentioned; see Griffin, *Russell's Idealist Apprentice*, especially Chap. 2 and 3.

10 Bertrand Russell, *An Essay on the Foundations of Geometry* (Cambridge: Cambridge University Press, 1897). For discussion of this work, see Griffin, *Russell's Idealist Apprenticeship*, and the present author's *Russell, Idealism, and the Emergence of Analytic Philosophy*, Chap. 3.

11 *My Philosophical Development* (London: Allen & Unwin, 1959), 42.

12 *Mind*, n.s., v. 6 (1897), 235–40.

13 See, for example, Russell's *My Philosophical Development*, p. 54: "Moore led the way, but I followed closely in his footsteps."

14 Bertrand Russell, *Principles of Mathematics* (London: Allen & Unwin, 1937; 1st ed. 1903); hereafter cited in the main body of the text.

15 Here I rely upon an interpretation of Hegel as building on, rather than wholly rejecting, the Kantian Copernican Revolution. I cannot defend this interpretation in this essay. See, for instance, Robert B. Pippin, *Hegel's Idealism* (Cambridge: Cambridge University Press, 1989).

16 *Kritik der Reinen Vernunft* (Riga: Hartknoch, 1781; 2nd ed. 1787). I have largely, but not wholly, taken my translations from Kemp Smith, *Critique of Pure Reason* (London: Macmillan, 1968; 1st ed. 1929). I follow the usual practice of citing the original page numbers of the first edition as A, those of the second as B.

17 Here, perhaps even more than elsewhere, I compress very complex material with inevitable distortions. I ignore, for example, the difficult but significant distinction between a form of intuition and a formal intuition.

   Note that Kant also suggests, in the Introduction to the *Critique*, that "the two stems of human knowledge," sensibility and understanding, "perhaps spring from a common, but to us unknown, root" (A 15–B 29). This suggestion, and the problematic nature of the distinction, was important to Kant's idealist successors.

18 *The Works of T.H. Green*, 3 vols. (London: Longmans, Green & Co., 1894), III, 146.

19 See Nettleship's "Memoir," ibid., vol. III, esp. p. lxx: "The teaching of philosophy in Oxford at this time centered round certain works of Aristotle, to which portions of Plato has recently been added. Modern philosophy was scarcely recognised officially as part of the course, but the writings of J.S. Mill, especially his *Logic*, were largely read, and . . . were probably the most powerful element in the intellectual leaven of the place."

20 See especially his long introduction to Hume's *Treatise*, which contains a lengthy discussion of Locke and a briefer discussion of Berkeley, as well as an exhaustive consideration of Hume. This Introduction is reprinted as pp. 1–371 of vol. I of Green's *Works*.

21 T.H. Green, *Prolegomena to Ethics*, ed. A.C. Bradley (Oxford: Clarendon Press, 1883). This book was left unfinished at Green's death and was completed, on the basis of Green's notes, by the editor. The parts that concern us were put in final form by Green.

22 For Hegel's criticism of Kant, see *Lectures on the History of Philosophy* vol. III, trans. E.S. Haldane and Frances H. Simon (London: Routledge and Kegan Paul, 1955), pt. 3, sec. 3; B (*Werkausgabe*, ed. Moldenhauer & Michel (Frankfurt: Surkampf, 1971), XX, 329–86; future references to Hegel in German are all to this edition); *G.W.F. Hegel's Logic, Being Part One of the Encyclopedia of the Philosophical Sciences*, trans. William Wallace (Oxford: Clarendon Press, 1975), sect. 42–60 (*Werkausgabe*, VIII, 112–47); *Hegel's Science of Logic*, trans. A.V. Miller (London; George Allen & Unwin, 1969), *passim*, e.g. pp. 46–47, 79–80, 396–97 (*Werkausgabe*, VI, 20, 254, 261).

23 Hegel frequently criticizes the Kantian thing in itself, an entity beyond all possible human knowledge. See, for examples, *Encyclopedia Logic*, sect. 44, 45 (*Werkausgabe*, VIII, 120–21); *Science of Logic*, pp. 489–90 (*Werkausgabe*, VI, 135–36). For Hegel's criticism of the Kantian distinction between intuition and the understanding, see *Science of Logic*, pp. 585–89 (*Werkausgabe*, VI, 488–493).

24 This representation of Green's view slides over what is, for Kant, a vital distinction. According to Kant, we cannot *know* of things as they are in themselves, but we can *think* of them. In Kant, however, this distinction presupposes that between intuition and understanding; Green, like Hegel and many other post-Kantian Idealists, did not accept this latter distinction.

25 *Science of Logic*, p. 491 (*Werkausgabe*, VI, 261); the same point is made in a number of other passages, such as *Encyclopedia Logic*, sect. 42 (addition) and 45 (addition) (*Werkausgabe*, VIII, 117–19 and 121–23), and throughout the discussion in *Lectures on the History of Philosophy*, Pt 3, sect. 3, B (*Werkausgabe*, XX, 322, 332, 333, 337, 351, 381).

26 *Lectures on the History of Philosophy*, p. 431 (*Werkausgabe*, XX, 337).

27 Moore wrote two versions of "Metaphysical Basis of Ethics," the first in 1897 and the second in 1899, and submitted each in the competition for a "Prize Fellowship" at Trinity College, Cambridge (the second version was successful). The manuscripts are owned by the Cambridge University Library; I consulted them when they were on loan to Trinity College, Cambridge. I thank the Librarian of Trinity College, Cambridge,

and the Syndics of Cambridge University Library. For discussion of this work, see Thomas Baldwin, *G.E. Moore* (London: Routledge, Chapman & Hall, 1990), Chap. I, and the present author's *Russell, Idealism, and the Emergence of Analytic Philosophy*, Chap. 4.

28 "The Metaphysical Basis of Ethics," 1897 version, Chap. 1. The only surviving copy of the dissertation is missing a number of pages at various points and is numbered in several inconsistent ways. If one numbers the surviving pages in sequence, beginning with the Preface and ignoring gaps, this passage occurs on p. 39.

29 This way of putting the matter presupposes Kant's distinction of formal from transcendental logic. Some of Kant's successors claimed the former cannot really exist as an independent subject, in which case the claim in the text is too simple. The crucial implication of Moore's use of the word "logical" here is in the idea that there need be no consciousness or experiencing subject involved; logical relations obtain between propositions, conceived of as independent and self-subsistent entities. Neither propositions nor the relations among them are to be thought of as in any way dependent upon thought, or experience, or anything mental. (Contrast this sense of "logical" with that used by Russell in the *Foundations of Geometry*; see p. 448, above.)

30 *A Critical Expositions of the Philosophy of Leibniz* (London: George Allen & Unwin, 1937; 1st ed. 1900).

31 See Russell, *Foundations of Geometry*, pp. 2–3, where he says that "to Kant *a priori* and *subjective* were almost interchangeable terms"; he also makes it clear that he takes the subjective to fall within the scope of empirical psychology.

32 Russell, *Principles of Mathematics*, p. 451. This quotation gives a good idea of the tone of Russell's extreme realism, but it hardly does justice to the doctrinal questions at issue. An Idealist may agree that numbers and islands and Indians all have the same ontological status, and that they are all discovered in any ordinary sense of that word. In fact, the doctrinal questions are surprisingly elusive and hard to formulate. Leaving aside the particular question of mathematics, a Kantian or Hegelian would agree that most of the objects of our knowledge are independent of us – in any ordinary sense of "independent of us." The real issue must be about the existence of a non-ordinary, or transcendental, sense of "independent of us." Russell and Moore do not explicitly confront this issue; they assume the ordinary sense of "independent of us" and take the only question to be whether objects have this property. This seems to leave the idealist view open to easy refutation.

33 Moore, *Principia Ethica*. The comparison between "good" and "yellow" also suggests the sense in which for Moore even ethics is a theoretical

matter – an issue of knowledge, not action. Ethics, for Moore, rests on the (non-sensuous) perception of the notion "good"; the relation of this perception to action is a further question.

34 Compare also Moore's statement about truth in "The Nature of Judgment" (*Mind*, 1899): 'If [the proposition that this paper exists] is true, it means only that the concepts, which are combined in specific relations in the concept of this paper, are also combined in a specific manner with the concept of existence. *That specific manner is something immediately known, like red"* (pp. 180–81; emphasis added). He also says "the nature of a true proposition is the ultimate *datum*" (in the same place).

35 In "The Nature of Judgment" (p. 183), Moore distinguishes his view from that of Kant precisely in this way, by saying that his theory "rejects the attempt to explain the "possibility of knowledge", accepting the cognitive relation as an ultimate *datum* or presupposition.

36 See notes 33, 34, above.

37 They clearly thought that the Idealists, if they had done nothing else, had shown that empiricism is false. Thus Moore, in "The Refutation of Idealism" (*Mind*, n.s. v. xii, 1903; reprinted in *Philosophical Studies* [New York: The Humanities Press, 1951]): "I consider it to be the main service of the philosophic school, to which the modern Idealists belong, that they have insisted on distinguishing 'sensation' and 'thought' and on emphasising the importance of the latter. Against Sensationalism or Empiricism they have maintained the true view." (*Philosophical Studies*, p. 7). Russell says quite bluntly: "empiricism is radically opposed to the philosophy advocated in the present work" (*Principles of Mathematics*, p. 493). This view of empiricism is no doubt a positive influence of Hegelianism on Platonic Atomism – although not in any very direct way on analytic philosophy as a whole.

38 I speak here of *ordinary* physical objects, because it was Russell's view that sense-data are themselves physical objects – although not, of course, ordinary physical objects. See Russell, "The Relation of Sense-Data to Physics" (*Scientia*, 4 [1914]; reprinted in *Mysticiam and Logic* (New York, Longmans, Green & Co., 1918), 145–79); see also Hylton, *Russell, Idealism, and The Emergence of Analytic Philosophy* Chap. 8, sect. 2.

39 Cf. Russell's *Leibniz:* "That all sound philosophy should begin with an analysis of propositions, is a truth too evident, perhaps to demand a proof" (p. 8).

40 In the final section of a 1906 essay, "The Nature of Truth" (*Proceedings of the Aristotelian Society*, n.s., v. VII), Russell discusses the multiple relation theory and declares himself uncertain of its correctness. The first two sections of this essay are reprinted in *Philosophical Essays* (London: George Allen & Unwin, 1966; 1st ed. 1910) under the title "The Monistic

Theory of Truth and Falsehood." The final section is replaced by a separate essay, "On the Nature of Truth and Falsehood," in which Russell advocates multiple relation theory, without his previous doubts. Vol. I of Whitehead and Russell's *Principia Mathematica* (Cambridge: Cambridge University Press, 1910) also puts forward the multiple relation theory.

41 This assumption may perhaps be explained in part by the fact that Frege and Russell were mathematicians. The idea that each sentence has, or ideally should have, a perfectly precise and definite content that can, in principle, be made fully explicit seems very natural if one takes the sentences of mathematics as one's paradigm. See W.D. Hart, "Clarity," *The Analytic Tradition*, ed. David Bell and Neil Cooper (Oxford: Basil Blackwell, 1990). It is also worth noting that the procedure of analysis, as described here, owes much to the logic of Frege and Russell, and to the idea that representing the content of a sentence in logical notation is not only clearer but also in some sense more accurate to the real nature of that content.

42 In G.E. Moore, *Philosophical Papers* (New York: Collier Books, 1962; 1st ed. 1959). W.D. Hart called to my attention the significance of Moore's procedure here.

43 Within analytic philosophy, as I have already indicated, it makes a decisive difference whether the primary source of "ordinary knowledge" is taken to be commonsense or science. G.E. Moore is of course an example of a philosopher for whom commonsense is primary. For others, such as Russell, Carnap, and, perhaps most notably, Quine, science plays this role. Quine, as we shall see, goes so far as to deny that philosophy is different in kind from any other sort of scientific knowledge; see note 58, below.

44 This is not, of course, to say that Kant's conception is without its difficulties; in particular, it must face the issue of how we can know the conditions of the possibility of experience – which may be either an epistemic question or a question about how it is possible even to think about such limits. These problems were important in the very earliest criticism of Kant, and thus in the development of post-Kantian Idealism (see F. C. Beiser, *The Fate of Reason* [Cambridge: Harvard University Press, 1987]); their analogue was, as we shall see, important also in the reaction to Wittgenstein's *Tractatus*.

45 "Kant never doubted for a moment that the propositions of logic are synthetic, whereas he rightly perceived that those of mathematics are synthetic. It has since appeared that logic is just as synthetic as all other kinds of truth" (*Principles of Mathematics*, p. 457). Russell makes a similar point nearly ten years later; see *Problems of Philosophy* (London: Oxford University Press, 1912), 79.

46 *Principles of Mathematics* does not discuss analyticity but refers us to *The Philosophy of Leibniz*. There Russell seems to deny that there are any analytic propositions; see pp. 16–17. Similarly Moore, in "Necessity" (*Mind*, n.s. 9, 1900) argues that allegedly analytic propositions are in fact synthetic (see p. 295). Hegel too argued against Kant's view that some truths are analytic; see section 115 of *Hegel's Logic*. Here, I suspect, there is clear Hegelian influence on Platonic Atomism – that Russell and Moore accepted the Hegelian criticism of Kant. Contrast the case of Frege, whose knowlege of Kant was not filtered through Hegelian critics, and who took the reduction of mathematics to logic to show that mathematics is analytic. I do not emphasize this Hegelian influence on Platonic Atomism, since it cannot be thought of as affecting analytic philosophy in general. The issue is further complicated by the fact that the synthetic status of mathematics is crucial for one aspect of Russell's use of logicism to argue against Idealism; see the present author's "Logic in Russell's Logicism" in *The Analytic Tradition*, ed. David Bell and Neil Cooper (Oxford: Basil Blackwell, 1990).

47 *Principles of Mathematics*, Preface, p. xv; see p. 462, above, where the rest of the sentence is quoted.

48 Russell, indeed, realized that the theory of types could not be based on the self-evidence of the axioms. One response was to say that the axioms are justified because they allow for the derivation of the theorems, and *they* are self-evident, so that there is "inductive evidence" for the truth of the axioms; see *Principia Mathematica*, vol. I, p. 59. But this view is not one that he could easily assimilate, since other views of his seem to demand that the status of logic is special, and quite different from that of non-logical truths.

49 Russell and Moore themselves were not among those who put great weight on the idea of necessity. See, for instance, *Principles of Mathematics*, p. 454; "The Nature of Judgment," pp. 188–89.

50 Wittgenstein, *Logische-Philosophische Abhandlung*, trans. D.F. Pears and B.F. McGuiness under the title *Tractatus Logico-Philosophicus* (London: Routledge & Kegan Paul, 1961, 1966). As is customary, I cite passages by numbered section.

51 See the present author's "Analyticity and the Indeterminacy of Translation," *Synthèse*, 1982, for related discussion.

52 This is, of course, a drastically incomplete account even of the issue of the *a priori* in the *Tractatus*. It is worth noting that just as it is characteristic of Idealism to sublime the notion of the mind (not your mind or my mind but The Mind – compare, most obviously, T.H. Green; see pp. 455–58, above), so the *Tractatus* may be said to sublime the notion of language (not English or Latin or German but *The* (underlying) Lan-

guage, or at least the structure that all languages must share). Then, to continue the crude analogy, just as a Kantian or post-Kantian Idealist can think of *a priori* truths as true in virtue of the nature of the mind, so Wittgenstein thinks of his *a priori* truths as true in virtue of the nature of language.

53 Carnap speaks of "Wittgenstein's mystical attitude, and his philosophy of the 'ineffable,' " *The Philosophy of Rudolf Carnap*, ed. P.A. Schilpp (LaSalle, Ill: Open Court, 1963), "Autobiography," 28. Carnap is speaking of Neurath's critical attitude toward Wittgenstein, but it is clear that on these points he sympathises with Neurath.

54 There is evidence that in the early days of the Vienna Circle some, at least, of its members did subscribe to something more like Wittgenstein's view. See Carnap, *Logical Syntax of Language* (London: Kegan Paul Trench, 1937), esp. 322.

55 Here see "Analyticity and the Indeterminacy of Translation," note 51, above.

56 See Carnap's response to Quine's "Carnap and Logical Truth," *The Philosophy of Rudolf Carnap*, pp. 915–22.

57 Besides "Carnap and Logical Truth" and the well-known "Two Dogmas of Empiricism" (in Quine's *From a Logical Point of View* [Cambridge: Harvard University Press, 1953]), see also Quine's reply to Charles Parsons in *The Library of Living Philosophers, volume XVIII, The Philosophy of W.V.O. Quine*, ed. L.E. Hahn & P.A. Schilpp (La Salle, Ill.: Open Court, 1986).

58 Quine's holism, and his rejection of any dualism of form and content, might remind one of Hegel. For Quine, as perhaps for Hegel, there can be no conception of the framework of knowledge that separates it from the substance of knowledge. In each case the result is a holistic attitude toward knowledge and a radical re-conception of the status of philosophy itself. The comparison cannot, of course, be pressed very far. Quine's emphasis on natural science, in particular, is a fundamental point of disanalogy.

A comparison between Quine and Hegel is also drawn by Richard Schuldenfrei, although on a rather different basis.. See his "Quine in Perspective," *Journal of Philosophy* LXIX (1972).

59 Quine's acceptance of the idea that knowledge is mediated is evident, I take it, in his insistence that we cannot avoid adherence to some theory of the world, even though there are alternatives to any such given theory. He holds that these facts do not prejudice the truth of what we say or the reality of what we talk about. Quine therefore denies that there is a fundamental contrast between the real and the theoretical; any such contrast would require a sense of "real" according to which the real is

independent of theory, but Quine denies that there is any such sense. Thus: "Everything to which we concede existence is a posit from the standpoint of the theory-building process, and simultaneously real from the standpoint of the theory that is being built. Nor let us look down on the standpoint of the theory as make-believe; for we can never do better that occupy the standpoint of some theory or other, the best we can muster at the time" (*Word and Object* Cambridge: Mass., M.I.T. Press, 1960], 22).

The issue of whether knowledge is mediated is, as our discussion of atomism suggested, related to the issue of holism versus atomism; thus it is not surprising that in Quine the insistence on the mediacy of knowledge goes with a holistic view of knowledge. The fact that those notions that one might think of as philosophical or framework notions – including the notion of experience itself – are supposed to be understood and justified in terms of ordinary, that is, for Quine scientific, knowledge suggests a sense in which his system closes on itself. This circularity is explicit in "Epistemology Naturalised," in *Ontological Relativity, and other essays* (New York: Columbia University Press, 1969). Here too we see, in more concrete form, an illustration of the comparison between Quine and Hegel made in the previous note.

BIBLIOGRAPHY

As we might expect for a philosopher of Hegel's stature, the literature on him is enormous. Since the 1960s it has been growing at an astronomical rate. The following bibliography is therefore necessarily selective. It concentrates on the most-recent literature on Hegel in French, German, and English. I have included older articles and books on Hegel only insofar as they have been of special interest, of proven worth, or filled a gap in the literature. Only important articles have been listed separately. If an article appears in a collection that has been already listed, it is not given a special entry. Whenever possible, English translations have been cited.

The aim of this bibliography is to provide a first working list of sources for the Hegel student or specialist. Students or specialists wishing to consult further literature should see Kurt Steinhauer, *Hegel Bibliographie* (Munich: Sauer, 1980), which lists almost all secondary sources published from 1802 to 1975. There are several other more-specialized bibliographies:

Brendenfeld, Hermann. "Dissertationen über Hegel und seine Philosophie: Deutschland, Österreich, Schweiz, 1842–1960." *Hegel Studien* II (1963): 424–441.

Gabel, Gernot. *Hegel: Eine Bibliographie der Dissertationen aus sieben westeuropäischen Ländern 1885–1975*. Hamburg: Edition Gemini, 1980.

Gründer, Karlfried. "Bibliographie zur politische Theorie Hegels." In Joachim Ritter, *Hegel und die franzöische Revolution*. Köln: Opladen, 1957.

Weiss, Frederick. "A Bibliography of Books on Hegel in English." In J. O'Malley, ed., *The Legacy of Hegel*. The Hague: Martinus Nijhoff, 1973.

HEGEL'S WORKS: GERMAN EDITIONS

Marheineke, Phillip, *et al*, ed. *G.W.F. Hegel's Werke*. 18 vols. Berlin: Duncker & Humblot, 1832–1845.

Glockner, Hermann, ed. *Sämtliche Werke. Jubiläumsausgabe*. 20 vols. Stuttgart: Fromann, 1927–1930.

487

Lasson, Georg, and Hoffmeister, Johannes, eds. *Sämtliche Werke. Kritische Ausgabe.* 30 vols. Leipzig: Meiner, 1911–1938 (incomplete).

Moldenhauer, Eva, and Michel, Karl, eds. *Werke. Werkausgabe.* 20 vols. Frankfurt: Suhrkamp, 1969–1972.

Deutsche Forschungsgemeinschaft im Verbindung mit Rheinisch-westfälishen Akadmie der Wissenschaften, ed. *Gesammelte Werke. Kritische Ausgabe.* 13 vols to date. Hamburg: Meiner, 1968f.

Nohl, Hermann, ed. *Hegels theologische Jugendschiften.* Tübingen: Mohr, 1907.

Lasson, Georg, ed. *Schriften zur Politik und Rechtsphilosophie.* Leipzig; Meiner, 1923.

Jenenser Logik, Metaphysik und Naturphilosophie. Leipzig: Meiner, 1923.

Wissenschaft der Logik. 2 vols. Hamburg: Meiner, 1966–67.

Erste Druckschriften. Hamburg: Meiner, 1928.

Hoffmeister, Johannes, ed. *Jenaer Realphilosophie I: Die Vorlesungen von 1803/04.* Leipzig: Meiner, 1932.

Jenaer Realphilosophie II: Die Vorlesungen von 1805/06. Leipzig: Meiner, 1932.

Briefe von und an Hegel. 5 vols. Hamburg: Meiner, 1952–1954.

Die Vernunft in der Geschichte. Hamburg: Meiner, 1955.

Dokumente zu Hegels Entwicklung. Stuttgart: Fromann, 1936.

Phänomenologie des Geistes. Hamburg: Meiner, 1952.

Nürnberger Schriften. Leipzig: Meiner, 1938.

Grundlinien der Philosophie des Rechts. Hamburg: Meiner, 1955.

Berliner Schriften, 1818–1831. Hamburg: Meiner, 1956.

Vorlesungen über die Philosophie der Weltgeschichte. 4 vols Hamburg: Meiner, 1955.

Ilting, Karl Heinz, ed. *Vorlesungen über Rechtsphilosophie.* 4 vols. Stuttgart: Fromann, 1973–1976.

Henrich, Dieter, ed. *Philosophie des Rechts: Die Vorlesung von 1819/20.* Frankfurt: Suhrkamp, 1983.

HEGEL'S WORKS: ENGLISH TRANSLATIONS

J.B. Baillie, trans. *The Phenomenology of Mind.* London: George Allen & Unwin, 1967.

Brown, Robert, ed. *Lectures on the History of Philosophy.* 3 vols. Berkeley: University of California Press, 1990.

Burbidge, J.S., trans. *The Jena System 1804/05: Logic and Metaphysics.* Montreal & Kingston: McGill/Queens University Press, 1986.

Butler, C., and Seiler, C. trans. *Letters.* Indianapolis: University of Indiana, 1984.

Dobbins, J., and Fuss, P., trans. *Three Essays 1793–1795*. Contains: "The Tübingen Essay," "Berne Fragments," "The Life of Jesus." Notre Dame, Ind.: University of Notre Dame Press, 1984.

Geraets, T.F., Harris, H.S., and Suchting, W.A. *The Encyclopedia Logic*. Indianapolis: Hackett, 1991.

George, Michael, and Vincent, Andrew, ed. *The Philosophical Propaedeutic*. Trans. A.V. Miller. Oxford: Basil Blackwell, 1986.

Giovanni, G., and Harris, H.S. *Between Kant and Hegel: Texts in the Development of Post-Kantian Idealism*. Albany: SUNY, 1985. Contains: "How the Ordinary Human Understanding Takes Philosophy," "Relationship of Skepticism."

Haldane, E.S., and Simpson, F.H., trans. *Lectures on the History of Philosophy*. 3 vols. London: Paul, Trench & Trübner, 1892–96.

Harris, H.S., and Cerf, W., trans. *Difference Between the Systems of Fichte and Schelling*. New York: SUNY, 1977.

Faith and Knowledge. New York: SUNY, 1977.

System of Ethical Life and First Philosophy of Spirit. New York: SUNY, 1979.

Hodgson, Peter, and Brown, R.F., trans. *Lectures on the Philosophy of Religion*. 3 vols. Berkeley: University of California Press, 1984–86.

Kaufmann, Walter, trans. *Hegel: Texts and Commentary. Hegel's Preface to his System in a New Translation*. Garden City, N.Y.: Doubleday, 1966.

Knox, T.M., trans. *Philosophy of Right*. Oxford: Clarendon Press, 1942.

Political Writings. Oxford: Clarendon Press, 1964.

Natural Law. Philadelphia: University of Pennsylvania Press, 1975.

Early Theological Writings. Chicago: University of Chicago Press, 1948.

Hegel's Aesthetics. Oxford: Clarendon Press, 1975.

Hegel's Introduction to the Lectures on the History of Philosophy. Oxford: Clarendon Press, 1985.

Miller, A.V., trans. *Science of Logic*. London: George Allen & Unwin, 1969.

Phenomenology of Spirit. Oxford: Oxford University Press, 1977.

Philosophy of Nature. Oxford: Oxford University Press, 1970.

Philosophy of Mind. Oxford: Oxford University Press, 1971.

Nisbet, H.B. *Lectures on the Philosophy of World History: Introduction: Reason in History*. Cambridge: Cambridge University Press, 1975.

Petry, M.J., trans. *The Berlin Phenomenology*. Dordrecht: Reidel, 1981.

Philosophy of Nature. 3 vols. London: George Allen & Unwin, 1970.

Philosophy of Subjective Spirit. 3 vols. Dordrecht: Reidel, 1978.

Rauch, Leo. *Hegel and the Human Spirit: A Translation of the Jena Lectures on the Philosophy of Spirit, 1805–06*. Detroit: Wayne State University Press, 1986.

Introduction to the Philosophy of History. Indianapolis, Ind.: Hackett, 1988.

Speirs, E.B., and Sanderson, J.B., trans. *Lectures on the Philosophy of Religion.* London: Paul, Trench & Trübner, 1895.

Wallace, William. *Hegel's Logic.* Oxford: Oxford University Press, 1975.

Waszek, Norbert. *Hegel's Habilitionsthesen.* A Translation with Introduction and Annotated Bibliography. In David Lamb, ed., *Hegel and Modern Philosophy.* London: Croom Helm, 1987.

Wood, Allen, ed. *Hegel's Philosophy of Right.* Trans. H.B. Nisbet. Cambridge: Cambridge University Press, 1991.

BACKGROUND AND CONTEXT

Aris, Reinhold. *A History of Political Thought in Germany.* London: Cass, 1936.

Beck, Lewis. *Early German Philosophy.* Cambridge: Harvard University Press, 1969.

Beiser, Frederick. *The Fate of Reason: German Philosophy from Kant to Fichte.* Cambridge: Harvard University Press, 1987.

Enlightenment, Revolution and Romanticism: The Formation of Modern German Political Thought, 1790–1800. Cambridge: Harvard University Press, 1992.

Breidbach, Olaf. *Das Organische in Hegels Denken: Studie zur Naturphilosophie und Biologie um 1800.* Epistemata: Reihe Philosophie vol. 10. Würzburg: Königshausen & Neumann, 1982.

Bruford, Walter. *Culture and Society in Classical Weimar.* Cambridge: Cambridge University Press, 1962.

Germany in the Eighteenth Century: The Social Background to the Literary Revival. Cambridge: Cambridge University Press, 1935.

Brunschwig, Henri. *Enlightenment and Romanticism in Eighteenth Century Prussia.* Trans. Frank Jellinek. Chicago: University of Chicago Press, 1974.

Butler, E.M. *The Tyranny of Greece over Germany.* Cambridge: Cambridge University Press, 1935.

Copleston, Frederick. *A History of Philosophy.* Vol. VII: Fichte to Hegel. Garden City, N.Y.: Doubleday, 1963.

Droz, Jacques. *L'Allemagne et la Revolution francaise.* Paris: Presses Universitaires de France, 1949.

Epstein, Klaus. *The Genesis of German Conservatism.* Princeton: Princeton University Press, 1966.

Esposito, Joseph. *Schelling's Idealism and Philosophy of Nature.* London: Associated University Presses, 1977.

Gray, Jesse. *Hegel and Greek Thought.* New York: Harper & Row, 1968.

Hartmann, Nicolai. *Die Philosophie des deutschen Idealismus.* Berlin: de Gruyter, 1929.

Haym, Rudolf. *Die romantische Schule.* Berlin: Weidmann, 1906. Reprint Darmstadt: Wissenschaftliche Buchgesellschaft, 1977.

Hegel, Hannelore. *Isaak von Sinclair zwischen Fichte, Hölderlin und Hegel.* Frankfurt: Klostermann, 1971.

Henrich, Dieter. *Hegel im Kontext.* Frankfurt: Suhrkamp, 1971.

Hinchmann, Lewis. *Hegel's Critique of the Enlightenment.* Gainesville: University Presses of Florida, 1984.

Hoffmeister, Johannes. *Goethe und des deutsche Idealismus.* Berlin: de Gruyter, 1929.

Huch, Ricarda. *Die Romantik: Blütezeit, Ausbreitung und Verfall* 2 vols. Leipzig: Haessel, 1908.

Kelly, George. *Idealism, Politics and History.* Cambridge: Cambridge University Press, 1969.

Kluckhohn, Paul. *Das Ideengut der deutschen Romantik.* 2nd ed. Halle: Niemeyer, 1942.

Die Auffassung der Liebe in der Literatur des 18 Jahrhunderts und in der deutschen Romantik. 3rd ed. Tübingen: Niemeyer, 1966.

Koselleck, Reinhart. *Preussen zwischen Reform und Revolution: Allgemeines Landrecht, Verwaltung und soziale Bewegung.* Stuttgart: Klett, 1967.

Kritik und Krise: Eine Studie zur Pathogenese der bürgerlichen Welt. 6th ed. Frankfurt: Suhrkamp, 1989.

Krieger, Leonhard. *The German Idea of Freedom: History of a Political Tradition.* Boston: Beacon Press, 1957.

Kronenberg, Moritz. *Geschichte des deutschen Idealismus.* 2 vols. Munich: Beck, 1912.

Kroner, Richard. *Von Kant bis Hegel.* Tübingen: Mohr, 1921.

Leube, Heinrich. *Das Tübinger Stift, 1770–1950.* Stuttgart, 1954.

Lovejoy, Arthur. *Reason, Understanding and Time.* Baltimore: Johns Hopkins University Press, 1961.

Metzger, Wilhelm. *Gesellschaft, Recht und Staat in der Ethik des deutschen Idealismus.* Heidelberg: Winter, 1917.

Nauen, Franz. *Revolution, Idealism and Human Freedom: Schelling, Hölderlin and Hegel and the Crisis of Early German Idealism.* Archivs Internationales d'Historie des Idees No. 45. The Hague: Martinus Nijhoff, 1971.

Pfleiderer, Otto. *The Development of Theology in Germany since Kant.* 2nd ed. Trans. J.F. Smith. London: Sonnenschein, 1893.

Rohr, David. *The Origins of Social Liberalism in Germany.* Chicago: University of Chicago Press, 1963.

Rosenberg Hans. *Bureaucracy, Aristocracy and Autocracy: The Prussian Experience 1660–1815.* Boston: Beacon Press, 1966.

Rosenkranz, Karl. *Geschichte der kantischen Philosophie.* Leipzig: Voss, 1840. Reprint ed. Stephen Dietzsch. Berlin: Akademie Verlag, 1987.

Royce, Josiah. *Lectures on Modern Idealism.* New Haven: Yale University Press, 1964.

The Spirit of Modern Philosophy. Boston: Houghton, Mifflin, 1892. Reprint New York: Dover, 1983.

Seth, Andrew. *The Development from Kant to Hegel.* Edinburgh: Williams & Norgate, 1882.

Simon, Walter. *The Failure of the Prussian Reform Movement, 1807–1819.* Ithaca, N.Y.: Cornell University Press, 1955.

Valjavec, Fritz. *Die Entstehung der politischen Strömungen in Deutschland, 1770–1815.* Munich: Oldenbourg, 1951.

HEGEL'S INTELLECTUAL DEVELOPMENT

Asveld, Paul. *La Pensée religieuse du jeune Hegel.* Paris: Desclee de Brouwer, 1953.

Axmann, Walter. *Zur Frage nach dem Ursprung des dialektischen Denkens bei Hegel.* Würzburg: Triltsch Verlag, 1939.

Baum, Manfred. *Die Entstehung der Hegelschen Dialektik.* Neuzeit und Gegenwart, vol 2. Bonn: Bouvier, 1986.

Betzendörfer, Walter. *Hölderlins Studienjahr im Tübinger Stift.* Salzer: Heibronn, 1922.

Beyer, Wilhelm. *Zwischen Phänomenologie und Logik: Hegel als Redakteur der Bamberger Zeitung.* 2nd. ed. Köln: Pahl-Rügenstein, 1974.

Bonsiepen, Wolfgang. *Der Begriff der Negativität in den Jenaer Schriften Hegels.* Hegel-Studien Beiheft 16. Bonn: Bouvier 1977.

"Zur Datierung und Interpretation des Fragments 'C: Die Wissenschaft.' " *Hegel Studien* XII (1977): 179–90.

Bormetter, Hugo. *Die Überwindung der blossen Vernunft: Hegels Auseinandersetzung mit Kant und Fichte in Tübingen und Bern.* Europäische Hochschulschriften Reihe 20, Philosophie vol 40. Frankfurt: Lang, 1979.

Bourgeois, Bernard. *Hegel à Francfort.* Paris: Vrin, 1970.

Bubner, Rüdiger. *Das älteste Systemprogramm: Studien zur Frühgeschichte des deutschen Idealismus.* Hegel-Studien Beiheft 9. Bonn: Bouvier, 1973.

Cain, Paul. *Widerspruch und Subjektivität: eine problem-geschichtliche Studie zum jungen Hegel.* Abhandlungen zu Philosophie, Psychologie und Pädagogik 130. Bonn: Bouvier, 1978.

Chamley, Paul. "Les origins de la pensée économique de Hegel." *Hegel-Studien* III (1965): 225–61.

Dickey, Laurence. *Hegel: Religion, Economics and Politics of the Spirit, 1770–1807.* Cambridge: Cambridge University Press, 1987.

Dilthey, Wilhelm. *Die Jugendgeschichte Hegels.* In *Gesammelte Schriften,* Vol 4: Stuttgart: Tuebner, 1962–65.

Düsing, Klaus. "Spekulation und Reflexion: Zur Zusammenarbeit Schellings und Hegels in Jena." *Hegel-Studien* V (1969): 95–128.

"Idealistische Substanz-Metaphysik. Probleme der Systementwicklung bei Schelling und Hegel in Jena." *Hegel-Studien Beiheft* 20 (1980): 25–44.

Fischer, Kuno. *Hegels Leben, Werke und Lehre.* 2nd ed. Heidelberg: Winter, 1911.

Gérard, Gilbert. *Critique et dialectique: l'itinéraire de Hegel à Iéna, 1801–1805.* Brussels: Facultés Saint Louis, 1982.

Glockner, Hermann. *Entwicklung und Schicksal der Hegelschen Philosophie.* Vol. II of *Hegel.* In *Sämtliche Werke* vol. 22. Stuttgart: Fromann, 1940.

Görland, Ingtraud. *Die Kantkritik des jungen Hegel.* Philosophische Abhandlungen 28. Frankfurt: Klostermann, 1966.

Haering, Theodor. *Hegel, sein Wollen und sein Werk.* Leipzig: Tuebner, 1929.

Hartknopf, Werner. *Der Durchbruch zur Dialektischen in Hegels Denken.* Meisenheim: Haim, 1876.

Kontinuität und Diskontinuität in Hegels Jenaer Anfängen Monographien zur philosophischen Forschung vol. 184. Königstein: Forum Academicum, 1979.

Harris, Henry. *Hegel's Development. Volume I: Toward the Sunlight 1770–1801.* Oxford: Oxford University Press, 1972.

Hegel's Development. Volume II: Night Thoughts. Jena 1801–1806. Oxford: Oxford University Press, 1983.

Haym, Rudolf. *Hegel und seine Zeit.* Berlin: Gaertner, 1857. Reprint Darmstadt: Wissenschaftliche Buchgesellschaft, 1962.

Helferich, Christoph. *G.W.F. Hegel.* Sammlung Metzler 182. Stuttgart: Metzler, 1979.

Henrich, Dieter, and Düsing, Klaus, eds. *Hegel in Jena: Die Entwicklung des Systems und der Zusammenarbeit mit Schelling. Hegel-Studien Beiheft XX.* Bonn: Bouvier, 1980.

Hyppolite, Jean. *Essays on Marx and Hegel.* Trans. J. O'Neill. New York: Basic Books, 1969.

Jamme, Christoph. "*Ein ungelehrtes Buch.*" *Die philosophische Gemeinschaft zwischen Hölderlin und Hegel in Frankfurt 1797–1800.* *Hegel-Studien Beiheft* XXIII. Bonn: Bouvier, 1983.

Kaufmann, Walter. *Hegel: A Reexamination.* Garden City, N.Y.: Doubleday, 1965.

Kimmerle, Heinz. 'Zur Chronologie von Hegels Jenaer Schriften." *Hegel-Studien* IV (1967): 125–67.

"Dokumente zu Hegels Jenaer Dozententätigkeit, 1801–1807." *Hegel-Studien* IV (1967): 21–100.

"Zur Entwicklung des Hegelschen Denkens in Jena." *Hegel-Studien Beiheft* 4 (1969): 33–48.

Das Problem der Abgeschlossenheit des Denkens: Hegels System der Philosophie in den Jahren 1800–1804. *Hegel-Studien Beiheft* VIII. Bonn: Bouvier, 1970.

Klaiber, Julius. *Hölderlin, Hegel und Schelling in ihren schwäbisches Jugendjahren.* Stuttgart: Cotta, 1877.

Krings, Hermann. *Die Entfremdung zwischen Schelling und Hegel 1801–1807.* Munich: Beck, 1977.

Legros, Robert. *La jeune Hegel et la naissance de la pensée romantique.* Brussels: Ousias, 1980.

Lukács, Georg. *The Young Hegel.* Trans. R. Livingstone. Cambridge; MIT Press, 1976.

Weist, Kurt. "Hegels Systemkonzeption in der frühen Jenaer Zeit." *Hegel-Studien Beiheft* XX (1980): 59–79.

Mueller, Gustav. *Hegel: Denkgeschichte eines Lebendigen.* Bern: Francke, 1959.

Nicolin, Georg, ed. *Hegel in Bericht seiner Zeitgenossen.* Hamburg: Meiner, 1970.

'Zur Situation der Biographischen Hegel Forschung: ein Bericht'. *Veröffentlichungen des Archivs der Stadt Stuttgart:* Sonderband 6. Stuttgart: Klett, 1975.

Peperzak, Adrien. *La jeune Hegel et la vision morale du monde.* The Hague: Martinus Nijhoff, 1960.

Plant, Raymond. *Hegel.* London: George Allen & Unwin, 1973.

Pöggeler, Otto. 'Hegels Jenaer Systemkonzeption'. *Philosophisches Jahrbuch* 71 (1963–64): 286–314.

"Hegel, der Verfasser des ältesten Systemprogramms des deutschen Idealismus." *Hegel-Studien Beiheft* IV (1969): 17–32.

Rohr-Moser, Günther. "Zur Vorgeschichte der Jugenschriften Hegels." *Zeitschrift für philosophische Forschung* XIV (1960): 182–208.

Schmidt, Gerhard. *Hegel in Nürnberg.* Tübingen: Niemeyer, 1960.

Schüler, Gisela. "Zur Chronologie von Hegels Jugendschriften." *Hegel-Studien* II (1963): 111–59.

Strahm, Hans. "Aus Hegels Berner Zeit." *Archiv für Geschichte der Philosophie* XII (1932): 514–33.

Trede, Johann. "Hegel's frühe Logik (1801–1803/04)." *Hegel-Studien* VII (1972): 123–68.

Wahl, Jean. *La Malheur de la conscience dans la philosophie de Hegel.* Paris: Editions Rieder, 1929.

EPISTEMOLOGY AND METAPHYSICS

Adorno, Theodor. *Drei Studien zu Hegel.* Frankfurt, Suhrkamp, 1963.

Ameriks, Karl. "Hegel's Critique of Kant's Theoretical Philosophy." *Philosophy and Phenomenological Research* XLVI (1985): 1–35.

Baum, Manfred. *Die Entstehung der hegelschen Dialektik.* Bonn: Bouvier, 1986.

Berthold-Bond, Daniel *Hegel's Grand Synthesis: A Study of Being, Thought and History.* Albany, N.Y.: SUNY, 1989.

Bloch, Ernst. *Subject-Objekt: Erläuterungen zu Hegel.* Frankfurt: Suhrkamp, 1962.

Bubner, Rüdiger. *Dialektik und Wissenschaft.* Frankfurt: Suhrkamp, 1962.

Caird, Edward. *Hegel.* Edinburgh: Basil Blackwood, 1883.

Clark, M. *Logic and System: A Study of the Transition from Vorstellung to Thought in the Philosophy of Hegel.* The Hague: Martinus Nijhoff, 1970.

Cunningham, Gustavus. *Thought and Reality in Hegel's System.* Cornell Studies in Philosophy No. 8. New York: Longmans, Green, 1910.

DeVries, William. "Hegel on Reference and Knowledge." *Journal of the History of Philosophy* 26 (1988): 297–307.

"Hegel on Representation and Thought." *Idealistic Studies* 17 (1987): 123–32.

"Hegel's Dialectic of Teleology." *Philosophical Topics* 19 (199): 51–72.

Dinkel, Bernhard. *Der junge Hegel und die Aufhebung des subjektiven Idealismus.* Münchener philosophische Forschungen vol 12. Bonn: Bouvier, 1974.

Findlay, J.N. *Hegel: A Re-examination.* London: George Allen & Unwin, 1958.

Forster, Michael. *Hegel and Scepticism.* Cambridge: Harvard University Press, 1989.

Glockner, Hermann. *Der Begriff in Hegels Philosophie.* Heidelberger Abhandlungen zur Philosophie und ihre Geschichte No. 2. Tübingen: Mohr, 1924.

Görland, Ingtraud. *Die Kantkritik des jungen Hegel.* Philosophische Abhandlungen XXVIII. Frankfurt: Klostermann, 1966.

Horstmann, Rolf-Peter, ed. *Seminar: Dialektik in der Philosophie Hegels.* Frankfurt: Suhrkamp, 1978.

Houlgate, Stephan. *Hegel, Nietzsche and the Criticism of Metaphysics.* Cambridge: Cambridge University Press, 1986.

Inwood, Michael. *Hegel.* London: Routledge, Kegan & Paul, 1983.

Kainz, Howard. *Paradox, Dialectic and System: A Contemporary Reconstruction of the Hegelian Problematic.* University Park, Penn.: Penn State University Press, 1987.

Lamb, David. *Hegel: From Foundation to System.* The Hague: Martinus Nijhoff, 1980.

Lauer, Quinton. *Essays in Hegelian Dialectic.* New York: Fordham University Press, 1983.

Hegel's Idea of Philosophy. 2nd ed. New York: Fordham University Press, 1983.

Maier, Josef. *On Hegel's Critique of Kant.* New York: Columbia University Press, 1939.

McRae, Robert. *Philosophy and the Absolute: The Modes of Hegel's Speculation.* Archivs internationales d'histoire des idées 109. The Hague: Martinus Nijhoff, 1985.

McTaggart, James. *Studies in Hegel's Dialectic.* New York: Russell & Russell, 1964.

Moran, Phillip. *Hegel and the Fundamental Problems of Philosophy.* Amsterdam: Grüner, 1988.

Mure, G.R.G. *An Introduction to Hegel.* Oxford: Clarendon Press, 1970.

Myers, Henry. *The Spinoza-Hegel Paradox.* Ithaca: Cornell University Press, 1944.

Pippin, Robert. *Hegel's Idealism.* Cambridge: Cambridge University Press, 1989.

Priest, Stephen, ed. *Hegel's Critique of Kant.* Oxford: Oxford University Press, 1987.

Rockmore, Thomas, *Hegel's Circular Epistemology.* Bloomington: Indiana University Press, 1986.

Röttges, Heinz. *Dialektik und Skeptizismus: die Rolle des Skeptizismus für Genese, Selbstverständnis und Kritik der Dialektik.* Frankfurt: Athenäum, 1987.

Rosen, Michael. *Hegel's Dialectic and its Criticism.* Cambridge: Cambridge University Press, 1982.

Rosen, Stanley, *G.W.F. Hegel.* New Haven: Yale University Press, 1974.

Schrader-Klebert, Karin. *Das Problem des Anfangs in Hegels Philosophie.* Vienna: Oldenbourg, 1969.

Sfard, David. *Du Rôle de l'Idée de Contradiction chez Hégel.* Nancy: Poncelet, 1934.

Smith, J. "Hegel's Critique of Kant." *Review of Metaphysics* 26 (1973): 438–60.

Soll, Ivan. *An Introduction to Hegel's Metaphysics.* Chicago: University of Chicago Press, 1969.

Stace, William. *The Philosophy of Hegel.* New York: Dover, 1955.

Stern, Robert. *Hegel, Kant and the Structure of the Object.* London: Routledge, 1990.

Taylor, Charles. *Hegel.* Cambridge: Cambridge University Press, 1975.

Westphal, Kenneth. "Hegel's Solution to the Dilemma of the Criterion." *The History of Philosophy Quarterly* 5 (1988): 173–88.

Werner, Jürgen. *Darstellung als Kritik: Hegels Frage nach dem Anfang der Wissenschaft.* Abhandlungen zur Philosophie Psychologie und Pädagogik 204. Bonn: Bouvier, 1986.

White, Alan. *Absolute Knowledge: Hegel and the Problem of Metaphysics.* Athens: Ohio University Press, 1983.

Wohlfahrt, Günter. *Der spekulative Satz: Bemerkungen zum Begriff der Spekulation bei Hegel.* Berlin: de Gruyter, 1981.

Wolff, M. *Der Begriff des Widerspruchs: Eine Studie zur Dialektik Kants und Hegels.* Königstein: Haim, 1981.

LOGIC

Baillie, J.B. *The Origin and Significance of Hegel's Logic.* London: Macmillan, 1901. Reprint New York: Garland, 1984.

Bole, T. "The Dialectic of Hegel's Logic as the Logic of Ontology." *Hegel Jahrbuch* 19/4 (1975): 152–59.

Bullinger, Anton. *Hegels Lehre vom Widerspruch.* Dillingen: Kolb, 1884.

Burbidge, John. *On Hegel's Logic: Fragments of a Commentary.* Atlantic Highlands, N.J.: Humanities Press, 1981.

DiGiovanni, George. "Reflection and Contradiction. A Commentary on Some Passages of Hegel's Science of Logic." *Hegel-Studien* VIII (1973): 131–62.

DiGiovanni, George, ed. *Essays on Hegel's Logic* Albany, N.Y.: SUNY, 1989.

Doz, André. *La logique de Hegel et les problems traditionels de l'ontologie.* Paris: Vrin, 1987.

Düsing, Klaus. *Das Problem der Subjektivität in Hegels Logik.* Bonn: Bouvier, 1976.

Falk, Hans-Peter. *Das Wissen in Hegels Wissenschaft der Logik.* Symposium No. 83. Freiburg: Alber, 1983.

Fleischmann, Eugène. *La science universelle, ou La Logique de Hegel* Recherches en sciences humaines no. 25. Paris: Plon, 1968.

Fulda, Hans. *Das Problem einer Einleitung in Hegels Wissenschaft der Logik.* Frankfurt: Klostermann, 1965.

Fulda, Hans, with Theunissen, Michael, and Horstmann, R.P., eds. *Kritische Darstellung der Metaphysik. Eine Diskussion der Hegels Logik.* Frankfurt: Suhrkamp, 1980.

Günther, Gotthard. *Grundzüge einer neuen Theorie des Denkens in Hegels Logik.* Hamburg: Meiner, 1978.

Hackenesch, Christa. *Die Logik der Andersheit: eine Untersuchung zu Hegels Begriff der Reflexion.* Frankfurt: Athenäum, 1987.

Harris, Errol. *An Interpretation of the Logic of Hegel.* Lanham, Md.: University Press of America, 1983.

Henrich, Dieter, ed. *Hegels Wissenschaft der Logik.* Veröffentlichen der Internationalen Hegel Vereinigung Nr. 16. Stuttgart: Klett, 1986.

Die Wissenschaft der Logik und der Logik der Reflexion. Bonn: Bouvier, 1987.

Hegels Wissenschaft der Logik: Formation und Rekonstruktion. Stuttgart: Klett-Cotta, 1986.

Johnson, Paul. *The Critique of Thought: A Re-examination of Hegel's Science of Logic.* Aldershot: Avebury, 1988.

Kemper, Peter. *Dialektik und Darstellung: eine Untersuchung zur spekulativen Methode in Hegels Wissenschaft der Logik.* Frankfurt: Fischer, 1980.

Lakebrink, Bernard. *Die Europäische Idee der Freiheit: 1 Teil, Hegels Logik und der Tradition der Selbstbestimmung.* Leiden: Brill, 1968.

Léonard, André. *Commentaire littéral de la logique de Hegel.* Bibliotheque Philosophique de Louvain 24. Paris: Vrin, 1974.

Marx, Wolfgang. *Hegels Theorie logischer Vermittlung.* Stuttgart/Bad Cannstatt: Fromann Holzboog, 1972.

McTaggart, James. *A Commentary on Hegel's Logic.* Cambridge: Cambridge University Press, 1910.

Mure, G.R.G. *A Study of Hegel's Logic.* Oxford: Clarendon Press, 1950.

Pechmann, Alexander. *Die Kategorie des Masses in Hegels Wissenschaft der Logik: Einführung und Kommentar.* Köln: Pahl Rügenstein, 1980.

Pinkard, Terry. *Hegels Dialectic. The Explanation of Possibility.* Philadelphia: Temple University Press, 1988.

"Hegel's Idealism and Hegel's Logic." *Zeitschrift für philosophische Forschung* 23 (1979): 210–25.

"The Logic of Hegel's Logic." *Journal of the History of Philosophy* 17 (1979): 417–35.

Puntel, L. "Was ist 'logisch' in Hegels *Wissenschaft der Logik*?" In W. Beyer, ed., *Die Logik des Wissens und das Problem der Erziehung.* Hamburg: Meiner, 1982.

Rademacher, Hans, *Hegels Wissenschaft der Logik: eine darstellende und erläuterende Einführung.* 2nd ed. Wiesbaden: Steiner, 1979.

Richli, Urs. *Form und Inhalt in G.W.F. Hegels Wissenschaft der Logik.* Vienna: Oldenbourg, 1982.

Rohs, Peter. *Form und Grund: Interpretation eines Kapitels der Hegelschen Wissenschaft der Logik.* Bonn: Bouvier, 1969.

Salomon, Werner. *Urteil und Selbstverhältnis: Kommentiernde Untersuchung zur Lehre vom Urteil in Hegels Wissenschaft der Logik.* Frankfurt: Fisher, 1982.

Schmid, Aloys. *Entwicklungsgeschichte der Hegel'schen Logik.* Regensberg: Joseph Mai, 1858. Reprint Hildesheim: Georg Olms, 1976.

Schmidt, Josef. *Hegels Wissenschaft der Logik und ihre Kritik durch Adolf Trendelenberg.* Pullacher philosophische Forschungen vol. 232. Munich: Berchmann, 1977.

Schubert, Alexander. *Der Strukturgedanke in Hegels Wissenschaft der Logik.* Königsstein: Haim, 1985.

Theunissen, Michael. *Sein und Schein: Die kritische Funktion der Hegelschen Logik.* Frankfurt: Suhrkamp, 1978.

Vos, Ludovocus. *Hegels Wissenschaft der Logik, die absolute Idee: Einleitung und Kommentar.* Bonn: Bouvier, 1983.

Wetzel, M. *Reflexion und Bestimmtheit in Hegels Wissenschaft der Logik.* Hamburg: Fundament, 1971.

PHENOMENOLOGY OF SPIRIT

Beaufort, Jan. *Die drei Schlüsse: Untersuchungen zur Stellung der "Phänomenologie" in Hegels System der Wissenschaft.* Epistemata: Reihe Philosophie Vol. 18. Würzburg: Königshausen & Neumann, 1983.

Becker, W. *Hegels Phänomenologie des Geistes: Eine Interpretation.* Stuttgart: Kohlhammer, 1970.

Bubner, Rüdiger. "Problemgeschichte und systematischer Sinn einer Phänomenologie." *Hegel Studien* V (1969): 129–59.

Claesges, Ulrich. *Darstellung des erscheinenden Wissens: systematisches Einleitung in Hegels Phänomenologie des Geistes.* Hegel-Studien Beiheft 21. Bonn: Bouvier, 1981.

Fink, Eugen. *Phänomenologische Interpretation der Phänomenologie des Geistes.* Frankfurt: Klostermann, 1977.

Flay, J. *Hegel's Quest for Certainty.* Albany: SUNY, 1984.

Forster, Michael. *Hegel's Idea of a Phenomenology of Spirit.* Cambridge: Harvard University Press, 1993.

Fulda, Hans, ed. *Materialien zu Hegels Phänomenologie des Geistes*. Frankfurt: Suhrkamp, 1973.

Gadamer, Hans, ed. *Beiträge zur Deutung der Phänomenologie des Geistes. Hegel-Studien Beiheft III*. Bonn: Bouvier, 1966. *Hegel's Dialectic: Five Hermeneutical Studies*. Trans. Christopher Smith. New Haven: Yale University Press, 1976.

Gauvin, Joseph. *Wortindex zu Hegels Phänomenologie des Geistes. Hegel-Studien* Beiheft 14. Bonn: Bouvier, 1977.

Guibal, Francis. *Dieu selon Hegel: essai sur la problématique de la Phénomenologie de l'esprit*. Paris: Aubier Montaigne, 1975.

Haering, Theodor. "Die Entstehungsgeschichte der Phänomenologie des Geistes." In *Verhandlungen des Dritten Hegelkongresses*, ed. B. Wigersma. Tübingen: Mohr, 1934: 118–138.

Hartmann, Klaus. *Die ontologische Option: Studien zu Hegels Propädeutik, Schellings Hegel-Kritik und Hegels Phänomenologie des Geistes*. Berlin: de Gruyter, 1976.

Heidegger, Martin. *Hegel's Concept of Experience*, New York: Harper & Row, 1970.

Heinrichs, J. *Die Logik der Phänomenologie des Geistes*. Abhandlungen zur Philosophie, Psychologie und Pädagogik 89. Bonn: Bouvier, 1974.

Hyppolyte, Jean. *Genesis and Structure of the Phenomenology of Spirit*. Trans. S. Cherniak and R. Heckmann. Evanston, Ill.: Northwestern University Press, 1974.

Jarczyk, Gwendoline. *Les premiers combats de la reconnaissance: maîtrise et servitude dans la phénoménologie de l'esprit de Hegel: text et commentaire*. Paris: Aubier, 1987.

Kainz, Howard. *Hegel's Phenomenology. Part I*. University: University of Alabama Press, 1976.

Hegel's Phenomenology. Part II. Athens: Ohio University Press, 1983.

Kimmerle, Gerd. *Sein und Selbst: Untersuchung zur Kategorialen Einheit von Vernunft und Geist in Hegels Phänomenologie des Geistes*. Abhandlungen zur Philosophie, Psychologie und Pädagogik 131. Bonn: Bouvier, 1978.

Kojeve, Andre. *Introduction to the Reading of Hegel*. Trans. J.H. Nichols. New York: Basic Books, 1960.

Labarriere, Pierre. *La phénoménologie de l'esprit de Hegel*. Paris: Aubier-Montaigne, 1979.

Structures et Mouvement Dialectique dans la Phénoménologie de l'Esprit de Hegel. Paris: Aubier-Montaigne, 1968.

Lauer, Quinton. *A Reading of Hegel's Phenomenology of Spirit*. 2nd ed. New York: Fordham University Press, 1976.

Loewenberg, Jacob. *Hegel's Phenomenology: Dialogues of the Life of the Mind*. La Salle, Ill.: Open court, 1965.

Maurer, Reinhart. *Hegel und das Ende der Geschichte: Interpretation zur Phänomenologie des Geistes.* Stuttgart: Kohlhammer 1965.

Marx, Werner. *Hegel's Phenomenology of Spirit: Its Point and Purpose.* New York: Harper & Row, 1975.

Norman, Richard. *Hegel's Phenomenology: A Philosophical Introduction.* London: Sussex University Press, 1976.

Pöggeler, Otto. "Zur Deutung der Phänomenologie des Geistes." *Hegel-Studien* I (1961): 255–294.

"Die Komposition des Phänomenologie des Geistes." *Hegel-Studien* III (1966): 27–74.

Hegels Idee einer Phänomenologie des Geistes. Freiburg: Alber, 1973.

Robinson, John. *Duty and Hypocrisy in Hegel's Phenomenology of Mind.* Toronto: Toronto University Press, 1977.

Scheier, Claus-Artur. *Analytischer Kommentar zu Hegels Phänomenologie des Geistes.* Freiburg: Alber, 1980.

Shklar, Judith. *Freedom and Independence: A Study of the Political Ideas in Hegel's Phenomenology of Mind.* Cambridge: Cambridge University Press, 1976.

Solomon, Robert. *In the Spirit of Hegel: A Study of G.W.F. Hegel's Phenomenology of Spirit.* Oxford: Oxford University Press, 1983.

Stiehler, Gottfried. *Die Dialektik in Hegels Phänomenologie des Geistes.* Berlin: Akademie, 1964.

Westphal, Kenneth. *Hegel's Epistemological Realism: A Study of the Aim and Method of Hegel's Phenomenology of Spirit.* Dordrecht: Kluwer, 1989.

Westphal, Merold, ed. *Method and Speculation in Hegel's Phenomenology.* Atlantic Highlands, N.J.: Humanities Press, 1982.

History and Truth in Hegel's Phenomenology. Atlantic Highlands, N.J.: Humanities Press, 1979.

SOCIAL AND POLITICAL PHILOSOPHY

Ahrweiler, Georg. *Hegels Gesellschaftslehre.* Marburger Beiträge zur Philosophie und Gesellschaftstheorie, vol. III. Darmstadt: Luchterhand, 1976.

Albrecht, Reinhardt. *Hegel und die Demokratie.* Abhandlungen zur Philosophie, Psychologie und Pädagogik 135. Bonn: Bouvier, 1978.

Angehrn, Emil. *Freiheit und System bei Hegel.* Berlin: de Gruyter 1977.

Ameriks, Karl. "The Hegelian Critique of Kantian Morality." In Marcia Moen, and Bernard den Ouden, eds., *New Essays on Kant.* New York: Peter Lang, 1987.

Avineri, Shlomo. *Hegel's Theory of the Modern State.* Cambridge: Cambridge University Press, 1972.

Bellamy, Richard. "Hegel and Liberalism." *History of European Ideas* 8 (1987): 693–708.

Bitsch, Briggitte. *Sollensbegriff und Moralitätskritik bei G.W.F. Hegel.* Abhandlungen zur Philosophie, Psychologie und Pädagogik 128. Bonn: Bouvier, 1977.

Bogdany, Armin. *Hegels Theorie des Gesetzes.* Freiberg: Alber, 1989.

Bolck, Franz, ed. *Hegel und die französische Revolution.* Wissenschaftliche Zeitschrift der Friedrich Schiller Universität, Jahrgang 21 (1972), Heft 1. 1–174.

Bourgeois, Bernard. *La droit naturel de Hegel, 1802–1803: commentaire.* Paris: Vrin, 1986.

Bülow, Friedrich. *Die Entwicklung der Hegelschen Sozialphilosophie.* Leipzig: Meiner, 1920.

Carrit, E.F. "Hegel's Sittlichkeit." *Proceedings of the Aristotelian Society* 36 (1935–36): 223–36.

Chamley, Paul. *Economie, politique et philosophie chez Stewart et Hegel.* Paris: Dalloz, 1963.

Cullen, Bernard. *Hegel's Social and Political Thought.* Dublin: Gill & Macmillan, 1979.

Denis, Henri. *Logique hégélienne et systèmes économiques.* Paris: Presses Universitaires de France, 1984.

D'Hondt, Jacques. *Hegel secret.* Paris: Presses Universitaires de France, 1968.

Hegel in His Time: Berlin, 1818–1831. Trans. John Burbidge. Peterborough, Ont: Broadview, 1988.

Doz, André. *Droit et liberté selon Hegel.* Paris: Presses Universitaires de France, 1986.

Drydyk, Jay. "Hegel's Politics: Liberal or Democratic?" *Canadian Journal of Philosophy* 16 (1986): 99–122.

Eber, Heinrich. *Hegels Ethik in ihrer Entwicklung bis zur Phänomenologie.* Strassburg: Elsass-Lothar, 1909.

Enskat, Rainer. *Die hegelsche Theorie des praktischen Bewußtseins.* Frankfurt: Klostermann, 1986.

Flechtheim, Ossip. *Hegels Strafrechtstheorie.* Schriften zur Rechtsphilosophie, Heft 42. Berlin: de Gruyter, 1975.

Fleischmann, Eugène. *La philosophie politique de Hegel.* Recherches en sciences humaines 18. Paris: Plon, 1964.

Forster, Michael. *The Political Philosophies of Plato and Hegel.* Oxford: Clarendon Press, 1935.

Haller, Michael. *System und Gesellschaft: Krise und Kritik der politischen Philosophie Hegels.* Deutscher Idealismus: vol. 3. Stuttgart: Klett-Cotta, 1981.

Hardimon, Michael. *The Project of Reconciliation: Hegel's Social Philosophy.* Cambridge: Cambridge University Press, 1993.

Heller, Hermann. *Hegel und der nationale Machtstaatsgedanke in Deutschland.* Leipzig and Berlin: Tuebner, 1921.

Henrich, Dieter, ed. *Hegels Philosophie des Rechts: die Theorie des Rechtsformen.* Stuttgart: Klett-Cotta, 1982.

Hocevar, Rolf. *Stände und Repräsentation beim jungen Hegel.* Munich: Beck, 1968.

Hegel und der preussischer Staat. Munich: Goldmann, 1973.

Hoy David. "Hegel's Critique of Kantian Morality." *History of Philosophy Quarterly* 6 (1989): 207–32.

Hoy, Joyce. "Hegel's Critique of Rawls." *Clio* 10 (981): 407–22.

Kaufmann, Walter, ed. *Hegel's Political Philosophy.* New York: Atherton Press, 1970.

Kelly, George. *Hegel's Retreat from Eleusius: Studies in Political Thought.* Princeton: Princeton University Press, 1978.

Lakeland, Paul. *The Politics of Salvation: The Hegelian Idea of the State.* Albany: SUNY, 1989.

Löwenstein, Julius. *Hegels Staatsidee.* Philosophische Forschungen No. 4. Berlin: Springer, 1927.

Lucas, Hans, and Pöggeler, Otto, eds. *Hegels Rechtsphilosophie im Zusammenhang der europäischen Verfassungsgeschichte.* Spekulation und Erfahrung: Abteilung II, Untersuchungen vol. I. Stuttgart/Bad Cannstatt: Fromann Holzboog, 1986.

Maker, William, ed. *Hegel on Economics and Freedom.* Macon, Georgia: Mercer University Press, 1987.

Marcuse, Herbert. *Reason and Revolution.* London: Routledge, Kegan & Paul, 1941.

Mayer-Moreau, Karl. *Hegels Socialphilosophie.* Tübingen: Mohr, 1910.

Mayinger, Josef. *Hegels Rechtsphilosophie und ihre Bedeutung in der Geschichte der marxistischen Staats- und Gesellschaftslehre.* Abhandlungen zur Philosophie, Psychologie und Pädagogik 189. Bonn: Bouvier, 1983.

Mitias, Michael. *The Moral Foundation of the State in Hegel's Philosophy of Right: Anatomy of an Argument.* Amsterdam: Rodopi, 1981.

Pelczynski, Z.A., ed. *Hegel's Political Philosophy: Problems and Perspectives.* Cambridge: Cambridge University Press, 1971.

Hegel and Civil Society. Cambridge: Cambridge University Press, 1984.

Peperzak, Adriann. *Philosophy and Politics: A Commentary on the Preface to Hegel's Philosophy of Right.* The Hague: Martinus Nijhoff, 1987.

Piontkowski, A.A. *Hegels Lehre über Staat und Recht und seine Strafrechtstheorie.* Berlin: Deutscher Zentralverlag, 1960.

Pinkard, Terry. "Freedom and Social Categories in Hegel's Ethics." *Philosophy and Phenomenological Research* 47 (1986): 209–32.

Popper, Karl. *The Open Society and Its Enemies.* London: Routledge, Kegan & Paul. Chapter 12: Hegel.

Reyburn, Hugh. *The Ethical Theory of Hegel: A Study of the Philosophy of Right.* Oxford: Clarendon Press, 1921.

Riedel, Manfred. *Theorie und Praxis im Denken Hegels.* Stuttgart: Kohlhammer, 1965.

Zwischen Tradition und Revolution: Studien zu Hegels Rechtsphilosophie. Stuttgart: Klett-Cotta, 1982. ed. *Materialien zu Hegels Rechtsphilosophie.* 2 vols. Frankfurt: Suhrkamp, 1974.

Ritter, Joachim. *Hegel and the French Revolution.* Cambridge: MIT Press, 1982.

Rosenkranz, Karl. *Hegel als deutscher Nationalphilosoph.* Leipzig: Duncker & Humblodt, 1870.

Rosenzweig, Franz. *Hegel und der Staat.* Berlin: Oldenbourg, 1920. Reprint Aalen: Scientia Verlag, 1962.

Sedgwick, S. "Hegel's Critique of the Subjective Idealism of Kant's Ethics." *Journal of the History of Philosophy* 26 (1988): 89–105.

"On the Relation of Pure Reason to Content: A Reply to Hegel's Critique of Formalism in Kant's Ethics." *Philosophy and Phenomenological Research* 49 (1988): 59–80.

Smith, Steven. *Hegel's Critique of Liberalism: Rights in Context.* Chicago: University of Chicago Press, 1989.

Steinberger, Peter. *Logic and Politics: Hegel's Philosophy of Right.* New Haven: Yale University Press, 1988.

Taminaux, Jacques. *La Nostalgie de la Grèce à l'aube de l'idéalisme allemand.* The Hague: Martinus Nijhoff, 1967.

Taylor, Charles. *Hegel and Modern Society.* Cambridge: Cambridge University Press, 1979.

Theunissen, Michael. *Hegels Lehre vom absoluten Geist als theologisch-politischer Traktat.* Berlin: de Gruyter, 1970.

Topitsch, Ernst. *Die Sozialphilosophie Hegels als Heilslehre und Herrschaftsideologie.* Munich: Piper, 1981.

Verene, Donald, ed. *Hegel's Social and Political Thought.* Atlantic Highlands, N.J.: Humanities Press, 1980.

Walsh, W.H. *Hegelian Ethics.* London: Macmillan, 1969.

Wasczek, Norbert. *The Scottish Enlightenment and Hegel's Account of Civil Society.* Dordrecht: Nijhoff, 1988.

Weil, Eric. *Hegel et l'état.* Paris: J. Vrin, 1950.

Westphal, Kenneth. "Hegel's Critique of Kant's Moral Worldview." *Philosophical Topics* 19 (1991): 133–76.

Wildt, Andreas. *Autonomie und Anerkennung: Hegels Moralitätskritik im Lichte seiner Fichte Rezeption.* Stuttgart: Klett-Cotta, 1982.

Wood, Allen. "The Emptiness of the Moral Will." *The Monist* 72 (1989): 454–83.

Hegel's Ethical Thought. Cambridge: Cambridge University Press, 1990.

ANTHOLOGIES ON VARIOUS TOPICS

Brinkley, Alan, ed. *Studies in Hegel.* The Hague: Martinus Nijhoff, 1960.

Cullen, Bernard, ed. *Hegel Today.* Aldershot: Avebury, 1988.

D'Hondt, Jacques, ed. *Hegel et la siècle des lumieres.* Paris: Presses Universitaires de France, 1974.

Fetscher, Iring, ed. *Hegel im Sicht der neueren Forschung.* Wege der Forschung vol. 52. Darmstadt: Wissenschaftliche Buchgesellschaft, 1973.

Heidtmann, Bernard, ed. *Hegel: Perspektiven seiner Philosophie heute.* Cologne: Pahl-Rügenstein, 1981.

Hospers, John, ed. "Hegel Today." *The Monist* 74, No. 3 (1991).

Inwood, Michael, ed. *Hegel.* Oxford: Oxford University Press, 1985.

Kaltenbrunner, Gerd. *Hegel und die Folgen.* Freiburg: Rombach, 1970.

Lamb, David, ed. *Hegel and Modern Philosophy.* London: Croom Helm, 1987.

MacIntyre, Alistair, ed. *Hegel: A Collection of Critical Essays.* New York: Doubleday, 1972.

O'Malley, J.J., ed. *The Legacy of Hegel: Proceedings of the Marquette Hegel Symposium 1970.* The Hague: Martinus Nijhoff, 1973.

Riedel, Manfred, ed. *Hegel und die antike Dialektik.* Frankfurt: Suhrkamp, 1990.

Ritter, Joachim, and Heede, Reinhard, eds. *Hegel-Bilanz: Zur Aktualität und Inaktualität der Philosophie Hegels.* Studien zur Philosophie und Literatur des neunzehnten Jahrhunderts, vol. 20. Frankfurt: Klostermann, 1973.

Travis, Don Carlos. *A Hegel Symposium.* Austin: University of Texas Press, 1962.

Vesey, Geoffrey, ed. *Idealism Past and Present.* Cambridge: Cambridge University Press, 1982.

Weiss, Frederick. *Beyond Epistemology: New Studies in the Philosophy of Hegel.* The Hague: Martinus Nijhoff, 1974.

NATURAL SCIENCES

Alexander, Samuel. "Hegel's Conception of Nature." *Mind* XI (1886): 495–523.

Beaumont, Bernard. "Hegel and the Seven Planets." *Mind* 62 (1854): 246–48.

Cohen, R.S., and Wartofsky, M.W. eds. *Hegel and the Sciences.* Dordrecht: Nijhoff, 1983.

Collingwood, R.G. *The Idea of Nature.* Oxford: Clarendon Press, 1949: pp. 121–132.

Engelhardt, Dietrich. *Hegel und die Chemie: Studie zur Philosophie und Wissenschaft der Natur um 1800.* Schriften zur Wissenschaftsgeschichte No. 1. Wiesbaden: Pressler, 1976.

Falkenberg, Brigitte. *Die Form der Materie: Zur Metaphysik der Natur bei Kant und Hegel.* Monographien zur philosophischer Forschung No. 283. Frankfurt: Athenäum, 1987.

Harris, E.E. "The Philosophy of Nature in Hegel's System." *Review of Metaphysics* III (1949/50): 213–28.

Kimmerle, Heinz. "Hegels Naturphilosophie in Jena." *Hegel-Studien* IV (1967): 125–76.

Petry, Michael John. *Hegel und die Naturwissenschaften.* Spekulation und Erfahrung, Abteilung 2, Band 2. Stuttgart-Bad Cannstaat: Frommann Holzboog, 1987.

Petry, Michael John. "Hegel's Dialectic and the Natural Sciences." *Hegel Jahrbuch* XIX (1975): 452–56.

Richter, Leonhard. *Hegels begreifende Naturbetrachtung.* Amsterdam: Rodopi, 1985.

Schleiden, Matthias. *Schellings und Hegels Verhältnis zur Naturwissenschaft.* Schriften zur Naturphilosophie vol 4. Weinheim, VCH, 1988.

Viellard-Baron, Jean Louis. "La notion de matèrie et la matérialisme vrai selon Hegel et Schelling a l'epoque d'Iena." *Hegel-Studien Beiheft* 20 (1980): 197–206.

Webb, Thomas. "The Problem of Knowledge in Hegel's Philosophy of Nature." *Hegel-Studien* 15 (1980): 171–86.

AESTHETICS

Bras, Gérard. *Hegel et l'art.* Paris: Presses Universitaires de France, 1989.

Bungay, Stephen. *Beauty and Truth: A Study of Hegel's Aesthetics.* Oxford: Oxford University Press, 1986.

Desmond, William. *Art and the Absolute: A Study of Hegel's Aesthetics.* Albany: Suny, 1986.

Fowkes, W.I. *A Hegelian Account of Contemporary Art.* Ann Arbor: UMI Research Press, 1981.

Fulda, Friedrich, ed. *Hegel und die Kritik der Urteilskraft.* Stuttgart: Klett-Cotta, 1990.

Gethmann-Siefert, Annemarie. *Die Funktion der Kunst in der Geschichte:*

Untersuchungen zu Hegels Aesthetik. Hegel-Studien Beiheft 25. Bonn: Bouvier, 1984.

Gombrich, Ernst. "Hegel und die Kunstgeschichte." *Neue Rundschau* 88 (1977): 202–19.

Harries, Karsten. "Hegel on the Future of Art." *Review of Metaphysics* 27 (1973–74): 677–96.

Helferich, Christoph. *Kunst und Subjektivität in Hegels Ästhetik.* Kronberg: Scriptor, 1976.

Henrich, Dieter. "Kunst und Natur in der idealistischen Äesthetik." In H.R. Jauss, ed., *Nachahmung und Illusion.* Munich: Eidos Verlag, 1964, pp. 128–134.

Henrich, Dieter. "Art and Philosophy of Art Today: Reflections with Reference to Hegel." In R.E. Amacher and V. Lange, eds. *New Perspectives in German Literary Criticism.* Princeton: Princeton University Press, 1979.

Horn, András. *Kunst und Freiheit: Eine Kritische Interpretation der Hegelschen Ästhetik.* The Hague: Martinus Nijhoff, 1969.

Jaeschke, Walter, ed. *Früher Idealismus und Frühromantik: Der Streit um die Grundlagen der Ästhetik, 1795–1805.* Hamburg: Meiner, 1990.

Kaminisky, Jack. *Hegel on Art.* Albany: SUNY, 1962.

Knox, Israel. *The Aesthetic Theories of Kant, Hegel & Schopenhauer.* Brighton: Harverster Press, 1988.

Koepsel, Werner. *Die Rezeption der Hegelschen Ästhetik im 20. Jahrhundert.* Abhandlungen zur Philosophie, Psychologie und Pädagogik 92. Bonn: Bouvier, 1975.

Kuhn, Helmut. *Die Vollendung der klassischen deutschen Ästhetik durch Hegel.* Berlin: Junker, 1931.

Lucas, Raymond. "A Problem of Hegel's Aesthetics." *Renaissance and Modern Studies* 4 (1960): 82–118.

Lukács, Gyorgy. *Aesthetik.* 2 vols. Berlin: Luchterhand, 1963.

Oelmüller, Will. "Hegels Satz vom Ende der Kunst." *Philosophisches Jahrbuch* 73 (1965–66): 75–94.

Paolucci, A., and Paolucci, H. *Hegel on Tragedy.* New York: Doubleday, 1960.

Pöggeler, Otto, and Gethmann-Siefert, Annemarie, eds. *Welt und Wirkung von Hegels Aesthetik. Hegel-Studien Beiheft* 27. Bonn: Bouvier, 1986.

Pöggeler, Otto. "Die Entstehung vom Hegels Ästhetik in Jena." *Hegel-Studien Beiheft* 20 (1980): 249–70.

Rosenkranz, Karl *Âsthetik der Häßlichen.* Königsberg: Bornträger, 1853. Reprint Darmstadt: Wissenschaftliche Buchgesellschaft, 1979.

Schüttauf, Konrad. *Die Kunst und die bildende Künste: eine Auseindersetzung mit Hegel.* Abhandlung zur Philosophie Psychologie und Pädagogik, No. 186. Bonn: Bouvier, 1984.

Wagner, Frank. *Hegels Philosophie der Dichtung*. Abhandlungen zur Philosophie, Psychologie und Pädagogik, No. 88. Bonn: Bouvier, 1974.

Zander, Hartwig. *Hegels Kunstphilosophie*. Ratingen: Henn, 1970.

PHILOSOPHY OF HISTORY

Barth, Paul. *Die Geschichtsphilosophie Hegels und der Hegelianer bis auf Marx und Hartmann*. Darmstadt: Wissenschaftliche Buchgesellschaft, 1967.

Collingwood, R.G. *The Idea of History*. Oxford: Clarendon Press, 1946.

Croce, Bendetto. *What Is Living and What Is Dead in the Philosophy of Hegel*. Trans. Douglas Ainslie. London: Macmillan.

Dannenberg, Friedrich. *Der Geist der Hegelschen Geschichtsphilosophie*. Langasalza: Beyer, 1923.

D'Hondt, Jacques. *Hegel, philosophe de l'histoire vivante*. Paris: Presses Universitaires de France, 1966.

Hyppolite, Jean. *Introduction à la philosophie de l'histoire de Hegel*. Paris: Rivière, 1948.

Lasson, Georg. *Hegel als Geschichtsphilosoph*. Leipzig: Meiner, 1920.

Leese, Kurt. *Die Geschichtsphilosophie Hegels*. Berlin: Furche, 1922.

Marcuse, Herbert. *Hegel's Ontology and the Theory of Historicity*. Trans. Seyla Benhabib. Cambridge: MIT Press, 1987.

Maurer, Reinhart. *Hagel und das Ende der Geschichte*. 2nd ed. Freiburg: Alber, 1980.

Meinecke, Friedrich. *Die Idee der Staatsräson in der Geschichte*. Munich: Oldenbourg, 1920.

O'Brien, G.D. *Hegel on Reason and History*. Chicago: University of Chicago Press, 1975.

Wilkins, B.T. *Hegel's Philosophy of History*. Ithaca, New York: Cornell University Press, 1974.

PHILOSOPHY OF MIND AND ACTION

DeVries, William. *Hegel's Theory of Mental Activity: An Introduction to Theoretical Spirit*. Ithaca, New York: Cornell University Press, 1988.

Elder, Crawford. *Appropriating Hegel*. Aberdeen: Aberdeen University Press, 1980.

Eley, Lothar, ed. *Hegels Theorie des subjektiven Geistes in der "Enzyklopädie der philosophischen Wissenschaften im Grundrisse."* Stuttgart-Bad Cannstatt: Frommann-Holzboog, 1990.

Henrich, Dieter, ed. *Hegels philosophische Psychologie*. *Hegel-Studien* Beiheft 19. Bonn: Bouvier, 1979.

Hespe, Franz, and Tuschling, Burkhard, eds. *Psychologie und Anthropologie oder Philosophie des Geistes Beiträge zu einer Hegel Tagung in Marburg 1989*. Stuttgart-Bad Cannstatt: Frommann-Holzboog, 1991.

Peperzak, Adrian. *Selbsterkenntnis des Absoluten: Grundlinien der Hegelschen Philosophie des Geistes*. Stuttgart: Fromann Holzboog, 1987.

Quelquejeu, Bernard. *La volonté dans la philosophie de Hegel*. Paris: Editions du Seuil, 1972.

Seeberger, Wilhelm. *Hegel oder die Entwicklung des Geistes zur Freiheit*. Stuttgart: Klett, 1961.

Stillmann, Peter, ed. *Hegel's Philosophy of the Spirit*. Albany: SUNY, 1987.

Weiss, Frederick, *Hegel's Critique of Aristotle's Philosophy of Mind*. The Hague: Martinus Nijhoff, 1969.

HEGELIANISM

Beyer, Wilhelm. *Hegel Bilder: Kritik der Hegel Deutungen*. 3rd ed. Berlin: Akademie Verlag, 1970.

Butler, Judith. *Subjects of Desire: Hegelian Reflections in Twentieth Century France*. New York: Columbia University Press, 1987.

Cromwell, Richard. *David Friedrich Strauss and His Place in Modern Thought*. Fairlawn, N.J.: Humanities Press, 1974.

D'Hondt, Jacques. *Hegel et l' hégélianisme*. Paris: Presses Universitaires de France, 1982.

Easton, Lloyd. *Hegel's First American Followers: The Ohio Hegelians*. Athens: Ohio University Press, 1966.

Glockner, Hermann. "Krisen und Wandlungen in der Geschichte des Hegelianismus." *Hegel-Studien Beiheft* 2 (1965): 211–28.

"Stand und Auffassung der Hegelschen Philosophie in Deutschland, hundert Jahr nach seinem Tode." *Hegel-Studien* Beiheft 2 (1965): 272–84.

"Hegelrenaissance und Neuhegelianismus." *Hegel-Studien* Beiheft 2 (1965): 312–49.

Goetzmann, William, ed. *The American Hegelians: An Intellectual Episode in the History of Western America*. New York: Alfred A. Knopf, 1973.

Haldar, Hiralal. *Neo-Hegelianism*. London: Heath Cranton, 1927.

Harris, Horton. *David Friedrich Strauss and His Theology*. Cambridge: Cambridge University Press, 1973.

Hook, Sidney. *From Hegel to Marx: Studies in the Intellectual Development of Karl Marx*. London: Victor Gollanz, 1936.

Höhne, Horst. *Der Hegelianismus in der englischen Philosophie*. Halle: Akademie Verlag, 1936.

Kamenka, Eugene. *The Philosophy of Ludwig Feuerbach*. London: Routledge, Kegan & Paul, 1970.

Knoop, Bernhard. *Hegel und die Franzosen.* Stuttgart: Kohlhammer, 1941.

Löwith, Karl. *From Hegel to Nietzsche: The Revolution in Nineteenth Century Thought.* Trans. David Green. Garden City, N.Y.: Doubleday, 1966.

Mackintosh, Robert. *Hegel and Hegelianism.* Bristol: Thoemmes, 1990.

Mah, Harold. *The End of Philosophy, the Origin of Ideology: Karl Marx and the Crisis of the Young Hegelians.* Berkeley: University of California Press, 1987.

McLellan, David. *The Young Hegelians and Karl Marx.* London: Macmillan, 1969.

Moog, Willy. *Hegel und die hegelsche Schule.* Munich: Reinhardt Verlag, 1930.

Negt, Oscar, ed. *Aktualität und Folgen der Philosophie Hegels.* Frankfurt: Suhrkamp, 1970.

Pepperle, Heinz, and Pepperle, Ingrid. *Die Hegelsche Linke: Dokumente zu Philosophie und Politik der deutschen Vormärz.* Frankfurt: Roderberg, 1986.

Rose, Gilliam. *Hegel contra Sociology.* London: Athlone, 1981.

Schacht, Richard. *Hegel and After: Studies in Continental Philosophy between Hegel & Sartre.* Pittsburgh: University of Pittsburgh Press, 1975.

Sussmann, H. *The Hegelian Aftermath: Readings in Hegel, Kierkegaard, Freud, Proust and James.* Baltimore: Johns Hopkins Press, 1982.

Toews, John. *Hegelianism: The Path Toward Dialectical Humanism, 1805–1841.* Cambridge: Cambridge University Press, 1980.

Wartofsky, Mark. *Feuerbach.* Cambridge: Cambridge University Press, 1977.

CHRONOLOGY

1770–1780: Hegel at Stuttgart
August 27, 1770: Born at Stuttgart
1773: attends Deutsche Schule
1780: attends Gymnasium Illustre
1788–1793: Hegel at Tübingen
October 1788: matriculates at Tübinger Stift.
1789–1790: shares a room with Hölderlin and Schelling and forms friendship with them.
September 1790: receives *Magister der Philosophie*.
September 1793: takes final examination.
1793–1797: Hegel at Bern
October 1793: becomes *Hauslehrer* to the family C.F. Tschügg
1797–1800: Hegel at Frankfurt
January 1797: becomes *Hauslehrer* at Frankfurt. Writes *Systemfragment, Spirit of Christianity and Its Fate*
1801–1807: Hegel at Jena
August 1801: Hegel habilitates at Jena with his dissertation "Dissertatio philosophica de Orbitis planetarum." Shortly afterward he publishes his first philosophical writing, *Difference between the Fichtean and Schellingian Systems of Philosophy*.
1802–1804: collaborates with Schelling and publishes *The Critical Journal of Philosophy*.
February 1805: named *außerordentlicher Professor*.
October 1806: Battle of Jena. Hegel flees the town with the manuscript of the *Phenomenology of Spirit*.
March 1807: Publication of the *Phenomenology of Spirit*.

1807–1808: Hegel at Bamberg

March 1807–November 1808: edits the *Bamberger Zeitung*.

1808–1816: Hegel at Nürnberg

1808: named Rector of the Ägidiengymnasiums in Nürnberg.

1811: marries Marie von Tucher.

1809–1811: lectures on the *Philosophical Propadeutic*.

1812: publication of the *Science of Logic*.

1816–1818: Hegel at Heidelberg

1816: named professor at Heidelberg.

1817: publication of the *Encyclopedia of the Philosophical Sciences*.

1818–1831: Hegel in Berlin

October 1818: gives *Antrittsvorlesung*.

1821: publication of the *Rechtsphilosophie*. Hegel lectures on religion and philosophy of history.

September to October 1822: journey to Brussels and the Netherlands.

September to October 1824: journey to Vienna through Prague.

August to October 1827: journey to Paris. Meets Goethe at Weimar upon return journey.

1829: Highpoint of his reputation. Influence in Prussia and all German universities.

November 14, 1831: Hegel dies in Berlin from cholera. Buried next to Fichte at the *Dorotheen-städtischen Friedhof,* Berlin.

INDEX